DICTIONARY OF
MEDICAL
BIOGRAPHY

EDITORIAL BOARD

DICTIONARY OF MEDICAL BIOGRAPHY

Volume 3, H–L

Edited by

W. F. Bynum *and* Helen Bynum

GREENWOOD PRESS
Westport, Connecticut • London

Library of Congress Cataloging-in-Publication Data

Dictonary of medical biography / edited by W. F. Bynum and Helen Bynum.
  p.   cm.
  Includes bibliographical references and index.
  ISBN 0–313–32877–3 (set : alk. paper) — ISBN 0–313–32878–1 (v. 1 : alk. paper) —
  ISBN 0–313–32879–X (v. 2 : alk. paper) — ISBN 0–313–32880–3 (v. 3 : alk. paper) —
  ISBN 0–313–32881–1 (v. 4 : alk. paper) — ISBN 0–313–32882–X (v. 5 : alk. paper)
  1. Medicine—Biography. 2. Healers—Biography. I. Bynum, W. F. (William F.), 1943– . II. Bynum, Helen.
  R134.D57   2007
  610—dc22   2006022953

British Library Cataloguing in Publication Data is available.

Library of Congress Catalog Card Number: 2006022953
ISBN: 0–313–32877–3 (set)
        0–313–32878–1 (vol. 1)
        0–313–32879–X (vol. 2)
        0–313–32880–3 (vol. 3)
        0–313–32881–1 (vol. 4)
        0–313–32882–X (vol. 5)

First published in 2007

Greenwood Press, 88 Post Road West, Westport, CT 06881
An imprint of Greenwood Publishing Group, Inc.
www.greenwood.com

Printed in the United States of America

The paper used in this book complies with the
Permanent Paper Standard issued by the National
Information Standards Organization (Z39.48–1984).

10   9   8   7   6   5   4   3   2   1

CONTENTS

CONTRIBUTORS

Göran Åkerström
Academic Hospital, Uppsala, Sweden
Sandström

Seema Alavi
Jamia Millia University, New Delhi, India
Aziz

Angelo Albrizio
Institut d'Histoire de la Médecine et de la Santé,
Geneva, Switzerland
De Giovanni

W. R. Albury
University of New South Wales, Sydney,
Australia
Bichat, Broussais, Corvisart des Marets, Magendie

Marta de Almeida
Museu de Astronomia e Ciências Afins,
Rio de Janeiro, Brazil
Ribas

Cristina Álvarez Millán
UNED, Madrid, Spain
*Ibn Buṭlān, Al-Majūsī, Ibn al-Nafis, Al-Rāzī, Ibn Rushd,
Ibn Zuhr*

Stuart Anderson
LSHTM, London, England
Beecham, Holloway, Squibb

Warwick Anderson
University of Wisconsin–Madison, Madison, WI,
USA
Burnet, Cleland

Jon Arrizabalaga
CSIC, Barcelona, Spain
Laguna, Sanches, Torrella

S. N. Arseculeratne
University of Peradeniya, Peradeniya,
Sri Lanka
M. Paul, Wickramarachchi

Mikel Astrain
Universidad de Granada, Granada, Spain
Lardizábal Dubois

Guy Attewell
Wellcome Trust Centre for the History of Medicine
at UCL, London, England
*Medical Traditions in South Asia, Abd ul-Hamīd,
M. Ajmal Khān, M. A'zam Khān, Saīd*

Nara Azevedo
Casa de Oswaldo Cruz, Fundação Oswaldo Cruz,
Rio de Janeiro, Brazil
Cruz

Søren Bak-Jensen
Medical Museion, Copenhagen, Denmark
Fibiger, Friderichsen, Gram, Hagedorn,
Pindborg, Salomonsen

Martha Baldwin
Stonehill College, Easton, MA, USA
Dionis

Marta Aleksandra Balinska
Institut national du cancer, Paris, France
Hirszfeld, Rajchman, Śniadecki

Rosa Ballester
Universidad Miguel Hernández, Alicante-Valencia, Spain
Martínez Vargas

Scott Bamber
UNICEF, Bangkok, Thailand
Jivaka

Richard Barnett
Wellcome Trust Centre for the History of Medicine
at UCL, London, England
Godlee, Knox, Long, W. Morton, Read, Simpson, Wakley

Josep Lluís Barona
Universidad de Valencia Blasco, Valencia, Spain
Ramón y Cajal, Trueta i Raspall

Penelope Barrett
Wellcome Trust Centre for the History of Medicine
at UCL, London, England
Li Shizhen

Alexander R. Bay
Chapman University, Orange Campus, CA, USA
Takaki

Elaine Beale
Cherhill, Wiltshire, England
Ingen Housz

Norman Beale
Cherhill, Wiltshire, England
Ingen Housz

Denise Best
California State University, Fresno, CA, USA
Pokrovskaia

Anne-Emanuelle Birn
University of Toronto, Toronto, ON, Canada
Morquio

Carla Bittel
Loyola Marymount University, Los Angeles, CA, USA
Baker, A. Jacobi, M. P. Jacobi, Van Hoosen

Johanna Bleker
ZHGB, Institut für Geschichte der Medizin,
Berlin, Germany
Henle, Schoenlein

Michael Bliss
University of Toronto, Toronto, ON, Canada
Cushing, Dandy

Hans Blom
Erasmus Universiteit, Rotterdam, the Netherlands
Mandeville

Michel Bonduelle
University of Paris, Paris, France
Duchenne de Boulogne, Guillain

Christopher Booth
Wellcome Trust Centre for the History of Medicine
at UCL, London, England
Haygarth, Hurst, Lettsom, Sherlock

Cornelius Borck
McGill University, Montreal, QC, Canada
Berger

Mineke Bosch
Universiteit Maastricht, Maastricht,
the Netherlands
Jacobs

David Bradley
LSHTM, London, England
Macdonald

Gunnar Broberg
University of Lund, Lund, Sweden
Linnaeus

Alejandra Bronfman
University of British Columbia, Vancouver,
BC, Canada
Finlay y Barres, Guiteras Gener

Linda Bryder
University of Auckland, Auckland, New Zealand
Gordon, King, Liley

Chris Burton
University of Lethbridge, Lethbridge, AB,
Canada
Burdenko, Fedorov, Semashko, Solev'ev

Helen Bynum
Shadingfield, Suffolk, England
Halsted, Harinasuta, Rogers, Snow, Steptoe

Ricardo Campos
CSIC, Madrid, Spain
Rubio Gali

Franco Carnevale
Azienda Sanitaria di Firenze, Florence, Italy
Devoto, Ramazzini

Ana María Carrillo
UNAM, Mexico City, Mexico
Montoya Lafragua

Ian Carter
University of Auckland, Auckland, New Zealand
M. Bell

Ramón Castejón-Bolea
Universidad Miguel Hernández, Alicante, Spain
Azúa y Suárez

Rafael Chabrán
Whittier College, Whittier, CA, USA
Hernández

Iain Chalmers
The James Lind Initiative, Oxford, England
Cochrane

Joël Chandelier
Ecole française de Rome, Rome, Italy
Gentile da Foligno

Rethy Chhem
University of Western Ontario, London, ON,
Canada
Yajnavaraha

Indira Chowdhury
Tata Institute of Fundamental Research,
Mumbai, India
*Chopra, Dharmendra, Mukerji, Pandit,
Ramalingaswami, P. Sen, Vakil*

Charlotte Christensen-Nugues
University of Lund, Lund, Sweden
Harpestreng

Amy Eisen Cislo
Washington University, St Louis, MO, USA
Gilbert the Englishman

Catherine S. Coleborne
Waikato University, Hamilton, New Zealand
Manning

Andrea Contini
University of Paris XII, Paris, France
Basaglia

Roger Cooter
Wellcome Trust Centre for the History of Medicine
at UCL, London, England
Braid, Charnley, Gall, R. Jones, Treves, Wells

Anne Cottebrune
Ruprecht-Karls-Universität Heidelberg,
Heidelberg, Germany
Fischer, Wagner

Christopher Crenner
KUMC, Kansas City, KS, USA
*Bowditch, Codman, Edsall, J. Jackson, Jarvis,
Minot*

Anna Crozier
University of Edinburgh, Edinburgh, Scotland
Atiman, Cook, Kasili, Spoerry, C. Williams

Ivan Crozier
University of Edinburgh, Edinburgh, Scotland
*Dickinson, Ellis, Haire, Hirschfeld, C. Mosher,
E. Mosher, Reich, Sanger, Stopes*

Marcos Cueto
Universidad Peruana Cayetano Heredia,
Lima, Peru
*Balmis, Candau, Horwitz Barak, Houssay,
Monge Medrano, Núñez Butrón, Paz Soldán,
Soper*

Michael Z. David
University of Chicago, Chicago, IL, USA
Pavlovskii, Sklifosovskii

Rosalie David
University of Manchester, Manchester,
England
Imhotep

Annemarie de Knecht-van Eekelen
CITO International, Arnhem, the Netherlands
De Lange

Ana Cecilia Rodríguez de Romo
Universidad Nacional Autónoma de México,
Mexico City, Mexico
*Arias de Benavides, Bernard, Bustamante
Vasconcelos, Chávez Sánchez, Izquierdo
Raudón, Liceaga, Martínez Báez, Montaña
Carranco*

Michelle DenBeste
California State University, Fresno, CA, USA
Pokrovskaia

Michael Denham
Wellcome Trust Centre for the History of Medicine
at UCL, London, England
M. Warren

Sven Dierig
Max-Planck-Institut, Berlin, Germany
Brücke, Ludwig

Derek A. Dow
University of Auckland, Auckland, New
Zealand
Buck, Gillies, Hercus, G. Robb, Scott

Alex Dracobly
University of Oregon, Eugene, OR, USA
Fournier, Ricord

Jean-Jacques Dreifuss
Centre Médical Universitaire, Geneva,
Switzerland
Coindet, Prevost

Ariane Dröscher
University of Bologna, Bologna, Italy
*Bassini, Bizzozero, Cotugno, Lombroso, Perroncito,
Rasori, Rizzoli*

Jacalyn Duffin
Queen's University, Kingston, ON, Canada
Laennec

Marguerite Dupree
University of Glasgow, Glasgow, Scotland
Anderson, Blackwell, Jex-Blake

Achintya Kumar Dutta
University of Burdwan, West Bengal, India
Brahmachari

William Eamon
New Mexico State University, Las Cruces, NM, USA
Nicholas of Poland

Myron Echenberg
McGill University, Montreal, QC, Canada
Brazil, Girard, A. Gregory, Jamot, Simond, Yersin

Wolfgang U. Eckart
Ruprecht-Karls-Universität Heidelberg,
Heidelberg, Germany
*Büchner, Dietl, Domagk, Sachs, Sauerbruch, Schwalbe,
Sennert, Skoda, Wundt, Zeiss*

Flávio Coelho Edler
Casa de Oswaldo Cruz, Fundação Oswaldo Cruz,
Rio de Janeiro, Brazil
Wucherer

Martin Edwards
Wellcome Trust Centre for the History of Medicine
at UCL, London, England
Balint

Kristen Ann Ehrenberger
University of Illinois, Urbana-Champaign, IL, USA
Drake

Antoinette Emch-Dériaz
University of Florida, Gainsville, FL, USA
Tissot

Eric J. Engstrom
ZHGB, Berlin, Germany
Kraepelin

Gunnar Eriksson
Uppsala Universitet, Uppsala, Sweden
Rudbeck

Bernardino Fantini
Institut d'Histoire de la Médecine et de la Santé,
Geneva, Switzerland
*Baglivi, Bovet, Celli, Dubini, Fabrizi da Acquapendente,
Golgi, Grassi, Lancisi, Pacini, Puccinotti, Redi, Sanarelli*

F. N. Fastier
University of Otago, Dunedin, New Zealand
Smirk

Morten Fink-Jensen
University of Copenhagen, Copenhagen, Denmark
Bartholin

Michael A. Flannery
University of Alabama at Birmingham,
Maylene, AL, USA
*J. Jones, Lloyd, McDowell, Newton, Nott, E. Warren,
D. Williams*

Yajaira Freites
IVIC, Caracas, Venezuela
Balmis, Beauperthuy, Gabaldón, Razetti

Charlotte Furth
University of Southern California, Los Angeles,
CA, USA
Zhu Zhenheng

Namrata R. Ganneri
Independent scholar, Mumbai, India
Joshi, Rakhmabai, Scudder

Michelle Garceau
Princeton University, Princeton, NJ, USA
Chauliac, William of Saliceto

Amy Gardiner
LSHTM, London, England
Burkitt

Nina Rattner Gelbart
Occidental College, Los Angeles, CA, USA
Du Coudray

Toby Gelfand
University of Ottawa, Ottowa, ON, Canada
*Bayle, Bernheim, Bourneville, Charcot, Desault, Hayem,
Lapeyronie, Lasègeu, Péan, Petit, Sée*

Jacques Gélis
University of Paris, Paris, France
Baudelocque

Dario Generali
Edizione Nazionale delle Opere di Antonio Vallisneri,
Milan, Italy
Vallisneri

Norman Gevitz
Ohio University, Athens, OH, USA
A. Still

James Gillespie
University of Sydney, Sydney, Australia
Argyle, Cilento

Florence Eliza Glaze
Coastal Carolina University, Conway, SC, USA
Constantine the African, Gariopontus

Christopher Goetz
Rush University Medical Center, Chicago, IL,
USA
Déjerine, Marie

Asaf Goldschmidt
Tel Aviv University, Tel Aviv, Israel
*Li Gao, Liu Wansu, Qian Yi, Wang Weiyi,
Xu Shuwei*

Christoph Gradmann
University of Oslo, Oslo, Norway
Klebs, Koch, Pettenkofer, Rabinowitsch-Kempner

John L. Graner
Mayo Clinic, Rochester, MN, USA
C. Mayo, W. Mayo

Joanna Grant
London, England
Wang Ji

Monica H. Green
Arizona State University, Tempe, AZ, USA
Trota

Samuel H. Greenblatt
Brown University, Pawtucket, RI, USA
Broca

David Greenwood
University of Nottingham, Nottingham,
England
Florey

Alberto Alonso Guardo
Universidad de Vallodolid, Vallodolid, Spain
Bernard of Gordon

Patrizia Guarnieri
Università degli Studi de Firenze, Florence, Italy
*Bufalini, Cerletti, Chiarugi, Concetti, De Sanctis,
Morselli, Mya*

Annick Guénel
LASEMA, Villejuif, France
Tùng Tôn Thất

Anita Guerrini
University of California, Santa Barbara, CA,
USA
G. Cheyne

Anne Y. Guillou
L'Université de Haute-Bretagne, Rennes, France
Pen

Bert Hall
University of Toronto, Toronto, ON, Canada
Guido da Vigevano

June Hannam
University of the West of England, Bristol, England
R. Paget

Caroline Hannaway
NIH History, Bethesda, MD, USA
Alibert, Cruveilhier, Dunglison, Dupuytren, Louis, Parran

Signe Lindskov Hansen
Copenhagen, Denmark
Finsen

Marta E. Hanson
Johns Hopkins University, Baltimore, MD, USA
Wu Youxing, Ye Gui, Zhang Jiebin

Susan Hardy
University of New South Wales, Sydney, Australia
Gillbee

Mark Harrison
Wellcome Unit for the History of Medicine, University of Oxford, Oxford, England
Carter, Christophers, Fayrer, Martin, Parkes, Ross

Joy Harvey
Independent scholar, Somerville, MA, USA
Bert, Bertillon, Brès, Edwards-Pilliet, Littré, Rayer, Tardieu, Trousseau, Vulpian

Mike Hawkins
Wellcome Trust Centre for the History of Medicine at UCL/Imperial College, London, England
Willis

E. A. Heaman
McGill University, Montreal, QC, Canada
Fleming, Sanderson, Wright

R. van Hee
Universiteit Antwerpen, Antwerp, Belgium
Depage, Vesalius

Jürgen Helm
Martin Luther Universität, Halle-Wittenberg, Halle, Germany
Brunfels, Erxleben, Frank, Gersdorff, Hoffmann, Stahl

John Henry
University of Edinburgh, Edinburgh, Scotland
Caius, Dubois, Fernel, Harvey, Linacre, Lower, Turquet, Winsløw

Volker Hess
ZHGB, Berlin, Germany
Behring, Frerichs, Kraus, Leyden, Traube, Wunderlich

Martha Hildreth
University of Nevada, Reno, NV, USA
Brouardel, Grancher

Caroline Hillard
Washington University, St Louis, MO, USA
Del Garbo, Mondino de' Liuzzi

Gilberto Hochman
Casa de Oswaldo Cruz, Fundação Oswaldo Cruz, Rio de Janeiro, Brazil
Barros Barreto, Chagas, Cruz, Fraga, Penna, Pinotti, Ribas, Wucherer

Hans-Georg Hofer
University of Manchester, Manchester, England
Krafft-Ebing, Wagner-Jauregg

Eddy Houwaart
Vrije Universiteit Medisch Centrum, Amsterdam, the Netherlands
Ali Cohen

Joel D. Howell
University of Michigan, Ann Arbor, MI, USA
Elliotson, Flick, Gerhard, Heberden, Herrick, Lewis

Elisabeth Hsu
University of Oxford, Oxford, England
Chunyu Yi

Christian Huber
Sigmund Freud-Privatstiftung, Vienna, Austria
Breuer, Jung

Rafael Huertas
CSIC, Madrid, Spain
Orfila i Rotger, Rodríguez Lafora

Teresa Huguet-Termes
Universitat Autònoma de Barcelona, Barcelona, Spain
Cardenal Fernández

Frank Huisman
University Medical Center, Utrecht/Universiteit Maastricht, Maastricht, the Netherlands
Einthoven, Hijmans van den Bergh, Loghem, Sylvius

Marion Hulverscheidt
Ruprecht-Karls-Universität Heidelberg,
Heidelberg, Germany
Basedow, Hegar

J. Willis Hurst
Emory University, Atlanta, GA, USA
White

Erik Ingebrigsten
Norwegian University of Science and Technology,
Trondheim, Norway
Holst

Lorentz M. Irgens
University of Bergen, Bergen, Norway
Hansen

Mark Jackson
University of Exeter, Exeter, England
Blackley, Down, Floyer, Freeman, Seguin, Tredgold

Bengt Jangfeldt
Center for the History of Science, Royal Academy of
Science, Stockholm, Sweden
Munthe

Mark Jenner
University of York, York, England
*Chamberlen, Clowes, Glisson, D. Turner, Wiseman,
Woodall*

William Johnston
Wesleyan University, Middletown, CT, USA
*Gotō Konzan, Hanaoka, Manse, Sugita, Yamawaki,
Yoshimasu*

Peter Jones
King's College Library, Cambridge, England
Arderne, Yperman

Eric Jorink
Constantijn Huygens Instituut, the Hague,
the Netherlands
*J. Heurnius, O. Heurnius, Lemnius, Piso,
Swammerdam*

Robert Jütte
Robert Bosch Stiftung, Stuttgart, Germany
*Auenbrugger, Hahnemann, Hirsch, Hufeland, Kaposi,
Rolfink, Rubner*

Oliver Kahl
University of Manchester, Manchester, England
Ibn at-Tilmīdh

Harmke Kamminga
University of Cambridge, Cambridge, England
Eijkman

Amalie M. Kass
Harvard Medical School, Boston, MA, USA
Cabot, Channing, Churchill, Dameshek, Kelly, Sims

Matthew Howard Kaufman
University of Edinburgh, Edinburgh, Scotland
Ballingall, C. Bell, Brodie, Guthrie, Liston, McGrigor

Amy Kemp
Indiana University, Bloomington, IN, USA
Souza

Helen King
University of Reading, Reading, England
*Agnodice, Archagathus, Hippocrates, Machaon,
Podalirius*

Stephanie Kirby
University of the West of England, Bristol, England
Nightingale

Rina Knoeff
Universiteit Maastricht, Maastricht,
the Netherlands
G. Bidloo, Boerhaave

Carl Henrik Koch
University of Copenhagen, Copenhagen,
Denmark
Stensen

Peter Koehler
Wever Hospital, Heerlen, the Netherlands
Babinski, Brown-Séquard, Winkler

Luuc Kooijmans
Universiteit van Amsterdam, Amsterdam,
the Netherlands
Ruysch

Maria Korasidou
Panteion University of Athens, Athens, Greece
Geroulanos, Goudas, Papanicolaou, Vouros, Zinnis

Jan K. van der Korst
Loosdrecht, the Netherlands
Camper, Swieten

Samuel Kottek
Hebrew University, Jerusalem, Israel
Astruc

Simone Petraglia Kropf
Casa de Oswaldo Cruz, Fundação Oswaldo
Cruz, Rio de Janeiro, Brazil
Chagas

Howard I. Kushner
Emory University, Atlanta, GA, USA
Gilles de la Tourette

Ann F. La Berge
Virginia Tech, Blacksburg, VA, USA
Parent-Duchâtelet, Villermé

Paul A. L. Lancaster
University of Sydney, New South Wales, Australia
Gregg

Øivind Larsen
University of Oslo, Oslo, Norway
Schiøtz

Christopher Lawrence
Wellcome Trust Centre for the History of
Medicine at UCL, London, England
*Cheselden, Culpeper, Lind, Mead, Pott, Pringle,
Salk, Sydenham, Trotter*

Sean Hsiang-lin Lei
National Tsing-hua University, Hsinchu, Taiwan
Yu Yan

Efraim Lev
University of Haifa, Haifa, Israel
Asaph

Milton James Lewis
University of Sydney, Sydney,
Australia
Cumpston

Shang-Jen Li
Institute of History and Philology, Academia
Sinica, Taipei, Taiwan
*Bruce, Hobson, Leishman, Lockhart, Manson,
Parker*

Kai Khiun Liew
Wellcome Trust Centre for the History of Medicine
at UCL, London, England
Chen Su Lan

Vivienne Lo
Wellcome Trust Centre for the History of Medicine
at UCL, London, England
Medicine in China

Stephen Lock
Aldeburgh, Suffolk, England
*The Western Medical Tradition, Beecher, Cooper,
Crile, Dale, Doll, Ferrier, Fishbein, Gull, Hart,
Hastings, G. Holmes, Keynes, Mitchell,
Pappworth, Pickles, Ryle, Saunders, Trudeau*

Winifred Logan
Glasgow, Scotland
Stephenson

Brigitte Lohff
Medizinische Hochschule Hannover,
Hannover, Germany
Autenrieth, Baer, Blumenbach, Müller, Oken, Reil

Jorge Lossio
University of Manchester, Manchester, England
Carrión, Espejo, Unanue

Ilana Löwy
CERMES, Villejuif, France
Aleksandrowicz, Bieganski, Biernacki, Korczak

Kenneth M. Ludmerer
Washington University, St Louis, MO, USA
Flexner

Joan E. Lynaugh
University of Pennsylvania Nursing School,
Philadelphia, PA, USA
L. Dock, L. Richards, I. Robb

Kan-Wen Ma
Wellcome Trust Centre for the History of Medicine
at UCL, London, England
Bian Que

Helen MacDonald
University of Melbourne, Carlton, Victoria,
Australia
W. MacKenzie

Andreas-Holger Maehle
University of Durham, Durham/Wolfson Research
Institute, Stockton, England
Moll

Susanne Malchau
Aarhus Universitet, Aarhus, Denmark
Mannerheim, Reimann

John Manton
University of Oxford, Oxford, England
Johnson, Lambo, Schweitzer

Predrag J. Markovic
Institute for Contemporary History, Belgrade, Serbia
Batut, Djordjević, Lazarević, Kostić, Nešić, Štampar, Subbotić

Shula Marks
SOAS, London, England
Gale, Gear, Gillman, Gluckman, Kark, Waterston

José Martínez-Pérez
Universidad de Castilla-La Mancha, Albacete, Spain
Calandre Ibáñez, Jiménez Díaz, Marañón Posadillo

Àlvar Martínez-Vidal
Universidad Autónoma de Barcelona, Barcelona, Spain
Gimbernat i Arbós, Giovannini

Romana Martorelli Vico
Università di Pisa, Pisa, Italy
Lanfranc, Ugo Benzi

J. Rosser Matthews
Williamsburg, VA, USA
Biggs, Bouchard, Bouchardat, Chapin, Greenwood, Hill

Janet McCalman
University of Melbourne, Melbourne, Australia
Balls-Headley, Bryce, Campbell, Macnamara, Scantlebury Brown

Louella McCarthy
University of Sydney, Sydney, New South Wales, Australia
D'Arcy

Laurence B. McCullough
Baylor College of Medicine, Houston, TX, USA
Hooker, Rush

Susan McGann
RCN Archives, Edinburgh, Scotland
Fenwick

James McGeachie
University of Ulster, Newtownabbey, Northern Ireland
Corrigan, Graves, W. Jenner, M. Mackenzie, Stokes, Wilde

Alessandro Medico
Washington University, St Louis, MO, USA
Peter of Abano

Rosa María Medina-Doménech
Universidad de Granada, Granada, Spain
Goyanes Capdevilla, Guilera Molas

Alfredo Menéndez
Universidad de Granada, Granada, Spain
Casal Julián

Sharon Messenger
Wellcome Trust Centre for the History of Medicine at UCL, London, England
Livingstone

Alexandre Métraux
Dossenheim, Germany
S. Freud, Goldstein

Dmitry Mikhel
Saratov State University, Saratov, Russia
Botkin, Erisman, Manassein, Molleson, Ostroumov, Zakhar'in

Bridie Andrews Minehan
Bentley College, Waltham, MA, USA
Ding Fubao, Yen

Consuelo Miqueo
Universidad de Zaragoza, Zaragoza, Spain
Piquer Arrufat

Néstor Miranda Canal
Universidad El Bosque y de la Universidad de Los Andes, Bogotá, Colombia
Vargas Reyes

Jorge Molero-Mesa
Universidad Autònoma de Barcelona, Barcelona, Spain
Sayé i Sempere

Laurence Monnais
Université de Montréal, Montreal, QC, Canada
Medical Traditions in Southeast Asia: From Syncretism to Pluralism

Maria Teresa Monti
CSPF-CNR, Milan, Italy
Spallanzani

Francisco Moreno de Carvalho
Independent scholar, São Paulo, Brazil
Amatus Lusitanus, Orta

Edward T. Morman
Baltimore, MD, USA
Bartlett, H. Bigelow, J. Bigelow, Billings, Da Costa, Pepper, Thayer, Welch

Barbara Mortimer
Edinburgh, Scotland
Sharp

Anne Marie Moulin
CNRS-CEDEJ, Cairo, Egypt
Bordet, Davaine, Laveran, Netter, Roux, Widal

Wolf-Dieter Müller-Jahncke
Hermann-Schelenz-Institut für Pharmazie und
Kulturgeschichte, Heidelberg, Germany
Paracelsus

Jock Murray
Dalhousie University, Halifax, Nova Scotia, Canada
Abbott, Banting, Bethune, Gowers, Grenfell, Huggins,
J. H. Jackson, Macphail, Osler, Parkinson, Penfield, Selye

Takeshi Nagashima
Keio University, Tokyo, Japan
Gotō Shinpei, Kitasato, Miyairi, Nagayo, Noguchi, Shiga

Michael J. Neuss
Columbia University, New York, NY, USA
Al-Anṭākī

Michael Neve
Wellcome Trust Centre for the History of Medicine
at UCL, London, England
Beddoes, Gully, Head, Prichard, Rivers, Winslow

Malcolm Nicolson
University of Glasgow, Glasgow, Scotland
Alison, Baillie, Donald, J. Hunter, W. Hunter, Lister, Smellie

Ingemar Nilsson
University of Gothenburg, Gothenburg, Sweden
Acrel

Sherwin Nuland
Yale University, New Haven, CT, USA
Beaumont, Bloodgood, Kubler-Ross, McBurney, Mott, Murphy

Eva Nyström
University of Uppsala, Uppsala, Sweden
Rosén von Rosenstein

Ynez Violé O'Neill
UCLA, Los Angeles, CA, USA
Paré

Diana Obregón
Universidad Nacional de Colombia Edificio Manuel
Ancizar, Bogotá, Colombia
Carrasquilla, García-Medina

Ambeth R. Ocampo
National Historical Institute, Manila, Philippines
Rizal

Guillermo Olagüe de Ros
Universidad de Granada, Granada, Spain
García Solá, Nóvoa Santos, Urrutia Guerezta

Jan Eric Olsén
University of Lund, Lund, Sweden
Gullstrand, Holmgren

Todd M. Olszewski
Yale University, New Haven, CT, USA
Cannon, D. Dock

Willie T. Ong
Makati Medical Center, Makati, Philippines
Acosta-Sison

Giuseppe Ongaro
Ospedale di Padova, Padova, Italy
Aranzio, Aselli, Bellini, Benivieni, Berengario da Carpi,
Borelli, Cardano, Cesalpino, Colombo, Cornaro,
Da Monte, Eustachi, Falloppia, Malpighi, Mattioli,
Mercuriale, Morgagni, Santorio, Scarpa, Severino,
Tagliacozzi, Valsalva, Zacchia

Ooi Keat Gin
Universiti Sains Malaysia, Penang, Malaysia
Danaraj, Lim Boon Keng, Wu Lien-Teh

Teresa Ortiz-Gómez
Universidad de Granada, Granada, Spain
Arroyo Villaverde, Soriano Fischer

Abena Dove Osseo-Asare
University of California, Berkeley, CA, USA
Ampofo, Barnor, De Graft-Johnson, C. Easmon

Nelly Oudshoorn
Universiteit Twente, Enschede,
the Netherlands
Laqueur

Caroline Overy
Wellcome Trust Centre for the History of
Medicine at UCL, London, England
Livingstone

Steven Palmer
University of Windsor, Windsor, Ontario,
Canada
Calderón Guardia, Durán Cartín,
Fernández y Hernández

José Pardo-Tomás
CSIC, Barcelona, Spain
Monardes

Lawrence Charles Parish
Jefferson Medical College, Philadelphia, PA, USA
Bateman, Duhring, Gross, Hutchinson, Shippen, Willan

Eldryd Parry
Tropical Health and Education Trust, London, England
Burkitt

Adell Patton Jr.
University of Missouri, St Louis, MO, USA
Boyle, J. Easmon, Odeku, Togba

Harry W. Paul
University of Florida, Gainesville, FL, USA
Pasteur, Rothschild

John Pearn
University of Queensland, Brisbane, Australia
Bancroft, Beaney, Coppleson, Fairley, Halford, MacGregor

Steven J. Peitzman
Drexel University College of Medicine,
Philadelphia, PA, USA
Addis, Bright, A. Richards, Scribner

Kim Pelis
National Institutes of Health, Bethesda, MD, USA
Barker, Councilman, Gorgas, Hammond, Nicolle, Reed, T. Smith

Concetta Pennuto
Université de Genève, Geneva, Switzerland
Ficino, Fracastoro

José Morgado Pereira
Universidade de Coimbra, Coimbra, Portugal
Egas Moniz

Jacques Philippon
Salpêtrière-Pitié Hospital, Paris, France
Mondor

Howard Phillips
University of Cape Town, Rondebosch, South Africa
Abdurahman, Barnard, Barry, Naidoo, Orenstein, Xuma

Jean-François Picard
CNRS, Paris, France
Debré, Delay, Hamburger, Leriche, Roussy, Vincent

Mikhail Poddubnyi
Voenno-meditsinskii Zhurnal, Moscow, Russia
N. Bidloo, Buial'skii, Dobroslavin, Gaaz, Inozemtsev, Pirogov, Pletnev

Hans Pols
University of Sydney, Sydney, Australia
Beard, Beers, Bowlby, Burton-Bradley, Grinker, Klein, Laing, Stillé

María-Isabel Porras-Gallo
University of Castilla-La Mancha, Madrid, Spain
Obrador Alcalde

Patricia E. Prestwich
University of Alberta, Edmonton, AB, Canada
Magnan, Moreau de Tours, Morel

Lawrence M. Principe
Johns Hopkins University, Baltimore, MD, USA
Helmont

Armin Prinz
Medizinische Universität Wien, Vienna, Austria
Wenckebach

Cay-Ruediger Pruell
Albert-Ludwigs-Universität, Freiburg, Germany
Aschoff, Cohnheim, Conti, Ehrlich, Rokitansky, Virchow

Constance Putnam
Independent scholar, Concord, MA, USA
Balassa, Bene, Duka, O. W. Holmes, Korányi, Markusovszky, Meigs, Morgan, Semmelweis, G. Shattuck, N. Smith, J. Warren

Emilio Quevedo
Universidad Nacional de Colombia, Bogotá, Colombia
Franco

Sean Quinlan
University of Idaho, Moscow, ID, USA
A. Louis, Quesnay

Camilo Quintero
University of Wisconsin–Madison, Madison, WI, USA
Mutis y Bosio

Roger Qvarsell
University of Linköping, Linköping, Sweden
Huss

Karina Ramacciotti
Universidad de Buenos Aires, Buenos Aires, Argentina
Carrillo, Mazza, Rawson

Mridula Ramanna
SIES College, University of Mumbai, Mumbai, India
Bentley, Choksy, Jhirad, Khanolkar, Lad, Morehead, J. Turner

Matthew Ramsey
Vanderbilt University, Nashville, TN, USA
*Civiale, Desgenettes, Fourcroy, Portal, Richerand, Velpeau,
Vicq d'Azyr*

Ismail Rashid
Vassar College, Poughkeepsie, NY, USA
Fanon, Horton

Carole Reeves
Wellcome Trust Centre for the History of Medicine
at UCL, London, England
*Abt, Battey, Buchan, Budd, Cole, Darwin, Holt, Keen,
Lane, S. Morton, Prout, Rock, Sabin, Scharlieb, Seacole,
Spock, Tait*

C. Joan Richardson
University of Texas Medical Branch, Galveston, TX,
USA
Barton

Philip Rieder
Université de Genève, Geneva, Switzerland
Bonet, De La Rive, Le Clerc, Odier, Reverdin, Tronchin

Ortrun Riha
Universität Leipzig, Leipzig, Germany
Isaac Israeli

Julius Rocca
University of Birmingham, Birmingham, England
*Aëtius, Aretaeus, Aristotle, Asclepiades, Caelius Aurelianus,
Celsus, Dioscorides, Empedocles, Erasistratus, Herophilos,
Pliny, Scribonius Largus, Soranus, Whytt*

Julia Rodriguez
University of New Hampshire, Durham, NH, USA
Aráoz Alfaro, Coni, Grierson, Ingenieros

Esteban Rodríguez-Ocaña
Universidad de Granada, Granada, Spain
Ferrán y Clúa, Pittaluga Fattorini

Volker Roelcke
Justus-Liebig Universität, Giessen, Germany
Alzheimer, Bleuler, Kretschmer, Mitscherlich, Rüdin

Hugo Röling
Universiteit van Amsterdam, Amsterdam,
the Netherlands
Rutgers

Naomi Rogers
Yale University, New Haven, CT, USA
Kenny

Anastasio Rojo
University of Valladolid, Valladolid, Spain
Bravo de Sobremonte, Mercado, Valles

Nils Rosdahl
Medical Museion, Copenhagen Denmark
Madsen

Barbara Gutmann Rosenkrantz
Harvard University, Cambridge, MA, USA
Hardy, L. Shattuck

Leonard D. Rosenman
UCSF, San Francisco, CA, USA
Frugard

Fred Rosner
Mount Sinai School of Medicine, New York,
NY, USA
Maimonides

Lisa Rosner
Richard Stockton College, Pomona, NJ, USA
*Bennett, Brown, Christison, Cullen, Ferriar, J. Gregory,
Laycock, Monro, Percival, Withering*

Frederic Roy
Université de Montréal, Montreal, QC,
Canada
Suvannavong

Marion Maria Ruisinger
Friedrich-Alexander-Universität,
Erlangen-Nuremberg, Germany
Heister

Han van Ruler
Erasmus Universiteit, Rotterdam,
the Netherlands
Blankaart, Bontekoe, Graaf

Andrea Rusnock
University of Rhode Island, Kingston,
RI, USA
*Arbuthnot, Bond, Boylston, E. Jenner, Jurin, Sutton,
Waterhouse*

Fernando Salmón
Universidad de Cantabria, Santander, Spain
Arnald, López Albo

Lutz D. H. Sauerteig
University of Durham, Durham/Wolfson
Research Institute, Stockton, England
Blaschko

Walton O. Schalick III
Washington University, St Louis, MO, USA
Gilles de Corbeil, Henry of Mondeville, John of Gaddesden, John of Saint-Amand, Peter of Abano, Peter of Spain, Richard the Englishman, Taddeo, William of Brescia

Volker Scheid
University of Westminster, London, England
Ding Ganren, Fei Boxiong, Yun Tieqiao

Aina Schiøtz
Universitetet i Bergen, Bergen, Norway
Evang

William Schneider
Indiana University, Indianapolis, IN, USA
Hirszfeld, Pinard, Richet, Tzanck

Heinz Schott
Rheinische Friedrich-Wilhelms-Universität, Bonn, Germany
Mesmer

Andrew Scull
University of California San Diego, San Diego, CA, USA
Brigham, Cotton, Dix, Earle, Haslam, Meyer, Ray, Tuke

Nikolaj Serikoff
The Wellcome Library, London, England
The Islamic Medical Tradition, Aḥmad, Ibn al-Bayṭār, Al-Bīrūnī, Clot Bey, Foley, Ḥaddād, Ibn al-Haytham, Mahfouz, Ibn al-Māsawayh, Meyerhof, Ibn Sīnā, Sournia, Van Dyck, Waldmeier, Al-Zahrāwī

Jole Shackelford
University of Minnesota, Minneapolis, MN, USA
Severinus

Sonu Shamdasani
Wellcome Trust Centre for the History of Medicine at UCL, London, England
Adler, Forel, A. Freud, Gesell, Janet, Menninger, Putnam, Sullivan

Patrick Henry Shea
Rockefeller Archive Center, Sleepy Hollow, NY, USA
Carrel

Sally Sheard
University of Liverpool, Liverpool, England
Bevan, Beveridge, Chadwick, Farr, Newman, Newsholme, Shuttleworth, T. S. Smith

Dongwon Shin
Korean Advanced Institute of Science and Technology, Taejon, Korea
Choe Han'gi, Heo, Sejong, Yi Jema

Barry David Silverman
Northside Hospital, Atlanta, GA, USA
Taussig

Mark E. Silverman
Emory University, Atlanta, GA, USA
Flint, Hope, J. Mackenzie

Jelena Jovanovic Simic
Zemun, Serbia
Batut, Djordjević, Lazarević, Kostić, Nešić, Štampar, Subbotić

P. N. Singer
London, England
Galen

Kavita Sivaramakrishnan
Public Health Foundation of India, New Delhi, India
G. Sen, P. Sharma, T. Sharma, Shukla, Vaid, Varier

Morten A. Skydsgaard
University of Aarhus, Aarhus, Denmark
Panum

Jean Louis De Sloover
Erpent (Namur), Belgium
Dodonaeus

David F. Smith
University of Aberdeen, Aberdeen, Scotland
Orr

F. B. Smith
Australian National University, Canberra, Australia
W. Thomson

Thomas Söderqvist
Medical Museion, Copenhagen, Denmark
Jerne

Marina Sorokina
Russian Academy of Sciences, Moscow, Russia
Al'tshuller, Briukhonenko, Haffkine, Ilizarov, Iudin, Negovskii, Semenovskii

David Sowell
Juniata College, Huntingdon, PA, USA
Perdomo Neira

Eduard A. van Staeyen
Leiden, the Netherlands
Guislain

Frank W. Stahnisch
Johannes Gutenberg-Universität, Mainz, Germany
Graefe, Griesinger, His, C. Vogt, O. Vogt, Warburg, Wassermann

Ida H. Stamhuis
Vrije Universiteit Amsterdam, Amsterdam, the Netherlands
Quetelet

Darwin H. Stapleton
Rockefeller Archive Center, Sleepy Hollow, NY, USA
Hackett

Jane Starfield
University of Johannesburg, Bertsham, South Africa
Molema, Moroka

Martin S. Staum
University of Calgary, Calgary, AB, Canada
Cabanis

Hubert Steinke
University of Bern, Bern, Switzerland
Haller

Oddvar Stokke
National Hospital, Oslo, Norway
Følling, Refsum

Michael Stolberg
Universität Würzburg, Würzburg, Germany
Bartisch, Fabricius, Fuchs, Platter, Rösslin, Scultetus

Marvin J. Stone
Baylor University Medical Center, Dallas, TX, USA
Coley, Ewing, Farber, E. Graham, Hodgkin, Wintrobe

Hindrik Strandberg
Helsinki, Finland
Willebrand, Ylppö

Karin Stukenbrock
Martin-Luther-Universität Halle-Wittenberg, Halle, Germany
Brunfels, Erxleben, Frank, Gersdorff, Hoffmann, Stahl

Charles Suradji
Jakarta, Indonesia
Soedarmo

Akihito Suzuki
Keio University, Yokohama, Japan
Medicine, State, and Society in Japan, 500–2000, Asada, Baelz, Conolly, Hata, Mori, Ogata, Pompe van Meerdervoort, Siebold, Yamagiwa

Mika Suzuki
Shizuoka University, Shizuoka, Japan
Ogino, Yoshioka

Victoria Sweet
UCSF, San Francisco, CA, USA
Hildegard of Bingen

Simon Szreter
University of Cambridge, Cambridge, England
McKeown

Cecilia Taiana
Carleton University, Ottawa, ON, Canada
Lacan

Ian Tait
Aldeburgh, Suffolk, England
Browne

Jennifer Tappan
Columbia University, New York, NY, USA
Trowell

Robert Tattersall
University of Nottingham, Nottingham, England
Abel, Addison, Albright, Doniach, Hench, Horsley, Joslin, Minkowski, Starling

Kim Taylor
Kaimu Productions, Shanghai, China
Hatem, Zhu Lian

Manuela Tecusan
University of Cambridge, Cambridge, England
Alcmaeon, Anaximander, Andreas, Democedes, Democritus, Diocles, Diogenes, Oribasius, Paul of Aegina, Philistion, Plato, Praxagoras, Rufus

Bert Theunissen
Universiteit Utrecht, Utrecht, the Netherlands
Donders

Michel Thiery
Stichting Jan Palfyn en Museum voor Geschiedenis van de Geneeskunde, Ghent, Belgium
Palfyn

C. Michele Thompson
Southern Connecticut State University,
New Haven, CT, USA
Lán Ông, Tuệ Tĩnh

Carsten Timmermann
University of Manchester, Manchester, England
Bauer, Grotjahn, McMichael, Pickering, D. Richards,
Rosenbach

Tom Treasure
St George's Hospital Medical School, London,
England
Beck, Blalock, C. E. Drew, C. R. Drew, Favaloro, Gibbon,
Hufnagel

Ulrich Tröhler
University of Bern, Bern, Switzerland
Bergmann, Billroth, Kocher, Langenbeck,
Mikulicz-Radecki, Nissen, Quervain

Arleen Marcia Tuchman
Vanderbilt University, Nashville, TN, USA
Zakrzewska

Marius Turda
Oxford Brookes University, Oxford, England
Babeş, Cantacuzino, Ciucă, Marinescu

Trevor Turner
Homerton University Hospital, London, England
Maudsley

Peter J. Tyler
Edgecliffe, New South Wales, Australia
W. Armstrong, Bland, Fiaschi, Mackellar, Skirving,
Stuart, Thompson

Michael Tyquin
Making History, Darlington, New South Wales,
Australia
Dunlop

Tatiana Ul'iankina
Institute of the History of Science and Technology,
Moscow, Russia
Mechnikov, Sechenov

G. van der Waa
Rotterdam, the Netherlands
Gaubius

Lia van Gemert
Universiteit Utrecht, Utrecht, the Netherlands
Beverwijck

Maria Vassiliou
University of Oxford, Oxford, England
Belios, Livadas

Jan Peter Verhave
UMCN, Nijmegen, the Netherlands
Swellengrebel

Joost Vijselaar
Trimbos-Instituut, Utrecht, the Netherlands
Schroeder van der Kolk

Jurjen Vis
Amsterdam, the Netherlands
Foreest

An Vleugels
National University of Singapore, Singapore
Kerr

Hans de Waardt
Vrije Universiteit Amsterdam, Amsterdam,
the Netherlands
Wier

Keir Waddington
Cardiff University, Cardiff, Wales
Abernethy, Brunton, Garrod, Gee, Lawrence,
J. Paget

Lisa K. Walker
University of California, Berkeley, CA, USA
Khlopin, Teziakov

John Walker-Smith
Wellcome Trust Centre for the History of
Medicine at UCL, London, England
G. Armstrong, G. Still, Underwood, West

Paul Weindling
Oxford Brookes University, Oxford, England
Verschuer

Dora B. Weiner
UCLA, Los Angeles, CA, USA
Esquirol, Larrey, Percy, Pinel, Tenon

Kathleen Wellman
Southern Methodist University, Dallas, TX, USA
La Mettrie, Patin, Renaudot

Ann Westmore
The University of Melbourne, Parkville, Victoria,
Australia
Cade

James Whorton
University of Washington, Tacoma, WA, USA
*Eddy, S. Graham, Kellogg, Lust, B. Palmer, D. Palmer,
S. Thomson, Trall*

Ann Wickham
Dublin City University, Dublin, Ireland
A. Jones

Elizabeth A. Williams
Oklahoma State University, Stillwater, OK, USA
Boissier de la Croix de Sauvages, Bordeu

Sabine Wilms
Paradigm Publications, Taos, NM, USA
Ge Hong, Sun Simiao, Tao Hongjing

Warren Winkelstein, Jr.
University of California, Berkeley, CA, USA
*Emerson, Frost, Goldberger, Hamilton, Kinyoun,
Lane-Claypon, Park, Paul, Wynder*

Michael Worboys
University of Manchester, Manchester, England
Allbutt, Bristowe, W. W. Cheyne, Moynihan, Simon, Syme

Jill Wrapson
University of Auckland, Auckland,
New Zealand
Barnett

Marcia Wright
Columbia University, New York, NY, USA
Park Ross

Rex Wright-St Clair (deceased)
Huntingdon, Hamilton, New Zealand
A. Thomson

Henrik R. Wulff
Medical Museion, Copenhagen, Denmark
Hirschsprung

Ronit Yoeli-Tlalim
Warburg Institute, London, England
Sangye Gyatso, Yuthog Yontan

William H. York
Portland State University, Portland, OR,
USA
Despars, Valesco of Tarenta

Benjamin Zajicek
University of Chicago, Chicago, IL, USA
Bekhterev, Korsakov, Pavlov

Soledad Zárate
Universidad de Chile, Santiago, Chile
Cruz-Coke Lassabe

Alfons Zarzoso
Museu d'Història de la Medicina de Catalunya,
Barcelona, Spain
Pedro-Pons, Puigvert Gorro

Franz Zehentmayr
Salzburg, Austria
Zhang Yuansu

Barbara Zipser
Wellcome Trust Centre for the History of Medicine
at UCL, London, England
Al-Mawṣilī

Patrick Zylberman
CERMES, Villejuif, France
Sand

ABBREVIATIONS

AMA	American Medical Association
ANB	*American National Biography*
BA	Bachelor of Arts
BCE	Before Common Era
BCG	Bacillus Calmette-Guérin (tuberculosis vaccination)
BM	Bachelor of Medicine
BMA	British Medical Association
BMJ	*British Medical Journal*
CBE	Commander, The Most Excellent Order of the British Empire
CE	Common Era
ChB	Bachelor of Surgery
ChD	Doctor of Surgery
ChM	Master of Surgery
CIE	Companion, The Most Eminent Order of the Indian Empire
KCIE	Knight Commander, The Most Eminent Order of the Indian Empire
CM	Master of Surgery
CMB	Combat Medical Badge (U.S. Army)
CMG	Companion, The Most Distinguished Order of St Michael and St George
CMO	Chief Medical Officer
CMS	Church Missionary Society
CSI	Companion, The Most Exalted Order of the Star of India
CSIRO	Commonwealth Scientific and Industrial Research Organization (Australia)
DAMB	*Dictionary of American Medical Biography*
DAuB	*Dictionary of Australian Biography* (available online)
DBE	Dame of the British Empire
DBI	*Dizionario Biografico degli Italiani*
DGMS	Director General Medical Service (military)

DMed	Doctor of Medicine
DNZB	*Dictionary of New Zealand Biography* (available online)
DPM	Diploma of Psychological Medicine
DSB	*Dictionary of Scientific Biography*
DSO	Distinguished Service Order (military British)
ECT	Electo-convulsive Therapy
EEG	Electroencephalogram
FAO	Food and Agriculture Organization (United Nations)
FRCP	Fellow Royal College of Physicians
FRCPEdin/FRCPEd	Fellow Royal College of Physicians Edinburgh
FRCS	Fellow of the Royal College of Surgeons
FRCSEdin/FRCSEd	Fellow Royal College of Surgeons Edinburgh
FRS	Fellow of the Royal Society
FRSEdin/FRSEd	Fellow of the Royal Society of Edinburgh
GBH	General Board of Health (England and Wales)
GMC	General Medical Council (UK)
GP	General Practitioner
ICN	International Council of Nursing
ICS	Indian Civil Service
IHB	International Health Board (Rockefeller Foundation)
IMS	Indian Medical Service
IOC	Institute Oswaldo Cruz
JAMA	*Journal of the American Medical Association*
KCSI	Knight Commander, The Most Exalted Order of the Star of India
LLD	Doctor of Laws
LMS	Licentiate in Medicine and Surgery
LRCP	Licentiate of the Royal College of Physicians
LRCPEdin/LRCPEd	Licentiate of the Royal College of Physicians Edinburgh
LRCSEdin/LRCSEd	Licentiate of the Royal College of Surgeons Edinburgh
LRFPS	Licentiate of the Royal Faculty of Physicians and Surgeons of Glasgow
LSA	Licentiate of the Society of Apothecaries
LSHTM	London School of Hygiene and Tropical Medicine
LSMW	London School of Medicine for Women
MA	Master of Arts
MB	Bachelor of Medicine
MBCM	Bachelor of Medicine Master of Surgery
MC	Military Cross
MD	Doctor of Medicine
mg	milligram
MMed	Master of Medicine
MO	Medical Officer
MoH	Medical Officer of Health
MRC	Medical Research Council
MRCNZ	Medical Research Council of New Zealand
MRCOG	Member of the Royal College of Gynaecologists
MRCP	Member of the Royal College of Physicians
MRCS	Member of the Royal College of Surgeons
MS	Multiple Sclerosis
NHMRC	National Health and Medical Research Council (Australia)
NSDAP	National Socialist Party (Nazi Germany)
NSW	New South Wales (Australia)
OAS	Organization of American States
OBE	Officer, The Most Excellent Order of the British Empire
Oxford DNB	*Oxford Dictionary of National Biography* (UK)
PASB	Pan American Sanitary Bureau

PhD	Doctor of Philosophy
QVJIN	Queen Victoria Jubilee Institute of Nursing
RACP	Royal Australasian College of Physicians
RACS	Royal Australasian College of Surgeons
RAMC	Royal Army Medical Corps (UK)
RBNA	Royal British Nurses Association
RCP	Royal College of Physicians
RCPEdin	Royal College of Physicians of Edinburgh
RCS	Royal College of Surgeons
RCSEdin	Royal College of Surgeons of Edinburgh
RMO	Resident Medical Officer
RSTMH	Royal Society of Tropical Medicine and Hygiene
SA	Sturm Abteilung [Storm Section] (Nazi Germany)
SLSAA	Surf Lifesaving Association of Australia
SS	Schutzstaffel [Protective Squadron] (Nazi Germany)
STD	Sexually Transmitted Diseases
UCH	University College Hospital (London, England)
UCL	University College London (England)
UNICEF	United Nations Children's Fund
UNRRA	United Nations Relief and Rehabilitation Administration
WHO	World Health Organization
YMCA	Young Men's Christian Association

LIST OF ENTRIES

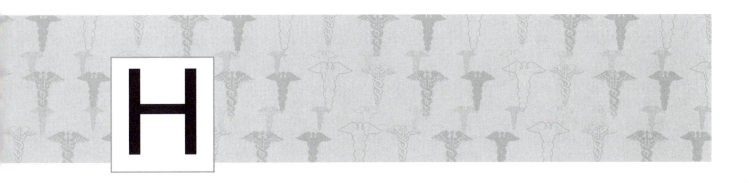

H

HACKETT, LEWIS WENDELL (b. Benecia, California, USA, 14 December 1884; d. Oakland, California, USA, 28 April 1962), *public health, malariology.*

Educated at the Belmont (CA) School where his father was an instructor, Hackett entered Harvard University at age sixteen and graduated *magna cum laude* in 1905. He returned to teach at Belmont for three years before entering Harvard Medical School. After receiving the MD in 1912, he pursued an additional year of studies in the new joint program in public health and in 1913 was awarded Harvard's first doctorate in that field. For the next year he was an instructor of preventative medicine at Harvard, as well as an assistant in the history of science.

Hackett was hired by the International Health Board (IHB), a Rockefeller philanthropy, in April 1914 and joined its field staff. He was sent to Panama to work in the anti-hookworm campaign, and during the next year carried out work in British Honduras (now Belize) and Guatemala. After demonstrating his administrative ability, Hackett was selected by the IHB to head its work in Brazil, where he arrived in 1916. Joining with the existing sanitarian movement there, Hackett promoted model anti-hookworm projects and later initiated a program of local health units intended to monitor endemic diseases and to provide basic care.

In 1923 the IHB reassigned Hackett to Italy, where the national government had just requested assistance with its antimalaria program: about half of the nation's provinces then reported an incidence of malaria. Hackett established a liaison with Alberto Missiroli, an Italian epidemiologist, and together (on the invitation of the city of Rome) they established the Stazione Sperimentale per la Lotta Anti-malarica [Experimental Station for the Fight against Malaria] and several related laboratories and field stations. They focused on establishing ways to control the disease vector, anopheline mosquitoes, rather than the disease itself, and adopted the widespread use of Paris Green (a double salt of arsenic and copper) as an insecticide. This environmental strategy was a significant shift from Italy's previous ameliorative program of widespread quinine distribution, and drew global attention to Hackett's and Missiroli's project. A global array of public health officials and epidemiologists collaborated in their work or observed it during their nine years of collaboration (1925–34) and were influenced to attempt similar environmental disease controls. Hackett summarized his experience and views in the Heath Clark lectures at the University of London in 1934, which were published as *Malaria in Europe* (1937). This volume effectively served as a textbook for a generation of malaria researchers.

After the new Istituto di Sanita Pubblica in Rome absorbed the Stazione Sperimentale in 1934, Hackett turned his attentions to malaria projects in the Balkans and other areas of the eastern Mediterranean, particularly Albania. In 1940 the Rockefeller Foundation (into which the IHB had merged in 1928) reassigned him to Buenos Aires to oversee public health projects in that region. World War II and the rise of the Peron government limited his accomplishments there.

Hackett retired from the Rockefeller Foundation in 1949. He served on the malaria expert committee of the World Health Organization from 1948. He subsequently served as editor of the *American Journal of Tropical Medicine and Hygiene*, 1951–57; as a visiting professor at the University of California, 1950–57; and as a lecturer at the Harvard School of Public Health, 1950–56. His accomplishments were recognized by the awarding of the Walter Reed Medal (Society of Tropical Medicine and Hygiene) in 1953 and the Bernard Nocht Medal (Hamburg Institut für Schiffs und Tropenkrankheiten) in 1957. He married Hazel Woods in 1912, and had two sons.

Bibliography

Primary: 1921. 'Personal Glimpses.' *Bulletin of the International Health Board* 2: 53–60.

Secondary: Farley, John, 2004. *To Cast Out Disease: A History of the International Health Division of the Rockefeller Foundation (1913–1951)* (Oxford); Stapleton, Darwin H., 1994. 'A Success for Science or Technology? The Rockefeller Foundation's Role in Malaria Eradication in Italy, 1924–1935.' *Medicina nei Secoli* 6: 213–228; 1962. 'Dr. Lewis Hackett, Medical Researcher.' *New York Times,* 30 April, p. 27.

Darwin H. Stapleton

ḤADDĀD, SĀMĪ IBRĀHĪM   (b. Jaffa, Ottoman Empire [now Tel Aviv–Yafo, Israel], 1890; d. Beirut, Lebanon, 5 February 1957), *medicine, history of medicine.*

Ḥaddād was born into an eminent Christian Palestinian family, which included, among other intellectuals, professionals, and merchants, the distinguished prelate and Patriarch of the Greek Orthodox Church of Antioch, Gregory Ḥaddād (1858–1928). A passionate book lover, the Patriarch was a model for Ḥaddād, who was able to remove a cataract for his mentor in 1928. Ḥaddād received secondary education in Jerusalem and in 1909 proceeded to advanced medical studies in Beirut at the Syrian Protestant College, which had established its teaching hospital only four years earlier.

After receiving his MD (1913), he occupied important posts in the Lebanese medical administration for several years, successfully combining this work with his medical practice and teaching. In 1920 he joined the Department of Surgery at the Syrian Protestant College (later the American University of Beirut). The recipient of numerous scholarly awards and fellowships, he traveled widely abroad. Though well-known as a cautious surgeon, skeptical of unproven novelty, he introduced to Lebanon—the medical center of the Middle East from the 1930s to the 1960s—newly developed methods of diagnosis and treatment, such as the cystoscope and the pyelogram.

Like many other leading Arabic personalities of his time, Ḥaddād was actively involved in the political ferment and the current of cultural revival that continued from late Ottoman times into the colonial period. He acted as physician and interpreter for the King-Crane Commission and, from 1920 until his death, played a significant role in decision-making at the American University of Beirut. In his spare time, he wrote extensively on the history of Arabic medicine and Middle Eastern hospitals and collected widely. His tastes were catholic and besides books, especially manuscripts, also included Roman surgical instruments, Phoenician and Roman glass, ancient pottery, precious stones, gems, stamps, watches, and coins. His manuscript collection comprised three hundred and thirty-five codices and included texts in Arabic, Persian, Turkish, Syriac, Armenian, and Hebrew. Medicine had a special place in Ḥaddād's collection, which included one hundred and twenty manuscripts on various aspects of Arabic medicine. In the preface to the Arabic catalog of Ḥaddād's collection, his son and cataloger Farid Ḥaddād wrote that his father took great care of his manuscripts. He ordered bindings to be made for manuscripts that had lost their previous bindings and a walnut cabinet with beautiful carvings in which to house them. He further mentions that the walnut cabinet was stolen in 1976 during the Lebanese civil war, when the Orient Hospital was practically destroyed. Eighty-seven manuscripts from his collection are now housed in the Wellcome Library for the History and Understanding of Medicine in London.

Bibliography

Primary: 1937. (with Keusséoglou, Anghélos) 'Un chapître oublié sur la circulation pulmonaire' in *Hippocrate. Revue d'humanisme medical* 5: 137–142.

Secondary: Serikoff, Nikolaj I., 2005. *Medical Arabic Manuscripts of the Wellcome Library. A Descriptive Catalogue of the Haddad Collection* (Leiden) pp. 9–10; Ḥaddād, F. S., 2001. *A First Class Man in Every Particular: Dr. Sāmī I Ḥaddād(1890–1957)* (Paradise Valley, AZ) (Contains a list of his works); Conrad, L. I., 1987. 'The *Sāmī Ḥaddād* Collection of Arabic Medical Manuscripts.' *Medical History* 31: 354–357.

Nikolaj Serikoff

HAFFKINE, WALDEMAR MORDECAI WOLFF   (b. Odessa, Russia, 15 March (27 March) 1860; d. Lausanne, Switzerland, 20 October 1930), *bacteriology, epidemiology.*

Haffkine was born as Vladimir (Mordechai Wolff) Aaronovich Khavkin to a Jewish family of limited means. He matriculated at the gymnasium in nearby Berdiansk, graduating in 1879, and then enrolled in the department of natural sciences at the Malorossiiskii University at Odessa. There he came under the influence of Elie Mechnikov, the microbiologist and future Nobel Prize winner.

After completing his studies in 1883, Haffkine joined the staff of the Zoological Museum in Odessa. He would be unable to advance beyond this position in Odessa. Despite his early scientific accomplishments Haffkine was denied a teaching position because he refused to be baptized. He was arrested three times by the Russian authorities for his political activities and finally left for Switzerland in 1888, where he worked at the medical school in Geneva. In 1889 Haffkine started working at the Pasteur Institute in Paris, where Mechnikov had already settled.

In 1892, when a cholera epidemic appeared in Europe, Haffkine began to work on producing a cholera inoculation. Seven years earlier Jaime Ferrán y Clúa from Spain had tried to make the same vaccine, but failed to find an effective dose. Haffkine proposed a method different from Ferrán's: he produced an attenuated form of the bacterium by exposing it to blasts of hot air. He tested the vaccine on himself and on Russian volunteers who were political emigrants. The results were encouraging, and so Haffkine proposed that within six days after the second inoculation the recipient was immune to cholera.

Lord Dufferin, the ambassador of Great Britain to France, suggested Haffkine try his vaccine in British India. From that time onward, Haffkine was deeply involved with this country. After initial criticism by the local medical bodies, his prophylactic inoculation became widely accepted and was applied during the Indian cholera epidemic of 1893. In 1896, when a bubonic plague epidemic overtook Bombay, Haffkine succeeded in developing a vaccine using dead bacteria ('Haffkine lymph'). The practical results were amazing: inoculated people fell ill seven times less than those who had not been inoculated, and died at a rate of only 10 percent of the former level.

Haffkine's achievements were highly appreciated in Great Britain. Lord Lister, President of the Royal Society, saluted him as a 'Savior of Humanity', and Queen Victoria made him a Companion of the Indian Empire. Haffkine was appointed a state bacteriologist of the Indian Government and the head of the Plague Laboratory, which became the main research center for infectious diseases in British India. In 1925 it was renamed the 'Haffkine Institute'.

However, Haffkine also had a lot of problems. From time to time he was called a Russian spy, and the medical community was also not very sympathetic toward him. In 1902 the bubonic plague vaccine apparently caused nineteen cases of tetanus. An inquiry commission indicted Haffkine, who was relieved of the position of director of the Plague Laboratory. A review of this commission's report by the Lister Institute in England overturned the decision, putting the blame on the doctor who administered the injections, and exonerated Haffkine. Because his Bombay position had by then been reoccupied, Haffkine moved to Calcutta, where he worked until his retirement in 1914.

Haffkine was elected an honorary member of many of the scientific societies and academies of Europe and Asia. His last

Cholera vaccination of the Third Gurkhas in India at the time of the 1893 epidemic. Reproduction of a wood engraving, 1894. Iconographic Collection, Wellcome Library, London.

years were devoted to setting aside much of his amassed wealth to foster Jewish education in Eastern Europe. The Haffkine Foundation, created in 1929 in Lausanne, was the last endowment of this great philanthropist to humanity.

Bibliography

Primary: 1899. *A discourse on preventive inoculation, delivered at the Royal Society, London, on June 8, 1899* (London); 1908. *On the present methods of combating the plague* (London); 1909. *La vaccination contre le cholera, la peste bubonique et la fièvre typhoïde et les expériences de bactériothérapie* (Calcutta); 1914. *On prophylactic inoculation against plague and pneumonia* (Calcutta).

Secondary: 1974. *Haffkine Institute Platinum Jubilee Commemoration Volume, 1899–1974* (Bombay); Waksman, Selman A., 1964. *The Brilliant and Tragic Life of W. M. W. Haffkine, Bacteriologist* (New Brunswick, NJ); Popovsky, M. 1963. *Sud'ba doktora Khavkina* [Doctor Khavkin's Fate] (Moscow); *DSB*; *Oxford DNB*.

Marina Sorokina

HAGEDORN, HANS CHRISTIAN (b. Copenhagen, Denmark, 6 March 1888; d. Copenhagen, 14 January 1971), *endocrinology, diabetes.*

Hagedorn's parents, the sea captain Jeppe Thomsen Hagedorn and his wife Karen Marie (née Barfred), were closely connected with the Danish folk high school. They were part owners of a freighter operated by the folk high school, and Hagedorn spent most of his childhood at sea. He studied medicine at the University of Copenhagen (1906–12), and upon graduation assisted at the physiological laboratory of the university (1912–13). He then left Copenhagen for a position as resident at Herning Centralsygehus, in the western part of Denmark, before taking up private practice in the nearby provincial town of Brande. There he married the dentist Marie Stavnstrup and started focusing his scientific interest on diabetes. Along with the pharmacist Birger Norman Jensen, Hagedorn developed a technically refined micro method for determining blood sugar levels, the Hagedorn-Jensen method, which won international acceptance. In 1919 Hagedorn returned to Copenhagen to continue his research, first at Rigshospitalet (1919–20), and later as resident at Kommunehospitalet (1920–24). He defended his thesis on blood sugar regulation in humans in 1921, establishing himself as a leading figure in Danish diabetes research and treatment.

Hagedorn established a private practice for metabolic diseases, and one of his first patients was the wife of Nobel laureate August Krogh, Marie, who suffered from diabetes. In 1922 August Krogh received license to produce insulin in Scandinavia, and he immediately invited Hagedorn to take part in this enterprise. Hagedorn accepted, and turned his family home north of Copenhagen into an insulin factory. In 1924 Krogh and Hagedorn joined with the pharmacist August Kongsted of Løvens Kemiske Fabrik (now Leo Pharma) and founded the Nordic Insulin Laboratory. Demand for insulin grew quickly, and Hagedorn devoted himself completely to optimizing its production and studying its clinical effects on diabetics. By the early 1930s, Hagedorn was responsible for 40 percent of the global production of insulin standard preparations. Profits were used to construct a private hospital, Niels Steensen Hospital, which opened in 1933 and set new architectural and technical standards, including an innovative design for hospital beds. Diabetics from the Nordic countries were treated without charge, and the hospital offered Hagedorn an opportunity to test new products.

From his earliest involvement with insulin, Hagedorn was concerned with the question of how to slow down and extend its effect. In 1932 he and Norman Jensen began experiments to combine insulin with protamine in order to protract absorption. Production and marketing of protamine insulin began in early 1936 and became an instant international success, earning Hagedorn widespread recognition as a leading figure in the field of diabetes. The protracted effect meant that diabetics could reduce their number of insulin injections, and the product marked the onset of a new era in insulin treatment.

The Nordic Insulin Laboratory expanded greatly in the 1930s, and Hagedorn fought to maintain a privileged position for the company in the face of competitors in the lucrative insulin market. He thus represented an unusual linkage between medical science and private industry, and was a controversial figure in Denmark, engaging in public discussions on patent laws and doctors' rights. After World War II Hagedorn had the huge task of rebuilding the company's international activities. Also, competition on the global insulin market greatly increased in the postwar years, coming mainly from Novo, a Danish insulin company established in 1925 by two of Hagedorn's earliest employees. The Nordic Insulin Laboratory went into decline while Novo grew to a dominant position internationally, and in 1989 Novo incorporated its Danish competitor, forming Novo Nordisk.

During the postwar years, Hagedorn withdrew from research and concentrated on the overall structuring of the company. Starting in the mid-1950s, he suffered from diabetes and was increasingly incapacitated by Parkinson's disease, and left his post as director of the Nordic Insulin Laboratory in 1963. In 1966 he was admitted to Niels Steensen Hospital, where he died five years later.

Bibliography

Primary: 1918. (with Norman Jensen, B.) 'Om kvantitativ Bestemmelse af minimale Glucosemængder, særlig i Blod.' *Ugeskrift for Læger* 80: 1217–1228; 1921. *Undersøgelser vedrørende Blodsukkerregulationen hos Mennesket* (Copenhagen).

Secondary: Deckert, Torsten, 2000. *H. C. Hagedorn and Danish Insulin* (Herning); Poulsen, Jacob E., 1978. 'Hans Christian Hagedorn. Læge—Videnskabsmand—Chef for Nordisk Insulinlaboratorium' in *Dansk medicinhistorisk årbog* pp. 9–45.

Søren Bak-Jensen

HAHNEMANN, SAMUEL (b. Meissen, Germany, 10 April 1755; d. Paris, France, 2 July 1843), *medicine, homeopathy.*

Hahnemann was the third child of Christian Friedrich Hahnemann, a porcelain painter, and Johanna Christiana, née Spiessen. His exact date of birth remains uncertain. The entry in the church register in the Frauenkirche in Meissen states that he was born on 11 April; however, Hahnemann himself always gave and celebrated 10 April as his birthday. Hahnemann's childhood was overshadowed by the economic aftermath of the Seven Years' War. His father, who worked as an artist in the local porcelain factory, had difficulties making ends meet due to a decline in production. Because of this, Samuel Hahnemann was taken away more than once from the town school and was forced to help contribute to the family income. While Hahnemann was a pupil at the grammar school in Meissen, the famous Prince School St Afra, he had to earn his living by coaching and teaching fellow students. Already as a schoolboy he showed unusual diligence and an exceptional talent for languages.

Medical Studies and Wayfaring Life

Hahnemann left school in 1775. Twenty years old and with only twenty *thalers* in his pocket, he enrolled at the University of Leipzig in order to study medicine. Very soon he found out that Leipzig was not the right place for training in practical medical science. He continued his medical education in Vienna, where he studied with Joseph Quarin, who was the personal physician to Empress Maria Theresa and afterward also to Emperor Joseph II. After nine months, Hahnemann had no money left and had to find a remunerative occupation. With the help of Quarin he became the family physician of Samuel of Brukenthal, the governor of Transylvania. Hahnemann moved to Hermannstadt, where he spent most of his time cataloging his patron's extensive library and valuable collection of coins, and hardly practiced medicine. He became a member of the local Freemason's Lodge. For the rest of his life he remained loyal to the Order, signing letters to fellow freemasons with the abbreviation 'Br.' (Brother). Less than two years later, Hahnemann left Hermannstadt in order to finish his medical studies. He went to Erlangen, where on 10 August 1779 he received a doctoral degree for his medical dissertation on 'Conspectus adfectuum spasmodicorum aetiologicus et therapeuticus' [A View of the Causes and Treatment of Cramp]. Homeopaths all over the world to this day celebrate this occasion, just as Hahnemann did during his own lifetime, underlining how important this formal recognition by the scientific community was to the founder of homeopathy and continues to be to his followers.

During the years from 1779 to 1805 Hahnemann moved twenty times. Among the many places where he stayed for short periods were a few bigger cities, such as Dessau (1781–82), Dresden (1785–88/89), and Hamburg (1800). In general, he preferred smaller towns (e.g., Gommern, Georgenthal, and Eilenburg), mainly because it was cheaper to live in them, and also because he thought it was easier to make a living as town physician in a smaller place. Only recently has it become known that in Gommern, where he stayed from 1783 to 1785, Hahnemann was obliged to write yet another dissertation in order to obtain the license allowing him to practice as a town physician. This second thesis, still unpublished, deals with obstetrical and forensic aspects of cutting the umbilical cord.

At that time Hahnemann was already married to Johanna Leopoldine Henriette Küchler (1764–1830), the daughter of an apothecary in Dessau, who would eventually gave birth to eleven children, two of whom died as infants. It soon proved difficult for Hahnemann to earn a good or even a moderate income from medical practice, and he broadened his activities, working also as an author and translator. This occupation proved to be more satisfactory than private practice in Hahnemann's wayward years. During the years from 1785 to 1789 he published more than 2,000 printed pages, including translations, original works on medical subjects, and essays. Due to his reputation as a writer on various medical and scientific subjects, Hahnemann was elected an honorary member by various distinguished societies, including the Academy of Science in Mayence in 1791.

Pioneering in Homeopathy and Psychiatry

While translating into German William Cullen's *Lectures on the materia medica* (published in English in 1772), Hahnemann developed a new method of healing. Disagreeing with Cullen's views on the medicinal effects of Peruvian bark, he made experiments on himself and discovered that Peruvian bark produced in him the symptoms of intermittent fever, with which he was familiar through a bout of malaria he had suffered in Transylvania. As this exotic plant had been used as an antipyretic remedy since the seventeenth century, Hahnemann deduced that 'substances which produce a form of fever resolve the types of intermittent fever'. Opponents of homeopathy still maintain that Hahnemann's strong physical reaction was entirely idiosyncratic and that his experiment cannot serve as evidence for the law of similars, which Hahnemann described at length in an article for Hufeland's medical journal in 1796—the founding year of homeopathy. By that time Hahnemann had recognized the total insufficiency and unreliability of 'heroic medicine', which included bloodletting, intestinal purging (calomel [mercury chloride]), vomiting (tartar emetic), profuse sweating (diaphoretics), and blistering. These medical treatments were well-meant, and widely propagated in the medical community, but they were actually harmful to the patient.

In his early professional career Hahnemann paid special attention to questions of psychiatry and nervous diseases. He developed a method of treatment for the mentally ill that was completely different from the one commonly employed at that time. Like Philippe Pinel in France, Hahnemann introduced humane treatment methods into Germany. His approach, which in modern terms can be labeled 'moral therapy', resulted in success, at least in the case of one patient, a high-ranking government officer by the name of Friedrich Arnold Klockenbring. Despite this successful cure Hahnemann failed to find other well-off patients for his private mental asylum in the castle of Georgenthal, which opened in 1792. After this failure, which was probably due to the rather high fee Hahnemann charged, he did not treat any other mental patients for any significant length of time, with one exception: his treatment of the insane German writer Johann Karl Wezel in Hamburg in 1800, which proved to be a total success, in both medical and economic terms.

Practicing a New Art of Healing

In 1796 Hahnemann published the manifesto of a new art of healing in an article entitled *Essay on a New Principle for ascertaining the curative powers of drugs, and some examinations of the previous principles*. In this seminal text, Hahnemann contrasted the traditional and hitherto almost universally applied axiom of healing, contraria contrariis, by another similarly formulated: similia similibus. In Hahnemann's own words, 'One should apply in the disease to be healed, particularly if chronic, that remedy which is able to stimulate another artificially produced disease, as similar as possible; and the former will be healed—*Similia similibus*—likes with likes.' Later on, in 1807, Hahnemann coined the word 'homeopathic' for his new art of healing, composed of the Greek *homoios* (similar) and *pathos* (disease, suffering). The form of therapy common in his time, based upon the opposing principle of contraria contrariis, he named 'allopathy', from the Greek *alloion* (of a different kind) and *pathos* (disease, suffering)—a term causing much dispute and anger among his fellow-physicians.

It would be wrong to assume that after the discovery and description of his new axiom of curing, Hahnemann completely stopped practicing medicine in the old vein. For a number of years he applied various methods, among them homeopathy. However, he tried to avoid mixtures of medicine, even while experimenting with allopathic means. Only four years after the foundations of the new curative doctrine were laid, Hahnemann's medical practice became more and more homeopathic, as can be seen from his medical casebooks, starting in 1801 and ending in 1843.

It was not for a lack of patients that Hahnemann moved from the little Saxonian town of Machern, where he stayed for a few months in 1801, to Eilenburg, twenty-four km northeast of Leipzig. In the formative years of homeopathy, Hahnemann was continually forced to find a place for his rapidly growing family to live, where the cost of living was not too high. And there can be no doubt that Hahnemann's temperament was also partly responsible for his restless wanderings. More than once he got into trouble with people, not only quarreling with colleagues, apothecaries, and medical officers, but also litigating over lodging against landlords or former owners of houses in which he had lived with his large family. It was not until 1805, when he established himself, after a short stay in Schilda (a small Saxonian town, hitherto not mentioned by his biographers), in Torgau on the river Elbe, that Hahnemann's restless years were interrupted for a considerable span of time (six years). From then on his life took a relatively quieter turn.

Systematic Elaboration of Homeopathic Therapy

In Torgau, Hahnemann continued to test homeopathy on an increasing number of patients who flocked to his medical practice. From 23 April 1806 to 9 September 1807, Hahnemann treated 507 patients, according to the entries in his medical casebook. He experimented with dilutions, though it was not until later that he would try out the high-potency tinctures (e.g., 30C) that have become the hallmark of homeopathy ever since. As early as 1807 he administered little globules or granules, approximately the size of a poppy seed, which were made of pure cane sugar and impregnated with homeopathic drugs.

Despite the increasing workload due to his growing reputation as a successful and unconventional healer, Hahnemann kept up his prolific activity as a writer. In 1806 he completed a translation of Albrecht von Haller's materia medica of German medicinal plants. His own medical writings of the Torgau period were concerned partly with defending himself against hostile attacks from colleagues on his tract on curing scarlet fever with belladonna, and partly with his agenda for a reform of the whole of medical science. In his treatise *On the Value of Speculative Systems of Medicine* (1808), he argued, 'Not one single founder or follower of any of the medical systems could or . . . would dare to carry out his system strictly and precisely into practice without doing his patients far greater injury than they would have suffered without medical aid.'

During his sojourn in Torgau, Hahnemann also managed to elaborate the theoretical foundations of homeopathy. His small book entitled *Heilkunde der Erfahrung* (1805), together with the first homeopathic materia medica, published under the Latin title *Fragmenta de viribus medicamentorum* (1805), attest that Hahnemann carried on his investigations during these years. In 1810 the first edition of the *Organon of Rational Healing* was published: many consider this to be the 'bible of homeopathy'. In the introduction to his famous book Hahnemann claims that hitherto, 'diseases of man were not healed in a rational way or according to fixed principles, but rather according to varied curative purposes, amongst others, according to the palliative rule: contraria contrariis curentur.' In contrast, his new art of healing based on the law of similars seemed to him to be the only rational therapy. The *Organon*, which was revised five times during Hahnemann's lifetime and has been translated into many languages, starts with the famous first paragraph reminding physicians that the 'doctor's sole object is to make sick men well'. What follows is a meticulous description of what homeopathy is about and how one has to practice it. The sixth edition, which Hahnemann revised shortly before his death, was not released for publication by his widow or by her heirs until the early 1920s. It was then that Hahnemann's biographer Richard Haehl managed to get hold of the manuscript and to publish it. It took another seventy years before the first critical edition of this much-debated work was finally published.

It is very likely that Hahnemann took the title for his magnum opus from the writings of two luminaries of science, Aristotle and Francis Bacon. The first is the author of a work entitled *Organon*, a compendium of his treatises on logic, and the second is the author of *Novum Organum*, a book outlining a better mode of investigating the truth. Despite the strong criticism that met the first edition of Hahnemann's *Organon*, this provocative guidebook to homeopathy became a classic, read and studied by his followers and patients alike. One of the few positive reviews by non-homeopathic physicians during Hahnemann's lifetime recognized at least one favorable aspect of the approach it described: the author's experiments with medicinal substances on healthy subjects.

Hahnemann at the University

In 1811, as the city of Torgau was preparing itself for a siege by the French army, Hahnemann moved to Leipzig. That this big city had a university seemed to him to be an advantage. However, before trying to become a member of the medical faculty there, with the right to teach students, he had opened a private medical institute where he meant to train graduated physicians in the art of homeopathy. The project failed due to a lack of students. He therefore decided to write yet another dissertation, hoping this would qualify him for teaching at the university level. The thesis, written in

Latin, was entitled *Dissertatio historico-medica de Helleborismo veterum*. Hahnemann sought to prove that the drug called hellebore by ancient medical authorities was actually *Veratrum album*. In 1812 he gave his first lecture at the university, reading paragraphs from the *Organon*. 'Unfortunately', as one of his first students recalled later, 'the lectures were not fitted to win friends and followers for his theories or himself.' Despite his failure as a teacher, he managed to gather a small group of young enthusiasts, with whom he undertook tests with various drugs. These early tests were of the greatest significance for the homeopathic science in general and the materia medica in particular.

Hahnemann's time was not completely taken up with lecturing and writing on homeopathy. He also had a prosperous medical practice and a growing reputation. His many successful cures had made him famous. Among his many patients were the wife of the chief justice of Leipzig, a prominent professor of philosophy at the local university, and, the most well-known of them all, Prince Karl Philipp of Schwarzenberg, an Austrian general who had won the battle of Leipzig in 1813. Unfortunately, the founder of homeopathy was not able to cure the latter. The field marshal died while being treated by Hahnemann. Shortly afterward Hahnemann left Leipzig, but not for the commonly supposed reason that the local apothecaries had driven him away because they resented his insistence on preparing homeopathic drugs himself. Rather, the medicinal laws of Saxony allowed only apothecaries to prepare medicines and to distribute them to patients. Conditions in Leipzig had become more and more unfavorable to Hahnemann's medical practice. He once more resolved this problem by migrating to another place.

During his stay in Leipzig, Hahnemann managed to finish another major work despite his heavy workload as medical practitioner: the *Materia medica pura*, appearing in six parts from 1811 to 1821. This multivolume work contains 'provings' by Samuel Hahnemann and his original 'provers' union' in their own words and records the various ways in which they prepared their medicines. It also contains an essay by Hahnemann on the central attributes of each medicine and its specific peculiarities.

Also, the year 1819 witnessed the publication of the second edition of the *Organon*. In this edition Hahnemann reviewed the advances made in homeopathy in the late 1810s. He made public his experience with the use of potencies such as 12C, 15C, and 18C. He also continued to dilute the remedies in water, as he found the liquid solution to be a more suitable medium for homeopathic remedies. It was easier when using a solution to adjust the original potency of the dosage to fit the judgment of the therapist and the constitution of the patient.

Physician-in-Ordinary to the Duke of Köthen

In 1821 Hahnemann left Leipzig and moved to Köthen, where the duke had granted him not only permission to settle but also the right to dispense his own remedies—a privilege he greatly cherished. He continued to work on another major publication entitled *Chronic Diseases*. Dissatisfied with the usual methods for the treatment of chronic diseases, he had started looking for a way to overcome their limitations. Hahnemann claimed that all chronic diseases (e.g., sycosis, syphilis, psora) have as their origin chronic miasms. His conception of these diseases, and in particular his psora theory, soon aroused the criticism of his foes and his followers alike. No other book by Hahnemann stirred up more excitement in the medical world.

At about the same time he introduced the method of homeopathic succussions, as he began to 'potentize' the remedies with a quick downward movement of the arm instead of merely shaking his dilutions. Each one of these downward jerks was called 'one succussion', and Hahnemann suggested in the second edition of *Materia medica pura* (published in the years from 1822 to 1827) that ten of these more powerful succussions be added for each additional level of dilution. In 1824 Hahnemann integrated his experiences of the previous six years into the third edition of the *Organon*, modifying, for example, the posology of his remedies. He advised against the use of drop doses of homeopathic dilutions and maintained instead that the proper amount was not a drop but 'the smallest part of a drop'. For this purpose he suggested the medication of poppy seed–sized sugar globules with the potentized liquid of the remedy. The use of the pellets made it much easier for the homeopath to control the exact amount of the dosage given to the patient. The gradual increase of the levels of his dilutions was a means of overcoming the toxic side effects caused by the physical doses of tinctures and powders. In treating patients with smaller doses, Hahnemann realized that the medicinal powers of his remedies were growing while the phenomenon of aggravation was increasing with the higher 'dynamization'. In the early 1830s he began experimenting with high potencies, going beyond 30C.

In 1831 the first cholera epidemic reached the eastern borders of the German Empire. The feared disease rapidly spread across all of Europe. At the same time there was much speculation about the origins of cholera. Hahnemann wrote four pamphlets on this disease, recommending camphor as both a curative remedy and a protective. The treatment recommended by Hahnemann proved so successful that even local governments and many physicians began to think differently about homeopathy.

Shortly after the anniversary of Hahnemann's doctorate in 1829, his anger was aroused by followers who did not practice homeopathy according to his rules. In an open letter he denounced the deviant colleagues as 'half homeopaths'. The result was that the 'pure' homeopaths began to attach themselves more closely to Hahnemann. The dispute was formally settled in 1833 but lingered on even after Hahnemann's death in 1843. Hahnemann's first wife died in 1830, aged sixty-six. A few years later he met his second wife, Mélanie d'Hervilly, a young French woman of noble origin who came to Köthen from Paris in order to be treated by the world-famous healer. They married in 1835 and moved to Paris, where Hahnemann spent the last years of his life.

The Evening of Life in Paris

Hahnemann continued to practice homeopathy despite the fact that he was already eighty years old when, together with his second wife, he settled in a posh area of the French capital. In fact, he introduced Mélanie to the art of homeopathy. During the Paris years Hahnemann's patients came from all over Europe, and among the most well-known were the British collector Lord Elgin and the Italian violinist Niccolò Pagani. Shortly before his death in July 1843, Hahnemann finished the sixth and final revision of the *Organon,* which contained details about a new method of dynamization, the fifty millesimal potency, i.e., the fifty-thousandth part of the 3C trituration of a homeopathic drug. Only after the publication of the sixth edition by the German homeopath Richard Haehl in 1920 did this highest range of potency become widely known in homeopathy.

Hahnemann died at the age of eighty-nine and was buried first at the Montmartre cemetery and later reburied. His tomb is now in the cemetery of Père Lachaise, next to those of other luminaries of medicine, the arts, and science. Today members of homeopathic societies and adherents of homeopathy all over the world work to ensure that Hahnemann's intellectual legacy is known, paying tribute to the short phrase the founder of homeopathy had chosen as his own epitaph: Non inutilis vixi [I have not lived in vain].

The Evolution of Homeopathy after Hahnemann

Before Hahnemann published the *Organon* in 1810 and started lecturing at the University of Leipzig in 1812, he had been the sole practitioner of homeopathy. Soon after its publication, he attracted a small group of followers, among them many young students and a few doctors, who assisted him in testing his drugs and then went off to practice the new art of healing. Among them was Johann Ernst Stapf, the founder of the first homeopathic journal (*Archiv für die homöopathische Heilkunst*) in 1822. Almost from the beginning, two distinct factions could be distinguished within the homeopathic camp. There were the 'true' followers of Hahnemann, to whom the teachings of the founder of homeopathy were dear, and those who considered themselves progressive, not willing to refrain completely from using non-homeopathic medicines. Despite this ongoing professional strife, homeopathy continued to flourish in nineteenth-century Germany. In 1900 there were about 550 homeopaths actively practicing in Germany.

A Danish physician, Hans Gram, who settled in New York City, brought homeopathy to America as early as 1824. The regular physicians in the large urban centers who were the first American practitioners to be attracted to homeopathy eventually developed a similar spectrum of divergent views on homeopathic therapeutics. The most prominent dissenter across the Atlantic was Constantine Hering, the founder of the homeopathic medical college in Allentown, Pennsylvania. The main barrier to harmony among Hahnemann's followers in the United States was disputes over the size of the dose to be used in homeopathic prescriptions. The 'high-dilutionists' used doses of drugs in reductions up to the thousandth dilution and more, whereas the 'low dilutionists' did not adhere to Hahnemann's later doctrine of infinitesimal doses. In 1880 the American homeopathic physicians separated into two major groups. A minority of American homeopaths, the 'purists' and high-potency advocates, had grown more dogmatic in reaction to the liberalism of the 'eclectics' and founded the International Hahnemannian Association.

In order to understand the transformation of homeopathy from a small sectarian movement to a professionally oriented alternative to orthodox medicine, one has to look at the growing number of patients (especially from the upper echelons of society) who sanctioned the new therapeutical system by demanding equal rights for homeopathic physicians and putting pressure on government bodies and other licensing agencies. They not only petitioned that homeopathic physicians be allowed to practice, but also demanded from the authorities that these doctors be granted the privilege of dispensing their own homeopathic medicines. Reigning princes, such as Hahnemann's patron, Prince Ferdinand of Anhalt-Köthen, or Queen Adelaide, the German wife of King William IV, were ardent supporters of homeopathy, too. Many of them had their own homeopathic physician-in-ordinary. Furthermore, in government circles it became almost a sign of good taste to be treated by a homeopathic doctor. Among the many influential state officials who made a definite and public stand for homeopathy was the Prussian state councilor Clemens von Bönninghausen, who became Hahnemann's favorite student and one of the leading homeopaths of the nineteenth century. Especially important was the homeopathic treatment undergone by two of the most popular war heroes in early nineteenth-century Austria and Germany, Count Schwarzenberg and Field Marshal von Radetzky. This was highly publicized in the press and thus helped to increase the reputation of the new art of healing, so violently attacked by many allopathic medical practitioners.

Even more importantly, homeopathy had 'zealous defenders in the general public who wished to be cured surely, painlessly, and cheaply', in the words of an allopathic physician. Its really steep rise in popularity, however, came during the 1830s, when Asiatic cholera struck Central Europe. There can be no doubt that this epidemic stimulated the general public's liking for homeopathy, as the news of the surprising results that had been achieved by the homeopathic cholera treatment spread quickly, especially among the upper and educated classes.

A similar phenomenon characterized the spread of homeopathy in the United States from its early beginnings in the

1820s. Unlike Grahamism and other comparable early nineteenth-century medical sects, homeopathy appealed not only to the urban working and lower–middle class population, but very soon also became extremely popular among the wealthy in many communities. One reason was that homeopathy was by that time very fashionable among the European nobility and upper classes, whose extravagant lifestyle was often copied by affluent Americans. Another was that the early American homeopathic physicians manifested an erudition that was rarely found among other alternative healers. Because these doctors were 'persons of the highest respectability and moral worth', as the editor of the *Boston Medical and Surgical Journal* put it, they appealed to a social elite seeking an alternative to regular medicine. By the end of the nineteenth century, the United States had approximately 10,000 homeopaths—about 8 percent of the total number of medical practitioners—and in 1883 the president of the American Institute of Homeopathy could claim that 'it is accurately safe to say that in the aggregate at the lowest calculation fully one-third of the taxable property is held by the people who employ homeopathic treatment'.

The fact that homeopathy is still available to patients under the National Health Service in the United Kingdom is to a great extent due to the strong royal and aristocratic patronage that began in the early decades of the nineteenth century, when Dr Frederick F. H. Quin became physician to Queen Victoria's uncle, Prince Leopold of Saxe-Coburg, who was later to become King of the Belgians. By the second half of the nineteenth century, homeopathy's institutional development was already well advanced in Great Britain. By the 1870s there were homeopathic hospitals not only in London, but also in Bath, Birmingham, Doncaster, Hastings, Manchester, and Southport. The number of homeopathic dispensaries had increased to 112. At about the same time, physicians openly practicing Hahnemann's 'art of healing' numbered 279, many of whom were members of the British Homeopathic Society, founded in 1844.

At the beginning of the twenty-first century homeopathy is still not fully recognized by the medical establishment, but it has millions of adherents all over the world, making it one of the most popular and widespread therapies in the growing field of complementary medicine.

Bibliography

Primary: 1810. (Wheeler, C. E., trans. and ed., *c.* 1913) *Organon of the rational art of healing* (London); 1811–21. (Hempel, Charles Julius, trans. and ed., 1846) *Materia medica pura* 3 vols. (New York); 1828–30. *The chronic diseases: their peculiar nature and their homoeopathic cure*, [trans. Tafel, Louis H., from the 2nd German edn., 1835. (Philadelphia, 1896)].

Secondary: Jütte, Robert, 2005. *Samuel Hahnemann. Begründer der Homöopathie* (Munich); Dinges, Martin, ed., 2002. *Patients in the History of Homoeopathy* (Sheffield); Jütte, Robert, Guenter B. Risse, and John Woodward, eds., 1998. *Culture, Knowledge and Healing. Historical Perspectives of Homoeopathic Medicine in Europe and North America* (Sheffield); Handley, Rima, 1990. *A Homeopathic Love Story. The Story of Samuel and Mélanie Hahnemann* (Berkeley); Haehl, Richard, 1927. *Samuel Hahnemann, His Life and Work* [trans. Wheeler, M. L., and W. H. R. Grundy 2 vols. (London)].

Robert Jütte

Samuel Hahnemann. Line engraving by L. Beyer after J. Schoppe, senior, 1831. Iconographic Collection, Wellcome Library, London.

HAIRE, NORMAN (b. Sydney, Australia, 21 January 1892; d. London, England, 11 September 1952), *gynecology, sexual reform.*

Haire was educated at Fort Street School, and graduated MB ChM at the University of Sydney. He developed his interest in gynecology and sexuality as a resident at Sydney Hospital and the Royal Women's Hospital. In 1919 he was dismissed as senior medical officer at Newcastle Hospital in New South Wales for his management of the influenza epidemic, though he seems to have been a scapegoat. He moved to London that year, changing his name onboard ship from Zions (the anglicized form of the Polish homophone for 'hare', zajc, chosen by his Polish father) to Haire. This name change disassociated him from the debacle at Newcastle Hospital, concealed his Jewish heritage, recalled the original meaning of his name, and may have reflected Haire's lifelong desire for a stage name—medical training had thwarted his ambition to become an actor.

After initially working as a house surgeon at Hampstead General Hospital, Haire quickly set up his own Harley Street practice. As an outsider (Australian, Jewish, homosexual, tee-totaler, overweight, interested in sex and birth control), Haire was atypical of the leading English medical practitioners, yet he ultimately had an appreciable impact on the development of sexual medicine and sexual reform in England.

Haire swiftly established himself as a sexologist, having read Havelock Ellis's *Studies in the Psychology of Sex* at the age of eighteen. He attended the British Society for the Study of Sex Psychology and wrote to Ellis, who introduced him to Magnus Hirschfeld in Berlin, a city he regarded as his 'spiritual home'. Through Hirschfeld, Haire became involved in the World League for Sexual Reform and was elected president of the English branch in 1930. He co-organized (with Dora Russell) the London Congress in 1929, and attended meetings in Berlin (1921), Copenhagen (1928), Vienna (1930), and Brno (1932); he was also a sometime resident at Hirschfeld's Berlin Institute for Sexology. Haire was famed for advocacy of a barrier method of contraception for women (the 'Haire cap'), and was a subscriber to the 'rejuvenation' methods of Eugene Steinach—the applications of which included an operation on the poet W. B. Yeats.

In the 1940s Haire returned to Australia, where his promotion of sexual matters in lectures and on the radio won him few friends. Matters were made worse when he contributed to the Australian popular press under the pseudonym 'Dr Wykeham Terris', giving liberal advice on birth control and sexual pleasure. He was surveilled by the Australian security services, vilified by the Catholic Church, and denounced in Parliament as a countercultural force. In his public engagements he tried to change puritanical attitudes toward sexuality, and he campaigned for proper birth control and an end to illegal and unprofessional abortions. Haire's most important contributions to medicine arose from his organizing powers. He toiled to bring contemporary sexual knowledge from the Continent to Britain and to Australia, through the organization of conferences and the translation of texts. Many of Magnus Hirschfeld's works were not available in English, except through précis made by Haire. He also founded, edited, and financed the *Journal of Sex Education*, which ceased publication after his death in 1952.

Bibliography

Primary: 1938. (ed.) *The Encyclopaedia of Sex Practice.* (London); 1938. (ed.) *Sexual Anomalies and Perversion: A Summary of the Works of the Late Magnus Hirschfeld.* (London).

Secondary: Wyndham, Diana, 2003. 'Versemaking and Lovemaking—W. B. Yeats' "Strange Second Puberty": Norman Haire and the Steinach Rejuvenation Operation.' *Journal of History of the Behavioral Sciences* 39: 25–50; Crozier, Ivan, 2003. '"All the World's a Stage": Dora Russell, Norman Haire, and the London Congress of the World League for Sexual Reform, 1929.' *Journal for the History of Sexuality* 12: 16–37; Crozier, Ivan, 2001. 'Becoming a Sexologist: Norman Haire, the 1929 London World League for Sexual Reform Congress, and Organising Medical Knowledge about Sex in Interwar England.' *History of Science* 39: 299–329; Wyndham, Diana, 2000. 'Misdiagnosis and Miscarriage of Justice? Dr Norman Haire and the 1919 Influenza Epidemic at Newcastle Hospital.' *Health and History* 2: 3–26.

Ivan Crozier

HALFORD, GEORGE BRITTON (b. Petworth, Sussex, England, 26 November 1824; d. Inverloch, Victoria, Australia, 27 May 1910), *anatomy, physiology, medical education.*

Halford, the son of Nancy Gadd and her husband James Halford, a merchant, studied medicine and surgery at St George's Hospital in London, qualifying MRCS 1852, LSA 1854, and MD (St Andrews) 1854. From 1852 to 1857 he held various appointments at Westminster Hospital, Liverpool Royal Infirmary and Lunatic Asylum (1856), Bridgnorth Infirmary, and the Royal Hospital for Diseases of the Chest, London (1857).

In October 1857 he commenced his life's career in medical research and medical education as Lecturer in Anatomy at the St George's Hospital Medical School. He was a dedicated comparative anatomist and was particularly interested in the relationship between the structure of the heart and blood flow on the one hand, and the sounds that emanated from the heart on the other, comparing these features in different species, including the ostrich, kiwi, python, elephant, eagle, and antelope. In 1860 he published *The Action and Sounds of the Heart; a Physiological Essay*, which established his reputation as a medical scientist.

In 1862 Halford applied for the combined chair of anatomy, physiology, and pathology at the new University of Melbourne Medical School, Australia's first school of medicine. Professor James Paget subsequently described Halford as 'one of the most distinguished experimental physiologists of the day'; and with this and other endorsements, particularly that from Sir Richard Owen of the British Museum, he was appointed to the position. Halford arrived in Melbourne on 22 December 1862 to begin a life of leadership in education, of service, and of controversy.

In his university life, Halford was embroiled in many academic battles. He insisted on the highest standards, both for matriculation and for curriculum content. He insisted, against much opposition, on physics being taught in the first year of the medical course. He fought, many decades before his time, for the admission of women. He was appointed foundation dean of the Faculty of Medicine in 1876, serving in that capacity from

1876–86 and again from 1890–96. He was an inspirational medical teacher.

He was a conservative personality, and Halford's medical research in Melbourne was naïve. He rejected Charles Darwin's paradigm of evolution. His scientific reputation was permanently damaged by his espousal of the intravenous injection of ammonia as a universal antidote for snakebite. His 'ammonia cure' enjoyed a brief public popularity, and for many years Halford insisted in a most subjective way that his observations of the microscopic appearance of the blood of experimentally envenomed animals proved his thesis. He finally retracted after a damning condemnation of his work by the editor of *Lancet* (1871): 'Professor Halford . . . urges on his medical brethren the duty of injecting into the veins of victims to snake bite even larger doses of liquid ammonia than he has hitherto prescribed. We adhere, however, to our opinion that Professor Halford's induction is not so scientifically complete as to warrant implicit confidence in this practice . . .' In 1864, two years after his arrival in Melbourne, he became embroiled in a matter of public outrage relating to the anatomical dissection of the corpse of an executed prisoner, Harrison, who was an insane murderer. Halford's behavior in this unsavory episode was impeccable, but mysterious rumors and untrue reporting in the public press spilled over into the professional columns of *Lancet*. An unfortunate article entitled 'Antipodal Polemics' (29 October 1864) besmirched his reputation, an injury that subsequent letters to *Lancet* never entirely erased. Although appointed (1882) to the Chair of Physiology and Anatomy at Melbourne University for life, Halford applied for extended leave at the age of seventy-two, and retired to Inverloch in southern Victoria. He lived in relatively impoverished circumstances and remained virtually forgotten until his death fourteen years later. There was no obituary, but his name has been commemorated since 1928 in the Halford Orations and in the fine genus of Australian tropical trees, *Halfordia*.

Bibliography

Secondary: Russell, K. F., 1977. *The Melbourne Medical School, 1862–1962* (Melbourne).

John Pearn

HALLER, ALBRECHT VON

HALLER, ALBRECHT VON (b. Bern, Switzerland, 16 October 1708; d. Bern, Switzerland, 12 December 1777), *medicine, physiology, botany, poetry.*

Haller was the fifth and youngest child of Niklaus Emanuel Haller, a jurist, and Anna Maria Engel. He studied medicine in Tübingen and especially in Leiden with Herman Boerhaave and Bernard Siegfried Albinus. After graduation in 1727, he visited England briefly and completed his anatomical and surgical studies in Paris. From 1729 to 1736 he worked as a physician in Bern and published some first, minor works in anatomy and botany. He achieved his first fame, however, with his *Versuch Schweizerischer Gedichte* [Essay of Swiss Poems] (1732), which served as the model for descriptive and philosophical poetry for the next generation and made Haller the most highly esteemed German poet of the 1730s and 1740s.

In 1736 he was called as professor of anatomy, botany, and surgery to the newly established University of Göttingen, where he stayed until 1753. In this period of intense scientific activity, he developed his main areas of research and laid the foundations of later works. In 1742 he published a massive flora of Switzerland and was soon acknowledged as one of the leading botanists and as the most important opponent of Linnean nomenclature. As an anatomist, he focused on the vascular system and set the new standard in this particular branch with his *Icones anatomicae* (eight parts, 1743–56). Haller's main interest, however, was physiology. His first major work was an annotated edition of Boerhaave's lectures on physiology (7 vols., 1739–44). In 1747 he published his own, short textbook of physiology, which ran through four original editions and was presumably the most widely used of all his scientific works. In recognition of his scientific contributions, Haller was ennobled by the emperor in 1749. More importantly, his standing was confirmed by his membership in the main European academies. In 1751 he was elected perpetual president of the newly founded Royal Academy of Sciences of Göttingen (Göttingen was at the time part of the Hanoverian empire). Haller was also busy as chief editor (1747–53) of the *Göttingische gelehrte Anzeigen*, the leading German review journal, for which he penned some 9,000 reviews in the years 1747–77.

Setting his hopes on a political career and aiming to secure the social and economic position of his family in Bernese patrician society, Haller returned to his hometown in 1753. He was never, however, elected to the Small Council (*Kleiner Rat*), the seat of political power. After some years in a modest position in Bern (*Rathausammann*), he was elected director of the salt mines in Roche, in the French part of the Bernese territories, where he could implement some of the agricultural reforms he promoted. In 1764 he returned to Bern and continued to work in various Bernese municipal bodies, such as the Economic Committee and the Medical Council. Haller's return to Switzerland was not a farewell to the Republic of Letters. He continued to maintain his vast correspondence, of which 3,700 letters to and 13,300 from 1,200 persons have survived. And he did not relent in his scientific activity. He proceeded with his embryological investigations, already started in Göttingen, and published his major works on the development of the chicken embryo in 1758 and 1767. His magnum opus, the *Elementa physiologiae*, appeared in eight volumes over a period of ten years (1757–66). Haller presented his views on anatomy and physiology to the wider public in Switzerland and in the supplements to the Paris *Encylopédie* (1772–77), for which he wrote some 200 articles. A second, considerably revised and enlarged edition of his volume on Swiss flora was published in 1768. Remote from major centers of academia, he continued to build up his large library, with eventually more than 23,000 titles, mostly belonging to the medical, botanical, and natural sciences. Haller devoted the last decade of his life to the editing of evaluative bibliographies of botany, anatomy, physiology, surgery, and the practice of medicine. In ten volumes, he presented and discussed some 50,000 works from all branches of medicine. Besides that, he wrote three novels on the principles of government, as well as religious works against the French freethinkers, notably Voltaire.

Physiology

Haller's main area of research was physiology, and it was his aim to base the subject on a more solid experimental foundation. Physiology, in his view, was animated anatomy ('anatomia animata'). With this expression he stressed the intimate correlation between structure and function, but he equally emphasized that the living body was animated and much more than a simple machine. Physiology could not, therefore, be a mere theoretical explanation of anatomical facts. It was the living, not only the dead, body that had to be studied. Haller intended to carry out animal experiments in all areas of physiology, but he did so only in selected subjects, partly due to his early leave from the university. These subjects were well defined, as it was his conviction that only the continuous performance of specialized research, and not the elaboration of great theories, would add to the advancement of science. In this ongoing process the use of hypotheses linking various fragments of knowledge was allowed as long as the hypotheses were clearly marked as such. It is the vast collection of facts and results combined with a cautious use of hypotheses that is characteristic of Haller's works, and notably of the *Elementa* (1757–66). This magisterial and extensive exposition of physiology served as a standard reference book into the early nineteenth century.

In his research, Haller focused on the questions of respiration, microcirculation of the blood, and various aspects of generation. His support for preformism was partly responsible for the predominance at the time of this model over an epigenetic explanation. Haller's most influential contribution was, however, his treatise *De partibus corporis humani sensibus et irritabilibus* (1753), in which he described and separated two fundamental bodily qualities: irritability, as the muscle's inherent ability to contract upon irritation, and sensibility, as the faculty of perception particular to nerves and the brain. He thus claimed the existence of a muscular power independent of the brain and the soul. Haller's new concept was based on a large number of animal experiments and presented a serious challenge to the reigning medical systems of mechanism and animism, as well as to the emerging vitalist theories. The experiments were repeated all over Europe, on a scale like never before. The results, however, were contradictory. Haller's concept was largely rejected, and animal experimentation could not be established as a major research method in physiology. Although Haller's description of an innate bodily faculty had a great impact on the evolution of physiological thought and fostered the development of vitalist

Haller (standing left) upholding a medical thesis. Engraving by Charles Domenique Joseph Eisen after P. F. Tardieu. Frontispiece to *Disputationes chirurgicae selectae . . .* Vol 1, Venice, 1755. Rare Books, Wellcome Library, London.

theories, only a few adopted his definition of the two qualities. The majority regarded irritability as a purely mechanical phenomenon or as a vital faculty extended beyond the muscular fibers, and conceived sensibility as an unconscious activity on a local or central nervous level. As a result, most subsequent authors did not consider the muscular and the nervous system to be entirely independent territories.

The Practice of Medicine

Besides physiology, Haller was busy in the areas of anatomy, botany, and poetry and criticism, and it is mainly in these branches that he was known and important. He contributed, however, also to the domain of medical practice. Haller regretted the fact that many and—as he believed— most of the important medical publications were inaccessible or unknown to the majority of physicians. He therefore collected and edited 436 significant dissertations on surgery (5 vols., 1755–56) and on the practice of medicine (1757–60). He also published bibliographies of surgery (2 vols., 1774–75) and of medical practice (1776–88) in which he recorded and to a large part commented on the whole literature from the earliest times to the present. In addition, Haller edited Boerhaave's medical consultations (1744, 1752) and lectures on eye diseases (1746, 1748). He also published various smaller works on clinical medicine, including a description of a small-pox epidemic (1736, 1755), a collection of pathological observations (1755, 1768), and a report on the effects of opium based on his own experience (1777).

More important, though, was Haller's concept of irritability and sensibility. He announced it as 'the source of a great many changes, both in physiology, pathology and surgery'. But he never explained what all these changes would be. Haller himself was cautious in the application of theoretical concepts to the practice of medicine and approved only of therapeutic methods that had been used successfully for some time. However, he applied his concept in the explanation of one of his favorite treatments. In case of nervous disorders like hysteria he argued that his acid mixture (containing equal doses of sulfuric acid and alcohol) would harden the nerves, which were too sensible. The 'Elixir acidum Haller'—as it was later called—was widely used in the late eighteenth and early nineteenth centuries and served mainly as an antiseptic, antipyretic, styptic, and tonic remedy. Haller considered his research to be also of relevance to surgical practice. It had been a dogma since antiquity that lesions of tendons—mainly occurring in bloodletting and war injuries—provoke intense pain and can cause dreadful accidents, with high fever, stupor, cramps, and often death. In his experiments, however, Haller had shown that the tendons are insensible. The pain and the accidents, he concluded, were actually due to the lesion of the nerve. One should no longer be afraid of the wounds of the tendons and their treatment with hot oil of turpentine should be dropped. He explained this general error, into which even the most respectable authors had fallen, through the fact that the ancients had used the word 'neuron' equally for nerve, tendon, and ligament. But the vast majority of surgical authors until the late 1780s doubted the insensibility of the tendons and considered their lesion to be a serious and potentially fatal accident that had to be treated accordingly.

Of greater consequence was Haller's description of irritability as an innate bodily faculty. The general idea of an active and a reactive power served not only as a physiological model, but also as a potent pathological model for explaining all kinds of disorders. Many pathologists—such as Jerome Gaub (Gaubius) or William Cullen—now described diseases quite generally as effects of an increase or decrease of a vital force. Like the physiologists, however, they did not accept Haller's clear separation between two different qualities, but thought that both the nervous and the muscular system participated in the process. Their theories made use not only of the ideas of Haller, but equally those of other authors, such as Robert Whytt and Théophile Bordeu. This is also true for the system of John Brown, which considered illness as a state of imbalance between external stimuli and the irritable body.

As a well-known medical authority, Haller was often consulted by physicians and patients. However, it was only during his early years in Bern (1731–36) that the practice of medicine was his main occupation. During this period Haller kept detailed patient records, which furnish insight into his therapeutic principles and the composition of his clientele.

Bibliography

Primary: 1757–60. *Disputationes ad morborum historiam et curationem facientes, quas collegit, edidit et recensuit Albertus Hallerus* 7 vols. (Lausanne); 1757–66. *Elementa physiologiae corporis humani* 8 vols. (Lausanne and Bern); 1776–88. *Bibliotheca medicinae practicae qua scripta ad partem medicinae practicae facientia a rerum initiis recensentur* 4 vols. (Bern and Basel).

Secondary: Steinke, Hubert, 2005. *Irritating Experiments. Haller's Concept and the European Controversy on Irritability and Sensibility 1750–1790* (Amsterdam and New York); Steinke, Hubert, and Claudia Profos, eds., 2004. *Bibliographia Halleriana. Verzeichnis der Schriften von und über Albrecht von Haller* (Basel); Boschung, Urs, 1996. 'Albrecht Haller's Patient Records (Berne 1731–1736).' *Gesnerus* 53: 5–14; Boschung, Urs, 1977: 'Albrecht von Haller als Arzt: zur Geschichte des Elixir acidum Halleri.' *Gesnerus* 34: 267–293; DSB.

Hubert Steinke

HALSTED, WILLIAM STEWART

HALSTED, WILLIAM STEWART   (b. New York, New York, USA, 23 September 1852; d. Baltimore, Maryland, USA, 7 September 1922), *surgery.*

Halsted, son of the cousins and strict Presbyterians William Mills Halsted, a businessman, and Mary Louisa Haines, attended Andover College (1863–69), Yale University (1870–74), and the College of Physicians and Surgeons, New York (1874–77), graduating MD. He interned early at Bellevue Hospital (1876) and served as house physician at New York Hospital before spending two years in Europe (1878–80), working in the laboratories and surgical clinics of Vienna, Leipzig, and Würzburg. Theodor Billroth, Anton Wölfler, Johann Mikulicz-Radecki, Albert Kölliker, Ernst Bergmann, and Richard Volkmann, among others, taught him during this time.

After returning to New York, Halsted combined private practice with six hospital posts (1880–85), concentrating on surgery. He demonstrated anatomy at the College of Physicians and Surgeons, and with others taught extramurally, preparing students for College examinations.

In 1884, following Carl Koller, he experimented with cocaine as a local anesthetic. He demonstrated the principle of nerve blocking: when cocaine is injected into a sensory nerve trunk, the area served by the nerve becomes insensitive. This is the basis of neuro-regional anesthesia. By 1885 his self-experimentation had become addiction, and he spent 1886 in a sanatorium in Providence, Rhode Island. He thereafter managed without cocaine but remained a user of morphine.

In December 1886 William Welch brought the recovering Halsted to the new Johns Hopkins Medical School. With Welch, William Osler, and Howard Kelly, he became one of Hopkins's

Johns Hopkins Hospital, 1890. Halftone reproduction from John Shaw Billings, *Description of the Johns Hopkins Hospital,* **Baltimore, 1890. Wellcome Library, London.**

promoting radical mastectomy (although the necessity of this is now debated). His research on the physiological effects of excising and transplanting thyroid and parathyroid glands in dogs led to the better treatment of exophthalmic goiter and improved understanding of the function of these glands.

Halsted contributed to the Hopkins ideal of excellence in medical education. His surgical residency program, with its levels of increasing responsibility, from assistant to resident to chief resident, produced many of the finest surgeons of early twentieth-century America, including such great academic surgeons as Harvey Cushing.

Bibliography

Primary: 1924. *Surgical Papers* 2 vols. (Baltimore).

Secondary: Harvey, A. McGehee, 1981. *Research and Discovery in Medicine: Contributions from Johns Hopkins* (Baltimore); Crowe, Samuel James, 1957. *Halsted of Johns Hopkins: The Man and His Men* (Springfield, IL); MacCallum, William George, 1930. *William Stewart Halsted, Surgeon* (Baltimore); *DAMB*.

Helen Bynum

'Big Four', establishing a reputation for exemplary surgical technique and for experimental and physiological surgery, and founding an internationally recognized school of surgery.

As an early Listerian he believed bacteria caused infected wounds, but moved toward aseptic surgery, avoiding exposure to germs, rather than attacking with antiseptics, and exercising extreme care when handling tissues. He had introduced nonadhering gutta percha dressings (1880) and silver foil as a dressing (1884), but during the Hopkins years, before the hospital opened (1889), he perfected additional techniques, e.g., the intestinal suture, which was ultimately demonstrated with painstaking care to his assistants. He eschewed unnecessary speed, which frequently caused damage, and sought to keep tissues healthy. He believed healthy tissue could combat minimal exposure to germs if the blood supply was unimpeded and if bruising, crushing, and dead spaces were prevented. Wounds must be closed carefully, layer by layer, and a surface blood clot encouraged, under which healing occurred. He invented several instruments and procedures to achieve his desired ends, e.g., metal bands and an applicator to occlude arteries in aneurysm (1905). Halsted's promotion of asepsis gradually resulted in the use of sterilized clothing and masks in Hopkins's operating theatres. In 1889 he famously asked Goodyear for rubber gloves to prevent dermatitis following exposure to antiseptics on his surgical nurse's hands. Nurse Caroline Hampton became Mrs Halsted in June 1890; they had no children.

In addition to these general innovations, his experimental animal work yielded important advances in the surgical treatment of specific diseases. He developed (simultaneously with Edoardo Bassini in Italy) a method of repairing inguinal hernias (1889): the operation cured a disabling condition, but was simple enough for a house surgeon to perform. He modified Volkmann's classic procedure for cancer of the breast,

HAMBURGER, JEAN (b. Paris, France, 15 July 1909; d. Paris, 1 February 1992), *nephrology.*

Hamburger was part of a new generation of French clinicians who enjoyed a double training in medicine and research and who combined the previously separate fields of clinical practice and biological research. He passed his certificate in general physiology at the Sorbonne in 1928 and enrolled in medical school, passing his internship exams in 1931. He was appointed assistant to Pasteur-Valléry-Radot (grandson of Pasteur), who studied kidney disease at the Broussais Hospital. In 1946 Hamburger passed the 'Agregation' to become a faculty professor and three years later was named chief of service at Necker Hospital, where he remained the rest of his career. His medical and scientific work covered three fields that he helped to define: resuscitation, which included transfusion and stabilization of the patients; nephrology, which included the physiology and pathology of the kidney; and organ transplantation.

In a manner that he admitted bordered on adventurous, Hamburger attempted in 1952 the first kidney transplant on a young brick mason seriously wounded by a fall from scaffolding. 'At this time it was terrible to see people with chronic nephritis living in horrible agony for three or four years. Our inability to treat them was unbearable, and it pushed us on in our research. At that time I had an attitude that some considered too bold, but it is in this manner that medical science progresses. When it concerns life-threatening illness, I think one has the right to try anything. Morality for the doctor in this instance consists in having every audacity' (Interview, 13 November 1990).

These first attempts at organ transplants revealed the serious problems of immunological incompatibility between donors and recipients. In 1955 Hamburger used one of the first dialysis machines, which proved very helpful in treating nephritis and severe uremia. Nonetheless the team at Necker Hospital was convinced that successful transplantation depended less on surgery than on immunology, and required better tissue compatibility between donor and patient. Accordingly, Hamburger and his collaborator Gabriel Richet achieved one of the first successful transplantations between nonidentical (heterozygous) twins. The other was done by John Merrill in Boston's Peter Bent Brigham Hospital. Later the development of a test by Jean-François Bach and Mireille Darden for inhibition of formation of red globules around lymphocytes marked a decisive step. On 12 February 1962 the first transplant in France between nontwins was performed. This success was demonstrated at a transplantation congress in New York in 1968. Jean Hamburger did not hide his disappointment when he was passed over for the 1990 Nobel Prize recognizing the first successful transplantations: 'There is no discontinuity between the research of a biologist analyzing the workings of an isolated cell and a doctor who studies the change in liver cells of alcoholic cirrhosis . . . . Research is thus indispensable to the quality of care because it determines the effectiveness of medical practice everywhere in the world' (Interview, 13 November 1990).

It was in this spirit that Hamburger organized medical research after the war. He used funds from the sale of a shipment of coffee brought from South America by his director, Pasteur-Vallery-Radot, to start an association for the promotion of medical research that in 1962 became the 'Fondation pour la recherche médicale' and is still active today. Similarly, at the beginning of the 1950s he formed the 'Club des Treize' along with his colleagues Jean Bernard and René Fauvert, who like him were concerned by the backwardness of French medical research. Officially known as the 'Cercle d'études clinique et biologique', they gathered once a month at the blood transfusion center of Necker Hospital. This group helped to start the 'Association Claude Bernard', an organization supported by the 'Assistance Publique', which supported the creation of laboratories in the Paris hospitals. Notable among these was Hamburger's Nephrology Research Center, which later became the Kidney and Transplant Immunology Research Unit of INSERM in 1970, a new French government organization dedicated to medical research that could legitimately claim Hamburger as one of its most important promoters.

Bibliography

Primary: 1952. (with Mathé, G.) *Physiologie normale et pathologique du métabolisme de l'eau* (Paris); 1968. (with Dausset, F., and G. Mathé) *Advance in transplantation: Proceedings of the First International Congress of the Transplantation Society, Paris 27–30 June 1967* (Copenhagen); 1971. (with Crosnier, Jean, Jean Dormont, and Jean-François Bach) *La Transplantation rénale: théorie et pratique* (Paris); 1972. *La puissance et la fragilité, essai sur les métamorphoses de la médecine et de l'homme* (Paris); 1976.

L'homme et les hommes: essai sur l'originalité biologique de l'individu (Paris); 1982. *Introduction au langage de la médecine.* (Paris).

Secondary: http://picardp1.ivry.cnrs.fr/Hamburger.html (including transcript of interview, 13 November 1990); http://www.renaloo.com/hamburger.htm; 1982. 'Jean Hamburger: Jubilee Issue. Homage to Professor Jean Hamburger.' *Kidney Int.* Suppl. 11: S1–S75

Jean-François Picard

HAMILTON, ALICE (b. New York, New York, USA, 27 February 1869; d. Hadlyme, Connecticut, USA, 22 September 1970), *toxicology, industrial hygiene, epidemiology.*

Hamilton was the third of five children, four girls and a boy, born to Montgomery and Gertrude Pond Hamilton. She grew up in Fort Wayne, Indiana, in a large compound composed of the houses of her grandparents, her parents, and her uncle's family. Like her siblings and cousins, she infrequently left the compound, except for weekly attendance at church. Until high school age, she and her siblings were taught by her parents and occasional hired instructors. In her autobiography she described her early education as comprising 'what our parents thought important: languages, literature, history. We had formal teaching only in languages; the other subjects we had to learn by ourselves by reading, and we did . . . Of science we had not even a smattering' (Hamilton, 1943). At seventeen, like all Hamilton girls, she was sent off to Miss Porter's 'finishing school' in Connecticut where, as she described, the teaching was 'some of the world's worst'. Despite the fragmentary nature of her primary and secondary education, Alice was determined to attain independence by acquiring a profession. Of the careers available to women in the late 1800s, she chose medicine. After a year at a local college to 'catch up' on the scientific training prerequisite to a medical education, she entered the University of Michigan, from which she received the MD degree in 1893. After an internship at the New England Hospital for Women and Children, she sailed in 1895 with her sister Edith, who subsequently became a renowned classics scholar, for Germany, where she spent a year of laboratory studies at the Universities of Leipzig and Munich. Her formal training was completed with a year at Johns Hopkins University, where she worked with Simon Flexner and came in contact with William Henry Welch and William Osler, all prominent medical scientists.

In 1897 Alice Hamilton moved to Chicago as professor of pathology and director of the histological and pathological laboratories of the Women's Medical School of Northwestern University. While in Chicago, inspired by a speech given by Jane Addams, the founder and director of Hull House who was later awarded the Nobel Peace Prize, Hamilton joined the 'settlement movement' and moved into Hull House, where she remained in residence for twenty-two years. Hull House, located in the midst of a poverty-stricken, overcrowded, unsanitary, criminal-infested, high-mortality, immigrant working-class neighborhood, exposed her to the harsh living conditions of the socially disadvantaged. Hull House also introduced her to the social reformers and the political and professional leaders who clustered around Jane Addams and who sparked the 'Progressive Era' of American history. It was these contacts that led to her appointment, in 1910, as medical director of a survey of industrial diseases in Illinois. Her findings, particularly the serious consequences of industrial exposure to lead in its various forms, resulted in legislative action and increased recognition of the potential for occupationally acquired disease.

During the ensuing twenty-five years, Hamilton investigated a number of industries and identified a range of toxic exposures with serious health consequences. As early as 1916, she chaired the industrial hygiene section of the American Public Health Association and became widely recognized as the leader of the field. In 1919 Alice Hamilton became the first woman to be appointed to the faculty of Harvard University.

In 1919 Hamilton attended, with Jane Addams, Emily Balch, and other peace advocates, the formative meeting in the Hague of the Women's International League for Peace and Freedom, of which she later became a national board member. In her later years, Alice Hamilton continued as a peace advocate and carried on a lively correspondence with Supreme Court Justice Felix Frankfurter and other prominent political figures.

Bibliography

Primary: 1925. *Industrial Poisons in the United States* (New York); 1934. *Industrial Toxicology* (New York); 1943. *Exploring the Dangerous Trades* (Boston).

Secondary: Sicherman, Barbara, 1984. *Alice Hamilton: A Life in Letters* (Cambridge, MA); *DAMB*.

Warren Winkelstein, Jr.

HAMMOND, WILLIAM ALEXANDER (b. Annapolis, Maryland, USA, 28 August 1828; d. Washington, D.C., USA, 5 January 1900), *neurology, military medicine.*

Hammond was the second son of John Wesley Hammond, a doctor, and Sarah Pinkney. Following early education at a Harrisburg, Pennsylvania, academy, he attended St John's College in his hometown of Annapolis. When he was sixteen, he moved to New York City to study medicine under William Holme van Buren. Hammond graduated MD from the University of the City of New York (1848) with a thesis on the 'Etiological and Therapeutical Influence of the Imagination'. He then moved to Philadelphia, where he was a resident medical student at the Philadelphia Hospital.

After moving to Saco, Maine, Hammond established a practice and soon passed the examination for army medical service. He was commissioned as an assistant surgeon on 3 July 1849, married Helen Nisbet (of Philadelphia) on 4 July, and moved with his wife to his first military post, in the New Mexico Territory, on 8 July. Suffering later from heart problems, he returned to the East Coast (1852–54); once improved, he was

again sent westward. At Fort Riley, Kansas, Hammond, with several other army surgeons, assisted Spencer Fullerton Baird in his grand ornithological survey (1854–57). Hammond had also brought along his microscope and a fascination with Justus von Liebig's chemical approach to understanding living matter. He soon established a small laboratory, where he tested some of Liebig's theories and commenced a study of urine—using himself as his own laboratory animal. When his health again declined (1857), he was granted extended leave from the army. Hammond settled in Philadelphia and quickly became active in the small but energetic circles interested in bringing European science to American medicine and biology. It was during this period that he made his first pilgrimage to the hospitals and laboratories of Europe (1858) and conducted experiments on poisons with Silas Weir Mitchell. In 1860 Hammond resigned from the army to become chair of anatomy and physiology at the University of Maryland. One might well conclude that Hammond was at heart a laboratory man, but this would be wrong. Upon moving to Baltimore, Hammond set up a private practice, and it would be his private practice that would bring him most of his fortune. His clinical approach would also inform the way he shaped neurology as a specialty in America.

Hammond had barely settled into his new positions when the Civil War began. He resigned from the university and returned to the army (May 1861), still as an assistant surgeon. Soon, however, he received a substantial promotion. The Union Army's Surgeon General, Clement A. Finley, had not impressed members of the influential U.S. Sanitary Commission. Hammond had. On 28 April 1862, Hammond was appointed Surgeon General, with the rank of brigadier general. Technically, he would hold the appointment until 18 August 1864. Reality was more complicated.

At the time that Hammond took charge of the Army Medical Department, both American military medicine and American medicine in general were in a state of disarray (the latter arguably more so than the former). Low professional status was a fundamental part of the problem with both. Standards had been fairly high for admission to army medical practice in peacetime. However, during the war, immediate need was the guiding force, and standards dropped considerably. Inexperienced doctors with MDs from America's dubious yet abundant proprietary medical schools were filling the ranks. Low educational standards and nonexistent licensing practices in civilian medicine did little to elevate the status of the 'profession'. At a time when hospital-based clinical training was central to the education of doctors in Europe, American doctors generally lacked hospital experience. Indeed, American hospitals had remained charity organizations, moral institutions guided by lay boards—not places of medical training and practice. The Civil War, and Hammond's organizational and scientific vision, helped to clear the path for broad change in this medical landscape.

Hammond's plans for transforming the medical department were sweeping, encompassing camp hygiene, medical education, battlefield evacuation, and hospital care. Some of these plans he realized personally; some he started, only to have others complete them. He devised a scheme for improving sanitation in the camps, detailing it in his popular 1863 *Treatise on Hygiene*. His efforts led to a decrease in intestinal diseases among the troops. The army medical school and medical museum that he envisioned to improve the quality of doctors were only instituted after he was out of the army; the records and reports he meticulously collected to document the medical history of the war were compiled, in accordance with his vision, under the direction of his successor, Joseph K. Barnes. The resulting *Medical and Surgical History of the War of the Rebellion* (1870–88) helped persuade European physicians that their American cousins had genuine contributions to make to their profession.

In his efforts to improve the evacuation of injured soldiers from the battlefield, Hammond sagely relied on Jonathan Letterman, whom he had appointed medical director of the Army of the Potomac (June 1862). Letterman devised an ambulance system that greatly facilitated timely evacuation to the hospitals that Hammond was personally helping to establish—and to make into respected institutions for quality care of the wounded. Not only did Hammond establish new hospitals, administered by doctors rather than by lay boards, he also brought in trained nurses, overseen by Dorothea Dix, to replace the convalescents who had halfheartedly tended to the work in the past. Moreover, at a time when specialization was still viewed with suspicion, he founded wards, and even hospitals, that provided specialized treatment. Most famously, he established Turner's Lane Hospital in Philadelphia, to tend to nervous disorders and the consequences of traumatic nerve injury. The hospital was run by his friend and collaborator S. W. Mitchell, along with George Reed Morehouse and W. W. Keen. The Turner's Lane trio not only treated soldiers whose injuries would otherwise have been misunderstood, they also conducted influential research on the special conditions exhibited by their patients: reflex paralysis and injuries to the nerves by gunshot wounds (1864). After the war ended, the positive experience of patients and doctors alike with well-run and efficient military hospitals, and the significance of the research conducted in those hospitals, did much to transform American civilian hospitals—and, eventually, to help raise the status of the American medical profession.

Hammond was supremely confident in the superiority of his efficient, autonomous, and scientific vision of medicine in both the military and civilian worlds. This confidence was essential to his numerous successes. It also brought about the eventual downfall of his military career. Hammond alienated many of his fellow medical practitioners when he issued his infamous 'Circular #6' (May 1863), removing the ever-popular but often abused medical treatments calomel and tartar emetic from the army supply table. (Doctors could still obtain the substances, but only through special requisition.) More ominously still, he quickly alienated Edwin M. Stanton, Lincoln's powerful secretary of war. In July 1863 Stanton took

Male with chronic spinal meningitis, probably of syphilitic origin, cured by potassium iodide and chloride of mercury. Lithograph from *A Treatise on the Diseases of the Nervous System*, 8th edition, New York, 1886. Wellcome Library, London.

action against his army's surgeon general. He appointed a civilian committee, headed by one of Hammond's old enemies, to examine the Medical Department. Meanwhile, he reassigned Hammond to New Orleans. By autumn, an exasperated—and still exiled—Hammond demanded that he be either returned to his office or court-martialed. Stanton granted the latter request. Formal proceedings against Hammond began in January 1864. Ultimately, Hammond was convicted of 'irregular' purchases, neglect of military discipline, and 'conduct unbecoming', charges that Hammond considered, and history has judged, to be largely unfounded. Hammond was dismissed from the army that August. The magnitude of his achievements as surgeon general becomes more impressive still when viewed within the context of the fifteen months he effectively had available to him. In 1878 Hammond funded an appeal of the case. The next year President Rutherford B. Hayes annulled the conviction, restoring Hammond's military status (now retired). Tactfully, Hammond declined the retirement pay to which he was entitled.

In the meantime, he had earned the funds for this eventual appeal by making a rather unconventional career decision: having been expelled from the army, he returned to New York and set up private practice in neurology. His hospital work in the war and his earlier local connections helped him not only to establish this practice, but also to obtain the appointments—some specially tailored to his interests—that enabled it to thrive. New York's College of Physicians and Surgeons appointed him lecturer on diseases of the mind and nervous system (1866–67), creating the post for him. Bellevue Hospital Medical College soon also established a position in neurology for Hammond (1867) and later, in 1872, moved him to a more conventional post, as professor of materia medica and therapeutics. The next year, he resigned his Bellevue professorship and then, in 1874, accepted two professorships: one at the University of the City of New York, in diseases of the mind and nervous system, the other (a summer position) at the University of Vermont. In the New York position, Hammond collaborated with medical colleagues interested in teaching their specialties to recent medical graduates—students who otherwise would have to go to Europe to study them—and established a postgraduate teaching facility. The group eventually became frustrated with the university, collectively resigned, and opened a school the following year (1882), the New York Post-Graduate Medical School, which Hammond was at the heart of and which enjoyed rapid success.

While in New York, Hammond not only amassed a decent personal fortune in private practice and taught medical and postgraduate students, he also consciously used his positions to further the establishment of neurology as a respectable medical discipline. To that end, he wrote textbooks (his *Treatise on the Diseases of the Nervous System* went through multiple editions and translations) and helped found societies (the New York Neurological Society [1872] and the American Neurological Society [1875]) and journals (including the *Journal of Nervous and Mental Diseases*). His clinical approach to the discipline was evident throughout. During this time, Hammond identified 'athetosis' as a neurological disorder. Also known as 'Hammond's disease', it is characterized by 'an inability to retain the fingers and toes in any position in which they may be placed, and by their continual motion' (Hammond, quoted in Blustein, 1991, p. 120). He was also involved with fellow neurologists in a five-year campaign (starting from 1878) against the monopoly of the Association of Medical Superintendents of American Institutes for the Insane over psychiatric treatment. Given his longstanding interest in the imagination, it is perhaps unsurprising that Hammond wrote several novels in this period as well. He also married his second wife, Ester Chaplin, in 1886.

In 1888 Hammond retired from the Post-Graduate Medical School and moved to Washington, D.C., where he opened a sanitarium for the treatment of nervous disorders. There he became fascinated with C. E. Brown-Séquard's therapeutic use of 'animal extracts'. Not only did he experiment with and publicly support the use of these extracts (he was particularly fond of a brain extract); he even helped organize the Columbia Chemical Company to manufacture them. This entrepreneurial project was controversial, as was his final novel, *The Son of Perdition*, which took as its subject a fictionalized retelling of the betrayal of Christ.

Hammond was a confident man; his booming voice and large stature—6'2" and 250 lbs.—helped him persuade others of his self-assured points (if his questionable diplomatic skills did not). He died suddenly of a heart attack in January 1900, and was buried in Arlington Cemetery.

Bibliography

Primary: 1863. *A Treatise on Hygiene, with Special Reference to the Military Service* (Philadelphia); 1871. *A Treatise on the Diseases of the Nervous System* (New York); 1873. 'Athetosis.' *Medical Record* 8: 309–311; 1879. *Fasting Girls; Their Physiology and Pathology* (New York); 1898. *The Son of Perdition* (Chicago).

Secondary: Blustein, Bonnie Ellen, 1991. *Preserve Your Love for Science: Life of William A. Hammond, American Neurologist* (Cambridge, MA); Miller, Mark D., 1987. 'William A. Hammond: Restoring the Reputation of a Surgeon General.' *Military Medicine* 152: 452–457; Key, Jack D., 1979. *William Alexander Hammond, M.D. (1828–1900)* (Rochester, MN); *DAMB*.

Kim Pelis

HANAOKA, SEISHŪ   (b. Hirayama, Kii domain [now Wakayama Prefecture], Japan, 30 November 1760; d. Hiyayama, Kii domain, Japan, 21 November 1835), *anesthesiology, surgery.*

Hanaoka Seishū was born in Kii domain (Kishū), in what is present-day Wakayama Prefecture. His father and grandfather both had practiced medicine, and after he demonstrated an aptitude for medicine while still young, his family sent him to study in Kyoto. There he became the pupil of several physicians and surgeons, including Yoshimasu Nangai (1750–1813), son of Yoshimasu Tōdō (1702–73), one of the most famous practitioners of the Kohōha, or 'Ancient Method School'. After several years of diligent study in Kyoto not only of medicine but also of the Chinese classics, Seishū returned to his family's home in Kishū and took over the family practice. Seishū became famous for the successful use of general anesthesia in major surgery in 1804. This was, above all, the result of his practical approach to medical theory and practice.

By the end of the eighteenth century in Japan, students of medicine often studied with practitioners of several schools and traditions in order to master the most effective therapeutic methods available. Although numerous physicians and surgeons remained dogmatic in their understanding of medical theory and practice, many more were practical and syncretic. Their motivation was not simply academic. Fortune and fame awaited the physicians and surgeons who could most effectively treat ailments—and medicine provided a rare opportunity to rise in a rigidly stratified social structure. Hanaoka Seishū, who studied both traditional and Western medicine and combined them to become one of the world's first surgeons to use a general anesthetic for major surgery, was a paragon of this trend toward pragmatic syncretism.

As a physician Seishū advocated the combined practice of internal and surgical medicine. Until then, in Japan the two practices had been separate, in much the same way as in Europe. He also advocated actively combining Chinese and Western approaches to medicine, with the goal of establishing the most effective therapeutic methods possible. He could hardly have been more successful. Seishū did his best to treat patients with even the most difficult and unusual of diseases and managed to cure many. His fame grew and patients traveled long distances to receive his treatments. At the same time, ever growing numbers of students came to study under him; he helped train over two thousand students over the course of his career and wrote numerous books that explained his treatment of a broad range of conditions.

This in itself would have been enough to earn Seishū an important place in Japanese medical history, but he attained his greatest fame, not only in Japan but worldwide, for developing a general anesthesia and performing major surgery in 1804. Seishū had scoured current pharmacopeia for effective sedatives so that he could further develop surgical procedures, and devised a formula based on the work of others that he called *tsūsensan* or *mafutsusan*. It contained several herbal ingredients, including eight parts of 'Korean morning glory' or *Chōsen asagao* (*Datura alba*), two parts of Japanese aconite (*Aconium japonicum*), two parts of Chinese angelica (*Angelica dahurica*), two parts of Norwegian angelica (*Angelica decursiva*), two parts of *Ligusticum wallichii*, and two parts of *Arisaema japonicum*, a form of Jack-in-the-pulpit. The most important active ingredients in the formula were atropine and scopolamine, both of which remain in use today. The ingredients were ground together, boiled in water, mixed with alcohol, and administered orally as a warm infusion. In two to four hours the patient would be anesthetized and remain that way from six to twenty-four hours, depending on the dose.

It is not clear what originally inspired Seishū to attempt the treatment of breast cancer, which was well-known as being impossible to cure. Several secondary sources attribute his inspiration to the work of an earlier physician, Nagatomi Dokushōan (1732–66), but this is impossible to verify. Seishū's younger sister did die from this disease, so her early death might have compelled him to attempt a surgical treatment for it. In any event, he used his anesthetic and operated on a sixty-year-old woman named Aiya Kan in 1804. His procedure was to open the breast and remove the tumor, then (as was common in treating open wounds in Japan at the time) wash the wound with a *shōchū*, a distilled alcoholic beverage, and bandage it with cotton cloth soaked in vinegar and egg whites. The patient seemed to suffer no ill effects from the surgery, but did die six months later.

In the following years, Seishū and his successors treated over 160 women at his clinic. Generally, Seishū's anesthetic and surgical methods were highly acclaimed, and he has been internationally remembered as a pioneer of modern anesthetics.

Bibliography

Primary: 1980. (Yoshinori, Ōtsuka, and Yakazu Dōmei, eds.) *Kinsen Kanpō igakusho shūsei* [Collected works of early modern Kanpō medicine] vols. 29 and 30 (Tokyo); 1986. (Hiromichi, Yasui, ed.) *Kinsei Kanpō chiken senshū* [Collected works of clinical Kanpō medicine in early modern period] vol.10 (Tokyo).

Secondary: Matsuki Akitomo, 2002. *Hanaoka Seishū no shin kenkyū* [New Studies of Hanaoka Seishū] (Tokyo); Kure Shūzō, 1994. *Hanaoka Seishū sensei oyobi sono geka* [On Hanaoka Seishū and His Surgical Practice] (Tokyo).

William Johnston

HANSEN, GERHARD HENRIK ARMAUER
(b. Bergen, Norway, 29 July 1841; d. Florø, Norway, 12 February 1912), *leprosy, microbiology, epidemiology, preventive medicine.*

Hansen, the son of Claus Hansen, a businessman, and Elisabeth Concordia Schram, had altogether fourteen siblings. After graduating MD from Royal Frederiks University (Oslo) in 1867, Hansen in 1868 started work on leprosy at the National Leprosarium no. 1 in Bergen. Despite growing differences of opinion on the etiology of leprosy, the head of the leprosarium, Daniel Cornelius Danielssen, provided Hansen with excellent facilities.

In 1869 and 1870 Hansen published preliminary results of his clinical and pathological studies, concluding that leprosy was a distinct nosological entity and not simply a 'degenerative' consequence of various causes.

In his main treatise, *On the Causes of Leprosy*, published in Norwegian (1874) and English (1875), Hansen presented epidemiological evidence that leprosy was an infectious disease and not a hereditary one, as claimed by Danielssen. Epidemiological evidence was obtained partially from the National Leprosy Registry of Norway, founded in 1856 and the first national register of any disease ever to have been established. Registry data suggested that the decrease in incidence of the disease had been particularly steep in the areas in which hospitalization, and thereby isolation of infectious cases, had been most strictly enforced. Next, Hansen described his microbiological findings. On 28 February 1873 he saw for the first time 'small staff-like bodies, much resembling bacteria, lying within the cells. Though unable to discover any difference between these bodies and true bacteria, I will not venture to declare them to be actually identical.'

No bacillus had previously been shown to be the cause of any chronic disease; among the acute infectious diseases, only the microbiological agent of anthrax had been discovered, in 1869. At first, Hansen examined his samples either unstained or stained by osmic acid, which was not adequate for visualization of the bacteria. In 1879 Hansen was visited by Albert Neisser from Robert Koch's laboratory in Breslau, Germany, who wanted to join Hansen in his efforts to stain the bacillus. After negative results in Bergen, Neisser succeeded back in Breslau, immediately publishing his findings, suggesting that these bacteria represented the infectious agent of leprosy. In subsequent papers, Neisser claimed the discovery for himself. In 1880 Hansen reacted by publishing his own claim of priority, providing further details about his discovery.

At the same time, Hansen met with another, more serious problem. Aware of Henle's postulates, requiring, among other things, that an infectious microorganism should induce a disease similar to that in man upon inoculation in an animal before proof of an infectious origin is established, Hansen reported twelve vain attempts to inoculate tissue from leprous nodules into rabbits, and later into other experimental animals. Thus, Hansen

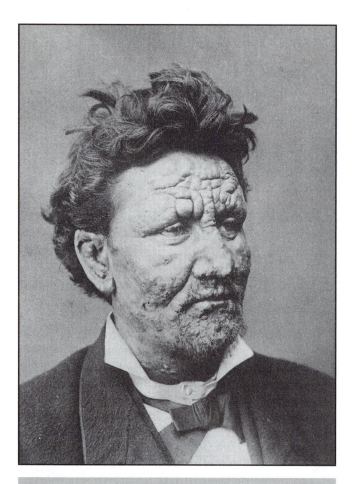

Portrait of a man suffering from tuberous leprosy. From *Leprosy in Its Clinical and Pathological Aspects*, 1895. Wellcome Library, London.

wanted to evaluate human models. Danielssen had already inoculated leprous material into himself, colleagues, and patients with other diseases, all with negative results. In 1880 Hansen inoculated leprous tissue from a patient with lepromatous leprosy (malignant) into two patients with tuberculoid leprosy (benign) to produce manifestations of lepromatous leprosy. This led to a legal charge against Hansen, who then had been appointed Chief Medical Officer for Leprosy. In spite of strong support from scientific and medical groups, Hansen was relieved of his post at the hospital where the experiment had been undertaken, but continued as Chief Medical Officer for Leprosy.

Thus established as an infectious disease, leprosy had to be controlled accordingly. Hansen predicted, based on time trend studies of the Registry, that the incidence was not decreasing as quickly as might be desirable. Isolation of all infectious patients seemed the most appropriate measure, and in 1877 an 'Act on the Maintenance of Poor Lepers etc.' was passed, stating that leprosy patients who were unable to maintain themselves were obliged to live in an institution. In 1885 more severe legislation was passed; an 'Act on Seclusion of Lepers

etc.' stated that all patients had to be isolated in a separate room at home, or they had to be admitted to a leprosy hospital. The Registry has provided firm evidence that the policy of isolation greatly contributed to the decline of the disease, which was more or less eradicated by 1920. At that time, more than 8,000 persons had been taken ill since 1850. At the first international leprosy conference in Berlin, in 1897, the Norwegian leprosy control program was recommended and Hansen was honored as the discoverer of the leprosy bacillus.

Bibliography

Primary: 1880. '*Bacillus leprae.*' *Virchows Arch. Pathol. Anat.* 79: 32–42; 1895. (with Looft, Carl) *Leprosy in Its Clinical and Pathological Aspects*, trans. Norman Walker (Bristol).

Secondary: Irgens, Lorentz M., 1984. 'The Discovery of *Mycobacterium leprae.*' *Am. J. Dermatopathol.* 6: 337–343; *DSB*.

Lorentz M. Irgens

HARDY, HARRIET LOUISE   (b. Arlington, Massachusetts, USA, 23 September 1906; d. Boston, Massachusetts, USA, 13 October 1993), *occupational medicine.*

Hardy was the eldest of two daughters born to Harriet Louise Decker (Wellesley College 1902) and Horace Dexter Hardy, a lawyer and state legislator who died of pneumonia in 1910. Two years later Hardy's mother remarried Charles Maxwell Sears, an engineer, and the family moved to Dorset, Vermont, to a countryside to which Hardy returned frequently throughout her working life for rest and relaxation and where she is now buried.

Hardy graduated from Wellesley College in 1928, completing her medical degree at Cornell University in 1932 and her postgraduate training at Philadelphia General Hospital (1932–34). Financial uncertainties during the Depression influenced her to promptly find employment, first at Northfield School for Girls (1935–39), and then at Radcliffe College (1939–45), where she headed medical services during a period of transformation in which the College assumed greater responsibility for students' health. At Radcliffe she made professional and personal connections that lasted throughout her life.

At the end of World War II Hardy directed her professional insight and interests toward occupational medicine, where few guidelines existed at the time. As the first medical consultant to the Division of Occupational Disease in the Massachusetts Department of Labor and as a junior investigator in the Industrial Medical Clinic run by Joseph Aub and Alice Hamilton at the Massachusetts General Hospital, Hardy concentrated on threats to health in the workplace, and soon developed a professional specialty that she called 'clinical preventive medicine'. Her reputation was first established in the investigation of severe respiratory illness reported by many of the young women employed in two factories that produced fluorescent light bulbs. Hardy's careful study showed the role of dust in spreading the poison beryllium, which was regularly used in manufacture. Her evidence was contested not only by the industry, but also by insurance investigators, company lawyers, and even in the United States Public Health Service. Hardy's significant disclosures of unexpected risks in the workplace also led to an appeal from the Atomic Energy Commission to review conditions at the facility in Los Alamos, New Mexico (1948). She returned to Cambridge to establish the Occupational Medical Service at the Massachusetts Institute of Technology (1949), and over the next two decades founded the national Beryllium Case Registry (1952) and continued to serve as consultant to the Atomic Energy Commission. Later challenged by representatives of the coal mining, cotton, and other chemical- and dust-laden manufacturing industries, Hardy stood her ground in court, conducting further investigations on benzol, asbestos, cadmium, and the anthrax bacillus. In 1975, on her own home ground, she addressed the Massachusetts Medical Society and charged doctors with responsibility to prepare their students for careers in occupational medicine.

Alice Hamilton, the leading figure in industrial and occupational medicine, asked Hardy to join her as coauthor of the revised (1949) edition of the classic text *Industrial Toxicology*. Hardy was also recognized internationally for her concern with the social as well as the medical consequences of the hazardous workplace. Hardy traveled widely for two decades, and lectured in Europe, South Africa, and Central America. Throughout her life she was easily fatigued and typically required periods of total rest. Hardy chose early retirement in the countryside that had always sustained her, and in this environment found the energy to complete and publish a memoir, *Challenging Man-Made Disease* (1983).

Bibliography

Primary: 1949. (with Hamilton, Alice) *Industrial Toxicology* 2nd edn. (New York); 1975. 'Risk and Responsibility. A Physician's Viewpoint.' *New England Journal of Medicine* 293: 803–806; 1983. *Challenging Man-Made Disease, the Memoirs of Harriet L. Hardy, MD* (New York).

Secondary: Hamilton, Alice, 1943. *Exploring the Dangerous Trades* (Boston).

Barbara Gutmann Rosenkrantz

HARINASUTA, KHUNYING TRANAKCHIT (b. Bangkok, Thailand, 6 May 1918; d. Bangkok, 29 April 1999), *tropical medicine.*

Harinasuta was the eldest daughter of Phraya Phadungviddayaserm and Khunying Rian. She attended Bangkok's Faculty of Medicine, Siriraj Hospital, University of Medical Science, and graduated (MD) in 1944. After a two-year internship (1944–46), she joined the department of internal medicine at the Siriraj Hospital as a lecturer.

In 1952 Harinasuta joined her husband in Liverpool, England. Chamlong Harinasuta was working toward a PhD at the Liverpool School of Tropical Medicine (LSTM) with funding from the Colombo plan. Harinasuta enrolled for the yearlong Diploma in Tropical Medicine and Hygiene (DTMH). The origin of this course lay in the supporting role medicine was supposed to play in Britain's domination of her tropical colonies. By the 1950s the DTMH hoped to help fill the gaps in the medical curricular of tropical countries, and increasingly the students attending came from abroad. With medical teaching often based on programs in the West, the infectious parasitic diseases prevalent in the tropics were poorly covered. Both husband and wife intended to increase their own knowledge and to use it constructively when they returned to Thailand.

In 1953 Khunying Harinasuta began working again at the Siriraj Hospital in Bangkok. After a military coup d'etat, Chamlong Harinasuta was offered the opportunity to lead an institution of his choice. He chose to open (1960) a postgraduate Faculty of Tropical Medicine (now School) in the University of the Medical Sciences (now Mahidol University) with a curriculum based on that at the LSTM, which was taught initially in Thai but switched to English (1966) after entry to the course was broadened to include the Southeast Asian region.

Harinasuta led the department of clinical tropical medicine (1960–78) and served as director of the Bangkok Hospital for Tropical Diseases (1961–78). In the course of her work, she came across patients whose malaria infections failed to respond to the antimalaria drug chloroquine. As part of Thailand's National Malaria Eradication Program (which was part of the WHO's global malaria eradication drive), this drug had been used extensively as the backup to spraying with the residual insecticide DDT, and in the late 1950s there were anecdotal reports from practitioners working in the endemic areas in northern Thailand, particularly near the border with Cambodia, of treatment failure. Harinasuta began more rigorous clinical and basic laboratory investigations, including counting malaria parasites. She also found employment for her discharged patients around the hospital in order to continue to follow up these cases. She announced her results about the incidence of chloroquine-resistant falciparum malaria at a UNESCO meeting in Singapore (1962): this was the first report based on an authoritative study. The audience was skeptical. In 1963 she traveled widely, demonstrating her slides, convincing more malariologists that Thailand was facing a serious problem of drug resistance. In 1966 a WHO investigation finally confirmed Harinasuta's work in Thailand.

Membership on the WHO Expert Committee on Malaria (1975–99) confirmed her prestige in the world malaria community. She also served as chairman of the Medical Scientific and Technical Advisory Committee for Refugees. This role was an indication of massive population displacements resulting from the political tensions in Southeast Asia, the importance of malaria in the health of refugees, and the problems their presence can pose for the countries receiving them.

Harinasuta's interest in research was matched by the activities of the cohort of colleagues who continued to study in Liverpool and to develop the research base of the Bangkok school, making it into a world-class institution. Her other contributions to the growth of medicine in Thailand included service as editor-in-chief of the *Southeast Asian Journal of Tropical Medicine and Public Health* (1971–99), president of the Thai Medical Women's Association (1970–76), and vice-president of the Medical Association (1973–74).

Bibliography

Primary: 1962. (with Migasen, S., and D. Bunnag) 'Chloroquine Resistance in *P. falciparum*' in UNESCO *First Symposium on Scientific Knowledge of Tropical Parasites* (Singapore) pp. 148–153; 1965. (with Suntharasamai, P., and C. Viravan). 'Chloroquine-resistant Falciparum Malaria in Thailand.' *Lancet* ii: 657–660.

Secondary: Power, Helen, 1997. 'Drug-Resistant Malaria: A Global Problem and the Thai Response' in Cunningham, Andrew, and Bridie Andrews, eds., *Western Medicine as Contested Knowledge* (Manchester) pp. 262–286.

Helen Bynum

HARPESTRENG, HENRIK (b. ?; d. Roskilde, Denmark, 2 April (?) 1244), *medicine, pharmacy.*

Harpestreng is known as the most influential medical writer in medieval Scandinavia. Details of his life are, however, scarce. We know that he served as a canon and as a physician in Roskilde (Denmark) during the first half of the thirteenth century, but nothing about his family or where and when he was born. He was probably educated at a foreign university, and he is normally referred to as 'mester' or 'magister' in the manuscripts. Two manuscripts from the fifteenth century describe him as physician to King Erik Plovpenning, who reigned from 1241 to 1250. According to the obituary notice found in *Liber daticus Roskildensis* (p. 47), he died 2 April 1244 as a canon of the cathedral of Roskilde, then the capital of Denmark.

Harpestreng's writings include works in Latin as well as in Danish. No relative chronology has been established, but a plausible assumption is that the Latin works date from his period abroad and the Danish from the time when he was established in Denmark. According to this chronology, Harpestreng's first known work would be *De simplicibus medicinis laxativis*, a treatise on the medical use of different herbs and drugs. Like his later writings, it shows the great influence on Harpestreng of the Salernitan School, and such authors as Galen, al-Rāzī, Ibn Sīnā, and Constantine the African are quoted. A later herbal for medical use, *Liber herborum*, is written in the same tradition, but also quotes from the *Regimen sanitatis*. Harpestreng's most influential work was another herbal or leech book, this one written in Danish and usually

called *Den danske Urtebog*. The majority of its 150 chapters are devoted to herbs and their medical uses, but it also contains some clinical observations and prescriptions for phlebotomy. Its principal sources are *De viribus herborum* by Macer Floridus (Odo de Meung) and *De gradibus liber* by Constantine the African. This book was copied throughout Scandinavia for centuries, and numerous manuscripts are available. Fragments of other medical writings, based on the same sources, have been found in different codices and are normally considered to be part of another leech book by Harpestreng. Some writings on medical astrology, phlebotomy (including prescriptions for King Erik), and other subjects are also usually ascribed to Harpestreng. Finally, several manuscripts indicate Harpestreng as the author of a leech book in Danish that treats different sicknesses and their remedies *a capite ad calcem*, but his authorship cannot be definitively ascertained.

Harpestreng can hardly be described as an original writer. He relies heavily in his Latin works on the writings of the Salernitan School, and his most influential book, *Den danske Urtebog*, consists for the most part of quotations from Macer Floridus and Constantine the African. The herbs and remedies that he mentions are largely the same that one finds in other leech books throughout Europe, even if there are some examples of exclusively Nordic herbs like *Angelica*, *Benedicta alba*, and *Benedicta ruffa*. However, this lack of originality does not diminish his influence on or his importance for the medical history of Scandinavia. Harpestreng's writings were enormously influential in the Nordic countries during the Middle Ages. They were copied, translated into other Nordic languages, and very often constituted the principal source in other writings on medicine. Harpestreng's knowledge of the classical medical tradition and his use of the vernacular to transmit this knowledge thus made him instrumental in the establishment of the learned classical medicine in the Nordic countries.

Bibliography

Primary: 1908–1920. (Kristensen, Marius, ed.) *Gamle danske Urtebøger, stenbøger og Kogebøger* 3 vols. (Copenhagen); 1914. (Johnsson, J. W. S., ed.) *De simplicibus medicinis laxativis* (Copenhagen); 1936. (Hauberg, Poul, ed.) *Liber herborum* (Copenhagen).

Secondary: Möller-Christensen, Vilhelm, 1944. *Middelalderens lægekunst i Danmark* (Copenhagen); Hauberg, Poul, 1919. 'Lidt om Henrik Harpestraengs Laegebog.' *Danske studier* 16: 111–128; *DSB*.

Charlotte Christensen-Nugues

HART, ERNEST ABRAHAM (b. Knightsbridge, London, England, 26 June 1835; d. Brighton, Sussex, England, 7 January 1898), *medical journalism, medical reform.*

Born to a dentist father, Hart was exposed early on to the anti-Semitic prejudices prevailing at the time. He could study at the City of London School, one of the few private schools that did not debar Jews, but his race prevented him from taking up a scholarship at Queens' College, Cambridge. Instead, he went to St George's Hospital Medical School, London, qualifying in 1856. He served as a house surgeon at another teaching hospital, St Mary's, then became a demonstrator in anatomy at Arbuthnot Lane's school and subsequently an ophthalmic and dental surgeon at St Mary's and dean of its medical school from 1863 to 1869. From 1863 he was also a part-time assistant editor of *Lancet*, writing many editorials. Nevertheless, he was unhappy there and in 1866 transferred to the *British Medical Journal* as its editor, where, save for a year's absence, he remained until his death.

Hart broadened the journal's appeal, remembering readers in the less prestigious aspects of medicine as well as those outside Britain, and cutting the space devoted to the humdrum affairs of the British Medical Association (BMA). He recruited many contributors, including war correspondents for conflicts such as the Franco-Prussian War, and initiated important sociomedical investigations, including air pollution and baby-farming, which often concealed the infanticide of foster children. Such persistent campaigns frequently resulted in legislation, encouraged by Hart's chairmanship of the BMA's Parliamentary Bills Committee (which in ten years considered no fewer than thirty-three subjects) as well as his membership in many influential outside bodies.

Nevertheless, success and Hart's pushiness and self-praise inevitably earned him many enemies, as did his promotion of unpopular causes, such as the Contagious Diseases Act (which called for the compulsory inspection of prostitutes), vivisection, and universal smallpox vaccination (his support of the last probably denying him election when he stood as a parliamentary candidate for the Mile End constituency). Just as he had reacted to suggestions (unlikely to be true) that he had been involved in his first wife's death (1861), he shrugged aside censure for publishing confidential comments made by the emperor of Germany while dying from laryngeal cancer and for failure to control heavy expenditure on what Hart claimed were outside contributors to the *British Medical Journal* (*BMJ*). The latter crisis possibly caused him to resign as editor and disappear for a year, but he was reappointed editor in 1870, against considerable competition. Hart's *BMJ* achieved enormous success, and he had few outside interests, apart from collecting Japanese art. When he was first appointed the circulation was 2,500; by his death it was 20,500—the largest of any medical journal anywhere, and providing more of the BMA's income than did subscriptions. He traveled widely, on journal business as well as for his health (he had developed diabetes, which was eventually to kill him), and was invited to the United States to advise the American Medical Association, first on how to set up a journal and again ten years later on how to improve it. His answer is still widely quoted: 'better papers, more condensation, and a large wastepaper basket'.

Apart from his social conscience, Hart's considerable achievements reflected three features of himself: he was a member of a loose-knit group of influential philanthropists that included Lord Shaftesbury and Baroness Burdett-Coutts, he held a powerful position within the BMA ('he *was* the BMA,' in one commentator's words), and he ran his campaigns deliberately to keep the issues before his readers but without boring them. All this should have ensured his place in the pantheon of great editors, but he remains little known, possibly because a promised biography was never written. Given the emphasis on his Jewishness in contemporary comments and even in his obituaries, however, the prevailing attitude toward race is quite probably another major reason.

Bibliography

Secondary: Bartrip, P. W. J., 1990. *Mirror of Medicine* (Oxford and London); *Oxford DNB*.

Stephen Lock

HARVEY, WILLIAM   (b. Folkestone, Kent, England, 1 April 1578; d. London or Roehampton, England, 3 June 1657), *anatomy, embryology, medicine, physiology.*

Life and Career

The oldest son of a yeoman farmer, Harvey went from the King's School in Canterbury to Gonville and Caius College, Cambridge (1593). An early interest in medicine is suggested, not only by this choice of college, but also by the fact that Harvey was awarded a scholarship endowed by Matthew Parker (1504–75), former Archbishop of Canterbury, to enable a Kent-born pupil of King's School to study medicine. Harvey took the BA (1597) and by early 1600 had enrolled at the University of Padua, then Europe's leading center for medical education. He was profoundly influenced there by the professor of surgery, Girolamo Fabrizi of Acquapendente (1537–1619). Instead of focusing on human anatomy, in the medical manner, Fabrizi was engaged upon a revived Aristotelian project to understand the way animals worked. This involved comparative anatomy across different species, and not only allowed, but also demanded, vivisection to understand how form related to function.

Harvey achieved the MD in April 1602 and incorporated it at Cambridge the same year. Intending to set up in practice in London, he applied for admission to the RCP. Although granted permission to practice straight away, he was not admitted to the College until 1604. It was in that same year that he married Elizabeth, daughter of Lancelot Browne (d. 1605), who was physician to James I and a leading fellow of the College. Browne died before he could help Harvey's career, but Harvey's brother, John, who was in the king's service, helped with his appointment as physician to St Bartholomew's Hospital (1609). Harvey subsequently became a prominent member of the College of Physicians, and was one of their censors in 1613, 1625, and 1627, an elect in 1627, and treasurer the following year. Perhaps most importantly, he was elected as their Lumleian Lecturer in 1615. These were lectures on surgery that had been endowed since the early 1580s by John, first Baron Lumley (c. 1533–1609), but Harvey gave them a natural-philosophical, rather than a surgical, focus by seeking to explain the way the body worked. It was the discussion of the function of the heart in these lectures, as he repeatedly modified them from 1616 to 1626, that was to lead Harvey to the discovery of circulation.

Harvey became one of the physicians to James I (1566–1625) about 1618, and continued as such for Charles I (1600–49), becoming his physician-in-ordinary in 1631 and senior physician-in-ordinary (the chief royal medical position) in 1639. In 1628 Harvey published *De motu cordis et sanguinis*, his discovery of the circulation of the blood, hinted at in the Lumleian Lectures years before, and became an internationally known, if controversial, figure. Harvey and Charles I became close friends, and Harvey often joined the king on official journeys. The king helped Harvey's ongoing research into animal generation by allowing him to dissect deer from the royal parks. He stayed with the king during the civil war, when the court moved to Oxford. He was briefly warden of Merton College during this time, but returned to London after the surrender of Oxford in 1646. Shortly after this, Harvey allowed his friend and admirer, George Ent (1604–89), to edit his papers on generation and to see them through the press as *De generatione animalium* (1651). Comparable studies on the generation of insects, together with other important studies, had evidently been lost early in the civil war, when Harvey's lodgings had been ransacked. While Ent was preparing *De generatione* for the press, Harvey published his only defense of the *De motu cordis*, responding to the criticisms of the leading French physician Jean Riolan, the younger (1580–1657), in his *Exercitatio anatomica de circulatione sanguinis* (1649).

Once back in London after his years with the king, he decided to renew his association with the College of Physicians, paying for a library, which was completed in 1654 (and which was largely destroyed in the Great Fire of London of 1666), and endowing an annual Harveian oration, which continues to be given in his honor. In 1654 he turned down the presidency of the College on account of his age. His friend John Aubrey (1626–97) reported that after the appearance of the *De motu cordis*, 'he fell mightily in his practise, and that 'twas believed by the vulgar he was crack-brained'. His innovations in physiological theory evidently brought similar suspicion from his fellow practitioners: 'All his profession would allow him to be an excellent Anatomist', Aubrey wrote, 'but I never heard of any that admired his Therapeutic way'. The theory met with significant opposition from medical practitioners, but proved more persuasive with natural philosophers, who immediately saw the need to reject Galenic physiology and to completely recast the understanding of the body. Harvey seems to have died as the result of a stroke, and was buried in the family vault at Hempstead Church, in Essex.

The Motion of the Heart and Blood

In the discussion of the heart in his Lumleian lectures, Harvey tried to decide between opposing views as to which was the heart's active stroke, systole (contraction) or diastole (dilation), whether the heart and arteries contract and dilate together or alternately, and whether the arteries have their own pulsific faculty, or are merely distended by the impulsion of material from the heart. These had become important issues as a result of the increasing acceptance of the pulmonary circulation, first announced by Realdo Colombo (1516–59) in 1559, which indicated that the traditional Galenic account of the heart was inadequate. Inspired by the work of Fabrizi, Harvey had been investigating these matters by vivisection, observing the beating hearts of cold-blooded creatures, which were simpler in structure and could be slowed by cooling, and of mammals in their dying moments, when their heart rhythms slowed down. Harvey became convinced that systole was the active stroke, so that the heartbeat consisted of a forceful contraction followed by a relaxation during which the ventricles dilated. During contraction the contents of the right ventricle were forced into the lungs (via the pulmonary artery), and the contents of the left ventricle were expelled into the aorta and the arterial system, the arteries responding passively.

It was evidently some time before Harvey realized the full implications of these conclusions. If the contractions of the left ventricle are pushing blood out of the heart at every beat, then the amount of blood sent from the heart to the arteries in a day, even on very conservative estimates of the amount of blood per beat, would have to be impossibly high. This constituted a crisis for Harvey's earlier conclusions, until he turned it into powerful evidence for the circulation of the blood.

Before Harvey it was assumed that only a small amount of venous blood, supposedly originating from the liver, found its way into the left ventricle of the heart, to be converted there into arterial blood, and then infused with a supposed vital spirit. Most of the venous blood was thought to be distributed to other parts of the body to deliver nutrients, and was consumed by those parts. This process was kept continuous by the consumption of food and its eventual conversion in the liver into venous blood, which was then distributed through the veins. Similarly, the venous blood that was successively converted in the left ventricle to arterial blood, and then to vital spirit, was distributed via the arteries and was consumed by the various parts of the body. Before the Harveian crisis there was no conception of the need for a circulating return, either to the liver or to the heart. What Harvey did was to unite the venous and the arterial systems, and to exclude the liver from this larger system. The arterial system was held to anastomose at its extremities with the venous system, so allowing an outflow from the heart into the arteries and a return via the veins. The cardiac throughput of blood could now be very high without demanding an impossible level of production of new blood.

Harvey used the quantitative argument (though only as a thought experiment—he made no attempt to measure actual quantities of blood expelled in systole) to point to the need for a circulation, but he also added further anatomical and vivisectional evidence. In particular, he was able to show that the valves in the veins, usually held merely to slow blood flow, actually ensured that blood could only flow toward the heart. One of his most elegant experimental demonstrations drew attention to the fact that a medium-tight tourniquet around the upper arm, designed to stop flow in the veins but not in the deeper-set arteries, caused the veins to swell on the side of the ligature opposite to that which would be expected if venous blood was flowing outward from the liver. Moreover, he was able to go on to show that the valves (visible as nodes in the engorged veins) only allowed flow back toward the heart.

A New Theory of Animal Generation

Harvey's interest in the blood perhaps grew out of the important role he ascribed to it in generation and development. Certainly, he was interested in generation very early in his career, even though *De generatione* was not published until 1651. Based on important observations, including his famous examination of the daily development of the chick in the egg and his dissections of the uteri of hinds at various stages after mating and conception, Harvey rejected the prevailing ancient theories of both Aristotle (384–322 BCE) and Galen (129–c. 210). These both involved the supposed shaping power of spermatic fluid working upon menstrual blood as the material principle of the developing embryo/fetus.

Finding no empirical evidence for the presence of spermatic fluid in eggs or wombs, Harvey concluded that the male contribution to reproduction was occult and indirect, and likened it to the principle of contagion in recent medical theory—notably that of Jean Fernel (1497–1558)—which was used to explain how one person's disease could cause another, who had simply been in contact with that person, to suffer the same disease (a seemingly occult circumstance according to the individualistic precepts of humoral pathology). Essentially, the male stimulated the female to a state of fecundity and she was then able to produce a primordium from which the already viable egg emerged. The egg itself was then solely responsible for producing the fetus through a process of epigenesis. For Harvey the egg represented a distinct and crucial phase in the life cycle of an individual, mediating between the parent and the offspring. So, although Harvey is credited with recognizing that all creatures, including the viviparous, emerge from eggs, his is not the same as our modern view. Harvey was also convinced by observation that the *punctum saliens* in the hen's egg developed into a pulsing thread, an incipient aorta, even before the heart emerged, and so concluded that blood was the primary vital principle in the egg, responsible for turning the egg into more blood, and for turning the blood into the body of the fetus. This in turn led Harvey to deny the existence of a vital spirit residing in, but distinct from, the blood, and somehow created by a process in the left ventricle.

Bibliography

Primary: 1616. *Lectures on the Whole of Anatomy* [O'Malley, C. D., F. N. L. Poynter, and K. F. Russell, trans., 1961 (Berkeley)]; 1628.

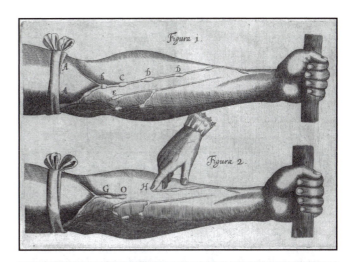

Harvey's demonstration of valves in the veins. Engraving from *Exercitatio anatomica de motu cordis* . . . Frankfurt, 1628. Rare Books, Wellcome Library, London.

An Anatomical Disputation concerning the Movement of the Heart and Blood in Living Creatures [Whitteridge, Gweneth, trans., 1976 (Oxford)]; 1649. *Exercitatio anatomica de circulatione sanguinis* (Cambridge); 1651. *Disputations touching the Generation of Animals* [Whitteridge, Gweneth, trans., 1981 (Oxford)].

Secondary: French, Roger K., 1994. *William Harvey's Natural Philosophy* (Cambridge); Bylebyl, Jerome J., ed., 1979. *William Harvey and His Age: The Professional and Social Context of the Discovery of the Circulation* (Baltimore); Pagel, Walter, 1967. *William Harvey's Biological Ideas* (New York); Keele, Kenneth D., 1965. *William Harvey, the Man, the Physician, the Scientist* (London); *DSB; Munk's Roll; Oxford DNB.*

John Henry

HASLAM, JOHN   (baptized London, England, 12 February 1764; d. London, 20 July 1844), *psychiatry.*

Haslam was born in obscurity, the son of another John Haslam, who must have been at least moderately prosperous to have funded his son's training. From an early age, the younger Haslam began to prepare to practice medicine, entering an apprenticeship (as was typical of the time) and then enrolling at St Bartholomew's Hospital, first as a student and then as a house surgeon. He attended George Fordyce's (1736–1802) lectures and worked as a physician's pupil under David Pitcairn (1749–1809). He then moved to Edinburgh (1785) and studied at the University there for more than two years. He was elected president of the Royal Medical, Natural History, and Chemical Societies. Thereafter, he pursued further studies at Uppsala in Sweden and at Cambridge University, though without obtaining a degree, a deficiency that precluded him entering the higher ranks of English medicine. He returned to London in the late 1780s, but his activities for the next several years remain mysterious.

In July 1795, however, he was elected as apothecary to Bethlem Hospital, the oldest and best-known institution for the treatment of mental disorders in the English-speaking world. A number of other medical men were also entering what was called 'the trade in lunacy' in these years, but Haslam's institutional position and his talents as a clinician soon won him a position of prominence among this emerging group of specialists. Bethlem's medical officers also included a visiting physician, Thomas Monro (1759–1833), and a surgeon, Bryan Crowther, but unlike them Haslam lived in the hospital. He quickly established lucrative connections with the proprietors of some of London's profit-making madhouses, especially Sir Jonathan Miles. In the meantime, he turned the opportunities for clinical observation to good account, publishing *Observations on Insanity* (1798), a book that was subsequently praised by both Philippe Pinel (1745–1826) and Samuel Tuke (1784–1857), proponents of moral treatment. There was much irony in this, for Haslam would soon become the *bête noire* of early nineteenth-century lunacy reformers, and he spent his career mocking and attacking those who promoted moral over medical treatment of the insane.

Haslam occupied a subordinate position at Bethlem, a situation he chafed under. He had a sharp tongue and pen, was convinced of his own intellectual superiority, and did not suffer fools gladly. His clinical experience had helped to convince him that insanity was a disorder of the body, and he was scornful of those who spoke of diseases of the mind. Yet in 1810 he published *Illustrations of Madness*, a remarkably detailed account of the delusions and hallucinations of one of his patients, James Tilly Matthews.

During the first fifteen years of the nineteenth century, Haslam's task at Bethlem was complicated by the poor physical state of the hospital, which by this time was quite literally collapsing. Soon, however, that was the least of his problems. A visit to the hospital in 1814 by a Quaker land agent, Edward Wakefield, keen to create a southern version of the Tukes' Retreat, led to a scandal that engulfed the institution, to the formation of a Select Committee of the House of Commons to study the state of madhouses, and to the dismissal in 1816 of both Haslam and his nominal superior, Thomas Monro. Indelibly linked to what the advocates of moral treatment alleged were the cruelties and harshness of the *ancien régime*, Haslam appeared to be a ruined man.

Instead, he exhibited a remarkable resilience. Selling his library to raise some capital, he purchased an MD from Marischal College, Aberdeen, and set about rebuilding his career as a physician. He acquired considerable repute as a witness in legal proceedings involving questions of insanity, and published regularly, stoutly defending medicine's prerogatives in the treatment of mental disorder, attacking what he saw as the cant and pretense of the advocates of moral treatment, and insisting, contrary to what was increasingly the received wisdom, that mechanical restraint was an essential element in the treatment of the insane. The proponents of lunacy reform were, he insisted, ignorant and misguided souls whose prescriptions were sure to make things worse. Two years before his death, he joined with Sir Alexander Morison (1779–1866) to form an organization dedicated to promoting these views, the Society for Improving the Condition of the Insane. His death came just twelve months before the reformers, led by Lord Shaftesbury, passed legislation enshrining the schemes of which he had been so bitterly critical.

Bibliography

Primary: 1798. *Observations on Madness* (London); 1809. *Observations on Madness and Melancholy* (London); 1810. *Illustrations of Madness* (London); 1817. *Medical Jurisprudence as It Relates to Insanity* (London); 1830. *A Letter to the Metropolitan Commissioners in Lunacy* (London).

Secondary: Scull, Andrew, Charlotte MacKenzie, and Nicholas Hervey, 1996. *Masters of Bedlam* (Princeton); Denis Leigh, 1955. 'John Haslam M.D. (1764–1844): Apothecary to Bethlem.' *Journal of the History of Medicine and Allied Sciences* 10: 17–44; *Oxford DNB*.

Andrew Scull

HASTINGS, CHARLES (b. Martley, Worcestershire, England, 11 January 1794; d. Worcester, England, 30 July 1866), *medicine, politics*.

Reputedly a cousin of Warren Hastings (1732–1818), the politician, Hastings was the sixth son and ninth child of a country parson. After a horseback accident, his father developed an incapacitating mental illness (though he eventually outlived his son), and hence Hastings's medical training started through an apprenticeship, for a few months to two surgeons in Stourport, Worcestershire, followed by some months' study in London. Three years after his appointment at the age of eighteen as house surgeon to the Worcester County Infirmary, however, he was able to go to Edinburgh University, where he graduated in 1818. Offered an immediate lectureship there in anatomy and physiology, he instead preferred to return to Worcester, where he was appointed physician to the Infirmary and spent the rest of his life in the city.

Hastings became preoccupied with improving provincial medical practice, and aimed to achieve this with the founding in 1826 of the *Midlands Medical and Surgical Reporter*. Nevertheless, only fifteen numbers were ever published, and four years later, when the publishers went out of business, Hastings changed tack and, though a new publication appeared after a few months, decided to start a new organization. In July 1832, in the midst of a threatened cholera epidemic, he called a meeting of fifty medical men in the Infirmary's boardroom to inaugurate the Provincial Medical and Surgical Association. With the stated aim of treating surgeons, physicians, and general practitioners equally, the proposed association had as its principal objective the increase of medical knowledge, and only secondarily the maintenance of the status of the profession in the provinces. Importantly, for many years the association and its successor was the major provider of postgraduate medical education outside the teaching hospitals.

With a lifelong, flourishing private medical practice, and a particular interest in chest diseases and industrial medicine, Hastings also threw himself into local affairs, presiding over an antislavery campaign and becoming a leading light in the natural history society and other societies. Nevertheless, he persisted with his medicopolitical activities, serving as secretary to the PMSA and taking a prominent role in the call for medical reform. The association was an enormous success, with the new railways enabling provincial doctors from all over Britain to attend its meetings, and there was strong pressure for it to change its name and move its operations to London. There had, however, been a previous, unsuccessful, British Medical Association, based in the capital, and initially Hastings resisted the proposals. Even so, in 1855 he bowed to the inevitable and, just as five years earlier its journal, the *Provincial Medical and Surgical Journal* (founded in 1840), had been renamed the *British Medical Journal*, so the organization became the British Medical Association.

Hastings was knighted in 1850 and received an honorary doctorate from the University of Oxford two years later, but achieved his second principal objective—the passage of the Medical Act and the formation of the General Medical Council—only in 1858, serving as Crown representative on the Council until he retired in 1862. Though the cynical might decry the medical reform movement as enlightened self-interest, the measures it advocated were all-important in the drive toward establishing a true medical profession. These included the identification of qualified doctors in a *Medical Register*, the laying down of standards for their training, and the protection of the public against quackery. Without the continual pressure from a powerful and prestigious organization led by an obviously first-class practitioner, who was not only a consummate medicopolitician but also pleasant and open-minded in debate, such evolution would have taken considerably longer and been more difficult to achieve—and the public would have been the loser.

Bibliography

Primary: 1832. 'Inaugural Address to the PMSA.' *Transactions of the PMSA 1832–33* 1: 5.

Secondary: Bartrip, P., 1996. *Themselves Writ Large* (London); McMenemy, W. H., 1959. *Charles Hastings and His Times* (London); *Oxford DNB*.

Stephen Lock

HATA, SAHACHIRŌ (b. Tomo, Iwami domain (now Shimane Prefecture), Japan, 23 March 1873; d. Tokyo, Japan, 22 November 1938), *bacteriology, medical chemistry.*

Sahachirō was the eighth son of Yamane Michiyasu and his wife Hide. Michiyasu was a wealthy farmer who also ran a successful brewery business. In 1887, when Sahachirō was fifteen years old, Hata Tokuta, who was a distant relative to the Yamane family and resided in the same village, adopted the promising young man. The Hata family had reputedly practiced medicine for eleven unbroken generations, and the adoption of Sahachirō was a means to continue the venerable family profession. With the prospect of inheriting the family's medical practice, Sahachirō matriculated in the preparatory course of the provincial Medical School of Okayama in 1890, graduated in 1895, and duly married Hata Tokuta's daughter Chiyo in the same year. He did not, however, fulfill the expectation of the Hata family. While working as an assistant doctor to the Prefectural Hospital of Okayama, the young Hata impressed Araki Torasaburō (1866–1942), who was the professor of medical chemistry at the Medical School of Okayama at that time and who later became an eminent biochemist. With the encouragement of Araki and the magnanimity of the family, Hata discarded the prospect of inheriting his family's medical practice and headed for Tokyo to join the frontier of medical scientific research. Hata's early career, in which he left a rural hometown to seek eminence in the capital, which had committed itself to modernization, thus embodied the ambition of the newly formed and aspiring nation. In 1898 he arrived in Tokyo to join the Institute for Infectious Diseases, headed by Kitasato Shibasabuō (1852–1931). At the Institute, Hata took responsibility for research and preventive activities on plague, which first hit Japan in 1899 and recurred in sporadic outbreaks during the following decade. From 1904 to 1905 he served as a medical and quarantine officer in the Russo-Japanese War.

The turning point came in 1907. Following the well-established career path for the Japanese medical elite, Hata left for Germany for further research. He first stayed at Robert Koch's Institute in Berlin for half a year, and then moved to Frankfurt to work under Paul Ehrlich (1854–1915). Having recently received a Nobel Prize in medicine in 1908, Ehrlich was then working on the new therapeutic principle of chemotherapy, trying to synthesize chemicals to destroy disease-causing organisms. Although Ehrlich's team had made progress in their attempt to develop chemotherapy against *Treponema pallida*, the causative agent of syphilis, the breakthrough was yet to come when the German scientist met the Japanese student. When Ehrlich learned that Hata had long worked on the plague organism, which, like spirochetes, posed a serious risk of infection to the laboratory scientist, Ehrlich chose Hata as the principal conductor of the research. Between 1908 and 1909, Hata conducted an extensive series of animal experiments: about one thousand chemical compounds, mainly arsenic-based, were synthesized and tested on thousands of animals that had been infected with the disease. One of the compounds, Preparation 606, turned out to be effective against the pathogens but not lethal to the animals. The compound was later named Salvarsan, and became the first effective chemotherapy. Hata's thorough, careful, and indefatigable work throughout the experiment earned special recognition from the grateful Ehrlich: Hata was arguably the greatest research assistant in the history of medicine.

In 1910 Hata returned to Japan crowned as the co-discoverer of Salvarsan. He was responsible for promoting

Hata Sahachirō with Paul Ehrlich (see biographical entry), 1910. Photogravure, Wellcome Library, London.

its use among Japanese medical practitioners and for its domestic production during World War I. In 1912 he was awarded an MD from the University of Tokyo for his work on Salvarsan. In 1920 he became professor of bacteriology at the newly established medical school of Keio University. He was invited to conferences across the globe, and national and international academic honors were showered upon him in his late years. Despite all these honors, he remained a modest, even low-profile, man: some would say he retained the mentality of a research assistant throughout his life. He died from arteriosclerosis in 1938 at the age of sixty-six.

Bibliography

Primary: 1981. *Hata Sahachirō ronsetsu-shū* [Collected Papers of Hata Sahachirō] (Tokyo); 1911. (with Ehrlich, Paul) *The Experimental Chemotherapy of Spirilloses* trans. A. Newbold and rev. Robert W. Felkin (London) (original German edition 1910).

Secondary: Hata, Fujiki, 1987. 'Hata Sahachirō no shōgai to gyōseki.' [Life and Works of Hata Sahachirō] *Nihon isigaku zasshi* 33; Hata, Yachiyo, 1952. *Hata Sahachirō shōden* [A Small Biography of Hata Sahachirō] (reprint, Tokyo, 1994).

Akihito Suzuki

HATEM, GEORGE **(aka MA HAIDE)** (b. Buffalo, New York, 26 September 1910; d. Beijing, China, 3 October 1988), *public health.*

Hatem was of Lebanese origin, but was born and brought up in the United States. He was educated in medicine at the American University in Beirut, Lebanon, and at the University of Geneva in Switzerland. He graduated in 1933 and traveled the same year to Shanghai at the recommendation of his wealthy Chinese roommate in Geneva, who wanted to go into private practice with him.

Shanghai in the 1930s represented a madhouse of foreign speculation and chaotic Chinese government. There was a healthy business to be made in treating venereal disease, which was Hatem's medical specialty, along with dermatology. Hatem, however, soon tired of the endemic corruption and flagrant lack of morals in Shanghai society and began to be influenced by a strong leftist movement led by such progressive foreigners as the American Agnes Smedley and the New Zealander Rewi Alley. He made the acquaintance of Madame Song Qingling, wife of the eminent Dr Sun Yatsen, founder of the Republic of China, and he began to learn more of, and identify himself more closely with, the goals and purpose of the Chinese Communist Party (CCP). In 1936 he closed his practice in Shanghai and, along with an intrepid American correspondent, Edgar Snow, crossed Guomindang lines and headed into the interior of China to Yan'an, the Communist Party's base camp. Here Hatem volunteered his medical services to Party leader Mao Zedong and for the next fourteen years served variously as medical consultant to the health department of the Central Revolutionary Military Commission, medical doctor to the CCP leaders, and as consultant to the foreign affairs office of the CCP Central Committee.

Hatem was the first foreign doctor allowed behind Communist lines and by far the longest serving. In 1937 he was honored with the distinction of being the first foreigner accepted into the CCP. While in Yan'an he married a Chinese lady, Zhou Sufei, and they had one son. Hatem came to be on close terms with some of the most powerful members of the future ruling elite of China, connections that were later to save his life.

In 1949, the year of the founding of the People's Republic of China, Hatem became a Chinese citizen, the first foreigner to be granted citizenship in the People's Republic. A year later, he was appointed to a public health position in the Ministry of Health. Here Hatem devoted himself to the eradication of syphilis and other sexually transmitted diseases in a nationwide series of mass sanitation campaigns that greatly improved basic health standards across the country. It was even claimed at the time that syphilis had been successfully removed from Chinese society. During the Cultural Revolution, the personal intervention of Premier Zhou Enlai allowed Hatem to remain in Beijing, while his wife and son were sent to reform through labor in the outlying province of Inner Mongolia. In 1977, a year after the end of the Cultural Revolution, Hatem turned his public health efforts to the eradication of leprosy in China. Demonstrating once again his lifelong determination to improve the health of the Chinese people, Hatem was eventually responsible for the establishment of three organizations on leprosy control in 1985: the China Association of Leprosy Prevention and Treatment, the China Welfare Foundation of Leprosy, and the China Research Center of Anti-Leprosy.

Bibliography

Secondary: Porter, Edgar A., 1997. *People's Doctor: George Hatem and China's Revolution* (Honolulu); Shapiro, Sidney, 1993. *Ma Haide: The Saga of American Doctor George Hatem in China* (San Francisco); Snow, Edgar, 1962. *The Other Side of the River: Red China Today* (New York).

Kim Taylor

HAYEM, GEORGES   (b. Paris, France, 25 November 1841; d. Paris, 29 August 1933), *hematology, pathology.*

The eldest of six children in a prosperous Jewish family, Hayem was intended for the commercial manufacturing enterprise founded by his father and mother, which was eventually taken up by a younger brother. Hayem opted for medicine instead, inspired, it was said, by the example of a revered ancestor who had intervened to save the desperately ill King Louis XV a century before. An outstanding student, Hayem placed first in the competition for internship in the Paris hospitals, and he rapidly ascended the academic hierarchy, becoming professor of therapeutics and materia medica at the Faculty of Medicine at the precocious age of thirty-eight. He worked under Vulpian at the Salpêtrière hospital, where he became close friends with Valentin Magnan, the future psychiatrist.

In 1878 Hayem won a post as physician to the Saint-Antoine hospital, where he would remain for the following thirty-three years. When he moved to a Faculty professorship of clinical medicine in 1893, he insisted that his courses remain at Saint-Antoine, where he had long since established an experimental and clinical laboratory. Hayem founded and for twenty-five years (1873–98) edited the *Revue des sciences médicales,* known as 'Hayem's journal', which contained an outstanding bibliography of contemporary publications from all countries, arranged by specialty.

Hayem's own prolific publications ranged over virtually all aspects of medical science and internal medicine: the nervous system (his MD thesis was on encephalitis), the heart and circulation, the liver, and the gastrointestinal system. Clinical investigator, animal experimentalist, physiologist, histologist, and pathologist, Hayem's most important contributions were in hematology, where his pioneering work made him a founder of the specialty. In his book, *Du sang et de ses altérations anatomiques,* he declared: 'the future belongs to hematology. It will bring us the solution to the great problems of disease' (1889, p. v).

From the 1870s Hayem embarked on a project described floridly by one of his students as constructing the 'magnificent edifice of the red corpuscle' (Dreyfus, p. 78). In a memoir to the Academy of Science, he identified the hematoblast as the blood element responsible for the formation and regeneration of erythrocytes. He classified various anemias and forms of hemorrhagic skin conditions (purpura). He had an apparatus constructed for counting red blood cells and devised an index of coloration. He studied the process of coagulation and the role of blood platelets, and he measured prolongation of bleeding times.

Hayem thus introduced quantitative methods into hematology, with important practical consequences for diagnosis and treatment, and he oversaw their application in his biweekly hospital teaching clinics as well as in his substantial private practice. He achieved good results treating cholera patients with intravenous solutions of isotonic saline (Hayem's serum). His contributions to the understanding of gastric pathology and chemistry were pioneering. Hayem trained a school of followers who described their mentor as outwardly somewhat cold and reserved, but generous and empathic underneath. Capable of devoting enormous energy to his work, erudite and dignified, Hayem was obliged to retire in 1911 at seventy, the mandatory retirement age for Faculty professors. He remained in good health until a very advanced age and continued to contribute actively to the medical literature and to professional societies. Hayem was spared the final indignity visited upon his Jewish colleagues within less than a decade of his death, that of being purged from the Academy of Medicine, the learned body of which he had been a member for nearly fifty years.

Bibliography

Primary: 1887–94. *Leçons de thérapeutiques* 5 vols. (Paris); 1889. *Du sang et de ses altérations anatomiques* (Paris); 1900. *Leçons cliniques sur les maladies du sang* (Paris).

Secondary: Dreyfus, Camille, 1957. 'Georges Hayem' in Dreyfus, Camille, *Some Milestones in the History of Hematology* (New York and London); Loeper, Maurice, 1933. 'Notice nécrologique sur M. Georges Hayem.' *Bulletins et mémoires de l'Académie nationale de médecine* 110: 145–155; Busquet, P., 1930. 'Hayem (Georges).' *Les biographies médicales* 6: 49–61.

Toby Gelfand

HAYGARTH, JOHN   (b. Swarthgill, Garsdale, Yorkshire, England, 1740; d. Bath, England, 10 June 1827), *medicine.*

Haygarth was the son of a yeoman farmer. He was educated at nearby Sedbergh School. He went up to Cambridge University in 1759 and then to Edinburgh, where he studied medicine. After a visit to the Continent, which included a stay at Leiden, he graduated MB at Cambridge in 1766.

A year later he was appointed physician to the Chester Infirmary. There he became a successful physician. In 1774 he was asked to investigate the population and diseases of

Chester. The resulting work, an excellent study of the population of every part of the city, was published by the Royal Society in 1778, and Haygarth was elected FRS a year later. Deeply concerned with the alarming mortality among the young from infectious fevers, particularly from smallpox, he published his *Inquiry How to Prevent the Smallpox* in 1784. He persuaded his fellow citizens to found a society for the prevention of smallpox using the technique of inoculation, in which material from a patient with smallpox was introduced into the arm of a healthy individual.

At the same time, he sought to prevent the spread of other infectious fevers by isolating sufferers, and he was responsible, in 1784, for setting aside separate wards at the Chester Infirmary for the treatment of fever patients. This pioneering development was to be followed in other cities throughout the land and led ultimately to the establishment of fever hospitals in nineteenth-century Britain. His friend and fellow student at Edinburgh, Thomas Percival of Manchester (1740–1804), was a close collaborator. Haygarth also knew the Quaker prison reformer, John Howard (1726–90), and sought to show how lazarettos for the prevention of the spread of plague should be managed. At the same time, he played an important role in extending the education of children at the Chester Bluecoat School to wider numbers from poor families.

In 1793 he published his monumental two-volume work, *A Sketch of a Plan to Eradicate the Casual Smallpox from Great Britain,* an ambitious and utopian attempt to extend his work at Chester on smallpox prevention to the entire country. It had little impact, being superseded in 1798 by Edward Jenner's (1749–1823) epoch-making discovery of the technique of vaccination.

In that same year, Haygarth retired from active medical practice and moved to Bath, where he lived at 15 Royal Crescent. He strongly supported Jenner's work, vaccination being initially considered highly controversial. At the same time, with his friend William Falconer, he successfully unmasked an American quack who sought to show that all manner of afflictions could be cured by the application of his 'Metallic Tractors', supposedly through the action of animal magnetism.

Haygarth had intended to spend his retirement writing up the voluminous records he had kept of his Chester patients, and he made a start in 1805 with studies of acute rheumatism. He particularly emphasized the use of the 'bark' (cinchona bark or quinine) in treatment. Other works include his *Letter to Dr Percival* (1801), in which he described in considerable detail the success of the fever wards at the Chester Infirmary.

He continued his philanthropic activities, contributing to the national debate on education by writing to Bielby Porteus, Bishop of London, in 1808 advising that schools should be established by the Church of England throughout the country, under the aegis of the Bishop in each diocese. He was also a prime mover in the founding of the Provident Institute at Bath for Savings in 1815, one of the earliest savings banks to be established in England.

In 1812 he moved to Lamridge House on the London Road, an elegant home where, after the death of his wife (1815), he lived with his daughter Mary. A staunch Anglican, John Haygarth worshipped at St Mary's Church in nearby Swainswick, a small village set among rolling hills, which must have reminded him of his native dale. He died in 1827. His tomb is in the churchyard at Swainswick.

Bibliography

Primary: 1784. *An Inquiry How to Prevent the Smallpox* (London); 1801. *A Letter to Dr Percival on the Prevention of Infectious Fevers* (Bath).

Secondary: Booth, Christopher, 2005. *John Haygarth FRS. A Physician of the Enlightenment* (Philadelphia); *Oxford DNB*.

Christopher Booth

IBN AL-HAYTHAM ABŪ 'ALI AL-ḤASAN IBN AL-ḤASAN AL-BASRĪ AL-MIṢRĪ (aka ALHAZEN) (b. Basra, Iraq, 965 ; d. Cairo, Egypt, 1039/1041), *optics*.

Ibn al-Haytham is regarded as the founder of physiological optics and its experimental science.

While living in Iraq, he wrote, among other books, a commentary on Euclid's 'Elements', in which he envisaged construction of a high dam on the river Nile, near Aswan, to regulate the water distribution. The fatimid Caliph al-Ḥākim (r. 996–1021) invited Ibn al-Haytham to visit Egypt and to construct the dam. On arrival, he realized that the insufficiency of the technical devices of that time made the dam impossible to build. In fact, the Dam of Aswan was constructed in the same place only in 1971. The Caliph al-Ḥākim was an exceptionally gifted but rather extravagant individual: he was persuaded that he himself was an incarnation of the Almighty. (Modern-day Druzes still consider him to be as such.) Therefore, nobody was safe at the Caliph's court. To try to save his life and be relieved from the task of building the dam, Ibn al-Haytham successfully played a madman. He was put under house arrest and his goods confiscated until the Caliph al-Ḥākim disappeared mysteriously on 13 February 1021. Only during the reign of subsequent Caliphs, al-Ẓāhir (r. 1021–36) and al-Mustanṣir (r. 1036–94), did Ibn al-Haytham reappear and recover his possessions, which later he probably endowed to the famous mosque and the University of al-Azhar. He settled in a small house there and earned his livelihood by transcribing books (he possessed beautiful handwriting).

In Europe, the works of Alhazen (as Ibn al-Haytham was known in the Latin West) became famous and were subsequently translated into Latin. His works are chiefly confined to geometry, stereometry, and astronomy. He introduced the theory of the gravity of the air and considered air density in conjunction with altitude. With regard to medicine, his works deal with the nature of light. Before Ibn al-Haytham, the teaching of optics was confined to the laws of light diffusion in the homogenous medium, the law of reflection of light, and the law of refraction. Following Galen's theories, he worked on the anatomy of the eye and disputed the ideas of Plato and Euclid with regard to sight. He pioneered the theory of sight and identified its nature as a process, whereby the rays form an image inside the crystalline lens of the eye.

Bibliography

Primary: Rashed, Roshdi, ed.,1993. *Les mathématiques infinitésimales du IXe au XIe siècle* (London).

Secondary: Rosenfeld, B. A., and E. Ihsanolğu, 2003. *Mathematicians, Astronomers and Other Scholars of Islamic Civilisation and Their Works (7th–19th c.)* (Istanbul); De Goeje, M. J., 1998. 'Notice biographique d'Ibn al-Haitham' in *Islamic Mathematics and Astronomy* vol. 57 *Texts and Studies* (Frankfurt am Main) pp. 186–188; Al-Kutubi, Z., 1972. *Al-Ḥasan bin al-Haytham* (Damascus); *DSB.*

Nikolaj Serikoff

HEAD, HENRY   (b. London, England, 4 August 1861; d. Reading, Berkshire, England, 8 October 1940), *neurology.*

Head, the son of an insurance broker (also called Henry Head) and his wife Hester Beck, daughter of a wine merchant, was educated at a Quaker school in north London and then at the elite private school Charterhouse before going to Trinity College, Cambridge (1880), to read natural sciences. From 1884 until 1886 he studied physiology in Prague and then qualified MB (Cantab) in 1890, taking his MD, also at Cambridge, in 1892. The MD thesis, on disturbances of sensation, was eventually published between 1893 and 1896. The combination of—or veering between—laboratory science and general medicine stayed with Head throughout his career.

In 1896 Head became assistant physician at the London Hospital in Whitechapel, the hospital he remained linked to for the rest of his life. While settling at the London, he brought with him an interest in the physiological basis of sensation, which was sustained through his observation of the dissociations produced by injury of the sensory nerve fibers. Head and a surgeon at the London realized that their patients who had such injuries were unable to accurately describe their sensations, partly through lay ignorance and partly because consultation time was inevitably short. There was only one solution: Head had to become the experimental subject himself. This experiment was performed in 1903, with the central presence of the psychologist W. H. R. Rivers (1864–1922), who helped to conduct the tests. The surgery excised small portions of Head's left radial and external cutaneous nerves, leaving him unaware of the nature of the stimuli applied and unable to recall the nature of his replies to questions asked by Rivers. The experiment was published in *Brain* in 1908 and was also featured in the multi-authored *Studies in Neurology* of 1920.

Head had, as it were, found a reliable witness in himself (as interpreted by Rivers), and this matter of finding reliable witnesses/patients was fundamental in his later work on aphasia. Although these researches were eventually written up in *Aphasia and Kindred Disorders of Speech* (1926), most of the work was done well before then. Head wanted to follow the example of John Hughlings Jackson (1835–1911) and investigate the psychological as well as the clinical aspects of speech disturbances. This required not only a new approach to aphasia (Head was scornful of almost all other previous work on aphasia since the 1860s), but also a new group of patients, who could make their own contribution to the research by being reliable self-witnesses, just as he himself had been in his study of sensory nerve injury. World War I brought such a group into being—intelligent young men, especially officers—who had been cut down in the full bloom of youth, often by gunshot, but who could understand the tests to be performed upon them and willingly collaborate. His patients participated as he himself had done, a reliable witness at his own point of injury; he became the figure to these patients that Rivers had been for him. Head thereby took the opportunity to apply very rigorous tests as a result—symbol testing, conversations, the ability to mime or to draw pictures of named objects—confident that his innovations in aphasic studies were partly based on a patient corps not rendered irrelevant in their own story by class, or bad education, or sheer age. Able to render into words the relevant parts of their own experience, Head's patients supplied data of a psychological dimension that was needed for a proper science of aphasia, allowing him to improve upon earlier and cruder accounts of the effects of lesions at various sites within the physical brain itself.

Elected FRS in 1899, Head was knighted in 1927. He married Ruth Mayhew in 1904: there were no children. His later years were disfigured by a chronic nervous disease, which came close to making him immobile.

Bibliography

Primary: 1920. (with Rivers, W. H. R., et al.) *Studies in Neurology* 2 vols. (London); 1926. *Aphasia and Kindred Disorders of Speech* 2 vols. (Cambridge).

Secondary: Jacyna, L. S., 2000. *Lost Words: Narratives of Language and the Brain, 1825–1926* (Princeton); Holmes, Gordon, 1941. 'Henry Head, 1861–1940.' *Obituary Notices of Fellows of The Royal Society* 3: 665–689; *Oxford DNB.*

Michael Neve

HEBERDEN, WILLIAM   (b. Southwark, London, England, 13 August 1710; d. London, England, 17 May 1801), *medicine.*

Heberden was the third child of Richard Heberden, an innkeeper, and Elizabeth Cooper. At the young age of fourteen he took a sizarship at St John's College, Cambridge, receiving a BA in 1728 and his MD in 1738. In 1752 he married Elizabeth Martin, daughter of John Martin, a member of parliament. She died in 1754, after bearing him two children, John (who died in infancy) and Thomas. In 1760 Heberden married again, to Mary Wollaston. The couple had eight children, only two of whom survived him,

Mary and William (William later became physician to the king).

After practicing medicine in Cambridge for ten years, Heberden moved to London in 1748, where he became one of the most distinguished physicians of the day. In 1746 he had been named a FRCP, and in 1749 he became a Fellow of the Royal Society. The first to differentiate chickenpox from smallpox, Heberden presented this finding in a paper that was typical of his life's work, both in the detailed clinical description it contained and in its being read to the College of Physicians. Benjamin Franklin (1706–90) asked Heberden to write a booklet giving instructions on how to inoculate for smallpox. Heberden carried on a busy clinical practice for almost thirty years; one of his last patients was George III, to whom he was summoned in 1788 on account of the king's mental derangement. Samuel Johnson (1709–84) called Heberden the 'ultimum Romanorum, the last of our learned physicians'.

Throughout his life Heberden took extensive notes on his clinical practice. Near the end of his life he used those notes to write his major work, *Commentaries on the History and Cure of Diseases*. His son, William, published the book in 1802, the year after his death. It is one of the last important medical books to be originally written in Latin, although an English translation also appeared the same year.

Heberden is best remembered today for his contributions to heart disease and to rheumatic disease. He was the first person to use the term 'angina pectoris' to describe a form of heart disease that is now thought of as part of the syndrome associated with 'heart attacks'. He described the syndrome with a fluency and precision that makes it unmistakable to twenty-first century physicians, and to patients who have the disease: 'Those who are afflicted with it, are seized, while they are walking, (more especially if it be up hill, and soon after eating) with a painful and most disagreeable sensation in the breast, which seems as if it would extinguish life . . . the moment they stand still, all this uneasiness vanishes . . . After it has continued a year or more, it will not cease so instantaneously upon standing still; and it will come on . . . when they are lying down' (Heberden, 1802, Chapter 30).

Heberden thus described inciting and relieving factors, the character of the pain, the emotions that accompany it, and its progression. Elsewhere he noted the various locations of the pain and the fact that it was more common in men, especially those older than fifty. He was, however, unaware of any association with coronary artery disease. It remains unclear whether he was describing a disorder that had already been recognized for some time, or whether he was noting a truly new disease.

Heberden is also remembered today for his thoughts on the rheumatic diseases. Gout was then a common disease, thought to render its sufferers free from more serious disease, although Heberden observed that 'this seems to be the favourite disease of the present age in England; wished for by those who have it not, and boasted of by those who fancy they have it; though

severely lamented by most who in reality suffer its tyranny' (*Commentaries*, 1802, p. 38). He did not agree with some of his colleagues' penchant for drastic treatment for gout, and for his reticence was labeled by Samuel Johnson 'Dr Timidorum Timidissimus'. Heberden saw no good in spa treatment and thought sea bathing far superior—thus encouraging the success of Brighton and its bathing machines.

The name of 'Heberden' today is most likely to evoke thoughts of the nodes that bear his name, affecting the joints at the end of the fingers. Heberden noted that these nodes were the size of a small pea, and had no connection with gout; they were usually not painful, but could be disfiguring. He associated these nodes with a disease he called 'chronic rheumatism', which we would now call 'osteoarthritis'.

Bibliography

Primary: 1768. 'On the chickenpox.' *Medical Transactions of the College of Physicians of London* 1: 427–436; 1772. 'Some account of a disorder in the breast.' *Medical Transactions of the College of Physicians of London* 2: 59–67; 1802. *Commentaries on the History and Cure of Diseases* (London).

Secondary: Silverman, Mark E., 2003. 'William Heberden and "Some Account of a Disorder of the Breast"' in Hurst, J. Willis, C. Richard Conti, and Bruce W. Fye, eds., *Profiles in Cardiology* (Mahwah, NJ) pp. 48–50; Michaels, Leon, 2001. *The Eighteenth-Century Origins of Angina Pectoris: Predisposing Causes, Recognition, and Aftermath* (London); *Oxford DNB*.

Joel D. Howell

HEGAR, (ERNST LUDWIG) ALFRED (b. Darmstadt, Germany, 6 January 1830; d. Oberried, near Freiburg im Breisgau, Germany, 4 August 1919), *gynecology*.

Hegar was the son of the Geheimer Obermedizinalrat August Hegar (1794–1882) and Caroline Stutzner (1800–34), the daughter of a lieutenant colonel. Hegar went to the gymnasium in Darmstadt and studied medicine in Giessen, Heidelberg, Berlin, and Vienna. He graduated as an MD in Giessen in 1852 and served as a medical practitioner in Darmstadt.

He was highly influenced by Gustav Simon, the professor of surgery in Heidelberg from whom he learned the techniques of plastic surgery and fistula operation. In 1864 he gained the professorship for obstetrics and gynecology in Freiburg im Breisgau, and stayed on there until his retirement in 1904.

Hegar is known as the founder of operative gynecology in Germany. In his textbook, which he published together with his disciple Rudolph Kaltenbach, he described all operations possible on the female genital organs. For example, Hegar mentioned the performance of clitoridectomy in three cases, as a therapy for masturbation or nymphomania. Following Semmelweis's work, he insisted on using antisepsis. An early indication of pregnancy (palpable softening of the collar of the uterus) was named after Hegar, but it lost its significance after hormonal testing for pregnancy became standard.

Dilatation pins used for widening the uterine collar are named after him (Hegar-Stifte).

During his days, Hegar gained a certain degree of fame for the performance of the oophorectomy of healthy ovaries as a surgical therapy for nervous disorders. He was first to perform this operation on 27 July 1872. Robert Battey (1828–95) soon followed, on 17 August 1872. Even though it was not disputed that Hegar had introduced this procedure, the operation was named after Hegar in German-speaking countries and after Battey in the English-speaking world. Indications for this operation were unbearable pains projecting onto the ovaries, painful menstruation, or palpable knots. Diagnostic methods were rare at that time, and the ambidextrous palpation of the inner organs was used, a diagnostic tool also introduced by Hegar. Hysteria was no indication for Hegar to operate on the ovaries, although he could not convince his colleagues from castrating women diagnosed as hysterics.

Hegar founded the journal *Beiträge zur Geburtshilfe und Gynäkologie* in 1898; he wrote articles and monographs about the role of women in society and their place in the world. He took a rather conservative point of view in his long answer to August Bebel's book *Die Frau und der Sozialismus* (first published in 1879), when he tried to downplay the assumed sex drive of women. He held the popular opinion attributing a stronger sex drive to black people, and he strongly argued for a certificate documenting the health of each family and its ancestors, in order to prevent reproduction in cases of pronounced 'degeneration' of an individual. These degenerations encompassed 'idiocy, insanity, epilepsy, congenital deaf-mutism, blindness and "instinctive" criminality'. He did not, however, advocate castration, as he was a strong believer in the effectiveness of regulation by law.

Hegar was honorary member of the Gesellschaft für Rassenhygiene, founded around Alfred Ploetz in 1905, a local chapter of which was installed by Eugen Fischer and Fritz Lenz in his immediate vicinity, in Freiburg im Breisgau. Hegar, together with a number of his contemporaries, advocated the necessity of social change through racial hygiene, a viewpoint that would later lead to genocide and the killing of 'unworthy' humans.

Bibliography

Primary: 1874. (with Kaltenbach, Rudolf) *Die operative Gynäkologie* (Erlangen) (4th edn., 1897); 1877. 'Die Castration der Frauen vom physiologischen und chirurgischen Standpunkt aus' in *Sammlung klinischer Vorträge* (Leipzig), pp. 136–138; 1894. *Der Geschlechtstrieb. Eine social-medicinische Studie* (Stuttgart).

Secondary: Spitzbart, H., 1985. 'Alfred Hegar (1830–1914).' *Zentralblatt Gynäkologie* 107(1): 58–60; Mayer, August, 1961. *Alfred Hegar und der Gestaltwandel der Gynäkologie seit Hegar.* (Freiburg im Breisgau); Lange, W., 1939. *Die Verdienste Alfred Hegars um die Entwicklung der Frauenheilkunde* (Düsseldorf).

Marion Hulverscheidt

HEISTER, LORENZ   (b. Frankfurt am Main, Germany, 19 November 1683; d. Bornum, Germany, 18 April 1758), *anatomy, surgery, medicine, botany.*

Heister, son of Johann Heinrich Heister, an innkeeper, and Maria Alleinsen, the daughter of a merchant, studied medicine in Giessen (1702–03) and in Wetzlar (1703–06). In 1706 he turned to the Netherlands. There he continued his training with the clinician Herman Boerhaave, the anatomists Frederik Ruysch and Goverd Bidloo, the surgeon Johann Jacob Rau, and the botanist Caspar Comelin. Eager to improve his surgical skills, Heister volunteered in the Spanish War of Succession during the summer seasons from 1707 to 1709. In May 1708 he obtained his MD at the University of Harderwijk.

Two years later Heister followed a call to the position of professor of anatomy and surgery at the University of Altdorf, near Nuremberg, where he arrived after a visit to England in November 1710. Here he married and established himself in the academic world. Nine years later he accepted the chair of anatomy, surgery, and physiology at the University of Helmstedt in the Duchy of Braunschweig-Wolfenbüttel. In May 1720 Heister set out for Helmstedt, where he spent the rest of his life, refusing calls to the universities of St Petersburg (1724), Kiel (1731), Göttingen (1734), and Würzburg (c.1748). In 1730 he exchanged the chair of anatomy for the chair of botany and the custody of the *Hortus medicus*. Heister, who had enjoyed robust health, died at the age of seventy-four during a visit to an out-of-town patient.

Heister was no reformer of medicine. He gained significance rather as an assiduous collector, a gifted teacher, and a prolific author. In 1717 he published his first 'best seller', the small *Compendium anatomicum*, which served generations of students as a reference book during dissection courses. The considerable popularity Heister enjoyed in his time, however, was due to his most successful work, the *Chirurgie* (1719). Based on his profound reading, his anatomical training, and his experiences in surgical practice, this handbook covered the whole field of surgery in a clear and expressive style and showed the relevant instruments in copper plates of high quality. Written in the vernacular, it found its way not only onto the scholarly bookshelves, but into the shops of the barbers and the salons of laymen as well. In the following decades it was translated into Latin (1739), Dutch, Spanish, English, Italian, and French. German ships' surgeons distributed it to Africa and Asia, and the Dutch edition even reached Japan. It was due to the uncommon success and the lasting impact of the *Chirurgie* that Heister has been labeled by later generations as the 'first academic surgeon in Germany'.

In the eyes of his contemporaries, however, Heister was not confined to surgery. In his correspondence, his casebooks (*Wahrnehmungen*, 1753, 1770), and his minor publications, he reveals himself as a well-established scholar with a wide field of activity and interest, including physic, obstetrics, forensic medicine, and anatomy. His medical advice was solicited in hundreds of consultation letters, and his scientific correspondence connected him with scholars from most European countries, including such renowned figures as Albrecht von Haller, Giovanni Battista Morgagni, and Christoph Jacob Trew. It was botany, above all, that dominated Heister's later scientific work. In open animosity to Carl Linnaeus, he created a botanical system of his own (*Systema plantarum*, 1748).

Bibliography

Primary: 1717. *Compendium anatomicum . . .* (Altdorf) (English edn., 1721); 1719. *Chirurgie . . .* (Nuremberg) (Latin edn., 1739; English edn., 1745); 1748. *Systema plantarum . . .* (Helmstedt); 1753, 1770. *Medicinische, Chirurgische und Anatomische Wahrnehmungen* 2 vols. (Rostock).

Secondary: Ruisinger, Marion Maria, 2003. 'Der flüssige Kristall. Anatomische Forschung und therapeutische Praxis bei Lorenz Heister (1683–1758) am Beispiel des Starleidens' in Helm, Jürgen, and Karin Stukenbrock, eds., *Anatomie. Sektionen einer medizinischen Wissenschaft im 18. Jahrhundert* (Stuttgart) pp. 101–125; Leporin, Christian Polycarpo, 1725. *Ausführlicher Bericht vom Leben und Schrifften des durch ganz Europa berühmten Herrn D. Laurentii Heisteri . . .* (Quedlinburg).

Marion Maria Ruisinger

VAN HELMONT, JOAN BAPTISTA (b. Brussels, Belgium, [baptized] 12 January 1579; d. Brussels, 30 December 1644), *medicine, chemistry, digestion, disease.*

Helmont was born into a noble Flemish family, the youngest child of Christiaan Van Helmont (d. 1580), a Brabant counselor, and Marie de Stassart. He attended the University of Louvain, but feeling that his studies were empty, refused his degree. He then studied astronomy, mathematics, law, and other subjects, and attended lectures offered by the Jesuits (particularly those by Martin del Rio, author of the *Disquisitiones magicae*), who had newly set themselves up in Louvain. All these studies he found unsatisfying. He then turned to medicine, took an MD in 1599, and lectured briefly in the Louvain medical faculty. He traveled through Switzerland, Italy, England, and France in1600–05, and claimed that everywhere he found only errors and ignorance in medical matters. In 1609 he married Margerite Van Ranst and settled on his wife's property at Vilvorde until moving permanently to Brussels in 1616. The couple had four daughters and one son, Francis Mercury Van Helmont (1614–99), who in 1648 produced the posthumous edition of his father's major work—the *Ortus medicinae* [The Dawn of Medicine]—and acquired his own fame as a courtier, author, and kabbalist.

Trouble started when Helmont involved himself in a dispute over the 'weapon-salve', a sympathetic cure, which was to be applied not to the wound but to the weapon that caused it. Helmont's *On the Magnetic Cure of Wounds* was

published in Paris in 1621, purportedly without his knowledge, and criticized both the Calvinist professor Rudolf Goclenius and the Jesuit Jean Roberti, who were involved in the dispute. Helmont's voluble defense of sympathetic magic and cures brought condemnation from the Louvain medical and theological faculties (1623–24 and 1633–34), the Spanish Inquisition (1625), and other bodies. Although he remained an orthodox Catholic and abjured his errors in 1627 and 1630, he was kept under house arrest in 1634–35. Although no further legal developments transpired after 1636, proceedings were not formally ended until 1642. His widow finally had his name cleared in 1646, two years after his death.

In 1624 Helmont published *Supplementa in spadanis fontibus*, a work on spa water that treated the origins of springs and showed that the transformation of iron into copper by the waters of some springs was not a transmutation, but rather a reciprocal dissolution of the iron and precipitation of copper naturally occurring in the water. In 1642 he published *De febribus* [On Fevers], for which he obtained the ecclesiastical imprimatur (as he had for *De spadanis*), and in 1644 reprinted this work in *Opuscula medica inaudita* [Little Unheard-of Medical Works], a collection also containing tracts on lithiasis, plague, and Galenic humors.

Intellectual Commitments

True to the spirit of the seventeenth-century *novatores*, Helmont vigorously rejected much of traditional learning. By 1607 he adopted Paracelsus as the renovator of a medicine that had been well-founded by Hippocrates but corrupted by Galen and his followers. In his maturity, however, Helmont criticized the Swiss iconoclast as much as he did Galen and Aristotle. Yet Helmont retained the Paracelsian stance that physiological functions were fundamentally chemical and that chemistry was paramount in understanding nature and in preparing medicines. To these ideas the Belgian philosopher added an emphasis on quantitative analysis and the use of the balance. Throughout his life Helmont practiced both medicine and 'pyrotechny', that is, the craft of the fire, or chemistry. He entitled himself 'philosopher by fire', implying that he had gained true knowledge, not from university studies, but only through chemical experiment. Helmont is undoubtedly one of the most important medical and scientific thinkers of the seventeenth century; his ideas exerted enormous influence well into the eighteenth century.

Helmont vehemently assailed Galenic medicine and Scholastic method. He rejected the humoral theory of health and disease along with the practices founded upon it, such as bleeding. He discarded the assignment of qualities and grades to medicaments (e.g., the idea that opium is 'cold in the fourth degree') as pseudomathematical, and rejected the concept of critical days. He denied direct astrological influence on human health or actions. He viewed Scholastic logi-

Joan Baptista van Helmont. Engraving from *Aufgang der Artzney-Kunst* ... Sultzbach, 1683. Rare Books, Wellcome Library, London.

cal practices as verbal juggling, and championed experiment and observation as 'ocular demonstrations' superior to syllogistic ones. It is clear that Helmont himself was an extremely acute and thoughtful observer of natural and medical phenomena. He argued that the *ratio* (reason) celebrated by Aristotle as characteristic of man is actually deceitful and common to lower animals. Following Neoplatonic and mystical thought, Helmont asserted that man's characteristic nature lies not in *ratio* but in *intellectus*, the true image of God in man, which can (though infrequently) gain knowledge instantaneously through exstasis, a divine way of knowing superior to the dull method of sequential logic. This was Adam's regular way of knowing before the Fall.

Natural Philosophy

Helmont's natural-philosophical, medical, and theological ideas form a comprehensive system. Rejecting both the

four elements of the Peripatetics and the *tria prima* (mercury, sulfur, and salt) of Paracelsus, Helmont argued that water is the basic material substratum of all substances. He based this water-theory upon both Genesis 1 and laboratory experiments, such as his famous 'willow-tree experiment' in which a five-pound sapling planted in 200 pounds of soil and given only rain or distilled water for five years gained 164 pounds in weight without any significant diminution in the weight of the soil—and thus water alone had been turned into all the substances of the tree.

According to Helmont, this transformation of water into the manifold forms found in nature occurs by the action of *semina* (seeds) produced by *fermenta* (ferments) implanted in the world by God. There is a resemblance here to the *rationes seminales* (seminal reasons) of St Augustine and the Stoics. The *semina*, however, must be guided by a directing principle; this *faber* (workman or smith) is the *archeus*, a quasi-spiritual entity containing within itself 'an image of the generated thing', which it impresses upon the newly developing object in the same way that strong images in the imagination of a pregnant woman can be imprinted upon the fetus.

Only fundamental changes, however, require *semina* and *archei*. Many transformations carried out in the laboratory—such as the dissolution of metals in acids to form salts—do not, however, involve the action of *semina*, but only a rearrangement of their minute particles. Such change was, for Helmont, superficial; the starting material receives only a *larva* (mask) but remains unchanged and recoverable in its original form. As one proof, he provided a workable experiment to re-isolate (in its original form and weight) even the sand out of glass.

In Helmont's economy of nature, substances can return to water through heat and cold. Fire can destroy many substances, allowing them to turn into *Gas* (a word coined by Helmont from *chaos*), a noncondensable substance more subtle than any vapor, but which retains some properties of the body from which it was produced. Burning sulfur produces a stinking *Gas sulphuris*, and burning charcoal a choking *Gas sylvestris*. Thus Helmont was the first to recognize the diversity of gaseous substances. Such *Gas*, exposed to extreme cold in the upper parts of the air, is subtilized into its smallest atoms, thus destroying the last vestiges of its origin, whereupon the *Gas* returns to elemental water. This return to water can also be accomplished by art using a fluid called the *alkahest*; when digested with any substance, the alkahest reduces it into its *primum ens* (first essence), and then into water. Helmont claimed to possess this substance, but declined to teach its preparation; scores of chemists after him eagerly sought to prepare it.

Physiology and Disease

Helmont's medical and natural philosophical ideas were inseparable. The human body is governed by a chief archeus, and individual organs have their own subordinate archei. The 'mouth of the stomach' is the seat of the immortal soul, which is linked to the sensitive soul, and thence to the chief archeus. The fact that sudden fear, surprise, and strong passions are felt first in the stomach testifies to this idea. The stomach and spleen (which Helmont called the body's *duumvirate*) are thus of primary importance. Helmont advanced a six-stage digestion process, each step further subtilizing food into a substance fit for assimilation. Recognizing the acidity of gastric juice, Helmont argued that food is first turned by an acidic ferment (originating in the spleen) into chyle. This 'cream' passes out of the stomach to receive a second ferment from the gall bladder, which converts the acid into salt. The mesentery then provides a third digestion, using a ferment from the liver to produce venous blood. In the heart, a fourth digestion converts venous blood into arterial blood, which by a fifth digestion becomes a vital spirit, which, diffused with the blood through the arteries, nourishing each part of the body in individual final digestions. Arterial blood, of which seven to ten ounces are produced daily, then volatilizes totally, expiring insensibly through the pores of the skin. Helmont seems to have been unaware of Harvey's theory of the circulation of the blood, and asserts the porosity of the heart's septum.

Diseases, like everything else, arise from specific *semina*; Helmont called disease 'an unknown guest' in the body. Some disease *semina* are hereditary, the image of the seed being impressed upon the offspring by its progenitor. Others arise when external forces irritate an archeus, so that owing to its anger or fury it impresses false or improper images upon the body, thus causing ulcers and cancers. In other cases, the archeus becomes lazy, fearful, confused, or weak, or is perturbed by a patient's troubled state of mind, and neglects or misdirects its activities. A neglectful archeus, for example, might allow food to remain too long in digestion, and thus putrefy, conceive foreign *semina*, and cause disease. Similar neglect could allow the *semina* of diseases impressed upon the body from outside to flourish, instead of being overwhelmed. Originally, the immortal soul was in direct and perfect command of the archeus, and so sickness was unknown. But after Adam's sin, the immortal soul withdrew from direct contact with the world, becoming enveloped within a mortal, sensitive soul that now governs the chief archeus, and because this soul is postlapsarian and thus subject to weakness and decay, disease and death have come into the world.

Effective medicines must therefore act to strengthen, pacify, or invigorate a disordered archeus, and to cleanse the body of improper or foreign *semina*. Because the Galenists are ignorant of the archeus, and thus of the true causes of disease, their medicaments treat only symptoms. Helmontian medicines must be prepared chemically to pass unharmed through the various digestions and arrive at the seat of the disease. Ideal for this purpose are saline materials, and especially the *prima entia* prepared from simples using

the alkahest, which frees them from all harmful qualities. Helmont especially commended the *primum ens* from the wood of the Cedar of Lebanon tree as a 'balsam of life'.

Bibliography

Primary: 1607. *Eisagoge in artem medicam a Paracelso restitutam* (in C. Broeckx, 1853–54. 'Le premier ouvrage de J.-B. Van Helmont.' *Annales de l'académie d'archéologie de Belgique* 10: 327–392; 11: 119–191); 1644. *Opuscula medica inaudita* (Cologne) (2nd edn., Amsterdam, 1648; reprint edn., Brussels, 1966); 1648. *Ortus medicinae* (Amsterdam) (reprint edn., Brussels, 1966); 1659. *Dageraad, ofte Nieuwe Opkomst der Geneeskonst* (Amsterdam) (reprint edn., Amsterdam, 1944).

Secondary: Porto, Paulo A., 2002. '*Summus atque felicissimus salium*: The Medical Relevance of the *Liquor Alkahest*.' *Bulletin of the History of Medicine* 76: 1–29; Debus, Allen, 2001. *Chemistry and the Medical Debate: Van Helmont to Boerhaave* (Canton, MA); Giglioni, Guido, 2000. *Immaginazione e malattia: Saggio su Jan Baptiste van Helmont* (Milan); Heinecke, Berthold, 1996. *Wissenschaft und Mystik bei J. B. Van Helmont (1579–1644)* (Bern and Vienna); Clericuzio, Antonio, 1993. 'From Van Helmont to Boyle: A Study of the Transmission of Helmontian Chemical and Medical Theories in Seventeenth-Century England.' *British Journal for the History of Science* 26: 303–354; Pagel, Walter, 1982. *Joan Baptista Van Helmont: Reformer of Science and Medicine* (Cambridge).

Lawrence M. Principe

HENCH, PHILIP SHOWALTER

(b. Pittsburgh, Pennsylvania, USA, 28 February 1896; d. Ocho Rios, Jamaica, 30 March 1965), *medicine, rheumatology.*

Hench, the son of Jacob Bixler Hench and Clara Showalter, graduated from Lafayette College, Pennsylvania, in 1916 and enlisted in the medical corps of the U.S. Army, completing his medical training at Pittsburgh (1920). He joined the Mayo Clinic in 1923 as assistant in the department of rheumatic diseases and in 1926 became the department's head. Between 1928 and 1929, he studied at the von Müller Clinic in Munich.

In 1929 a man with rheumatoid arthritis told him that within a week of developing jaundice, his symptoms had been relieved and he did not relapse until several weeks after the jaundice had disappeared. During the next five years Hench confirmed the relief of rheumatic symptoms in sixteen other jaundiced patients and began to think that, contrary to received wisdom, rheumatoid arthritis might be reversible. Artificially induced jaundice also brought relief, but not bile salts or transfusions of jaundiced blood. Thus, it seemed that the antirheumatic factor was an epiphenomenon of the illness causing jaundice, a hypothesis that was strengthened by Hench's observation that pregnancy had the same effect. He thought the unknown 'factor X' might be a hormone, albeit a unisexual one, because men received the same relief from it as women. His observations during the war years suggested that other diseases, such as psoriasis, asthma, migraine, hay fever, and myasthenia gravis, also remitted during pregnancy and/or jaundice.

In 1938 Hench began a close collaboration with the chemist Edward C. Kendall (1886–1972), who had isolated thyroxine (1914) and was now deeply involved in adrenal research. Of twenty-eight compounds that Kendall had isolated from tons of adrenal glands, one, Compound E, seemed to be particularly effective in preserving the life of adrenalectomized animals, and by 1941 Hench and Kendall thought it might be their substance X, but could not test this because of the miniscule amounts available. At this point the U.S. government, spurred by rumors that Luftwaffe pilots had unusual stamina from injections of adrenal extract, began supporting research on adrenal steroids. Merck continued this work after the war, and by April 1948, after having spent $14 million, had 9 g of Compound E, which was allocated for studies of Addison's disease or for basic research. By September 1948, Hench had managed to get some. His first patient, a twenty-nine-year-old woman who had been chair-bound with rheumatoid arthritis for five years, was able to walk after four injections. Fifteen more patients were treated, and the dramatic results were documented on 'before and after' cinefilms. The findings were trumpeted in the press as 'cures', although it soon became obvious that the benefit only lasted as long as the hormone, cortisone, was continued. Furthermore, it was a double-edged sword, because high doses produced iatrogenic Cushing's syndrome.

Hench was awarded the Nobel Prize in 1950 jointly with Kendall and Tadeus Reichstein (1897–1996) of Switzerland. Apart from his role in the development of cortisone, he was a highly regarded clinician and his teachings on arthritis, known as 'Hench's axioms', emphasized the importance of broad medical knowledge in the assessment of patients. He overcame a severe cleft palate to become a fine lecturer. In addition, he was a medical historian, and a member of the Sherlock Holmes Society.

Bibliography

Primary: 1933. 'Analgesia Accompanying Hepatitis and Jaundice in Cases of Chronic Arthritis, Fibrositis and Sciatic Pain.' *Proc. Staff Meet. Mayo Clin.* 8: 430–437; 1950. (with Kendall, E., C. H. Slocumb, and H. F. Polley) 'Effects of Cortisone Acetate and Pituitary ACTH on Rheumatoid Arthritis, Rheumatic Fever and Certain Other Conditions.' *Arch. Int. Med.* 85: 545–666; 1950. 'The Reversibility of Certain Rheumatic and Non-Rheumatic Conditions by the Use of Cortisone or the Adrenocorticotrophic Hormone.' [Nobel Prize lecture] *Annals of Internal Medicine* 36: 1–38.

Secondary: Hetenyi, G., and J. Karsh, 1997. 'Cortisone Therapy: A Challenge to Academic Medicine in 1949–1952.' *Persp. Biol. Med.* 40: 426–438; Marks, H. M., 1992. 'Cortisone, 1949: A Year in the Political Life of a Drug.' *Bulletin of the History of Medicine* 66: 419–439; *DAMB*.

Robert Tattersall

HENLE, FRIEDRICH GUSTAV JACOB (b. Fürth, Germany, 19 July 1809; d. Göttingen, Germany, 13 May 1885), *anatomy, histology, pathology.*

Henle came from a Jewish family that converted to Protestantism when he was a boy of twelve. His father, Wilhelm Henle, was a merchant and his mother, Helene Dorothea Diesbeck, was the daughter of a rabbi. At Koblenz, where Henle attended a classical secondary school, he became socially acquainted with Johannes Müller, then a newly appointed professor of anatomy at Bonn, who kindled Henle's interest in medical research.

From 1827 to 1831 Henle studied medicine at Bonn and Heidelberg, and received his MD at Bonn in 1832. When Müller took over the chair for anatomy and physiology at Berlin in 1833, Henle became his assistant. His first attempt to qualify as a lecturer failed in 1835, because a political denunciation of his earlier membership in a students' association sent him to prison. Through the intervention of Alexander von Humboldt, he was set free after four weeks, but was finally sentenced to six years' imprisonment in 1837. After a few weeks he was pardoned and so at last could resume his academic career.

In 1840 Henle was appointed professor for anatomy and physiology at the new university at Zurich, and in 1841 he published his famous *Allgemeine Anatomie* [General Anatomy], which was based on the chemical and microscopic investigation of the human (and animal) body. In 1844 he founded, together with the clinician Carl Pfeufer, the *Zeitschrift für rationelle Medizin,* a journal intended to bridge the gap between clinical empiricism and new scientific knowledge.

In Zurich Henle fell in love with his first wife, Elise Egloff, a young seamstress who worked as a nurse in the house of a colleague. They kept their engagement secret while he had her educated to fit into the position of a professor's wife. They married in 1846. She gave him a son and a daughter and died from tuberculosis in 1848. In 1849 Henle married Marie Richter; they had four daughters and a son.

Meanwhile Henle had moved to Heidelberg (1844) as professor of anatomy and physiology, where he strove to separate the two disciplines of anatomy and physiology. During this period he wrote his *Handbuch der rationellen Pathologie* (1846–53), in which he tried to bring together the newest findings in chemistry, physiology, histology, and morbid anatomy, and to evaluate their significance for pathology. In 1852 he took over the chair of anatomy at Göttingen, where he stayed for the rest of his life, and over a period of sixteen years composed his comprehensive *Handbuch der systematischen Anatomie des Menschen* (1855–71).

Because of his pioneering work in histology and his many contributions to microscopic anatomy (including 'Henle's loop'), Henle is rightly considered to be one of the greatest anatomists of his time. Of equal importance was his impact on general pathology because of a paper called 'Von den Miasmen und Kontagien', which was published among others under the title *Pathologische Untersuchungen* in 1840. By submitting the evidence of contagious diseases to logical reasoning, Henle pointed out that infection must be caused and spread by invisible living organisms. This was the basis upon which more than thirty years later Robert Koch, a former student of Henle, set up his medical bacteriology.

Bibliography

Primary: 1840. 'Von den Miasmen und Konatigien und von den miasmatisch-kontagiösen Krankheiten' in *Pathologische Untersuchungen* (Berlin) pp. 1–82, also in Marchand, Felix, ed., 1910. *Sudhoffs Klassiker der Medizin* No. 3 (Leipzig), English trans. by Rosen, George, 1938. *Bulletin of the History of Medicine* 6: 907–983; 1841. *Allgemeine Anatomie* (Leipzig); 1846–53. *Handbuch der rationellen Pathologie* 2 vols. (Leipzig); 1855–71. *Handbuch der systematischen Anatomie* 3 vols. (Braunschweig).

Secondary: Tuchman, Arleen M., 1993. *Science, Medicine, and the State in Germany: The Case of Baden 1815–1871* (Oxford and New York); Merkel, Friedrich, 1891. *Jacob Henle* (Braunschweig); *DSB*.

Johanna Bleker

HENRY OF MONDEVILLE (aka HENRI DE AMONDAVILLA, DE HERMONDAVILLA) (b. Émondeville, France, ?; d. Paris, France, *c.* 1320), *surgery, pharmacology, medicine.*

Originally from Émondeville (Manche), rather than Mondeville (Calvados), but certainly Norman, Henry was reputedly a student of a fellow Norman, John Pitart, who was surgeon to the kings of France from 1298 to 1327. It is unlikely that he studied with the bishop-surgeon Theodoric in Italy, as some have suggested. Henry himself describes studying both surgery and medicine in Paris and Montpellier, where he also practiced and taught. In Montpellier, Henry's teaching was on both surgery and medicine, and in Paris, on surgery alone. He acknowledges association with the surgical confraternity of Saints Cosmas and Damian, although it is unlikely this was a venue for surgical education, as some believe. From his preface, it is also likely that Henry had some connection to the Faculty of Medicine at the University of Paris, but just how is unclear.

His affiliation with John Pitart indicates an early association with the royal court (*c.* 1298), where starting from 1301 he was caring for the children of king Philip the Fair. About 1306 he began writing his magnum opus, despite duties at court. By 1312 the king had sent him to Artois, England, and throughout the French kingdom, both for court matters and as a medical aid to the French armies. That same year he also lectured in Paris and read the first two books of his surgical text. Henry refers to embalming the bodies of two kings of France, possibly Philip III, Philip the Fair, or Louis X. He also received patronage from Philip IV's brother, Charles, Count of Valois. Henry doubtless died of a pulmonary condition, the symptoms of which provoked complaint in his text.

The *Chirurgia* was written sometime between *c.* 1306 and Henry's death, although it remained incomplete. A portion was translated into French in 1314. Written in five books, it nevertheless has three gross portions: an anatomy, the core of the surgical text, and a list of drugs. These three parts circulated separately during the Middle Ages and survive in more than twelve manuscripts starting from the fourteenth century. Book One offers an anatomy, in which Henry advocated the use of both an artificial cranium and anatomical drawings to convey anatomical principles to students. Books Two and Three present wounds and their healing, as well as the usual potpourri of surgical conditions that were not wounds, ulcers or osseous. Book Four was never written, but was intended to discuss fractures and subluxations. In the fifth book, Henry deployed the newfangled Italian surgical antidotary of Lanfranc to complete his treatise. The only other text associated with Henry's name is a commentary by an 'Albertus', which survives in one fifteenth-century manuscript at Cambridge, England.

Henry's position for the field of surgery emphasized the value of the learned, literate surgeon, familiar with medicine, over the practicing lay surgeon; his rhetoric also suggests that he saw medicine proper as inferior to surgery, contrary to the precepts of the day. Stressing his textual facility, Henry based his surgery on Avicenna (Ibn Sīnā), Theodoric, Lanfranc, and other authors. Most famously, Henry characterized the contemporary tripartite schools of thought on wound-healing, advocating the position of Theodoric and Pitart before him on a minimalization of pus in acute wounds. In addition, he used recent authors and informatic techniques, such as those of John of Saint-Amand and his innovative concordance.

Henry was acutely aware of the niceties of clinical practice, caviling against the needs of the surgeon to pander to women and their cosmetic needs at court in order to maintain one's practice. Yet he was also sensitive to the appropriate bounds of surgical care, because during his tenure at court, the royal surgeon was placed in charge of overseeing surgical practice throughout Paris. This model of surgical regulation and training doubtless frustrated Henry's ambitions for his field.

Bibiography

Primary: Pagel, Julius Leopold, 1892. *Die Chirurgie des Henrich von Mondeville (Hermondaville) nach Berliner, Erfurter und Pariser Codices* (Berlin); Nicaise, Victor, 1893. *Chirurgie de Maître Henri de Mondeville, chirurgien de Philippe le Bel, roi de France, composée de 1306 à 1320* (Paris); Wernicke, Robert, 1897. *Aus dem Antidotarium des Henri de Mondeville (14. Jahrhundert)*, Inaugural-Dissertation, Medicinischen Facultät der Friedrich-Wilhelms-Universität zu Berlin (Berlin).

Secondary: Macdougall, Simone C., 2000. 'The Surgeon and the Saints: Henri de Mondeville on Divine Healing.' *Journal of Medieval History* 26: 253–267; Jacquart, Danielle, 1998. *La médecine médiévale dans le cadre parisien XIVe–XVe siècles* (Paris); Jacquart, Danielle, 1994. 'Medical Practice in Paris in the First Half of the Fourteenth Century' in García-Ballester, Luis, et al., eds., *Practical Medicine from Salerno to the Black Death* (Cambridge) pp. 186–210; Pouchelle, Marie-Christine, 1990. (Morris, Rosemary, trans.) *The Body and Surgery in the Middle Ages* (New Brunswick, NJ).

Walton O. Schalick III

HEO, JUN 渚栅 (b. Korea, 1539; d. Seoul, Korea, 1615), *Korean medicine, epidemiology.*

Heo Jun is the most famous physician in Korean history. A royal doctor by his early thirties, he served the Royal Hospital for more than forty years and wrote at least seven medical treatises, including the internationally known *Dong'uibo'gam* 镲捷咽鏌 [Treasured Collections of an Eastern (Korean) Physician]. After its first publication in 1613, *Dong'uibo'gam* saw more than ten reprints in Korea, more than thirty in China, and at least two in Japan.

Though his father was a county governor, Heo Jun's mother was a concubine. Because the children of concubines were legally barred from taking office in the civil service or the military, the only professions open to a boy of Heo Jun's birth were astronomy, the law, the interpretation of Chinese and Japanese texts, and medicine.

Nothing is known about Heo Jun's medical training. In 1581, while working at the Royal Hospital, King Seonjo (r. 1567–1608) ordered him to revise an important book on diagnosis, which medical students had been using as a basic text for at least a century.

Heo Jun became famous in 1590 for curing thousands of smallpox patients, among them the crown prince, Goang'haegun. At that time he was the only royal physician to ignore the religious prohibition against treating people for the disease. He refused to accept the contemporary belief that the god who brought smallpox would kill any patient who sought medical treatment. This success encouraged him to write a medical text aimed at putting an end to the practice of not treating smallpox patients, *Oenhaedu'chang'jip'yo* 惠滬飲探桦帽 [Essentials of Smallpox with Korean Translation].

Dong'uibo'gam, completed in 1610, brought Heo Jun long-lasting fame. After the first Japanese invasion of Korea in 1592, King Seonjo ordered him to compile a medical book to expose the effects of war upon medicine. Work began with a team of six doctors, five of them royal doctors, but after the second Japanese invasion in 1597, his colleagues scattered and he had to finish the treatise alone. It took Heo Jun ten years to complete this twenty-five-volume work. Meanwhile, as the first royal doctor, he was impeached for King Seonjo's death and exiled between 1608 and 1609 to Uiju, at the northern frontier of Korea. Although the exile was painful, it gave Heo Jun the time that he needed to complete most of the work, which was finally published in 1613.

Dong'uibo'gam consists of five sections: inner-body physiology and symptoms, outer-body symptoms, common diseases, pharmacology, and acupuncture and moxibustion. This book had three distinctive features. First, it attached more importance to cultivation of the mind and body than to external medical treatment. The popularity of Neo-Confucian and Taoist self-cultivation techniques among the ruling *yangban* class in Korea was influential in this regard. Second, it made an attempt to resolve apparent contradictions within traditional East Asian medical discourse, such as those between knowledge and practice that were highlighted between the four great doctors of Jin and Yuan. Between the Han and Ming dynasties, Chinese medical texts and remedy collections were widely disseminated throughout the territory equivalent to modern-day Korea, together with their opposing viewpoints. Third, it emphasized the benefits of using locally produced drugs, according to Korean tradition.

During 1601, while working on *Dong'uibo'gam*, Heo Jun also wrote manuals on obstetrics, emergency treatments, and smallpox. All of these books, originally written in Chinese script, as was conventional in Korean literature, were also translated into vernacular Korean to allow easy access for a popular audience. Heo Jun spent his last days studying the prevention of typhus and scarlet fever. As the leading doctor in Korea he championed preventive health care, writing two short books on infectious diseases. His book on scarlet fever, *Byuk'yeok'sinbang* 径嫄筧 [Divine Remedies for Treating Contagious Illness], later attracted serious attention from medical historians for his unique and original observations, which were unprecedented in both China and Korea. The Japanese medical historian Sakae Miki insists that Heo Jun was the first person to study the disease in East Asian countries. His descriptions of the symptomatology, including fever, headache, sore throat, dropsy, rash, and desquamation, seem so accurate that they have been compared to those in Daniel Sennert's 1627 European treatise on fever.

Heo Jun died in 1615. In an honor unprecedented in Korean history, the king posthumously conferred upon him the highest court rank.

Bibliography

Primary: 1601. *Oenhaedu'chang'jip'yo* [Essentials of Smallpox with Korean Translation] (Seoul); 1613. *Dong'uibo'gam* [Treasured Collections of an Eastern (Korean) Physician] (Seoul); 1615. *Byuk'yeok'sinbang* [Divine Remedies for Treating Contagious Illness] (Seoul).

Secondary: Dongwon, Shin, 2004. *Hoyeolja, Choson'eul Seup'kyok'hada: Momgoa Ui'hak'ui Hankuk'sa* [Cholera Invaded Korea: A Korean History of Body and Medicine] (Seoul); Dujong, Kim, 1966. *Hankuk Ui'hak'sa* [History of Korean Medicine] (Seoul); Sakae, Miki, 1962. *Chosen Igakusi Kyu Sitsubeisi* [History of Korean Medicine and of Disease in Korea] (Osaka).

Dongwon Shin

HERCUS, CHARLES ERNEST   (b. Dunedin, New Zealand, 16 June 1888; d. Dunedin, 26 March 1971), *medical research, medical education.*

Hercus, son of Canadian-born Elizabeth Jane Proctor and Peter Hercus, a Scottish-born warehouseman or merchant, was schooled at Christchurch Boys High. He then qualified in both dentistry (1911) and medicine (1914) at the University of Otago before joining the New Zealand Medical Corps; he was supposedly the only man to disembark at Gallipoli carrying a microscope. Hercus retained a lifelong affection for army service; his death certificate described him as a retired dean of medicine and an ex-serviceman.

Hercus's interest in preventive and social medicine stemmed from his wartime experiences. In 1922 he became professor of public health and bacteriology at Otago, and within three years he was faculty subdean. Such was his stature that no one stood against him when the deanship fell vacant in 1937. From 1928 until 1938 he was the driving force behind the Clinical Club of Dunedin, which would become a casualty of the time that he later devoted to university and research activities after 1937.

Hercus revolutionized public health teaching at Otago, in collaboration with senior officials in the New Zealand Health Department and local authorities. An admirer of Sir George Newman, he helped establish a health clinic in the Home Science Department, where students gained an awareness of social, economic, and community influences on health; undergraduate class examinations were discarded in favor of a public health thesis.

Surviving theses (some 3,300 in total) show the changing scope of Hercus's research agenda. The earliest comprise numerous local studies, often with a focus on housing, infectious diseases (notably tuberculosis and sexually transmitted diseases), industrial health, and aspects of the dairy and meat industries. Topics from the 1930s included Maori health, health camps, and infant and preschool health. The emphasis was very much on the community.

Hercus had a profound influence on New Zealand health research. In 1921 he began to study links between endemic goiter and iodine deficiency in New Zealand soils. Murray Drennan, professor of clinical pathology at Otago, instigated this project, but it was Hercus who convinced the Health Department in 1923 that 'the greatest encouragement should be given to research work'. As a member, and later chairman, of the Medical Research Council of New Zealand, he ensured the creation, at its foundation in 1937, of an endocrinology committee; this reflected his commitment to employing full-time researchers on problems of particular concern to New Zealand. His contribution was acknowledged with an invitation to deliver the 1952 Banting Memorial Lecture in Toronto, one of his most cherished moments.

Hercus facilitated ongoing research into hydatids, another area of special local interest, initially pursued by Louis Barnett. He also demonstrated a concern for indigenous health, dating from his brief time as a district health officer, and encouraged student theses in this field. He actively promoted medical research in neighboring Polynesia, first through the aegis of the South Pacific Health Board (1944) and then as chairman of the Island Territories Research Committee from 1946 onward, and he personally led a medical expedition to the Cook Islands during the university's long vacation of 1949–50.

These activities were in addition to the demands placed upon him as dean from 1937 to 1958. One obituarist noted that '[he] was the last of a generation that was expected to and was able to run single-handed a faculty of medicine', while the Otago University Council paid tribute to his achievement in transforming 'an efficient training centre for general practitioners . . . into a modern institution that achieved a more appropriate balance between teaching and research'.

Bibliography

Primary: 1921. (with Baker, E.) 'Statistical Study of the Incidence of Goitre Amongst the School Children of Canterbury and the West Coast.' *New Zealand Medical Journal* 20: 116–121; 1936. 'War Memories.' *Digest* 1(3): 26–30.

Secondary: Hercus, C., and G. Bell, 1964. *The Otago Medical School under the First Three Deans* (Edinburgh).

Derek A. Dow

HERNÁNDEZ, FRANCISCO   (b. La Puebla de Montalbán, near Toledo, Spain, *c.* 1517; d. Madrid, Spain, 28 January 1587), *botany, natural history, medicinal plants.*

The exact date and year of Hernánadez's birth are unknown, but most scholars agree it was *c.* 1517. Nothing is known of Hernández's family or of his early life and education. Like the famous Golden Age author of *La Celestina*, Fernando de Rojas, he was born in La Puebla de Montalbán, and like him was most probably of *converso*-Jewish origin.

Significance of Hernández's Work

Hernández identified and described more than 3,000 plants that were not then known in Europe. His work included important descriptions of cacao, chili, corn, tobacco, and tomato and of their medicinal uses. Through his work, some European botanists, physicians, and pharmacists turned their attention away from Old World medicinal plants and toward the plants of the New World as sources for new materia medica. In addition to being an active and important botanist, he was also an active physician with clinical and experimental experience.

Education and Medical Practice

Hernández was educated at the Renaissance University of Alcalá de Henares, where other important Spanish physicians also studied, among them Nicolás Monardes (*c.* 1492/

1508–88), Francisco Vallés, Juan Barrios, and Francisco de Arceo. Among the latter, Monardes is of special interest in that he was one of the first Spanish physicians to be interested in and write about New World materia medica. He also cultivated American plants in his famous garden located in Seville. Between 1565 and 1574 he published his *Historia medicinal,* in which he included New World plants. Unlike Hernández, he never visited the New World.

After completing his medical education in Alcalá de Henares, Hernández practiced medicine for several years in Toledo and Seville. By the 1560s, he had risen to the position of royal surgeon, with prestigious appointments at the hospitals of Guadalupe (Extremadura) and the Hospital de la Santa Cruz Toledo in Spain. While working at the famous hospital of Guadalupe he performed many autopsies, thereby perfecting his knowledge of human anatomy. During this time he is believed to have come into contact with the famous anatomist Andreas Vesalius.

In addition to his work in medicine, botany, and material medica, Hernández is also known for his translation and commentaries on Pliny's *Natural History,* which he began in 1567 and finished while working in Mexico in the 1570s. This was one of the first Spanish translations of Pliny, and, like all of his works, it was not published in his lifetime.

Expedition to New Spain

Hernández was court physician to Philip II, and in 1570 he was named *Protomédico de las Indias*—a kind of surgeon general or chief medical officer of the Spanish American colonies—and principal investigator of a scientific expedition to New Spain. In his instructions to Hernández in 1570, Philip II declared: 'wishing that our subjects should enjoy a long life and preserve health, [I] take care of providing them with physicians and teachers, who will direct, teach and cure illness'. The Crown was very keen not only on the use of medicinal plants but also on the economic implications of the trade in American drugs. Of particular interest was guaiacum, which was used in the treatment of syphilis and was a source of wealth for many Europeans.

As his title indicates, while in New Spain Hernández was, by order of the King, to act as *protomédico* and carry out inspections and certifications of local physicians, hospitals, and medical practitioners. However, because of impediments from the local *Audiencia* (local governing court), he was not able to carry out these administrative duties and instead turned to his botanical investigations.

Hernández's fame begins with his 1570 trip to New Spain. His charge was to lead a scientific expedition, one of the first of its kind, to undertake a detailed study of native materia medica, especially with respect to medicinal plants and their uses. The main purpose of this expedition was to gather information from native medical men in New Spain about 'herbs, trees, and medicinal plants', with the objective of learning uses, doses, as well as the conditions for cultiva-

tion, so that the medicinal plants could be grown in Spain. Hernández was also expected to carry out the same research in Peru, a task that he was not able to complete.

Hernández set out to create what was then called 'a moral and natural history'. In doing so, he compiled a series of ethnographic materials on the Valley of Mexico, which today we would describe as 'medico-botanical-anthropological' in nature. Hernández spent more than six years traveling throughout Mexico, studying and chronicling information related to native medical knowledge and practices. He not only collected information, but also investigated and did field work in the areas where the plants grew. In addition, he experimented on himself as to the effectiveness of the plants and other medicinal remedies. In addition to plants, Hernández also studied the use of animals and minerals as materia medica. While in Mexico, Hernández worked in the Hospital Real de Indios, located in Mexico City, and experienced firsthand the terrible epidemic of the 'cocolitzli', and subsequently wrote a treatise on the epidemic and disease.

Hernández's investigations culminated in a work known as *The Natural History of the Plants of New Spain*, which was completed by 1577 but was never published in his lifetime. In its original form, it consisted of sixteen folio volumes written in Latin and contained descriptions and illustrations of plants, animals, and minerals that were used as materia medica in Mexico. The majority of the botanical information found in Hernández's work was not known in Europe at the time.

In 1577 Hernández, who had recently turned sixty years old, returned to Spain, extremely ill but with the high hopes of seeing his work published and well received. He turned over his work to the King; however, it was given over to one Nardo Antonio Recchi, a Neapolitan physician and one of Philip II's court physicians, who was called upon to draw up a shorter version of Hernández's work and organize it in such a manner that the information might be more useful. It was deposited in the library of El Escorial where, sadly, it was destroyed in the terrible fire of 1671.

However, drafts, fragments, editions, and translations of Hernández's work survived in Spain and Mexico and in other places. Generations of scholars, scientists, physicians, botanists, and pharmacists have published editions of Hernández's original works as well. His work remains, even to this day, an extensive and exhaustive body of research and source of information on medicinal plants from the New World. It has been called 'one of the most original works on materia medica of the Renaissance'. His research is considered to be the most extensive ever done concerning the plant, animal, and mineral materia medica of Mexico.

Hernández and Aztec Medicine

There is no doubt that Hernández had close contact with native Mexican healers. Hernández viewed Aztec medicine and the use of medicinal plants through the lenses of European humoral pathology and therapeutics. His critique of Aztec medicine can be found throughout his work and especially in his *De antiquitatibus Novae Hispaniae* [On the Antiquities of New Spain], which bears some similarities to Bernardino de Sahagún's work in that it deals with Aztec religious ceremonies, customs, laws, and medicine. Bernardino de Sahagún (1499–1590), a Franciscan missionary, was educated at the University of Salamanca, and then went on to spend the greater part of his life in Mexico carrying out significant ethnographic and anthropological investigations. Much of this work is found in his famous encyclopedic Florentine Codex, which contains a great deal of information on medicinal plants and their uses. There is no record of Hernández and Sahagún ever meeting, nor do we have any information on Hernández's knowledge of the Codex Cruz Badiano (1552), a primary source on Aztec plants and their uses. This manuscript was prepared at the College of the Holy Cross of Tlatelolco, near Mexico City, where Sahagún taught and carried out his important research using native informants.

Studies on Hernández

One of the earliest references to Hernández is found in the work of the Jesuit missionary and theologian José de Acosta (1540–1600), *Historia natural y moral de Indias* (2nd edn., Barcelona, 1590), which treats the natural and moral history of the New World. In his book, Acosta refers to a number of useful plants, but because he was not trained as a scientist, he does not describe them from a botanical or scientific perspective.

A significant amount of Hernández's work appeared in Francisco Ximénez's *Quatro libros de la naturaleza y virtudes de las plantas y animals que estan recevidos en el uso de la medicina en la Nueva España* (Mexico, 1615). Francisco Ximénez was a lay hospital brother who worked with Bernardino Alvarez, a key figure in the history of Mexican hospitals. Ximénez worked at the Hospital of the Holy Cross in what is now the state of Morelos, where he came into contact with Hernández. Ximénez' s work deals with the so-called Four Books of Nature and the virtues of the plants and animals that were used in New Spain (Mexico) as medicines and the manner in which they were prepared and administered. This book is based on the Latin work of Hernández, translated by Fray Francisco Ximénez of the Convent of St Dominic in Mexico City. María de Espinosa López Dávalos, widow of Diego López Dávalos, printed Ximénez's work in Mexico City. The primary object of Ximénez's work was to provide practical medical information, especially on the use of medicinal plants for people living in places with no access to physicians or prepared medicines.

In addition to Ximénez, Hernández also came into contact with other physicians working in Mexico who were to produce some of the first of the so-called Mexican medical classics, among them the work of Gregorio López (*c.* 1542–*c.* 1596), author of the *Tesoro de las medicinas*, of Agustín Farfán (1532–

1604), author of *Tractado breve de anathomía y chirugía* (Mexico, 1579), and of Alfonso López de Hinojoso (1534–97), who is known for his *Summa y recopilación de chirugía* (Mexico, 1578). A significant amount of information on Hernández was also published in the work of Fray Agustin de Vetencourt (1620–1700) and is found in his *Teatro mexicano*.

Unfortunately Hernández's work remained unpublished in his native Spain during the seventeenth century, even when it was known in Mexico, Italy, the Netherlands, Britain, and France. Portions of Hernández's writings first appeared in Juan Barrios's *Verdadera medicina cirugía astrología* (Mexico, 1607), and in the writings of the seventeenth-century Jesuit theologian and professor of natural history Juan Eusebeo Nieremberg (*c.* 1595–1658), including his *Historia naturae, maxime peregrinae* (1635).

The Rome Edition

For almost fifty years from 1603 to 1651, the Accademia dei Lincei was involved in the publication of Francisco Hernández's *Mexican Treasury*. This work, often referred to as 'the Rome Edition', is one of the most important, if not the most important, editions of Hernández's work. It is most certainly the most important in terms of the dissemination of Hernández's writings. In 1603 Federico Cesi (1585–1630) founded the Accademia dei Lincei, which was one of the first scientific societies of the modern period. The Accademia dei Lincei was at once a scientific society, a scientific brotherhood, and a philosophical militia. The purpose of this society or brotherhood was to engage in free inquiry into the natural sciences. It sought to investigate and study the many mysteries of nature and to reorganize knowledge and produce a visual theater of nature. In the words of its founder, the principal objective of this young men's intellectual club was to 'read the great and true and universal book of the world'. This scientific society was a secular counterpart to religious institutions, such as the Jesuits, which also had a firm commitment to scientific investigation. The Accademia dei Lincei was a scientific fraternity that stressed the acquisition and mutual exchange of knowledge. They also formed an international scientific network for the transmission and reception of knowledge, although it was not as extensive as that of the Jesuits. The Accademia dei Lincei and its scientific research also must be contextualized in the aftermath of the Counter-Reformation in Rome.

The two principal flagship projects of the new Academia dei Lincei were the publication of the works of Galileo and of Francisco Hernández. Galileo became a member of the Accademia dei Lincei in 1611, and from that date the Accademia fostered the publication of his works. Francesco Stelutti was especially influential in publishing and collaborating with Galileo. Galileo, in turn, was aware of the work of Francisco Hernández and of the Lincei's publication of the *Mexican Treasury*.

Members of the Accademia dei Lincei came into contact with work of Francisco Hernández via two paths: first through Federico Cesi's visit to Naples in 1603, where he came into contact with the noted Neapolitan scholar Giambattista Della Porta (1538–1615) and Della Porta's attempts to acquire Recchi's copy of the Hernández manuscript, and second through the study of the Hernández manuscripts at El Escorial. At least three of the Lincei visited or attempted to visit the Escorial Library in order to see and study Hernández's texts. These include the visits of Johannes Schreck (c. 1577–1653), also known as 'Terrentius', of Eck (Heck or Herkius), and of Cassiano dal Pozzo.

Cassiano dal Pozzo (1588–1657) was a seventeenth-century patron of the arts and sciences and a famous antiquarian. In 1622 he became a member of the Accademia dei Lincei. While in Rome he came into the service of Cardinal Francesco Barberini (1597–1679), who was nephew to Pope Urban VIII. Cassiano was also instrumental in commissioning the copy of the Codex Cruz Badiano, which is known today as the 'Erbario Messicano' and housed in the Royal Collection in Windsor Castle, England. Cassiano dal Pozzo also visited the Escorial Library, where he came into contact with the librarian Andrés de los Reyes. Andrés de los Reyes was the principal archivist and librarian of the Escorial from 1622 to 1638. Cassiano asked the librarian for permission to copy several important Hernández works. Among them were Hernández's treatise on animals and minerals, later published by J. Faber, and the most important *Index alphabeticus plantarum Novae Hispaniae*, which was used for the Rome Edition and is of great importance in reconstructing the works of Hernández lost in the Escorial fire of 1671.

Hernández in the Netherlands

In 1625 the Dutchman Jan (or Joannes) de Laet (1582–1691), the director of the Dutch West India Company and a noted geographer, became interested in Hernández. His work *Nieuwe Wereldt ofte Beschrigvingh van West-Indien* (Leiden, 1625) and *Novus orbis descriptionii Indiae occidentalis* (1633) incorporated a great deal of material based on Hernández's writings. These works described the plants, geography, climate, and customs of the Caribbean and of Central and South America. The primary purpose of these works was to serve as a guide for the employees of the Dutch West India Company. Other men from the Low Countries who were important for the spread of Hernández's work include Willem Pies or Piso (c. 1611–78), who was a Dutch physician and worked at the Dutch settlement in Brazil (1636–44), and the natural historian and geographer Georg Margraff (d. 1643). This work is found in their *Historiae rerum naturalium Brasiliae libri octo*, which is part of *Historiae naturalis Brasiliae* (1648) and includes Pies's *De medicinia Brasilensi libri quattuor*.

Hernández in England

In addition, Hernández's work also appeared in the works of John Ray, Robert Morison, and Hans Sloane in

Title page of *Rerum Medicarum Novae Hispaniae Thesaurus . . .* 1651. Engraving. Rare Books, Wellcome Library, London.

England. John Ray's *Historia plantarum*, 3 vols. (London, 1686–1704) contains many portions based on Hernández's research. Robert Morison (1620–83) was a Scottish botanist and the author of *Plantarun historia universalis oxoniensis* (1699), which along with Ray's work served to develop the systematic classification of plants and also contains numerous references to Hernández. Of greater importance are the references found in the writings of Sir Hans Sloane (1660–1753). Sloane was a noted physician, scientist, and collector. His collection became part of the founding core of the British Museum. Sloane cited Hernández extensively in his *Catalogus plantarum quae in insula Jamaica sponte proveniunt* (London, 1696), as well as in his famous *A Voyage to Jamaica* (1725).

Hernández in France

During the early part of the eighteenth century, Hernández's work was made known in France through the writings of Joseph Pitton de Tournefort (1656–1708), Charles Plumier, Pierre Pomet, and Antoine-Laurent Jassieu (1748–1836).

Tournefort, the noted French botanist, physician, and director of the Jardin des Plantes in Paris, is remembered for his system of classification of plants and his interest in New World plants. His interest in the work of Hernández is seen in his *Institutiones rei herbari,* 3 vols. (Paris, 1700). Charles Plumier (1646–1704), a French botanist, a member of the Order of Minims, and a student of Tournefort, used Hernández in both his *Description des plantes de l'Amerique* (Paris, 1693) and his *Nova plantarum americanarem genera* (Paris, 1703–04). Another Frenchman, Etienne François Geoffroy (1672–1731), a physician, chemist, and pharmacist, mentions Hernández extensively in his *Tractatus de materia medica* (1741) and in his *Traité de la matiere medicale,* 3 vols. (Paris, 1743). We also find references to the work of Hernández in Pomet's *A Compleat History of Druggs* (trans. London, 1712).

Linnaeus and Pehr Löfling

Carl (Carolus) Linnaeus (1707–78), the famous Swedish biologist known for his system of naming and classifying living organisms, was also very interested in the work of Hernández, especially through the work of his star student Pehr Löfling (1729–56). In 1751 Löfling moved to Spain. Four years later he participated in a scientific expedition to Venezuela under the command of José Iturriaga. He died during this expedition and Linnaeus subsequently published his work. This work, titled *Iter Hispanicum* (1758), contains many references to Hernández.

Hernández in Spain

In Spain the noted Spanish botanist, pharmacist, and chemist Casimiro Gómez Ortega (1741–1810), who was also director and professor of the Real Jardín Botánco (Royal Botanic Garden) and royal pharmacist to Charles III, published Hernández's *Opera, cum edita tum inedita, ad autographi fidem et integritatem expressa,* 3 vols. (Madrid, 1790), based on manuscripts discovered in the Jesuit Colegio Imperial in Madrid in 1767 by Juan Bautista Muñoz. Gómez Ortega's *Opera,* also known as 'the Madrid Edition', was printed by Joaquin Ibarra (1725–95). While not a true 'complete works', it was the first attempt at such an endeavor. During the eighteenth century, the work and traditions of Hernández were continued by three important scientific expeditions commissioned by Charles III of Spain. The first included expeditions of Híploito Ruiz and José Pavón to Peru and Chile. The results of these expeditions were published in their famous *Flora Peruviana et Chilensis* (1777-1788). The second was José Celestino Mutis's (1783–1810) exploration of what is now Colombia, which culminated in his famous *Flora Nueva Granada.* The third major expedition was headed by Martín Sessé y Lacasta (1751–1808) and José Mariano Moçiño (1757–1820) and is summarized in their *Catálogo de animales y plantas mexicanas,*

Guaiacum tree of the West Indies, the bark of which was used to treat syphilis. Woodcut from *Rerum Medicarum Novae Hispaniae Thesaurus . . .* 1651. Rare Books, Wellcome Library, London.

Plantae Novae Hispaniae and *Flora mexicana.* The purpose of this expedition was '. . . to make drawings, collect natural products, and to illustrate and complete the work of Dr. Francisco Hernández'. At this time we also find the important work of the Mexican Jesuit teacher and Aztec scholar, Francisco Javier Calvijero or Calvigiero (1731–87), who included significant information from Hernández in his *Ancient History of Mexico* (1780–81).

Hernández in the Twentieth Century

At the end of the twentieth century a significant amount of research on Hernández was carried out in Mexico. Research by the Instituto de Biología of the National University of Mexico (UNAM), as well as the first edition of the *Complete Works of Francisco Hernández (Obras completas),* contributed significantly to research on Hernández. The most complete Hernández bibliography has been compiled by and is a part of the *Complete Works* by the UNAM. During the latter half of the past century the 'Francisco Hernández Project' housed at UCLA's Center for Medieval and Renaissance Studies and the Instituto de Estudios Documentales e Históricos sobre la Ciencia at the University of Valencia has also greatly expanded research on Hernández. Originally working separately, in time the UCLA team and the group from Valencia came together and worked jointly. The work of the Francisco Hernández Project was headed by Simon Varey and Rafael Chabrán, and culminated in the publication of two volumes by Stanford University Press in 2000. These volumes brought together the most recent research on the life and work of Francisco Hernández, including an anthology and English translations of his work.

Bibliography

Primary: 1960–84. *Obras completas* (Mexico); 1590. Codex Pomar; Barrios, J., 1607. *Verdadera medicina* (Mexico); Ximénez, F., 1616. *Quatro Libros de la naturaleza* (Mexico); De Laet, J., 1625. *Nieuwe Wereldt ofte Beschrigvingh van West-Indien* (Leiden); 1626. *Index alphabeticus plantarum Novae Hispaniae*; De Laet, J., 1633. *Novus Orbis descriptionii Indiae occidentalis* (Leiden); Nieremberg, J. E., 1635. *Historia naturae, maxime peregrinae* (Antwerp); 1651. *Rerum medicarum Hispaniae thesaurus* (Rome); 1790. *Opera* (Madrid); 1888. *Cuatro libros de la naturaleza* (Mexico); 1888. *Cuatro libros de la naturaleza* (Morelia); 1926. *Antigüedades de la Nueva España* (Mexico); 1942–46. *Historia de las plantas de Nueva España* (Mexico); 1945. *Antigüedades de la Nueva España* (Mexico); 1959. *Historia de las plantas de Nueva España* (Mexico); 1966–76. *Historia natural* (Mexico) (translation of Pliny's *Natural History*); 1998. *De materia medica Novae Hispaniae libri quatuor* (Aranjuez and Madrid); 2000. (Varey, Simon, ed., with the assistance of Rafael Chabrán and Cynthia L. Chamberlin) *The Mexican Treasury: The Writings of Dr. Francisco Hernández* (Stanford).

Secondary: Freedberg, David, 2002. *The Eyes of the Lynx* (Chicago); Varey, Simon, Rafael Chabrán, and Dora Weiner, eds., 2000. *Searching for the Secrets of Nature: The Life and Works of Dr. Francisco Hernández* (Stanford); Chabrán, Rafael, 2000. 'The Classical Tradition in Renaissance Spain and New Trends in Philology, Medicine and Materia Medica' in Varey, S., et al., *Searching for the Secrets of Nature: The Life and Works of Dr. Francisco Hernández* (Stanford) pp. 21–32; Chabrán, Rafael, and Simon Varey, 2000. 'The Hernández Text in the Mexican Treasury' in Varey, S., et al., *Searching for the Secrets of Nature: The Life and Works of Dr. Francisco Hernández* (Stanford) pp. 3–25; Varey, Simon, ed., and Rafael Chabrán and Cynthia Camberlin, trans., 2000. *The Mexican Treasury: The Writings of Dr. Francisco Hernández* (Stanford); Chabrán, Rafael, 1996. 'López Piñero y la historia de la historia natural: Las aportaciones de Francisco Hernández.' *Arbor* 153(604–605): 161–196; López Piñero, J. M., and José Pardo Tomás, 1996. *La influencia de Francisco Hernández (1515–1587) en la constitución de la botánica y la materia médica modernas* (Valencia); Chabrán, Rafael, and Simon Varey, 1995. 'Mexican Medicine Comes to England.' *Viator: Medieval and Renaissance Studies* 26: 333–353; Chabrán, Rafael, and Simon Varey, 1995. 'An Epistle to Arias Montano: An English Translation of a Poem by Francisco Hernández.' *The Huntington Library Quarterly* 55(2): 621–634; López Piñero, J. M., and José Pardo Tomás, 1994. *Nuevo materiales y noticias sobre la Historia de las plantas de Nueva España de Francisco Hernández* (Valencia); Varey, Simon, and Rafael Chabrán, 1994. 'Medical Natural History in the Renaissance: The Strange Case of Francisco Hernández.' *The Huntington Library Quarterly* 47(2): 125–151; Somolinos D'Ardois, Germán de, 1960. *Vida y obra de Francisco Hernández* (Mexico City); *DSB.*

Rafael Chabrán

HEROPHILUS OF CHALCEDON   (b. Chalcedon, Asia Minor [now Kadiköy, Turkey], *c.* 330 BCE; d. *c.* 260 BCE) **and ERASISTRATUS OF CEOS** (b. Iulis [now Kéa], Ceos, Greece, *c.* 315 BCE; d. Mycale, Asia Minor [now Turkey], *c.* 240 BCE), *anatomy, medicine, physiology, vivisection.*

Herophilus was born in the small town of Chalcedon on the Bosporus. At some time in his youth he studied medicine under Praxagoras of Cos. He may even have worked in Athens for a time, but it is in Alexandria that he spent the most productive part of his career. Erasistratus, his younger contemporary, was born in Iulis on Ceos. He was initially active at the court of the Selucids at Antioch, as was his father, Cleombrotus, and his teacher, Chrysippus of Cnidus. The evidence suggests that the bulk of his career was also spent in Alexandria.

Herophilus and Erasistratus practiced medicine in Alexandria at a unique period in history and were responsible for a set of remarkable advances in anatomy and physiological theory. Their chief and revolutionary innovation is that they practiced, for the first and only time in Western Antiquity, systematic human dissection and probably also human vivisection. Although Herophilus and Erasistratus carried out these practices on animals as well, the former has given them their fame and notoriety. Celsus reported, through a utilitarian argument that he did not endorse, that human vivisection, while admittedly cruel, might be considered useful in that future lives could be saved by the knowledge gained. However, the Patristic writer Tertullian condemned Herophilus as a 'butcher' (*lanius*) and a 'dissector of adults' (*maiorum prosector*). Galen, our chief source for Herophilus and Erasistratus, mentioned animal vivisections carried out by both men, and states that Herophilus made most of his new advances in anatomy not by dissecting animals but by dissecting human beings, though Herophilus himself was silent on the question of human vivisection. The balance of evidence does suggest that human vivisections were carried out and that the subjects were likely Egyptians who had been condemned to death by the Ptolemaic state and thus were beneath consideration by the new Greek rulers.

The circumstances probably helped loosen the traditional Greek strictures against mutilation of the dead. That these values were further weakened by exposure to Egyptian embalming practices is possible, but unlikely. It should also be noted that political patronage exercised by the newly established Hellenistic Ptolemaic rulers (specifically the first two Ptolemies) enabled Herophilus and Erasistratus to undertake their groundbreaking researches. Such patronage, Galen noted, was mandatory for conducting research into the human body. In addition, sponsorship was a means for a ruler to increase his prestige and status, and Herophilus's arrival in Alexandria coincided with the state's acquisition of the services of other representatives of the intelligentsia of the Greek world, such as Aristarchus and Euclid. At any event, human dissection and vivisection began and ended in antiquity with Herophilus and Erasistratus. By the second century, Galen urged his students to visit Alexandria if possible in order to augment their anatomical training in osteology, where specimens of the human skeleton were available for study.

Herophilus's Works

Herophilus wrote at least eight books on medical subjects, of which only fragments survive, although many were transmitted, in more or less intact form, to Galen's day. In antiquity, some believed that Herophilus was the author of the Hippocratic treatise *On Nutriment*, but that text was composed at least one hundred years after Herophilus (and the so-called *Letter of Herophilus to the King of Antioch* is a medieval forgery). The first book of Herophilus's *Anatomy* examined the brain and nerves; Book II described the liver and abdominal contents; Book III the reproductive system; and Book IV discussed the blood vessels, the heart valves, and the blood supply of the brain. Herophilus's description of the liver is meticulous and accurate, and based on the human organ. His term for the duodenum is still in use, and he seems to have described the retina accurately for the first time. But it is Herophilus's work on the brain and nerves that is arguably his greatest achievement. Herophilus reaffirmed the distinction, first made by Aristotle, between cerebrum and cerebellum. He also gave a description of part of the venous sinuses of the brain, the *torcular Herophili*. Another part of the brain's vascular system that Herophilus seems to have described for the first time is the *retiform plexus*, a relatively inaccessible, symmetrical arrangement of small arteries found in the base of the brain in certain animals. That the retiform plexus does not exist in man (or ape) is evidence that Herophilus's anatomical work relied far more on animals than on human beings. Herophilus described the ventricles of the brain, noting that within them lay a complex of arteries and veins, which he thought resembled the fetal chorion, and so he termed them *choroid twisted clusters* or *choroid plexuses.*

Herophilus seems to have regarded the posterior (or fourth) ventricle, the ventricle of the cerebellum, as the most important. He described in detail the floor of the fourth ventricle, likening it to a reed pen (*calamus scriptorius*). We do not know how Herophilus experimented on the ventricles in order to reach his conclusion concerning the importance of the fourth ventricle. Galen, however, in a discussion that implies Herophilus knew of the other ventricles, stated that Herophilus thought that it was not the middle (third) ventricle, but the fourth ventricle that was the most important and essential for life. Observation of how butchers killed animals by cutting through the base of the brain (in the region of the upper cervical vertebrae), together with knowledge of the anatomical relationships of the fourth ventricle to the cerebellum and spinal cord, may have given Herophilus the basis for his ventricular experimental work.

Herophilus held that the motor nerves arise from the brain and spinal marrow, but he did not completely distinguish between nerves, tendons, and ligaments, apparently placing all of them under the umbrella of structures that collectively exercise the same physiological function. Herophilus seems to have considered pneuma as a physiological medium for nervous action, but exactly how he employed it for this purpose is uncertain. He did not depart from the Praxagorean concept that the arteries contained pneuma (as well as blood), and therefore the Herophilean theory of physiology does not exclude the vascular system from consideration as a medium for sense transmission. In the extant work of Herophilus, the brain assumed anatomical and physiological prominence for the first time, and a causal relationship was established between the brain and the nerves on the basis of empirical research.

None of the discussion of Herophilus's anatomical achievements is meant to diminish his accomplishments in other fields of medicine. His *On Pulses* elaborated an increasingly complex system of pulse classification, much emulated and elaborated upon by later medical authors. His *Midwifery* was the first text specifically devoted to this subject (although, like Erasistratus, he held that there were no diseases specific to women); and *On Eyes* may well have considered the eye from the anatomical, physiological, and therapeutic points of view. *Therapeutics* showed a wide-ranging approach to the subject, and the beginnings of later polypharmacy can be traced to him. *Against Common Opinions* was as much directed against common notions in medicine as it was a way for Herophilus to promote views of the medical art. Herophilus apparently elaborated a tripartite classificatory framework for the theory and practice of medicine. This consisted of 'knowledge of things concerning health', into which fell matters related to anatomy and physiology; 'knowledge of things concerning disease', which dealt with pathological conditions; and 'knowledge of neutral things', concerned with surgery, therapeutics, and dietetics. Clearly, such a framework would be highly adaptable.

Erasistratus's Achievements

The anatomical and physiological work of Erasistratus was based on a similar, Herophilean, program of dissection and experimental vivisection. Erasistratus also investigated the brain in some detail. He held that the anterior ventricles communicated with each other at their point of contact and that from there, a passage (the aqueduct) led to a cavity in the cerebellum (the fourth ventricle). It is likely that the aqueduct was Erasistratus's discovery. Several sources speak of Erasistratus placing the controlling center of the body, not in a ventricle or ventricles of the brain, but in the covering layers of the brain (or at least in the dura mater). The reason is linked to the question of the source of the nerves, for according to Galen, Erasistratus, until late in life, maintained that the nerves originated in the brain's meningeal layers. He subsequently regarded the brain substance as the source of the nerves.

Broadly speaking, if Herophilus can be assigned credit for major discoveries in anatomy, then Erasistratus, although responsible for genuine accomplishments in anatomical science, especially his depiction of the heart valves and his elucidation of their function, was the more wide-ranging and investigative physiologist of the two. Erasistratus's lost *General Principles* can be considered the first comprehensive textbook on human physiology, discussing the function of the body in broadly mechanistic terms based on the principle of matter 'moving towards that which is being emptied'. Thus, air had to enter the lungs after exhalation in order to fill a potential empty space. Pneuma was a mainstay of Erasistratean physiology. In the heart, pneuma from outside air was refined into 'vital' pneuma. This in turn was further processed by the brain into a 'psychic' form, which entered the nerves. This is broadly similar to Galen's later conception of pneumatic differentiation, but for Erasistratus these changes were quantitative, not qualitative as they were for Galen. And for Erasistratus, pneuma was carried in the arteries as well as in the nerves, which is similar to the view of Herophilus's teacher, Praxagoras, who held that pneuma carried by the arteries alone was the agent for voluntary motion. For Erasistratus, the veins only carried blood. Erasistratus also differed from Galen (and mainstream Hippocratic practices) in his aversion to venesection. Erasistratus favored a more holistic approach to illness and disease, also avoiding purgation as far as possible, but seems to have countenanced venesection in extreme cases. Pathological states could in some instances be explained by a blockage of pneuma (for example, the effects of apoplexy were deemed to be caused by phlegm blocking the nerves from the brain, so impeding the passage of psychic pneuma). In others, an excess (or 'plethora') of blood in the veins might have been responsible for a wide range of disease states.

Conclusion

After Herophilus and Erasistratus, there was little systematized anatomical study until the beginning of the second century, when anatomy entered a period of revival. During this period of almost 400 years, increasing emphasis was placed on codification of existing medical knowledge. How-

Herophilus and Erasistratus. Detail of a woodcut depicting classical herbalists and medical scholars, from the title page to Lorenz Fries, *Spiegel der Artzney* . . . 1532. Iconographic Collection, Wellcome Library, London.

ever, the innovations of Herophilus and Erasistratus in clinical medicine and therapeutics resulted in continuing developments in pulse theory, pharmacology, surgery, and orthopedics. Herophilus and Erasistratus also bequeathed to posterity eponymous medical sects, and the Erasistrateans in particular were influential even in Galen's time. There is no doubt that Herophilus and Erasistratus pushed forward the frontiers of understanding of the human body, making possible the anatomical and physiological work of later medical authors, especially Galen's, as well as those of the Renaissance anatomists. But for all their revolutionary advances in broadening medical science in this field, Herophilus and Erasistratus gained these insights in part by utilizing living human subjects. Such practices bear comparison to those carried out by Nazi Germany and Imperial Japan, both of which defined the condemned as less than human. It is a sobering legacy.

Bibliography

Primary: Garofalo, Ivan, 1988. *Erasistrati fragmenta* (Pisa); Von Staden, Heinrich, 1989. *Herophilus. The Art of Medicine in Early Alexandria. Edition, Translation and Essays* (Cambridge).

Secondary: Guerrini, Anita. 2003. *Experimenting with Humans and Animals. From Galen to Animal Rights* (Baltimore); Von Staden, Heinrich, 1992. 'The Discovery of the Body: Human Dissection and Its Cultural Contexts in Ancient Greece.' *Yale Journal of Biology and Medicine* 65: 223–241; Longrigg, James, 1981. 'Superlative Achievement and Comparative Neglect: Alexandrian Medical Science and Modern Historical Research.' *History of Science* 19: 155–200; Lonie, Iain, 1975. 'The Paradoxical Text "On the Heart".' *Medical History* 17: 1–15, 136–153; Lonie, Iain, 1964. 'Erasistratus, the Erasistrateans, and Aristotle.' *Bulletin of the History of Medicine* 38: 426–443; *DSB*.

Julius Rocca

HERRICK, JAMES BRYAN   (b. Oak Park, Illinois, USA, 11 August 1861; d. Chicago, Illinois, USA, 7 March 1954), *medicine, cardiology.*

Herrick was the son of Origen White Herrick, a banker, and Dora Ellen Kettlestrings. He married Zellah P. Davies in 1889; they had two children. Herrick graduated from the University of Michigan in 1882. An English professor at Michigan introduced Herrick to Chaucer, sparking a love for Chaucer that remained with Herrick throughout his life. (He once gave an after-dinner talk entitled 'Why I Read Chaucer at Seventy.') Herrick was for a time a high school teacher in Oak Park and Peoria, Illinois. While there, his interest in teaching the students physiological functioning in a living dog earned him a public warning from the American Society for the Prevention of Cruelty to Animals.

In 1888 Herrick received his MD from Rush Medical College in Chicago; he spent the following year as an intern at Cook County Hospital, also in Chicago. Herrick spent his career at Cook County Hospital and Presbyterian Hospital, the latter of which he served as its president from 1908–13. He was also on the internal medicine faculty at Rush Medical College. Herrick found time early in his career to attend additional clinics in Berlin, Vienna, and Prague in order to advance his understanding of the latest findings in clinical medicine. He never stopped wanting to learn more, and at the age of forty-three returned for a time to the classrooms at the University of Chicago to study new developments in biological, physical, and organic chemistry.

Starting the year after he graduated from medical school, Herrick put his clinical observations into print, publishing at least one paper in most years, and as many as eleven in 1896. Herrick was said to be a master at bedside diagnosis, and his first book was a manual of physical diagnosis. His early habit of writing about his clinical observations may have prepared him for his case discussions of the two diseases for which he is most often remembered: sickle cell anemia and coronary thrombosis.

Sickle Cell Anemia

In 1904 Walter Noel, a twenty-year-old dental student from Grenada, was admitted to Presbyterian Hospital, suffering from recurrent, nonhealing skin lesions. When Herrick's intern, Ernest Irons, examined the blood he saw numerous deformed, sickle-shaped cells. The very decision to look microscopically at the patient's blood was somewhat unusual in 1904. Moreover, Herrick did not rely on the hospital laboratory, but instead based his conclusions on personal observations by himself and the intern who was working with him. Herrick and Irons followed Noel for two years, until he returned to Grenada to practice dentistry. Herrick did not publish his observations until 1910, and they are probably the first description of the disease we now know as sickle cell anemia. Herrick proposed that 'some unrecognized change in the composition of the [red blood cell] corpuscles itself

may be the determining factor', a prescient suggestion in light of our current understanding of the disease.

This case description raised questions about whether clinical presentation or laboratory findings ought to take precedence in making a diagnosis. Herrick's generation of clinicians primarily saw laboratory findings as only part of larger picture, not as the determining piece of information. This emphasis would change for future generations. As sickle cell anemia came to be diagnosed far more often in people of color, this disease also raised new questions about how much importance to assign to skin color—often coded as 'race'—in making a diagnosis.

Coronary Thrombosis

By 1910 Herrick had written a good deal about heart disease. He was well acquainted with previous discussions in the medical literature about 'coronary thrombosis', the occlusion of one or more of the 'coronary arteries' supplying the heart with blood. Most people thought that occlusion of a coronary artery would prevent blood from supplying a large part of the heart and would lead to immediate death of the patient, although some observers had suggested that the syndrome could be clinically recognized immediately prior to death. In 1910 Herrick was called upon to care for a banker who had taken ill after returning home from the theater. Herrick stayed at the patient's house, caring for the patient until he finally succumbed, fifty-five hours after the onset of pain. Herrick suspected that the cause of death was an acute obstruction of a coronary artery. The autopsy proved him correct. When reviewing his previous cases, Herrick realized that he had seen patients before with a similar condition, and came to believe that, contrary to generally received wisdom, the affliction need not prove immediately fatal. He suggested that part of the reason why some patients survive coronary thrombosis was that parts of the heart could be supplied by more than one source of blood, and that when one coronary artery was obstructed blood might still reach the area through another artery. Yet when Herrick read his paper describing coronary thrombosis at the annual meeting of the Association of American Physicians, it attracted little attention. Herrick later recalled that it 'fell flat as a pancake'. It attracted only one question, and that by a man 'who discussed every paper read there that day'. The paper was published in 1912.

Six years later, Herrick came back to the same organization and again presented another discussion of coronary thrombosis, this time describing use of a new tool, the electrocardiograph machine. This new device had been invented in 1902 by Willem Einthoven of the Netherlands. Most of the work with the machine had concentrated on its use for diagnosing abnormal cardiac rhythms. In 1915, at the annual meeting of the Association of American Physicians, Herrick had asked what was the significance of an inversion in the last wave of the tracing, the 'T' wave, and had been told that this wave was of little importance. A few years later Herrick was working with Fred

Smith, a resident at Rush Medical College. Through the generosity of a benefactor, Mrs Cyrus H. McCormick, Presbyterian Hospital had recently acquired an electrocardiograph machine. Herrick suggested that Smith produce a coronary occlusion in a dog (by ligating the coronary artery) and record the electrocardiographic changes. When he did so, Smith observed inverted T waves and suggested that this would be the typical change in a myocardial infarction, or 'heart attack', caused by obstruction of a coronary artery. Later in 1918 Herrick described the same findings in patients with the disease. Unlike his purely clinical diagnosis in 1912, this finding immediately attracted significant attention. In contrast to the impact of the 1912 paper, diagnosis of myocardial infarction was made far more often in U.S. hospitals after the 1918 paper was published in 1919. Clinicians found the electrocardiogram useful when they wished to eliminate heart disease from other possible causes of pain, such as gallbladder or ulcer disease. The finding of characteristic electrocardiogram changes in connection with coronary occlusion also stimulated widespread interest in other uses of the electrocardiograph machine.

Honors and Wider Interests

Herrick lived to see his work honored in a variety of venues. He received honorary degrees, was president of the Association of American Physicians (1923) and of the American Heart Association (1927), and received the George M. Kober Medal from the Association of American Physicians in 1930 and the Distinguished Service Medal from the American Medical Association in 1939.

Herrick wrote *A Short History of Cardiology* (1942), which was praised by no less an expert than Sir Thomas Lewis (although Lewis objected to the term 'cardiology'). An active member of the Chicago Literary Club, Herrick spent much of his time trying to convince physicians to become more cultured, and he himself wrote many historical essays.

Bibliography

Primary: 1910. 'Peculiar Elongated and Sickle-Shaped Red Blood Corpuscles in a Case of Severe Anemia.' *Archives of Internal Medicine* 6: 517–521; 1912. 'Clinical Features of Sudden Obstruction of the Coronary Arteries.' *Journal of the American Medical Association* 59: 2015–2020; 1919. 'Thrombosis of the Coronary Arteries.' *Journal of the American Medical Association* 72: 387–390; 1942. A *Short History of Cardiology* (Springfield, IL); 1949. *Memories of Eighty Years* (Chicago).

Secondary: Wailoo, Keith, 1991. ''A Disease *Sui Generis*'': The Origins of Sickle Cell Anemia and the Emergence of Modern Clinical Research, 1904–1924.' *Bulletin of the History of Medicine* 65: 185–208; Howell, Joel D., 1984. 'Early Perceptions of the Electrocardiogram: From Arrhythmia to Infarction.' *Bulletin of the History of Medicine* 58: 83–98; Holmes, William H., 1935. *James Bryan Herrick: An Appreciation* (Chicago); *DAMB*.

Joel D. Howell

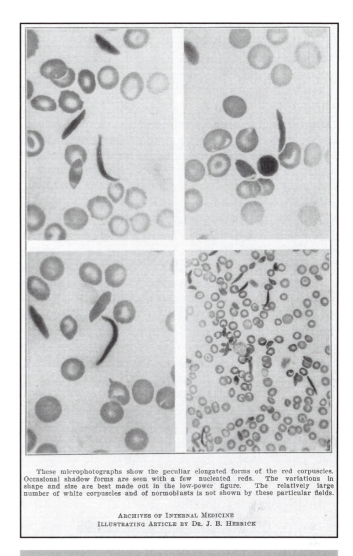

These microphotographs show the peculiar elongated forms of the red corpuscles. Occasional shadow forms are seen with a few nucleated reds. The variations in shape and size are best made out in the low-power figure. The relatively large number of white corpuscles and of normoblasts is not shown by these particular fields.

ARCHIVES OF INTERNAL MEDICINE
ILLUSTRATING ARTICLE BY DR. J. B. HERRICK

Photomicrographs illustrating the flat crescent-shaped red blood cells in sickle-cell anemia. Halftone reproduction from 'Peculiar elongated and sickle-shaped red blood corpuscles in a case of severe anemia', *Archives of Internal Medicine,* **1910, vol 6, pp. 517-21.**

HEURNIUS, JOHANNES (b. Utrecht, the Netherlands, 4 February 1543; d. Leiden, the Netherlands, 11 August 1601) **and OTTO** (b. Utrecht, the Netherlands, 8 September 1577; d. Leiden, the Netherlands, 14 July 1652), *medicine, anatomy, philosophy.*

Johannes Heurnius was born in 1543. After studying in, among other places, Louvain and Paris, he obtained his MD in 1571 at the famous University of Padua. After returning to Utrecht in 1573, he converted to Protestantism and was appointed town physician. In 1581 he accepted the chair of *professor institutiones medicinae* at the newly founded University of Leiden (1575). He acquired fame as a teacher who held Hippocrates in high esteem. As physician, he served two Princes of Orange: Willem and his son and successor Maurits. The senior Heurnius was a professor in the best humanist tradition: well versed in the ancients, but little interested in the new empirical approach, as advocated at the universities of Northern Italy and Leiden. The latter institution established a *hortus botanicus* and a *theatrum anatomicum* in 1594.

Better known than his father is Otto Heurnius, who matriculated at Leiden University in 1592, to become *magister artium* seven years later. Following a career path that was obviously pointed out by his father, he was appointed Reader in Logic in 1600. In July 1601 he took his MD. When the father was on his deathbed a month later, he recommended young Otto as his successor. Two weeks after his father's funeral, the curators willingly appointed Otto *professor extraordinarius* at the medical faculty. Otto frequently issued reprints of his father's works, and was to edit the *Opera omnia* of the latter. In 1611 he obtained an ordinary professorship. From 1617 on, Otto Heurnius held the chair of anatomy as well, as successor to Petrus Pauw (1564–1617). This implied that Otto Heurnius was now keeper of the already famous Leiden *theatrum anatomicum*, known not only for its dissections, but also for its collection of curiosities. Among other things, Heurnius displayed the stone he himself had cut from the bladder of his late father. Moreover, he spent exorbitant sums on the purchase of all kinds of curiosities, mostly artifacts from ancient Egypt, including an impressive mummy in its sarcophagus. He received an indemnification from the Leiden curators to write an exhaustive work on mummification, ancient and present. The book would never appear in print. In 1650, at the age of seventy-three, Otto Heurnius resigned from his duties. He died on 14 July 1652.

Otto's fame mainly rests on the initiative he took in 1636 to start a *collegium medico-practicum*. The introduction of clinical demonstrations into the academic curriculum was an extremely important innovation, and Heurnius and his Leiden colleague Ewaldus Screvelius were the first in Northern Europe to undertake this enterprise. Clinical lessons took place on a weekly basis at the Leiden municipal hospital, the *Caecilia gasthuis* (now the Boerhaave Museum). The clinical course established by Otto would later bring European fame to his successors Dele Boë Sylvius and Boerhaave.

However, Otto Heurnius certainly was not a 'modern'. He vehemently opposed Harvey's theory of the circulation of the blood. Moreover, he was an inspired advocate of the *prisca scientia*, the 'Knowledge of the Ancients'. His expensive acquisitions for the anatomical theatre were mainly intended to illustrate the wisdom of ancient Egypt, 'the Cradle of Science' as Otto Heurnius called it. One of the very few books Otto published, the *Barbaricae philosophiae antiquitatum* (1600; reprint 1619), is a homage to the wisdom of the Egyptians, and one of the very few Dutch works in which hermeticism is embraced.

Bibliography

Primary: [Johannes Heurnius] 1609. *Opera omnia. Edidit auctoris filius Ottho Heurnius* (Leiden); 1587. *Praxis medicinae nova ratio* (Leiden); 1592. *Institutiones medicinae* (Leiden); 1594. *De morbis qui in singulis partibus humani capitis insidere consueverunt* (Leiden); 1609. *In Hippocratis Coi De victus ratione in morbis acutis librum I et II commentarius* (Leiden); [Otto Heurnius] 1600. *Barbaricae philosophiae antiquitatum libri duo* (Leiden, reprint 1619).

Secondary: Jorink, E., 2006. *Het Boek der Natuur in de Gouden Eeuw. Nederlandse geleerden en de wonderen van Gods schepping 1575–1715* (Leiden); Otterspeer, W., 2000. *Het bolwerk van de vrijheid. De Leidse universiteit 1575–1672* (Amsterdam); Beukers, H., 1987–88. 'Clinical Teaching in Leiden from Its Beginnings until the End of the Eighteenth Century.' *Clio Medica* 21: 139–152; Lunsingh Scheurleer, Th. H., 1975. 'Une amphithéâtre d'anatomie moralisée' in Lunsingh Scheurleer, Th. H., ed., *Leiden University in the Seventeenth Century: An Exchange of Learning* (Leiden) pp. 217–278.

Eric Jorink

HIJMANS VAN DEN BERGH, ABRAHAM ALBERT
(b. Rotterdam, the Netherlands, 1 December 1869; d. Utrecht, the Netherlands, 28 September 1943), *biochemistry, clinical chemistry, internal medicine.*

Born Abraham Albert Hijmans, the son of Benjamin Hijmans, a merchant, and Berdina van den Bergh, he studied at the science faculty of Ghent between 1888 and 1890, after his parents had moved from Rotterdam to Antwerp. On 10 October 1890 Hijmans matriculated at Leiden University, to study medicine. In 1895 he became the assistant of Willem Nolen, who was professor of internal medicine. On 21 May 1896 he acquired the doctorate *cum laude* with a thesis called *De giftigheid der urine en de leer der auto-intoxicatie*, an experimental toxicological study on the theory of auto-intoxication, which he rejected. After studying in Prague and Breslau, Hijmans was appointed first physician of the municipal Coolsingel Hospital in Rotterdam in 1899. In May 1900 he married Catharina Maria Hudig, with whom he had a son and two daughters. During these years, Hijmans started the research in clinical chemistry that was to occupy him all his life. On 20 January 1912 he accepted his appointment as professor of internal medicine at Groningen University (becoming the successor of his friend and colleague Karel Frederik Wenckebach), with an inaugural address called *Het denken in pathologie en kliniek*, in which he held up the example of Claude Bernard.

His publications during his Groningen professorship made Hijmans van den Bergh's name. Internationally, he is known for his research on bilirubin, the decomposition product of hemoglobin. Together with Isidore Snapper, he developed a quantitative method to determine bilirubin in blood (1913). Around 1910 he became convinced of the existence of two types of bilirubin: one that is found in case of liver disorders and one in case of increased blood hemoglobin decomposition. With P. Muller, a chemist who was the head of his Groningen laboratory, he succeeded in tracing the two types that correspond with two types of jaundice (1916). Henceforth, the seriousness of jaundice could be established by doing blood tests.

Hijmans van den Bergh did not focus exclusively on laboratory medicine, but took an interest in the wider dimensions of the discipline as well. He decided to accept the invitation of the National Life Insurance Bank in Rotterdam to write a handbook on life insurance medicine (1916), which he co-authored with Nolen and Jan Siegenbeek van Heulekom. The book—which was translated into German in 1925—laid the foundations of life insurance medicine in the Netherlands.

On 5 October 1918 Hijmans van den Bergh delivered his inaugural address at Utrecht University (*Over het gestel*), where he was the successor of Sape Talma. In Utrecht, he carried on his experimental research on hemoglobin, porphyrins, lipochromes, and bilirubin, while his clinical studies covered the whole field of internal medicine. In a book on diabetes—which was also translated into German—he outlined the therapeutic possibilities of insulin, which had recently become available. In 1940, two years after his deteriorating health had forced him into retirement, Hijmans van den Bergh published the first volume of his handbook on internal medicine, co-authored with Snapper and C. D. de Langen, his successor in Utrecht. It was to remain in use until long after World War II.

By combining biochemical and clinical research, Hijmans van den Bergh greatly contributed to the development of Dutch internal medicine. His honorary doctorates, two royal distinctions, and his membership in several learned societies bear witness of his wide recognition. In addition, his students praised him for his didactic skills, his undogmatic and scientific attitude, and his modesty. Proof of his nuanced attitude is to be found in a speech called 'Balans der geneeskunde' [Drawing Up the Balance of Medicine] (1932), in which he presented his views on medicine and the organization of the health care system. As a Jew, Hijmans van den Bergh was forced to go into hiding during the German occupation. He found shelter in the home of de Langen, where he died in 1943.

Bibliography

Primary: 1916. (with Nolen, W., and J. Siegenbeek van Heulekom) *Levensverzekeringgeneeskunde. Een leidraad voor artsen en voor studenten in de geneeskunde* (Groningen); 1918. (with Snapper, I., and P. Muller) *Der Gallenfarbstoff im Blute* (Leiden); 1925. *Voordrachten over suikerziekte* (Utrecht); 1940–42. (with de Langen, C. D., and I. Snapper) *Leerboek voor de inwendige geneeskunde* 2 vols. (Amsterdam).

Secondary: Wagenaar, J., 2002. 'A. A. Hijmans van den Bergh (1869–1943), Internist' in Kaandorp, C. J. E., et al., eds., *Erflaters van de geneeskunde. Beroemde Nederlandse artsen beschreven door hun (kinds)kinderen* (Alphen aan den Rijn) pp. 94–105; Lieburg, M. J. van, 1989. 'Hijmans, Abraham Albert' in Charité, J., ed, *Biografisch woordenboek van Nederland* vol. 3 (the Hague) pp. 283–285.

Frank Huisman

HILDEGARD OF BINGEN   (b. Bermersheim, Germany, 1098; d. Bingen, Germany, 17 September 1179), *monastic medicine, medicine, folk medicine.*

Hildegard of Bingen was born in 1098 in Germany, in the village of Bermersheim. Her father, Hildebert, was an unfree but noble servant to Emperor Henry IV, and her mother, Mecthilde, was related to some of the most powerful families in Germany. At eight Hildegard was sent away to be educated by a young relative, Jutta, and at twelve she entered the newly re-established double (male and female) monastery of Disibodenberg in the Rhineland. She became a nun and lived the usual life of a Benedictine until her early forties, when she began to experience complex spiritual visions and a 'call' to write. She completed her first book of theology, *Scivias*, at fifty; shortly thereafter she left Disibodenberg to establish a new, all-female monastery eighteen miles away at Rupertsberg, just across from Bingen on the Rhine.

At Rupertsberg Hildegard continued to write, as well as to compose music and to create remarkable illuminations of her spiritual experiences. As her reputation spread, she began to correspond via letters with people from all over Europe, including most of its crowned heads, and to preach in numerous towns and monasteries of Germany and northern France. By the time of her death at the age of eighty-one, the sum of her work was prodigious: three large volumes of theology including spectacular illuminations, two musical dramas and over seventy liturgical pieces, two saintly biographies, a commentary on the Benedictine Rule, the glossary of a private language, and more than three hundred letters. Following her death, her supporters pushed to have her declared a saint, and for that reason an investigative team was sent by the pope to her monastery to interview those who had known her. Records of that investigation were sent to the Vatican. Although Hildegard was never officially declared a saint, she did become a kind of unofficial saint, and her nuns guarded the original copies of her work with great care. Popular excerpts were made of her spiritual writings, and in the following centuries there was a quiet but deep acknowledgment of her spiritual achievements.

This is an unusual though not completely surprising history for a medieval nun, but how did Hildegard become a character in medical history?

In 1862 a manuscript was unearthed in Copenhagen by the medical-botanical historian Karl Jessen, *Causae et curae Hildegardis Bingensis*. It turned out to be a practical manual of twelfth-century medicine, and is the earliest surviving text of this type that can be attached to a specific person, place, and time. It was known that Hildegard had written about how people could be helped by various substances, and one such natural science text, *Physica*, had been printed as early as 1532. *Physica*, however, fell into a more explicable tradition (for a work authored by a nun) than did *Causes and Cures*, because its chapters on plants, minerals, and animals conformed to the literary format of the medieval encyclopedia. Although some of its recipes were surprising (for impotence and infertility, for example), the text itself could be explained as a florilegium, a medieval collection or 'bouquet' of texts, which Hildegard could have culled from other texts.

Causes and Cures was a different matter entirely. It was inescapably *practical*. Although it began with a traditional description of the universe as a spiritual hierarchy (from God to sun, stars, and humans), its second chapter revolved around the body—the workings of liver, lung, and heart, and the physical sexuality of both men and women—and included instructions for bleeding and cupping, and even treatments for farm animals. Its third and fourth chapters were given over to practical recipes: for headaches, eye pain, cough, constipation, and diarrhea, and even for infertility, impotence, and childbirth. In its final chapter there was material on diagnosis and prognosis: how to know if a patient would live or die by looking at his eyes, face, urine, or stool, or by taking his pulse. It even gave a *lunarium*, a lunar-based horoscope for determining the character of offspring.

Causes and Cures was not only a practical text, it was also original. That is, although its information was not different from the kind of practical information on herbs, bloodletting, diagnosis, and prognosis to be found in other texts, none of it had been precisely *copied* from known texts. The conclusion was inescapable: *Causes and Cures* had been written by someone who had practiced medicine.

But how could the *Causae et curae Hildegardis Bingensis* be squared with the Blessed Hildegard of Bingen? Many scholars simply held that Hildegard had not written the text. But because its style was unmistakably Hildegardian, they hypothesized that an admirer had written it in her style and then surreptitiously placed the pastiche into the library at Bingen. This hypothesis had problems, however. For one thing, there was no good reason for someone to have produced a pastiche of such a book that was so difficult to square with Hildegard's recognized persona; for another, Hildegard's nuns had sworn to the papal commission that she had, indeed, composed *Causes and Cures*. Most importantly, Hildegard's other work demonstrated that practical medicine was indeed an important part of her worldview, to be found not only in the glossary of her private language but even in her spiritual metaphors.

What seems to have occurred is that a medical Hildegard evolved into a saintly Hildegard. She probably began her career as the infirmarian for the women's side of Disibodenberg. The male infirmarian taught her the techniques and practices of medieval medicine, and she supplemented this knowledge with textual material from the monastic library, as well as with oral folk knowledge gleaned from Disibodenberg's many ill visitors. When she left Disibodenberg and became abbess of the new monastery at Rupertsberg, she trained a replacement, a nun-infirmarian; *Causes and Cures* is the record of that training.

That is how Hildegard ended up in medical history. As the oldest surviving practical medical text that can be ascribed to a particular person, place, and time, her *Causes and Cures* gives a unique insight into the worldview of the medieval practitioner of medicine.

Hildegard's Achievements

Still, Hildegard would be surprised to find herself in the *Dictionary of Medical Biography*. Medicine and science were not her vocation, and from her point of view, her main achievement was to have carried out God's will during her lifetime. To be sure, she does list among her achievements her works on the subtleties of the different natures of created beings, perhaps because these works portrayed all created beings as gifts of God to humans. Whether she included *Causes and Cures* under this rubric is unclear, because the practice of medicine by monastics was frowned upon by 1162. Perhaps she did mean to include it among her other accomplishments, as one of the first things she'd written, and as the useful thing it was—a training manual for her student, detailing her own personal and idiosyncratic method of medicine.

Did Hildegard come up with anything new or original in medicine? She did, but in a limited way. Many of her uses of herbs appear (without attribution) in later herbal texts and cookbooks, and Book IV of *Physica* has been called the most complete work on fish in the Rhineland until the mid–nineteenth century. Still, she did not invent any new technology or discover any radically new use of plants. She *did* reconceptualize an ancient botanical concept—*viriditas* (green sap)—as a bodily liquid with many of the characteristics we attribute today to 'hormone', but this led to no discoveries, no inventions, and no new science. Hildegard was not an academic, and her medicine was far out of the mainstream, a little tributary of the Rhine; 800 years passed before the mainstream to changed its bed and wended its way to her. Why did it do so? What are her achievements from the point of view of medical history?

Hildegard's work demonstrates the existence of an indigenous Western medical holism that was intrinsic to the premodern West. This was a medical holism cognate with, but distinct from, Chinese and Indian medicine; like them, it was based on a geocentric cosmos, whose revolution caused the seasons and the consequent fluctuation of bodily elements, qualities, and humors. It was a system that, after millennia of success, disappeared from view in the West in the late 1800s, to reappear more recently in alternative medicines, such as homeopathy, naturopathy, and anthroposophy, although usually misunderstood. In Hildegard's medical work, however, we have a snapshot of this ancient Western medicine in action, at a particular place and a particular time.

This is, to be sure, not Hildegard's achievement, but it is her legacy. Although her medicine survived only parenthetically, by virtue of her fame as a mystic, it nevertheless preserves a picture of a different but still Western way of understanding and treating the body. Thus, it calls into question the West's own way of parsing itself as mechanistic, rational, and linear. Hildegard demonstrates a Western medicine in which the body is as much a plant to be nurtured as a machine to be fixed, or a code to be broken; where the doctor is as much a gardener as a mechanic or a programmer. Her medicine implies that behind the modern Western view of body is an older, equally Western view, indigenous and complementary to the cellular, code-based mechanism, the development of which is traced in these volumes. It is a radial and horticultural model of the body.

Does Hildegard's work provide any new, useful facts? It would be difficult to hold that it does. Merely identifying the ingredients in her recipes is problematic, and correlating a cure with the syndrome for which it was used, even when it can be ascertained (as a liver or thyroid disorder, for instance), is too wide a gap to bridge. Although there are today many lay proponents of a new 'God-given' Hildegardian medicine, what they have discovered is simply a premodern medicine that resonates because it exhibits the same philosophical outlook as most alternative medicines.

What Hildegard *does* give us is access to the implicit worldview of her time and place, which still structures the language that we speak and the concepts that we use today. The goal toward which to strive was in her case a heavenly paradise; in ours, it is an earthly one, where every disease is curable and death comes only to the deserving.

Bibliography

Primary: Migne, Jacques-Paul, ed., 1855. *S. Hildegardis Abbatissae Opera Omnia.* Vol. 197, *Patrologiae Cursus Completus. Series Latina* (Paris); 1996. (Palmquist, Mary, and John Kulas, eds.) *Holistic Healing* (Collegeville, MN); Throop, Priscilla, 1998. *Hildegard Von Bingen's Physica: The Complete English Translation of Her Classic Work on Health and Healing* (Rochester, VT); Moulinier, Laurence, ed., 2003. *Beate Hildegardis Bingensis Causae et cure* (Berlin).

Secondary: Sweet, Victoria, 2006. *Rooted in the Sky: Premodern Medicine in Hildegard of Bingen's 'Causes and Cures'* (New York); Sweet, Victoria, 1999. 'Hildegard of Bingen and the Greening of Medieval Medicine.' *Bulletin of the History of Medicine* 73: 381–403; Burnett, Charles, and Peter Dronke, eds., 1998. *Hildegard of Bingen: The Context of Her Thought and Art* (London); Flanagan, Sabina, 1998. *Hildegard of Bingen, 1098–1179: A Visionary Life* 2nd edn. (London); Newman, Barbara, ed., 1998. *Voice of the Living Light: Hildegard of Bingen and Her World* (Berkeley).

Victoria Sweet

HILL, (AUSTIN) BRADFORD [TONY]   (b. London, England, 8 July 1897; d. Ambleside, Westmorland, England, 18 April 1991), *medical statistics, epidemiology.*

Hill was the third son of the physiologist Sir Leonard Hill. Although he initially planned to become a doctor, his ambitions were thwarted when he contracted tuberculosis during World War I. During his convalescence, he earned a degree in economics from London University by correspondence. In

Hildegard von Bingen. Line engraving by W. Marshall. Iconographic Collection, Wellcome Library, London.

1922 he was offered a post with the Industrial Fatigue Research Board, which had ties to the Medical Research Council. There he received his early training in epidemiology and benefited from the support of the medical statistician Major Greenwood (1880–1949), who had once worked for his father. In 1927 Greenwood became the first professor of epidemiology and medical statistics at the London School of Hygiene and Tropical Medicine, and Hill joined his staff. In 1933 Hill became reader in epidemiology and vital statistics and, upon Greenwood's retirement in 1945, he succeeded him as professor of medical statistics and director of the Statistical Research Unit of the MRC. He was knighted in 1961.

Hill's fame rests on three achievements: the publication of a widely-used textbook on medical statistics, the design of the first randomized controlled clinical trial, and the articulation of a set of criteria (now known as the 'Bradford Hill criteria'), which enabled epidemiologists to draw inferences about the etiology of chronic disease. In 1937 the editors of *Lancet* asked Hill to write a series of articles on how to apply statistics to medicine. These articles were subsequently published in book form as *Principles of Medical Statistics* and translated into many languages. It remained in print for decades; the twelfth edition was published in 1991, the year of Hill's death.

In designing clinical trials, Hill introduced the practice of randomly assigning the patients either to the group receiving the experimental therapy or to the control group. Drawing on the work of Sir Ronald Fisher (1890–1962), who had introduced randomization in the context of agricultural experiments, Hill applied the technique in a 1946 clinical trial to test the efficacy of the drug streptomycin on tuberculosis; the rationale behind randomization was that there would be less likelihood of bias in the results if the patients were randomly assigned. The results of the trial were reported in the *British Medical Journal* in 1948, with a noticeably smaller number of the patients who received streptomycin dying during the course of the trial. Some commentators have argued that this randomized, controlled clinical trial has been the model against which all subsequent trials have been judged.

In 1951 Hill and his associate Richard Doll (1912–2005) launched a major prospective epidemiological study to determine whether there was a relationship between cigarette smoking and lung cancer. By sending out a questionnaire to British physicians on their personal smoking habits and later determining the cause of death when the respondents passed away, Hill and Doll tried to determine whether cigarette smoking could be implicated a causal factor leading to lung cancer. Their study reached conclusions that were consistent with earlier retrospective studies—namely, cigarette smoking increased one's risk of contracting cancer. In 1965 Hill generalized from his epidemiological studies and those of others to develop criteria that would indicate when an association between two phenomena could be construed as implying an underlying causal relationship.

At the time of his death, Hill was regarded as one of the world's leading medical statisticians.

Bibliography

Primary: 1937. *Principles of Medical Statistics* (London); 1950. (with Doll, W. R. S.) 'Smoking and Carcinoma of the Lung: Preliminary Report.' *British Medical Journal* ii: 739–748; 1965. 'The Environment and Disease: Association or Causation?' *Proceedings of the Royal Society of Medicine* 58: 295–300; 1990. 'Memories of the British Streptomycin Trial in Tuberculosis: The First Randomised Clinical Trial.' *Controlled Clinical Trials* 11: 77–79.

Secondary: Magnello, Eileen, 2002. 'The Introduction of Mathematical Statistics into Medical Research: The Roles of Karl Pearson, Major Greenwood, and Austin Bradford Hill' in Magnello, Eileen, and Anne Hardy, eds., *The Road to Medical Statistics* (Amsterdam) pp. 95–123; Doll, Richard, 1994. 'Austin Bradford Hill.' *Biographical Memoirs of Fellows of the Royal Society* 40: 128–140; 1993. 'Sir Austin Bradford Hill, 1897–1991.' *Statistics in Medicine* 12: 795–808; 1982. *Statistics in Medicine* 1(4): 297–375 (issue celebrating Hill's 85th birthday); *Oxford DNB*.

J. Rosser Matthews

HIPPOCRATES OF COS (b. Cos, Greece, *c.* 460 BCE; d. Thessaly, Greece, *c.* 370 BCE), *medicine.*

Virtually nothing is known of the historical Hippocrates. His traditional date of birth comes from an ancient source who claimed to have consulted the archives on Cos, but there is no way of knowing how reliable this, or any other piece of information provided in antiquity, is. The earliest mentions of Hippocrates' name in extant primary sources suggest that, at the very least, he was famous as a physician in his lifetime. Plato's two brief references to him, written at the beginning of the fourth century BCE, assumed that he would be known in Athens, which is the setting of the dialogues containing these references. However, as Plato used Hippocrates to make specific points of his own, we cannot regard him as a transparent source. In the *Protagoras*, Socrates was represented as referring to 'Hippocrates of Cos, the famous physician' when offering an example of what one should expect to learn from a paid teacher. This dialogue is set in around 430 BCE, which suggests that Hippocrates was already well-known at this date and that he had paying pupils. His association, in this dialogue and elsewhere, with the island of Cos led to later attempts to divide up the treatises of the Hippocratic corpus into 'Coan' and 'Cnidian' categories, according to their medical theories and favored therapies, with 'Coan' medicine as the superior form, but recent scholarship has come to regard such a division as unhelpful.

Plato's later *Phaedrus* gave a near-contemporary view of the content of the medicine of 'Hippocrates the Asclepiad', characterizing it by its emphasis on the need for knowledge of 'the whole' in order to understand the constituent parts of the body; the epithet may refer to a specific family-group of medical practitioners, or more generally to those who, regardless of profession, claimed descent from the healing god Asclepius. What is meant by 'the whole' has been extensively debated; it could mean the whole body or, even more broadly, the whole environmental context in which that body functions. Many attempts to identify the elements of the Hippocratic corpus representing the 'genuine work of Hippocrates'—a formulation made famous by Francis Adams in his 1849 edition of those works he singled out as authored by the historical Hippocrates—have therefore taken as their starting point a quest for a text that says something about 'the whole'. Forty years after Plato's *Phaedrus*, Aristotle (*Politics* 1326a15-17) briefly mentioned Hippocrates without referring to his birthplace or family, which suggests that his fame was such that his name alone would suffice to identify him, and that the use of the term 'great' when applied to Hippocrates concerned his reputation, rather than his (small) physical stature.

The Anonymus Londinensis papyrus, acquired by the British Museum in 1890, provides another piece of early evidence, as it summarizes what it called 'Aristotle's view of Hippocrates'. It may derive from Aristotle's pupil Meno, who, according to Galen, compiled a work giving a précis of the theories of many ancient physicians. In the papyrus, Hippocrates occupies a place second only to Aristotle himself, and the writer summarized 'Aristotle's view' as being that Hippocrates regarded the cause of disease as lying in the 'breaths' (Greek *physai*) that arose from residues in the body, caused by a failure of digestion to heat the foods properly; the analogy of digestion as cooking was common in the Hippocratic texts. The writer of the papyrus, however, disagreed with Aristotle, and characterized the position of Hippocrates as being, instead, that disease came from the loss of balance in the body, and he cites as genuinely Hippocratic *On the Nature of Man*—the treatise from which Galen later took what he claimed to be the 'Hippocratic' four-humor theory—and, more surprisingly, *Diseases* 1, a treatise that was not central to the Galenic construction of Hippocrates. When the papyrus was first published, it caused a stir because the extant medical treatise under the title of *Breaths* had previously been rejected as an inferior work by a 'second-rate Sophist, indeed . . . a mere gossipmonger' (Jouanna, 1999, p. 60), which was under no circumstances to be linked with the historical Hippocrates.

Later sources add much detail to the biography of Hippocrates, but should be treated with great caution; they contradict each other on many points. In antiquity, it was common to compose imaginary speeches and letters involving famous people, often linking contemporaries by suggesting circumstances in which they could have met. Because Hippocrates was recognized as a great doctor, people wanted to know more about his life, and so he was the subject of such compositions from as early as 350 BCE. It is unclear whether these texts codify traditional stories, perhaps local to Cos, or invent new ones in order to give authority to the medical school there. Medical writers—most notably Galen—made allusions to details of Hippocrates' life, but these depended on the pseudepigrapha. In around 100 a *Life of Hippocrates* was written by a Soranus—perhaps Soranus of Ephesus—and this was seen as so useful and authoritative that it was copied at the beginning of many manuscripts, and of early printed editions, of the Hippocratic corpus. At the beginning of the twentieth century, another early biography was discovered; written in Latin, the *Brussels Life* contains some new details, but there is no reason to think it is any more reliable than others.

In the main tradition that grew up around the 'Father of Medicine', his mother was named as a midwife called Phaenerete, and his father as Heraclides. An alternative tradition has his mother as Praxithea, the daughter of Phaenerete. His training may therefore have occurred within what was already a medical family, and some ancient sources stated that his grandfather had written medical treatises; according to Galen, in his day it was disputed whether these should be identified as the treatises *On Joints* and *Fractures*. However, it is also possible that the biographical traditions arose at times when medical training normally passed through families, and that Hippocrates was being (re)created in the image of those who wrote about him. Also listed as his teachers in the ancient biographies were the philosophers Gorgias of Leontini, Democritus of Abdera, and the physician Herodicus, but there is no reliable evidence for their role in Hippocrates' training; indeed, *Epidemics* 6.3.18 condemns a Herodicus who killed feverish patients by making them undertake excessive exercise.

Writing in the first century BCE, the geographer Strabo introduced another influential thread into the biographical accounts of Hippocrates, claiming that Hippocrates had copied his remedies from the votive inscriptions at the temple of Asclepius on Cos. Greek temple medicine coexisted with Hippocratic medicine, and both traditions continued for many centuries, with the experiences of the second-century orator Aelius Aristides showing clearly that, at least in the Roman Empire, sanctuaries of Asclepius had doctors-in-residence. Although there are occasional similarities between the treatments described on the temple inscriptions and those in the Hippocratic texts, there is no evidence that medical writers copied the texts; indeed, the opposite route of transmission is also possible, with temple medicine changing in order to keep up with the expectations of patients.

Career and Achievements

The different place names mentioned in the seven volumes of *Epidemics*—of which Books 1 and 3 have traditionally been seen as 'genuine works'—and the interest of *Airs, Waters, Places* in helping the physician to predict what the dominant diseases in a new town will be, based on its location and the prevailing wind, have been used to argue that Hippocrates traveled widely within the Greek world. In the second century, Aulus Gellius (*Attic Nights* 17.21) characterized the period of the Greek 'intellectual revolution' as being when Sophocles and Euripides were famous as tragic poets, Hippocrates as a physician, and Democritus as a philosopher. The Hippocratic pseudepigrapha also noticed the overlap, and included exchanges of letters between Hippocrates and Democritus, whose laughter even at the misfortune of others made the people of Abdera wonder if he was mad. After writing to him, Hippocrates realized that Democritus was only laughing at human folly, and the two men became friends. In another story told by the biographers, Hippocrates was called to help the Macedonian King Perdiccas, and interpreted 'by certain signs'—specified as changes in skin color—that the cause was love-sickness; this he was able to cure.

Stories of the life of Hippocrates emphasized his moral virtues as well as his medical skills. He was supposed to have been approached by King Artaxerxes I of Persia to stop plague from spreading in the lands under his control; because Herodotus (3.130) had described the king's grandfather, Darius, as using the Greek doctor Democedes of Croton, and Artaxerxes himself had used the Greek Apollonides of Cos as a court physician, such an approach is not entirely incredible. In the story, Hippocrates refused, rating wisdom above gold, and declined to help the enemies of Greece. Though praised by Galen, this positive narrative of patriotism was used by Romans in an entirely negative way, to emphasize that Greek doctors were determined to kill their Roman employers. Nineteenth-century political reformers also linked Hippocratic patriotism to *Airs, Waters, Places*, in which the health benefits of Greek freedom are contrasted with the effects of the despotic rule of the Eastern monarchs. The appeals to patriotism in the Hippocratic legend could be challenged, for should not a doctor treat anyone needing his help, regardless of race or circumstances?

In the traditions that grew up around Hippocrates, the overlap between his putative dates and the timing of the most serious disease to affect the Greek world cannot be ignored. However, the plague in Persia was eventually conflated with the one that affected Athens and much of the Greek world in 431/430 BCE. The earliest stories of Hippocrates curing a plague in Greece described an epidemic spreading from the north, whereas the plague of Athens was described by Thucydides as coming from the south; however, by the sixth century the two outbreaks had been conflated, and Byzantine writers even suggested that Hippocrates had found a cure for the condition. Earlier sources have Hippocrates lighting bonfires to purify the air, and his use of fire to cure epidemics was mentioned in the first century by Pliny (36.79).

However, there are also three occasions on which the ancient biographers linked him to fire in a more negative sense, presenting him as responsible for arson: burning the temple of Cos after plagiarizing the cures listed on its votive inscriptions, then burning the library at Cnidus, and finally burning the medical works at the library of Cos. All these hostile accounts have in common the idea that he buried any evidence of the true source of his theories and therapies, and demonstrate that, while most ancient physicians respected Hippocrates as their intellectual ancestor, there were also others who rejected his influence.

Transmission

Whatever their individual views, everyone who wrote about medicine in antiquity was engaged in debate over Hippocrates' ideas; for example, Herophilus of Chalcedon wrote a work against the Hippocratic *Prognostic*, whereas several Hellenistic writers wrote commentaries, or compiled glossaries to explain difficult terms in Hippocratic texts. In the first century, Aretaeus of Cappadocia still wrote in the Ionian dialect, in homage to Hippocrates; the Hippocratic treatises had been written in Ionic, as the dialect of philosophy. By the time of Galen, knowledge of Hippocratic texts was not restricted to medical writers, but also existed among the educated elite; Plutarch mentioned Hippocrates eleven times in his *Moralia*, with the *Aphorisms* alone being cited four times. In Italy, especially at Ravenna, Hippocratic texts were translated into Latin from the sixth century onward, and then traveled into Syriac and Arabic circles, as well as finding a place in the medical curriculum of late antiquity. The Byzantine encyclopedists of the tenth century added further material to the growing biographical tradition, and in the twelfth century Joannes Tzetzes produced a list of the ancestors of Hippocrates, tracing his descent from Asclepius in seventeen generations.

In the history of medical education, Hippocrates' *Aphorisms* has been one of the most influential texts, as it is more easily committed to memory than other treatises. Traditionally seen as the culmination of the experiences of Hippocrates' long lifetime, it held a central place in both the medieval and the Renaissance university, appearing with *Prognostic* and *Regimen in Acute Diseases* in the medical curricula of both Paris and Oxford in the fifteenth century. The translation of the entire Hippocratic corpus into Latin by Marco Fabio Calvi in 1525 was responsible for a movement back to Hippocrates later in the sixteenth century, although Hippocrates continued to be read through a Galenic filter. In gynecology, however, where there was no obvious work of Galen to guide practice, Hippocrates was seen as the more useful writer, with two Hippocratic volumes on *Diseases of Women*, another *On the Nature of Woman*, and a fourth *On Barren Women*.

Works

Much of the Hippocratic corpus dates from the lifetime of Hippocrates, but the wide range of language, style, and theoretical content indicates that the work of more than one man was represented therein. Soranus's *Life of Hippocrates* argued that variation could be due to shifts in style over a long lifetime, but the biographical tradition more commonly accounts for obvious differences in the works associated with his name by attributing some of them to other members of his family; he was supposed to have had two sons, Thessalus and Dracon, both of whom named their own sons 'Hippocrates', as well as a daughter who, in a medieval romance, was turned into a dragon until her prince came to her rescue. Scholars attempting to explain why Anonymus Londinensis appeared to be describing *Breaths* suggested that Meno might have confused the great Hippocrates with another member of the family with the same name. Wesley Smith proposed that a librarian in Alexandria in around 200 BCE was responsible for grouping together as 'Hippocratic' all medical texts in Greek, and argued that it was then Galen, fighting to achieve superiority in the competitive context of Roman medicine in the second century, who made the greatest contribution to the construction of 'Hippocrates'. Galen used the name of Hippocrates over 2,500 times, wrote commentaries on eighteen Hippocratic texts, labeled those texts that resonated with his own ideas 'genuinely Hippocratic', and elevated to prominence *On the Nature of Man*, where the four-humor theory was most developed; other Hippocratic texts worked with three humors, or two principles. While Galen regarded the description of the humors as the work of Hippocrates himself, on the authority of Aristotle the rest of *On the Nature of Man* was linked with the name of Polybus, Hippocrates' son-in-law and pupil. One of the treatises that Galen found most genuinely Hippocratic, *Nutriment*, has now been shown conclusively to be from the Hellenistic period, on the grounds of vocabulary and its Stoic roots.

Some of the variation in the treatises of the Hippocratic corpus derives from the texts having being composed for several very different audiences: for fellow physicians, for lay people, and even for the writer himself. They represent the earliest surviving examples of Greek prose known to us, and exhibit signs consistent with the first stages of literacy; for example, listing and then grouping together similar items. The seven books of case histories known as the *Epidemics* gave detailed case histories and appear to have been written down so that the physician could look for emerging patterns; however, they could also have been put together in order to prove an existing theory. Some treatises present a reasoned argument, and may have originated in public speeches, whereas others focus more on therapy without much explicit interest in causes. Many are interrelated; several appear to be by the same author and to have been separated at some point in the history of the texts (most notably *On Generation/Nature of the Child/Diseases IV*), and others to have been joined together artificially (e.g., *Diseases I–IV*). Others are different versions of the same material; *Aphorisms* repeats sections from the gynecological treatises, whereas some books of the *Epidemics* and the *Diseases of Women* and *On the Nature of Woman* share material in common. The gynecological treatises refer to a text on the disease of virgins; such a text survives, but it does not include the material cited, so it is not clear whether there is another, lost, treatise on this topic, or whether the text that survives is incomplete.

The surviving treatises give us a clear sense of how physicians in antiquity constructed and defended their authority over the body. They attacked their rivals—the philosophers (*On Tradition in Medicine*) and the religious healers (*On the Sacred Disease*)—but they were also capable of arguing from first principles, and regarded themselves as pious people. In a world in which there was no formal medical education or licensing system, they relied on their ability to explain the workings of the body, their wide range of healing methods, and their personal integrity.

Ethics

The best-known document associated with the name of Hippocrates is the *Oath*, but this seems to have very little connection with the historical person, probably dating after the death of Hippocrates. It recommends that medical knowledge should be kept within a family, or quasi-familial, structure, yet Plato informed us that the historical Hippocrates taught medicine for a fee. It prohibits surgery, even 'for the stone', yet surgery is heavily represented elsewhere in the Hippocratic corpus. Sixteenth-century writers reinterpreted this ban by saying that Hippocrates was aware that the technique was not yet at a sufficiently high level; i.e., the embargo was not intended to endure forever. The *Oath*'s prohibition on giving a woman a pessary that caused abortion must be read alongside the description in *On Generation/Nature of the Child* of how to provoke a miscar-

Portrait of Hippocrates after an ancient sculpture. Engraving by Paulus Pontius, 1638, after Sir Peter Paul Rubens. Iconographic Collection, Wellcome Library, London.

riage by jumping up and down with the heels touching the buttocks, suggesting perhaps that some methods of abortion were seen as more dangerous than others, or perhaps that variation on this issue existed among Greek physicians. Alternatively, the fear may have been that the woman might ask for the drug, then use it on someone else for whom it was not appropriate. Similarly, the *Oath*'s insistence that no fatal drugs were to be given may be less about euthanasia than about the control of potentially lethal substances. The injunction to keep silent about all one may have learned about a patient is more analogous to modern notions of patient confidentiality. In *On Decorum*—a Hippocratic text that is so difficult to date that it has been assigned to the early third century BCE or to the second century—we read of the physician paying attention to all features of the patient's environment, remaining calm, cheerful, and ready to reprove or comfort as appropriate, has been taken as the ideal of the 'bedside manner'. Yet other Hippocratic ethical texts seem, to modern eyes, to be more about deception than about ethical behavior—*On Decorum* itself also explains how to dress and talk in order to give patients the impression that one is a trustworthy physician.

Images

Visual depictions of Hippocrates also depend heavily on the late biographical tradition. The *Life* by Soranus (12) stated that many likenesses show him with his head covered by either a felt cap or by his cloak. This iconographic convention is explained as showing noble birth, or as covering baldness, or as a statement that the head is the site of the brain, seen as the governing organ of the body. Soranus added other possible interpretations: a sign of his love of travel, a sign of his works' lack of clarity, a sign of the need to guard against injuries, or an attempt to keep his cloak away from his hands in order to perform surgery more conveniently. This format is used in a famous Byzantine miniature, found in a fourteenth-century manuscript which included the *Life* at the beginning of the Hippocratic corpus (BN gr. 2144); here, Hippocrates is bearded, clearly bald, and also has the edge of his cloak over his head. However, a rather different convention is used by Roman coins issued on Cos, which have on one side an image of Heracles or Asclepius, and on the other give a portrait or seated image of their famous resident bearded and bald, but with his head uncovered. This convention is also used by the bust of Ostia, dating to the first century and only discovered in 1940, which shows Hippocrates as a bearded and bald old man.

Conclusion

If we cannot confidently assign any text of the Hippocratic corpus to Hippocrates, is it reasonable to talk of 'Hippocratic medicine' at all? Classical Greek medicine was clearly not the work of only one man. Recent work on Hippocrates' contemporaries, such Diocles of Carystus, whose treatises only survive in fragments cited in later works, raises such questions in a particularly acute way. The preeminence of Hippocrates in classical studies may therefore badly skew our view of medicine in the fifth and fourth centuries BCE.

But the very range of ideas in the Hippocratic corpus also accounts for the popularity of Hippocrates in the history of medicine; every new approach, from the Paracelsian to the homeopathic, or from environmental medicine to patient-centered medicine, has been able to find in this heterogeneous collection an appropriate forebear, thus allowing medical novelty to be presented as a return to the true principles of the Father of Medicine. Hippocrates was left untouched by Paracelsus's attacks on the medical writers of the past, instead being described as 'a master of the light of Nature', and Paracelsus's views on the value of travel echoed the Hippocratic *Airs, Waters, Places*. In proposing the theory of circulation of the blood, William Harvey praised the short—and late—Hippocratic treatise *On the Heart*. In the seventeenth century Thomas Sydenham, the 'English Hippocrates', focused on the empirical Hippocrates, praising the principles of observation in the *Epidemics*, whereas a hundred years later it was *Airs, Waters, Places* that was in vogue, with the rise of climatology. In France, Hippocrates was associated with Montpellier, Galen with Paris. One of the most disturbing features of the history of Hippocratism was its enthusiastic use in Nazi Germany to support eugenics, experiments on humans, and even racial extermination. The health of 'the whole' was here interpreted to mean that the well-being of the *Volk* should be valued above that of the individual.

Even during the many centuries when Galenic medical theory was dominant, it was Hippocrates who remained the model of the ideal physician. Although Galen was often seen as representing theoretical medicine, Hippocrates became the patron of observation; but, as Cantor has pointed out, this eventually led to Hippocrates's downfall, as it suggested that 'the accumulated experience since Hippocrates also had claim to a place in medicine' (Cantor, 2002, p. 6). Hippocrates is not only the Father of Medicine, but also a resource on which medicine has been able to draw for its continual self-definition.

Bibliography

Primary: Plato, *Protagoras* (311b-c); Plato, *Phaedrus* (270c); 1839–61. (Littré, Emile, ed.) *Oeuvres completes d'Hippocrate* 10 vols. (Paris); Loeb Classical Library, 1923– (in progress). *Hippocrates* (Cambridge, MA, and London); Lloyd, G. E. R., ed. and introd., 1983. *Hippocratic Writings* (Harmondsworth).

Secondary: Cantor, David, ed., 2002. *Reinventing Hippocrates* (Aldershot); Jouanna, Jacques, 1999. *Hippocrates* (Baltimore) (originally in French, 1992); Rubin Pinault, Jody, 1992. *Hippocratic Lives and Legends* (Leiden); Langholf, Volker, 1990. *Medical Theories in Hippocrates. Early Texts and the 'Epidemics'* (Berlin); Smith, Wesley D., 1979. *The Hippocratic Tradition* (Ithaca, NY); Edelstein, Ludwig, 1967. *Ancient Medicine. Selected Papers of Ludwig Edelstein* (Baltimore); *DSB*.

Helen King

HIRSCH, AUGUST (b. Danzig [now Poland], 4 October 1817; d. Berlin, Germany, 28 January 1894), *hygiene, medical history.*

Hirsch was born as Aron Simon to a Jewish merchant and his wife Pauline Friedländer. He changed his name when he converted to Christianity. At the age of fifteen he became an apprentice to a merchant in Berlin. After following commerce for three years, he decided to take the German school-leaving examination (Abitur). In 1839 he began the study of medicine at the University of Leipzig and completed his course in Berlin in 1843, where he received his MD, writing a doctoral dissertation on croup. The following year he established himself as a physician in Elbing, West Prussia, and two years later he moved to Danzig. Because he had considered entering the Anglo-Indian service as a surgeon, he gave special attention to geographic-pathological studies. The results of his research were published in the *Hamburger medizinische Zeitschrift* in 1848 under the title 'Ueber die Geographische Verbreitung von Malariafieber und Lungenschwindsucht und den Räumlichen Antagonismus dieser Krankheiten'. These investigations led him to a new field, that of historical pathology. His *Handbuch der historisch-geographischen Pathologie* soon became a standard work both in tropical medicine and in medical history.

In 1863 he was offered the chair of pathology and medical history at the University of Berlin, a position he held until his death. Hirsch was active in the fight against epidemic diseases. In 1865 he was sent by the government to the Vistula districts in West Prussia to report on the epidemic of cerebrospinal meningitis. His report was published as *Die Meningitis Cerebro-Spinalis Epidemica* (Berlin, 1866). During the Franco-Prussian war (1870–01) he was in charge of a sanitary train. The following year he was the cofounder of the *Deutsche Gesellschaft für Öffentliche Gesundheitspflege*, of which he was president until 1885. As a member of the imperial commission on cholera, Hirsch was sent again to West Prussia. His official report was published in 1873 and reprinted separately in 1874. In 1878 he was the German representative at the international sanitary congress in Vienna. In 1879 he was sent by the German government to Russia to report on the prevalence of cholera in the province of Astrakhan. From 1866 onward Hirsch acted with Virchow as editor of *Jahresbericht über die Fortschritte und Leistungen in der Medizin*.

Hirsch was a prolific writer, publishing not only on hygiene and tropical medicine, but also on medical history. In 1865, for example, he edited the history of epidemic diseases in the Middle Ages written by his predecessor in the chair, J. F. K. Hecker. He believed that history could serve as a standard for measuring medical progress. He was among the first hygienists who realized the importance of Ignác Semmelweis's work on puerperal fever. From 1884 to 1888 he was one of the editors of the *Biographisches Lexikon der hervorragenden Aerzte aller Zeiten und Völker* (Vienna). He also contributed many medical biographies to the *Allgemeine Deutsche Biographie*. In 1892 he was admitted to the prestigious German academy of science, the Leopoldina.

Bibliography

Primary: 1859–64. *Handbuch der Historisch-Geographischen Pathologie* 2 vols. (Erlangen) [English trans., New Sydenham Society, 1883 (London)]; 1864. *Ueber die Anatomie der alten griechischen Aerzte* (Berlin); 1866. *Die Meningitis Cerebro-Spinalis Epidemica* (Berlin); 1874. *Das Auftreten und der Verlauf der Cholera in den preussischen Provinzen Posen und Preussen (Mai–September, 1873)* (2nd edn., Berlin, 1876); 1875. *Über Verhütung und Bekämpfung der Volkskrankheiten* (Berlin); 1877. *Geschichte der Augenheilkunde* (Leipzig); 1880. *Mittheilungen über die Pest-Epidemie im Winter 1878-79 im Russischen Gouvernement Astrachan* (Berlin); 1894. *Geschichte der medizinischen Wissenschaft in Deutschland* (Munich and Leipzig).

Secondary: Barrett, Frank A., 2000. 'August Hirsch: As Critic of, and Contributor to, Geographical Medicine and Medical Geography' in Rupke, Nicolaas, ed., *Medical Geography in Historical Perspective, Medical History, Supplement No. 20* (London); Lauer, Hans H., 1971. 'Hirsch, Max.' *Neue deutsche Biographie* vol. 9 (Berlin) pp. 212-213; Kagan, Solomon R., 1952. *Jewish Medicine* (Boston) p. 554; Singer, Isidore, 1904. 'Hirsch, Max' in *The Jewish Encyclopedia*, vol. 6 (New York and London) p. 409.

Robert Jütte

HIRSCHFELD, MAGNUS (b. Kolberg [Kolobrzeg], Poland, 14 May 1868; d. Nice, France, 14 May 1935), *sexology, homosexual rights advocacy.*

Hirschfeld was born in the Prussian Baltic port of Kolberg into a conservative Jewish family. He studied modern languages in Breslau, and then medicine in Strasbourg, Munich, Heidelberg, and Berlin, where he took his degree in 1892. In 1894 he began his medical practice, and by 1896 had begun his work in sexology with the pseudonymous publication of *Sappho und Sokrates*, which argued for the fair treatment of homosexuals because they were members of a 'third sex', an idea he took from German legal reformer, Karl Heinrich Ulrichs. In 1897 Hirschfeld founded the Wissenschaftlich-Humanitäre Komitee [Scientific-Humanitarian Committee], an organization that aimed to change paragraph 175 of the Prussian legal code, by which homosexuality was deemed illegal. Hirschfeld served as committee president until 1929, when it was disbanded.

Although Hirschfeld's specific contributions to sexology were not especially ground-breaking, he was a great organizer and promoter of sexual science. In 1908 he was a cofounder of the Berlin Association for Psychoanalysis, although his writings cannot be considered psychoanalytical. In 1913 he was cofounder of the Physicians' Society for Sexual Science and Eugenics in Berlin. In 1919 he opened the Institute for Sexology, and in 1921 he organized the first international sexological congress. In 1928 he cofounded the World League for Sexual Reform, with himself, Havelock Ellis, and Auguste Forel as presidents.

Hirschfeld was also famous for traveling widely through Europe and the rest of the world to promote his work. In 1926 he traveled to Moscow and Leningrad on the invitation of the government of the USSR. Between 1930 and 1932, Hirschfeld gave public lectures on aspects of sexology from the United States to the Far East, including Tokyo, Shanghai, Manila, Djakarta, Calcutta, Cairo, and Tel Aviv. After this world tour, Hirschfeld returned to Vienna, but due to German political problems went into exile in Switzerland.

Hirschfeld used his writings to popularize sexology. Between 1899 and 1923, he was editor of the *Jahrbuch für sexuelle Zwischenstufen* [Yearbook for Sexual Transitions], and in 1908 became editor of *Zeitschrift für Sexualwissenschaft* [Journal of Sexology]. His work on homosexuality began with a strong biological premise; his *Geschlechtsübergänge: Mischungen männlicher und weiblicher Geschlectscharaktere (Sexuelle Zwischenstufen)* [Sexual Malformations: Mixtures of Male and Female Sexual Characteristics (Sexual Intermediate Types)] (1905) emphasized homosexuality as a part of a spectrum of sexual types. In 1910 he wrote *Die Transvestiten*, which was the first treatment of transvestism disassociating it from homosexuality. Hirschfeld was also a great collector of case histories—a 130-part questionnaire filled in by 10,000 men formed the basis of his *Die Homosexualität des Mannes und des Weibes* [Male and Female Homosexuality] (1914). Hirschfeld's theories of *Sexualzwischenstufen* linked hermaphrodites to homosexuality and postulated biological theories of homosexuality based on hormones, which were later to be used to 'treat' male homosexuals with androgen injections. Serious questions related to these works have been raised concerning the manner in which he gathered funds for his institutes. It is claimed that Hirschfeld would threaten to blackmail homosexuals after taking their clinical histories if they did not contribute some of their wealth to his efforts of emancipation.

On a personal front, Hirschfeld was well-known as a homosexual, referred to in the gay clubs of Nollendorfplatz by the name of 'Tante Magnesia'. He also aided the section for sex offenses in the Berlin Police Department. He had two main relationships—with the archivist of the Institute, Karl Giese, and with his Chinese disciple Li Shiu Tong, both of whom were named in his will. He attracted a variety of other followers, such as the Australian sexologist Norman Haire and the Hungarian author Arthur Koestler, although Havelock Ellis preferred to keep his distance and would pretend to be ill whenever Hirschfeld was in London. Hirschfeld also engaged in various disputes with the Prussian sexologist Albert Moll.

In 1933 Hirschfeld, who was living in exile in Paris, heard that the Nazis had plundered and closed his institute and burned his books in a three-day incineration on Opernplatz. A total of 10,000 books and documents were destroyed, including a vast archive of case histories. Unable to return to Germany for fear of Nazi persecution for his homosexual tastes, his political activism, and his Jewish origin, he died in French exile in Nice on his birthday in 1935.

Bibliography

Primary: 1905. *Geschlechtsübergänge* (Leipzig); 1910. *Die Transvestiten: Eine Untersuchung über den erotischen Verkleidungstrieb, mit umfangreichem kasuistischem und historischem Material* (Berlin); 1914. *Die Homosexualität des Mannes und des Weibes* (Berlin).

Secondary: Charlotte Wolff, 1986. *Magnus Hirschfeld: A Portrait of a Pioneer in Sexology* (London); James D. Steakley, 1975. *The Homosexual Emancipation Movement in Germany* (New York).

Ivan Crozier

HIRSCHSPRUNG, HARALD (b. Copenhagen, Denmark, 14 December 1830; d. Copenhagen, 11 April 1916), *pediatric gastroenterology*.

Hirschsprung was the younger son of Abraham Marcus Hirschsprung and Petrea, née Hertz. The father, who as a young man had fled Germany to avoid conscription by the advancing Napoleonic Army, had founded a cigar factory in Copenhagen and expected his son to join the business. Harald, however, refused and insisted on studying medicine; he graduated from Copenhagen University in 1855.

From the beginning of his career Hirschsprung took an interest in clinical research. As a houseman at the Royal Frederik's Hospital, he wrote papers on a number of topics, including carcinoma of the bladder and the sigmoid mesocolon, and in 1861 he defended his doctoral thesis on congenital atresia of the esophagus and the small bowel. He had himself observed four cases and had found ten additional reports in the archives of the hospital and in the international literature.

In 1870 he joined the staff of a small pediatric hospital, and in 1876 he published the first of a series of papers on intussusception, recommending hydrostatic pressure and external manipulation. In 1894 he reviewed the results of this treatment in 107 cases.

In 1877 Hirschsprung became titular professor at Copenhagen University and in 1879 he was appointed chief physician at the new Queen Louise Children's Hospital. He held this position until retirement in 1904, and under his leadership the hospital gained an international reputation for pediatric research. He was an efficient fund-raiser and established outpatient clinics in the poorer districts of Copenhagen. He lost, however, the support of the hospital's royal patron, Queen Louise, who had suggested that there should be biblical texts over each bed. Hirschsprung preferred pictures of animals, and the Queen was so offended that she never visited the hospital that bore her name.

In 1886 Hirschsprung addressed the Gesellschaft für Kinderheilkunde in Berlin, reporting the fatal course of a rare disease in two children aged eleven months and seven months. He demonstrated a preparation of the large gut of the first of these patients. The sigmoid and, even more so, the transverse colon were enormously dilated, whereas the rectum was neither dilated nor narrowed. Hirschsprung was not aware of the neurogenic origin of the disease, but realized that it was congenital. By 1904 Hirschsprung had reported ten cases of the disease, which came to be known as 'Hirschsprung's disease'. Hirschsprung was the first to describe the clinical picture and the pathology of the disease systematically, but it was found later that some reported cases, predating Hirschsprung's first paper, are compatible with a diagnosis of Hirschsprung's disease. They include a report by Ruysch from 1691.

Hirschsprung also made other contributions to pediatrics, including careful studies of congenital pyloric stenosis. He became 'Docent' at Copenhagen University in 1891, but was not popular as a teacher. He chose to give his lectures on Sunday mornings from 9 to 11 A.M. and preferred to lecture on rare children's diseases rather than on those common conditions that the students would encounter in general practice.

In 1862 Hirschsprung married Mariane, née Hertz. They had two daughters and, all members of the family having musical talents, the home became a meeting place for musicians and music lovers. He received international fame during his lifetime and made lasting contributions to our knowledge of congenital diseases of the gastrointestinal tract.

Bibliography

Primary: 1861. Den medfødte Tillukning af Spiserøret samt Bidrag til Kundskaber om den medfødte Tyndtarmstillukning (thesis) (Copenhagen); 1876. 'Et Tilfælde af subakut Tarminvagination.' *Hospitalstidende* 3: 321–327; 1888. 'Stuhlträgheit Neugeborener in Folge von Dilatation und Hypertrophie des Colons.' *Jahrbuch für Kinderheilkunde* 27: 1–7.

Secondary: Roed-Petersen, Karsten, and Gunna Erichsen, 1988. 'The Danish Pediatrician Harald Hirschsprung.' *Surgery, Gynecology and Obstetrics* 166: 181–185; Lister, James, 1977. 'Hirschsprung: The man and the disease.' *Journal of the Royal College of Surgeons of Edinburgh* 22: 377–384; Monrad, Svenn, 1931. 'Harald Hirschsprung' in Kraft, Ludvig, ed., *Lægeportrætter fra det 19. Aarhundrede* (Copenhagen) pp. 57–66.

Henrik R. Wulff

HIRSZFELD, LUDWIK   (b. Warsaw, Poland, 5 August 1884; d. Wroclaw, Poland, 7 March 1954), *immunology.*

Hirszfeld was one of the leading figures of immunology in the first half of the twentieth century. Co-discoverer of the inheritance of ABO blood types and co-author of the first large-scale study of human population genetics, Hirszfeld went on to establish a laboratory of experimental medicine at the National Institute of Hygiene in the new Polish state between the wars. He survived the Warsaw ghetto during Nazi occupation and settled in Wroclaw (formerly Breslau) after the war, where he headed the Microbiology Department and founded an Immunological Institute.

Hirszfeld, son of the banker Stanislaw, was born into a Jewish family of the Warsaw intelligentsia and grew up in the industrial town of Lodz. He left Russian-occupied Poland to study medicine in Germany, first in Würzburg (1902–04) and subsequently in Berlin, where he completed his doctorate in 1907. He was appointed to the Cancer Research Institute in Heidelberg (1907–11), where he worked under Emil von Dungern. Together, they proved that the blood groups recently discovered by Landsteiner were inherited according to Mendelian laws and established the present-day nomenclature of ABO blood groups.

In 1911 Hirszfeld moved to the Department of Hygiene at the University of Zurich, but when World War I began he volunteered first to join the fight against the typhus epidemic in Serbia, and then went on to establish a central medical laboratory for the Allied army in Salonica. It was there that he and his pediatrician wife, Hanna Kasman, laid the groundwork for the new field of human population genetics through their discovery of the distribution of ABO blood groups, based on testing of over 8,000 individuals from the diverse populations represented within the *Armée d'Orient.*

In 1920 Hirszfeld returned to Poland and directed the serology laboratory of the National Institute of Hygiene, of which he became *de facto* scientific director once Ludwik Rajchman was appointed to the League of Nations. Hirszfeld was also professor at the University of Warsaw and traveled widely, notably in his capacity as a member of the League of Nations' biological standardization committee. In 1928 he published *Konstitutionsserologie,* which presented a theory of inheritance of predisposition to disease.

Other research by Hirszfeld and his students on blood types and on specific diseases such as diphtheria led him to study fetal-maternal compatibility, which came tantalizingly close to the discovery of Rh disease. In 1938 he published *Les groupes sanguins,* which gave Western readers full access to his thirty years of research in serology.

After the German invasion of Poland in 1939, Hirszfeld was deprived of all his positions and eventually forced into the Warsaw ghetto, where he was named to the Jewish Health Council and set up blood donor banks, a medical school, and a research laboratory. In 1943 he escaped from the ghetto with his wife and daughter and spent the remainder of the war hiding in the Polish countryside.

In 1944 Hirszfeld was called upon by the provisional Polish government to Lublin, where he co-organized the Maria Sklodowska Curie University. In 1945 he moved to Wroclaw and established the University's medical school and directed the department of microbiology. Shortly before his death, he founded the Institute of Immunology and Experimental Therapy, which now bears his name.

In 1946 Hirszfeld published his memoirs, which dwell less on scientific research than on his experience as a scientist, a Pole, and a Jew caught up in the tumult of the twentieth century. Beyond being a unique account of wartime experiences, it is also a powerful warning against the perversion of science to political ends.

Bibliography

Primary: 1928. *Konstitutionsserologie* (Berlin); 1938. *Les groupes sanguins, leur application à la biologie, à la médecine et au droit* (Paris); 1946. *Historia jednego zycia* [The Story of One Life] (Warsaw).

Secondary: Milgrom, Felix, 1987. 'Fundamental Discoveries in Immunohematology and Immunogenetics by Ludwik Hirszfeld.' *Vox Sang* 52: 149–151; Jaworski, Marek, 1980. *Ludwik Hirszfeld, sein Beitrag zu Serologie und Immunologie* (Leipzig); 1935–98. 'Ludwik Hirszfeld' in *Polski Slownik Biograficzny* (Wroclaw).

Marta Aleksandra Balinska and William Schneider

HIS, WILHELM (THE ELDER)   (b. Basel, Switzerland, 9 July 1831; d. Leipzig, Germany, 1 May 1904), *anatomy, histology, embryology.*

His, descended from the old patrician family 'Ochs', was the son of a silk industrialist. In 1818 the family had changed its name to 'His'. He studied medicine at the universities of Basel, Bern, Würzburg, and Berlin, where Rudolf Virchow, Johannes Müller, and Robert Remak were his teachers. In 1854 he graduated MD at Basel with his dissertation *Zur Histologie der Cornea* (1854). After an elective period at the Paris Medical School, where he worked with Charles Edouard Brown-Séquard and Claude Bernard, he commenced his internship under the ophthalmologist Albrecht von Graefe at the latter's private clinic in Berlin. After receiving the 'Venia legendi' from the Friedrich-Wilhelm University in 1857, His was called to the chair of anatomy and physiology at the University of Basel. In 1872 he was made 'Ordinarius' at the Institute of Anatomy at Leipzig, where he stayed until his death. This newly constructed institute, which had been created after His's own plans, reopened in 1875. It was one of the most modern institutes of its time and was the site of the Leipzig school of microscopical anatomy.

His worked extensively on the histology of the cornea, on the lymphatic system, on the mucous membranes, on the cavities of the human body, and in the area of embryology. He used ingenious micro-techniques, such as the Oschatz-microtome, for successive slicing of different morphological growth stages. For His, embryology was essentially based on histological methods and an epistemology of close comparison. He objected fervently to the evolutionary theories of Charles Darwin and Ernst Haeckel, defending the view that the germ disc was already morphologically determined and subject to an inborn formative program. This view is also visually reflected in the excellent His-Steger models, which were to represent the ontogenetic forms of the embryo in pronounced naturalistic magnification. After the introduction of microphotography in Germany by Joseph von Gerlach, His began to experiment with histological photography and the production of serial images of embryonic development.

In 1884 he discovered the 'neuroblasts'—progenitor cells of the central and peripheral nervous system. This discovery was a landmark contribution to the general 'neuron' theory of brain morphology and function. For His, neuroblasts behaved as independent elements and built up various kinds of neuroanatomical centers. Nevertheless, he was a careful scientist, stating that the brain was more than just an assembly of optimally distributed contact points and that in the makeup of neuronal cable structures the nerve cell also served other purposes than as a mere relay (1893).

Together with Joseph Hyrtl of Vienna and Wilhelm von Waldeyer-Hartz of Berlin, His was one of the key figures in the commission of the newly funded Anatomical Society for *Nomina anatomica*. His engagement with medical terminology and anatomical nomenclature cannot be overemphasized, as he contributed extensively to the scientific ideal of a research-based type of medical teaching. In 1895 His published a rather curious book entitled *Johann Sebastian Bach, Forschungen über dessen Grabstätte, Gebeine und Antlitz*, in which he described the identification of the skeleton and the

representation of the face of the German baroque composer Johann Sebastian Bach. This piece of work stands within the broader tradition of anthropological, anatomical, and forensic research into the nature of human genius.

The overall scientific and social influence of His is highlighted by his membership in many eminent societies of the time, including the Internationale Anatomische Gesellschaft, where he was founding governor in 1886, and the Internationale Assoziation der Akademien. His served on the editorial boards of *Archiv für Anthropologie* and *Zeitschrift für Anatomie und Entwicklungsgeschichte*, which was later called *Anatomische Abteilung des Archivs für Anatomie und Physiologie* (from 1878).

Bibliography

Primary: 1880–85. *Anatomie menschlicher Embryonen* 3 vols. (Leipzig); 1893. 'Ueber den Aufbau unseres Nervensystems.' *Verhandlungen der Gesellschaft der deutschen Naturforscher und Aerzte* 1: 39–67; 1895. *Johann Sebastian Bach, Forschungen über dessen Grabstätte, Gebeine und Antlitz* (Leipzig).

Secondary: Rasmussen, A. T., 1953. 'Wilhelm His' in Haymaker, Webb, ed., *Founders of Neurology* (Springfield, IL) pp. 49–51; His, W. d. J., 1931. *Wilhelm His der Anatom. Ein Lebensbild* (Berlin and Vienna); Rabl, Carl, 1909. *Geschichte der Anatomie an der Universität Leipzig* (Leipzig); *DSB*.

Frank W. Stahnisch

HOBSON, BENJAMIN   (b. Welford, England, 2 January 1816; d. Forest Hill, England, 16 February 1873), *surgery, missionary medicine.*

Benjamin Hobson was the son of Rev Benjamin Hobson, an Independent minister. After an apprenticeship at Birmingham General Hospital, Hobson enrolled in medicine at University College London in 1835 and sat for the membership examinations of the Royal College of Surgeons (England) in 1838. He received his MB from the University of London in 1839 and was appointed a medical missionary to China by the London Missionary Society. Hobson arrived in Macao in December 1839 and took charge of the hospital founded by Peter Parker of the Medical Missionary Society in China. Hobson then moved to Hong Kong (1843), where he continued his medical missionary work. He failed, however, to realize his goal of establishing a medical school for the Chinese in the colony. Disagreements between the American missionaries and their British colleagues led to the split of the Medical Missionary Society in China in 1845. In the same year, the deteriorating health of his wife, Jane Abbey, compelled Hobson to return to England. She died just before their ship reached Dover. Hobson sailed to China again in 1847 after his remarriage to Mary Rebecca Morrison, daughter of Robert Morrison, the pioneering Protestant missionary to China. He resumed medical work in Hong Kong, and soon moved to Canton (Guangzhou) in February 1848.

Hobson concentrated on treating surgical conditions, especially diseases of the eyes. He usually selected patients with good prospects of recovery because any perception of failure by the Chinese would damage the missionary enterprise. Hobson's medical practice was apparently popular among the Chinese, but his proselytizing efforts were much less successful.

Hobson considered Chinese medicine far inferior to European medicine. He wrote his first Chinese medical book, *Quanti xinlun* [Outline of Anatomy and Physiology], in 1851 as part of his grand project of educating the Chinese. Hobson attempted to provide accurate translations of terms such as nerve, artery, and vein, whose previous Chinese translations had been confusing. Hobson imported an anatomical model to instruct his Chinese collaborator, Chen Xiutang. In *Quanti xinlun* Hobson also presented the typical arguments of natural theology, that the human body revealed God's ingenious design and divine wisdom.

Hobson was forced back to Hong Kong in 1856 because of the unrest in Canton on the eve of the Second Opium War. He moved to Shanghai in February 1857 to work with William Lockhart and took charge of the missionary hospital when Lockhart returned to England at the end of that year. Hobson wrote prolifically while in Shanghai. He composed *Xiyi luelun* [First Lines of the Practice of Surgery in the West] in 1857. *Neike xinshuo* [Practice of Medicine and Materia Medica] and *Fuying xinshuo* [Treatise on Midwifery and Diseases of the Children] followed in 1858. All three books were written with the collaboration of the Chinese literati Guan Mao-cai. The last two books were written partly in response to the Chinese opinion that whereas European medicine excelled in surgical operations, Chinese medicine was better at treating internal diseases. Rather than translate particular works, Hobson always drew from several sources for his Chinese medical treatises. These books, sought after not only by Chinese readers but also by Japanese and Korean scholars, were reprinted several times. At least four Japanese editions of *Quanti xinlun* with commentaries were published.

Toward the end of 1858, Hobson's health deteriorated. He returned to England in early 1859. He soon resumed medical practice at Clifton and then Cheltenham. A facial paralysis, however, forced Hobson to retire in 1864.

Bibliography

Primary: 1851. 全體新論 *Quanti xinlun* [Outline of Anatomy and Physiology] (Guangzhou); 1857. 西醫略論 *Xiyi luelun* [First Lines of the Practice of Surgery in the West] (Shanghai); 1858. 婦嬰新說 *Fuying xinshuo* [Treatise on Midwifery and Diseases of the Children] (Shanghai); 1858. 內科新說 *Neike xinshuo* [Practice of Medicine and Materia Medica] (Shanghai).

Secondary: Wong, K. Chimin, and Wu Lien-teh, 1936. *History of Chinese Medicine* (Shanghai).

Shang-Jen Li

HODGKIN, THOMAS (b. Pentonville, England, 17 August 1798; d. Jaffa, Ottoman Empire, 4 April 1866), *medicine, pathology.*

Hodgkin was born into a devout Quaker family in a village near London. His upbringing imbued him from early life with honesty, discipline, and concern for social justice. As a Quaker, Thomas wore plain clothes and spoke in a formal manner. At the age of twenty-one he wrote an 'Essay on the Promotion of Civilization', which criticized the imperialistic behavior of colonists resulting in degradation or death of North American Indians and other native peoples. Thomas also developed an interest in science. He served as apprentice to an apothecary and walked the wards at Guy's Hospital prior to attending medical school in Edinburgh. During 1821–22 he visited European medical centers and met René Laennec in Paris, who instructed him on the use of the newly devised stethoscope. Hodgkin received his MD from Edinburgh (1823) and the same year met Moses Montefiore (1784–1885), a philanthropist who was to become his patient and close friend. In 1826 Hodgkin was appointed the first lecturer in morbid anatomy and the museum curator at Guy's Hospital. Between 1826 and 1837, he performed hundreds of autopsies and cataloged over 3,000 specimens. He presented the first systematic lectures on pathology in England, which were published in two volumes. In 1827 Hodgkin and Joseph J. Lister (1786–1869) studied various tissues with the microscope. Using Lister's improved achromatic lenses, they discovered the biconcave shape of human erythrocytes and the striations in skeletal and cardiac muscle. This paper has been termed the 'foundation of modern histology'. Hodgkin described aortic regurgitation five years before Dominic Corrigan (1802–80). Hodgkin's paper, 'On Some Morbid Appearances of the Absorbent Glands and Spleen', appeared in 1832. He reported seven patients with gross enlargement of lymph nodes and spleen, but without inflammation or other significant pathology. Two of the cases were patients of Richard Bright (1789–1858) and one was a patient of Thomas Addison (1793–1860). Hodgkin recognized that tuberculosis coexisted in some of the patients, but felt that the findings he identified were distinct from tuberculosis. He pointed out that the disease spread to contiguous lymph node groups in an orderly manner and that splenic involvement was a late development. He noted that Marcello Malpighi (1628–94) had described a similar condition in 1666. Despite his previous work with Lister, Hodgkin apparently did not examine these abnormal tissues under the microscope. The reason is unclear, though it may have been due to the primitive status of microtechnique and specimen preparation around 1830.

Hodgkin brought the first stethoscope to Guy's Hospital and taught Laennec's method for its use to medical students and physicians. The museum for which he served as first curator was a landmark contribution to medical science and helped make Guy's one of the leading teaching institutions in England. The preservation and availability of specimens from his original lymphoma cases enabled others to confirm the entity that became known as Hodgkin's disease a century later.

Another well-known Guy's Hospital physician, Samuel Wilks (1824–1911), published a paper on 'lardaceous disease' (amyloidosis) and other underlying conditions in 1856 in which he unknowingly redescribed some of Hodgkin's original cases. Wilks became aware of Hodgkin's initial work on lymph nodes and spleen through an 1838 citation by Richard Bright. In 1865 Wilks published a more detailed paper on enlargement of the lymphatic glands and spleen and, for the first time, used the eponym 'Hodgkin's disease', thereby immortalizing his predecessor. Like Hodgkin, Wilks did not provide a histologic description. Subsequently multiple articles on the microscopic appearance of the disorder appeared, culminating with the reports by W. S. Greenfield in 1878, Carl Sternberg in 1898, and Dorothy Reed in 1902, of the multinucleate giant cells characteristic of Hodgkin's disease.

In 1926 Herbert Fox confirmed histologically that two of three cases described by Hodgkin in 1832 did in fact have Hodgkin's disease. One patient had what was then called lymphosarcoma, now included among the non-Hodgkin's lymphomas. Thus Hodgkin's name echoes in the halls of major medical centers throughout the world every day in association with both categories of malignant lymphoma.

Hodgkin, Richard Bright, and Thomas Addison were contemporaries and became known as the 'three great men of Guy's'. All correlated clinical with postmortem findings. All had diseases named for them, but Hodgkin's remains by far the most familiar. Bright's disease no longer survives as a distinct clinical entity, and Addison's disease is rare.

Hodgkin's outstanding academic career came to an abrupt halt in 1837 when he was rejected for the post of clinical staff physician at Guy's Hospital. He immediately resigned. He had incensed the autocratic chief hospital administrator, Benjamin Harrison, Jr., who held that post from 1797 to 1848. Harrison was also deputy chairman of the board of the Hudson's Bay Company. According to Hodgkin, Hudson's Bay Company had given guns and alcohol to the Indians in exchange for furs, which brought large profits. In a letter to Harrison, Hodgkin had criticized the Hudson's Bay Company for its exploitation of Indians by colonists. Not surprisingly, these views did not sit well with Harrison and some others in Victorian England. The clinical appointment at Guy's went instead to Benjamin Babington (1794–1866), a well-connected physician who had invented the 'glottiscope', an instrument which Hodgkin renamed the 'laryngiscope'. Hodgkin's heartfelt but somewhat naïve views collided with those of Benjamin Harrison in an explosive confrontation that effectively ended Hodgkin's medical research and teaching activities. The result was a tragedy for Hodgkin and an irreplaceable loss for Guy's.

Hodgkin endured major disappointment in his personal as well as his professional life before the age of forty. He was not permitted to marry his true love, Sarah Godlee, because

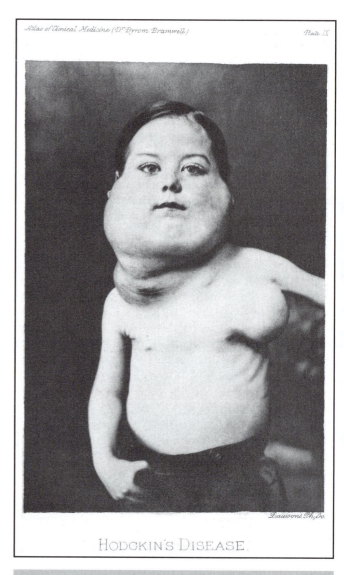

Child aged seven with Hodgkin's disease of five years' duration. He died within weeks of the photograph being taken, 1888. Halftone reproduction from Sir Byrom Bramwell, *Atlas of Clinical Medicine*, Edinburgh, 1892. Wellcome Library, London.

they were first cousins. Even though he petitioned the Society of Friends to make an exception on two separate occasions, he was refused. Later, but too late for Hodgkin, the rule was repealed. He finally married Sara Scaife, a widow and not a Quaker, in 1849.

Hodgkin's activities as a social reformer and physician continued after he left Guy's Hospital. His efforts on behalf of underprivileged and oppressed peoples throughout the world were lifelong. He took part in organizing the new University of London and its medical school, the first nonsectarian institution of its kind in England. Hodgkin declined the prestigious FRCP in 1836 because he felt the criteria for selection were unfair. He cared for the poor in London, especially Jews, often not charging fees. In addition, he traveled to many countries with Moses Montefiore, in order to help Jews and Christians as a medical missionary. He was a strong advocate of sanitary measures and protection of factory children. He championed education of laypersons about personal, social, and occupational health issues. In four lectures given in 1829 (published in 1835) he emphasized the importance of clean air, proper bathing, prompt disposal of sewage, and the dangers of tobacco. He also stressed the need for regular exercise and adequate education (for girls as well as boys). He studied the new sciences of ethnology and anthropology, and belonged to many organizations dedicated to improving of the lives of less fortunate people, holding leadership positions in some of them. During a trip to Palestine (then under Ottoman rule) with Montefiore in 1866, Hodgkin became ill with dysentery and died in Jaffa, where he is buried. His gravestone bears the inscription 'nothing of humanity was foreign to him'.

Hodgkin was an exceptional and compassionate physician who first described the malignant lymphoma that bears his name. During his brief career at Guy's Hospital, he made other major contributions in clinical medicine and pathology. He served as first curator of the museum at Guy's, which became and remains one of the front-rank medical museums in the world. His adherence to Quaker precepts and strong reformist penchant were constant features of his life. Some of his altruistic efforts were too impractical and unpopular to be successful. Nevertheless, Thomas Hodgkin's life continues to serve as a beacon for social justice and human rights inspiring to physicians and laypersons alike.

Bibliography

Primary: 1827. (with Lister, J. J.) 'Notice of some microscopic observations of the blood and animal tissues.' *Philosphical Magazine* (n.s.) 2: 130–138; 1829. *Catalogue of the Preparations in the Anatomical Museum of Guy's Hospital* (London); 1829. 'On the retroversion of the valves of the aorta.' *London Medical Gazette* 3: 433–443; 1832. 'On some morbid appearances of the absorbent glands and spleen.' *Medico-Chirurgical Transactions* 17: 68–114; 1835. *Lectures on the Means of Promoting and Preserving Health Delivered at the Mechanics' Institute, Spitalfields* (London); 1836/1840. *Lectures of the Morbid Anatomy of the Serous and Mucous Membranes* 2 vols. (London).

Secondary: Rosenfield, Louis, 1993. *Thomas Hodgkin. Morbid Anatomist & Social Activist* (Lanham, MD); Kass, A. M., and E. H. Kass, 1988. *Perfecting the World. The Life and Times of Thomas Hodgkin* (Boston); Rose, Michael, 1981. *Curator of the Dead. Thomas Hodgkin (1798–1866)* (London); Kaplan, Henry S., 1980. *Hodgkin's Disease* 2nd edn. (Cambridge) especially chapter 1, pp. 1–15; Wilks, Samuel, 1909. 'A short account of the life and works of Thomas Hodgkin, M.D.' *Guy's Hospital Gazette* 23: 528–532; Wilks, Samuel, 1865. 'Enlargement of the lymphatic glands and spleen (or, Hodgkin's Disease) with remarks.' *Guy's Hospital Reports* 11: 56–67; *Oxford DNB*.

Marvin J. Stone

HOFFMANN, FRIEDRICH   (b. Halle, Germany, 19 February 1660; d. Halle, 12 November 1742), *medicine.*

Hoffmann's father Friedrich Hoffmann (the Elder) practiced as a physician in Halle while serving as the personal doctor of the Protestant administrator of the Duchy (*Erzstift*) of Magdeburg. From 1678 Hoffmann was a student at the University of Jena, where he studied under the well-known iatrochemist Georg Wolfgang Wedel. After a short period of study in Erfurt, Hoffmann earned the Dr med degree in Jena in 1681. After teaching for a short time in Jena, Hoffmann went to Minden as a general practitioner. In 1683 he took an educational trip through Belgium, Holland, and England, where he met Robert Boyle. After his return to Germany in 1684, he was initially active again in Minden. In 1685 he took up a post there as garrison physician, and then went to Halberstadt in 1687, where he worked as a district physician.

In 1683 Hoffmann was appointed by the Brandenburg Elector Frederick III, later King Frederick I of Prussia, to the first chair in medicine at the newly established University of Halle. Hoffmann lectured on anatomy, surgery, therapy, physics, and chemistry, and proved to be a very successful academic teacher, attracting many students to Halle. Under the direction of Hoffmann and Georg Ernst Stahl, the medical faculty in Halle became the leading German center for the training of academic doctors at the beginning of the eighteenth century. In 1709 Frederick summoned Hoffmann to Berlin as his personal physician. Due to intrigues at the royal court, Hoffmann left this service three years later and returned to Halle. There he lived and taught until his death, with a short interruption in 1734, when he was called once again to Berlin.

Hoffmann was, along with Herman Boerhaave in Leiden, the most consistent representative of a direction in medicine that sought, building on Descartes's mechanical philosophy of nature, to explain the functions of the human body solely via principles of mechanics. The human body was considered an artfully constructed machine whose individual components moved as was necessary in keeping with their form, size, location, and interaction. This movement, especially the circular movement of the blood, was the most important principle of the living body. Life meant nothing other than constant motion. To come to a stop led to ruin and was synonymous with death.

Hoffmann postulated a fine material substance as the origin of motion. It was taken in with the breath and mixed in the organism with a portion of the blood. This ether, which was reminiscent of the *spiritus* of ancient classical and medieval medical tradition, was the source, via a power it contained, for the continual motion of the heart, which supported the circulation of blood. The movement of the other muscles in the body was also based on a *spiritus*-like substance, a nerve liquid formed in the brain. This was transmitted via the nerves to the muscles in order to provide the impulse for motion. In the opposite direction, the nerve liquid transmitted perceptions to the brain as wavelike movements. Hoffmann, for religious reasons, did not deny the existence of a soul. But in his eyes, its relation to the mechanical events in the body was of no importance for the theory of medicine or the practical activity of the physician.

Hoffmann saw diseases as disturbances in the normal movements of the solid and liquid parts of the body. The task of the doctor was thus to assist the organism to normalize its sequences of movement. Hoffmann's therapy was conservative and mild: it basically consisted of measures in diet and the prescription of simple medications. The painkiller developed and sold by Hoffmann, the so-called *Liquor anodynus mineralis,* is famous as 'Hoffmann's drops'.

Hoffmann was one of the most famous medical specialists in the first half of the eighteenth century in Europe. He was a member of the Berlin Academy of Sciences, the Royal Society of London, and the Russian Academy of Sciences. His consistent attempts to derive bodily functions from mechanical principles was, in its simplicity, doomed to failure. But inter alia it was Hoffmann's thinking that paved the way for the technical view of the human organism that characterizes modern medicine.

Bibliography

Primary: 1718–20. *Medicina rationalis systematica* 2 vols. (Halle); 1721–39. *Medicina consultatoria* 2 vols. (Halle); 1738. *Medicus politicus* (Leiden); 1974. (King, Lester, trans. and intro.) *Fundamenta medicae* (New York).

Secondary: Lanz, Almut, 1995. *Arzneimittel in der Therapie Friedrich Hoffmanns (1660–1742) unter besonderer Berücksichtigung der Medicina consultatoria (1721–1723)* (Braunschweig); Müller, Ingo W., 1991. *Iatromechanische Theorie und ärztliche Praxis im Vergleich zur galenistischen Medizin* (Stuttgart); Rothschuh, Karl Eduard, 1976. 'Studien zu Friedrich Hoffmann.' *Sudhoffs Archiv* 60: 163–193, 235–270; *DSB.*

Jürgen Helm and
Karin Stukenbrock

HOLLOWAY, THOMAS (b. Plymouth Dock, Devon, England, 22 September 1800; d. Sunninghill, Surrey, England, 26 December 1883), *patent medicines, philanthropy.*

Holloway was the eldest of six children of Thomas Holloway and his wife, Mary Chellow, who ran a bakery and several inns in Plymouth Dock. He received his early education in Camborne. In 1811 the family moved to Penzance to run the Turks Head Inn. In 1816 they opened a grocery and bakery, where Thomas got his first experience of retail trade.

He began an apprenticeship as a chemist and druggist with William Harvey in Penzance. In 1828 he left Cornwall to seek his fortune. He spent three years in France, and on his return took up a post as secretary and interpreter for a firm of importers and exporters in London.

In 1837 he was approached by an Italian trader, Felix Albinolo, proprietor of *Albinolo's Ointment.* Albinolo found himself in a debtors' prison, and Holloway saw an opportunity to produce his own ointment. He made a batch using his mother's saucepan, and in 1837 placed his first newspaper advertisement for *Holloway's Ointment.* In 1839 he began to also manufacture pills, moving to bigger premises at 244 Strand.

Holloway's business was built on mass advertising. In 1838 he spent £1,000 on posters and inserts in newspapers and periodicals. By 1842 this had risen to £5,000, by 1845 to £10,000, by 1855 to £30,000, and by 1883 to £50,000. His advertisements made extensive use of testimonials, and he used a wide range of other ploys to promote his products.

Two houses were erected at the rear of 224 Strand to provide more space, and in 1867 he acquired bigger premises at 533 New Oxford Street. In 1851 he employed five clerks, twelve men, nine boys, and three women. By 1883 there were over one hundred workers employed in the factory and warehouse, together with dozens of salesmen, agents, and distributors.

Thomas became a shrewd speculator in stocks and shares, and started to buy fine paintings. He also developed a keen interest in property. He owned Elm House at Winkfield near Windsor, later purchasing Tittenhurst Park in Sunninghill, and another country house, Broomfield. He also acquired the Whitbourne estate and owned property in Cornwall.

As his fortune grew Thomas had the problem of what to do with it. In 1840 he had married Jane Pearce Driver, the elder daughter of a Rotherhithe shipwright, but he and his wife had no children. His chosen cause, largely on the advice of the social reformer Lord Shaftesbury, was to provide for 'the treatment of mental illness among the less prosperous middle classes'.

William Henry Crossland won a competition in 1871 that was held to find an architect for the sanatorium, which was to have a neo-Gothic design. Holloway himself took responsibility for its planning. He insisted that the building should be spacious, comfortable, and welcoming, and that each patient should have his or her own room. Mrs Holloway laid the first brick in May 1872. To avoid unnecessary delay, Thomas bought the brickworks. Nevertheless, progress was slow, and he eventually died before the sanatorium opened.

In June 1873 he began his second philanthropic project, a college for the education of women, following a meeting with the prime minister, Gladstone, and his wife. Crossland was again appointed architect, and he suggested that it be modeled on the chateau of Chambord in Loir-et-Cher, France. In 1874 Holloway acquired the Mount Lee estate in Egham, Surrey, but it was not until 14 September 1879 that the first brick was laid. The Royal Holloway College was formally opened by Queen Victoria on 30 June 1886.

On his death Thomas left his remaining fortune and the business to his wife's sister. It remained in family hands until 1930. Papers relating to Thomas Holloway and his family (1863–1965) are housed at Royal Holloway, University of London Archives (RHC RF100-103).

Bibliography

Secondary: Harrison-Barbet, Anthony, 1994. *Thomas Holloway: Victorian Philanthropist* (Egham); Bingham, Caroline, 1987. *The History of Royal Holloway College 1886–1986* (London); *Oxford DNB*.

Stuart Anderson

HOLMES, GORDON MORGAN   (b. Castlebellingham, County Louth, Ireland, 22 February 1876; d. Farnham, Surrey, England, 29 December 1965), *neurology.*

Son of a farmer, Holmes studied at Trinity College, Dublin, graduating in 1897. A Stewart Scholarship then enabled him to go to Frankfurt, where he studied neuroanatomy and histology under Karl Weigert (1845–1904) and Ludwig Edinger (1855–1918). Nevertheless, his research was cut short when projected funds were diverted to Paul Ehrlich (1854–1915) for his research on Salvarsan, and Holmes proceeded to the National Hospital for Nervous Disease, Queen Square, London, where he was successively house physician, resident medical officer, and pathologist. Between 1900 and 1911 he published papers on neuroanatomy and neuropathology, including an early description of the symptoms of cerebellar tumor. He then joined Henry Head (1861–1940) to work on the role of the cerebral cortex in sensory perception, and also helped to delineate the function of the thalamus and its relation to the cerebral cortex, and introduced into neurology precise methods of mapping the skin.

The opportunity to extend this work, particularly on the cerebellum and visual pathways, occurred when Holmes served as consulting neurologist to the British Army during World War I, holding the rank of lieutenant colonel. Here he saw hundreds of gunshot injuries in men who had been previously healthy, so that the findings could not be influenced by degenerative or other conditions. Even on cold nights in France, after a heavy daily routine, Holmes would sit up late working on his research material, and he published no fewer than eighteen papers based on his wartime experiences between 1915 and 1918. In 1919 his Montgomery Lectures in Dublin, again owing much to this wartime research, were considered to be a milestone in the physiology of vision. His work emphasized that primary visual perception, including color vision, is subserved by the cortex of the striate area. On the other hand, more highly differentiated visual functions, such as the identification of objects, the recognition of spatial relationships, and local visual attention, are subserved by other, more remote, portions of the brain.

Holmes's research between the world wars concentrated on the slow deterioration of brain function with age. After retiring in 1941, he continued to work as a consultant with the Emergency Medical Service, and in 1946 produced *An Introduction to Clinical Neurology,* followed eight years later by a history of the National Hospital, Queen Square, the penultimate of his 174 articles published during his lifetime. He edited the journal *Brain* from 1922 to 1937. He was elected FRS in 1933. In the view of C. G. Philips, Dr Lee's Professor of Anatomy at Oxford and editor of Holmes's *Collected Papers,* Holmes has probably never been surpassed as a clinical examiner of normal and disordered neurological function. After scrupulous history-taking and routine tests, he would then devise special procedures to measure the degree of lost function in a patient. His work shows how an acute mind can harness the study of even the most dreadful of battle injuries toward the ultimate amelioration of human disease.

Bibliography

Primary: 1979. (Philips, C. G., ed.) *Collected Papers* (Oxford).

Secondary: Breathnech, C. S., 1975. 'Sir Gordon Holmes.' *Medical History* 19: 194–200; Walshe, F. M. R., 1966. 'Gordon Morgan Holmes.' *Biographical Memoirs of Fellows of the Royal Society* 12: 311–319; *Munk's Roll; Oxford DNB*.

Stephen Lock

HOLMES, OLIVER WENDELL   (b. Cambridge, Massachusetts, USA, 29 August 1809; d. Boston, Massachusetts, USA, 7 October 1894), *medicine, medical education, physiology, anatomy, belles lettres.*

From the point of view of medical history, the most curious thing about Holmes, the physician, is that people generally think of him first and foremost as Holmes, the poet and essayist. Nor are they wrong. It has been said that Holmes's medical contributions were not recognized until the 1940s, but that is not altogether accurate. He was the widely-respected professor of anatomy at Harvard Medical School for thirty-six years, during six of which he also served as dean. (He was also very much in the public eye in that latter role for a time, having had the misfortune to be dean and to have to deal with the media when one of his medical school colleagues—John Webster—was convicted of and hanged for the murder of another distinguished medical school colleague, George Parkman.) However, although Holmes was a popular medical educator for decades and wrote a handful of significant medical essays, the fact remains that his primary influence on the life and letters of the United States comes from his literary output rather than his medical career.

The son of the serious-minded pastor of the Congregational Church in Cambridge, Massachusetts, and a socially involved mother, Wendell—as he was called—was very much a product of New England. Despite his stern upbringing, he evidenced, while still very young, a fun-loving spirit, a talent for talk, and an irrepressible inclination to rhyme whatever could be rhymed. He was an indifferent pupil in the early years of his schooling, already showing the signs of the restless imagination and quick wit that would dog him, and make him famous, later in life. Following a year at Phillips Academy, he went to Harvard as a matter of course (born into the social and cultural elite of Boston and Cambridge, he could hardly have done otherwise). Expected by the family to follow in his father's footsteps, Holmes seems to instead have had more worldly tastes; when it came time to choose a profession after earning his BA at Harvard (1829), he spent a year studying law before deciding he would rather become a physician. He also began more earnestly to write poetry—something he had been doing sporadically for years.

Studying medicine first at Harvard and then in Paris, Holmes there came under the spell of Pierre-Charles-Alexandre Louis. Returning to Boston full of enthusiasm for microscopy and for Louis's numerical methods, he still had to satisfy Harvard's graduation requirements. With the acceptance of his thesis ('A Dissertation on Acute Pericarditis)' and a successful oral examination, he earned his MD in early 1836. That same year, he was appointed to a position at the Boston Dispensary and then—with Jacob Bigelow and two other colleagues—he established the Tremont Medical School in Boston. The four physicians offered a more systematically ordered curriculum than was customary, and each of them taught in two (and only two) subject areas. Also in 1836, while waiting to get himself established, Holmes entered the prestigious annual Boylston Prize Medal essay contest sponsored by Harvard Medical School. Like George Cheyne Shattuck before him, he won on his first attempt, then submitted papers on both contest topics the following year, and won both prizes that year. Again like Shattuck, he promptly published his essays in a slim volume (*Boylston Prize Dissertations for the Years 1836-7*). The third of those essays may have been the introduction for some American physicians to the French methods of 'direct exploration'—auscultation and percussion—that increased diagnostic precision. An inveterate tinkerer, Holmes also adapted the microscope he had brought back from Paris for use in the classroom.

In 1838 and 1839 Holmes honed his teaching skills at Dartmouth Medical School. His introductory lectures there provide evidence that he was earnest about his responsibility as a teacher and eager to add breadth to his students' education. Holmes also began to practice medicine in Boston, whether desultorily or merely unsuccessfully may be a matter of interpretation. What is clear is that he was writing and publishing more poetry—as well as medical essays—and seeing very few patients. Many people thought it undignified for a prospective physician to be dabbling in verse, and Holmes periodically swore he would stop writing poetry. But from the time he published 'Old Ironsides' (1830) through his years of membership with other men of letters in the Saturday Club, during which he wrote what would become his famous 'Autocrat' series of essays for the *Atlantic Monthly* (a new magazine for which he proposed the name), lectured on literary topics for the Lowell Institute (a kind of 'Open University'), and accepted virtually every proffered invitation to give celebratory speeches or write dedicatory poems, he was a force to be reckoned with in literary Boston.

He was, moreover, something of an eccentric, in a society where that was not always an asset. He loved performing, whether on a public stage, in clubs, or in private drawing-rooms. Not surprisingly, then, at the time of his death he

Oliver Wendell Holmes. Colored lithograph by Sir Leslie Ward (Spy), 1886. Iconographic Collection, Wellcome Library, London.

was known less for having been a physician than as a poet, biographer, novelist, and lecturer. He modeled himself on Dr Samuel Johnson, with whom he loved to be compared, and to compare himself—he was not without vanity.

Only in a few instances, in the medical essays that indeed occasionally flowed from his pen, did Holmes's literary and medical activities merge. Early in his career, Holmes became agitated over quackery and what he considered the irresponsible treatment modes of homeopaths. His disdain and complete contempt were clear in his ringing attack on their practices ('Homeopathy and Its Kindred Delusions'). He was also a therapeutic nihilist, suggesting at one point in characteristically dramatic style that patients would be better off if physicians were to throw all their medicaments into the sea.

By far the most notable contribution Holmes made to medical literature, however, was his paper on the contagiousness of puerperal fever. He read the paper before the Boston Society for Medical Improvement in January 1843 (when he was still a young man of thirty-four). Three months later, the essay was published in what turned out to be the final issue of a short-lived journal, the *New England Quarterly Journal of Medicine and Surgery*. Given the rash of cases of puerperal fever in Boston just then, it is no surprise that the article received a fair amount of attention locally. Summaries of its key points, or references to it, appeared in a few professional journals and venues. (For example, later that year, Samuel Kneeland, while finishing his medical studies at Harvard Medical School, chose to take up the same topic in his MD dissertation—for which he won the Prize Medal when he submitted it to the Boylston contest. He may have been inspired by Holmes, whom he quoted freely.) But by no means did everyone find convincing Holmes's insistence that puerperal fever was contagious, any more than the same theory was universally accepted when promoted (with a solid underpinning of statistical data) by Ignác Semmelweis in Budapest and Vienna a few years later.

Outspoken opposition to the contagion theory from two well-known professors of the diseases of women in Philadelphia, Hugh L. Hodge and—especially—Charles Delucena Meigs, troubled Holmes, but it was twelve years before their attacks became so vigorous (and personal) that he felt moved to respond. He then republished his essay in 1855 in pamphlet form, with an introduction full of criticism of 'Two widely known and highly esteemed practitioners, Professors in two of the largest Medical Schools in the Union, teaching the branch of art which includes the Diseases of Women' (Holmes, 1855, p. 9). The new version of the paper was almost twice as long as the original essay. Holmes acknowledged both that the 'teachings of the two Professors in the great schools of Philadelphia are some to be listened to' (p. 23) and that, although he opposed Hodge's conclusions, at least the tone and language in Hodge's lecture 'On the Non-Contagious Character of Puerperal Fever' were 'unobjectionable' (p. 9). Meigs's *On the Nature, Signs and Treatment of Childbed Fever* infuriated Holmes, however. Credulity is not stretched by surmising that Meigs's attack is largely responsible for the fact that we have Holmes's longer and more discursive essay at all.

Holmes's re-issuing of his essay was a curiously belated action. He had published nary a word on puerperal fever during the dozen years between 1843 and 1855 (nor after 1855, except that the later version of his essay was frequently republished, and Holmes himself often included it in collections of his papers). Thus, although Holmes wrote eloquently and passionately on the subject, it seems generous to rank him among the major contributors to the solving of the puzzle of the disease that killed so many women. Nonetheless, this single paper was influential, and Holmes's reputation for having made a valuable contribution to medical science rests largely on it.

On the other hand, it must be conceded that Holmes's puerperal fever essay—though generally referred to (certainly in the United States) as a 'classic of medical literature'—was not the product of any original research. Holmes himself acknowledged that the information in his paper was not novel, but he insisted that it was nonetheless worth presenting. Also, like his earlier homeopathy lectures, the puerperal fever paper demonstrated unequivocally that Holmes, the *bon vivant*, wit, and charming poet could write seriously, clearly, and argumentatively—effectively marshaling and weighing evidence. He brought before the profession a uniquely detailed catalogue of cases that he culled from the literature or were shared with him by colleagues. The resulting paper could not fail to impress its auditors (and, later, its readers); it was an impassioned and vigorous bit of work, an outstanding example of what would today be called a review essay. After collecting information from his many sources, Holmes drew conclusions (which others had also reached), and then summarized the results in a bold rhetorical style. He pointed a finger directly at the physicians who were, he said, themselves carrying a 'private pestilence' to their patients.

The most important feature of this particular essay by Holmes may well have been that he made the case for the contagiousness of puerperal fever in a manner that rendered the point impossible to ignore—thanks above all to his skill as a writer. William Osler later called Holmes 'the most successful combination which the world has ever seen of the physician and the man of letters' (Osler, 1908, p. 57).

Bibliography

Primary: 1842. *Homeopathy and Its Kindred Delusions; Two Lectures* (Boston); 1843. 'The Contagiousness of Puerperal Fever.' *New England Quarterly Journal of Medicine and Surgery* 1(4): 503–530; 1855. *Puerperal Fever as a Private Pestilence* (Boston); 1888. *Medical Essays* (Boston).

Secondary: Hoyt, Edwin P., 1979. *The Improper Bostonian: Dr. Oliver Wendell Holmes* (New York); Tilton, Eleanor M., 1947. *The Amiable Autocrat: A Biography of Dr. Oliver Wendell Holmes* (New York); Osler, William, 1908. *An Alabama Student and Other Biographical Essays* (New York and London); Morse, John Torrey, 1896. *The Life and Letters of Oliver Wendell Holmes* 2 vols. (Boston).

Constance Putnam

HOLMGREN, ALARIK FRITHIOF (b. Västra Ny, Östergötland, Sweden, 22 October 1831; d. Uppsala, Sweden, 14 August 1897), *physiology*.

Holmgren, son of Anders Holmgren, court chaplain, and Gustava Nordwall, was the youngest of twelve children. He spent a good deal of his childhood roving in the forests with his brothers. Later on in his career, Holmgren would stress, both in his teaching and in his many poems, the importance of learning through nature; open-air activities encouraged an alert mind and a vigorous body. Holmgren began school only at the age of thirteen. Later on he studied in Uppsala and graduated in medicine in 1857. Holmgren assisted during the cholera epidemic in Norrköping and Söderköping in 1853 and worked as a house surgeon at the water-cure establishment in Söderköping in 1855. After obtaining his doctor's degree in 1861, Holmgren set off for Vienna, where he received training in experimental physiology under the supervision of Ernst Brücke and Carl Ludwig. He completed his studies abroad with a stay at Emil du Bois-Reymond's laboratory in Berlin.

In 1862 a temporary physiological laboratory was established at the Faculty of Medicine in Uppsala. Here Holmgren began giving classes in physiology. He introduced animal experiments into the medical curriculum and initiated his students into the use of new instruments such as the kymograph, the sphygmograph, and the galvanometer. Through Holmgren, the scientific ideals of the so-called organic physicists (Ludwig, du Bois-Reymond, Brücke, and Helmholtz) were brought to Sweden. In 1864 he was appointed professor of physiology. In 1867 the department of physiology moved to a suitable building of its own in Uppsala.

Besides teaching and introducing experimental physiology to his medical colleagues, Holmgren devoted his time to laboratory research. Although his methods bore witness to the reductionistic style of his German teachers, Holmgren also engaged in some spectacular researches. In the late 1860s, he carried out a series of experiments, consisting of feeding pigeons with meat and hawks with vegetables, intended to demonstrate Darwin's theory of evolution. This unfortunate attempt to revert carnivores into herbivores and vice versa was followed in the 1870s by a number of studies of decapitations.

Holmgren's true contribution to the science of medicine concerns the physiology of vision. His discovery of the retina current in 1865 (published in Swedish in 1871 and in German in 1880), proved that the electrophysiological theories of Emil du Bois-Reymond were valid also for the sense of sight. His examination of the iris asserted that the contractions and dilatations of the pupil most certainly were reflex movements, at a time when anatomists still had not identified the existence of intraocular ganglions. In the early 1870s Holmgren's research shifted focus from animal experiments to methods adjusted to human beings. Fascinated by the intriguing nature of color perception, Holmgren dedicated his remaining career to problems concerning our ability to perceive colors. At first, his interest in color perception was wholly theoretical. In 1875, though, a railway accident in Sweden gave him reason to believe that the engine driver had been unable to distinguish the color of the light signal. This became the starting point for Holmgren's grand project, the mapping of color blindness among the Swedish population by means of testing using colored wools.

Bibliography

Primary: 1877. *De la cécité des couleurs dans ses rapports avec les chemins de fer et la marine* (Uppsala); 1879–80. 'Ueber die Retinaströme' in *Untersuchungen aus dem Physiologischen Institute der Universität Heidelberg,* vol. 3 (Heidelberg); 1889–92. 'Studien über die Elementaren Farbenempfindungen I–II.' *Skandinavisches Archiv für Physiologie* vol. 1 and 3 (Leipzig).

Secondary: Olsén, Jan Eric, 2004. *Liksom ett par nya ögon. Frithiof Holmgren och synsinnets problematik* (Malmö); Granit, Ragnar, 1964. 'Frithiof Holmgren: minnesteckning.' *Levnadsteckningar över Kungl. Svenska vetenskapsakademins ledamöter* (Stockholm); Granit, Ragnar, 1945. 'Frithiof Holmgren och upptäckten av näthinnans elektriska belysningsreaktion' in *Lychnos 1944–1945* (Uppsala); *DSB.*

Jan Eric Olsén

HOLST, AXEL (b. Kristiania, Norway, 6 September 1860; d. Oslo, Norway, 26 April 1931), *hygiene, nutrition.*

Holst was born into a family with a medical tradition. His father was Chief Army Surgeon Axel Holst (1826–80), and his grandfather was Frederik Holst (1791–1871), who taught pharmacology, toxicology, and hygiene at the Royal Frederik University in Christiania (1824–60). Holst graduated from Christiania Cathedral School in 1877 and received his medical degree in 1884. During the following years he made several trips abroad, studying, among other topics, the production of pure yeast and bacteriological methods. After appointment to a position in the Health Commission of Christiania in 1890, he traveled again for two years, studying bacteriology and hygiene in Germany, England, and France. He visited Robert Koch in Berlin during the tuberculin frenzy of 1890. Holst received his Medical Doctorate in 1892 with a thesis on streptococcus bacteria. In that same year he was appointed Chief Medical Officer of Christiania, and in the following year professor of hygiene and bacteriology, as well as director of the new Institute of Hygiene at the University in Christiania. During the next decade his research focused on bacteriology, particularly on various forms of tuberculosis.

Following a trip to Asia in 1901 his interest turned toward the research for which he is most recognized by posterity, i.e., the etiology of beriberi and scurvy. While visiting Christian Eijkman's laboratory in Dutch East India, Holst had witnessed diet-based experiments provoking beriberi in chickens. After his return, he wished to continue this research on mammals, choosing guinea pigs as the subjects of his experiments. This was a lucky choice, as the guinea pig is one of only a few mammals, in addition to man, that develop scurvy due to inability to synthesize ascorbic acid. After initial studies showing tissue alterations in the guinea pigs similar to those occurring in children suffering from scurvy, Holst started his collaboration with pediatrician Theodor Frølich (1870–1947). Their results were published internationally in the *Journal of Hygiene* (1907), concluding on the etiology of scurvy that 'the disease originates in these animals as well as in man as a result only of certain special diet'. The novelty in this conclusion was that a specific disease was caused by a particular type of one-sided diet, and that its prevention or treatment could be accomplished by minute changes to this diet, e.g., with the addition of small doses of lemon juice. Holst's extrapolations from observations of guinea pigs to humans, as well as the proposed dietary etiology of scurvy, were heavily criticized both by his fellow professors and by the polar explorer and national hero Fritjof Nansen. This criticism, in addition to funding problems, led to Holst giving up this line of research in 1913.

In the following decades, Holst held numerous leading positions in international and national organizations, and served as rector of the University (1919–21). , Holst was instrumental in establishing the first professional training in Norway for chief medical officers, as a joint venture between the newly formed State Institute of Public Health, Holst's Institute of Hygiene, and the Rockefeller Foundation. For this purpose, he was granted a traveling fellowship from the Rockefeller Foundation, to visit and study various schools for medical officers and public health nurses in Central Europe. The school resulting from these preparations was opened after Holst's retirement in 1930.

Bibliography

Primary: 1888. 'Investigations on Bacteria in Suppurative Processes, in Particular Streptococcus pyogenes.' *Norsk magasin for Lægevitenskap* 3: 188–240; 1907. (with Frölich, T.) 'Experimental Studies Relating to Ship-Beri-Beri and Scurvy.' *The Journal of Hygiene* 7: 634–671.

Secondary: Norum, Kåre, and Hans J. Grav, 2002. 'Axel Holst and Theodor Frølich—Pioneers in the Combat of Scurvy.' *Tidsskrift for den Norske Lægeforening* 122: 1686–1687; 1996. 'Axel Holst, 1860–1931' in Larsen, Ø., ed., *Norway's Physicians* (Oslo); Carpenter, Kenneth J., 1986. *The History of Scurvy and Vitamin C* (Cambridge).

Erik Ingebrigtsen

HOLT, LUTHER EMMETT (b. Webster, New York, USA, 4 March 1855; d. Peking, China, 14 January 1924), *medicine, pediatrics.*

Holt, the youngest of three children of Horace Holt, a farmer, and Sabrah Curtice, was raised in a staunchly Baptist environment, where he worked around the farm as a boy, and attended Webster Academy (*c.* 1867–71) and Rochester University (graduated 1875). While training as a teacher at Riverside Academy, Wellsville (1875–76), he read books on anatomy and physiology. Following an anatomy course at Buffalo University Medical College (1876–77), he was apprenticed for eight months to J. W. Whitbeck of Rochester before securing an internship at The Hospital for the Ruptured and Crippled, New York (1878) and enrolling at the College of Physicians and Surgeons (later affiliated with Columbia University), from which he graduated (1880) among the top ten in his class. A surgical internship at Bellevue Hospital introduced him to William H. Welch, who had established the bacteriology laboratory. Active membership in the Baptist community brought him into contact with the Rockefeller family.

Holt opened a private medical practice (1881), also obtaining staff appointments at the Northwestern Dispensary and the New York Infant Asylum, which housed 300 city foundlings. Of these patients he kept meticulous medical records, performed autopsies on every fatal case, and sent specimens to Bellevue for microscopical analysis. He helped found the *Archives of Pediatrics* (1884), and became its assistant editor. During a three-month tour of Europe (1884), Holt made many career contacts and attended classes on obstetrics and pathology at Vienna's Allgemeine Krankenhaus. He married Linda Mairs (April 1886) and they had five children, of whom a son, Luther Emmett Jr., became a pediatrician. He and his wife made a further visit to Europe (1903) and also to Egypt (1912). Small in stature and solemn of countenance, Holt was nevertheless a talented and animated teacher, running quiz classes for medical students, and establishing a training school for nursemaids at the New York Babies Hospital, an institution for pauper infants (founded 1887), of which he became medical director (1889–1923). Under his leadership, the Hospital pioneered a program of sending visiting nurses to inspect and instruct mothers at home. His celebrated advice manual, *The Care and Feeding of Children* (1894), went through twelve revisions and was translated into Spanish, Russian, and Chinese during his lifetime. Similarly, *The Diseases of Infancy and Childhood* (1897) went through eight editions.

Holt was appointed professor of pediatrics at the New York Polyclinic Hospital and Medical School (1891–1901) before succeeding to Abraham Jacobi's chair at Columbia University (1901–21). A founder member of the American Pediatric Society (1887), he served as its president (1897, 1923), and was the only clinician on the first board of scientific directors of the Rockefeller Institute (1901), which funded laboratory facilities and two biochemists at the Babies Hospital (1910). He nevertheless suffered adverse publicity after introducing the Pirquet tuberculin test to the Hospital, and was accused by the Hearst press of 'Human Vivisection' (1914). Holt and his colleagues personally financed the commercial production of clean modified milk to counteract the contaminated milk that he believed was a cause of much infant illness, particularly diarrhea, and with Helen L. Fales he devised standards of nutrition based on detailed dietary analyses of a large series of healthy children. This was published as *Food, Health and Growth* (1922). Holt was a prime mover in organizing the Association for the Study and Prevention of Infant Mortality (1911), and he became director of the Child Health Organization (1918), which aimed to improve children's nutrition through school activities, health clubs, and games and comic characters. The idea spread internationally. As a representative for child hygiene, Holt was involved in the formation of the League of Red Cross Societies (1919), which was later incorporated into the Health Organization of the League of Nations (1923). In the fall of 1923, he went to China as a visiting professor at Peking Union Medical College, founded by the

Rockefeller Foundation (1921), to help organize the pediatric service at its 225-bed teaching hospital. It was here that he suffered a fatal heart attack.

Bibliography

Primary: 1891. 'The diarrhoeal diseases: acute and chronic.' in Keating, John M., ed., *Cyclopaedia of the Diseases of Children*, vol. III, part I (Edinburgh and London) pp. 61–162; 1894. *The Care and Feeding of Children: A Catechism for the Use of Mothers and Children's Nurses* (New York); 1897. *The Diseases of Infancy and Childhood: For the Use of Students and Practitioners of Medicine* (New York); 1904. (ed. with Flexner, Simon) *Bacteriological and Clinical Studies of the Diarrheal Diseases of Infancy with Reference to the Bacillus Dysenteriae (Shiga): From the Rockefeller Institute for Medical Research* (New York); 1922. *Food, Health and Growth: A Discussion of the Nutrition of Children* (New York).

Secondary: Jones, Kathleen W, 1983–84. 'Sentiment and Science: The Late Nineteenth Century Pediatrician as Mother's Advisor.' *Journal of Social History* 17: 79–96; Duffus, R. L., and Luther Emmett Holt, Jr., 1940. *L. Emmett Holt: Pioneer of a Children's Century* (New York); *DAMB*.

Carole Reeves

HOOKER, WORTHINGTON (b. Springfield, Massachusetts, USA, 3 March 1806; d. New Haven, Connecticut, USA, 6 November 1867), *medicine, medical ethics.*

Hooker attended Yale College in New Haven, Connecticut, from which he graduated in 1825, going on to obtain his MD from Harvard Medical School in Boston, Massachusetts, in 1829. He practiced medicine in Norwich, Connecticut, until 1852, when he became professor of the theory and practice of medicine at Yale Medical School, a position that he held from 1852 to 1867. He was an attending physician at the State Hospital (the New Haven Hospital) and later became a member of its board of directors. He served as a vice-president of the American Medical Association in 1864. Hooker was opposed to homeopathy and to quackery in its various forms, taking particular exception to drugs compounded of many ingredients. He also defended the medical profession against its many critics of the time. In his published work, he was especially concerned to 'protect patients and physicians from the delusions that were (often honestly) presented by physicians as if they were medical truths' (Beauchamp, 1995, p. 114). He also wrote scientific books aimed at a youthful audience.

His most important book was *Physician and Patient* (New York, 1849), which made a major contribution to the history of medical ethics. Hooker defended the 1847 *Code of Ethics* of the American Medical Association, the first modern, national code of ethics of a national association of physicians. He included the *Code* in *Physician and Patient* and championed the *Code* as an antidote to quackery and as a means to advance the standing and reputation of the medical profession.

In this book he gave particular and extended attention to the ethics of truth-telling to patients. Hooker understood physicians in the past to have claimed the privilege to exercise discretion in informing patients, especially those who were seriously ill, about their condition, and to decide how much information was to be provided and when it was to be provided. Hooker argued that experience teaches that honest communication with patients does not always result in harmful consequences to them and that, even when there are such consequences, they are not as harmful as the consequences of patients later discovering that they have been deceived or suspecting that they have been deceived. Hooker focused not simply on the effects of such deception on an individual patient, but also on its effects on society generally. He did place some limits on the ethical obligation to be forthcoming with patients, e.g., when the physician is uncertain about the outcomes of clinical management and communicating this uncertainty could be reliably expected to confuse the patient. Hooker's ethics of truth-telling has been described as 'the most original contribution to medical ethics by an American author in the nineteenth century' (Beauchamp, 1995, p. 106).

Bibliography

Primary: 1844. *Dissertation, on the Respect Due to the Medical Profession, and the Reasons That It Is Now Awarded by the Community* (Norwich, CT); 1849. *Physician and Patient; or, a Practical View of the Moral Duties, Relations and Interests of the Medical Profession and Community* (New York); 1850. *Lessons from the History of Medical Delusions* (New York); 1852. *Homeopathy: An Examination of Its Doctrines and Evidences* (New York); 1852. *Inaugural Address: The Present Mental Attitudes and Tendencies of the Medical Profession* (New Haven); 1857. *Rational Therapeutics: or the Comparative Value of Different Curative Means and the Principles of their Application* (Boston).

Secondary: Beauchamp, Tom L., 1995. 'Worthington Hooker on Ethics in Clinical Medicine' in Baker, Robert, ed., *The Codification of Medical Morality: Historical and Philosophical Studies of the Formalization of Western Medical Morality in the Eighteenth and Nineteenth Centuries: Volume Two: Anglo-American Medical Ethics and Medical Jurisprudence in the Nineteenth Century* (Dordrecht) pp. 105–199; Musto, David F., 1984. 'Worthington Hooker (1806–1867): Physician and Educator.' *Connecticut Medicine* 48: 569–574; Burns, Chester R., 1967. 'Worthington Hooker: Physician, Teacher, Reformer.' *Yale Medicine* 2: 17–18; *DAMB*.

Laurence B. McCullough

HOPE, JAMES (b. Stockport, England, 23 February 1801; d. Hampstead, England, 13 May 1841), *medicine, cardiology.*

Hope, the tenth child of a wealthy merchant, studied medicine at the University of Edinburgh (1820–25) and surgery at St Bartholomew's in London. He spent 1826 in the renowned hospitals of Paris and assisted Auguste Chomel (1788–1858), René Laennec's (1781–1826) successor at La Charité Hospital. The Paris school emphasized clinical-autopsy correlations, and Hope proved to be an apt student. After a European tour, he returned to London (1828) to practice at the Marylebone Infirmary. In 1831 he married Anne Fulton, who would later write a touching memoir about his career.

Hope's burning ambition was to become the leading physician in London, and he realized that this could best be attained through his special knowledge of stethoscopy. Laennec's 1819 *Treatise on Mediate Auscultation* had been translated into English in 1821 by John Forbes (1787–1861), who stated in his introduction 'That it will ever come into general use, not withstanding its value, I am extremely doubtful . . . its whole hue and character are foreign, and opposed to all our habits and associations' (Forbes, 1821, p. xix). Most physicians were distrustful of this novel technique, which they found confusing. Hope would become directly responsible for securing its acceptance in England.

He slavishly devoted himself to writing two illustrated textbooks and demonstrating the value of auscultation. He staged demonstrations showing that novice medical students, after only ten minutes of instruction, could match his stethoscopic conclusions on unknown patients. By publicly disclosing through an intermediary that his diagnoses were invariably correct at autopsy, he gained a reputation as a fine clinician and for self-promoting theatrics. Hope also performed ingenious experiments to elucidate the cause of the heart sounds, a controversial subject that had puzzled Laennec and other early ausculators. By inserting a hook to interfere with the semilunar valves in the donkey heart, Hope was the first to prove the relation of the second sound to valvular closure.

His 600-page textbook, *Treatise on the Diseases of the Heart and Great Vessels*, published in 1831 when he was aged thirty, is one of the finest early textbooks on the heart. Based on his minute clinical notes, 1,000 autopsies, and his own anatomic illustrations, the text includes some of the best early descriptions of the auscultatory and pathologic findings of valvular disease, arteritis, and cardiac asthma. He also provided physiological insights into the causes of hypertrophy and the etiology of murmurs, and emphasized remedies. This magnificent accomplishment, translated into German and Italian, boosted his reputation. He was elected FRS (1832) and in 1834 received a desired appointment to St George's Hospital, where his practice prospered. That year he also published *Morbid Anatomy*, an atlas with 260 color plates beautifully drawn by Hope.

Jealous, short-tempered, and fiercely determined to guard his reputation—it was said that he was 'Fond of righteousness but too fond of being right'—he eagerly entered into rancorous printed conflict with Dominic Corrigan (1802–80), Robert Graves (1796–1853), Jean Bouillaud (1796–1881), and his former friend C. J. B. Williams over the priority of his discoveries. He suffered from tuberculosis, which became symptomatic in 1837 and rapidly impaired his health. He continued his practice at St George's until March 1841, dying two months later, aged forty. His effective promotion of auscultation and his two scholarly textbooks fully realized his ambition to be a leading physician of his time.

Bibliography

Primary: 1831. *A Treatise on the Diseases of the Heart and Great Vessels* (London); 1834. *Principles and Illustrations of Morbid Anatomy* (London); 1838. 'Reply to Drs. Graves' and Stokes' remarks on Dr. Hope, in reference to auscultation.' *London Medical Gazette* 127–130.

Secondary: Bluth, Edward I., 1970. 'James Hope and the Acceptance of Auscultation.' *Journal of the History of Medicine* 25: 202–210; Flaxman, Nathan, 1938. 'The Hope of Cardiology.' *Bulletin of the History of Medicine* 6: 1–21; Forbes, John, 1821. *A Treatise on the Diseases of the Chest and Their Diagnosis* (London); *Oxford DNB*.

Mark E. Silverman

HORSLEY, VICTOR ALEXANDER HADEN

HORSLEY, VICTOR ALEXANDER HADEN (b. Kensington, London, England, 14 April 1857; d. Amara, Mesopotamia, 16 July 1916), *endocrinology, neurosurgery.*

Horsley was the son of the artist John Callcott Horsley and had strong medical connections on his mother's side. He was educated at Cranbrook school and wanted to become a cavalry officer, but his father persuaded him that medicine would be cheaper. In 1875 he entered the medical school at University College Hospital, London, where he was influenced by the physiologists John Scott Burdon Sanderson (1828–1905) and Edward Schafer (Sharpey-Schafer). The latter claimed that it was Burdon Sanderson's training in experimental physiology that determined Horsley's future career as 'a physiologist and as a scientific surgeon'. His student career was an unbroken series of academic successes, and he qualified MB, BS in 1881, winning the University scholarship and the gold medal in surgery. He was surgical dresser to John Marshall and clinical clerk to Henry Bastian, who first interested him in the nervous system. After a postgraduate year in Germany, Horsley returned as surgical registrar at University College Hospital. Two years later he became assistant surgeon and in 1886 was elected to the staff of the National Hospital, Queen Square, London.

Experimental Work

Between 1883 and 1891 Horsley was professor superintendent of the Brown Institution. This facility, of which Burdon Sanderson had been the first head, was founded by a bequest for 'research into maladies of quadrupeds and birds useful to man'. It consisted of a (veterinary) hospital and laboratory, the only place at the time where experiments could be done on large animals, such as monkeys. Here Horsley performed a long series of experiments on localization of brain function (with Charles Beevor, 1849–1921) and on the innervation of the larynx (with Felix Semon, 1854–1908).

In 1886 he became secretary to a commission to investigate Louis Pasteur's (1822–96) method for preventing

Sir Victor Horsley with friend. Photograph, Iconographic Collection, Wellcome Library, London.

rabies, which at the time caused around fifty deaths a year in England. He was the moving spirit of the investigation, and visited Pasteur in Paris and confirmed his results. He investigated an outbreak among deer in Richmond Park and observed some of the animals at the Brown Institution. His advice formed the basis of the Muzzling Order (1896), which, together with six-months quarantine for imported animals, stamped out the disease.

One of his relatively few experimental failures came in 1886 when he reported that he had removed the pituitary from two dogs, which then lived in good health for five and six months. He was, however, in good company, because until the work of Nicholas Paulesco in 1908, only four of fifteen physiologists who had done experimental hypophysectomies believed the gland was essential to life.

His work on the thyroid gland was more productive. At a meeting of the Clinical Society of London in 1883, a case of myxedema was presented and Semon drew attention to the fact that Theodor Kocher (1841–1917) of Bern had found that thyroidectomy led to a condition he called 'cachexia strumipriva', which was likened to cretinism in children and myxedema in adults. Semon proposed that cretinism and myxedema were due to the absence or degeneration of the

thyroid, a suggestion that was met with 'polite scepticism'. Nevertheless, the society set up a committee of thirteen, including Horsley, to investigate the problem. Horsley did thyroidectomies in monkeys and observed muscular twitchings and convulsions at first, and later myxedema. He concluded that myxedema was due to failure of thyroid function and this was agreed upon in the 200-page committee report published in 1888. In an article in the *British Medical Journal* in 1890, Horsley suggested treating myxedema by transplanting a sheep's thyroid. He never did it, but the next year George Murray (1865–1939) reported successful treatment with hypodermic injection of sheep thyroid extract.

Neurosurgery

Horsley is often described as the father of neurosurgery, but the first intracranial operations were carried out by Sir William Macewen (1848–1924) in Glasgow in 1879, Gustave Durante in Rome in 1884, and John Rickman Godlee (1849–1925) in London in 1884. Horsley's first intracranial operation was performed in 1886, three months after he joined the staff of the National Hospital. The patient was a twenty-two-year-old with Jacksonian epilepsy from an accident at age seven. There was no operating theater and Horsley, watched by David Ferrier (1843–1928) and John Hughlings Jackson (1835–1911), worked in a corner of the ward shut off by screens. After removal of the scar, the man's fits were cured. By the end of his first year at Queen Square, Horsley had done eleven intracranial operations, with only one death. In 1887 he performed what Osler called 'the most brilliant operation in the whole of surgery'. The patient was a forty-two-year-old businessman who had been diagnosed with a spinal tumor. After initially finding nothing, Horsley lengthened his incision and finally located a tumor at the level of the third and fourth dorsal roots. The patient made a complete recovery. In 1889 he was the first to expose a pituitary tumor by a transcranial approach, and in 1891 described an operation for the treatment of trigeminal neuralgia in which the Gasserian ganglion was removed. Around the turn of the century he did ten operations for pituitary tumor, but never wrote them up. An obituarist in *Lancet* suggested that, in general, Horsley was selective about publication and only reported his successes. The same obituarist lamented that he never produced a textbook of neurosurgery.

A significant technical problem in neurosurgery at that time was bleeding from the cranial vault. In animal experiments Horsley showed that ordinary modeling wax reduced the blood loss and he devised a preparation of seven parts beeswax and one part almond oil, known as 'Horsley's Wax'. He also invented a number of instruments and a head-holding device. The success of Horsley's neurosurgical operations was attributed by contemporaries to his 'minute familiarity with the experimental physiology of the nervous system' and to his speed and manual dexterity. He also made his own diagnoses, which led to conflict with some of his colleagues.

Public Work

Between 1891 and 1897 Horsley was president of the Medical Defence Union at a particularly difficult time for that organization, and from 1897 to 1907 he sat on the General Medical Council. When he was knighted in 1902, he was an internationally known physiologist and surgeon, and yet he retired from University College Hospital in 1906 when only forty-nine, although he continued private practice and research on the cerebellum with Robert H. Clarke. He had always been extraordinarily energetic, and it may have been that his scientific creativeness had begun to wane or that he just sought new pastures.

To the wider public he was probably best known for his ardent espousal of temperance. This dated from his student days, when he found that beer at mealtimes made him sleepy. As a result he decided that it was a toxin, not a stimulant. He caused great offense by referring to colleagues who drank socially as 'drunkards' or 'alcoholics'. In 1907 he published *Alcohol and the Human Body* with Dr Mary Sturge, a store of information on the subject. He felt deeply on questions of medical and social reform and tried to enter politics as a liberal, championing free trade, female suffrage, and universal health insurance. It is perhaps providential that he failed, because he was temperamentally unsuited to politics through his impatience and dogmatism. He was incapable of compromise and those who differed from him were apt to be dismissed as 'ruffians and scoundrels'.

During World War I he attracted further notoriety by condemning the rum ration and engaging in controversy about the treatment of war wounds with Sir Rickman Godlee. He was sent to Egypt, where he complained bitterly about the medical facilities. When he learned of the breakdown of medical services in Mesopotamia (now Iraq), he immediately volunteered to go there and on arrival wrote to the commander in chief that 'it is a misuse of language to say that the sick and wounded are being cared for'. In Mesopotamia he worked with his usual vigor, and probably died of heat stroke because he refused to wear a sun helmet. It was later claimed that he had often insisted that teetotalers could not get heat stroke!

Harvey Cushing (1869–1939), who disliked Horsley, described him as a gladiatorial figure in the neurosurgery of the 1880s, and to William Osler (1848–1919) he was 'a hard hitter with a fanatical conviction of the justice of his cause'.

Bibliography

Primary: 1885. 'The Brown Lectures on pathology.' *British Medical Journal* i: 11–115, 211–213; 1887. 'Remarks on ten consecutive cases of operations upon the brain and cranial cavity to illustrate the details and safety of the method employed.' *British Medical Journal* i: 863–865.

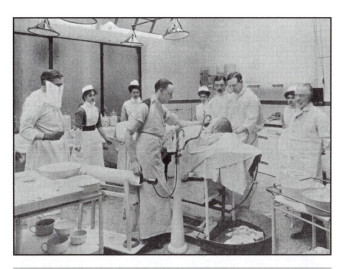

Sir Victor Horsley in the operating theatre, Queen Square, 1906. On the right is Theodor Kocher (see biographical entry). Horsley is on the left wearing the mask, his apparent bulk the result of wearing a large antiseptic dressing to sterilize the skin; he was to undergo an appendectomy the next morning. Halftone reproduction from Stephen Paget, *Sir Victor Horsley . . .* London, 1919. Wellcome Library, London.

Secondary: Hanigan, W. C., 1994. 'Obstinate Valour: The Military Service and Death of Sir Victor Horsley.' *Br. J. Neurosurg.* 8: 279–288. Lyons, J. B., 1966. *The Citizen Surgeon: A Biography of Sir Victor Horsley, F.R.S., F.R.C.S., 1857–1916* (London); Jefferson, Sir Geoffrey, 1957. 'Sir Victor Horsley, 1857–1916.' *British Medical Journal* i: 903–910; Paget, Stephen, 1919. *Victor Horsley, A Study of His Life and Work* (London); DSB; *Oxford DNB.*

Robert Tattersall

HORTON, JAMES AFRICANUS BEALE (b. Gloucester, Western Area, Sierra Leone, 1 June 1835; d. Freetown, Western Area, Sierra Leone, 15 October 1883), *general practice, surgery.*

Horton, the only surviving son of James Horton (1791–1867), a carpenter, and his wife, Nancy, attended Fourah Bay College (1853–55) and King's College, London (1855–58), where he qualified as member of the Royal College of Surgeons (MCRS). He also attended the University of Edinburgh (1858–59), graduating MD. His doctoral thesis, 'The Medical Topography of the Coast of West Africa including sketches of its Botany', which was subsequently published as a book (1859), argued that climate, vegetation, and soil strongly influenced human health in West Africa. This argument was to influence most of his subsequent research on tropical diseases and health in West Africa. After his education abroad, Horton returned to West Africa, where he devoted twenty-one years to colonial military service (1859–80) in the Gold Coast (now Ghana) and in the Gambia. He complemented his official work with private medical practice and extensive research into tropical diseases, climate, and geology. Though he disagreed with some of the latter's theories, Horton's research and writings were influenced by Sir James Ranald Martin (1793–1874), another colonial army doctor, who had written on tropical diseases in India. Like Martin and many of his contemporaries, Horton thought that lethal tropical diseases such as malaria and yellow fever were caused by deadly vapors from the soil.

Horton's research established that, contrary to the views of many European medical practitioners, peoples of African descent did not possess natural immunity to malaria. He also showed that people living in coastal areas were as prone to malaria as those living inland. This observation was confirmed after his death, when it was discovered that some species of anopheline mosquito could also breed in salt water. Horton recommended quinine as an antimalarial prophylactic.

Horton campaigned for improvements in the public health policies of colonial cities such as Freetown in Sierra Leone and Banjul in the Gambia. He called for proper sewage disposal and the development of piped water systems. He also recommended (especially near large settlements) the planting of large trees such as palm and coconut in swampy areas to reduce the incidence of malaria. By the end of the nineteenth century, the British colonial government in Sierra Leone had acted on some of Horton's suggestions.

Horton suggested that to reduce the prevalence of tropical fevers among Europeans, they should wear cotton clothing, drink alcohol temperately, and exercise frequently. He criticized bloodletting and excessive use of mercury to treat fevers by European doctors, arguing that the latter's effects were toxic and potentially fatal.

Based on the observation of his patients, Horton speculated that Guinea worm was transmitted through contact. He suggested applying poultices for the infected areas, and *Assafoetida*, a nauseating mixture, to eliminate the parasite. Between 1866 and 1874, his scientific observations and recommendations were published in a series of medical treatises. In 1874 Horton published a comprehensive medical guide on fevers, abdominal ailments, and other tropical illnesses, describing their symptoms, causes, and remedies. In 1875 he was promoted to surgeon-major, and in 1879 the British Colonial Office appointed him head of the army medical department of the Gold Coast. In 1880 Horton retired from colonial service.

By the end of the nineteenth century, most of the assumptions and theories on which Horton based his scientific research had been proved erroneous. However, he remains a pioneering figure in the history of research into tropical diseases and is especially remembered for his advocacy of progressive public health strategies in West Africa.

Bibliography

Primary: 1859. *The Medical Topography of West Africa* (London); 1868. *Guinea Worm or Dracunculus* (London); 1874. *The Diseases of Tropical Africa and Their Treatment* (London).

Secondary: Fyfe, Christopher, 1972. *Africanus Horton: 1835–1883: West African Scientist and Patriot* (New York); Davidson, Nicol, 1969. *Africanus Horton: The Dawn of Nationalism in Modern Africa: Extracts from the Political, Education, Scientific and Medical Writings of JAB Horton MD 1835–1883* (London), *Oxford DNB*.

Ismail Rashid

HORWITZ BARAK, ABRAHAM (b. Santiago, Chile, 25 December 1910; d. Washington, D.C., USA, 10 July 2000), *international health.*

A native of Chile, Horwitz was one of five children of Russian immigrants who escaped the persecution of Jews under the Czarist regime, seeking security and a better future in the Americas. He studied medicine in the University of Chile and received his degree in 1936. His laboratory career began as an assistant to Hugo Vaccaro, who held the chair of bacteriology. A year after his graduation he worked on infectious diseases in the Hospital Barros Lucos of Santiago. For a number of years thereafter he continued to specialize in infectious diseases. His work on meningitis received wide recognition in his home country.

In the mid-1940s Horwitz's interests turned to public health, partly due to a Rockefeller Foundation fellowship that allowed him to spend a year at the Herman Kiefer Hospital in Detroit and later study for a Master of Public Health (MPH) degree from Johns Hopkins University (1944). Upon his return to Chile he became director of the School of Public Health, and served as professor of infectious diseases, bacteriology, and immunology at the University of Chile. This was one of the first schools of its kind in Latin America and became one of the pillars of the Chilean National Public Health Service.

Horwitz eventually became second-in-command in this institution and demonstrated remarkable skill in the administration of public health services. At the same time, starting in 1950, he was recruited by the Pan American Health Office and initiated a distinguished career in international health. At this agency he was in charge of the smallpox vaccination programs and served as head of the field office in Lima (which directed the agency's activities in five Andean countries).

In 1959 he was elected director of the inter-American health agency, and later was re-elected for four consecutive terms, remaining at the head of the Pan American Health Office until 1975. He was the first Latin American to occupy this high position in the agency, which was created in 1902 (before then, U.S. surgeons general or American physicians had been directors). He brought a perspective that linked the planning and development of health services with an emphasis on research and the practice of epidemiology and the idea that health was a tool for economic modernization. In different publications he repeated the phrase 'without high-quality human energy there can be neither efficient production nor sufficient consumption', which reinforced the belief that Latin America's underdevelopment was a result of a vicious cycle: low productivity leads to inadequate income, resulting in deficient diet and inadequate housing, which in turn leads to poor health and low productivity. According to Horwitz modernization would break this cycle. He sought large capital investments in health and sanitation services in the Americas from a series of donors and bilateral agencies. Thanks to his activities, and to his friendship with the president of the Interamerican Development Bank, a number of health projects were made possible.

Horwitz was also internationally known for his expertise on malnutrition and vitamin A deficiency. From 1982 to 1995, he was chairman of the Subcommittee on Nutrition of the United Nations Administrative Committee on Coordination. Horwitz received many distinctions, including the Bronfman Prize of the American Public Health Association, the International Health Leadership Award of the Global Health Council, and honorary doctorates from Johns Hopkins University and the University of Chile. Presently, one of the main prizes of the Pan American Health Organization carries his name.

Bibliography

Primary: 1942. *Infección meningocócica en Chile.* (Santiago); 1975. 'The 10-Year Health Plan for the Americas.' *American Journal of Public Health* 65(10): 1057–1059.

Secondary: Cueto, Marcos, 2004. *El Valor de la Salud: Historia de la Organización Panamericana de la Salud.* (Washington, DC); Jiménez de la Jara, Jorge, 2003. 'Abraham Horwitz (1910–2000) Padre de la Salud Pública Panamericana.' *Revista Médica de Chile* 131(8): 929–934; Kraljevic, Roque O., 2001. 'Profesor Dr. Abraham Horwitz Barak (1910–2000).' *Revista Médica de Chile* 129(4): 456–460.

Marcos Cueto

HOUSSAY, BERNARDO ALBERTO   (b. Buenos Aires, Argentina, 10 April 1887; d. Buenos Aires, 21 September 1971), *physiology.*

Born to French immigrant parents, Houssay was a precocious student who first studied pharmacy (which gave him a foundation in chemistry) and then medicine at the University of Buenos Aires (where he graduated in 1910). His father was a lawyer. Breaking the tradition of talented Latin American medical students' pursuing graduate studies in Europe, Houssay completed his education in Argentina. He was self-taught in modern physiology. During the first years of his career, Houssay had a private medical practice and held a number of concurrent positions: professor of physiology at the School of Veterinary Medicine, clinician at the Alvear Hospital, and researcher at the Institute of Bacteriology of Buenos Aires, a center organized along European lines. At the Institute he met—and later married—the chemist María Angelica Catán. They had three children, all of whom became physicians.

In 1919 Houssay won in an open contest the chair of physiology in the Buenos Aires Medical School and organized a

Albert Houssay (front row, second left) with colleagues outside the Instituto de Biología y Medicina Experimental Buenos Aires, 1930s. Courtesy of Rockefeller Archive Center.

fully fledged Institute of Physiology that emphasized laboratory work and incorporated the chairs of physiology, biochemistry, and biophysics. In the same year he was elected president of the Argentine Society of Biology, an umbrella organization for medical research in the life sciences. The governmental support for these activities was made possible by a period of political stability, and by the public perception that science was crucial for Argentina's progress and medicine. From the 1920s Houssay's research concentrated on the hypophysis (pituitary) and its link with diabetes mellitus, reframing the disease as a general metabolic disorder. The holistic idea that an endocrine equilibrium was necessary for health was coincident with Walter B. Cannon's work at Harvard. With Rockefeller Foundation fellowships, Houssay sent to Boston some of his best students to train under Cannon. By the early 1940s Houssay's Institute was central to the School of Medicine. He was portrayed as a severe chief who taught the staff not to squander time. Houssay and his disciples published a celebrated textbook in human physiology used all over Latin American medical schools.

Argentine physiology's fortunes shifted in 1943 when a military coup, which would later open the door for the authoritarian regime of Colonel Peron, took control of the universities, dismissing Houssay and a number of other pro-Allied professors. Despite receiving offers from abroad to move with his laboratory, Houssay remained in his country at the private Institute of Biology and Experimental Medicine, supported by the Argentine Sauberan Foundation and the Rockefeller Foundation. Although he would not be definitively reinstated as Director of the University's Institute of Physiology until 1955, he never lost connection with the private center. During those difficult years, he received the 1947 Nobel Prize in Physiology and Medicine (shared with G. T. and C. F. Cori) for his finding that the anterior lobe of the hypophysis produces a hormone that blocks the effect of insulin in glucose metabolism. This was the first time that the science award had been given to a Latin American. In the late 1950s Houssay became involved with the organization of the new Argentine National Council for Scientific and Technical Research.

Houssay was a remarkable and disciplined researcher, responsible for placing Argentina on the world map of medical science. He demonstrated that scientific excellence was possible under adverse conditions.

Bibiography

Primary: 1918. *La acción fisiológica de los extractos hipófisiarios* (Buenos Aires); 1942. 'The Hyphophysis and Secretion of Insulin.' *Journal of Experimental Medicine* 75: 547–566; 1989. (Barrios Medina, Ariel, and Alejandro C. Paladín, eds.) *Escritos y Discursos del Dr. Bernardo A. Houssay* (Buenos Aires).

Secondary: Cueto, Marcos, 1994. 'Laboratory Styles and Argentine Physiology.' *Isis* 85: 228–246; Cerejido, Marcelino, 1990. *La Nuca de Houssay. La ciencia argentina entre Billiken y el exilio* (Mexico City); Barrios Medina, Ariel, 1987. 'Bernardo Alberto Houssay (1887–1971): un esbozo biográfico.' *Interciencia* 12: 290–299; Foglia, Virgilio G. 1980. 'The History of Bernardo Houssay's Research Laboratory, Instituto de Biología y Medicina Experimental: The First Twenty Years, 1944–1963.' *Journal of the History of Medicine and the Allied Sciences* 35: 380–396; Young, Frank, and V. G. Foglia, 1947. 'Bernardo Alberto Houssay, 1887–1971.' *Biographical Memoirs of Fellows of the Royal Society* 20: 247–270; *DSB*.

Marcos Cueto

HUFELAND, CHRISTOPH WILHELM (b. Langensalza, Germany, 12 August 1762; d. Berlin, Germany, 25 August 1836), *medicine.*

Hufeland received his early education in Weimar, where his father held the office of court physician to the grand duchess. He was a child of the Enlightenment with a pietist background. In 1780 he enrolled at the University of Jena, studying anatomy with Johann Ch. Locher. A year later he went to Göttingen, where he was introduced to the ideas of vitalism by his teacher Johann Friedrich Blumenbach. In 1783 he graduated in medicine, writing a medical dissertation on apparent death.

After assisting his ailing father for some years at Weimar, he was called in 1793 to the chair of medicine at Jena, receiving at the same time the appointment as court physician and councilor at Weimar. Goethe, Schiller, and Herder were not only among his friends, but also became his patients. By the turn of the century Hufeland was celebrated as the most eminent practical physician of his time in Germany. In 1785 he spoke out against mesmerism, debunking animal magnetism as a 'fabric of empty words'. He was less critical about homeopathy. In fact, Hahnemann's seminal article on the law of similars was published in a journal (*Journal der practischen Arzneikunde und Wundarzneikunst*) of which Hufeland was the founder and chief editor. Hufeland ardently supported vaccination and contributed to the spreading of Edward Jenner's method in German lands. Due to his interest in the problem of apparent death, he advocated the building of mortuaries. A seminar that Hufeland taught in Jena was so popular among his students that he turned it into a bestseller: *Macrobiotics or the Art of Prolonging Human Life* focuses on dietetics in the classical sense, demanding moderation in all aspects of life. Hufeland maintained that medicine aims at achieving health, whereas macrobiotics aims at achieving a long life. The first edition of this popular health care guide (which saw many reprints and translations) was dedicated to one of the luminaries of the German Enlightenment, the physicist and writer Georg Christoph Lichtenberg. Another bestseller was Hufeland's guidebook for mothers, published in 1799. He advised pregnant mothers to put alcohol aside, to get plenty of fresh air, and to avoid overexcitement. This little manual for mothers was, indeed, one of the new breed of inexpensive books sold to common folk. The first volume of his influential medical textbook (*System der practischen Heilkunde*) was conceived in Jena, too.

In 1798 Hufeland moved to Berlin, where he was placed at the head of the medical college and became medical superintendent of the Charité, the famous teaching hospital founded by King Friedrich Wilhelm I in 1727. Later he was appointed to the chair of pathology and therapeutics in the University of Berlin, and in 1810 he became councilor of state and member of the Prussian academy of science. In the same year he founded a learned society of physicians and surgeons in Berlin, which in 1833 was named after him. He also initiated a charity organization that cared for physicians in need, known as the Hufeland Foundation.

Bibliography

Primary: 1791. *Über die Ungewißheit des Todes und das einzig trügliche Mittel sich von seiner Wirklichkeit zu überzeugen und das Lebendigbegrabenwerden unmöglich zu machen* (Weimar); 1794. *Gemeinnützige Aufsätze zur Beförderung der Gesundheit, des Wohlseyns und vernünftiger medicinischer Auflärung* (Leipzig); 1795. *Ideen über Pathogenie, und Einfluss der Lebenskraft auf Entstehung* *und Form der Krankheiten* (Jena); 1796. (English trans., 1797) *Makrobiotik, oder die Kunst, das menschliche Leben zu verlängern* (Jena); 1799. *Guter Rath an Mütter über die wichtigsten Punkte der physischen Erziehung der Kinder in den ersten Jahren* (Berlin); 1800–05. *System der practischen Heilkunde* 2 vols. (Jena); 1822. *Kleine medizinische Schriften* (Berlin).

Secondary: Pfeiffer, Klaus, 2000. *Medizin der Goethezeit. Christoph Wilhelm Hufeland und die Heilkunde des 18. Jahrhunderts* (Cologne and Vienna); Baymann, Ernst, 1964. 'Christoph Wilhelm Hufeland und die praktische Medizin' (Medical dissertation, Düsseldorf).

Robert Jütte

HUFNAGEL, CHARLES ANTHONY   (b. Louisville, Kentucky, USA, 15 August 1916; d. Washington, D.C., USA, 31 May 1989), *thoracic surgery.*

As a houseman at Peter Bent Brigham Hospital, Hufnagel started laboratory work in Boston with Robert Edward Gross (1905–88). He is best known for the development of a valve that he placed in the aorta remote from the heart as a partial solution for severe incompetence of the aortic valve. This innovation was something of a cul-de-sac, because later, after the development of cardiopulmonary bypass, valves could be replaced directly within the heart. However, this was not until the 1960s. Hufnagel's exploratory laboratory work surely supplied many leads and contributions to later developments.

Hufnagel's first degree was earned at Notre Dame, and he then went to Harvard and studied medicine in New Jersey. His laboratory work started in 1938 at the age of twenty-two. He was put to work on the problem of coarctation, a congenital narrowing of the aorta high in the chest. There was a great fear of paraplegia if the aorta was clamped in that area. The risks and the relative safety that might be obtained by cooling were explored in dogs. This was before the better-known work on brain and total-body cooling was conducted. In the event, the collateral blood supply, which was part of the human problem of coarctation, provided its own protection. Robert Edward Gross (1905–88) (Hufnagel's chief) did the first operation applying Hufnagel's laboratory work in June and July 1945, with the second child surviving. Clarence Crafoord (1899–1984) had done the same operation in Stockholm, Sweden, in October 1944 and received the historical credit for being the 'first' but for Hufnagel it was part of his work on a broad front.

Hufnagel had performed some kidney transplants in the laboratory, and observed that even if the kidney were rejected, the artery connecting it to the recipient's circulation functioned. He experimented with all sorts of material, but in this phase seems to have been interested in rigid tubes, made of methyl methacrylate, tied or otherwise fixed into the vessels.

It was in such a rigid tube that Hufnagel constructed the nonreturn valve for which he is particularly remembered. He started work on this project around 1946, did his first operation on a patient in September 1952, and reported results in twenty-three patients in 1954. This was the window between closed and 'open' cardiac surgery. Relief of narrowed valves within the beating heart had entered practice, but the means of operating within the heart had not. Although Hufnagel's method of a valve interposed in the descending aorta was quickly superseded, it is certain that what he had learned in hundreds of animal experiments about materials, blood clotting, and the noise of these mechanical valves contributed to the subsequent flurry of heart valve designs in the 1960s and 1970s.

Interest in mechanical solutions continued. Again in that window between closed heart and 'open heart' surgery, Hufnagel was one of the surgeons who devised a means of closing an atrial septal defect (the less severe form of hole in the heart). In 1958 he published on replacing the esophagus with a rubber and wire mesh prosthesis. Hufnagel's contributions were all ingenious, the product of extensive laboratory work, some in themselves blind alleys but certainly providing a large amount of knowledge about materials and techniques, bricks to be used in the walls of others' endeavors.

Bibliography

Primary: 1954. (with Harvey, W. Proctor) 'Surgical Correction of Aortic Insufficiency.' *Surgery* 35: 674–675.

Secondary: Meade, R. H., 1961. *A History of Thoracic Surgery* (Springfield, IL); *DAMB.*

Tom Treasure

HUGGINS, CHARLES BRENTON   (b. Halifax, Nova Scotia, Canada, 22 September 1901; d. Chicago, Illinois, USA, 12 January 1997), *urology, cancer research.*

Born in Halifax, Nova Scotia, Huggins earned his undergraduate degree at Acadia University and his degree in medicine at Harvard, graduating in 1924. While doing an internship and surgical residency at the University of Michigan, he met Margaret Wellman, a nurse, and they married in 1927 and eventually had two children. The year they married they moved to Chicago, and Huggins spent the next forty years as a urologist and researcher at the University of Chicago Medical School.

In his early experiments he used fascia patches to cover bladder wounds, and made the observation that, unlike the response to patching in other hollow viscera, the bladder patch developed bone calcification. He noted that the fibroblasts transform into osteoblasts when placed on the bladder. Huggins was excited about the potential of research to answer important questions and determined to become a clinical scientist. He was granted a period of study abroad to visit various centers, and worked for a time in Robert Robison's laboratory at the Lister Institute, but found it less interesting to be involved in other people's research.

On returning to Chicago he concentrated his research on prostate cancer, and it was a lucky chance that he chose dogs for his experimental work, as dogs are the only animals besides humans that spontaneously develop cancers of the prostate. He observed that dogs with cancer of the prostate had very high levels of testosterone and that orchidectomy caused the tumors to regress. Huggins showed that the tumors were not autonomous, self-perpetuating masses of cells, but were affected and controlled in their growth by various chemical signals, such as hormones. Applying the concept to therapy, he showed that many tumors, even very advanced and widespread malignancies, could regress if the source of the chemical or hormonal signal were removed.

His classic paper showing that deprivation of male hormones could cause metastatic prostate cancer to regress in men was published in 1941, and over the next decade he also demonstrated that removal of female hormones could cause regression of breast cancer. In the 1960s he published papers showing that aromatic compounds and pigments could prevent and suppress some leukemias and breast cancer. He related this effect to oxidative enzymes that play a role in the development and control of cancer growth.

Supported generously by an Alabama businessman, he established the Ben May Laboratory for Cancer Research, which had the motto 'Discovery is our Business'. He was a constant worker, in his laboratory seven days a week. He wrote about the research process, and believed in small productive laboratories. He recruited a small team of creative individuals, with a small number of research students, and focused on a small number of questions. He said that great events do not happen if many pigeons are flying about the room. His admonitions for beginning scientists were to avoid meetings, as they are a waste of time; to not write books, as they are too soon out of date; to avoid the library; to work on problems that are not in the books; and to discover first, then do library research to see if your discovery can be connected to established ideas, and then write a concise paper. He also talked about elegant science and about how excellence in work engenders excellence in life: A talented investigator has a nose for a good and noble problem. A question should be proposed as simply as possible so that Nature must provide an unequivocal answer.

Huggins advanced research on cancer by developing animal models of rapid cancer development. He also made important contributions to the field of bone growth, and developed chromogenic substrates for simple enzyme assays that are now used worldwide to determine how sulfhydryl groups alter the structure and properties of hormones. He applied the concept of hormonal and chemical effects on cancer growth to the treatment of advanced cancer of the testes, ovaries, and adrenal glands. He has been referred to as the founder of chemical urology and as the founder of endocrinology of cancer.

Huggins shared the 1966 Nobel Prize with Francis Peyton Rous, who did work on the viral causes of cancer. The citation noted his 'fundamental discoveries concerning the hormone dependence of normal and neoplastic cells in experimental animals and their immediate practical application to the treatment of human prostatic and breast cancer'.

Huggins became the William B. Ogden Distinguished Service Professor Emeritus of Surgery at the University of Chicago. He was the recipient of many awards, honorary degrees, and fellowships. After retirement he became Chancellor of Acadia University, his undergraduate alma mater. He died at age ninety-five at his Hyde Park home in Chicago in 1997.

Bibliography

Primary: 1941. (with Hodges, C. V.) 'Studies on Prostatic Cancer. The Effect of Castration, of Estrogen and of Androgen Injection on Serum Phosphatase in Metastatic Carcinoma of the Prostate.' *J. Urol.* 167: 948–951, 168: 9–12; 1965. 'The Business of Discovery in the Medical Sciences.' *JAMA* 194: 1211–1215.

Secondary: Bullough, Vern, 1990. 'Charles Brenton Huggins' in Fox, Daniel M., et al. eds., *Nobel Laureates in Medicine or Physiology* (New York); Haddow, Alexander, et al., eds., 1982. *On Cancer and Hormones: Twenty-Seven Essays Presented to Charles Huggins* (Chicago).

Jock Murray

HUNTER, JOHN   (b. Long Calderwood, East Kilbride, Lanarkshire, Scotland, 14 February 1728; d. London, England, 16 October 1793), *surgery, anatomy, comparative anatomy.*

Hunter was the youngest child of John Hunter, farmer, and Agnes Paul. He received little formal education and, his father having died in 1741, remained at home until he was nearly twenty. For a short time, he assisted his brother-in-law, who was a timber merchant and cabinet-maker in Glasgow. Hunter knew, however, that his brother William (1718–83) had established himself as a surgeon and anatomy teacher in London, and in 1748 he wrote to William asking to be allowed to join him. William offered John a position as his assistant and Hunter rode to London on horseback in September of that year.

John was ten years younger than his sibling, and the brothers had not seen one another for more than seven years. William was now a sophisticated metropolitan gentleman, who had effaced his speech and behavior of Scotticisms; John was a rough, largely unschooled, country boy. But William quickly recognized that his brother had a real aptitude for anatomical work. By teaching and employing John, William could honor his obligations as head of the family while simultaneously gaining a valuable colleague. John began working as a demonstrator in his brother's school from as early as 1750. He seems also to have been in charge of securing the supply of fresh corpses upon which William's method of anatomical teaching depended, a task for which his down-to-earth manner evidently suited him. In 1749 William acquired premises in Covent Garden, and the two brothers lived and worked together there until 1756.

To complement the instruction that he was giving his brother in anatomy, William arranged that John should begin the study of surgery, first under William Cheselden (1688–1752) at the Chelsea Hospital and, later, under Percivall Pott (1714–88) at St Bartholomew's. Cheselden, who was regarded as the finest operator in London, stressed the importance of good surgical technique, both to achieve a satisfactory treatment outcome and to minimize the pain suffered by the patient. Pott emphasized that wound management should follow the natural processes of healing as closely and as conservatively as possible. Hunter's own surgical practice would later be built upon these two central principles.

In 1754 John Hunter entered St George's Hospital as a surgical pupil. The next year he matriculated at St Mary's Hall, Oxford, but, unwilling to submit to a classical education, left after a few months to return to St George's, where, in May 1756, he was appointed house surgeon. In the autumn of that year, however, Hunter left to resume assisting his brother with his anatomy teaching. Also in 1756, William took up residence in Jermyn Street, but John remained at their original premises in Covent Garden. Around this time, William offered John a partnership in his anatomy school but the younger man refused, unsure of his abilities as a lecturer.

Throughout the 1750s, Hunter worked intensively in the family business of teaching anatomy and dissection. He assisted his brother in his researches and was increasingly sought after for his expertise in postmortem investigations. Hunter was also developing his skills as a surgeon—he recorded that in 1752 he treated a chimney sweep with urethral stricture, 'the first patient I ever had with this disease', for whom he invented a new method of applying caustic to the blockage. However, in acquiring practice as a surgeon in London, Hunter was handicapped by his not having completed a formal apprenticeship.

Sometime in 1759 Hunter suffered a period of severe ill health, which was attributed to overwork. He was forced to rest for several months. In October 1760, on returning to active employment, he signed up as an army surgeon. The Seven Years' War (1756–63) was in progress and surgeons were in demand. In March 1761 Hunter sailed with the British expedition that had been sent to take Belle-Île, an island off the Atlantic coast of Brittany. In the course of a bloody campaign, which lasted several weeks, he gained considerable experience of military surgery and of wound management. The following year, Hunter was assigned to the British forces in Portugal. Here there were few British casualties and he was engaged more with the administration of the surgical service and the army hospitals rather than with practical surgery. His military service also gave him opportunities to make many natural-historical observations and to begin collecting in the field.

The treaty of Paris, signed in February 1763, ended the war, and Hunter returned to London on half pay. Although his military experience had made him a professional surgeon, Hunter still found it difficult to establish a successful practice in the competitive medical environment of the capital. He worked for a time with James Spence, a London dentist. Dentistry was regarded as the lowest rung of the surgical hierarchy at this time. However, as well as bringing some welcome remuneration, dental surgery also provided a focus for Hunter's long-standing interest in the anatomy of the skull and the jaws. He drew upon this experience when preparing his first major publication, *A Treatise on the Natural History of the Human Teeth*, which appeared in 1771 and which was the first scientific treatise on dental surgery to be published in English.

Hunter's discussion of the teeth was based firmly upon his detailed knowledge of the muscles and bones of the jaws and face. He was thus able to analyze how the movements of mastication are produced by the combined action of several muscle groups. Hunter also studied the development of the teeth in the fetus and in the child, and refuted the older opinion that the deciduous teeth are pushed out of the gums by the mechanical pressure of the growing permanent teeth. Rather, as he put it, the means by which the milk teeth are loosened, and partially reabsorbed, is a 'particular process of the animal oeconomy'. He noted the differences between human teeth and those of, on the one hand, a carnivore, and, on the other, a grazing animal, concluding that a human being 'ought therefore to be considered as a compound, fitted equally to live upon flesh and upon vegetable'. This connection between the bodily structures associated with digestion and the life of the animal was a theme that Hunter would return to many times in his later work.

Hunter's treatment of his subject matter, although that of a very experienced anatomist, was nevertheless intended to be of use to working dentists. He emphasized, for example, the adverse effect of diseased dentition upon general health and drew attention to how 'calcareous deposits' could cause gum disease, if not regularly removed. He considered, from an anatomical perspective, the best method of extracting the teeth, and commented on the inadequacy, for this task, of the dental instruments then available. Hunter was a considerable advocate of the transplantation of teeth and his *Treatise* contains accounts of some of his famous transplantation experiments, such as implanting a tooth into the comb of a cockerel. In 1778 Hunter published a supplement to the *Treatise*, in which he dealt more specifically with the diseases of the teeth and the appropriate modes of treatment. He was the first author to write on malocclusion and its correction.

At the somewhat advanced age of forty, Hunter took the examination for the Diploma of the Company of Surgeons and was duly admitted. Later in 1768 he was elected to the position of surgeon at St George's, thus establishing his place in the capital's surgical circles. His reputation increased rapidly and, within ten years of his return to London, he had gained a large and lucrative practice. It was, doubtless, his improved financial circumstances that allowed him to marry (1771). His bride, Ann Home, the twenty-nine-year-old daughter of a surgical colleague, was a cultivated, well-educated woman, a musician and a published poet whose verses were admired by Robert Burns. By this time, Hunter was already spending more than he could afford building up his collection of animals, living and dead, and of anatomical material. He acquired a second house in Earl's Court, then a rural location, where his menagerie was kept.

In 1770 William Hunter moved his teaching establishment to Great Windmill Street, and John took over the lease of the premises at Jermyn Street. Now he began to take on paying pupils, the first of whom was Edward Jenner (1749–1823), upon whom Hunter was a lifelong influence. Hunter's nephew, Matthew Baillie (1761–1823), and his brother-in-law, Everard Home (1756–1832), were also pupils. Early in the 1770s, Hunter began to teach a course of formal lectures on the 'Principles and Practice of Surgery, in which will be introduced so much of the Animal Oeconomy as may be necessary to illustrate the Principles of those Diseases which are the Object of Surgery'. Nervous and unduly tied to his (very detailed) notes, Hunter was never a truly successful lecturer, although several of the coming generation of young surgeons, such as Astley Cooper (1768–1841) and Anthony Carlisle (1768–1840), listened to him to great advantage. Hunter was nevertheless an outstanding teacher when he could engage with a student on a sustained and individual basis and when he could make the experience of learning one of joint experiment and discovery.

In 1783 Hunter acquired premises on Leicester Square, in which he could, for the first time, properly organize and display his anatomical museum. The vast collections were arranged thematically to reveal the variety of means by which animals and plants maintain and reproduce themselves. There were sections on motion, digestion, reproduction, and so forth. The specimens were grouped not by taxon but by living function. Thus, the hinge of an oyster shell was placed beside a preparation of the ligament that extends from the back of the head to the neck in humans. Likewise, examples of the xylem and phloem of vascular plants were juxtaposed to the lymphatic system of mammals. Hunter studied the lower forms to understand the higher ones better, and in each section the specimens were arranged so as to highlight the increased complexity and more complete differentiation of the more advanced types. In the natural history section of the museum, Hunter displayed more than 5,000 wet preparations, 3,000 stuffed or dried animals, 1,200 fossils, and nearly a thousand osteology specimens, comparative and human. The pathological section contained almost a thousand diseased human organs, arranged to illustrate not only the effects of disease but also the processes of healing and restoration of function. Hunter's museum was not merely an exceptional feat of collecting, even by eighteenth-century standards, its organization also constituted a vivid display of his conception of the unity of life. One nineteenth-century commentator described it very aptly as Hunter's 'Great Unwritten Book'.

Hunter was appointed surgeon-in-extraordinary to George III in 1776. From his point of view, this brought with it the enormous advantage of easier access to the monarch's menagerie. When one of the royal elephants died, the King donated the carcass to Hunter's collection. He and his assistants performed the first-ever thorough dissection of an elephant and made the first mounted skeleton of the animal. Hunter was also interested in the mode of growth of antlers, which he understood to be different to that of bone. In July 1785 he ligated a carotid artery of one of the King's stags in Richmond Park, expecting that the procedure would impair the growth of the antler. However, some days later, he discovered that the velvet was warm and the antler growing as strongly as before. On dissection he found that some of the smaller arteries, above and below the ligature, were enlarged. Hunter then instructed Everard Home to ligate the femoral artery of a dog. Again it was found that the function of the tied artery was taken over by its tributaries. From these observations, Hunter enunciated the principle of collateral circulation.

It was not long before he put this discovery to practical use. Four months later, a coachman was admitted to St George's with a large popliteal aneurysm. The customary response to this painful and life-threatening condition was to ligate the artery above and below the sac and empty its contents, but this operation was seldom successful and amputation was often resorted to. Hunter proposed instead to ligate the artery well above the aneurysm, hoping that the collateral circulation would maintain blood supply to the lower leg. He left the sac itself untouched, believing its contents would be reabsorbed. The operation was a complete success, and the coachman returned to work six weeks later. He died, of an unrelated condition, the following year, and his leg duly found its way into Hunter's museum. Hunter later refined the procedure and operated on a further three cases. His fourth patient, a man of thirty-seven, survived for a further fifty years. Nevertheless, some of Hunter's contemporaries were skeptical of the utility of this operation, believing that dilations of the arterial wall were a sign of general, rather than localized, disease. However, the procedure was widely adopted in the nineteenth century and became the standard technique for dealing with aneurysm.

Hunter's next major publication was *A Treatise on the Venereal Disease*, which appeared in 1786. The treatment of venereal disease was, evidently, a major part of Hunter's business, as it was of most eighteenth-century surgeons. His discussion of the subject displays his considerable clinical experience of gonorrhea and what he termed 'lues venerea'. He argued that the course of gonorrhea was little affected by the remedies then available but that the disease was usually self-limiting. Syphilis, on the other hand, generally required vigorous treatment with mercury. Hunter was convinced, however, that syphilis and gonorrhea were caused by the same poison—the former being the pathological effect produced on a 'secreting surface', such as a mucous membrane, and the latter the effect produced on a 'non-secreting surface', such as the skin. He supported this opinion by the evidence of an inoculation experiment, probably performed on himself, and by his doctrine that two diseases could not affect the same body part simultaneously. (It is odd that, elsewhere in the *Treatise,* Hunter noted that patients loaded with mercury for the treatment of lues venerea might yet contract gonorrhea.)

A Treatise on the Venereal Disease was a popular book in its day: the first edition rapidly sold out, and a revised second edition was published only two years later. However, the long-term importance of Hunter's *Treatise* lies largely in its being an attempt to discuss, in a rational and nonjudgmental manner, a subject that has been, before and since, too often the province of obfuscation, hypocrisy, moralizing, and quackery. The *Treatise* also revealed Hunter's impatience with conventional views and his insight into the importance of the psychological condition of his patients. He expressed skepticism that masturbation could reasonably be regarded as a cause of impotence. Regretting that many men 'are miserable from this idea', he wrote, 'I am clear in my own mind that the books on this subject had done more harm than good.' Hunter's authoritatively stated opinion did not sway his nineteenth-century editors, however, who appended footnotes reaffirming the harmfulness of the practice. Hunter stressed that sexual response was not under voluntary control. In a famous anticipation of twentieth-century sex therapy, he advised a male patient who was having difficulties consummating a relationship to share a bed with the woman in question but to desist from any sexual activity. Relieved of anxiety to perform, the man found himself unable to adhere to his surgeon's prohibition.

It might be said that *A Treatise on the Venereal Disease* does not represent the best of Hunter's work. The arguments for this position are often speculative and sometimes unclear. The subject matter was not ideally suited to the modes of inquiry at which Hunter most excelled. Experimentation on animal subjects proved to be impossible—Hunter tried, but failed, to infect a variety of species. He was often forced to draw conclusions based on observations he could not personally corroborate, in an area where the veracity of his patients was very problematic. Anatomical investigation provided little new information, although by dissecting executed criminals who were known to have had severe gonorrhea, Hunter established that, even in cases of copious discharge, the urethra was not ulcerated. He was also able to give some precise indication of the damage to the major organ systems that 'lues venerea' could cause in the long term.

Hunter's exceptional talents were much better displayed in the second book he published in 1786, *Observations on Certain Parts of the Animal Oeconomy.* This was a collection of short papers, most of which had been originally read to the Royal Society, to which Hunter had been elected in 1767. An extraordinary variety of subjects were covered, including the manner in which the testes descend into the scrotum, the genitalia of freemartins, the organs of hearing in fish, the gizzard of the gillaroo trout, the secretions of the crop of

John Hunter's menagerie. Drawing by Barlow from Jessé Foot, *The Life of John Hunter*, London, 1794. Rare Books, Wellcome Library, London.

breeding pigeons, and the course of the olfactory nerve. What unified Hunter's approach to this diversity of subject matter was his commitment to painstaking comparative anatomy, supplemented by carefully designed and ingenious experiments. The essay on animal heat, which was a pioneering investigation of hibernation, among much else, describes forty-one numbered experiments and many unnumbered ones. Over this vast range of subject matter, most of Hunter's observations were original. He provided, for example, the first description of the gubernaculum testis, and showed that the fluid contained in the seminal vesicles was not identical to semen. Hunter was always concerned, not merely to describe anatomical structure, but to comprehend living function. Nor were more practical concerns neglected—Hunter noted, for example, how knowledge of the descent of the testes assisted the surgeon to understand congenital hernia. Overall, *Observations* was a dazzling display of Hunter's skill in dissection and experimentation, his relentless curiosity, and his unremitting industry.

In 1785 Hunter was appointed deputy surgeon-general of the army and, in 1790, surgeon-general and inspector-general of army hospitals. Motivated by his personal experiences of the shortcomings of military surgery in Belle-Île and in Portugal, Hunter proved a committed administrator and a very active reformer, quickly instituting a promotion system based more upon merit than upon patronage. His workload greatly increased when war was declared with France in February 1793.

It would seem to have been his renewed professional association with the army that prompted Hunter finally to bring to publication materials that he had first begun to put together while serving at Belle-Île. *A Treatise on the Blood, Inflammation and Gun-Shot Wounds* was completed in his lifetime but appeared posthumously in 1794, with an account of his life by his brother-in-law, Everard Home. Hunter's experience of the management of gunshot wounds in Belle-Île had led him to doubt the received wisdom that the wound should be dilated to locate and remove the ball. Only when the foreign object pressed on a vital part, or the damage to the surrounding health was incompatible with restoration of health, did Hunter proceed to surgery. And even then he advocated waiting until the initial inflammation had subsided and the patient had rallied his strength. The custom of military surgeons at this time was to operate as soon as possible after the injury occurred. The practical sections of the book are accompanied by long and detailed discussions of inflammation, granulation, and so forth. Overall, *A Treatise on the Blood* was Hunter's most substantial addition to the literature on the theory and practice of operative surgery.

For the last three or four decades of his life, Hunter was the most active medical researcher in London. He gave a total of twenty-seven papers to the Royal Society. His first was on the autodigestion of the stomach wall by the gastric juices after death; one of his last was on the 'oeconomy of bees', the fruit of twenty years of observation. He also shed light on the growth of bones. By an extensive series of experiments in which he feed madder root to pigs, which caused new bone formation to be pigmented, and by implanting pins into the shafts of the bones of living pigs, he was able to reveal where new bone is deposited. Hunter gave the Croonian Lectures, on muscular motion, from 1776 to 1782, and was awarded the Copley medial in 1787. However, many of his findings were not published until after his death. The geological observations he made in Portugal and his work on fossils, in which he controversially conjectured a time frame of 'thousands of centuries', did not appear in print until 1859.

Hunter died in 1793, after having suffered from angina pectoris for some years. He may have been a martyr to his venereal inoculation experiments. His zeal for collecting left his estate with many debts and, for a time, his family was in financial difficulties. However, his collection was eventually bought for the nation and housed in the RCS. The Hunterian Museum was extensively damaged by bombing during World War II but has recently been restored and handsomely rehoused by the College. The College also supports regular Hunterian Lectures.

In his lifetime, Hunter was not universally popular among his surgical colleagues. He could speak harshly to them and did not hide his opinion that the surgery of his day was in a defective state. He was not a natural stylist. He received a considerable amount of editorial help with his writing, possibly from Tobias Smollett and William Combe, and certainly from Gilbert Blane, George Fordyce, and David Pitcairn. But his prose is still heavy and his meaning sometimes obscure. Nevertheless, Hunter's immense achievements and his sustained application of scientific principles to the improvement of surgery made him a hero to many of those surgeons who sought to enhance the status of the craft in the nineteenth century. Initially placed in the vault of St Martin-in-the-Fields, Hunter's coffin was moved to Westminster Abbey in 1859.

Bibliography

Primary: 1835–49. (Palmer, J. F., ed.) *The Works of John Hunter F.R.S. with Notes* 4 vols. (London).

Secondary: Moore, Wendy, 2005. *The Knife Man* (London); Jacyna, L. S., 1983. 'Images of John Hunter in the Nineteenth Century.' *History of Science* 21: 85–108; Qvist, George, 1981. *John Hunter 1728–1793* (London); Dobson, Jessie, 1969. *John Hunter* (Edinburgh); Kobler, John, 1960. *The Reluctant Surgeon: The Life of John Hunter* (London); Gloyne, Stephen Roodhouse, 1950. *John Hunter* (Edinburgh); *DSB*; *Oxford DNB*.

Malcolm Nicolson

HUNTER, WILLIAM (b. Long Calderwood, East Kilbride, Lanarkshire, Scotland, 23 May 1718; d. London, England, 30 March 1783), *anatomy, midwifery*.

Hunter was the seventh child of John Hunter, a farmer, and Agnes Paul. Hunter's father intended that he should train for the ministry and, having attended the local Latin school, he matriculated at Glasgow University in 1731. In the skeptical environment of the University, however, Hunter developed doctrinal misgivings and decided against becoming a clergyman. He left in 1736 without graduating. William Cullen (1710–90), then in practice in Hamilton and a friend of the Hunter family, offered Hunter an apprenticeship, which he accepted. In order to improve his medical knowledge, Hunter attended the anatomy lectures of Alexander Munro primus in Edinburgh (1739). The next year Hunter went to London to learn midwifery from William Smellie (1697–1763), in whose house he resided. He also carried a letter of introduction to James Douglas (1675–1742), who shortly offered Hunter a post as his anatomy assistant and tutor to his son, William George. Douglas also arranged for Hunter to become a surgical pupil at St George's Hospital. Hunter took up residence with the Douglases in 1741. He had previously undertaken to enter a partnership with Cullen in Hamilton when his medical education was finished but, in the light of the opportunities opening for him in London, Cullen released Hunter from the obligation.

James Douglas died in 1742, but Hunter continued to live with the family until 1749. In 1743 he and William George

Douglas traveled to Paris. There Hunter heard Antoine Ferrein (1693–1769) lecture on anatomy and Henry-François Le Dran (1685–1770) on surgery. He returned to London in 1744 but traveled to the Continent again in 1748, visiting Leiden, where he was very intrigued by anatomical preparations of the uterus and the placenta, and Paris. Later in the same year, he was joined in London by his younger brother, John, and in 1749 the Hunters established their own household, with facilities for teaching, in Covent Garden. The Company of Surgeons admitted Hunter in 1747 and, in the following year, he was appointed surgeon and man-midwife to the Middlesex Hospital. In 1749 he secured a similar appointment to the newly founded British Lying-in Hospital. During a visit to the family properties in Scotland (1750), he obtained an MD from Glasgow University.

From at least the time of his return from his first visit to Paris, Hunter practiced surgery and midwifery in London. Initially, his scientific interests followed those of James Douglas, as exemplified by his work on the structure and pathology of the atricular cartilages. By the mid-1740s, Hunter had begun detailed anatomical investigations of the lymphatic system and the female reproductive organs. In 1746 Hunter advertised his first anatomy course, which was modeled upon the Parisian style of teaching, in which the students themselves dissected human material. This initiative was very successful and Hunter quickly became one of the foremost teachers of anatomy in London, a pre-eminence he would retain for the rest of his life.

In 1750 Hunter was able to dissect, for the first time, a full-term human gravid uterus. He employed the artist Jan van Rymsdyk (d. 1790) to make drawings of several of his dissections of this specimen. These were engraved and exhibited in 1752, with a view to attracting subscribers to support their publication. Rymsdyk's drawings of the full-term specimen eventually supplied the first ten plates of Hunter's *Anatomy of the Human Gravid Uterus Exhibited by Figures* (1774). A magnificent elephant-folio volume, Hunter's *Anatomy* illustrated, in thirty-four plates, all the stages of pregnancy. Its only text, however, was the descriptions of the plates. Hunter prepared a more comprehensive account of the anatomy of pregnancy, the draft of which was found after his death and edited for publication by his nephew, Matthew Baillie. It appeared as *Anatomical Description of the Human Gravid Uterus and Its Contents* (1794). The detailed text of the latter publication admirably complements the accurate and beautifully crafted images of the earlier one, and it is likely that Hunter's original intention was to publish the two together.

Hunter was the first to describe the decidua reflexa, one of the membranes that envelope the fetus, and the condition of retroverted uterus. His investigations also established that the placenta was supplied with both fetal and maternal blood, but that the two circulations were entirely separate. Previously Alexander Munro primus (1697–1767) had denied that the placenta received maternal blood but, when

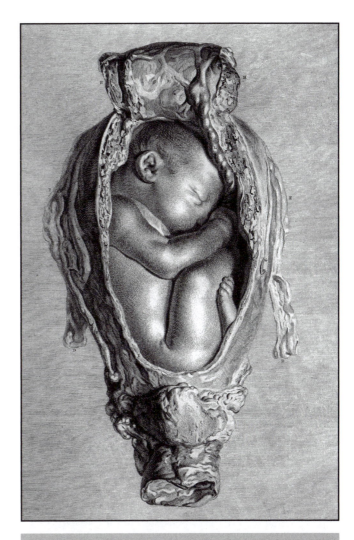

Fetus in utero in the breech position. Engraving from *The Anatomy of the Human Gravid Uterus . . .* London, 1774. Rare Books, Wellcome Library, London.

in Holland, Hunter had seen injected preparations that seemed to indicate the opposite. Hunter also undertook important work on the lymphatic system, which he viewed as an absorbent system, but the results of these inquiries were not published until the appearance of William Cruickshank's *Anatomy of the Absorbing Vessels of the Human Body* (1786). As was the custom of the period, Hunter used his anatomical lectures to disseminate many of his original findings, a practice that resulted in his involvement in several priority disputes.

As a man-midwife, Hunter's polished manners, his discretion, and his sympathetic and confident demeanor at the bedside all equipped him well for the cultivation of an exclusive, upper-class clientele. Throughout the 1750s, wealthy and aristocratic families sought his services with increasing regularity. At this time, Sir Reginald Manningham and Dr Francis Sandys still largely dominated the fashionable practice of man-midwifery in London. However, the death, in

1759, of the former and the retirement of the latter left the field open for Hunter. His successful supervision, in 1762, of the first confinement of Queen Charlotte, was a personal and professional triumph, leading to Hunter's appointment as physician-in-extraordinary to the Queen. By this time, Hunter had established himself as the leading man-midwife of the day.

Like all male midwives before him, William Smellie was generally summoned to perform surgical interventions once it had become clear that labor was seriously obstructed. His specialty was, thus, emergency obstetrics. By contrast, Hunter's wealthy clients tended to engage his services earlier, either at the onset of labor or even in the later stages of pregnancy. As a result of this pattern of consultation, the bulk of Hunter's practice consisted of the supervision of normal confinements. As is understandable under such circumstances he usually recommended patience, rather than active intervention, in the management of labor. He cautioned against the too ready application of instruments and was particularly opposed to the unnecessary or unduly forceful use of the forceps. Hunter also reformed the practice of delivering the placenta digitally or by pulling on the umbilical cord, preferring to await its natural expulsion, except in cases where serious hemorrhage supervened.

Hunter never married (although he may have been engaged to Douglas's daughter, Martha, who died in 1744) but was, nevertheless, the quasipatriarchal head of what was effectively a family business of anatomy teaching. He was assisted in London not only by his younger brother, John, but also by his older brother, James, and by his nephew, Matthew Baillie. Hunter also employed William Hewson (1739–74) and William Cruickshank (1745–1800) in this capacity.

By the 1760s, with the success of his practice and his teaching, Hunter was a wealthy man. He devoted much of his surplus income to collecting. In addition to the enormous number of anatomical preparations he acquired for use in teaching and research, he also collected coins, books, minerals, and natural history specimens. He also sought to establish a permanent home for his collections, proposing to the government that, if land were provided from public funds, he would build and equip a national school of anatomy. State support was not forthcoming, however. Hunter then commissioned the architect James Mylne to design a house in Great Windmill Street that could accommodate the teaching of anatomy and house his collections. Hunter began lecturing in the new premises in 1767.

In 1756 Hunter left the Company of Surgeons and became a licentiate of the Royal College of Physicians. He found, however, that he was excluded from the Fellowship of the College because of his midwifery practice, and so joined the rival body, the Society of Collegiate Physicians, which he served as its treasurer and, latterly, its president. He was elected FRS in 1767. Hunter was also a member of the Society of London Physicians, in whose journal, *Medical Observations and Inquiries,* he published several of his most

important papers, including a very influential study of the 'signs of murder in bastard children'. Hunter's testimony, particularly the consideration he gave to the mother's state of mind and the doubt he was able to place on the reliability of the hydrostatic test, was crucial in several capital court cases. His remarks on the place of the expert medical witness, 'physical people who are called in to settle questions in science', remain apposite: 'In general, I am afraid that too much has been left to our decision. Many of our profession are not so conversant with science as the world may think; and some of us are a little disposed to grasp at authority in a public examination by giving a quick and decided opinion, where it should have been guarded with doubt . . .' (Hunter, 1784, p. 281). Hunter suggested standards for the degree of experience required to make reliable judgments in cases of suspicious neonatal death.

Hunter died in 1783, after collapsing while teaching at Great Windmill Street. He was buried in St James Church, Piccadilly, where a monument was raised to his memory. His will left his various collections and his library to Glasgow University, where they remain in the Hunterian Museum and Art Gallery. Hunter had a reputation as a difficult man—he was estranged from his brother John for many years and quarreled also with Hewson—but there can be no doubting the genuine affection and gratitude of those who studied anatomy or midwifery at his schools in Covent Garden and Great Windmill Street. He raised both the scientific and the social standing of obstetrics. He was a major force in the transformation of the surgically-trained birth attendant from an object of fear to a respected and reassuring provider of skilled support and assistance: 'I have seen the private, as well as the public virtues, the private as well as the more public frailties of women in all ranks of life. I have been in their secrets, their counsellor and adviser in the moments of their greatest distress in body and mind. I have been a witness to their private conduct when they were preparing themselves to meet danger . . .' (Hunter, 1784, p. 269).

Bibliography

Primary: 1774. *The Anatomy of the Human Gravid Uterus, exhibited in figures* (Birmingham); 1784. 'On the uncertainty of the signs of murder, in the case of bastard children.' *Medical Observations and Inquiries* 6: 266–290; 1794. *An Anatomical Description of the Human Gravid Uterus, and its contents* (London).

Secondary: Wilson, Adrian, 1995. *The Making of Man-Midwifery* (London); Brock, Helen, 1994. 'The Many Facets of Dr William Hunter (1718–83).' *History of Science* 32: 387–408; Brock, C. Helen, 1985. 'The Happiness of Riches' in Bynum, W. F., and Roy Porter, eds., *William Hunter and the Eighteenth-Century Medical World* (Cambridge) pp. 35–54; Porter, Roy, 1985. 'William Hunter: A Surgeon and a Gentleman' in Bynum, W. F., and R. Porter, eds., *William Hunter and the Eighteenth-Century Medical World* (Cambridge) pp. 7–34; *DSB*; *Oxford DNB*.

Malcolm Nicolson

HURST, ARTHUR FREDERICK

HURST, ARTHUR FREDERICK (b. Bradford, England, 23 July 1879; d. Birmingham, England, 17 August 1944), *medicine, gastroenterology.*

Hurst (formerly Hertz) was the third son of William Martin Hertz, wool merchant, and his wife Fanny Mary, daughter of Julius Baruch Halle, merchant of Clapham Park, London. Hurst was educated at Bradford and Manchester Grammar Schools, then at Magdalen College, Oxford, where he graduated with first class honors (1901). After further education at Guy's Hospital, he graduated BM (Oxon) in 1904. With the help of a Radcliffe traveling scholarship, he then studied in the United States, Munich, and Paris. He was appointed assistant physician to the neurological department at Guy's Hospital in 1906, remaining there until his retirement as senior physician in 1939. In 1912 he married Cushla Harriette Strotter, daughter of a New Zealand farmer. They had one son and two daughters.

Hurst soon established a national reputation as a physician, with a large private consulting practice. At the same time he studied the physiology of the alimentary tract in health and disease, using the newly developed technique of radiology. His first studies involved the sensibility of the gastrointestinal tract, and the findings were delivered as the Goulstonian Lectures of the RCP in 1911. During the World War I he served first in Salonika, and then at Netley, where he achieved remarkable results in the treatment of shell shock by suggestion. Much of his research was directed to constipation and the treatment of peptic ulcer, conditions that were extremely common in the days between the two world wars. He did, however, also introduce the concept of achalasia, or absence of relaxation, which might cause troublesome dilatation of organs such as the esophagus. Tiring of the demands of a single-handed consulting practice, Hurst set up the New Lodge Clinic at Windsor, where he concentrated on his investigative work. Although highly regarded as a physician and investigator in his day, Hurst made no great contribution to gastroenterology itself and he left no *magnum opus*. He edited *Guy's Hospital Reports* between 1921 and 1939. He was an enthusiastic member of the Association of Physicians of Great Britain and Ireland, and a founding member of the Medical Pilgrims Club, an amiable group of well-heeled physicians who enjoyed traveling together. His most enduring achievement, however, was undoubtedly the foundation of the Gastroenterological Club in 1937. Starting with forty members, by the end of the twentieth century it had become the British Society of Gastroenterology, with more than 2,500 members, the leading association for its subject in Europe. The society's most prestigious lecture is named the Arthur Hurst Lecture.

Hurst was rewarded with many honors. At the RCP, he was Goulstonian Lecturer (1911), Croonian Lecturer (1920), Harveian Orator (1937), and Moxon Medallist (1939). He was knighted in the Coronation Honors of 1937.

After his retirement from Guy's Hospital (1939), Hurst went to live in Oxford. There he undertook ward rounds at the Radcliffe Infirmary, which drew enthusiastic audiences. He had the misfortune to suffer throughout his later life from severe deafness, which did, however, spare him from much committee work and from examining. He had the disconcerting habit of switching off his hearing aid, then a cumbersome apparatus, if he considered a presentation to a medical meeting to be not worth listening to. He also suffered from intractable asthma, for which he treated himself with injections of adrenaline. It was at the home of T. L. Hardy, first professor of gastroenterology in England and the secretary to the newly founded Gastroenterological Club, that Hurst suddenly died, in the garden, on 17 August 1944.

Bibliography

Primary: 1909. *Constipation and Allied Intestinal Disorders* (London); 1917. *Medical Diseases of the War* (London); 1949. *A Twentieth Century Physician: Being the Reminiscences of Sir Arthur Hurst* (London); 1969. (Hunt, Thomas, ed.) *Selected Writings of Sir Arthur Hurst (1879–1944)* (London).

Secondary: Jones, F. A., 1987. 'Gastroenterology in Britain before 1937 and the Founding of the Gastro-enterological Club.' *Gut* Golden Jubilee edition: 3–6; Mann, W. N., 1979. 'Arthur Hurst: A Personal Note.' *Guy's Hospital Gazette* 94: 281–286; *Oxford DNB*.

Christopher Booth

HUSS, MAGNUS

HUSS, MAGNUS (b. Torp, Medelpad, Sweden, 22 October 1807; d. Stockholm, Sweden, 22 April 1890), *medicine, public health.*

Huss grew up as a son of a vicar in a cultivated family in the northern part of Sweden. He went to the gymnasium in Hernösand after being taught at home, and at the age of seventeen he became a student at the University of Uppsala. He started with botany and chemistry, but after that medicine became his main commitment. In the late 1820s the teaching of medicine was very theoretical, and he therefore, like many other students, moved to Stockholm for the more practical part of the education. In Stockholm he came under the influence of the professor of anatomy Anders Retzius. During the 1830s he had several appointments as a doctor and wrote articles for Swedish medical journals, and in the years of 1837 and 1838 he traveled around Europe, visiting Vienna and Paris, among other cities.

After returning to Sweden in 1839 he was appointed as senior physician at the largest and most important hospital in Stockholm, Serafimerlasarettet. In the next year he was also appointed as professor of medicine at the Karolinska Institut. With these positions he became one of the most influential medical men in Sweden during the following decades. As professor of medicine he located most of his teaching at the hospital and introduced the students into the methods of physical diagnostics. Besides the bedside teaching, he also stressed the importance of laboratory examinations and how to learn from autopsies carried out when patients died.

A large number of the patients at the hospital had symptoms that Huss thought were caused by the extensive use of alcohol. He described and analyzed a large number of these cases and published the results in the book *Alcoholismus chronicus* (1849–51). The concept of alcoholism was not new, but his documentation of the medical consequences of the use of alcohol had a great impact on contemporary medicine. Huss thought of alcohol as a kind of poison to the body, and he gave clinical and pathological descriptions of how the heart, the brain, the liver, and so on were damaged by it. But he was also interested in the various causes of the drinking habits, including the cold Swedish climate, the severe housing conditions in the capital city, and bad examples from parents. Huss emphasized the importance of individual responsibility and published a number of articles and booklets about the social and medical consequences of the use of alcohol. As a well-known doctor and medical official, he wrote important works for the Swedish temperance movement.

In the late 1850s Huss left his positions at the hospital and the medical institute and started a new career as a medical official. He applied for a less demanding position as chairman of the national board of health (Sundhetskollegiet). He was later an inspector for all the mental hospitals in the country, which demanded a lot of traveling, and he was also, among other appointments, chairman of the national school of nursing.

In 1857 he married, at the age of fifty, and became a nobleman in the same year, perhaps due to the fact that several members of the royal family had consulted him as a practitioner. Most of the time during the 1860s and 70s Huss and his wife lived in the countryside in the southeastern part of Sweden. Starting from 1883 Huss was back in Stockholm, participating in the debate about the consumption of alcohol, writing a book about the education of nurses, and working on a autobiography, which was published in the year of his death, 1890.

Bibliography

Primary: 1849–51. *Alcoholismus chronicus eller kronisk alkholsjukdom* 2 vols. (Stockholm); 1852. *Om Sveriges endemiska sjukdomar* (Stockholm); 1890. *Några skizzer och tidsbilder från min lefvnad* (Stockholm).

Secondary: Sournia, Jean-Charles, 1990. *A History of Alcoholism* (Oxford).

Roger Qvarsell

HUTCHINSON, JONATHAN (b. Selby, Yorkshire, England, 23 July 1828; d Haslemere, Surrey, England, 23 June 1913), *medicine, dermatology, neurology, ophthalmology, pathology, surgery.*

Hutchinson was the second son of twelve children born to Jonathan Hutchinson, a prosperous businessman in the flax trade, and Elizabeth Massey. The families had long been prominent Quakers and had started by farming increasingly large estates. As was the custom among Yorkshire Quakers,

Jonathan was educated at home by the Misses Proctor. While his older brother, Massey, chose dentistry, Jonathan selected medicine as a profession. He began a five-year apprenticeship on 22 January 1845 with Caleb Williams of York, who was a surgeon-apothecary, as well as a minister to the Society of Friends. Young Hutchinson also attended lectures at the York School of Medicine and visited the wards at the York County Hospital.

Early Years

In 1850 Hutchinson went to London to study under James Paget (1814–99) at St Bartholomew's Hospital Medical School, where he was elected to the Abernethian Society. After four months, he passed his MRCS examinations and, the next month, those for the LSA. An interlude of several months as house surgeon at the York County Hospital followed, before he would permanently return to London, enrolling for a year's term (1851) at the Moorfields Hospital for Diseases of the Eye.

Although his first hospital appointment was as a clinical assistant at the Liverpool Street Chest Hospital, he aspired to become a consulting surgeon. Within a few years, he had been elected to the Pathological Society and the Hunterian Society, each of which he would later serve as its president. His delivered his first scientific paper, *Dyspepsia and Phthisis*, to the latter in 1855. Over the next sixty years, he would read innumerable papers to medical societies and would become known as a superb debater.

Hutchinson was one of the most energetic workers in London, or for that matter, in the world of medicine. For example, in 1857 he was instrumental in starting the New Sydenham Society (NSS) (1857–1911), whose purpose was to publish medical works that might not be easily accessible and which was based upon the recently closed Sydenham Society (1843–55). The NSS produced such works as *An Atlas of Illustrations of Pathology*, and the English translation of Hebra's and Kaposi's texts. A lexicon project, an enormous undertaking, was not very successful. Curiously, while Hutchinson wanted uniformity in medical terminology, he often named newly described entities after the patient, e.g., Branford legs (erythema induratum) or Mortimer's malady (sarcoidosis).

London Medicine

In 1859 Hutchinson was elected as assistant surgeon to The London Hospital, ultimately rising to surgeon (1863) and consulting surgeon (1883). During this time he also enjoyed appointments at the Metropolitan Free Hospital, Blackfriars Hospital for Skin Diseases (1854), and the Royal London Ophthalmic Hospital (1863). He continued on the staff of Moorfields, and developed an extensive private practice at his home first in Finsbury Square and then in Cavendish Square. From 1867 to 1869, Hutchinson was dean of The London Hospital Medical College. He also edited the *British Medical Journal* (1869–70), after having previously served on the *Medical Times and Gazette* (1855).

Hutchinson was elected president of the RCS and Hunterian Professor in Surgery and Pathology for a five-year term, beginning in 1879. In 1875 he had started his large folio atlas, *Illustrations of Clinical Surgery*, which was completed in five installments over the next decade, and was widely received in England as well as in America and in Germany. Beginning in 1889 he edited all the volumes—or more correctly, wrote them, as every paper was his own—of the *Archives of Surgery*. He received honorary degrees from a number of universities and recognition from many international societies, and was elected as FRS (1882).

Contributions

Hutchinson was a prodigious worker and would eventually serve as president of six professional societies. He was also president of the Third International Congress of Dermatology when it met in London (1896), and he was Lettsomian Lecturer (1886) and president (1892) of the Medical Society of London. Hutchinson served on two royal commissions: on capabilities of London hospitals to treat smallpox and fever patients (1881) and on compulsory vaccination (1890–96). For his extensive work, he was knighted (1908).

Among the diseases he described are arsenical zoster (1861); cheiropompholyx (1871), which had been previously described as dyshidrosis by Tilbury Fox in 1868; varicella gangrenosa (1882); dermatitis gangrenosa infantum (1882); arsenical keratosis (1887); and craterform ulcer of the face (1899, keratoacanthoma).

A myriad of other diseases or signs are associated with his name: 'Hutchinson's congenital syphilis triad'—interstitial keratitis, notched incisor teeth, and eighth nerve deafness; 'Hutchinson's masked-like face'—tabes dorsalis; 'Hutchinson's melanotic whitlow'—melanoma in the nailbed; 'Hutchinson's freckle'—lentigo maligna (melanoma); 'Hutchinson's chronic skin plaques'—sarcoidosis; 'Hutchinson's prurigo'—summer prurigo, recurrent summer eruption; 'Hutchinson's type of erythema induratum'; 'Hutchinson's unequal pupils'—meningeal hemorrhage; 'Hutchinson's sign'—eye involvement of herpes zoster when the nasal tip shows herpetic lesions. He described signs in terms that could easily be remembered: the 'apple jelly' nodule of lupus vulgaris, or the 'screwdriver' peg teeth of congenital syphilis.

Other Activities and Ideas

Hutchinson collected a number of pathological illustrations and specimens that the Royal College of Surgeons refused. He then opened his own museum at 1 Park Crescent, Regent's Park (1893), that later became part of the short-lived Medical Graduate College and Polyclinic (1898) at Chenies Street. After his death, the medical components were acquired by Johns Hopkins University School of Medicine in Baltimore, USA. He also developed a natural history museum at his country seat in Haslemere, where he often lectured on Sundays.

Although he was an early proponent of antiseptic surgery and of the tenets of Joseph Lister (1827–1912), he refused to change his thoughts on the causation of leprosy. Even after the mycobacterium was demonstrated in Hansen's disease, Hutchinson adhered to his fish-eating theory (in which ingesting decomposed fish was the etiology). He was a strong proponent of isolating lepers. As to the treatment of syphilis before Paul Ehrlich's (1854–1915) drug '606', he was emphatic about 'drenching' the syphilitic with mercury until salivation occurred. He also thought that alopecia areata might have a fungal background, despite contrary proof.

Hutchinson did not believe that women should be in medicine. Although he permitted men to have an occasional glass of wine, he was against women consuming any alcoholic beverage.

Hutchinson and his wife, Maud Jane Pyrset West, had ten children, three of whom followed him into medicine. His last years were mostly spent at the country home in Haslemere, where he continued to swim almost daily in the cold-water streams. Until the end, he was a prodigious worker, and was so often serious that there is no record of his having any humor.

Bibliography

Primary: 1863. *A Clinical Memoir on Certain Diseases of the Eye and Ear, Consequent on Inherited Syphilis; with an appended chapter of commentaries on the transmission of syphilis from parent to offspring, and its more remote consequences* (London); 1869–93. *Addresses and Papers* 2 vols. (London); 1869–75. *A Descriptive Catalogue of the New Sydenham Society's Atlas of Portraits of Diseases of the Skin* 2 vols. (London); 1878–88. *Illustrations of clinical surgery. Illustrating surgical diseases, symptoms and accidents, also operative and other methods of treatment* 2 vols. (London); 1887. *Syphilis* (London); 1889–1911. *Archives of Surgery* 11 vols. (London); 1895. *A smaller atlas of illustrations of clinical surgery* (London).

Secondary: Crissey, J. T., and L. C. Parish, 1981. *The Dermatology and Syphilology of the Nineteenth Century* (New York); Jackson, R., 1980. 'Jonathan Hutchinson on Syphilis.' *Sex. Transm. Dis.* 7(2): 90–96; Wales, A. E., 1963. 'Sir Jonathan Hutchinson, 1828–1913.' *Br. J. Vener. Dis.* 39: 67–86; McCleary, J., and E. M. Farber, 1952. 'Dermatological Writings of Sir Jonathan Hutchinson.' *AMA Arch. Derm. Syphilol.* 65(2): 130–136. McKusick, V. A., 1952. 'The Clinical Observations of Jonathan Hutchinson.' *Am. Jyph. Gonorrhea Vener. Dis.* 36(2): 101–126; Hutchinson, Herbert, 1946. *Jonathan Hutchinson, Life and Letters* (London); *Oxford DNB*.

Lawrence Charles Parish

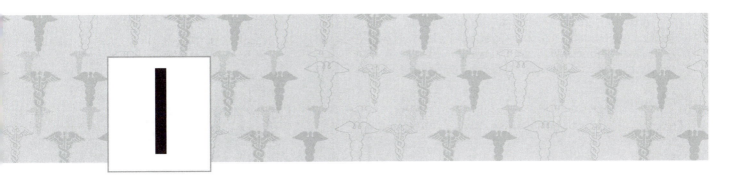

I

ILIZAROV, GAVRIIL ABRAMOVICH (b. Belovez, Russia, 15 June 1921; d. Kurgan, Russia, 24 July 1992), *surgery, traumatology, orthopedics.*

Ilizarov, a highland Jew from the Northern Caucasus, was born by accident on the western border of Soviet Russia, where his family was starving during the Civil War. Soon after Gavriil's birth, they returned to their native village of aul Kusary, where Ilizarov graduated from school and, in 1941, entered the Crimean Medical Institute in Simferopol. In 1944 he was directed as a country doctor to the village of Dolgovka, 150 miles from the Siberian town of Kurgan.

The only educated physician for hundreds of miles around, Ilizarov helped local people with a wide range of diseases. The treatment of disabled Soviet soldiers of World War II suffering from severe limb trauma, with large bone defects, was one of the most urgent tasks. Ilizarov considered that an unfavorable biomechanical environment was the principal cause of continuing fractures. He suggested a new curative system: transosseous osteosynthesis based on a tension-wire circular external fixator that he invented in 1951 ('Ilizarov's apparatus').

Ilizarov argued that bone was one of the most active tissues and could grow intensively under appropriate conditions of stabilization, realignment, and compression. These could be created by minimal surgical intervention and by the versatility of his apparatus, consisting of various supporting elements (half-rings, arches, and long connecting plates), wires, wire fixators, and threaded rods.

The method of transosseous osteosynthesis was not new. Over the years, a number of devices had been proposed for improving the interfragmentary compression of fractures treated in external skeletal fixation. The years during and after World War II were especially productive for the development of external equipment (by J. Charnley, P. Hoffmann, H. Greifensteiner, and others). In distinction from its predecessors, the Ilizarov apparatus applied force to the fragments in all the needed directions, and ensured stable fixation while retaining joint motion. A surgeon, using the various elements, could assemble the individual components into any configuration needed to deal with a patient's specific problem.

In 1955 Ilizarov was appointed head of the department of surgery in the Kurgan regional hospital for disabled soldiers of World War II. There he began to broaden the use of his apparatus for aligning and lengthening limbs. He managed to thicken the shin and increase the length by as much as 50 cm, and to elongate the spine to increase stature. Despite a positive evaluation of Ilizarov's apparatus in 1955 by the Central Institute for Traumatology and Orthopedics in Moscow, its clinical implementation was delayed for a decade because Ilizarov's colleagues in the central clinics could not believe the Siberian surgeon had achieved such tremendous results.

Not until 1966 did Ilizarov receive a small laboratory in Kurgan. To promote his innovations, he summarized the results in his doctoral thesis defended at the Perm Medical Institute in 1968, 'Kompressionnyi osteosintez apparatom avtora (eksperimental'no-klinicheskoe issledovanie)' [Transosseous compression osteosynthesis with the author's apparatus. Experimental and clinical investigation]. Official recognition followed in 1969 when, by decree of the government of the Russian Federation, Ilizarov's laboratory was transformed into the branch of the Leningrad Institute for Traumatology and Orthopedics. It later became an independent institution; then in 1987 it was reorganized into the Kurgan Scientific Center of Reconstructive Orthopedics and Traumatology. In 1991 Ilizarov was elected a full member of the USSR Academy of Sciences, and an honorary member of many medical societies in Europe. Many enthusiastic articles and novels were written about 'the magician from Kurgan', and he became a hero and the subject of movies and documentary films.

Bibliography

Primary: 1992. (ed. and trans. Green, Stuart A.) *Transosseous Osteosynthesis: Theoretical and Clinical Aspects of the Regeneration and Growth of Tissue* (Berlin).

Secondary: Green, Stuart A., ed., 1992. *Ilizarov Method* (Philadelphia); Bianchi Maiocchi, A., and J. Aronson, eds., 1990. *Operative Principles of Ilizarov: Fracture Treatment, Nonunion, Osteomyelitis, Lengthening, Deformity Correction* (Baltimore); Nuvakhov, B., 1987. *Doctor Ilizarov* (Moscow).

Marina Sorokina

IMHOTEP (b. Egypt, Dynasty 3 [*c.* 2686 BCE]; d. Egypt, Dynasty 3 [*c.* 2630 BCE]), *credited with founding medical science in Egypt.*

Described by Sir William Osler as 'the first figure of a physician to stand out clearly from the mists of antiquity' (Osler, 1923, p. 10), Imhotep was deified as the Egyptian god of medicine some two thousand years after his death. However, there is no specific evidence to prove that he ever practiced medicine in his lifetime.

Early Life and Career

In his own account, Constantine the African (Africanus) stated that, according to the *History of Egypt* written by Manetho (a priest who lived in Egypt in the reign of Ptolemy II Philadelphus, 285–246 BCE), King Djoser 'because of his medical skill, has the reputation of Asklepios [the Greek god of medicine] among the Egyptians'. However, this is most probably a reference to Djoser's Chief Minister, Imhotep, rather than to the king himself.

The only contemporary reference to Imhotep survives on the base of a statue discovered near the entrance to the Step Pyramid at Sakkara. This statue belonged to King Djoser, and

I-EM-HETEP
(Imhotep)
Ca. 650 B.C.   Saite Period

Statuette of Imhotep. Photogravure, Iconographic Collection, Wellcome Library, London.

the inscription describes Imhotep as 'the seal-bearer of the King of Lower Egypt . . . ruler of the Great House . . . the High Priest of Heliopolis . . . the Chief of Sculptors, of the masons and of the producers of stone vessels' (Wildung, 1977a, pp. 31–32).

Little is known of Imhotep's early life. Apparently, he was the son of a builder, Kanofer, and his wife, Kherednankh, and was probably born *c.* 2686 BCE at Memphis. Later, he may have entered one of the great temples, where, as a priest, he would have served the resident god by performing the daily rituals and would have also gained training and knowledge in mathematics and astronomy.

Kings frequently drew their senior political advisors and administrators from the priesthood, and Imhotep was ultimately chosen and appointed as Vizier or Chancellor. In this role, he exercised great influence as the king's political counselor and second-in-command.

Achievements as the Royal Architect

The most tangible and enduring evidence of Imhotep's genius is provided by his work as Djoser's architect. The Step

Pyramid at Sakkara, which he designed and constructed for Djoser, is the world's earliest-known large-scale monument built in dressed stone. As the first named architect of a stone building, Imhotep can also probably be accredited with the invention of the pyramid as a royal burial place.

Several stages in the development of the pyramid form can be observed in the Step Pyramid at Sakkara.

Originally, Djoser's burial place had been designed as a traditional *mastaba*-tomb, but it was subsequently enlarged with the addition of five graduated layers, with decreasing base measurements, to form a stepped structure. Imhotep may have conceived the idea of the pyramid as a staircase to give the king access to heaven. The grandeur of this concept must have been equaled by Egypt's determination and ability, at this early date, to assemble the requisite manpower, skills, and resources.

A book reputedly kept in the temple library at the Temple of Horus at Edfu recorded that Imhotep also built the original building on this site, following divine instructions and using a plan of the temple that 'fell from the sky'. This early temple was apparently the model for the much later Ptolemaic structure (237–57 BCE), where a wall relief shows Imhotep as a scribe-priest, with a scroll in his hands. Elsewhere in the temple, an inscription describes him as 'great god, residing at Edfu, at whose order everyone lives, who cures any illness in Egypt' (Worth Estes, 1989, p. 129).

Sage and Writer

Although none of his writings have been discovered, Imhotep is attributed with the authorship of several books, including an *Instruction in Wisdom*. In Dynasty 11 (*c.* 2133–1991 BCE), another writer referred to Imhotep's architectural achievements to demonstrate that even monumental burial structures cannot ensure the owners' continued existence after death.

As a priest, he would have been trained as a scribe, and in late Egyptian history, there was widespread manufacture of small statues of Imhotep, representing him in this role. Several hundred examples have survived, showing him as a seated figure, dressed in a pleated kilt and skullcap and holding an open papyrus roll on his lap.

Deification

The tomb of Imhotep's contemporary, Hesy-Re, has been found at Sakkara, where the inscriptions confirm that he was 'Chief of dentists and doctors'. However, because Imhotep's own tomb has never been discovered (although he was most probably buried at Sakkara, and the site may well have become a place of pilgrimage soon after his death), there is no inscriptional confirmation that he was Djoser's physician as well as his architect, or that he held the title of medical practitioner during his lifetime. This title (*swnw*) appears after his name only in very late texts.

Nevertheless, although no contemporary evidence of his medical status has survived, Imhotep was later deified and revered by the Egyptians as their god of medicine, and today he is credited as a pioneer of medical science. He may have enjoyed a semi-divine status as early as Dynasty 5 (*c.* 2400 BCE), and his apotheosis as god of medicine possibly dates to Dynasty 19 (*c.* 1300 BCE).

By Dynasty 27 (*c.* 500 BCE), inscriptions referred to him as a god, and his divinity was well established. However, until he was deified, it was not customary for Egyptians to worship a single god of medicine; they preferred to offer their prayers to various deities who had responsibility for different areas of medicine.

Also, it was very rare for nonroyal mortals to achieve individual deification. However, by this period, both Imhotep and Amenhotep, son of Hapu (a sage who had lived in Dynasty 18, *c.* 1400 BCE) were regarded as divine healers, and their shrines became centers of pilgrimage, although there is no conclusive evidence that either was a medical practitioner in life. They shared several healing shrines and are shown together in a Late Period (525–332 BCE) relief on the outside of the east (rear) wall of the Temple of Ptah at Karnak. By this time, officials had started to build their own tombs near the Step Pyramid, in order to gain Imhotep's blessing and support.

Imhotep also acquired divine parentage. An inscription on one of his statuettes states that he was the offspring of a human mother, Kherednankh, and a divine father—Ptah, god of Memphis. Elsewhere, he was attributed with two divine parents—Ptah, god of Memphis, and Sekhmet, goddess of war and disease—while his human mother, Kherednankh, became one of his divine supporters. Ptah, Sekhmet, and Imhotep were now regarded as an important divine triad at Memphis.

In the Ptolemaic Period (332–30 BCE), the Greek rulers of Egypt enhanced Imhotep's position further, by identifying Imouthes (the Greek version of his name) with their own god of healing—Asklepios—whose cult had started in the third century BCE.

Role of the Temple in Healing

The temples played an important part in the cult of Imhotep/Asklepios. The sick made pilgrimages to the god's shrines, where they participated in rituals and ceremonies, in the hope of receiving a cure. Incubation was an important aspect of this treatment: the sick slept in the temple precinct and, often through a dream, encountered the deity, who gave reassurance and healing to the patient.

Various Egyptian shrines and sanctuaries were associated with Imhotep. The largest and most famous temple, which the Greeks called the 'Asklepion', was at Sakkara and may have marked either the actual or supposed site of Imhotep's tomb. This became a great center of pilgrimage, but in 380, the Roman emperor Theodosius ordered the destruction of the temple.

The god Imhotep possessed smaller shrines at Thebes. One was located at the mortuary temple of Ramesses III at Medinet Habu. Also, there were two small shrines built by Ptolemy VIII Euergetes (second century BCE) on the upper terrace of Queen Hatshepsut's mortuary temple at Deir el-Bahri (c. 1500 BCE); a temple at Deir el-Medina, built by Ptolemy IV (221–204 BCE) and dedicated to Hathor, Imhotep, and Amenhotep, son of Hapu; and a shrine in the Temple of Ptah at Karnak.

On the island of Philae, adjacent to the Temple of Isis, Ptolemy V Epiphanes (204–180 BCE) built a shrine to commemorate an event he had requested in his prayers to Imhotep—the birth of his son, Ptolemy VI Philometor.

Imhotep's reputation as a god of healing brought the sick to these shrines from all over Egypt and from abroad. Graffiti at some of the sites provides a record of the patients' visits and their success in obtaining cures.

Literary Sources

Surviving documents containing references to Imhotep add to knowledge of the god's mythology and attributes. A *Hymn to Imhotep*, inscribed in the Temple of Ptah at Karnak, describes details of his worship at Thebes. It dates to the Roman Period (30 BCE onward), when the cult of Imhotep/Asklepios reached its zenith.

Another text, the 'Famine Stela', carved on the Island of Sehel in the First Cataract, dates to the Ptolemaic Period (332–30 BCE), but describes events set in Dynasty 3 (c. 2660 BCE). It purports to be a decree issued by King Djoser to a 'Governor of the South', in which the king refers to a seven-year famine and his consultation with a priest of Imhotep.

The priest informs the king that the god Khnum controls the flow of the Nile inundation, and the god then appears to the king and promises to end the famine. As a thank-offering to the god, Djoser grants the god's temple at Elephantine a share of the revenue from a tract of land in Lower Nubia.

An inscription on the Stela of Taimhotep (British Museum No.147) dates to the reign of Cleopatra VII (51–30 BCE) and records how Imhotep responded to Taimhotep, the wife of a High Priest of Memphis and mother of three daughters, by granting her request for the birth of a son.

Another text (Oxyrhynchus Papyrus 1381) describes an episode during a temple incubation, when Imhotep appeared as a vision to the mother of a suffering patient. As a result of the god's intervention, the pain and fever left the man, who expressed his gratitude to the god by recording his experience in writing.

Contributions

In antiquity, Imhotep enjoyed a reputation as a distinguished polymath and early intellectual who was renowned for his wisdom. However, there is only circumstantial evidence to support the claim that he contributed to medical science. Also, it is unclear why the Egyptians chose to promote Imhotep as their first major god of medicine, or why the Greeks subsequently assimilated him with Asklepios and promoted his cult. Possibly Imhotep's reputation as a renowned scribe and sage and his consequent close association with Thoth, god of wisdom and writing, may have facilitated his adoption as god of medicine.

Imhotep became the deified embodiment of the priest-physician, closely associated with temple medicine. His widespread cult was only finally extinguished by the arrival of Christianity and the consequent closure of the temples.

Bibliography

Secondary: Nunn, John F., 1996. *Ancient Egyptian Medicine* (London); Worth Estes, J., 1989. *The Medical Skills of Ancient Egypt* (Canton, MA); Risse, G. B., 1986. 'Imhotep and Medicine: A Reevaluation.' *Western Journal of Medicine* 144: 622–624; Lichtheim, Miriam, 1980. *Ancient Egyptian Literature*, vol. 3 (Berkeley); Wildung, Dietrich, 1977a. *Egyptian Saints: Deification in Pharaonic Egypt* (New York); Wildung, Dietrich, 1977b. *Imhotep und Amenhotep. Gottwerdung in Alten Agypter* (Munich); Hurry, J., 1926. *Imhotep: The Vizier and Physician of King Zoser* (London) (repr. Chicago, 1978); Osler, Sir William, 1923. *The Evolution of Modern Medicine* (New Haven); Sethe, Kurt, 1902. *Imhotep, der Asklepios der Agypter* (Leipzig) (repr. Hildesheim, 1964).

Rosalie David

INGEN HOUSZ, JAN (b. Breda, the Netherlands, 8 December 1730; d. Bowood House, Calne, Wiltshire, England, 7 September 1799), *medicine, smallpox inoculation.*

The medical career of Ingen Housz was launched when he was twelve. The younger son of a widower leather merchant and apothecary, he was renowned for his schoolboy prowess in the classical languages. John Pringle, physician with the English continental army, met the Ingen Housz family when he was garrisoned near Breda in 1743, and encouraged Jan to train as a physician, guiding his later progress.

At sixteen, Ingen Housz, a Catholic, left the Netherlands to study at Louvain and graduated MD on 24 July 1753. He continued his studies at Leiden with Bernhard Siegfried Albinus, and also at Paris and Edinburgh. Back in Breda, he built a medical practice linked to his father's dispensary. He maintained his interest in physics, particularly electricity, pioneering the flat disc generator. In July 1764 his father died and, exhibiting strength of character, Ingen Housz insisted on opening the body to prove that his father's demise had been needlessly accelerated by treatments based on the wrong diagnosis.

Later that year, anxious to learn smallpox inoculation, he traveled to London. Pringle, now a Royal Physician, introduced him into a circle of doctors and enlightenment 'philosophers' that included William Heberden, George Baker, and Benjamin Franklin. After a clinical refresher at Edinburgh, Ingen Housz was taken to the London Foundling Hospital by William Watson, honorary physician and board member, and taught how to inoculate. Over the winter of 1767–68 he stayed with Thomas Dimsdale, a physician at Hertford (near London), who practiced one of the simplest and best inoculation methods. While Ingen Housz was there, a smallpox epidemic threatened, and he helped administer a successful mass inoculation. This invaluable experience convinced him to promote inoculation in the Netherlands, and he published a letter to Rev Charles Pierre Chais, its main protagonist there.

In London, the character and new skills of Ingen Housz were attracting notice. At Pringle's suggestion, King George III proposed the Dutch doctor to Maria Theresa, Holy Roman Empress of Austria, when she requested an English inoculator for Vienna where smallpox was rife, even at the Royal Court. Ingen Housz arrived on 14 May 1768, and was invited to demonstrate his inoculation practice to the Empress personally. About a hundred poor children were willingly volunteered by their parents and treated successfully. Ingen Housz then safely inoculated those Royals still prone to smallpox in both Vienna and Florence. Ingen Housz was awarded a sizeable annuity and promoted to Royal Physician. Meanwhile, admirers in London arranged his election to the Royal Society.

For the next twenty years Ingen Housz was based in Vienna, introducing smallpox inoculation throughout the Habsburg Empire, and taking satisfaction in seeing it become accepted practice. Liberated from regular medical practice by his new financial security, he spent the rest of his life in scientific experimentation. In true eighteenth-century fashion, his interests were eclectic: air purity, inhaled oxygen therapy, phosphorus, platinum, heat conduction in metals, manures, and carbonated water for bladder stones. He also invented the cover slip for microscopy, but his most significant contribution was the first revelation (in England, 1779), by characteristically ingenious experiments, of the essentials of photosynthesis.

Near the end of his life, Ingen Housz disputed publicly with Edward Jenner, provoking Jenner to publish an appendix to his famous 'cowpox paper' with better-defined terms and techniques.

In 1775 Ingen Housz married Agatha Jacquin, sister of the Professor of Botany at Vienna. The couple had no children and lived apart for their last decade, with Ingen Housz marooned in England by the French Revolution and its aftermath. He developed a terminal illness in the spring of 1799 but retained his remarkable intellect until the last week of his life.

Bibliography

Primary: 1782. (Molitor, Niklas Karl, ed.) *Vermischte Schriften phisisch-medizinischen Inhalts* (Vienna); 1768. *Lettre de Monsieur Ingenhousz, Docteur en médecine, à Monsieur Chais, Pasteur de l'Église Wallonne de la Haye* (Amsterdam).

Secondary: Ingen Housz, Jan Maarten, Norman Beale, and Elaine Beale, 2005. 'The Life of Dr Jan Ingen Housz (1730–99), Private Counsellor and Personal Physician to Emperor Joseph II of Austria.' *Journal of Medical Biography* 13: 15–21; Beale, Norman, and Elaine Beale, 2005. 'Evidence-based Medicine in the Eighteenth Century: The Ingen Housz-Jenner Correspondence Revisited.' *Medical History* 49: 79–98; Wiesner, Julius, et al., 1905. *Jan Ingen-Housz. Sein Leben und sein Wirken als Naturforscher und Arzt* (Vienna); *DSB.*

Norman Beale and
Elaine Beale

INGENIEROS, JOSÉ (b. Palermo, Italy, 24 April 1877; d. Buenos Aires, Argentina, 31 October 1925), *psychiatry.*

Ingenieros, Argentina's leading neurologist, psychiatrist, and criminologist at the turn of the century, was born in Palermo, Italy, in 1877. (In his early career Ingenieros used his family's original Italian name *Ingegnieri* or the intermediate *Ingegnieros* until he fully Hispanicized it in 1913.) Son of an Italian journalist, he spent his childhood in Montevideo, Uruguay, and moved to Buenos Aires as a youth to study at the prestigious boys' high school *Colegio Nacional.* Entering the university at age fifteen, he became the star pupil of two prestigious figures at the Medical School of the University of Buenos Aires, José María Ramos Mejía and Francisco de Veyga, the one an expert in neurology and the other in hygiene. By 1900 Ingenieros had earned his medical degree at the University of Buenos Aires, with his doctoral thesis, 'The Simulation of Madness', honored by the medical faculty's top prize. It was a Darwinian interpretation of the psychological state of 'malingering', the feigning of illness. Upon Ingenieros's graduation, his mentor Veyga appointed him chief of the neurology clinic at the University of Buenos Aires.

Ingenieros was influential in ushering in expanding specialization of various aspects of criminal justice and 'clinical' examinations of individual offenders, with an emphasis on laboratory studies, patient observation, and recommendations for treatment. In 1907, supported by the National Penitentiary, he founded and directed its new Criminology Institute. The following year he was a founding member of the Argentine Psychology Society, and he became president of the Argentine Medical Association in 1909.

From his clinical post Ingenieros pioneered the first clinical studies of hysteria in Argentina. In the first two decades of the twentieth century, he published two full-length manuscripts on hysteria, as well as numerous articles focused on specific cases. He also did research on other forms of mental illness and crime, applying the most current European theories to the Argentine population. Between 1904 and 1911, when he served as Director of the *Servicio de Observación de Alienados* (Lunatic Observation Service) of the Buenos Aires Police, his reputation spread abroad. The Parisian *Société Medico-Psychologique* named him a corresponding member, and he was selected as Argentine representative to the Fifth International

José Ingenieros lecturing and pointing at a patient. Photograph, early twentieth century. Archivo General de la Nación, Buenos Aires.

Congress of Psychology in Rome, where he served as president of the Pathological Psychology Section. Like most Argentine physicians at the turn of the century, the young Ingenieros twice enacted the ritual of extended residency abroad, spending a number of years studying and lecturing in France, Italy, and Germany. During a European tour, he married, bringing his Swiss bride, Eva Rutenberg, back to Buenos Aires in 1911.

Above all, Ingenieros was an institution builder in the rapidly developing city of Buenos Aires. One of his signal contributions to medicine there was his 1902 founding of the *Archivos de Psiquiatría, Criminología, y Ciencias Afines* [Archives of Psychiatry, Criminology, and Related Sciences]. He envisioned it a repository for new research findings, a platform for the new Argentine criminology, and a forum for international scientific debate. Its prestigious pages provided for the first time in Argentina a unified ground for criminological science, expanding the space devoted to publication and discussion of local crime data. The *Archivos* quickly became Argentina's leading vehicle for European theory, the chief arena of internal debate and innovation, and, ultimately, a prized exemplar of scientific excellence for the nation. Building on French, Italian, and British theories, Ingenieros and colleagues proposed a comprehensive new methodology, an 'Argentine school' of psychopathology that sought to make assessments of abnormal people more precise. For many years the *Archivos* was the only Latin American journal exclusively dedicated to criminological science.

Bibliography

Primary: 1903. *Simulación de la locura* (Buenos Aires); 1904. *Histeria y sugestión* (Buenos Aires): 1907. *Criminología* (Buenos Aires).

Secondary: Rodriguez Kauth, Angel, 1996. *José Ingenieros* (Buenos Aires); Terán, Oscar, 1986. *José Ingenieros: pensar la nación* (Buenos Aires).

Julia Rodriguez

INOZEMTSEV, FEDOR IVANOVICH (b. Belkino, Kaluga province, Russia, 12 February 1802; d. Moscow, Russia, 6 August 1869) *surgery.*

Inozemtsev was born to a manager's family originating in the Caucasus (by some evidence, from Persia). He took his schooling and undergraduate studies in Khar'kov, graduating from the medical faculty of Khar'kov University in 1828 and the Professorial Institute in Derpt (Tartu) in 1833, where he had studied along with N. N. Pirogov, G. I. Sokol'skii, and A. M. Filomafitskii. He was a student of professors I. F. Moier and I. F. Erdman.

In 1833 Inozemtsev defended his dissertation, 'De lithotomiae methode bilaterali', and then spent two years in Berlin, Dresden, and Vienna, training in the surgical clinics of I. Dieffenbach, A. Graefe, I. Rust, and others. From 1835 he was an adjunct professor, and from 1837 an ordinary professor of the department of practical (operative) surgery at the surgical clinic of Moscow University. In 1839–40 he undertook a second scientific assignment, visiting leading surgical and therapeutic clinics of Germany, France, and Italy.

From 1846 to 1859 Inozemtsev served as creator and director of the Moscow University surgical clinic. The program he developed there was one of the first in Russia to teach so-called 'applied or surgical anatomy'. He participated actively in the reforming of university clinical training. He was one of the founders of topographic anatomy and operative surgery as an independent research and teaching discipline, and developed an anatomical-physiological orientation in surgery. Inozemtsev used his own apartment to teach this orientation for out-patient admissions of the sick. He was the first in Russia to conduct an operation under ether (1 February 1847), and during the following four months undertook forty-two operations under ether.

Inozemtsev was a leading proponent of a conservative surgical approach, and spoke out against broadening the range of radical operations. He was known widely as a practical doctor, and treated the writers N. V. Gogol, N. M. Iazykov, and N. S. Turgenev, as well as General A. P. Ermolov and actor M. S. Shchekin.

He participated in the struggle with the cholera epidemic in 1847–48, and advised a complex infusion for the treatment of cholera, also using it for gastro-intestinal disorders. In the book *Ob anatomiko-patologicheskom znachenii kholery* [About the anatomical-pathological significance of cholera] (1847), he generalized his experience and gave a series of useful therapeutic recommendations.

He also introduced measures from folk medicine into therapeutic practice. In 1853 he proposed a complex infusion from rhubarb, which became known as 'Inozemtsev drops' and was used with success in gastrointestinal disorders for the lessening of pain and for peristalsis. This infusion was still employed in the USSR until the 1940s.

Inozemtsev was a strong supporter of treatment by milk, believing that it cured by acting on the central nervous system. In his monograph *O lechenii molokom prostudnykh i prostudnymi sopriazhennykh boleznei kholodno-likhoradochnogo svoistva* [About the treatment of milk for colds and cold-related illness with cold-fever qualities] (1857), he reported successfully treating with milk illnesses of the lungs, gastro-intestinal tract, skin, and nervous system. Thanks to Inozemtsev, treatment by milk was broadly practiced by Russian doctors from the 1860s to the 1880s.

Inozemtsev was the founder, editor, and publisher of the *Moskovskaia meditsinskaia gazeta* [Moscow Medical Newspaper], launched in 1858 and published until 1878, and the organizer of the 'Society of Russian Doctors in Moscow' (1861). This society grew from his circle of friends and students and quickly became an influential public organization, promoting the rights of Russian doctors against the opposition of ethnic Germans. In 1861 Inozemtsev transferred the *Moscow Medical Newspaper* to the society. In 1865 he opened a clinic for nonresident patients.

Inozemtsev actively inculcated a whole generation of doctors, and indoctrinated them on humane relations with the patient. The range of memoirs concerning Inozemtsev is evidence of his popularity among his contemporaries and confirms his devotion to the idea of humanism.

Bibliography

Primary: Rossiiskaia gosudarstvennaia biblioteka [The Russian State Library]. Nauchno-issledovatel'skii otdel rukopisei [The Scientific-research department of manuscripts]. Fond 41, op. 162, d. 24; 10, 21, 129; d. 743; 31, 2; Ven. V. 150, 1; Pog-II, 14, 4–5 (Letters to M. Pogodin); chizh., 31, 18 (Letters to F. V. Chizhov) (Moscow).

Secondary: Mirskii, M. B., 2000. 'Fedor Inozemtsev—khirurg-konservator.' ['Fedor Inozemtsev—surgeon-conservative.'] *Istoricheskii vestnik Moskovskoi meditsinksii akademii imeni I.M. Sechenov*, XI: 147–159; Arkhangel'skii, G. V., 1959. *F.I. Inozemtsev i ego znachenie v razvitii russkoi meditsiny* [F. I. Inozemtsev and his significance in the development of Russian medicine] (Moscow); Guberti, N. N., 1898. 'Vospominaniia o F.I. Inozemtseve.' [Recollections about F. I. Inozemtsev] *Russkii arkhiv*, 2: 230–238; Smirnov, S. A., 1872. *Vospominaniia o Fedore Ivanoviche Inozemtseve* [Recollections about Fedor Ivanovich Inozemtsev] (Moscow).

Mikhail Poddubnyi

ISAAC ISRAELI (aka ISHAQ IBN SULAYMAN AL-ISRA'ILI, ISAAC JUDAEUS, ISAAC THE JEW)

(b. Egypt, c. 840; d. Tunisia, 932), *medicine, ophthalmology, philosophy.*

Not much is known about Isaac's life. His biographers, Ibn Gulgul and Sa'id, mention his Jewish origin, his renunciation of marriage, offspring and wealth, and his long life. Isaac started his career as an eye specialist in al-Fustat (Cairo). In his later years he worked at the Aglabidian court in Kairouan (Tunisia). After Ziyadat Allah III's death (r. 903–09), Isaac served the Fatimid successor Ubaid Allah al-Mahdi (r. 910–34) as his personal physician. In those years, Isaac had two promising pupils: the Jew Dunas Ibn Tamim and Constantine the African (Constantinus Africanus). The former took over Isaac's post, and the latter translated Ibn al-Gazzar's *Zad al-mustafir* [Medical Advice for Travelers] into Latin (along with the major medical works of Isaac); it was well known in medieval Europe under the title *Viaticum.*

Isaac's writings also treated ethical and philosophical topics. His four theoretical treatises (*Definitions and Descriptions, Spirit and Soul, The Substances, The Elements*) can be regarded as having established Jewish Neoplatonism. Isaac might also be the author of fifty aphorisms on medical ethics and decent behavior.

The huge number of citations in Isaac's writings shows his wide reading and his profound knowledge of ancient and current medical literature that, presumably, he had the luck to find in the library of Kairouan. He followed Hippocrates's concept of humoral pathology as explained in Galen's commentaries. To the concepts of Hippocrates and Galen, his main sources, Isaac added therapeutic recommendations of his own, thus combining theory and practice.

Since prevention was of great importance in ancient medicine, it is not surprising that Isaac wrote four volumes (about 1,200 hand-written pages) on dietetics in general, and on various kinds of food in detail. The legend of his living for 100 years might have been intended as proof of the effectiveness of his advice. Isaac was one of the first writers in Arabic whose works were translated into Latin. This enabled his comprehensive monograph, *Kitab al-Baul* (*Liber de urinis* [Book of Urine]), to have great influence in the West and prepare the way for the uptake of urinary analysis—the most common diagnostic method in medieval medicine. Isaac described the basic ideas of uroscopy, interpreting the variety of urine colors, compositions, suspended matter and sediment. For more than 500 years, his book was required reading at the universities, and as early as the late thirteenth century, the text even found its way into the German vernacular.

Isaac's *Book on Fevers* made him a celebrity among Arabic scholars. The author himself regarded it as his most precious estate. The book was divided into five parts. First, Isaac dealt with the nature and cause of fever in general; then he wrote about the 'one day fever'. The third chapter described the 'hectic fever', or consumption, and makes suggestions for its treatment, most of them derived from Isaac's own experience. The fourth chapter addressed acute fevers and their somatic and psychic complications, and the last chapter dealt with 'purulent' and 'putrid' fevers. Modern readers should not expect much equivalence with modern terms; the *Book on Fevers* was strictly based on the concept of four humors and their causal imbalance in the human body.

Bibliography

Primary: 1962. *Musar harofe'im, Guide for Physicians*, trans. Bar-Sela, Ariel and Hebbel Edward Hoff, 'Isaac Israeli's Fifty Admonitions to the Physicians.' *The Journal of the History of Medicine and*

Allied Sciences 17: 245–257; 1981. *Kitab al-Hummayat, Liber febrium, On Fevers.* Third discourse (On consumption), Latham, John D. and Haskell D. Isaacs, eds. and trans. (Cambridge); 1986. (Sezgin, Fuat, ed.) *Kitab al-Aghdhiya, Diaetae universales et particulares, Book on Dietetics* 3 vols. (Frankfurt am Main).

Secondary: Veit, Raphaela, 2003. *Das Buch der Fieber des Isaac Israeli und seine Bedeutung im lateinischen Westen* (Stuttgart); Sezgin, Fuat ed., 1996. *Ishaq ibn Sulayman al-Isra'ili. Texts and Studies* (Frankfurt am Main); Altmann, Alexander, and Samuel M. Stern, 1979. *Isaac Israeli, a Neoplatonic Philosopher of the Early 10th Century* (Westport, CT).

Ortrun Riha

IUDIN, SERGEI SERGEEVICH (b. Moscow, Russia, 27 September [9 October] 1891; d. Moscow, Russia, 12 June 1954), *surgery.*

A great surgeon whose reputation spread far beyond the boundaries of the USSR, Iudin was born into a big family of famous Russian Orthodox merchants. His father was a technical director of a factory and provided a very good education for all of his four sons and three daughters. Sergei was the eldest. He studied foreign languages with home tutors, and every summer traveled to Europe to improve his linguistic knowledge. The Iudins had a home zoo and home laboratories for the children, who also played violin and sang in chorus together.

In 1911 Iudin graduated from the Second Moscow Gymnasium and entered the department of natural sciences at Moscow University, moving into the medical faculty the following year. The gynecological clinic of professor A. Gubarev and the surgical clinic of professor R. Venglovsky were his favorite places at that time.

World War I interrupted Iudin's education and changed his plans. He joined the Russian Army as a physician (1914) and was wounded three times. One of these injuries involved the spine and rendered him paralyzed and bedridden for nine months. However, Iudin came back to military service and served at Tula hospital. In 1916 he passed his exams and received a diploma from Moscow University.

The years after the Bolshevik Revolution (1917) were devoted to intensive medical practice in the Zakharino hospital for disabled Russian soldiers returning from the front. Because the hospital was not far from Moscow, its staff could maintain and improve existing professional contacts, as well as develop new ones. While working at Zakharino, Iudin invented devices for the immobilization and amputation of limbs, started writing his thesis on spinal anesthesia, and actively studied extensive thoracoplasty for chronic pleural empyema. Based on this last work, he was elected a member of the Russian Surgical Association.

In 1922 Iudin began his surgical sojourn at the hospital in Serpukhov (Moscow region). During these years he focused on the problems of anesthesia, visited A. Bier at his clinic in Germany and, after flirting with Braun's technique

Sergei Sergeevich Iudin. Cartoon by 'Kukryniksy', 1942. Image supplied by author.

for the solar plexus, published his first monograph, *Spinomozgovaia anesteziia. Istoriia, osnovanie, tekhnika i klinicheskaia otsenka metoda i ego primeneniia* [On spinal anesthesia] (Serpukhov, 1925), and dedicated it to Bier.

Iudin was one of the few Russian surgeons who managed, for professional reasons, to travel extensively following the Bolshevik Revolution. He eagerly acquainted himself with recent work and innovations of technique emanating from physicians of other countries. In 1926 he visited the United States and the clinics of G. W. Crile (Cleveland, Ohio), H. Cushing (Boston, Massachusetts), W. W. Babcock (Philadelphia, University of Pennsylvania), and John M. T. Finney (Baltimore, The Johns Hopkins Hospital). The Mayo Clinic invited Iudin to perform a gastrectomy, and the Russian surgeon received an offer to stay in the Unites States. Iudin refused because of his patriotism. After returning to Russia, he described his impressions from America in a series of articles that proved very popular among Soviet physicians (see *Novyi khirurgicheskii arkhiv*, 1927, vols. 12–14). Twenty years later, in 1948, these articles would be obliterated from Soviet libraries and their author arrested, accused of promoting the 'cult' of American medical achievements.

Despite working in the provinces to the end of the 1920s, Iudin became well known as a surgeon and famed for his innovations. Many visitors came to Serpukhov to observe his operations and to exchange ideas and techniques. Finally, in 1928, he was appointed to the famous Sklifossovskii Institute for Emergency Medicine at Moscow (formerly Sheremetiev Hospital) and was made the director of its surgery, a position he held for more than twenty years. Iudin's organizing abilities, dynamic energy, and excellent contacts helped to equip the Sklifossovskii surgery with modern medical equipment, post-operative wards, and special traumatological apartments. He was adored by the staff at the Sklifossovskii Institute as well as by his patients, among whom were foreign ambassadors, dignitaries and their wives, and members of the Soviet government.

Iudin performed intensive surgery on a wide range of operable conditions, but his main interest was the physiology and pathology of digestion, with special reference to perforated ulcers of the stomach and duodenum. The radical surgical treatment of acute perforated ulcers was one of his most brilliant conceptions. Motivated by the death in 1922 of the famous Russian theatrical producer, E. Vakhtangov, after two unsuccessful operations had been performed in Zakharino hospital by his colleagues, Iudin insisted on the resection of a part of the stomach together with the ulcer. By 1943 he had handled more than 2,000 cases of perforated ulcers and had performed more than 100 complete gastrectomies, including one such operation on his own mother.

In the first half of the twentieth century, the acceptance of surgery as a cure for peptic ulcer was widespread in the majority of Western countries. But many Soviet surgeons did not share this view and became Iudin's opponents. His *Etude sur les ulcéres gastriques et duodénaux perforés* was published in 1939 in Belgium. However, it was not published in the Soviet Union until 1955, after Iudin's death, when his students published the original version in Russian.

Iudin carefully followed all the innovations of his colleagues and was profoundly interested in the problems of blood transfusion, one of the most urgent topics in medical science at the beginning of the twentieth century. Blood studies developed intensively in Soviet Russia, too. In 1926 the Institute for Blood Transfusion was established in Moscow. In September 1928, at the Third Ukrainian Surgery Congress, V. Shamov announced the discovery (by himself and M. Kostuikov) that blood remained viable for use after remaining for eleven hours in the body of a dead animal. Iudin immediately noted this announcement, and after preparations on 23 March 1930, the same year K. Landsteiner received a Nobel Prize for discovering the first three blood groups, Iudin made the world's first transfusion of corpse blood. In 1933 his book *La transfusion du sang de cadavre a l'homme* was published in Paris. Before the beginning of World War II, Iudin constantly exchanged information and experiences of new cases of corpse-blood transfusion with Western colleagues who published reports in the Western medical press. In 1938 he reported about 2,500 successful cases. But not until 1962, after the death of both, did Iudin and Shamov receive the highest Soviet award, the Lenin Prize, for the development and introduction of corpse blood.

Esophagoplasty was another important initiative actively promoted by Iudin. He modified the technique of the operations of constriction and obstruction of the esophagus, suggested at the beginning of the twentieth century by E. Rou and P. Herzen, and invented a special instrument (a metal heart) and procedures for producing the artificial esophagus. Iudin advocated that a segment of small intestine be brought up in front of the sternum to replace the blocked esophagus; he preferred to 'bypass' the stomach at the abdominal termination of this new food tube and insert the intestinal esophagus into the jejunum. By 1947 Iudin completed 150 cases of full esophagoplasty and summarized the results in his monograph *Vosstanovitel'naia khirurgiia pri neprokhodimosti pishchevoda* [Restoration Surgery in Cases of Esophagus Obstruction] (1954).

World War II marked a new period in Iudin's personal and professional life. Despite a coronary thrombosis at the end of 1941, he was appointed a consulting surgeon at the front and feverishly wrote war-related manuals and bulletins for the instruction of those new to surgical practice. In 1942 Iudin received a Stalin Prize for his works on field medicine and the artificial esophagus; two years later he was elected a full member of the USSR Academy of Medical Sciences. With this full acknowledgment of Iudin's worthiness, he appeared to be established as a patriarch of Soviet medicine.

Iudin's personality was captivating; he was a poet, fisherman, and lover of all things beautiful. Not only medical students, close colleagues and patients adored him; so did a considerable number of the Russian artistic elite. He was portrayed many times with special reference to his long, thin, supple fingers and large, clever, attentive eyes. The great Iudin's contributions to medicine were recognized by colleagues throughout the world who elected him into medical professional societies in Europe and the United States.

Yet all his awards, national and international, did not save Iudin from the terrible persecution of Stalin's regime. On 22 December 1948, the eve of the Cold War, Iudin was arrested by the Soviet intelligence service and accused of espionage for Great Britain. The secret police prosecuted the surgeon for supposedly transferring files concerning corpse-blood transfusion, and for informal meetings with English journalists. Iudin spent more than three years in Moscow prisons. Finally, by extralegal decision (without court decree), he was deported to Siberia (Berdsk, Novosibirsk province) for a sentence of ten years. However, immediately after Stalin's death in March 1953, Iudin was discharged, fully rehabilitated, restored to all his ranks, and in the summer of 1953 he returned to Moscow. Unfortunately, just nine months later he passed away.

Bibliography

Primary: 1991. *Selected Papers* (Moscow); 1960. *Izbrannye proizvedeniia* [Selected Papers] Vols. 1–3 (Moscow); 1931. *L'Anesthésie locale pour les grandes opérations de l'estomac* (Paris); 1933. *La transfusion du sang de cadavre a l'homme.* Preface by Prof Gosset

(Paris); 1939. *Etude sur les ulcères gastriques et duodénaux perforés* (Brussels); 1968. *Razmyshleniia khirurga* [Surgeon's Reflections] (Moscow).

Secondary: Iudin, I. Iu., 2003. 'Preface' to Iudin, S. S. *Etiudy zheludochnoi khirurgii* [Studies of Stomach Surgery] (Moscow) pp. 5–31; Kulikovskaia, G., 1990. *Pravda o professore Iudine* [The Truth about Professor Iudin] (Moscow); Arapov, D. A., 1960. 'Zhizneopisanie S.S. Iudina' [The Life of S. S. Iudin] in Iudin, S. S. *Selected Papers* (Moscow) vol. 1, pp. 5–20.

Marina Sorokina

IZQUIERDO RAUDÓN, JOSÉ JOAQUÍN (b. Puebla, Mexico, 8 May 1893; d. Mexico City, Mexico, 16 January 1974), *physiology, history of medicine.*

Izquierdo Raudón was the eldest of four children of an esteemed aristocratic family in Puebla. As a child, he showed interest in reading and studied in prestigious private schools, such as San Pedro y San Pablo. He studied medicine at the Antiguo Colegio de Puebla (now the University of Puebla) and at the San Pedro y San Pablo Hospital. For financial and family reasons, he moved to Mexico City in 1917, where he studied the physiology of the Indians of Teotihuacán and high-elevation polyglobulia. As well, he began his career as professor of physiology at the National University's Medical School, which he never left, continuing to work there until his death.

In 1922 the Institute of Hygiene awarded Izquierdo a scholarship to study vaccinations in the United States, and the opportunity to visit physiology laboratories at Harvard, Cornell, Columbia, Johns Hopkins, and Pennsylvania universities. Later the Rockefeller Foundation funded his research in the physiology departments at Harvard, Cambridge, and Cologne, and in Marine Biology at Plymouth. Although he was always grateful to Joseph Barcroft and Walter Cannon, the work of French physiologist Claude Bernard (1813–78) exercised a profound influence on Izquierdo's career. Indeed, his translation of Bernard's *Introduction to the Study of Experimental Medicine* [*Introducción al Estudio de la Medicina Experimental*] is the finest one in Spanish.

Upon his return to Mexico, Izquierdo devoted all his efforts to modernizing the teaching of physiology. Although at the time Fernando Ocaranza had implanted what he called 'physiological thinking' in the Faculty of Medicine, there were no laboratories where students could practice, and the program did not include new topics in the discipline. Despite bureaucratic obstacles, Izquierdo succeeded in creating the Department of Physiology, modernizing the program of study, organizing experimental instruction, and equipping experimental laboratories. He was convinced that medicine had to be taught through experimentation, following the precepts of the scientific method as formulated by Bernard. In addition, he believed that physiology professors not only required solid training in their chosen field, but should also be adept field researchers. Students had to repeat crucial experiments related to cardiac functioning, digestion, the nervous system, and mechanisms of intoxication. More than just experimental physiology, Izquierdo promoted the actual discipline as he also organized laboratories dedicated to scientific research.

For 100 years (1857–1957), the School of Medicine occupied a beautiful, seventeenth-century building in Mexico City's Historical Center. Izquierdo participated in its move to the National University. He was allowed to plan the laboratories and classrooms according to his criteria. Also, he established a beautiful library with the best journals and books on physiology and medicine, and a collection of historical medical books from the sixteenth to the nineteenth centuries. A collection of Izquierdo's papers is held at the Archivo Histórico de la Facultad de Medicina (AHFM), Universidad Nacional Autónoma de México (UNAM), Mexico City.

Although trained as a physiologist, he stood out as a historian of science, known for his scrupulous use of sources, his rigorous references, the profundity and seriousness of his analyses, and his ability to consult texts in their original languages. He wrote prolifically in this field.

Izquierdo served as president of numerous scientific academies and societies in Mexico and belonged to many associations of physiology and the history of science.

Bibliography

Primary: 1934. *Balance cuatricentenario de la fisiología en México* (Mexico City); 1939. *Análisis experimental de los fenómenos fisiológicos fundamentales* (Mexico City); 1942. *Claudio Bernard, creador de la medicina científica* (Mexico City).

Secondary: Castañeda López, Gabriela, 2004. José Joaquín Izquierdo, 1893–1974. MA thesis; Rodríguez de Romo, Ana Cecilia, 1996. 'J. J. Izquierdo, historiador de la Medicina' in Rodríguez-Sala, M. L., and I. Guevara, eds., *Tres etapas del desarrollo de la cultura científico-tecnológica en México* (Mexico City) pp. 85–108.

Ana Cecilia Rodríguez de Romo

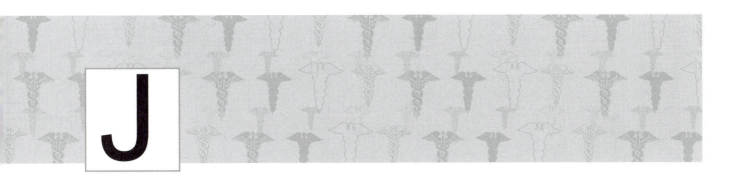

J

JACKSON, JAMES (b. Newburyport, Massachusetts, USA, 3 October 1777; d. Boston, Massachusetts, USA, 27 August 1867), *medicine.*

Jackson got his early education in Boston among a privileged cohort, attending Boston Latin School and later Harvard College. Upon his graduation from college in 1796, he briefly took a position teaching English at Leicester Academy but soon determined to pursue medicine. In the following year he attended a course of lectures at the Medical Institution of Harvard University; the larger part of his education, however, came through his two-year apprenticeship with Edward Augustus Holyoke, who was a son of the president of Harvard University and himself the first president of the Massachusetts Medical Society.

In 1799 Jackson learned that his brother, Henry, was to captain the *Thomas Russell* sailing for London and that Jackson could have free passage. Jackson stayed abroad a year, studying anatomy at Guy's and St Thomas's hospitals and renewing an acquaintance with his college friend, the future surgeon John Collins Warren, who was also in England studying. Jackson's arrival in London immediately followed the publication of Edward Jenner's famous study of vaccination to prevent smallpox. Jackson made his way to the Smallpox and Inoculation Hospital at St Pancras, where he learned the new technique under the tutelage of William Woodville.

On his return to Boston, Jackson quickly spread word of his experience with vaccination and established a local rep-

utation that earned him a notable $150 in his first month of practice. He became a promoter of vaccination and a source for the precious vaccine-material. Still, Jackson was only twenty-five, a newcomer to Boston's medical community, and he sagely chose to ally himself with a more senior physician, Benjamin Waterhouse, who was an early and ardent champion of vaccination in Boston.

As Jackson established his practice, he also became a leader in reforming medical education. In 1802 he obtained a position at the charitable Boston Dispensary serving the city's poor. Part of this arrangement included the ability to offer clinical instruction for medical students at the Dispensary. In 1809 Jackson obtained a similar position at the Leverett Street Almshouse. When Harvard set out to reorganize its medical school and moved it to a new location in Boston, Jackson was able to combine these posts and provide the systematic clinical instruction that was difficult to offer to an apprentice in a private medical office.

Meanwhile, Jackson had joined with his friend and classmate John C. Collins to set up a new proprietary hospital for the city. They had already proven their collaborative skills in the shared project reforming the Massachusetts Medical Society beginning in 1802. In 1810 they sent out a letter soliciting contributions for the foundation of Massachusetts General Hospital, thus inaugurating the city's preeminent medical institution. Jackson was appointed in 1812 as the Hershey Professor of Physic at Harvard Medical

School, succeeding the first occupant of the position, Benjamin Waterhouse. This appointment permitted the early alignment of the hospital and medical school. The war with Britain in 1812 delayed development of Massachusetts General. But when the doors of the new hospital finally opened in 1821, Jackson had charge of medicine and Collins of surgery.

Among Jackson's contributions to medical scholarship, the most frequently cited is his clarifying observation on nerve damage resulting from chronic alcohol abuse, which he published in 1822. As a popular medical educator, he also penned the widely celebrated *Lectures to a Young Physician*.

Bibliography

Primary: 1822. 'On a peculiar disease resulting from the use of ardent spirits.' *New England Journal of Medicine and Surgery* 11: 351–353; 1855. *Letters to a Young Physician* (Boston).

Secondary: Putnam, James Jackson, 1905. *A Memoir of Dr. James Jackson: with sketches of his father, Hon. Jonathan Jackson* (Boston); *DAMB*.

Christopher Crenner

JACKSON, JOHN HUGHLINGS   (b. Providence Green, Green Hammerton, York, England, 4 April 1835; d. London, England, 7 October 1911), *neurology*.

Born to Yorkshire yeoman farmer and brewer Samuel Jackson and his Welsh wife, Sarah Hughlings, the youngest of five children, Jackson had a rudimentary education in local small schools. He apprenticed to a local physician, Dr Anderson, who was a lecturer in a small York medical school that had been attended seven years earlier by Jonathan Hutchinson (1828–1913). He then studied under James Paget (1814–99) at St Bartholomew's Hospital in London, qualifying MRCS and LSA (1856), and later received his MD from St Andrew's.

Early Career

On returning home to work at the York Dispensary, he was influenced by Thomas Laycock (1812–76), who had an interest in neurology and consciousness. Jackson had a growing interest in philosophy and was impressed, as was Charles Darwin, with Herbert Spencer's concept of evolution and dissolution. He was considering changing careers to move toward philosophy, but when he was introduced to Hutchinson in London, he was persuaded to stay in medicine. Charles Édouard Brown-Séquard (1817–94) encouraged him to focus his interest on neurology and made him aware of a vacancy at the recently opened National Hospital for the Paralysed and Epileptic in Queen Square, where Brown-Séquard was the senior physician. Hutchinson became a close friend and provided Jackson with funding to join his medical publishing venture, the *Medical Times and Gazette*, which produced a series of papers on interesting medical cases.

John Hughlings Jackson. Halftone reproduction from James Taylor (ed.), *Selected Writings of John Hughlings Jackson*, London, 1931–32. Wellcome Library, London.

He was associated with four hospitals. The National Hospital for the Paralysed and Epileptic, founded by the Chandler sisters in 1860, provided him with access to neurological cases for forty-five years. Many of his early contributions to the medical literature were in ophthalmology from his experience at Moorfield's Eye Hospital, where he was an early proponent and instructor in the use of the ophthalmoscope. At the London Hospital and the Metropolitan Free Hospital, he had access to many patients, and at the London Hospital, he taught pathology and the use of the microscope, which was just finding a general place in hospital practice. He obtained clinical material and experience from each institution, which became the basis of his writings. He was a master at clinical observation, but rather than describing cases, he wished to develop concepts of organization and functioning of the nervous system. He was elected FRS in 1878.

Jackson's Writings and Concepts

Jackson's approach was to observe carefully and in detail the patients he saw, aiming to understanding the underlying mechanism at a time when neurology was characterized by cataloging neurological features and classifying diseases.

He was more interested in exploring broad ideas about the organization and hierarchy of the nervous system made evident when disease altered function. He brought Spencer's hypothesis of evolution and dissolution to an understanding of how the nervous system evolved and broke down in disease, thus providing a broad framework for the empirical descriptions provided by his colleagues. Others were good at finding facts, he said, but he wanted to provide a unified structure, a doctrine that harmonized the many observations about how the brain worked.

He outlined the organization of the nervous system into levels, from the most primitive and simple, mainly involved with reflex action (cord, medulla, and pons), to the middle Rolandic region and to the highest level in the prefrontal cortex. Each level would have a representation of the level below it. His framework for function in the nervous system included the evolutionary concepts of evolution and dissolution, the compensatory mechanisms the brain might use when damage occurs, the localization patterns in the brain and the degree of laterality of various functions, and the development of speech and patterns of speech abnormality in neurological disease.

He devoted a great deal of time to understanding epilepsy and how the patterns of excessive periodic discharges provided a means of explaining how the brain was organized and functioned, adopting Robert Bentley Todd's earlier ideas. His best-known case of epilepsy was his wife, who developed a pattern of marching epileptic movements after a cerebral thrombosis, which he called uncinate seizures and which Charcot renamed Jacksonian seizures. He conceptualized the idea of graduation of movements from voluntary to involuntary, evolution from automatic to purposeful movements, and dissolution from purposeful to the automatic.

He wrote over 300 papers, often publishing them in obscure journals. As he drafted his papers, each rewrite would be longer and longer because he was fearful of making unwarranted claims. He would explain each idea in more complex and detailed descriptions, often repeating the argument in different ways so that the reader might be unsure if he was repeating a concept or pursuing a new idea. His writings are often verbose, repetitive, and unclear, punctuated by long footnotes. He took eleven pages to define the word 'epilepsy'. He took pains to credit the ideas and work of others, including his students.

He resisted writing a book, saying that his colleagues would find him out. Sir William Osler (1849–1919), Silas Weir Mitchell (1829–1914), and James Putnam (1846–1918) wrote to encourage him to publish a collection of his writings, but he answered that many of his writings were likely outdated. A collection would only appear many years after his death.

It is interesting that his obtuse and obscurely published writing was so popular. One reason was that there was a growing cadre of bright neurological clinicians who knew they were in a vibrant and advancing field, and they understood Jackson's ideas. Individuals such as Charles Édouard Brown-Séquard, William Gowers (1845–1915), Jean-Martin Charcot (1825–93), David Ferrier (1843–1928), and Henry Head (1861–1940) were in awe of Jackson's capacity to explain brain function and broadcast his ideas widely.

Later Career

Despite his dislike of socializing, he was courteous to his colleagues and students, who referred to him as 'The Sage' and regarded him warmly. He involved many clinicians in discussions of his cases, forming a 'committee' to address phenomena that interested him. He wrote clear instructions to the registrar for experiments and tests on the patients under study. However, he was not a good lecturer, and his weak voice and need to explain were tiresome, so his lectures were poorly attended. On the other hand, he did not think lectures were the way to learn medicine and believed that students should learn by observation and experience with real patients on the wards.

As a member of the London consulting community, he tended to go his own way, applying himself entirely to his work. He did collaborate on the formation of the journal *Brain* (1878), becoming one of the first editors. He also initiated the Neurological Society (1885) and as the first president delivered the address 'On the Scope and Aims of Neurology'. In 1911 this organization became the neurology section of the Royal Society of Medicine.

He delivered the Gulstonian, Croonian, and Lumleian lectures to the RCP and was awarded the Moxon medal. Among other honors, he received honorary degrees from Yorkshire, Glasgow, Leeds, Bologna, and Edinburgh universities.

On his retirement (1894) a portrait by Lance Calkin was unveiled, and his former teacher Sir James Paget remarked that he provided 'lucidity to physiology and guidance to surgery'. In 1907 a bust by Herbert Hampton was presented to the National Hospital, Queen Square, by subscribers.

Personal Life

When Jackson moved to London, he lived at Finsbury Circus, moved a number of times, and settled at 3 Manchester Square after his marriage (1885) to his first cousin, the accomplished Elizabeth Dade. After she died, he was a lonely widower, and he led an increasingly eccentric solitary life.

His restlessness and fear of boredom were legendary, and he apparently left the theater, dining tables, or meetings after a short time. He would sometimes see the first act of a play and return another night to see act two, but never stayed or returned for act three. He read constantly but indiscriminately: important novelists or works of philosophy, pulp novels, and 'any rubbish that was handy'. He would tear sheets from the books as he read, tossing the pages aside as he walked or traveled in his carriage. He didn't consider whether the books belonged to him or his friends. It is often told that he would tear the cover off a book and split it in two, putting one half in each jacket pocket, to be further stripped as he read. In company he would often excuse himself and begin reading.

He had no interest in socializing or social events and no hobbies. He had little interest in cultural pursuits or sports and claimed he was grateful that his educational and intellectual interests were limited because it gave him greater focus for his work. It was said that on a nice day he would invite a registrar to ride in his carriage to discuss patients, but would then let him out somewhere in the city, from where he would have to make his way back to the hospital. He loved sitting by a fire and would do so even in the summer, yet he didn't mind the cold and seldom wore a coat.

In his later years he became increasingly deaf, suffering from migraines and vertigo. He died of pneumonia and was buried in Highgate Cemetery. His obituary in the *British Medical Journal* unusually ran to five pages. Many eponymous awards, lectureships, and prizes followed.

Jackson's Legacy

In 1935, the centenary of his birth, there was a publication of a Hughlings Jackson memorial volume and many lectures devoted to his work, all indicating that his ideas had advanced neurology remarkably and still stood the test of time. The two-volume collection of his works totals over 1,000 pages with sixty-nine of his more than 300 articles selected to put forward his most important ideas.

His writings are difficult for the current reader, as they were for the readers of his time, but the basic concepts changed how neurologists saw the nervous system and changed the course of neurology. He is referred to as the 'Father of British Neurology', but more often as the 'Father of Modern Neurology', an indication of his stature among his colleagues.

Bibliography

Primary: 1925. (Taylor, J., ed.) *Neurological Fragments of J. Hughlings Jackson* (London); 1931-1932. (Taylor, J., ed.) *Selected Writings of John Hughlings Jackson*, 2 vols. (London) (Vol. 2 includes a bibliography of his work).

Secondary: Critchley, M., and Eileen Critchley, 1998. *John Hughlings Jackson: Father of English Neurology* (Oxford); Dewhurst, Kenneth, 1982. *Hughlings Jackson on Psychiatry* (Oxford); Lassek, A. M., 1970. *The Unique Legacy of Doctor Hughlings Jackson* (Springfield, IL); Lennox, W. G., 1970. 'Hughlings Jackson' in Webb, Haymaker, and Francis Schiller, eds., *Founders of Neurology*, 2nd edn., (Springfield, IL) pp. 456–459; Broadbent, W., 1903. 'Hughlings Jackson as a Pioneer in Nervous Physiology and Pathology.' *Brain* 26: 305–336; *DSB*; *Oxford DNB*.

Jock Murray

JACOBI, ABRAHAM (b. Hartum, Westphalia, Germany, 6 May 1830; d. Bolton Landing, New York, USA, 10 July 1919), *medicine, pediatrics.*

Jacobi was the son of working-class parents: Eleaser Jacobi, a cattle trader, and Julie Jacobi, a shopkeeper in the village of Hartum. They were a secularized family of German Jewish descent. As a young man, Abraham studied in the gymnasium near Minden. He then studied at the University of Greifswald and at Göttingen University and received his MD at the University of Bonn in 1851. He was an activist during the German revolutions of 1848 and joined Karl Marx's Communist League. Jacobi was arrested in 1851, was tried at the Cologne Communist Trial, and spent two years in prison. Upon release, he fled to Great Britain, where he stayed with Karl Marx in London and Friedrich Engels in Manchester. After struggling to establish a medical practice, he decided to leave for the United States and arrived in Boston in 1853. He soon moved to New York City and set up a practice in the German district of the Lower East Side, Kleindeutschland. Jacobi began work at the German Dispensary of New York, where he joined other like-minded German physicians to provide free health care to poor families in the community. He established the Children's Clinic at the Dispensary, the first of its kind in America. Here, Jacobi began a long career that combined pediatric medicine with social reform, becoming the American 'Father of Pediatrics'.

During his early years in New York, Jacobi set out to create specialized health care for children while maintaining his involvement in socialist politics. He became a member of the German labor movement and a leader in the American Worker's League. He soon gave most of his political energy to medical reform. Most influenced by the German physician Rudolf Virchow, Jacobi pursued a rational therapeutic model based on physiological and cellular pathology. Also like Virchow, he saw a direct connection between poverty and disease, believing that the roots of childhood illness rested in social inequality. As Russell Viner has shown, Jacobi believed that medicine and politics were inseparable and went on to develop a pediatric specialty based on socialist, democratic, and egalitarian principles.

Jacobi built a strong reputation as a physician and became involved in the medical reform movement at mid-century, arguing for the integration of physiological and chemical sciences into medical school curricula. He also set out to create at medical schools a discipline focused on children's health and with that a system of therapeutics based on identifying specific diseases and treatments for children. He received his first faculty appointment as professor of infantile pathology and therapeutics at the New York Medical College (1860–64), the first chair of diseases of children in the United States. Jacobi then moved to the University of the City of New York (1865–70). But it was during his long career at Columbia, as professor of the diseases of children at the College of Physicians and Surgeons

Abraham Jacobi. Halftone reproduction from *Medical Life* 1928, vol. 35 (no. 5). Wellcome Library, London.

from 1870 to 1902, that he was most productive in building a foundation for his specialty. Also in these years, he served on the staff at several New York hospitals, including the German Hospital (Lenox Hill); Mount Sinai Hospital, where he was a founder of the pediatric department; the Nursery and Child's Hospital; and Roosevelt Hospital.

Jacobi was instrumental in the founding of pediatric journals and medical societies. In 1868 he helped start the *American Journal of Obstetrics and the Diseases of Women and Children.* He went on to be the first chair of the Section on Diseases of Children of the American Medical Association and founded the Section for Pediatrics of the New York Academy of Medicine. He was also a founding member of the American Pediatric Society in 1888. Jacobi held leadership positions in several medical societies, serving as President of the American Pediatric Society (twice), the New York Academy of Medicine, the American Medical Association, the Association of American Physicians, and the American Climatologic Association, among others. While president of the New York County Medical Society, he met his third wife in 1871, physician Mary C. Putnam Jacobi (1842–1906).

Abraham Jacobi's first wife, Fanny Meyer, was a fellow German radical who followed him to New York. Their first and only child, Julius, died of meningitis in 1855, and Fanny died one year later in childbirth. He lost his second wife, Kate Rosalie, in 1871 because of complications of a miscarriage; the couple had already lost four children. In 1873 he married Mary Putnam, who shared his interest in socialism, scientific medicine, and political activism. The couple had a professional and political partnership that lasted more than three decades. Pediatric medicine was also a very personal matter for the Jacobis. Their first child died a day after her birth in 1874, but their next two children, Ernst and Marjorie, survived past infancy. Ernst, however, died at age seven of diphtheria, a disease his father had studied and combated in the city for several years. Losing seven children in his lifetime, Abraham Jacobi's personal experiences with childhood death remained an important influence on his professional work.

Jacobi was one of the most prolific writers of his time on pediatric medicine, authoring numerous articles and books on a variety of subjects, including hygiene, tuberculosis, typhoid fever, and influenza. His *Treatise on Diphtheria* (1880) was one of the main sources on the prevention, control, and treatment of the disease, until the coming of bacteriology; at first Jacobi rejected simple bacteriological explanations for diphtheria and lamented 'bacteriomania', but he later reconsidered his position. Jacobi also focused a great deal of his work on childhood nutrition. In response to the high disease and mortality rate of infants linked to diet, particularly cholera infantum, Jacobi developed a treatise on the subject. In *Infant Diet* (1873), he argued that breast milk was the absolute best source of nutrition for infants, followed by diluted and specially treated cow's milk. One year later, Mary Putnam Jacobi helped him revise the text for 'popular use' and became active in pediatric medicine herself. *Infant Diet* was an effort to make nutritional information easy and accessible and to improve the material conditions, and thus the survival rate, of poor children through securing their diets. In the early 1890s, Abraham Jacobi was involved in the development of milk stations in New York and contributed to the expansion of several public health programs for children. He helped develop a 'Summer Corps' of physicians to treat poor children in the tenements and joined in the child welfare movements, participating in the Society for the Prevention of Cruelty to Children.

Beyond his medical activism, Jacobi applied his socialist principles to new movements and political concerns in the American context. During the Civil War era, Jacobi supported the Republicans, condemning slavery and allying himself with his close friend and fellow German émigré, Carl Schurz. He went on to associate himself with many social science and Progressive era programs, including tenement-house reform, restrictions on child labor, and antituberculosis campaigns. Most of all, Jacobi concentrated his political activism within the content, practice, policies, and research of pediatric medicine itself, arguing that the pediatrician was as important as the politician in the progress of reform and the maintenance of democracy.

Abraham Jacobi is remembered as the most important leader in the founding of American pediatrics. His biography reveals the significant influence of German immigration on American medicine. Jacobi is counted among the great figures of post–Civil War medicine and is revered for successfully merging scientific ideals with child welfare. Several New York hospitals at one time have had children's wards named in his honor, and Jacobi Hospital in the Bronx still bears his name. Abraham Jacobi died in 1919, after a very long career, at the age of eighty-nine.

Bibliography

Primary: 1874. *Infant Diet; Revised, Enlarged, and Adapted to Popular Use by Mary Putnam Jacobi, M.D.* (New York); 1880. *Treatise on Diphtheria* (New York); 1893. *Aufsätze, Vorträge, und Reden* (New York); 1909. (Robinson, William J., ed.) *Doctor Jacobi's Works: Collected Essays, Addresses, Scientific Papers, and Miscellaneous Writing* (New York).

Secondary: Hammonds, Evelyn, 1999. *Childhood's Deadly Scourge: The Campaign to Control Diphtheria in New York City, 1880–1930* (Baltimore); Viner, Russell, 1998. 'Abraham Jacobi and German Medical Radicalism in Antebellum New York.' *Bulletin of the History of Medicine* 72: 434–463; Viner, Russell, 1997. 'Healthy Children for a New World: Abraham Jacobi and the Making of American Pediatrics.' PhD dissertation, University of Cambridge; Harvey, Joy, 1996. 'Clanging Eagles: The Marriage and Collaboration between Two Nineteenth-Century Physicians, Mary Putnam Jacobi and Abraham Jacobi' in Pycior, Helena M., Nancy G. Slack, and Pnina G. Abir-Am, eds., *Creative Couples in the Sciences* (New Brunswick, NJ) pp. 185–195; *DAMB*.

Carla Bittel

JACOBI, MARY CORINNA PUTNAM (b. London, England, 31 August 1842; d. New York, New York, USA, 10 June 1906), *medicine, pediatrics, women's health.*

Mary Corinna Putnam was the first child of New York publisher George Palmer Putnam and his wife, Victorine Haven Putnam. Born in London, she moved back to the United States with her family in 1848 and grew up in the rural suburbs of New York. Although she was raised in the world of letters, Putnam decided to pursue a medical education and studied at three institutions. She received her first degree from the New York College of Pharmacy (1863) and then her first MD from the Female (later Woman's) Medical College of Pennsylvania (1864). She served briefly as an intern at the New England Hospital for Women and Children in Boston. To strengthen her education, Putnam traveled to Paris and was the first woman admitted to the École de Médecine, graduating with high honors and her second MD in 1871. Shortly afterward, she returned to New York City, where

Mary Putnam Jacobi. Halftone reproduction from *Mary Putnam Jacobi, M.D, a Pathfinder in Medicine . . .*, **New York, 1925. Wellcome Library, London.**

she first set up a private practice. Putnam quickly turned her attention to teaching, serving as a lecturer and then professor of materia medica and therapeutics at the Woman's Medical College of the New York Infirmary from 1871 to 1889. Later, she also taught at the New York Post-Graduate Medical School, giving lectures on Diseases of Women and Children from 1882 to 1885. For thirty years, she practiced medicine in Manhattan, working as an attending physician at the New York Infirmary, establishing the Pediatric Clinic at Mt Sinai, and serving as a visiting physician at St Mark's Hospital. She simultaneously conducted experimental research and published nine books and over 120 articles on a wide range of topics. One of the leading women physicians of her time, she fought to expand women's medical education and had a long career of political activism that went hand in hand with medicine.

Mary Putnam Jacobi devoted a large portion of her career to studying the health of women. Her most significant medical studies challenged prevailing ideas about the pathological nature of the female body. Her physiological and neurological studies argued that women were physically and mentally capable of being active members in the public sphere. She is most famous for her essay *The Question of Rest for Women During Menstruation* (1877), winner of the Harvard Boylston Prize in 1876. She also studied hysteria, the 'female malady' of the nineteenth century, condemning the rest cure and advocating therapies based on mental and physical activity. Jacobi also studied anemia, uterine and ovarian diseases, and several other diseases of women and children. A vocal supporter of scientific models of medicine, she favored a close connection between laboratory studies and clinical care and advocated many forms of experimentalism, including vivisection.

Jacobi's work as a physician and researcher was closely tied to her role as a political activist, for matters of health intertwined with questions about the status of women. She worked on behalf of women's higher education and co-education in American medical schools and was particularly active in the call for the admission of women to the medical schools at Harvard and Johns Hopkins. In addition, she played a strong role in promoting women in the medical profession, holding leadership positions in several societies, such as the Association for the Advancement of the Medical Education of Women, the Women's Medical Association of New York City, and the Alumnae Association of the Woman's Medical College of Pennsylvania. In the latter half of her career, Jacobi teamed up with activists such as Florence Kelley and Josephine Shaw Lowell in the Consumer's League to advocate for improved conditions for working women. She also became a leader in the struggle for woman suffrage, leading the New York State campaign in the 1890s, and was furthermore deeply interested in the health and welfare of children.

After returning from Paris in 1871, Putnam met Abraham Jacobi, the eminent physician and socialist regarded later as the 'Father of Pediatrics' in America. They married in 1873 and had two children. The couple became intellectual and political partners and shared a lifelong commitment to using medicine for social reform. They collaborated on *Infant Diet* (1874), a manual of childhood nutrition, composed originally by Abraham and revised for 'popular use' by Mary. Childhood illness became a personal matter for the Jacobis when their only son, Ernst, died of diphtheria, after Abraham had fought to control the disease in the city for years. Moreover, both physicians believed children's health was of great social and political consequence.

Mary Putnam Jacobi was one of the most distinguished and important women physicians of the late nineteenth century, remembered for her impressive medical training, her high standards for medical education, her extensive body of research and writing, and her advocacy of science in medicine. Jacobi was highly respected beyond the women's medical community, and she earned the support of many medical men, who welcomed her into the profession's most prestigious medical societies. She was a member of the New York County Medical Society, the Medical Library and Journal Association, the New York Pathologi-

cal Society, the New York Neurological Society, and the Therapeutical Society of New York; she was also the first woman admitted to the New York Academy of Medicine, and she chaired its Section on Neurology. Moreover, she applied her medical knowledge to offer new interpretations of female physiology and used her credentials as a physician to advocate for women's rights. She stood as an important symbol of women's ability to practice medicine and carry out rigorous scientific work. She died in 1906 from a meningeal tumor.

Bibliography

Primary: 1877. *The Question of Rest for Women During Menstruation* (New York); 1925. *Life and Letters of Mary Putnam Jacobi* (New York); 1925. (Women's Medical Association of New York City, ed.) *Pathfinder in Medicine* (New York).

Secondary: Wells, Susan, 2001. *Out of the Dead House: Nineteenth-Century Women Physicians and the Writing of Medicine* (Madison, WI); Harvey, Joy, 1996. 'Clanging Eagles: The Marriage and Collaboration between Two Nineteenth-Century Physicians, Mary Putnam Jacobi and Abraham Jacobi' in Pycior, Helena M., Nancy G. Slack, and Pnina G. Abir-Am, eds., *Creative Couples in the Sciences* (New Brunswick, NJ) pp. 185–195; Morantz-Sanchez, Regina, 1985. *Sympathy and Science: Women Physicians in American Medicine* (New York); *DAMB*.

Carla Bittel

JACOBS, ALETTA HENRIETTE   (b. Sappemeer, the Netherlands, 9 February 1854; d. Baarn, the Netherlands, 10 August 1929), *general practice, women's rights.*

Jacobs was born the eighth daughter of eleven children of a Jewish country doctor, Abraham Jacobs, and his wife, Anna Jacobs-de Jongh. By the age of six Jacobs had decided that she wanted to become a doctor as well. She compensated for the lack of formal education available to girls by taking the assistant pharmacist exam in 1870. The following year she wrote a letter to the liberal prime minister, Johan Rudolf Thorbecke, asking permission to enter the University of Groningen. At first, Thorbecke granted her only provisional permission. One year later, and two days before he died, he converted this into a formal assent.

After her medical studies in Groningen and Amsterdam, Jacobs earned her state license as general practitioner in 1878. On 8 March 1879 in Groningen, she defended her doctoral thesis on localization in the brain. Immediately afterward, she left for a postgraduate stay in London, where each morning she visited the Hospital for Sick Children in Great Ormond Street. In addition, she attended lectures and practical training sessions for the students of the London School of Medicine for Women in the Royal Free Hospital. She was also a regular visitor at the small hospital for women in Marylebone Road, supervised by Elizabeth Garrett Anderson, the second woman to officially register as a doctor in the United Kingdom.

At the international medical conference in Amsterdam in September 1879, Jacobs was widely acclaimed and decided to stay in the Netherlands. The general practice she opened in Amsterdam immediately attracted many female patients; at the time, the treatment of men by women doctors was still taboo. In 1882 she started a free clinic for poor women and children in the slums of Amsterdam. During this period she introduced the contraceptive device of the German doctor Mensinga, the pessary still known as 'the Dutch cap'. In 1898 Jacobs published a popular book on the female body (*De vrouw*). In the 1920s she earned world fame for her activities in this area, in great part thanks to the American birth control movement, which honored her as a pioneer.

In 1884 she engaged in a 'free marriage' with the politician and merchant, Carel Victor Gerritsen. He was active in radical politics, at first in Amsterdam, later on a national level. In 1892 their marriage became official, and a year later Aletta Jacobs gave birth to a child that lived for only one day. In 1905, just after his reelection to Parliament, Gerritsen died.

Perhaps Jacobs's most important contribution to the world was her continuous effort on behalf of women's rights. In 1883 her attempt to register as a voter was turned down by the authorities. She fought her case all the way to the High Court (the Supreme Court of the Netherlands), but to no avail. In 1894 she helped found the Dutch Women's Suffrage Association, and became its president in 1903. In this function—which she held until Dutch women earned active suffrage in 1919—she worked tirelessly, including travel to Africa, Asia, China, and Japan in 1911–12.

Jacobs translated two major feminist works into Dutch: Charlotte Perkins Gilman's *Women and Economics,* and Olive Schreiner's *Woman and Labour.* She herself wrote miscellaneous essays on subjects such as women's labor, the women's movement, prostitution, and peace. In 1915 she took the initiative for a Women's Conference at The Hague. The final decision of this conference—to present its resolutions to the governments of belligerent and neutral countries—brought Jacobs before the Pope and the president of the United States.

Bibliography

Primary: 1898. *De vrouw, haar bouw en haar inwendige organen. Een populaire schets* (Deventer); 1899. *Vrouwenbelangen* (Amsterdam); 1924. *Herinneringen* (Amsterdam) [Harriet Feinberg, ed., and Wright, Annie, trans., 1996. *Memories. My Life as an International Leader in Health, Suffrage, and Peace* (New York)].

Secondary: Bosch, Mineke, 2005. *Een onwrikbaar geloof in rechtvaardigheid. Aletta Jacobs, 1854–1929* (Amsterdam); Bosch, Mineke, 1999. 'Colonial Dimensions of Dutch Women's Suffrage. Travel Letters from Africa and Asia.' *Journal of Women's History* 11(2): 8–34; Bosch, Mineke (with Annemarie Kloosterman), 1990. *Politics and Friendship. Letters from the International Woman Suffrage Alliance, 1902–1943* (Columbus, OH).

Mineke Bosch

JAMOT, EUGÈNE (b. Saint-Sulpice-les-Champs, Creuse, France, 14 November 1879; d. Saint-Sulpice-les-Champs, 26 April 1937), *medicine, bacteriology.*

The brilliant son of a Limousin farming family, Jamot taught in an Algiers secondary school before finishing his medical degree at Montpellier (1908). After two years as a rural physician near his birthplace, he enrolled in the Pharo, the French military's school of tropical medicine in Marseilles. A suspended sentence for assaulting his mother's second husband prompted this abrupt change in career.

As a new medical officer in the French colonial health service, Jamot traveled to Chad in French Equatorial Africa (FEA) as a physician in a medical battalion (1911). Upon his return to France, he studied at the Pasteur Institute in Paris, where he first encountered the trypanosome protozoa which caused trypanosomiasis, or sleeping sickness.

Appointed director of the Pasteur Institute in Brazzaville, capital of FEA, in 1916, Jamot persuaded Governor-General Merlin that only an all-out campaign carried to the remotest corners of the vast French colony would succeed in eradicating trypanosomiasis. Between 1917 and 1919 Jamot traveled many thousands of miles, treating more than 5,300 cases of trypanosomiasis from among 100,000 people examined. News of Jamot's success spread widely. By 1922 he had created his own center at Ayos, Cameroun, and was ready to launch a full attack on the disease, using what soon became known as the Jamot method of 'mobile medicine'.

The Ayos training center prepared doctors, nurses, and sanitary agents to follow the Jamot motto: 'go everywhere'. Seven teams of 400 members, each armed with up to fourteen microscopes, fanned out to virtually every corner of FEA. The plan called for the transmission of trypanosomiasis to be eliminated by recurring visits. By 1931 Jamot was able to state that he and his teams had eliminated the disease as a major health threat in FEA.

Not all ventures were successful. One disaster occurred in Bafia, Cameroun (1931), when a young physician administered too strong a dose of Atoxyl, a powerful arsenic-based medication, and almost 900 Africans went blind. Though not informed by the doctor of what had transpired, Jamot took the blame, and was sentenced to house arrest in Dakar for several weeks. Africans often resisted Jamot's teams, dreading Atoxyl and the lumbar punctures, which constituted part of the testing for the presence of trypanosomes.

Jamot was outspoken and brash, and several times incurred the ire of the colonial administration. He criticized the harsh labor recruitment practices of the French regime, and of private concessionaire companies involved in rubber gathering. He was also shocked to find the health service had not even begun to address such basic public health problems as syphilis, leprosy, and tuberculosis. He believed that good medical care for Africans was equitable compensation for the spread of trypanosomiasis caused in part by France's conquest and early colonial rule. His private reports to the French colonial administration were suppressed for fear of international criticism.

Having worn out his welcome in FEA, Jamot turned his attention (1931–32) to trypanosomiasis in French West Africa (FWA). With a minuscule budget and at the age of fifty-three, Jamot again traveled widely, identifying 70,000 sufferers, of whom 37,000 lived in what is now western Burkina Faso.

When a 1934 French sanitary conference at Bobo-Dioulasso rejected Jamot's call for an autonomous and permanent trypanosomiasis service for FWA, Jamot, sick and unhappy, retired to France, where he died three years later. His warnings proved correct. The epidemic continued to spread until, in 1939, FWA finally created the Muraz center in Bobo-Dioulasso and made significant gains against trypanosomiasis, especially after 1945.

Bibliography

Primary: 1929. *La maladie du sommeil au Cameroun. Comment nous la combattons* (Archives of the Centre Muraz, Bobo-Dioulasso).

Secondary: Bado, Jean-Paul, 1996. *Médecine coloniale et grandes endémies en Afrique, 1900–1960* (Paris); Ducloux, M., 1988. 'Eugène Jamot (1879–1937): Un fils du Limousin.' *Bulletin de la Société de Pathologie Exotique* 81: 419–426; Sanner, L., 1979. 'Eugène Jamot: l'homme.' *Médecine Tropicale* 39: 479–484.

Myron Echenberg

JANET, PIERRE (b. Paris, France, 30 May 1859; d. Paris, 24 February 1947), *psychological medicine, psychiatry.*

Janet came from a middle-class family. In his youth, his interests were drawn to philosophy by his uncle, Paul Janet (1823–99), a representative of Paul Cousin's school of eclecticism and professor of philosophy at the Sorbonne. In 1879 Pierre entered l'École Normale Supérieure, where he formed a lifelong friendship with Henri Bergson. At the urging of his uncle, he combined his philosophical studies with medicine. In 1883, he became a professor of philosophy at the lycée in Le Havre, where he remained for seven years.

The subject of hypnosis had recently been rehabilitated in medicine by Charles Richet and Jean-Martin Charcot, and Paul Janet had been much interested in issues relating to post-hypnotic suggestion. At Le Havre, Pierre Janet made the acquaintance of Joseph Gibert. Janet intended to write his medical thesis on hallucinations, and Gibert drew his attention to other interesting psychological cases. He introduced him to Léonie Boulanger, who had been observed to present interesting phenomena with clairvoyance, suggestion and hypnotism. This led Janet into the rapidly developing field of abnormal psychology. In 1885 his paper detailing his experiments with Boulanger on hypnotism at a distance (from Paris) was read by Paul Janet at

Pierre Janet. Photograph by Eugene Pirou, Paris. Iconographic Collection, Wellcome Library, London.

the newly founded Société de Psychologie Physiologique. The paper attracted the interest of Charcot, Richet, and the English psychical researchers Frederic Myers and Edmund Gurney, who came to Le Havre to do further experiments with Pierre Janet. At this time telepathy was considered an important subject in the new scientific psychology. While drawing on some of the methods and conceptions of the psychical researchers, Janet later distanced himself from any attribution of supernormal capacities to the trance state, and from spiritualistic interpretations of such states.

Léonie Boulanger had previously been treated by magnetists, and Janet came to view her hypnotic performances as the re-enaction of her magnetic experiences. It was during this period that he commenced historical studies of animal magnetism and hypnosis and concluded that Bernheim and Charcot had neglected to acknowledge the earlier magnetists. Beginning in 1886 Janet published a series of articles in the *Revue Philosophique* on hypnosis that established his reputation. He presented a position between that of the Nancy and

Salpêtrière schools. He articulated his model of the dissociation of consciousness and the role of the subconscious. Although these terms were already in use, they became firmly associated with Janet. For Janet, hypnosis offered an experimental means to study the personality. It demonstrated the existence of separate memory chains, or 'automatisms', which could go so far as to form alternate or double personalities. For Janet, the dissociation of consciousness explained suggestion, hypnotic and post-hypnotic states, as well as hysteria. Janet referred to the subconscious as opposed to the unconscious because the acts in question, while not 'conscious' to the primary consciousness, were 'conscious' to the secondary consciousness.

He drew these studies together in his philosophy thesis. Paul Janet was one of the examiners. Charcot created a psychological laboratory at the Salpêtrière for Pierre Janet, who was appointed a lecturer in psychology at the Sorbonne and commenced his medical studies. Janet regarded Charcot and Théodule Ribot as his two 'masters', from whom he gained his basic orientation: to study mental pathology to illuminate general psychology and, in turn, to use notions from experimental psychology to treat mental disturbances. Janet viewed mental disorders as a form of 'natural' experiment.

During this period he became drawn to the study of neuroses. In 1893 he defended his medical thesis, *Contribution à l'étude des accidents mentaux chez les hystériques*, which formed part of his work published the same year, *L'Etat mental des hystériques*. It was one of the last dissertations under Charcot, who wrote a preface to Janet's book. Developing Charcot's research, Janet viewed hysteria as a psychogenic disorder, characterized by a narrowing of the field of personal consciousness and a tendency to dissociate sensations and memories. These dissociated memories and sensations continued to exist in the subconscious, and have effects. Janet laid particular emphasis on the pathogenic effect of traumatic events, and believed patients could be led to recollect such events under hypnosis, automatic writing, and crystal gazing.

During this period Janet focused on the role of dreams and subconscious reveries. The therapeutic significance of the former was that they often revealed the pathogenic event, and brought to light subconscious 'fixed ideas' that could subsequently be liquidated. With the sick, subconscious reveries became involuntary, and Janet characterized hysterics as individuals who, not content to dream at night, dreamed all day long. Neurotics needed to be directed, and this role had to be assumed by the physician in order for the patient to regain his or her self-mastery. Janet called his method 'psychological analysis'. In Vienna, Breuer and Freud drew upon Janet's work, and a priority dispute later broke out between Janet and the two of them. Subsequent historical research has tended to support Janet's claims.

After Charcot's death in 1893, Janet continued to work at the Salpêtrière, now directed by Fulgence Raymond, and also developed a private psychological practice. In 1894 he married Marguerite Duchesne, with whom he would have three children. In the same year he published his textbook of philosophy. In 1896 he published a *Manuel du Baccalauréat*, which went through several revised editions. In 1898 he was appointed to the Sorbonne, and in 1900 he presided over the international congress of experimental psychology in Paris, an indication of his status in the profession.

In addition to hysteria, Janet took up the study of depression, phobias, and obsessions. The results of these studies were published in *Névroses et Idées Fixes* (1898) and also in *Obsessions et Psychasthenie* (1903). (Janet understood 'fixed ideas', a syndrome he had coined, as persistent emotional as well as ideational states.) He defined psychasthenics as patients on the limits of insanity with varied symptoms, including deliriums of doubt, obsessions, impulsions, and phobias. In hysteria, the psychological phenomena were clearly separated or dissociated into independent groups and, at times, into independent personalities. In psychasthenia, the deliriums did not remain subconscious, but formed the content of the patient's obsessions and ruminations. Psychasthenia was characterized by three factors: the 'sense of incompleteness', the loss of the 'function of the real', and the physiological symptoms of nervous exhaustion. This led Janet to present a new model of the hierarchy of mental functioning. The function of 'the real' represented one of a hierarchy of mental functions. Each function was characterized by a level of psychological tension, the superior functions having the highest level. Janet claimed that the superior mental functions, such as the function of the real, were the most complicated and hardest to perform, and hence the first affected by psychological difficulties, leading to a reversion to inferior functions. Janet's works were marked by the provisional and hypothetical nature of his theoretical constructions, which he repeatedly subjected to extensive revision and copious clinical illustrations. For example, the second volume of his *Obsessions et Psychasthenie* exceeded 500 pages and presented 236 cases.

During this time Janet played an important role in the institutional development of the new scientific psychology in France. In 1901 he founded the Société de Psychologie. In 1902 he succeeded Théodule Ribot at the Collège de France, where he would lecture until 1935. In 1904, with George Dumas, he founded the *Journal de Psychologie*. Throughout this period Janet's work became widely known, and he was viewed as the most important French psychologist. Janet did not, however, court followers or build up a movement. As a result, his reputation during his lifetime greatly exceeded his legacy.

In the United States, William James viewed Janet's work as the epitome of the functional psychology now required. In 1906 James invited Janet to give a course of fifteen lectures on hysteria (in English) at Harvard. Janet's presentations had greater contemporary significance than did

Freud's famous visit to Clark University three years later. Janet's work played a central role in the rise of the Boston school of psychotherapy, and in the development of psychotherapy and psychopathology in the United States. His conception of the dissociation of consciousness was widely taken up. In many respects, the pathological psychology he developed had its greatest impact on the burgeoning field of psychotherapy, and much that should have been attributed to his work was ascribed to psychoanalysis.

In 1910 Jules Déjerine succeeded Raymond as director at the Salpêtrière. Déjerine, a critic of Janet's work, deprived him of his hospital laboratory. Aside from the Collège de France, Janet now had no institutional position. At the Collège he was free to pursue his research interests, but he was not part of the university and did not develop a group of students or followers.

From the time of his presentation at the International Congress for Psychiatry and Neurology at Amsterdam in 1907, Janet became increasingly critical of psychoanalysis, and what he took to be Freud's illegitimate claims for originality. In 1913 at the International Congress of Medicine in London, he presented a detailed and nuanced critique of psychoanalysis, asserting his priority in the cathartic treatment of the neuroses, and calling into question Freud's symbolic interpretations, his sexual theory of the neuroses, and his general tendency toward overgeneralization from insufficient clinical material.

During this period Janet focused his attention on the study of the hierarchical functions of the mind and of psychological energetics. Interestingly, while Janet's early work played a significant part in William James's essay 'The Energies of Men', James's essay played an important role in Janet's late work in psychotherapy, inspiring his concept of psychological mobilization. Janet conceptualized psychological force as the quantity of energy required to accomplish psychological acts. Psychological tension represented the capacity to utilize this force at a high level in the hierarchy of mental functions. Psychotherapy, he claimed, assisted the patient in balancing psychological 'expenditures' with 'income', and in restoring the power to mobilize reserves of energy. Janet's *Les Médications psychologiques* presented an important account of the history of psychotherapy combined with a recasting of his earlier studies in the context of his new system. His account of the relations of magnetic tradition to the hypnotic tradition provided one of the main templates for how this area has been subsequently viewed.

In 1926 Janet published *De l'angoisse à l'extase*. At the center of this work was the case of 'Madeleine', whom Janet had been studying for twenty-two years. Madeleine experienced states of ecstasy, stigmata, and encounters with the Devil. Janet regarded her as a case of psychasthenic delirium, and one that provided a prime opportunity for studying the nature of belief. This led him to begin his studies on the evolution of intellectual tendencies, and to present a new conceptual synthesis, drawing on child psychology, ethnology, and animal psychology. Janet became increasingly taken up with the psychology of religion, and at the time of his death in 1947, he was working on a book on the psychology of belief. Janet's late work, however, never attained anything like the attention earned by his earlier studies.

Henri Ellenberger's *The Discovery of the Unconscious* (1970) revived interest in Janet's contributions and led to his work being taken up by contemporary clinicians. Contested readings of his early work have played important roles in recent formulations of trauma, dissociative disorders, and multiple personality. At the same time, his work has increasingly piqued the interest of historians, leading to a series of reissues of his writings.

Bibliography

Primary: 1889. *L'Automatisme psychologique* (Paris); 1893. *L'État mental des hystériques* (Paris); 1919. *Les Médications psychologiques* (Paris); 1926. *De l'angoisse à l'extase* (Paris).

Secondary: Brooks, John I., 1998. *The Eclectic Legacy: Academic Philosophy and the Human Sciences in Nineteenth-century France* (Newark, DE); Maître, Jacques, 1993. *Une inconnue célèbre: Madeleine Lebouc/Pauline Lair Lamotte (1863–1918)* (Paris); Ellenberger, Henri, 1970. *The Discovery of the Unconscious: The History and Evolution of Dynamic Psychiatry* (New York); Institut Pierre Janet, http://Pierre-Janet.com

Sonu Shamdasani

JARVIS, EDWARD   (b. Concord, Massachusetts, USA, 9 January 1803; d. Dorchester, Massachusetts, USA, 31 October 1884), *psychiatry, public health.*

Edward Jarvis was a leader in the collection of vital statistics for the improvement of the public health. Jarvis's *Report on Insanity* for the legislature in Massachusetts in 1855 was the most significant statistical survey of mental illness of its time.

Jarvis grew up in Concord, Massachusetts, a town he later regarded as a norm for a healthful, civic community. Born to Francis Jarvis and Millicent Hosmer, Edward, like his father, was apprenticed young to a woolen manufacturer, but he soon returned home and convinced his family to let him prepare for college. In 1822 he entered Harvard College. Jarvis was drawn to the study of botany and taxonomy, which seemed to demonstrate the rational orderliness of a world consonant with his Unitarian upbringing.

After graduation, Jarvis became engaged to Almira Hunt, and they married in 1834. Jarvis considered the clergy, but turned hesitantly to medicine, a less prestigious occupation. His start as a physician's apprentice left him dissatisfied. He managed to obtain a loan and set out for Harvard Medical School, which offered the modest advantage of formal lectures and a chance to observe on the wards at Massachusetts General Hospital.

To gain a foothold in this competitive medical world, Jarvis moved next to the small town of Northfield and purchased a practice from a local physician. He was surprised to find that his erstwhile colleague remained in town after the sale as a successful competitor. He replicated his failure in private practice twice more: in Concord, Massachusetts, and then in Louisville, Kentucky.

All this time, however, Jarvis was developing his interest in the care of the mentally ill and in the statistical study of disease. He read and was strongly influenced by the French physician Pierre Louis, who championed a new statistical approach to medicine. In practice, Jarvis favored the treatment of the mentally ill through personal supervision and moral guidance, often taking private, paying patients into his home and following the model of his senior colleagues, Thomas Kirkbride and Pliny Earle.

When his practice in Louisville flagged, Jarvis returned to Dorchester, Massachusetts, outside Boston, in 1842 and again set up practice caring for people with mental illness. For Jarvis, moral rectitude and personal health were a continuum, linked by mutual direct influence. State regulation of the public health required the conditioning of moral behavior, through education and guidance. But Jarvis argued that this project faced the immediate obstacle of an inadequate statistical basis that obscured the true connections among environment, individual habits, and ill health. Jarvis turned his attention to collection of vital statistics and gradually became a leader of wide influence.

He rose to national attention in the contentious debate following the federal census of 1840, which had indicated an abnormally high rate of insanity among those categorized as free colored persons. Proslavery advocates such as Secretary of State John C. Calhoun held up this finding as evidence in support of slavery. Jarvis entered the fray as a critic of the census. He betrayed little interest in slavery, but expressed indignity over the flaws of the data, which counted, for example, more free blacks with mental illness in some areas than the total black population. Jarvis became expert at rooting out and addressing methodological flaws. His survey of insanity in Massachusetts in 1855 pioneered the collection of detailed, aggregate statistics on the occurrence of mental illness by ethnicity and class. Jarvis became a critical advisor to the federal decennial census of 1850 and helped to establish categories for health statistics. One platform for exercising his influence was his tenure for thirty-two years as president of the American Statistical Association.

Bibliography

Primary: 1844. 'Insanity among the Coloured Population of the Free States.' *American Journal of the Medical Sciences* 7: 71–83; 1855. *Report on Insanity and Idiocy in Massachusetts, by the Commission on Lunacy* (Boston).

Secondary: Davico, Rosalba, ed., 1992. *The Autobiography of Edward Jarvis, 1803–1884* (London); Grob, Gerald N. 1979. *Edward Jarvis and the Medical World of Nineteenth-Century America* (Knoxville, TN); *DAMB*.

Christopher Crenner

JENNER, EDWARD (b. Berkeley, Gloucestershire, England, 17 May 1749; d. Berkeley, Gloucestershire, 26 January 1823), *general practice, smallpox vaccination*.

Jenner, the eighth of nine children and fourth son of Reverend Stephen Jenner (1702–54), vicar of Berkeley, and Sarah Jenner née Head, was raised by his siblings after the death of both of his parents (1754). At age eight he boarded with the Reverend Thomas Clissold and attended the Wotton-under-Edge Free Grammar School. In 1758 he studied the classics with the Reverend Washbourne at the Cirencester Grammar School and spent his free time collecting fossils. At Cirencester he made lifelong friends with Caleb Hillier Parry (later a doctor in Bath), Charles Brandon Trye (later a surgeon in Gloucester), and John Clinch (who became a clergyman and missionary in Newfoundland). Jenner left the Cirencester Grammar School when he was twelve. He did not follow his two elder brothers to Oxford University, but instead, at the age of thirteen, began a six-year apprenticeship with the surgeon-apothecary Daniel Ludlow of Chipping Sodbury.

At the end of his apprenticeship, Jenner chose to go to London to further his studies (his family was wealthy enough to support this decision). Beginning in the fall of 1770, he boarded with John Hunter (1728–93), chief surgeon at St George's Hospital. Jenner enrolled as a student at St George's and at the private surgical school of John's older brother, William Hunter (1718–83), on Great Windmill Street. He also attended lectures given by the Scots physician George Fordyce (1736–1802) on physics, chemistry, and materia medica. During this period John Hunter recommended Jenner to Sir Joseph Banks (1743–1820), who sought help in preserving, classifying, and cataloging the thousands of specimens he had collected while accompanying Captain James Cook on the world voyage of the Endeavour. This experience established a friendship between the two men and proved to be beneficial to Jenner later in his life. Banks asked Jenner to accompany him on Cook's upcoming second voyage, but Jenner declined the offer.

After two years of study with some of the most eminent physicians and surgeons in England, Jenner returned home to Berkeley, and at the age of twenty-three he established a successful medical practice that extended over 400 square miles. He traveled on horseback in all weather, including snowstorms. He initially lived with his brother Stephen for several years in Berkeley. On 6 March 1788 he married Catherine Kingscote (1760/61–1815), and they lived in Chauntry Cottage (The Chantry) in Berkeley, which Jenner had purchased in 1785 (now the Jenner Museum). They had three children: Edward (1789–1810), Catherine (1794–1833), and Robert Fitzhardinge (1797–1854).

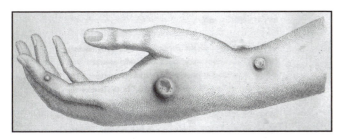

The hand of Sarah Nelmes infected with the cowpox. Color plate from *An Inquiry into the Causes and Effects of the Variolae Vaccinae . . .* London, 1798. Rare Books, Wellcome Library, London.

Jenner's interest in cowpox dates to his apprenticeship with John Ludlow, when he became aware of cowpox and how some milkers believed it to be a preventive against smallpox. Although Jenner appreciated the many benefits of smallpox inoculation, his own experience perhaps spurred him to look for alternative methods. While he was attending the Wotton-under-Edge Grammar School, he was inoculated against smallpox during a local outbreak of that disease. As was typical of the procedure at mid-century (before the Sutton family innovations), Jenner underwent a six-week preparation of bleeding and purging prior to inoculation and then was isolated in an 'inoculation stable' with other inoculees for the actual procedure, in order to prevent the spreading of infection. The whole experience left him weak and filled him with horrible memories.

Jenner maintained a steady, if interrupted, interest in cowpox throughout his career. During the 1770s and 1780s he kept accounts of individuals who had had cowpox and, when later exposed to smallpox, remained healthy. In 1788 he showed drawings of cowpox pustules on milkers' hands to medical men in London, including Everard Home (1756–1832). The following year, he inoculated three individuals (including his infant son) with what he believed to be swinepox; he later decided that the disease was a mild form of smallpox. One of the major difficulties Jenner faced in pursuing his research on cowpox was the relative infrequency of the disease: cowpox could only occasionally be found in the dairy herds around Berkeley. At some point he decided to test the possibility of transferring cowpox from an infected person to a healthy person, much the same way that inoculated smallpox was passed from arm to arm. This would help overcome the problem of supply.

In May 1796 Sarah Nelmes, daughter of a local farmer near Berkeley, contracted cowpox through a thorn scratch on her hand while milking cows. Seizing this opportunity, Jenner selected a healthy eight-year-old boy, James Phipps, son of a local laborer, and on 14 May he made two incisions on the boy's arm and inserted cowpox taken from the pustule on Nelmes's hand. Four days later, there was redness around the incision, and eight days after the incision, two pustules with reddish edges and a bluish center were observed. Phipps had fever for one to two days and otherwise weathered the cowpox inoculation with few symptoms. On 1 July Phipps was inoculated with smallpox to no effect.

Eager to share his findings, Jenner traveled to London in 1796 with a paper announcing his discovery. He sought to have it published in the *Philosophical Transactions* of the Royal Society, with the support of the president of the Royal Society, Sir Joseph Banks, and Everard Home. Banks gave the manuscript to Lord Somerville, president of the Board of Agriculture, who in turn shared it with Mr. Dolland, a surgeon who lived in dairy country. Dolland confirmed Jenner's observations, but in the end, Banks decided not to publish Jenner's paper because he thought there was insufficient proof to support his claim.

Jenner returned to Berkeley in October 1796. By that time, cowpox had disappeared from Berkeley and did not re-emerge until spring 1798. During this time Jenner circulated his manuscript among local friends who likely urged him to publish it privately. In March 1798 Jenner inoculated over twelve individuals with cowpox, some of whom were subsequently inoculated with smallpox with no reactions. At the end of April, Jenner once again left Berkeley for London with a new version of his manuscript, including colored drawings of the cowpox pustule, and a quill with dried vaccine lymph from Hannah Excell, one of the girls Jenner had inoculated with cowpox. Jenner and his family stayed in London for almost three months. During that time he could not persuade anyone to try cowpox inoculation with the lymph he had brought from Berkeley. Only after he left London did one of his friends, the surgeon Henry Cline (1740–1827), inoculate a patient with success.

Jenner's *An Inquiry into the Causes and Effects of the Variolae Vaccinae, a Disease discovered in some of the Western Counties of England, particularly Gloucesterhire, and known by the name of the Cow Pox* was published privately in September 1798. In this seventy-five-page pamphlet, Jenner discussed the possible origins of cowpox (he thought it was a horse disease called grease), its symptoms in humans, and its protective qualities against smallpox. The bulk of the pamphlet was a series of case histories detailing accounts that Jenner had recorded of individuals who had accidentally caught the cowpox and of those whom he had deliberately inoculated with cowpox. Jenner's pamphlet gained a quick and geographically widespread readership. London physician George Pearson first reviewed it in November 1798. By January 1799 copies had been sent to America, and by 1801 translated editions were available in Dutch, French, German, Italian, Latin, and Spanish.

The majority of readers embraced what came to be known as vaccination (a term coined in 1803), but there were criticisms. Some objected to the introduction of animal diseases into humans, and several cartoons captured this fear of 'bovinization'. Others objected to Jenner's claim that cowpox originated from the horse disease grease. Still others doubted whether vaccination provided lifelong immunity (it did not), which Jenner had claimed. Jenner published two further pamphlets that addressed some early criticisms. In *Further Observations on the Variolae Vaccinae* (1799), he sought to distinguish between true and spurious cowpox: the former provided protection against smallpox whereas the latter did not. In *A Continuation of Facts and Observations Relative to the Variolae Vaccinae or Cowpox* (1800), Jenner clarified the types of pustules that were distinctive to cowpox in contrast to those typical of smallpox.

These three publications form the core of Jenner's work on vaccination. He continued to publish on the subject throughout his life and maintained an extensive correspondence network with vaccinators throughout the world. He met with British royalty, including George II, Queen Charlotte, and the Prince of Wales, and with the Tsar of Russia and the King of Prussia during visits to London. He corresponded with Napoleon, despite the fact that Britain was at war with France. Royal patronage helped establish vaccination. So, too, did the British military's quick adoption of the procedure (Jenner received a gold medal from the British navy in 1801). In 1803 the Royal Jennerian Society was created (Jenner served briefly as its president), which later became the National Vaccine Establishment.

Although urged by some friends to keep vaccination secret and thereby profit financially, Jenner chose to share his work freely. In recognition of his contribution, Parliament awarded two grants to Jenner: £10,000 in 1802 and £20,000 in 1807. Moreover, he received numerous honors and awards from societies and universities throughout the world (Jenner's first biographer, John Baron, lists these awards in the second volume of *Life of Edward Jenner*). He was made Physician Extraordinary to George IV in 1820 (an honorary position), but he was not knighted.

In addition to his work on vaccination, Jenner pursued natural history throughout his life. He began collecting fossils as a child and developed a fine collection, including a specimen of a plesiosaur. He later was made an honorary member of the Geological Society of London in 1809. After his studies in London, Jenner maintained a close working relationship with John Hunter and carried out numerous investigations at Hunter's request, including measuring the temperature of a hibernating hedgehog (the only animal that hibernates in Britain). For Banks, he investigated the use of blood as manure. He helped organize the launching of a hot air balloon near Berkeley (1784), just one year after the initial launch made by the Montgolfier brothers in France. On his own, he avidly studied the behavior of the cuckoo. The female cuckoo lays its eggs in the nests of other birds, which raise the chicks as their own. The original eggs and chicks are pushed out of the nest. Jenner determined that the newly hatched cuckoo was responsible for displacing the other chicks, and he described a unique anatomical feature in the infant cuckoo that disappeared in maturity

and that made this behavior possible (Jenner's discovery was confirmed in 1921 with the use of motion pictures). His paper on this topic was read to the Royal Society in 1788 and led to his election as FRS in 1789.

Jenner's later years were marked by illness and depression. In 1815 his wife Catherine died of tuberculosis; five years earlier, his son Edward had died of the same disease. Jenner's own health had been weakened by two serious attacks of either typhus or typhoid in 1794 and 1811. In 1821 he had a minor stroke, and on 26 January 1823 he died of a stroke at his home in Berkeley.

Writings about Jenner have been hagiographic (John Baron and Paul Saunders), or highly critical (Charles Creighton). Richard Fischer's biography provides a more balanced account of his life and work.

Bibliography

Primary: 1798. *An Inquiry into the Causes and Effects of the Variolae Vaccinae, a Disease discovered in some of the Western Counties of England, particularly Gloucestershire, and known by the name of the Cow Pox* (London); 1799. *Further Observations on the Variolae Vaccinae* (London); 1800. *A Continuation of Facts and Observations Relative to the Variolae Vaccinae or Cowpox* (London).

Secondary: Bazin, Hervé, 2000. *The Eradication of Smallpox: Edward Jenner and the First and Only Eradiation of a Human Infectious Disease*, trans. Andrew and Glenise Morgan (San Diego); Fisher, Richard B., 1991. *Edward Jenner 1749–1823* (London); Saunders, Paul, 1982. *Edward Jenner: The Cheltenham Years 1795–1823* (Hanover, NH); Baxby, Derrick, 1981. *Jenner's Smallpox Vaccine: The Riddle of Vaccinia Virus and Its Origin* (London); Razzell, Peter E., 1980. *Edward Jenner's Cowpox Vaccine: The History of Medical Myth*, 2nd edn. (Firle); Creighton, Charles, 1889. *Jenner and Vaccination: A Strange Chapter in Medical History* (London); Baron, John, 1827–1838. *The Life of Edward Jenner* 2 vols. (London); *DSB*; *Oxford DNB*.

Andrea Rusnock

JENNER, WILLIAM (b. Rochester, Kent, England, 30 January 1815; d. Bishop's Waltham, Hampshire, England, 11 December 1898), *medicine.*

Shortly after University College Hospital in London first opened to receive patients on 1 November 1834, the medical student William Jenner 'walked the hospital' and thereby began a lifelong association with that institution and the surrounding area, dying as the original hospital building was being demolished.

Apprenticed at age sixteen to a Marylebone apothecary, Jenner quickly established his own successful Marylebone practice after becoming LSA (1837). General practice was, however, merely a stepping-stone to a hospital career. The MRCS (1837) and earning a London University MD followed a period of working as surgeon-accoucheur to the Royal Maternity Charity, before he opted for pathology under the tutelage of Sir Robert Carswell (1793–1857) and others at University College.

His election to MRCP (1848) came as he was beginning the study of some 1,000 acute cases at the London Fever Hospital, which culminated in his definitive contribution to the contemporary debate on whether typhus and typhoid were related or distinctly separate diseases. His paper 'Typhoid and typhus fevers: An attempt to determine the question of their identity or non-identity, by an analysis of the symptoms and of the appearances found after death, in sixty-six fatal cases of continued fever, observed at the London Fever Hospital from January 1847 to February 1849' appeared in the *Monthly Journal of Medical Science* (April 1849) and as a monograph (1850).

'The publication of this paper undoubtedly marks an epoch' (*British Medical Journal*, 1898, ii, p. 1849); until then the two fevers had been generally thought to be similar or related. Earlier work in the United States, Britain, and France had distinguished between the violently contagious typhus or jail fever and typhoid fever, which French researches had shown to present distinct intestinal lesions but rarely to be infectious, but it was Jenner's 'minute clinical and pathological study of 66 fatal cases, in 23 of which ulceration of Peyer's patches existed, while in the remainder it was absent' and his demonstration of how 'this difference in the *post-mortem* appearances corresponded with differences in the clinical features—the course, eruption, and duration—of the two sets of cases' that 'established the non-identity of typhoid and typhus fevers so completely that the question has never since been disputed' (*British Medical Journal*, 1898, ii, p. 1849).

The publication accelerated Jenner's progress through a series of teaching and hospital posts: professor of pathological anatomy, University College (1849); first physician, Hospital for Sick Children, Great Ormond Street (1858–61); physician, London Fever Hospital (1853–61); professor of clinical medicine, University College, and, from 1862, professor of principles and practice of medicine there; and physician-extraordinary to the Queen (1861), attending Prince Albert prior to his death from typhoid and successfully treating the Prince of Wales for typhoid (1871). He was honored by Queen Victoria with a Baronetcy in 1868 and as a Knight Commander (1872) and subsequently a Grand Commander of the Order of the Bath (1889), and she mourned his passing as 'not only a most able physician but a true and devoted friend of Her Majesty's who deeply mourns his loss' (cited in *British Medical Journal* 1898 ii, p. 1851). In the prodigiously successful private practice, which came to occupy much of his time after 1878, he was the most fashionable London consultant.

Jenner had a formidably intimidating presence as a clinical teacher. His 1869 Address in Medicine to the British Medical Association in Leeds exemplified his sense of the duty the practitioner owed to his patient, reiterating the opening words of his Course of Systematic Medicine: 'The great aim of the physician is to prevent disease; failing that, to cure; failing that to alleviate suffering and prolong life' (cited *British Medical Journal*, 1898, ii, p. 1852).

A member of what *Lancet* called 'a veritable galaxy of brilliant men at this period . . . [who] formed the staff of University College Hospital' on both the medical and surgical side, Jenner was successively elected president of the RCP seven times from 1881. The best of his published work can be found in the *Lectures and essays on fever and diphtheria* (1893), which contains his essays on fevers and 'acute specific diseases' together with his 1861 treatise on diphtheria and the *Clinical lectures and essays on rickets, tuberculosis, abdominal tumours and other subjects* (1895). His Great Ormond Street lectures (on rickets) and 1868 University College lectures (on abdominal tumors) contained within the latter volume are, like the fever and diphtheria papers, definitive masterpieces of Victorian medical writing; his Goulstonian lectures encapsulating his teaching more generally.

Bibliography

Primary: 1850. *On the identity or non-identity of typhoid and typhus fevers* (London); 1893. *Lectures and essays on fever and diphtheria, 1849–1879* (London); 1895. *Clinical lectures and essays on rickets, tuberculosis, abdominal tumours and other subjects* (London).

Secondary: Anon., 1898. 'Obituary.' *British Medical Journal* ii: 1849–1853; Anon., 1898. 'Obituary.' *Lancet* ii: 1674–1676; Anon., 1898. 'Obituary.' *Edinburgh Medical Journal* n.s. 5: 1899; *Munk's Roll*; *Oxford DNB*.

James McGeachie

JERNE, NIELS KAJ (b. London, England, 23 December 1911; d. Castillon-du-Gard, France, 7 October 1994), *immunology*.

Jerne was the fourth of five children of an émigré Danish industrialist. During Word War I the family moved to Rotterdam, where Jerne's father became reasonably wealthy. After completing high school in 1928 with average grades, Jerne was employed as a clerk in Elders & Fyffes banana company, and only five years later did he receive financial support to attend university.

Jerne began studying chemistry at the University of Leiden, but failed; then he attempted to study medicine in Copenhagen. He was married to a Czech painter, Ilse 'Tjek' Wahl, dropped out of university again, and did not resume his studies until 1939. To support his growing family he took a part-time position in the Department of Standardization at Statens Seruminstitut in Copenhagen, one of the world's leading institutions for serology and vaccinology, where he discovered his aptitude for statistical analysis.

His wife's death in the fall of 1945 was a decisive turn in Jerne's life. He finally finished his medical degree in 1947 and decided, after internship and remarriage, to go into research. Using the reaction between diphtheria toxin and antitoxin in a rabbit skin assay system, he studied the phenomenon of antibody avidity ('binding strength'). After his dissertation in 1951, he adopted a much more sensitive bacteriophage-antiphage system to study how antibody avidity increases during the early stages of immunization. After a period of inconclusive experimentation, he was struck, in the summer of 1954, by an experiment that allegedly demonstrated the existence of preformed antibodies. Although their existence was a highly disputed issue in serology, Jerne used this finding to formulate a new theory of the formation of antibodies in opposition to the dominant instruction theories (especially Linus Pauling's).

Jerne's theory was positively received by the Darwinistically inclined molecular biologists, but the reaction of the immunologists was lukewarm, and Jerne felt discouraged. In 1956 he left his family and a permanent job in Copenhagen to work as a scientific officer in the Section of Biological Standardization at the WHO. In Geneva Jerne drew up international guidelines for the production of vaccines and sera, and in 1960 he was assigned the responsibility for organizing WHO's new Immunology Program.

In the meantime, the selection theory had won the attention of a growing number of immunologists after Macfarlane Burnet formulated a cellular version of it (the clonal selection theory) in 1957. Jerne began to consider making a scientific comeback. In 1962, after he had moved to the department of microbiology in Pittsburgh, he utilized his former bacteriophage research experiences to construct a simple plaque assay for the quantification of antibody-producing cells *in vitro*, which became one of the most widely used immunological methods in cellular immunology.

Jerne received offers from Harvard and Copenhagen, but in 1966 chose the position as director of the Paul-Ehrlich-Institut in Frankfurt am Main to build up a European counterpart to U.S. dominance in the field. Two years later, the multinational pharmaceutical company Hoffman-La Roche asked him to become director of a new institute for immunological research in Basel, Switzerland. The Basel Institut für Immunologie opened in 1971 with a staff of 150. Jerne had a knack for selecting talented young immunologists and, in the course of the 1970s, the Basel Institut became the world's leading immunological research institute. Jerne's own theoretical work centered on the problem of the regulation of the immune system. In 1973 he proposed the idiotypic network theory of the immune system, in which all antibodies and lymphocyte receptors are conceived as mutually independent parts of a steady-state system. This theory remains a matter of dispute among immunologists.

After his retirement in 1980, Jerne withdrew (with his third wife) to his country home in Languedoc, France. He continued to develop his ideas about the immune system as a cybernetic network; he became increasingly fascinated by semiotics and the analogies between linguistics and immunology. He received a multitude of honorary degrees and prizes, including the 1984 Nobel Prize in Physiology or Medicine.

Bibliography:

Primary: 1955. 'The Natural-Selection Theory of Antibody Formation.' *Proceedings of the National Academy of Sciences* 41: 849–857; 1963. (with Nordin, A. A.) 'Plaque Formation in Agar by Single Antibody-producing Cells.' *Science* 140: 405; 1985. 'The Generative Grammar of the Immune System' in *Les Prix Nobel 1984: Nobel Prizes, Presentations, Biographies and Lectures* (Stockholm) pp. 157–171.

Secondary: Söderqvist, Thomas, 2003. *Science as Autobiography: The Troubled Life of Niels Jerne* (New Haven).

Thomas Söderqvist

JEX-BLAKE, SOPHIA LOUISA (b. Hastings, Sussex, England, 21 January 1840; d. Mark Cross, Sussex, England, 7 January 1912), *medical education, medicine, women's health.*

Jex-Blake was the youngest of the three surviving children of Thomas Jex-Blake, a lawyer, and Maria Emily Cubitt. Educated at boarding schools in Sussex and London, Jex-Blake planned a career as a schoolteacher, though she did not need to earn a living. She trained at Queen's College in London (1858–59). A gifted mathematician, she became a tutor at the College while still a student, continuing until 1861, sharing a house with Octavia Hill (1838–1912). In 1862, while studying with private tutors in Edinburgh, she helped Elizabeth Garrett (1836–1917) prepare her unsuccessful application to Edinburgh University for admission as a medical student. Later that year, Jex-Blake traveled in Europe and taught at the Grand Ducal Institute in Mannheim.

In 1865 Jex-Blake toured progressive co-educational educational institutions in the United States, gathering information for her book *A Visit to Some American Schools and Colleges* (London, 1867). During her visit, she met Lucy Sewall, resident physician at the New England Hospital for Women and Children, and Jex-Blake worked there as a clerk and nursing assistant. The experience shifted her ambitions from teaching to medical practice. Failing to gain admission to Harvard Medical School, she studied briefly at Elizabeth Blackwell's (1821–1910) new medical school for women in New York City before her father's death required her return to Britain late in 1868.

In the UK in 1869, the medical register included only two women, and all routes to join them appeared closed. Nevertheless, encouraged by Edinburgh supporters of women's higher education, Jex-Blake applied to Edinburgh University for admission as a medical student. A ruling that mixed classes were impossible and that special classes for one woman were impractical left the door open for a group of women. Jex-Blake placed newspaper advertisements. In total ten women matriculated as medical students in November 1869, the first women to do so in a British university. Although Jex-Blake's account focuses on the seven,

'*Septem contra Edinam*', who signed a petition to the managers of the Edinburgh Royal Infirmary for access to its wards for clinical training, thirty-nine women matriculated with her between 1869 and 1873. Jex-Blake and others completed the required classes and examinations, but bitter disputes and court cases left the University unable to grant the women degrees.

In 1874 Jex-Blake's campaign shifted to London. She promoted parliamentary action to resolve legal barriers to women's access to medical qualifications; Russell Gurney's Act of 1876 permitted examining bodies to accept women candidates for registrable qualifications. In 1877 Jex-Blake received her MD from Bern and passed the examination in Dublin for the qualification, enabling her to become the fifth woman on the medical register. Also, in 1874 her efforts led to the foundation of the London School of Medicine for Women (LSMW). Serving as the LSMW's unofficial secretary between 1874 and 1877, she was disappointed when the Council found her forthright, militant approach no longer appropriate and failed to appoint her honorary secretary.

In 1878 Jex-Blake moved to Edinburgh, established a successful medical practice, and opened a dispensary treating poor women. Depressed after the death of her mother in 1881, she gave up practice for two years, before reopening her practice and adding beds to the dispensary to create the Edinburgh Hospital for Women. After the RCPSEdin opened its examination to women in 1885, she founded the Edinburgh School of Medicine for Women. Opposition to her strict rules led to the secession in 1889 of a group of students who established another school—the Medical College for Women. Jex-Blake's school closed in 1898, the year before she retired to Sussex, but the hospital expanded, providing a valuable service to Edinburgh's women.

Jex-Blake's drive and determination, if not her diplomacy, opened opportunities for all medical women who followed.

Bibliography

Primary: 1872. *Medical Women: Two Essays* (Edinburgh).

Secondary: Elston, M. A., 2004. 'Edinburgh Seven (*act.* 1869–1873).' *Oxford DNB*; Roberts, S., 1993. *Sophia Jex-Blake: A Woman Pioneer in Nineteenth-Century Medical Reform* (London); Todd, M., 1918. *The Life of Sophia Jex-Blake* (London); *Oxford DNB*.

Marguerite Dupree

JHIRAD, JERUSHA (b. Shimoga, India, 1890, d. ?, 1983), *obstetrics, maternal health.*

Jhirad, an Indian Jew, had her early education at the High School for Indian Girls at Poona, and matriculated in 1907. When she was eleven, her sister fell seriously ill in Bombay but made a marvelous recovery under treatment by Annette Benson, the medical officer of Cama and Alb-less Hospitals. This so impressed Jhirad that she decided to become a doctor. She studied at the Grant Medical College, Bombay, winning scholarships and prizes, and graduated in 1912. Her next endeavor was to seek an MD from London, which was the prescribed qualification for the position of medical officer, her desired goal. She found that scholarships to pursue an MD were open only to men. Since residents' posts were also not available to women, she had to start general practice in Bombay. Subsequently, she managed to secure a loan scholarship from the industrial house of Tatas to pursue her MD in obstetrics and gynecology from the London School of Medicine for Women. Six months into her stay there, the Government of Bombay awarded her a five-year scholarship. She completed her internship at the Elizabeth Garrett Anderson Hospital, London, and worked as house surgeon for a couple of years.

When Jhirad returned to India after World War I, she served at the Lady Hardinge College and Hospital, Delhi, and then as senior surgeon, Bangalore Maternity Hospital. Finding the facilities in Bangalore limited, she started private practice in Bombay. She worked as honorary surgeon at Cama Hospital (1925–28) and in 1928 was appointed Superintendent, realizing her dream of an Indian holding the highest position at the institution. Under her guidance, the work of the hospital expanded, and undergraduate and postgraduate training facilities for women medical students were provided. A fund for a library at Cama Hospital, named after her, was created on the occasion of her eightieth birthday. She was both a fellow and a member of the syndicate of the University of Bombay. She maintained that there should be medical facilities and education exclusively for women, to promote their acceptance in the field. Accordingly, she joined in the protests against the move to convert Lady Hardinge College into a coeducational school.

Jhirad was a founding member of the Federation of Obstetrical and Gynaecological Society of India. While she contended that *dais* (Indian midwives) would have to unlearn their traditional and unhygienic obstetric practices, she held that they could be trained and were an asset in rural areas where other facilities were nonexistent. She was also hopeful that with the increasing education of men, a change could be brought about in the thinking of the superstitious women of their families. She recommended that classes for fathers could be a part of welfare work. Under the aegis of the Indian Research Fund Association, Jhirad conducted a statistical inquiry into the causes of maternal deaths in Bombay. She showed that the highest mortality was among the poor, and consequently urged better living conditions and a balanced diet to tackle the problem. She was very active with the Association of Medical Women in India and served as its president. For several years (until 1954), she was chairperson of the Maternity and Child Welfare Advisory Committee of the Indian

Council of Medical Research. She was awarded the MBE (1945) and in 1962 the *Padmashri*, a civilian honor bestowed by the Government of India for distinguished achievers.

Bibliography

Primary: 1929. 'Medico Social Work' in Gedge, Evelyn C., ed., *Women in Modern India: Fifteen Papers by Indian Women* (Bombay) pp. 133–137; 1941. *Report on an Investigation into the Causes of Maternal Mortality in the City of Bombay* (New Delhi); 1957. *University of Bombay Centenary Souvenir (1857–1957)* (Bombay).

Secondary: Ramanna, Mridula, 2005. 'Women's Health in Colonial Bombay, 1850–1920' in Shah, K. K., ed., *History and Gender Some Explorations* (Jaipur) pp. 155–170.

Mridula Ramanna

JIMÉNEZ DÍAZ, CARLOS   (b. Madrid, Spain, 9 February 1898; d. Madrid, 18 May 1967), *internal medicine.*

The son of a shopkeeper, Jiménez Díaz studied at the Faculty of Medicine of the Madrid Central University (1913–19). After completing his PhD (1919), he applied for a professorship in Medical Pathology at the University of Barcelona. The rejection of his application brought about great protest by those who criticized the selection system for university teaching staff. After obtaining a grant to further his studies abroad, he went to Germany (1921), where he widened his clinical knowledge with Carl von Noorden (1858–1944), studied physical chemistry with Leonor Michaelis (1875–1949), and experimental medicine with Adolf Bickel.

Upon his return to Spain, he obtained the chair in medical pathology at the University of Seville (1922), and later the same chair at the Madrid Central University (1926). Here he was fortunate enough to enjoy the new building of the Faculty of Medicine and the extensive laboratories built alongside the classrooms. These facilities inspired Jiménez Díaz to conceptualize the joining of teaching, research, and healthcare within his department. Realizing that there were insufficient funds for equipment and staff, he managed to win over a group of financiers (1934), enabling him to set up his own institution, the *Instituto de Investigaciones Clínicas y Médicas* [Institute for Medical Research].

Following the Civil War (1936–39), Jiménez Díaz won the backing of the new government to rebuild the *Instituto*, and he founded (1940) and ran the journal, *Revista Clínica Española,* as a vehicle for his publications. After being appointed medical head of staff at the Provincial Hospital in Madrid (1943), he founded the *Boletín del Instituto de Investigaciones Médicas* (1945), and also set up the Spanish Cardiology Society (1947), and the Spanish Society for Allergies (1948).

In 1953 Jiménez Díaz reorganized the *Instituto* in order to carry out clinical work and thereby increase postgraduate teaching and the training of specialists. With both pub-

lic and private backing he managed to have a new building constructed to house the clinical work—the *Clínica de Nuestra Señora de la Concepción.* This building was extended to provide sufficient space for teaching, as well as to allow the section of the institute dedicated to research to be moved from the Faculty of Medicine (1956). In 1964 the *Fundación Jiménez Díaz* was founded, incorporating the *Instituto* and the association set up to protect the development of the former. This last great change at the *Instituto* during its creator's lifetime was carried out to improve its economic viability and guarantee its future.

Jiménez Díaz was a key figure in the twentieth-century development of medicine in Spain. Through his *Instituto* he developed the system of resident physicians for postgraduate training, introduced specialist areas, and championed the need to link clinical observation and laboratory work to improve diagnosis. His research made important contributions to the study of various diseases, particularly to allergies and those related to nutrition. His work on the diseases of hemp workers and diseases produced by eating vetch flour are renowned examples. He is also considered a pioneer of the ideas of autoimmunity, autoantibodies, and immunosuppressant therapy. Moreover, he transmitted his medical thinking and clinical experience through numerous publications, among the most well-known being *Lecciones de Patología Médica* (1935–52) and *Tratado de la Práctica Médica* (1959, 1963, 1964).

Bibliography

Primary: 1952. *La investigación científica y la enseñanza y orientación de la Medicina* (Madrid); 1953. *El asma y enfermedades afines: normas prácticas de diagnóstico y tratamiento* (Madrid); 1954. *Los métodos de exploración clínica y su valoración: El médico explorando a su enfermo* (Madrid).

Secondary: Peset, José L., 1999. 'Carlos Jiménez Díaz, maestro de la Medicina española.' *Eidon. Revista de la Fundación de Ciencias de la Salud* 5: 22–25; Jiménez Casado, Mariano, 1993. *Doctor Jiménez Díaz: Vida y obra: la persecución de un sueño* (Madrid); Peset, José L., 1973. 'Carlos Jiménez Díaz y el ejercicio de la Medicina.' *Medicina & Historia,* 1ª serie, 23.

José Martínez-Pérez

JIVAKA, KOMARABHACCA   (b. Magadha, India, sixth or fifth century BCE, d. ?, ?), *Thai traditional medicine, pediatrics.*

Jivaka Komarabhacca was a medical practitioner who lived in Magadha, an ancient Indian Kingdom in the area of the modern Bihar state. Jivaka's life and healing work are described in the Buddhist canon, in the *Mahavagga* of the *Vinaya Pitaka,* and he is said to have been the Buddha's physician. Jivaka is perhaps better known today in relation to Thai traditional medicine where, under the name Chiwok Komaraphat, he is referred to as 'the father of Thai medicine'. According to Thai sources, Jivaka Komarabhacca was the person who compiled the texts on which Thai traditional medicine is based. Prefaces to Thai traditional medical texts generally include a dedication to him; e.g., *Tamra Prathom Chinda*, a famous text on pediatrics, begins, 'I have paid homage to the Lord Buddha the refuge of the world and also made special obeisance to Jivaka Komarabhacca the doctor whose greatness can be compared to that of the illustrious Lord Indra, the greatest of all the kings of the gods.'

Jivaka Komarabhacca is said to have been born to a courtesan of Rajagraha and abandoned, then subsequently found and raised by Abhaya, a son of King Bimbisara. This is given by many scholars as the reason for the name Komarabhacca, which means 'adopted by a prince'. However, the name Komarabhacca can also be translated as 'child doctor', leading some writers to conclude that the name Komarabhacca refers instead to the fact that he was a pediatrician. This is supported by evidence from Thai traditional medicine, where the longest descriptions of Jivaka appear in texts on pediatrics.

Apart from these details, little information is available on Jivaka's family background and his life. Buddhist texts mention that Jivaka went to the city of Taksila to study medicine for seven years. The Thai medical text *Tamra Prathom Chinda* adds that Jivaka Komarabhacca was a student of the esteemed doctor Rogamrtindra, referred to as 'the venerable Tamyae' (in modern Thai meaning 'traditional midwife'), who possessed great healing skills and, due to his great merit, knew the properties of all medicinal plants. It is said that wherever Rogamrtindra went, each tree and medicinal plant would call out to him and tell him its name and the afflictions it could cure. He compiled texts containing descriptions of his medicines so that they could be passed down from one doctor to another.

Jivaka established a reputation as a skillful doctor, initially at Taksila and then back in Rajagraha, where he treated King Bimbisara and was appointed physician to the king, his wives, and to the monks, with the Buddha as head. Jivaka treated many wealthy and influential people, including kings, and later became the Buddha's personal doctor. According to the accounts, he healed the Buddha for one unspecified illness by administration of a purgative and treated a foot injury caused by a splinter of rock. The texts attribute to Jivaka the Buddhist Sangha's regulation that men with certain types of diseases should be refused entry into the order. This was a measure to deter the many people afflicted with disease who were joining the Sangha in order to receive free treatment from Jivaka rather than from an interest in the Buddha's teachings.

Jivaka's contribution to medicine extends far beyond his own time and place. Although it is impossible to determine how much of the healing work attributed to him in the canonical accounts is that of Jivaka himself, a composite drawn from the work of several practitioners, or simply an invention, the legend of Jivaka in the Buddhist canon nevertheless constitutes one of the key sources of information about the history and practice of the ayurvedic medical tradition. The legend also serves an important function in the Buddhist canon, establishing the basis for rules pertaining to ordination and behavior of Buddhist monks. In addition, Jivaka occupies an important place in other medical systems influenced by Indic medicine, especially those of Southeast Asia, for example that of the Thai, where to the present day his contributions remain influential, serving as examples to inspire, guide, and legitimize the work of practitioners of Thai traditional medicine.

Bibliography

Secondary: Bamber, Scott, 1998. 'Medicine, Food and Poison in Traditional Thai Healing.' *Osiris* 13: 339–353; Mulholland, Jean, 1989. *Herbal Medicine in Paediatrics: Translation of a Thai Book of Genesis* (Canberra); Zysk, Kenneth G., 1982. 'Studies in Traditional Indian Medicine in the Pali Canon: Jivaka and *Ayurveda.*' *The Journal of the International Association of Buddhist Studies* 5(1): 70–86; Mulholland, Jean, 1979. 'Thai Traditional Medicine: Ancient Thought and Practice in a Thai Context.' *Journal of the Siam Society* 67(2): 80–115; Wat Pho Traditional Medical Association, ed., 1961–76. *Phaetsat Songkhro* (Bangkok) (in Thai); Beyer, C, 1907. 'About Siamese Medicine.' *The Journal of the Siam Society* 4: 1–22; Bradley, Dan Beach, 1865. 'Siamese Practice of Medicine.' *Bangkok Calendar* (reprinted 1967, *The Social Science Review Quarterly* 5:3: 83–94).

Scott Bamber

JOHN OF GADDESDEN (aka ANGLICUS, GATESDEN, GADESDENE, GADDISDYN) (b. Little Gaddesden, Buckinghamshire, England, *c.* 1280; d. 1349), *medicine, surgery.*

Although he was one of the most significant English medical writers of his day, there are few details of John's life. He may have undertaken his early studies at St Albans, and he was at Oxford from 1305, studying medicine as late as 1309. It is less certain that he was also a student of theology at Oxford in 1320, at which time he was a fellow at Merton College while also in medical practice. By 1332 he was listed as a doctor of medicine and describes having students himself. There is no support for a theory that he trained at Montpellier. He is noteworthy as the first physician of consequence trained completely in England.

John's medical practice was distinguished by an early association with the royal house. He describes curing Edward (born 1313), son of Edward II, of smallpox by encircling him with a red cloth. In 1332 he was a clerk of Edward III and continued to attend the royal children. The Black Prince in 1346 gave him a golden rose, which became the metaphor for his principal work. It appears he also attended students, clergy, canons and, at one time, the monks at Abingdon Abbey. Although he mentions a female patient and injured knights, it is not clear that his practice was so all-encompassing. For his royal service, at least, he held many prebends, including London and Chichester. From 1307 to 1316 he was rector at St Nicholas, Abingdon.

His principal work, *The English Rose of Medicine* (1305/ 14/17), was mentioned by Geoffrey Chaucer (*Canterbury Tales*, Prologue, 436) and translated into Irish in the Middle Ages, and volumes of his work were bequeathed in English wills. By reputation, he was probably well respected in his day and after in England, but by Guy of Chauliac's (*c.* 1300–68) time, his work was viewed by elite Continental authors as rather derivative.

A popular Latin text intended for physicians and surgeons alike, the *Rose* was divided into five parts for the petals of the flower: fevers, injuries, hygiene, diet, and drugs. Its name no doubt evoked the gift of the golden rose from the Black Prince, as well as Bernard of Gordon's continental *Lily of Medicine*. John derived his material from Bernard of Gordon, Henry of Mondeville, John of Saint-Amand, Gilbert the Englishman, Richard the Englishman, Avicenna (Ibn Sīnā), Averroes (Ibn Rushd), Galen, Dioscorides, and others. His work was part of a fourteenth-century movement to link theory and specific conditions in a practical fashion, although he broke with the Continental tradition and favored Galen over the Aristotelian assimilation of medicine into the philosophical arts.

He displayed a fair understanding of the nature of the translations with which he worked, at one time comparing two separate versions of Avicenna on leprosy. He probably performed lesser kinds of surgery himself, including reducing a dislocated jaw and removing ranula from his father's mouth. Some have reported that John was the first to have passed a urinary catheter, although this does not seem likely.

His other texts include *On the Regimen and Diet of Acute Diseases*; *On Simple Medicines*; *On Digestibles and Evacuations*; *On the Instruments of the Art*; *Quid pro quo*; *On Phlebotomy*; and perhaps *Practical Medicine* and *For Diets*.

While often misinterpreted by modern critics looking for examples of medieval 'ignorance', John remains an excellent example of a medieval author who assimilated a large variety of sources with his own experience.

Bibliography

Primary: 1492. *Rosa Anglica practica medicine a capita ad pedes* (Pavia).

Secondary: Getz, Faye Marie, 1998. *Medicine in the English Middle Ages* (Princeton, NJ); Talbot, Charles H.,1967. *Medicine in Medieval England* (London); Talbot, Charles H., and E. A. Hammond, 1965. *The Medical Practitioners in Medieval England: A Biographical Register* (London) pp. 148–150; Lennox, William G., 1939. 'John Gaddesden on Epilepsy.' *Annals of Medical History* (3rd series) 1: 283–307.

Walton O. Schalick III

JOHN OF SAINT-AMAND (b. Belgium, *c.* 1230; d. Tournai, Belgium, 1303), *medicine, pharmacology, medical education*.

A prominent cleric, teacher, physician, and author in northern France, John helped establish the 'New Galen' at the turn of the thirteenth century. With Taddeo Alderotti and Arnald of Vilanova, John was one of the three most important medical authors in the late thirteenth century for adapting Arabic and ancient medical texts and ideas into Latin.

His birth and youth are shrouded by a paucity of sources, but he was probably born in Saint-Amand en Pouelle to a family of modest means. He almost certainly studied the liberal arts, philosophy, and medicine at the University of Paris. His university affiliation thereafter is less certain. Although we have no contemporary reference to John's status as a professor, his surviving texts abound in incidental phrasing and references corroborating this position. Like a typical example of a successful northern European academic, John held a number of ecclesiastical positions as prebends. All five of his were within nine miles of Saint-Amand, and included the canonacy of the cathedral of Notre-Dame de Tournai, where he was memorialized after his death. John died between 14 March and 7 May 1303.

Asides in his written works indicate that John saw patients as well as teaching students. Among those to whom he offered advice were women, children, and potentates, like the Bishop Gautier de Croix. As were some of his colleagues, John was sensitive to the activities of other kinds of practitioners, from pharmacists to 'old women'. John's writings reflect the first century of university practitioners attempting to situate themselves within a robust marketplace.

But it is for his learning that John is best remembered. He wrote more than twenty Latin medical works. The two most famous works are *Exposition on the Antidotary of Nicholas*, and *Revocativum*, which is divided into three parts: *The Concordance*, *The Areolae*, and *Abbreviations of the Books of Galen*. The *Concordance* adopted the then recent textual device invented by Parisian theologians for biblical exegesis and applied it to words found in the works of Galen, Hippocrates, Avicenna (Ibn Sīnā), and others. The *Abbreviations* condensed seventeen texts of Galen and Hippocrates. *Areolae* was a list of simple medicines and short descriptions of a variety of compounds stemming therefrom. Its popularity is attested to in at least thirty-two manuscript witnesses.

However, the *Expositio* was John's most popular work. A commentary on the Salernitan *Antidotary of Nicholas*, John wrote it sometime between 1290 and 1303. The *Antidotary*'s author is unknown, but this text was frequently copied and used by both pharmacists and doctors. By the middle of the fourteenth century, the *Antidotary* was mandated by law as the source of pharmaceutical activities in Paris. Each copy was to be corrected regularly, and one source for those corrections was John's commentary. It survives in whole or in part in more than seventy manuscripts

Hippocrates' Regimen of Acute Diseases; and a commentary on the *Additiones of Mesue*. These commentaries were joined by other texts on more pharmacological and pharmaceutical texts: *An Abbreviation of the Antidotary*; *Addition to the Tacuinum (regimen of health)* as well as *On the Means of Healing, On Remedies*; and, uncertainly, *On the Book of Surgical Medication*. Hints of his popularity also survive in various collections of recipes, excerpts, and marginalia. At least two of his texts are lost: *On the Conservation of Health and the Delaying of Old Age,* and *On the Powers of Plants*.

One reason for John's popularity was his reception of newly translated Arabic texts, as well as his use of a variety of textual strategies to ease the burdens of students struggling to find the growing number of Galenic and Hippocratic medical comments. But John was also a crucial transitional figure between the more conservative *Articellan* system of his own educational youth and the much broader curricula that followed.

While John's commentaries are typical of the leading scholars of his day, his emphasis on pharmacology and medical educational techniques mirrored the Salernitan scholar, Gilles de Corbeil, who came to teach in Paris at the beginning of the century. But John's work was far more philosophically nuanced and intellectually stimulating. In essence, he was a second step in the *via scolaris* embraced by the new-fangled medieval universities. Undoubtedly, his focus on pharmacological subjects reflected a growing sensitivity within the Medical Faculty for the importance of this subject, both as a topic of medical instruction and investigation, and as a theme of medical practice within the environs of Paris and northern France. Within a few years of John's death, the French kings began issuing regulations of spice and drug sales.

John's writings were influential beyond their copies and the bounds of the University and the royal court. The elite surgeon, Henry of Mondeville, embraced John's innovative system for dividing and citing the works of Galen. In addition, some fifty years later, Peter of St Flour augmented some of John's work in his *Compilation of the Flowers of Medicine (Concordance)*.

His creative interpretations of pharmacologic theories, like that of the specific form, reflected both his own close readings of his predecessors, and the use his successors would make of his ideas. While John's pharmacologic ideas were highly integrative and original, they were simultaneously philosophical compared to those of the rest of the known faculty. John addressed a controversy in pharmacology head on—how do simple drugs behave when compounded (i.e., is the sum of the parts less than the whole?)?—suggesting that the measures of the key characteristic (*radix*) of drugs, in the form of simples, could be quantified, weighed, or measured. Following along an Avicennan model, he also argued that a process of fermentation occurred in the mixing of simples, creating a new formulation in the compound.

John of Saint-Amand. From a fifteenth-century illuminated manuscript, a commentary upon the *Grabadin [compendium] medicinarum particularium*. CLM 733, fo. 32r, *Additiones mesue* (32r-238v). Courtesy of Bayerische Staatsbibliothek.

from the thirteenth to the sixteenth centuries; multiple editions were printed from the late fifteenth to the seventeenth centuries. The Parisian Medical Faculty maintained its own copy, still held in its library.

John wrote the first academic commentary on part of Avicenna's *Canon* (Book I, fen 3 and Book IV). His role as an interpreter of the burgeoning Arabic-to-Latin translations of his day also gave him familiarity with the ninth-century Arabic author, Serapion. But the majority of John's nine commentaries were on more conventional texts from the solidifying medical curriculum: *On the Diets of Isaac; On the Fevers of Isaac; A Little Gloss on the Isagoge of Johanitius; Commentary on Philaretus' Book of the Pulses; Commentary on Theophilus' Book of the Urines; Commentary on*

At the same time, John did not ignore practically relevant subjects then receiving attention in Paris, such as phlebotomy and cosmetics, each of which had noteworthy places in the minds of patients at court and among the elite of the day. In addition, he stressed the side effects of drugs, laxatives prominent among them, in a volume unusual for the day. Such descriptions were doubtless useful to those who tried to increase the influence of the University faculty in the regulatory actions of the day.

Along with those scholars at Bologna and Montpellier, John's scholastic shadow was one of the farthest reaching in the late Middle Ages. In Paris it was not to be eclipsed until Jacques Despars in the fifteenth century. John's impact was at once theoretical and practical, synthetic and regulatory, in the setting of the most influential of northern European universities.

Bibliograhy

Primary: 1549. *Expositio super Antidotarium Nicholai* in *Mesue et omnia quae cum eo imprimi* . . . (Venice), fo. 230v–72r; Pagel, Julius Leopold, 1893. *Die Areolae des Johannes de Sancto Amando (13.Jahrhundert)* (Berlin); Pagel, Julius Leopold, 1894. *Die Concordanciae des Johannes de Sancto Amando* (Berlin).

Secondary: Schalick, Walton O. (forthcoming). *Marketing Medicine: Medical and Pharmaceutical Regulation in Paris, 1200–1400*; Garcia-Ballester, Luis, 1998. 'The New Galen: A Challenge to Latin Galenism in Thirteenth-century Montpellier' in Fischer, Klaus-Dietrich, Diethard Nickel, and Paul Potter, eds., *Text and Tradition: Studies in Ancient Medicine and Its Transmission: Presented to Jutta Kollesch* (Leiden) pp. 55–83; Schalick, Walton O., 1997. 'Add One Part Pharmacy to One Part Surgery and One Part Medicine: Jean de Saint-Amand and the Development of Medical Pharmacology in Paris, c. 1230–1303.' The Johns Hopkins University, PhD dissertation (Baltimore); Jacquart, Danielle, 1994. 'L'oeuvre de Jean de Saint-Amand et les méthodes d'enseignement à la Faculté de Médecine de Paris à la fin du XIIIe siècle' in Hamesse, Jacqueline, ed., *Manuels, programmes de cours et techniques d'enseignement dans les universités médiévales* (Louvain-la-Neuve) pp. 257–275; Arnald of Vilanova, 1975. *Aphorismi de gradibus* in McVaugh, Michael R., ed., *Arnaldi de Villanova Opera Medical Omnia* vol. II (Granada and Barcelona).

Walton O. Schalick III

JOHNSON, OBADIAH (b. Hastings, Freetown, Sierra Leone, 29 June 1849; d. London, England, 12 September 1920), *medicine, surgery.*

Johnson was the fourth child of seven born to Henry Johnson, a descendant of eighteenth-century Oyo ruler Abiodun, and Sarah, both freed Yoruba slaves who had settled in Sierra Leone. Henry's association with the Church Missionary Society (CMS) brought the family to Ibadan, Nigeria, in 1857, and Obadiah was educated at Kudeti, Ibadan, until his father's death in 1865, then until 1868 at Faji School in Lagos, where he moved with his mother.

After an apprenticeship to a Lagos carpenter and contractor, he entered the CMS Grammar School in Freetown, and from 1874 to 1877 taught at Holy Trinity School, Freetown.

Remaining in Sierra Leone, he entered Fourah Bay College on a CMS scholarship. The College had recently affiliated with the University of Durham, and in 1879 Johnson became one of its first three students to be presented for a BA degree. He then went to London to pursue medical studies at King's College. He became MRCS in 1884 and MB (Edinburgh), winning all available science and surgery prizes, before returning to general practice in Lagos in 1886. He married Mabel Emily Maxwell and took up a post as Assistant Colonial Surgeon at Sherbro, Sierra Leone, in 1887.

By 1888 he had returned to private practice in Lagos, rapidly building up a reputation and a clientele among Europeans and Africans, and was appointed Assistant Colonial Surgeon in Lagos in 1889, the same year as he earned an Edinburgh MD for his thesis on the therapeutics of West Africa. In racially tense late nineteenth-century Lagos, with the pan-Africanism of Edward Blyden and the African Church movement forming a new cultural nationalist vanguard, Europeans, fiercely protective of their social and professional standing, resisted moves for African political advancement. Johnson and his African colleague, John Randle, found themselves stranded on a lower pay scale than that of their European counterparts, on the spurious grounds that 'these gentlemen are in their own country and as regards living are not subject ordinarily to the same monetary calls as their European colleagues'. Furthermore, avenues to advancement were repeatedly and routinely blocked (Adeloye, 1985, p. 79).

Discouraged by a spiteful report from a more rapidly promoted European colleague, Johnson left the Colonial Medical Service to enter private practice in 1897, and he began to devote more time to writing and to community and church affairs. He was appointed to the Lagos Legislative Council in 1901 and served there for thirteen years, working on the all-African committee responsible for the 1910 *Report on the Yorubas*. He presented a paper on Lagos history in 1901, recognizing the impact of the slave trade on Yoruba history, and presenting a clear periodization of this history. He also edited the remaining drafts and notes of his brother Samuel's lost manuscript, *The History of the Yorubas*, culminating in the eventual publication of Samuel's work in 1921. By then, Obadiah had died, leaving a legacy as a brilliant and trailblazing African doctor and as an important cultural nationalist amid the ferment of colonial Lagos.

Bibliography

Primary: 1921. (by Samuel Johnson, edited by Obadiah Johnson) *The History of the Yorubas from the Earliest Times to the Beginning of the British Protectorate,* (London); 1982. (Singer, Philip, and Elizabeth A. Titus, eds.) *An Essay on West African Therapeutics* (Reproduction of 1889 Edinburgh MD thesis.) (Owerri).

Secondary: Ajayi, J. F. Ade, 2000. 'Samuel Johnson and Yoruba Historiography' in Jenkins, Paul, ed., *The Recovery of the West African Past: African Pastors and African History in the Nineteenth Century* (London) pp. 57–68; Doortmont, Michel, 1991. 'Samuel Johnson (1846–1901): Missionary, Diplomat, Historian' in Falola, Toyin, ed., *Yoruba Historiography* (Madison, WI) pp.167–182; Adeloye, Adelola, 1985. *African Pioneers of Modern Medicine: Nigerian Doctors of the Nineteenth Century* (Ibadan); Hopkins, A. G., 1969. 'A Report on the Yoruba, 1910.' *Journal of the Historical Society of Nigeria* 5(1): 67–100.

John Manton

JONES, AGNES ELIZABETH   (b. Cambridge, England, 10 November 1832; d. Liverpool, England, 19 February 1868), *nursing reform.*

Jones was born in England to Colonel Joseph Jones of Kildare, Ireland, and his wife, Elizabeth Smyth. However, her family returned to Ireland, where they were members of the Protestant ascendancy, and she lived at the family home at Fahan, County Donegal, with an interlude in Mauritius when her father's regiment was posted there. She grew up a devout Christian and looked for a way to live a practical religious life.

In 1850 the family moved to Dublin and from there made a series of visits to the continent. In 1853 the family visited Kaiserswerth, and Jones and an aunt spent a week there examining the work of the institution in more detail. This institution where devout female evangelical Christians controlled numerous activities, including nursing and the training of teachers, evidently made a considerable impression, and in 1860 Jones was allowed by her family to return to Kaiserswerth and to a role as a probationer in the hospital there. Her time there convinced her that her vocation was in nursing, although she did not wish to remain in Kaiserswerth, and in 1862 she entered St Thomas's Hospital as a Nightingale probationer.

As was the case with many of the women who entered nursing from the upper and middle classes in this period, she immediately went from her year of training to the running of a hospital, taking charge of the London Great Northern Hospital (1863). It was from here in 1865 that she was recruited by William Rathbone (1787–1868) to introduce trained nurses into the workhouse hospital in Liverpool, one of the largest in the country.

At this time the treatment of the sick inhabitants of workhouses was appalling. In Liverpool, as elsewhere, the workhouse hospital was staffed by healthy women paupers, assisted by a group of cleaners, none of whom had any training in nursing. Supervision came from three paid but untrained parish officers. The number of patients could often exceed 1,200, and at night, wards were locked or, in some cases, patrolled by police to keep order. Neglect and abuse of patients in workhouses was not uncommon. Rathbone, a noted philanthropist, convinced the Liverpool Vestry, which controlled the workhouse and of which he was a member, that reforms were necessary and offered to pay for trained nurses for three years at his own expense. Jones, regarded by Florence Nightingale (1820–1910) as 'her best and dearest pupil', arrived to take charge. Within a month she had sacked thirty-five of the existing workhouse 'nurses' for drunkenness, and to assist her in her transformation of the hospital, she had twelve trained nurses and seven Nightingale probationers.

In her work in nursing, Jones retained her evangelical religious commitment, regarding Christian training of nurses to be primary and hospital skill as secondary. However under her control, cleanliness increased, medical instructions were more closely obeyed, and patients were treated with kindness and consideration. Her work also demonstrated clearly the impact of properly trained nursing superintendence. This pilot scheme in Liverpool, thanks to Jones, was regarded as a remarkable success—so much so that in 1867 the Vestry agreed to make the system permanent and take over financial responsibility for it. The reforms she introduced spread elsewhere as other Boards of Poor Law Guardians accepted the need to introduce teams of trained nurses under trained Superintendents.

Jones, however, was not to see the fruit of her labors. There were frequent epidemics in Liverpool, nursing staff were often ill, and she died at age thirty-five, having contracted typhus from one of her nurses.

Bibliography

Secondary: Summers, A., 1989. 'Ministering Angels.' *History Today* 53–59; Ross, J. C., and J. Ross, 1988. *A Gifted Touch: A Biography of Agnes Jones* (Worthing); Higginbotham, J., 1872. Memorials of Agnes Elizabeth Jones by her Sister (*London*); Oxford DNB.

Ann Wickham

JONES, JOSEPH   (b. Liberty County, Georgia, USA, 6 September 1833; d. New Orleans, Louisiana, USA, 17 February 1896), *medicine, medical history.*

After receiving a classical education at South Carolina College and later Princeton, Jones chose a medical career and enrolled at the prestigious University of Pennsylvania, where he received his degree in 1856. In 1858 he accepted a position first as professor of chemistry at Savannah Medical College and then at the Medical College of Georgia prior to the Civil War. One year later, Jones met and married Caroline Smelt Davis, with whom he had four children.

The Civil War would bring Jones to prominence. Given that Jones was an ardent secessionist, there was no question that his sympathies lay with the South. He promptly joined the Confederate Army and, rising from the ranks, transferred into the Medical Department, where he caught the eye of Surgeon-General Samuel Preston Moore. Moore enlisted Jones to investigate the camp diseases plaguing the troops. Jones launched extensive studies into a variety of illnesses, especially malaria, tetanus, and hospital gangrene; his descriptions of those diseases remain some of the most detailed accounts in existence from a Southern physician.

After the war Jones moved to New Orleans, where he practiced medicine before accepting the chemistry chair at the University of Louisiana. Caroline died in 1868, and in 1870 Jones married Susan Rayner Polk. They had three children together. Jones rose to positions of prominence within the state, serving as president of the Louisiana State Board of Health and president of the state's medical society in 1887.

But he is best remembered as perhaps the most prominent physician-spokesman for the idealized Lost Cause. Jones helped found the Southern Historical Society on 1 May 1869, drafting its constitution and becoming its first Secretary. Throughout the postwar years, Jones engaged in an indefatigable effort at compiling war-related statistics designed to confirm the notion that the South was simply overwhelmed by the North. According to Jones, the total number of Confederates in the field never exceeded 600,000, of which a third perished from disease and injury. Jones estimated that another third were taken prisoner, and disability discharges and desertions cost the South another 100,000. By war's end, he believed there were no more than 100,000 Confederates in the field, suggesting that the Confederacy was outmanned three or four to one. This estimate fit in well with that of a mythical defeated South, a noble agricultural yeomanry outgunned by northerners caricatured as driven by Mammon, industry, and immigrant hordes. Because many of the statistical records of the Confederacy were lost with the burning of Richmond in April 1865, Jones's figures became oft-quoted and assumed an air of officialdom. Thomas L. Livermore disagreed, however, suggesting that Jones's figures were suspect and that the alleged three-to-one or four-to-one advantage of the Union army was grossly inaccurate. Nevertheless, the publication of Jones's medical history of the Confederacy in 1892 did much to further establish the defeat-by-sheer-numbers thesis and ensconce the cult of the Lost Cause as a persistent American myth. Although Jones may have exaggerated the disparity of Confederate-to-Union troops, his medical statistics unquestionably establish the fact that the Union's ability to call upon a steady supply of reinforcements made indiscriminant disease its greatest ally.

Bibliography

Primary: 1867. *Researches upon 'Spurious Vaccination': or the Abnormal Phenomenon Accompanying and Following Vaccination in the Confederate Army during the Recent American Civil War, 1861–1865.* (Nashville); 1876–1890. *Medical and Surgical Memoirs*, 3 vols. in 4 (New Orleans); 1892. 'The Medical History of the Confederate States Army and Navy.' *Southern Historical Society Papers* 20: 109–166.

Secondary: Vandiver, Frank E., 1977. *Biographical Dictionary of the Confederacy* (Westport, CT); Breeden, James O., 1975. *Joseph Jones, M.D.: Scientist of the Old South* (Lexington, KY); Cunning-ham, H. H., 1960. *Doctors in Gray: The Confederate Medical Service*, 2nd end. (Baton Rouge); *DAMB*.

Michael A. Flannery

JONES, ROBERT (b. Rhyl, Denbighshire, Wales, 28 June 1857; d. Llanfechain, Montgomeryshire, Wales, 4 January 1933), *orthopedics.*

Acknowledged as the father of modern orthopedics, Jones was the eldest child of the freelance journalist Robert Jones (1836–75) and his wife, Mary. He spent three years at Sydenham College, London, before being sent to Liverpool in 1873 to apprentice with his uncle Hugh Owen Thomas (1834–91), an expert in locomotor injuries and deformities, and at the same time begin studies at the Liverpool school of medicine, from which he graduated in 1878. In 1881 he was appointed honorary assistant surgeon to the Stanley Hospital, Liverpool, rising to full surgeon in 1886. A year later, he married Susannah (d. 1918), the daughter of a Liverpool merchant with whom he had a son and a daughter.

In 1888, three years after establishing his own private practice, Jones was invited by the Manchester Ship Canal Company to act as its consulting surgeon during the construction of the thirty-five-mile canal to Liverpool. Responsible for the well-being of the 10,000–20,000 navvies annually employed on this five-year project, he designed a comprehensive accident service that provided near-continuity of care for patients, from the moment of injury to recovery.

In the course of this work, in 1889, Jones was elected honorary surgeon and dean of the clinical school at Liverpool's Royal Southern Hospital. There in 1906 he established one of the first hospital orthopedic outpatient clinics in Britain, the only one at the time to deal both with injured workers and with disabled children. As at his Nelson Street Clinic, which he inherited from his uncle upon the latter's death in 1891 and turned into an internationally famous showcase for scientifically managed orthopedic surgery, Jones devised a meticulous division of labor among his surgical assistants that enabled him to undertake staggeringly heavy caseloads.

He was also involved with the care and curative provision for children with chronic conditions such as polio and tuberculosis of the bone and joints. In 1898 he cofounded a rural hospital for such children at Heswell, Liverpool, which was the first of its kind in Britain. Shortly thereafter, he was recruited by the nurse Agnes Hunt to act as the consulting surgeon to her children's convalescent home in Oswestry, which Jones soon transformed into an internationally renowned orthopedic hospital, earning him the lifelong devotion of Hunt.

Jones' greatest plaudits—including his CB (1917) and KBE (1919)—were gained for his work during World War I. With 65 percent of war casualties being impairments to the locomotor system, the war afforded him the opportunity to implement on an even larger scale the kind of organization he had provided for the Manchester Ship Canal project. Appointed director of military orthopedics in March 1916, he initiated the rationalization and standardization of military orthopedic procedures and techniques, while at the same time organizing more than twenty special military orthopedic centers in Britain and staffing them with young orthopedists from the United States and the Commonwealth. The flagship of these centers was the one established in May 1916 at Shepherd's Bush, London, where no fewer than 1,000 of the first 1,300 disabled recruits were rehabilitated to active military duty.

Hitherto, outside of Liverpool, the orthopedic specialism mostly had comprised the treatment of disabled children and, institutionally, the treatment of clubfoot. Jones expanded the specialism, redefining it to encompass the treatment of acute locomotor injuries. He also played a part in founding the British Orthopedic Association in February 1918, over which he presided from 1920 to 1925. However, he had no interest in developing an autonomous specialism. He wanted to see orthopedics integrated in the structure of medical education and the voluntary hospitals. Although from about 1910 almost all of his work was confined to the treatment of locomotor disorders, he remained a general surgeon committed to surgical expertise within a conceptually unified medical system. Blessed with a generous, open personality and immense vitality, he was able to pull it off.

Bibliography

Primary: 1922. 'Orthopaedic Surgery.' *Encyclopaedia Britannica*, 1922 supplement to the 11th edition, covering the period 1911–21.

Secondary: Watson, F., 1934. *The Life of Sir Robert Jones* (London); *Oxford DNB*.

Roger Cooter

JOSHI, ANANDI GOPAL   (b. Kalyan, India, 31 March 1865; d. Pune, India, 26 February 1887), *medicine.*

Anandi (originally named Yamuna) was the daughter of Ganpatrao Amriteshwar Joshi, a Brahmin landlord. In straitened circumstances, the family arranged the marriage of nine-year old Anandi to Gopalrao Vinayak Joshi, a clerk in the Post and Telegraph Department. The twenty-nine-year-old widower agreed to marry Anandi only on the condition that he could tutor her. Obsessed with the idea of women's education, Gopalrao was a peculiar groom, refusing to accept a dowry but wanting his wife to be educated when female education was taboo, especially for married women.

Gopalrao made unceasing attempts to teach his young wife, moving out of Anandi's natal household to Alibaug, where she began her education in earnest. At the age of twelve, Anandi had a son who lived only for ten days. There were no more children. She began learning Marathi, and soon was reading Sanskrit as well as English. His wife's intelligence and thirst for knowledge emboldened Gopal-

rao to suggest that she pursue medical education. Thereafter, the Joshis pursued a single goal: Anandi's becoming a doctor. They approached Christian missionaries who attempted to arrange passage to America for the Joshis, only to disappoint them. The related correspondence was published in an American newspaper, and communication opened between Anandi and Mrs Theodicia E. Carpenter, who became a friend.

In the quest for formal education for Anandi, Gopalrao took a transfer to Bombay, but the move was unsuccessful. Constantly in penury, they moved to Bhuj, Jammnagar district, and finally to Calcutta. The Joshis abandoned their initial plans of migrating to America together and made arrangements for Anandi to go alone. At the age of seventeen, Anandi sailed from Calcutta to New York—the first Indian woman to do so.

Anandi lived with the Carpenters in Roselle, and she decided to enroll at the Philadelphia Medical School because it offered a grant of $600. The curriculum at Philadelphia included surgery, perceived as an added advantage. Anandi entered the college on 7 March 1883. After staying with the Carpenters for four months, Anandi moved to an accommodation near her college. In America, she adhered to all norms of Hindu Brahmin womanhood, remaining a strict vegetarian. She surprised many Americans by her public defense of the custom of child marriage. Nevertheless, her persistence and academic zeal won her the admiration of the dean of her college, Rachel Bodley, who wrote to Queen Victoria about her student's achievements.

The poor diet, excessively hard conditions, and the cold had begun to take a toll on her health, and the behavior of the eccentric Gopalrao, who had managed to reach America in 1885, compounded her woes. Anandi presented her thesis on 'Obstetrics among the Aryan Hindu Women' and was awarded her MD degree on 11 March 1886. The famous Pandita Ramabai attended her graduation ceremony.

Anandi decided against settling in America and on 9 October 1886 sailed from New York. Even before she returned to India, the princely state of Kolhapur appointed her Physician-in-charge of the female ward of the Albert Edward Hospital.

In India, Anandi's health deteriorated, and she insisted on being treated by a local doctor; but he refused to treat a female doctor trained in western medicine. She succumbed to tuberculosis of the lungs in 1887. Anandi's achievements despite difficult circumstances made an impression on many of her contemporaries. As India's first woman doctor, she was regarded as an exemplary and virtuous Hindu woman, and was appropriately lauded.

Bibliography

Secondary: Joshi, S. J., 1992. (trans. and abridged by Asha Damle) *Anandi Gopal* (Calcutta); Kanitkar, Kashibai, 1912. Dr *Anandi Gopal: Yanche Charitra va Patre* (Bombay); Dall, Caroline Healey, 1888. *The Life of Dr Anandibai Joshee* (Boston).

Namrata R. Ganneri

JOSLIN, ELLIOTT PROCTOR   (b. Oxford, Massachusetts, USA, 6 June 1869; d. Brookline, Massachusetts, USA, 28 January 1962), *medicine, diabetes.*

Joslin was the most prominent diabetes specialist of the twentieth century. His father, Allen, was a partner in a shoe factory, and his mother, Sarah, was related to the founders of Procter and Gamble. His childhood was spent in the small town of Oxford, Massachusetts, where he lived for the rest of his life. His first presentation as a student was on a diabetic, Mary Higgens, and his first paper on the disease was given to the Boylston Medical Society in 1893. He graduated from Harvard in 1895 and, after a year in Germany and Austria (1896–97), interned at the Massachusetts General Hospital. In 1898 he again visited Europe, where he met many of the great men of diabetes, including Bernhard Naunyn (1839–1925), whom he particularly admired. In all he made seventeen trips to Europe, the first in 1888 at age nineteen and the last in 1961 when, at age ninety-two, he participated in the International Diabetes Federation meeting in Geneva.

The first edition of his famous textbook *The Treatment of Diabetes Mellitus* was published in 1916, and for it he managed to trace 97.5 percent of the thousand patients he had seen during the previous twenty years. The first four editions (1916, 1917, 1924, and 1928) were single-author books. Before insulin, Joslin was an enthusiast for the undernutrition treatment of Frederick Allen, claiming that 'we no longer nurse diabetics, we treat them.' Nevertheless, virtually all his patients under age twenty died, whereas between 1923 and 1925, with the benefit of insulin, 94 percent recovered from diabetic coma. He was one of the first doctors in the twentieth century who not only preached the importance of patient education but also practiced it. In 1918 he produced the first edition of his *Diabetic Manual for the Mutual Use of Doctors and Patients*, the last edition of which was published in 1959. In the mid-1920s he set up a foot clinic and joint medical–surgical service. This included a 'beauty parlor' for prophylactic foot care because, as Joslin wrote, 'Gangrene is not heaven sent but earth born'.

He took great interest in the activities of his patients, especially children, many of whom he kept in touch with through yearly letters. He organized summer camps for children in the hope that their general health would be improved by the country air and that they would learn to become independent.

His work with statisticians from the Metropolitan Life Insurance Company in the 1930s was one of the first investigations of the epidemiology of diabetes. He had become interested in this in his hometown, where six of seven people living in adjoining houses had died of diabetes. Nobody spoke of an epidemic, but as he noted, the reaction of the local health authorities would have been different had it been typhoid or scarlet fever; 'because the disease was diabetes and occurred over a considerable interval of time, the fatalities passed unnoticed'.

After insulin he was a staunch proponent of good diabetic control, writing in 1928 that 'success in the treatment of diabetic children lies in keeping their urine sugar-free. If sugar appears, a penalty follows.' This view was controversial for the next sixty years but has now been vindicated.

Throughout his life he was deeply religious and had a puritanical zeal, tempered by charm, warmth, and optimism so that patients adored him. He had a spare frame and frugal habits and regarded obesity as an evil. When lecturing about obesity, he used to enter the room carrying two gallon pails of water in each hand as a graphic illustration of the strain that being overweight imposes on the body.

Bibliography

Primary: 1916. *The Treatment of Diabetes Mellitus: With Observations Based upon One Thousand Cases* (Philadelphia); 1918. *A Diabetic Manual for the Mutual Use of Doctors and Patients* (Philadelphia).

Secondary: Feudtner, C., 2003. *Bitter Sweet: Diabetes, Insulin and the Transformation of Illness* (Chapel Hill, NC); Holt, Anna C., 1969. *Elliott Proctor Joslin: A Memoir, 1869–1962* (Worcester, MA).

Robert Tattersall

JUNG, CARL GUSTAV   (b. Kesswil, Switzerland, 26 July 1875; d. Küsnacht, Switzerland, 6 June 1961), *psychiatry, psychoanalysis, analytical psychology.*

Jung was the son of the pastor Johann Paul Achilles Jung and grandson of Carl Gustav Jung (1794–1864), a famous physician and rector of the University of Basel. After studying medicine at the University of Basel, Jung was an intern under Eugen Bleuler at the Burghölzli psychiatric clinic in Zurich (1900–05), where he was occupied with the treatment of psychoses and with association studies. Jung was able to prove that delayed responses in association tests are an indicator for emotional impressions, which he referred to as 'complexes' and saw as objective substantiation for Freud's theory of repression.

From 1905 to 1909 Jung was a senior physician at Burghölzli, and until 1913 a docent at the University of Zurich. His correspondence with Freud began in 1906. Freud courted Jung, meeting with him in person from 1907 onward, and seeing in him the ideal international representative of the psychoanalytic movement.

Jung left Burghölzli in 1909 and established a private practice in Küsnacht. In 1910 he became the first president of the International Psychoanalytical Association. His first differences with Freud arose with the publication of *Wandlungen und Symbole der Libido* (1912), wherein Jung defined the libido as a universal, undifferentiated psychical energy, whereas for Freud, libido was a strictly sexual drive. The scientific dispute eventually led to a break with Freud in 1913, and in 1914 Jung resigned the presidency of the International Psychoanalytical Association.

Jung's position as president of the International General Medical Society for Psychotherapy, an organization founded in 1934 in Germany (Jung served as president until 1939), as well as several questionable remarks about Judaism, earned him the hostility of some critics.

Between 1933 and 1942 Jung taught as a docent (honorary professorship in 1935) at the Swiss Federal Institute of Technology in Zurich. He became professor at the University of Basel in 1943 but resigned a year later due to illness.

After his split with Freud, Jung developed his own approach to depth psychology, which he termed analytical (complex) psychology. It incorporated elements of gnosis, mythological research, symbolism, religious studies, hermeticism, and alchemy, and differs markedly from Freud's naturalistic-positivistic psychoanalysis.

The central concepts of Jung's thinking were individuation, the self, the archetype, and the collective unconscious. He understood individuation as the realization of all developmental possibilities residing in the self, a process having the goal of developing the person into a whole individual. The self encompasses all of the conscious and unconscious elements of the psyche, and consists of the ego, the individual unconscious, and the collective unconscious. The collective unconscious is the psychical heritage gathered in the course of humanity's phylogenetic development and the sum of all archetypes, which are innate, inherited patterns of the psychical functioning, common to all humans and activating typical patterns of behavior and experience. Among the archetypal structures are ego, persona (social mask), shadow (repressed, split-off partial personalities), and animus and anima (unconscious gender differentiation, i.e. the image of the man in the woman's psyche and vice versa).

Jung dealt with the 'type' problem in *Psychological Types* (1921), where he differentiated two attitude types: introversion and extraversion, and four functional types: thinking, feeling, sensation, and intuition.

In the last years of his life, Jung devoted himself intensively to the study of alchemical and hermetic texts, the symbols and images of which he interpreted as projections of the collective unconscious and the archetypal.

Jung's works made a key contribution to the meeting of Eastern and Western thought. His ideas have found especially strong resonance among artists and writers, and have been taken up by myth research, psychotherapy, and the New Age movement.

Bibliography

Primary: 1953–1992. (Read, Herbert, Michael Fordham, Gerhard Adler, eds., McGuire, William, exec. ed., trans. Hull, R. F. C.) *The Collected Works of C. G. Jung* 20 vols. (Princeton); 1963. (Jaffé, Aniela, ed.; trans. Winston, Richard, and Clara Winston) *Memories, Dreams, Reflections* (Princeton); 1973–75. (Adler, Gerhard, ed. and selected, with Aniela Jaffé, trans. Hull, R. F. C.) *Letters* 2 vols. (Princeton); 1974. (McGuire, William, ed., trans. Manheim, Richard, and R. F. C. Hull) *The Freud/Jung Letters* (Princeton).

Secondary: Bair, Deirdre, 2003. *Jung. A Biography* (Boston, New York, and London); Shamdasani, Sonu, 2003. *Jung and the Making of Modern Psychology. The Dream of a Science* (Cambridge).

Christian Huber,
trans. Christopher Barber

JURIN, JAMES   (baptized London, England, 15 December 1684; d. London, 29 March 1750), *medicine, natural philosophy, smallpox inoculation.*

Jurin was the son of John Jurin, a member of the Dyers Company and a London freeman of Huguenot descent, and Dorcas Cotesworth, sister of London physician Caleb Cotesworth. Jurin was educated at the Royal Mathematical School at Christ's Hospital and earned a full scholarship to Trinity College, Cambridge, where he received his BA (1705) and his MA (1709). In 1709 he studied at Leiden University, but did not receive a degree. At the end of 1709, he returned to England and assumed the position of headmaster at the Newcastle-upon-Tyne Public School. While in Newcastle, he offered a course of lectures on mathematics and mechanics, thereby becoming one of the first public lecturers on Newtonian natural philosophy outside of London.

In 1715 Jurin left Newcastle because of disagreements with the town council regarding school fees. He relocated to Cambridge, where he studied medicine and received his MD (1716). He moved to London and quickly established a successful private practice there and in Tunbridge Wells, a spa town some fifty kilometers southeast of London. In 1724 he married Mary Douglas (née Harris), the wealthy widow of a Northumbrian landowner. They had six children who survived to adulthood, five daughters and one son.

Jurin enmeshed himself in the medical and natural philosophical circles of early eighteenth-century London. He became secretary to the Royal Society (1721) and held that position until 1727, when Isaac Newton, president of the Royal Society, died. As Secretary, he corresponded with leading natural philosophers throughout Europe and the North American colonies. In 1719 he became FRCP, and in 1722 he lectured on anatomy to the Surgeons' Company. In 1725 he was elected physician to the newly established Guy's Hospital; in 1731 he became a Governor of that institution. Late in life, he was five times elected Censor to the RCP and briefly served as its president for three months before his death.

Jurin's most significant contribution to medicine was his statistical evaluation of the risks associated with smallpox inoculation. The procedure entailed inserting a small amount of pus from a smallpox pustule into an incision made on the arm or leg of a healthy individual. Inoculation had been introduced to England from Turkey through the efforts of Lady Mary Wortley Montagu (1689–1762) and had been reported by physicians in the *Philosophical Transactions*. A mild case of the disease generally resulted and protected the inoculated individual from a subsequent attack of smallpox. Occasionally, patients contracted a severe case of smallpox and sometimes died. It was this risk of death that Jurin sought to evaluate numerically. As secretary to the Royal Society, he collected reports of the successes and failures of inoculation from physicians and surgeons throughout England, Scotland, and the New England colonies. He calculated the risk of dying from inoculation as one in ninety-one (this risk decreased substantially in the last quarter of the eighteenth century, as improvements to the procedure were made). Using data from the London Bills of Mortality, Jurin calculated the chances of dying from natural smallpox as one in seven or eight. He concluded that the chances of dying from natural smallpox were so much greater than the chances of dying from inoculation that it was in the best interests of individuals and parents to seek inoculation. Jurin published a series of pamphlets summarizing his results. These pamphlets were cited frequently by contemporaries throughout Europe as evidence to support inoculation. They also provided the first statistical evaluation of a medical procedure.

Jurin was a staunch supporter of Newtonian natural philosophy and defended Newtonian ideas in several pamphlet disputes so characteristic of the period. He penned anonymous contributions to the *Analyst* controversy, begun with a 1734 pamphlet written by Bishop George Berkeley, who asserted that the calculus was as much an article of faith as was religion. Under the pseudonym Philalethes Cantabrigiensis, Jurin used satire to defend Newtonianism. He took a similar approach a decade later in a dispute over *vis viva*, or how to measure the quantity of motion. In addition to his satirical defenses of Newton, Jurin published many papers on hydrodynamics, optics, and iatrophysics.

Near the end of his career, Jurin became embroiled in a dispute about his role in the death of the Prime Minister Robert Walpole. Walpole suffered from bladder stones and was unable to find relief. Jurin was called in as a consulting physician, and he recommended a medication that he had developed for treating stones called lixivium lithontripticum. Walpole took the medicine for eights weeks and then passed a large stone and fifteen small fragments. Despite these evacuations, Walpole's condition worsened, and he died one month later. Shortly before his death, he blamed Jurin's lixivium for his poor health. Jurin defended himself from a panoply of printed attacks and was able to maintain his professional standing. He died in London at age sixty-six and was buried in St James's Church, Garlick Hill, London.

Bibliography

Primary: 1723. *A Letter to Caleb Cotesworth, M.D., containing a Comparison between the Mortality of the Natural Smallpox and that given by Inoculation* (London); 1734. *Geometry No Friend to Infidelity; or a Defense of Sir Isaac Newton & the British Mathematicians,* by Philalethes Cantabrigiensis (London); 1996. (Rusnock, Andrea, ed. and introd.) *Correspondence of James Jurin 1684–1750* (Atlanta and Amsterdam).

Secondary: Rusnock, Andrea, 1995. 'The Weight of Evidence and the Burden of Authority: Case Histories, Medical Statistics and Smallpox Inoculation' in Porter, Roy, ed., *Medicine in the Enlightenment* (Amsterdam) pp. 289–315; *Oxford DNB.*

Andrea Rusnock

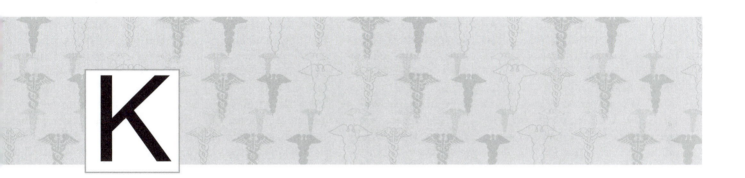

K

KAPOSI (formerly KOHN), MORITZ (b. Kaposvár, Hungary, 23 October 1837; d. Vienna, Austria, 6 March 1902), *medicine, dermatology.*

Kaposi was born Moritz Kohn in Hungary, the son of poor Jewish parents. Nevertheless, he was eventually able to leave his hometown and start his medical studies in Vienna in 1856. In 1861 he received his medical degree and was shortly afterwards appointed assistant to Ferdinand von Hebra (1816–80). He worked with the well-regarded Austrian dermatologist from 1862 to 1867. Kohn fell in love with and later married von Hebra's daughter, Martha. In order to marry his Catholic bride, and to pursue a university career, he converted to Christianity and changed his name from Kohn to Kaposi—a wordplay on his place of birth, Kaposvár. His son, Hermann Kaposi, born in 1872, would become a professor of surgery in Breslau. In 1866 Kaposi finished his Habilitation thesis on the effects of syphilis on mucous membranes in the nose and throat and was appointed Privatdozent.

Together with his mentor and father-in-law, he completed von Hebra's textbook on dermatology, published in 1872. Three years later he became associate professor at the University of Vienna. After von Hebra's death, Kaposi was appointed director of the university hospital and head of the dermatology department. In 1893 he assumed von Hebra's dermatology chair at the University. In 1882 he became a member of the prestigious German academy of science, the Leopoldina. He was appointed Hofrat in 1899.

Kaposi made a number of original contributions to clinical dermatology. His *Pathologie und Therapie der Hautkrankheiten* (1879) proves that he looked at dermatology from clinical, pathological, and therapeutic aspects. Kaposi was very interested in syphilis—its lesions to the skin and mucosa, its etiology, and its treatment. He established dermatitis herpetiformis (first described by von Hebra) as an entity, and also lymphoderma perniciosa and lichen ruber moniliformis. With von Hebra and others he published some of the early descriptions of lupus erythematosus of the skin. He also described rhinoscleroma and rhinophyma. His list of publications up to 1899 numbered 122 larger works and special publications. In 1872 Kaposi published an article on the strange case of a man from Burma who was tattooed on almost every square inch of his body, including his genitals. The illustrations to this case appeared in volume eight of von Hebra's *Atlas der Hautkrankheiten*.

In 1876 Kaposi described the disease that bears his name, calling it 'idiopathic multiple pigmented sarcoma of the skin'. For many years thereafter, Kaposi's sarcoma was considered to be a relatively rare, slow-growing malignancy, most commonly seen in middle-aged and elderly men. The epidemic form of Kaposi's disease, called Kaposi-AIDS, was first described in 1981. The diagnosis was made on the basis of epidemiological, clinical, biological, radiological, endoscopic, and histological evidence. Kaposi's sarcoma is now one of the diagnostic markers of the acquired immunodeficiency syndrome. Over the past several years, however, the incidence of HIV-associated Kaposi's sarcoma has declined, and the reasons for this are uncertain.

Bibliography

Primary: 1866. *Die Syphilis der Schleimhaut der Mund-, Rachen-, Nasen-, und Kehlkopfhöhle* (Erlangen); 1872. 'Idiopathisches multiples Pigmentsarkom der Haut.' *Archiv für Dermatologie und Syphilis* 4: 265–273. English translation in *CA: A Cancer Journal for Clinicians* (New York, 1982) 32: 342–347; 1875. *Die Syphilis der Haut- und der angrenzenden Schleimhäute* (Vienna); 1876. 'Bösartige Neubildungen' in Virchow, Rudolf, ed., *Handbuch der speciellen Pathologie und Therapie* vol. III, 2nd part (Erlangen) pp. 379–475; 1880. *Pathologie und Therapie der Hautkrankheiten in Vorlesungen für praktische Ärzte und Studirende* (Vienna and Leipzig) [1895. English trans. Johnston, James C., reprinted in Classics of Medicine Library (Birmingham, AL, 1985)]; 1880. *Handbuch der Syphilis* (Stuttgart); 1882. 'Über Xeroderma pigmentosum' in *Medizinische Jahrbücher* (Vienna) pp. 619–633; 1885. 'Über eine neue Form von Hautkrankheit: Lymphodermia perniciosa' in *Medizinische Jahrbücher* (Vienna) pp. 129–147; 1898–1900. *Handatlas der Hautkrankheiten für Studierende und Ärzte* 3 vols. (Vienna and Leipzig).

Secondary: Crissey, John Thorne, and Lawrence Charles Parish, 1981. *The Dermatology and Syphilology of the Nineteenth Century* (New York); Sailer, Karl Ludwig, 1977. 'Kaposi, Moritz' in *Neue Deutsche Biographie* 11: 133–134; Siegl, Norbert, 1971. *Personalbibliographien von Professoren und Dozenten der ersten Wiener Hautklinik im ungefähren Zeitraum von 1845–1969.* Medical Dissertation (University of Erlangen) pp. 15–27.

Robert Jütte

KARK, SIDNEY

KARK, SIDNEY (b. Johannesburg, South Africa, 22 October 1911; d. Jerusalem, Israel, 18 April 1998), *social medicine, preventive medicine, family medicine, community-oriented primary care.*

The son of Lithuanians who emigrated to South Africa in the 1880s, Kark attended Parktown Boys' High School in Johannesburg before studying medicine at the University of the Witwatersrand (Wits) (1929–35). Both he and his wife, Emily, who was to be his lifelong partner in the development of community-oriented primary health care, attributed the importance of the ferment of liberal and radical ideas at Wits to their 'development towards a philosophy of life' (Kark and Kark, 1999, p. 7). The stark inequalities and racial disparities of South Africa, exacerbated by the world depression and the rise of fascism in Europe, gave a particular edge to student life in the 1930s, and at university the young Karks began to question the blinkered racial attitudes of the time, and to seek a deeper understanding of South African society and its impact on health. His encounter with a remarkable group of staff and students in the Wits Medical School and Arts Faculty led to Kark's recognition of the importance of anthropology, history, and political economy for an understanding of ill health, and his use of participant observation in clinical and epidemiological practice throughout his life.

Alerted to the social injustices and inequities of contemporary South African society, Kark saw these reflected in the health conditions of the majority of South Africa's people. As a member of the Bantu Studies Society and a leading member of the Labour Party on the campus, he helped found a Society for the Study of Medical Conditions among the Bantu, and wrote pioneering articles for the medical student journal, *The Leech* (e.g. Kark, 1934).

Thanks to Eustace Cluver, then Secretary for Health and Chief Medical Officer (1938–40), Kark was appointed with Harding le Riche, a physical anthropologist, to conduct a year-long survey of the nutrition and health of African school children in South Africa, a matter of growing concern to both the state and the Chamber of Mines in the 1930s. In all they examined 7,000 children in nine urban and rural regions, and revealed the high incidence of malnutrition and chronic infectious diseases. Detailing the list of afflictions discovered, they concluded, 'The outstanding fact is that they are all preventable' (Kark and Kark, 1999: p. 13). Their report underlined the Department of Health's growing realization that African health was being compromised by the diseases of uneven industrialization, South Africa's migrant labor system, and rural dispossession. This sense of a health crisis underlay the Department's 1939 decision to establish four experimental rural health centers. Kark was appointed to head the first of these (and, as it transpired, the only one until after World War II) in Pholela, in rural Natal.

At Pholela, the Karks developed both the concept and practice of social medicine, which has been widely recognized as underpinning the famous Alma Ata Declaration of 1978. Health centers and primary health care were not particularly new ideas in the 1930s. What distinguished the health center at Pholela were both the comprehensive and integrated notion of medicine it embraced, and Kark's insistence on the measurement of outcomes through intensive monitoring, evaluation and research. At the same time, the Karks recognized their own ignorance of local beliefs about health and illness and the role of indigenous healers, and saw the need to gain the confidence and solicit the advice not only of chiefs and elders, but also of a wide range of church, community, and school groups.

Local people were enlisted as members of the health team. Working with the community served not only to disseminate health education, but also to educate the health team itself. The activities of this center were multifaceted, designed to promote health education and prevent ill health as well as to provide a curative service when needed. In addition to a daily clinic with separate prenatal and infant sessions, immunizations, and health education, all part of the normal running of the center, its activities included a school health service, which conducted clinical examinations, nutritional assessments, and immunizations. Health talks ranged from 'personal hygiene, fly control and the importance of pit latrines, to gardening for diet improvement' (Kark and Kark, 1999, p. 30). Talks were accompanied by practical demonstrations, a vegetable garden at the health center being an early innovation.

Confronted by the absence of vital statistics, Kark and his team defined a selected research area based on a local population census conducted by specially trained community health workers, within which they conducted more intensive family and community health programs. This demographic and epidemiologic survey was complemented by the addition of historical, ethnographic, sociological, and psychological data, to produce a rounded profile of the community. The usual division between the clinic and the fieldwork of the health team was bridged through the coordination of clinical (individual and family) and community-based public health records. As their defined area expanded, so differences between the older defined areas and the newly incorporated ones could be compared. Importantly, by defining the community and collecting information in this way, Kark was also able to track the effectiveness of the center's activities. Within a few years he was able to demonstrate significant improvements in the health of the Pholela community, as measured by mortality statistics, infant deaths, the incidence of kwashiorkor, attendance at prenatal clinics, the decline in STDs, and improved diet (Kark and Steuart, 1962).

It was the conclusive demonstration of the effectiveness of the Pholela health center in reducing mortality and morbidity that impressed Henry Gluckman when he was introduced to the work at Pholela, and led to the recommendation of the National Health Services Commission, which he chaired, that health centers based on the Pholela model should provide the foundation for a national health service in South Africa (UG30, 1944). Pholela became the first training base for the health workers needed for this ambitious project (1945).

It soon became evident, however, that to implement the Commission's recommendations, a larger national training and research center was necessary, and at the end of 1945 the Karks were transferred to Durban to establish this initially in temporary property at the King George V Tuberculosis Hospital, then later at the Institute for Family and Community Health (IFCH) at Clairwood, with rural Pholela and three urban and suburban sites designated for practical training and research purposes. The Clairwood Institute was incorporated into the newly established Durban Medical School, and Kark was appointed professor of preventive community and family medicine (1945). He and the then dean, George Gale, ensured that preventive medicine was integrated into all the students' years of clinical study.

Given the radical nature of Kark's approach, it is not surprising that it was opposed by more conservative members of the profession, even before the electoral victory of the National Party in 1948 put an end to any serious attention to African health. By that time only forty of the proposed 400 health centers had been established, and these were now removed from the IFCH administration and starved of funds. By 1960, most had either closed down or been transformed into curative polyclinics under provincial administration. The Karks were under sustained pressure from the state, their activities labeled 'communist'. Many of their closest colleagues had left for Israel, North America, and Australia, taking Kark's concept of community health with them. With the impending passage of the Extension of Universities Act (which threatened to bring the Durban Medical School under state control), Kark accepted a temporary appointment as the first chair of the department of epidemiology in the School of Public Health at the University of North Carolina at Chapel Hill (1958), before departing for Jerusalem on a three-year WHO appointment as visiting professor of social medicine in Hadassah Medical School the following year.

With support from the WHO, the Medical School, and the Hebrew University, Kark established a Department of Social Medicine (formalized in 1982 as the School of Public Health and Community Medicine), attracting several colleagues he had trained in South Africa to join him. Within two years he had organized an MPH, which soon attracted students from all over the world. The Kiryat Hayovel Community Health Centre in Jerusalem (which Kark had advised since its inception in 1953) provided the arena for the teaching, testing, and practice of Community Oriented Primary Care (COPC). Always insistent on understanding the specificity of local culture and local health institutions and practices, Kark adapted the lessons of Pholela to the conditions he found in Jerusalem.

Throughout his career, Kark was concerned with what he conceived of as 'community health syndromes . . . a complex of disease and other health conditions in a specific community, its causal factors, and the interrelationships among these health conditions and between the health conditions and other factors' (Kark and Abramson, 2003, p. 882). His approach was holistic, based on integrating curative, preventive, and promotive care, and individual and family care with community care; he stressed the connections between the social and health sciences and worked with multidisciplinary health teams. His practice was also 'evidence-based', with a firm epidemiological underpinning. These ideas of what he called Community Oriented Primary Care were spread through the dispersal of his South African trainees, and later by the hundreds, if not thousands, of international students he and they trained. Despite the contemporary emphasis in developed countries on tertiary care and drugs, Kark's methods and ideas have continued relevance and resonance in the rest of the world.

Bibliography

Primary: 1934. 'The Economic Factor in the Health of the Bantu in South Africa.' *Leech* 5: 18–22; 1949. 'The Social Pathology of Syphilis in Africans.' *South African Medical Journal* 23(5): 77–84; 1962. (with Steuart, G. W. eds.) *A Practice of Social Medicine. A South African Team's Experiences in Different African Communities* (Edinburgh and London); 1974. *Epidemiology and Community Medicine* (New York); 1981. *The Practice of Community Oriented Primary Health Care* (New York); 1999. (with Kark, Emily) *Promoting Community Health. From Pholela to Jerusalem* (Johannesburg).

Secondary: Kark, J. D., and J. H. Abramson, 2003. 'Sidney Kark's Contribution to Epidemiology and Community Medicine.' *International Journal of Epidemiology* 32: 882–884; Marks, Shula, 1997. 'South Africa's Early Experiment in Social Medicine: Its Pioneers and Politics.' *American Journal of Public Health* 87: 452–459; [Various], 1993. 'Tributes to Sidney Kark.' *American Journal of Public Health* 83: 946–948, 1037–1050.

Shula Marks

KASILI, EDWARD GEORGE (b. Bungoma, Western Province, Kenya, 9 June 1942; d. Nairobi, Kenya, 26 December 1994), *pediatrics, oncology.*

Kasili, son of a teacher and farmer, Bartholomew Walubengo, and his wife Salome, spent his early life in Bungoma, Western Province. Educated initially in this area and later at Alliance High School, Kikuyu, Kasili was inspired to study medicine through seeing the suffering of his younger brother, Joseph, a victim of the polio epidemic of the 1950s. Spurred on by this experience, Kasili attended Makerere University, Kampala, Uganda, graduating MB ChB (1968). Upon qualification, he returned to his homeland and became a medical intern at the King George Hospital (now Kenyatta National Hospital (KNH)), Nairobi (1968–69). Although humble by nature, Kasili was a man of action, and would spend the vast majority of his professional life dedicated to improving the health of cancer patients in Kenya.

Appointed in 1972 as a lecturer in the Faculty of Medicine, University of Nairobi, Kasili began his teaching and research career in pediatric oncology (appointed senior lecturer 1975, associate professor 1980, and professor 1982). He continued his education while working at the University, achieving the MRCPath (1974), MD (Nairobi, 1979), and FRCPath (1982, the first Kenyan to be elected). Although cancer treatment had begun at KNH in the 1960s, it was Kasili's MD thesis on leukemia that was the first full-scale research report to come out of Kenya. In this work, Kasili was the first to disprove (through a detailed study of 456 cases at KNH) a commonly held theory that Kenyan Africans were somehow less susceptible to leukemia than others elsewhere. He was able to build on this research later in his career to eventually prove that 'the incidence of some childhood cancer in Africa is one of the highest recorded in the world' (Kasili, 1986, p. 3). As well as extensive research into malignancies, Kasili would also become a key player in the founding and building of various facilities for the care of children with cancer. He established the Pediatric Oncology Ward at the KNH (1985), and also the Nairobi Hospice Charitable Trust (1989)—the first institution in Tropical Africa specializing in care for those with terminal cancer.

Kasili held many prominent positions throughout his career: he was the founding chairman and professor of the department of hematology and blood transfusion at the University of Nairobi (1985–1994), and a Fellow of the Kenyan National Academy of Sciences. He also undertook various editorial duties, serving as the Editor-in-Chief of the *East African Medical Journal* (1987–1994) and as a member of the editorial board of the *Journal of Pediatric Oncology/Hematology*. He was also the founding chairman of Bungoma Professionals Group (BPG), a group of local professionals founded in 1990 dedicated to giving back to their community. This group was instrumental in setting up medical camps, providing treatment, and distributing food and clothing for displaced victims of the land clashes in Western Kenya that resulted from the introduction of multiparty politics in the early 1990s.

Kasili, who had devoted his professional career to caring for underprivileged children with cancer in the developing world, eventually died in 1994 after his own struggle with the illness. He was survived by his wife, Speranza (whom he married in Nairobi on 28 February 1970), and his five children. During his lifetime he enjoyed jogging, cycling, reading, and tennis.

Bibliography

Primary: 1984. (with Kyambi, J. M., and J. N. Onyango) 'The Treatment of Childhood Malignancies in Kenya.' *East African Medical Journal* 61: 663; 1986. 'Children's Cancer Ward at KNH.' *Medicus* August: p. 3; 1991. *A Synopsis of the Management of Some Cancers in Kenya* (Nairobi); 1993. 'Evolution of Paediatric Oncology over the Years: Overview with a Focus on Sub-Saharan Africa and Examples from the Kenyan Experience.' *East African Medical Journal* 70: 343–347.

Secondary: Iliffe, John, 1998. *East African Doctors* (Cambridge).

Anna Crozier

KEEN, WILLIAM WILLIAMS (b. Philadelphia, Pennsylvania, USA, 19 January 1837; d. Philadelphia, 7 June 1932), *medicine, surgery.*

Keen, the sixth of eight children of William W. Keen, a merchant, and Susan Budd, was educated at Central High School, Philadelphia (1849–53), and Brown University (1855–59). Intended for the Baptist ministry, he remained a devout Christian but was drawn to medicine. After a year at Jefferson Medical College (1860–61), he left at the outbreak of the Civil War to join the Fifth Massachusetts Regiment as assistant surgeon, returning to complete his MD (1862). Reentering the U.S. Army as a civilian surgeon, he served the war (1862–64) under Silas Weir Mitchell and George R. Morehouse at Turner's Lane military hospital, Philadelphia. 'My serving with Weir Mitchell was the chief turning point of my whole professional life . . . our war work laid the foundation of modern neurological surgery' (Keen, 1927, pp. 22–23). Keen's description of cervical sympathetic syndrome in a soldier wounded in the neck predated Johan Friedrich Horner's account by six years, being published in *Gunshot Wounds and other Injuries of Nerves* (1864). During most of his army service, he collected specimens for the Army Medical Museum, Washington.

A tour of Europe (1864–66) included Paris, studying with Guillaume Duchenne de Boulogne and Alfred Velpeau; and Berlin, working in the laboratories of Rudolf Virchow and Bernhard von Langenbeck. Keen taught surgical pathology at Jefferson (1866–75) and was appointed head of the Philadelphia School of Anatomy (1866–75), his course of lectures on pathological anatomy (1866–67) being the first ever given in that city. He married Emma Corinna Borden (1867), and they had four daughters. Corinna died in 1886, and as bereavement therapy, he edited *Gray's Anatomy* (1887). He held the posts of professor of artistic anatomy, Pennsylvania Academy of the Fine Arts (1876–90); professor of surgery, Woman's Medical College of Pennsylvania (1884–89); and professor of surgery at Jefferson (1889–1907). He traveled extensively in Britain (1881), India, Persia (1901–02), and Europe (1908), where he found many former students.

At St Mary's Hospital, Philadelphia, Keen performed the first successful removal of a brain tumor in the United States (1887), the patient being still alive in 1915. Other innovative neurosurgical procedures included decompression of the skull and drainage of the lateral ventricles in hydrocephalus, for which he established the procedure. On Joseph Lister's visit to Philadelphia (1876), Keen became converted to Lister's antiseptic system of surgery, and with James William White, he wrote *An American Text-Book of Surgery* (1892), the first such text in the United States to incorporate Listerian principles. This was superseded by his edited work, *Surgery: Its Principles and Practice* (1906–21). Keen assisted in the secret operations performed on President Grover Cleveland (1893) for malignant maxillary tumor, later writing a detailed description of the procedure (1917). His successor at Jefferson, J. Chalmers DaCosta, claimed that in the worst surgical situations, Keen always became calmer, quieter, kinder, and more pleasant. In later life, he was a popular and entertaining after-dinner speaker.

Increasing eminence brought honorary degrees from American and foreign universities, including Edinburgh, Paris, and Uppsala; and honorary fellowships from the American College of Surgeons, the Italian Surgical Society, the German Surgical Society, and the Royal Colleges of Surgeons of England, Edinburgh, and Ireland. The first American surgeon to be elected President of the International Society of Surgery (1920), he presided over its meeting in Paris (1923) and was variously president of the American Surgical Association (1899), the American Medical Association (1900), the College of Physicians of Philadelphia (1900), the Congress of American Physicians and Surgeons (1903), and the American Philosophical Society (1908). Other honors included Order of the Crown of Belgium (1920), the Légion d'Honneur, France (1923), and the Bigelow Medal of Boston Surgical Society (1922). During World War I, he was the oldest member of the Medical Reserve Corps (rank of major) and a member of the National Research Council (1917–18). Despite his religious beliefs (lifelong member of the First Baptist Church, Philadelphia), Keen was a fervent spokesperson for evolutionary theory and the importance of animal experimentation. He believed that the greatest medical discoveries were vaccination, anesthesia, and antisepsis.

Bibliography

Primary: 1864. (with Mitchell, Silas Weir, and George R. Morehouse) *Gunshot Wounds and Other Injuries of Nerves* (Philadelphia); 1892. *An American Text-Book of Surgery: For Practitioners and Students* (Philadelphia); 1905. *Addresses and Other Papers* (Philadelphia and London); 1906–21. (ed.) *Surgery: Its Principles and Practice*, 8 vols. (Philadelphia); 1914. *Animal Experimentation and Medical Progress* (Boston); 1917. *The Surgical Operations on President Cleveland in 1893* (Philadelphia); 1917. *The Treatment of War Wounds* (Philadelphia and London); 1923. *Selected Papers and Addresses* (Philadelphia); 1927. *Address. Celebration of the Ninetieth Birthday of William Williams Keen, M.D.* (Philadelphia); 1990. (James, W. W. Keen, ed.) *The Memoirs of William Williams Keen, M.D.* (Doylestown, PA).

Secondary: Soria, Emilio D., and Edward J. Fine, 1993. 'On Dalton's Cat: The History of Cervical Sympathetic Syndrome.' *Journal of the History of the Neurosciences* 2(4): 303–313; Geist, D., and G. R. Erikson, 1976. 'The Writings of William Williams Keen: A Selective Annotated Bibliography.' *Transactions and Studies of the College of Physicians of Philadelphia* 43: 337–371; *DAMB*.

Carole Reeves

KELLOGG, JOHN HARVEY (b. Tyrone Township, Michigan, USA, 26 February 1852; d. Battle Creek, Michigan, USA, 14 December 1943), *health reform.*

The son of John Kellogg and Ann Stanley, Kellogg married Ella Eaton in 1879; they had no children. He first studied hydropathy at the Hygeio-Therapeutic College in Florence, New Jersey (1872), and then attended medical lectures at the University of Michigan and Bellevue Hospital College of Medicine in New York City, receiving his MD from the latter (1875).

Reared in the Seventh Day Adventist Church, Kellogg adopted the health teachings of the Church's leader, Ellen White, a set of precepts supposedly received through divine revelation that included abstinence from alcohol, tobacco, and meat. In 1875 Kellogg became the editor of the *Adventist Health Reformer*, which in 1878 became *Good Health*, one of the most popular health periodicals in America. He served as its editor until his death. In 1876 he assumed the directorship of the church-administered Western Health Reform Institute in Battle Creek, Michigan, which in 1878 he renamed the Medical and Surgical Sanitarium. Under the popular name of the Battle Creek Sanitarium, the institution prospered as one of the country's best-known medical facilities from the late 1800s until the 1930s. In 1942 the U.S. Army purchased the sanitarium for use as a military hospital.

Sanitarium clients were offered a program of 'biologic living' that combined vegetarian diet, exercise, fresh air, and other components of good hygiene with curative measures such as hydrotherapy, electrotherapy, phototherapy, and, in extreme cases, surgery (Kellogg was highly respected as a surgeon). He also delivered thousands of lectures on the laws of health to both sanitarium residents and lay audiences around the country and was a prolific publisher of books and articles on all aspects of health behavior. Of particular concern to him was the great pathological fad of the early 1900s, 'autointoxication', a form of self-poisoning supposed to result from bacterial decomposition of protein residues in the colon. The result of constipation, autointoxication was blamed for all manner of physical complaints, from headaches to cancer. Several of Kellogg's books were devoted entirely to the dangers of autointoxication, which he argued could be prevented by vegetable diet.

Kellogg was equally concerned about the damages done by sexual excess and masturbation, and through his interest in sexual hygiene, he became a leader in the early twentieth-century eugenics movement. He was convinced that the deleterious effects of flesh food, alcohol, tobacco, and other impurities could be passed on to offspring, and in 1905 he founded the Race Betterment Foundation in order to promote a more vigorous population. He was also a founder of the Health and Efficiency League of America and was active in the Committee of One Hundred, a group of prominent citizens that campaigned for a cabinet-level department of health. From 1895 to 1910, he ran the American Medical Missionary College.

Kellogg is best known for his development of precooked breakfast cereals, beginning with a product he called Granola (1878) and followed by a succession of flaked cereals marketed from 1894 onward. He also pioneered in the creation of nut- and gluten-based meat substitutes, including peanut butter, introduced in the early 1890s. All were promoted as beneficial for health, and soon other cereal manufacturers were opening factories in Battle Creek, establishing the city as the health food capital of the United States. One such manufacturer was Kellogg's own brother Will Keith, and it was the W. K. Kellogg Company that grew into the leader of today's breakfast cereal industry.

Bibliography

Primary: 1923. *The Natural Diet of Man* (Battle Creek, MI); 1877. *Plain Facts about Sexual Life* (Battle Creek, MI); 1918. *Autointoxication or Intestinal Toxemia* (Battle Creek, MI).

Secondary: Engs, Ruth, 2003. *The Progressive Era's Health Reform Movement: A Historical Dictionary* (Westport, CT) pp. 192–195; Whorton, James, 1982. *Crusaders for Fitness: The History of American Health Reformers* (Princeton) pp. 201–238; Schwarz, Richard, 1970. *John Harvey Kellogg, M.D.* (Nashville); *DAMB*.

James Whorton

KELLY, HOWARD ATWOOD   (b. Camden, New Jersey, USA, 20 February 1858; d. Baltimore, Maryland, USA, 12 January 1943), *gynecology*.

Kelly was the son of Henry Kuhl Kelly, a businessman, and Louise Warner Hard, whose influence was responsible for his intense religious beliefs and passion for nature. He wanted to be a naturalist but chose medicine as a more reliable profession, graduated from University of Pennsylvania Medical School (1882), and continued training at Kensington Episcopal Hospital, near Philadelphia.

He developed a private practice and founded Kensington Hospital for Women, performing operations that attracted attention from Agnew, Osler, and other luminaries. In 1888–89 he was associate professor and professor of obstetrics at his alma mater. During brief trips to Europe, he visited noteworthy surgeries and studied anatomy. While in Germany (1889), he married Letitia Bredow; eventually, there were nine children.

In 1889 Kelly went to Baltimore as chief of gynecology at the newly established Johns Hopkins Hospital, joining Welch, Osler, and Halsted to form the Hopkins' famous 'Four Doctors'. When the Johns Hopkins Medical School opened (1893), Kelly was named professor of obstetrics and gynecology. Kelly had little interest in obstetrics, which soon became a separate department.

Kelly established a long-term residency program in gynecology that helped develop the specialty and produced several protégés who achieved fame. He was a superb operator, precise and careful; his operating room was usually crowded with Hopkins students and visiting surgeons for whom he skillfully described his cases. He developed surgical instruments, including the Kelly clamp, Kelly pads that facilitated drainage from the operating table, and an air cystoscope. He also developed new techniques for diagnosis and treatment of bladder, ureter, and kidney diseases.

In 1892 Kelly acquired a small private clinic that he enlarged and renamed Howard A. Kelly Hospital, serving as physician in chief until 1938. There he experimented with radium in cancer treatment. He resigned from Hopkins in 1919 when the hospital adopted the 'full time' policy, but remained emeritus professor and honorary consultant in gynecology. He continued to operate at the Kelly Hospital until 1940, when he retired and the hospital closed.

Kelly was a prolific author with a bibliography of nearly 550 titles. *Operative Gynecology* (2 vols.) appeared in 1898 with illustrations by Max Brödel, establishing gynecology as a surgical specialty and illustration as an important component of medical publishing. Other notable works include *The Vermiform Appendix and its Diseases*, with Elizabeth Hurdon (1905); *Gynecology and Abdominal Surgery*, with Charles P. Noble (2 vols., 1907–08); *Medical Gynecology* (1908); *Myomata of the Uterus*, with Thomas S. Cullen (1909); and *Diseases of the Kidney, Ureters, and Bladder*, with F. R. Burnham (1914).

Kelly never lost his interest in natural science. He was an expert in mycology. Summers were spent in the backwoods of Canada, where he pursued this hobby as well as botany and ornithology. In 1914 he published *Some American Medical Botanists*. A man of limitless energy and interests, he also produced *Cyclopedia of American Medical Biography* (1912), *American Medical Biographies* (1920), and *Dictionary of American Medical Biography* (1928), the last two with Walter L. Burrage.

Devotion to his Christian faith was an important part of his life. He delivered Sunday sermons, was active in social reform, supported missionaries, and founded a summer camp for poor boys. He was reputed to have made philanthropic contributions exceeding one million dollars, being especially generous to Hopkins.

Kelly's accomplishments were recognized with honorary degrees, membership in foreign medical societies, and awards from foreign governments. He was president of the Southern Surgical and Gynecological Society (1907) and the American Gynecological Society (1912).

Bibliography

Secondary: Davis, Audrey W., 1959. *Dr. Kelly of Hopkins, Surgeon, Scientist, Christian* (Boston); Corner, George W., 1943. 'Howard Atwood Kelly (1858–1943) as a Medical Historian.' *Bulletin of the History of Medicine* 14: 191–200; Cullen, Thomas S., 1943. 'Dr. Howard Atwood Kelly, the Last of the Johns Hopkins "Big Four".' *Johns Hopkins Alumni Magazine* 31 (3–4); *DAMB*.

Amalie M. Kass

KENNY, ELIZABETH   (b. Warialda, New South Wales, Australia, 20 September 1880; d. Toowoomba, Queensland, Australia, 30 November 1952), *physical therapy, rehabilitative medicine.*

The daughter of Michael Kenny and Mary Moore, Kenny attended rural primary schools, followed by informal nursing apprenticeships. Her main mentor was Toowoomba physician and surgeon Aeneas McDonnell. Kenny worked first as a bush nurse in southern Queensland (1910–15), founding and directing a small private hospital, St Canice's in Clifton. From 1915 to 1919 she served with the Australian Army Nursing Service, being promoted to the rank of Sister in 1916.

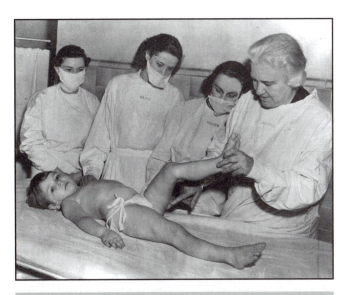

Kenny (right) demonstrates her therapy techniques at the Sister Kenny Institute. Photograph *c.* 1942. Minnesota Historical Society.

After the war she worked for more than a decade (1920–32) as a private nurse, specializing in patients paralyzed by poliomyelitis. Based on this experience, she obtained federal and state government support (1933–39) to found polio clinics in Queensland, New South Wales, Victoria, and Tasmania. However, her innovative methods increasingly antagonized local physicians, and in 1940 she relocated to Minneapolis, Minnesota where, until 1942, she treated polio patients and directed courses for doctors, nurses, and physical therapists in the 'Kenny method' at Minneapolis General Hospital and the University of Minnesota Hospital, with funding from the National Foundation for Infantile Paralysis (March of Dimes).

In 1942 she established and directed the Elizabeth Kenny Institute in Minneapolis. The Elizabeth Kenny Foundation, launched in 1943 and the primary financial support for her work throughout the United States, became an explicit competitor for public support against the March of Dimes campaigns. Her major textbook, *The Kenny Concept of Infantile Paralysis and Its Treatment* (1943), was published in collaboration with Minneapolis physician John Florian Pohl. She also produced three clinical films demonstrating her methods (1943–49).

Kenny organized numerous Kenny clinics across the United States while continuing to train former nurses or physical therapists as 'Kenny therapists'. In 1948 she was an expert witness at Congressional hearings on the National Science Foundation. Although she retired in 1949 from the directorship of the Kenny Institute and returned to Toowoomba, she continued to travel to North America and Europe. Kenny never married, although in 1926 she adopted Lily Stewart (renamed Mary Kenny).

RKO Studios released a Hollywood movie, *Sister Kenny* (1946), based on her autobiography and starring Rosalind

Kenny (right) and her niece Mary are met by Cary Grant at the opening of the movie *Sister Kenny*. Kenny was played by Rosalind Russell. Photograph 1946, Minnesota Historical Society.

Russell. In 1952 Elizabeth Kenny was ranked by a Gallup poll as America's most admired woman, outranking former first lady Eleanor Roosevelt.

Elizabeth Kenny's new methods of treating patients paralyzed by polio had become standard care by the 1940s. Opposed to the orthodox use of splinting and orthopedic surgery, Kenny argued that muscle movement could be restored through careful muscle training and the use of 'hot packs' of moist heat. She developed a new conception of polio paralysis in which so-called 'normal' muscles were in fact in 'spasm', while opposing flaccid muscles were not paralyzed but were dissociated from motor neurons and needed to be 're-educated'. Her 'Kenny method' was adopted by doctors, nurses, and physical therapists, and promoted by women's and businessmen's clubs, the press, and the families of patients. She sought to gain scientific interest in her theory of polio as a non-neurotropic, systemic disease, but as a nurse she lacked scientific authority, and this concept was accepted only after the work of David Bodian, Isabel Morgan, John Enders, and other virologists in the late 1940s. Major collections of Elizabeth Kenny Papers are held at the Minnesota Historical Society and at Fryer Library and Department of Special Collections, University of Queensland.

Bibliography

Primary: 1937. *Infantile Paralysis and Cerebral Diplegia: Methods Used for the Restoration of Function* (Sydney); 1943. (with Ostenso, Martha) *And They Shall Walk: The Life Story of Sister Elizabeth Kenny* (New York); 1955. *My Battle and Victory: History of the Discovery of Poliomyelitis as a Systemic Disease* (London).

Secondary: Rogers, Naomi, 2004. 'Sister Kenny Goes to Washington: Polio, Populism and Medical Politics in Postwar America' in Johnston, Robert D., ed., *The Politics of Healing: Histories of Alternative Medicine in Twentieth-Century North America* (New York) pp. 97–116; Gould, Tony, 1995. *A Summer Plague: Polio and Its Survivors* (New Haven, CT); Wilson, John R., 1995. *Through Kenny's Eyes: An Exploration of Sister Elizabeth Kenny's Views about Nursing* (Townsville); Cohn, Victor, 1975. *Sister Kenny: The Woman Who Challenged the Doctors* (Minneapolis).

Naomi Rogers

KERR, NORMAN SHANKS (b. Glasgow, Scotland, 17 May 1834; d. Hastings, Sussex, England, 30 May 1899), *addiction medicine.*

Born in Glasgow as the eldest son of a Glasgow merchant, Kerr attended a Glasgow high school. Supporting himself as a journalist with the *Glasgow Mail*, he studied medicine at the University of Glasgow, where he established a Total Abstinence Society. After graduating (1861), Kerr worked for a few years as a surgeon on Allan Canadian Mail steamers. In 1871 he practiced in Dunstable, where he was public vaccinator, and in the same year, he married Eleanor Henderson. Three years later, the couple settled in St Johns Wood, London, and Kerr became the Medical Officer of Health of St Marylebone, a post he held for twenty-four years, encountering many cases of working-class drunkenness. His interest in drunkenness, however, extended beyond that of the traditional temperance movements and included the United Kingdom Alliance, of which he was a long-standing member. It also covered the less obvious and more problematic issue of abuse by middle-class and upper-class patients, whom Kerr encountered in his private practice, and he was particularly interested in the problem of female middle-class drinking. He promoted the concept of 'inebriety' or 'dipsomania' to refer to the craving for drink as a medical problem; habitual drinking was for him a mental disease affecting willpower.

Kerr succeeded in organizing medical opinion in a campaign for legislation to provide institutional care for habitual drunkards. He became president of the Society for Promoting Legislation for the Control and Cure of Habitual Drunkenness, founded (1876) to petition Parliament to establish a legal institutional framework for the care of habitual drunkards. The Habitual Drunkards Act 1879 was passed, which provided government licenses for private homes. Kerr became senior consulting physician of the Dalrymple Home in Rickmansworth, Hertfordshire (1883). This was a model sanatorium offering care to recovering middle-class and upper-class alcoholics who had entered treatment voluntarily.

Because the Habitual Drunkards Act 1879 did not provide legal endorsement for compulsory confinement for alcoholics, Kerr set up the Society for the Study and Cure of Inebriety (1884), aimed at promoting the notion of habitual drunkenness as a medical condition. Kerr was corresponding secretary of the American Association for the Cure of Inebriates, and the association's program influenced the emphasis on the need for medical institutional care. Kerr served as the president of the Society for the Study and Cure of Inebriety until his death, and he edited its *Proceedings*.

His efforts resulted in the Inebriates Act 1898, which granted the State powers to provide asylums in which habitual drunkards could be forcibly detained.

Two years after his first wife's death (1892), which left him with four daughters and a son (Arthur, d. 1933, a rector in the Church of England), Kerr remarried Edith Jane Henderson (d. 1922), who fully supported her husband's temperance work as vice president of the British Women's Total Abstinence Union. Ill health led Kerr to retire to Hastings in Sussex, where he died. He was buried at Paddington Cemetery, London.

Kerr was Britain's leading specialist on alcoholism in the late nineteenth century. He regarded habitual drinking as a medical rather than a moral problem. He led the way to the understanding of what is now known as addiction, and his efforts placed alcohol dependence firmly within the realm of medicine.

Bibliography

Primary: 1888. *Inebriety, Its Aetiology, Pathology, Treatment, and Jurisprudence* (London, 2nd edn. 1889, 3rd edn. 1894); 1895. *Alcoholism and Drug Habits* in vol. 3 of Stedman, Thomas L., ed., *Twentieth Century Practice* 20 vols. (London).

Secondary: Berridge, Virginia, 1990. 'The Society for the Study of Addiction, 1884–1988.' *British Journal of Addiction* 85(5); MacLeod, Roy M., 1967. 'The Edge of Hope: Social Policy and Chronic Alcoholism. 1870–1900.' *Journal of the History of Medicine and Allied Sciences* 22: 215–245; *Oxford DNB*.

An Vleugels

KEYNES, GEOFFREY LANGDON   (b. Cambridge, England, 25 March 1887; d. Brinkley, Cambridgeshire, England, 5 July 1982), *surgery, bibliography*.

After studying at Cambridge University, Keynes trained at St Bartholomew's Hospital, London, winning a scholarship in surgery and qualifying in 1914. On the outbreak of World War I, he joined the Royal Army Medical Corps and was immediately posted to France. He spent the entire war there, at first in the trenches and then in casualty clearing stations. The experience gave him vast surgical experience, as well as an interest in pioneering blood transfusion, on which he subsequently wrote the first textbook published in Britain (1922) and helped establish the blood transfusion service in London.

After the war, Keynes returned to a post on the new surgical professorial unit at St Bartholomew's, gaining higher qualifications in surgery (FRCS, 1920) and being appointed assistant surgeon in 1928. He specialized in hernia repair, thyroid and gastric surgery, and especially cancer of the breast. For the last he employed the new radiation treatment, at first using radium needles and then radiotherapy—either as well as conventional surgery or as a substitute for it in advanced cases. So good were the results that Keynes started to abandon the conventional radical mastectomy—then much-feared for its extensive mutilating effects—in favor of

simple 'lumpectomy' and radiation. Though this then challenged orthodox management, much later it came to be preferred as an equally curative approach. In World War II, Keynes served in the Royal Air Force, becoming acting air vice-marshal. He continued research, however, helping to pioneer excision of a thymic tumor to cure myasthenia gravis

Retiring in 1952, Keynes continued his other life. He was elected FRCP (1953) and knighted (1955). He had received a copy of his first book, a bibliography of John Donne (1572–1631), while in the trenches in 1914. For the rest of his life, he wrote about and edited his favorite authors—especially William Blake (1757–1827), John Evelyn (1620–1706), William Harvey (1578–1657), and Rupert Brooke (1887–1915, a friend until his death), often publishing with the Nonesuch Press, being a great friend of its founder, Francis Meynell. He was also a member of the prestigious bibliographic coteries, the Roxburghe Club and Grolier Club. A lover of the ballet, Keynes also wrote the program for *Job*, a masque for dancing based on works by Blake, whose graphic work he numbered among his extensive collection. The music was by Ralph Vaughan Williams (1872–1958), another friend, and the scenery by his sister-in-law, Gwen Raverat, a celebrated engraver. Keynes was also a trustee, and later chairman, of the National Portrait Gallery, using his knowledge to discover an unknown portrait of Harvey in a derelict mansion, which the gallery later acquired.

In all this his family connections and friends helped Keynes, for he was part of a great Cambridge intellectual dynasty. His father was a university lecturer and later a senior administrative official; his great-uncle was the pediatrician John Langdon Down (1828–96, describer of Down syndrome); his brother Maynard Keynes (1883–1946) was an economist; his sister married the physiologist Archibald Vivian Hill; and his son married a daughter of E. D. Adrian, who, like Hill, was a Nobel Prize winner for physiology or medicine. Through Maynard, Keynes knew many of the Bloomsbury Group, though he always denied being part of it, and indeed in 1913 he saved the life of the author Virginia Woolf (1882–1941), who had taken an overdose, by rushing her to the casualty department at St Bartholomew's for urgent treatment. Nevertheless, Keynes always said that surgery gave him the greatest satisfaction of all his vocations, and countless women have to thank him for his courage in introducing and persisting with a nonmutilating procedure to treat the commonest tumor to affect them.

Bibliography

Primary: 1922. *Blood Transfusion* (London); 1932. *The Radium Treatment of Carcinoma of the Breast* (Bristol); 1981. *The Gates of Memory* (Oxford).

Secondary: Osler Club, 1961. *Geoffrey Keynes, Tributes on the Occasion of his 70th Birthday: with a bibliographical check list of his publications* (London); *Munk's Roll; Oxford DNB; Plarr's Lives*.

Stephen Lock

KHĀN, MUHAMMAD AJMAL (b. Delhi, India, 12 February 1863; d. Rampur, India, 29 December 1927), *hakīm, physician of unani tibb.*

Ajmal Khān, son of Ghulām Mahmūd Khān and great-grandson of Muhammad Sharīf Khān, belonged to an illustrious Delhi-based family of practitioners of tibb who had migrated from Herat (Afghanistan) with Babur, the founder of the Mughal dynasty in 1526. Ajmal Khān studied Persian, Arabic, and the subjects of traditional Islamic learning. He studied tibb under his father and elder brothers, Hakīms Abdulmajīd Khān and Wāsil Khān. In 1884 Ajmal Khān married the daughter of Hakīm Ghulāmullāh Khān, who bore two daughters and a son. The family physicians ran a renowned clinic from their ancestral home in Delhi. In 1883 Abdulmajīd Khān established the first independent institution of unani tibb in India, Madrasa Tibbiya, which was formally opened in 1889.

Ajmal Khān was appointed as physician to the Nawāb of Rampur (1892), where he remained until 1901. During this time he composed his first work in Urdu, on plague (*al-Tā'ūn*), which struck Bombay in 1896. The work advocated a learned unani profession accessible to ordinary people. Ajmal Khān returned to Delhi upon the death of Abdulmajīd Khān, to set up his own clinic. He acquired fame for his pulse and urine diagnosis and dispensed free medicines to the poor, Hindus and Muslims alike, but charged 1,000 rupees for visits outside Delhi. Ajmal Khān subsequently took over the Madrasa and its journal, *Majalla-i Tibbiya*. The school imparted education in tibb and elements of the Western medical disciplines of surgery, anatomy, and physiology. The Sharīfi practices also reflected the composite (ayurvedic and unani) culture of unani practice in India in their preparation of medicinal calces (*kushtajāt*).

Keeping abreast with pressures for the commercialization of quality unani medicines, and in order to help meet the expenses of the school, Ajmal Khān took over his elder brother's 'Unani and Vedic Medicines Limited Company' (1904) and founded the successful (and still operating) Hindustānī Davākhāna [Hindustani dispensary]. Ajmal Khān's initiative to provide formal medical education for women in midwifery and unani tibb, paralleling the activities of Christian medical missions and Western women's health organizations in India, led to the establishment of the Madrasa Tibbiya Zenāna va Shifākhāna [Unani Women's School and Clinic] (1909).

By 1910 Ajmal Khān's plans for a forum representing a united front of ayurvedic and unani practitioners, in the light of the proposals for a Medical Registration Act in the Bombay legislature, came to fruition as the All India Vedic and Unani Tibbi Conference, which convened in Delhi in 1910 and played a leading role for the promotion of unani and ayurvedic interests into the 1920s.

By 1916 Ajmal Khān secured college status for the Madrasa Tibbiya; the Viceroy Lord Hardinge laid the foundation stone and Mahatma Gandhi inaugurated the Ayurvedic and Unani Tibbi College in 1921. This did not reflect unqualified support for tibb from the British government in India or from Gandhi, but it did indicate Ajmal Khān's political stature. Ajmal Khān's life in politics intersected with his medical activities. He was active in the 1910s and 1920s in movements against British rule and in the Indian National Congress, reflecting his ideal of a composite Hindu and Muslim national culture in India. He founded the university Jamia Millia in Delhi (1920). Between 1905 and 1925 Ajmal Khān visited several countries in Europe and West Asia, mostly in connection with his medical and political pursuits.

Ajmal Khān planned for the establishment of a research laboratory for the chemical analysis of medicinal plants, a plan realized posthumously (1928). Working there from 1929, Dr. Salimuzzaman Siddiqui (1897–1994) analyzed *pāgal būtī sarpangadha* (*Rauwolfia serpentina*), commonly used in indigenous medicine for snakebite and mental ailments, naming an active ingredient he isolated—ajmaline—in honor of his patron.

Bibliography

Primary: 1315 Hijri [1898]. (*al-Tā'ūn*) (Delhi); [n.d.]. *Hāziq* (Delhi); 1991. *Rasā'il Masīh al-Mulk* (ed., trans. M. Razi ul-Islam Nadvi) (Aligarh).

Secondary: Nizami, Zafar Ahmed, 1988. *Hakim Ajmal Khan* (Delhi); Metcalf, Barbara D., 1986. 'Hakim Ajmal Khan: Rais of Delhi and Muslim Leader' in Frykenberg, R. E. ed., *Delhi through the Ages: Essays in Urban History, Culture and Society* (Delhi) pp. 299–315; Metcalf, Barbara D., 1985. 'Nationalist Muslims in British India: The Case of Hakim Ajmal Khan.' *Modern Asian Studies* 19: 1–28; Abdul Ghaffar, Qazi Muhammad, 1950. *Hāyāt-i Ajmal* (Aligarh).

Guy Attewell

KHĀN, MUHAMMAD A'ZAM (b. Rampur, India, 1813; d. Indore, India, 13 April 1902), *hakīm, physician of unani tibb.*

Hakīm A'zam Khān was the son of Hakīm Shāh A'zam Khān. His ancestors were originally from Sistan (Afghanistan), but his family had made their home in various locations in Uttar Pradesh (northern India) over many generations. A'zam Khān's forefathers had long-standing ties to the military, and had been granted land (*jāgīr*) for their service to Nawāb Sayyid 'Ali Muhammad Khān of Rohilkhand. A'zam Khān's father broke with the family tradition of soldiery to take up medicine as a profession, which he learned from a disciple of a line of physicians who traced their studentship back to the distinguished early eighteenth-century physician Hakīm 'Alavī Khān (d. 1749). A'zam Khān was fourteen when his father died but continued his studies of Persian and Arabic, logic, and religious studies. He studied tibb under Hakīm Maulvī Nūrulislām.

Hakīm A'zam Khān moved to the wealthy Princely State of Bhopāl during the rule of Nawāb Qudsiya Begum (1835) and became physician of Nawāb Jahāngīr Muhammad Khān. In 1837 A'zam Khān gained promotion, earning a monthly salary of 200 rupees and land yielding 3,000 rupees annually, and he was awarded the title *Nāzim-i Jahān* ('the adjuster of the world') after successfully treating his patron for renal pain when other reputed physicians had failed. After the death of his patron in 1841, A'zam Khān left for Ujjain (Madhya Pradesh), where he worked as chief physician and judge to Bījā Bījā'ī. In 1844 he was appointed as the chief physician of Māhārāja Tukojī Rāo Holkar of the Princely State of Indore, where he remained for the rest of his long life, retiring under Sivājī Rāo Holkar, Tukojī's successor. In Indore he occupied several important positions in the state in addition to his services as a physician, including high court judge.

Known in Indore as *Masīh-i A'zam* (A'zam (lit.) 'the messiah') for his remarkable qualities as a healer, A'zam Khān was appointed examiner for the employment by the state of *hakīm*s, *vaid*s (ayurvedic practitioners), and *jarrāh*s (surgeons). In 1856 the Tukojī Rāo granted him extensive land for housing and gardens, in which he grew medicinal plants.

A'zam Khān was a renowned teacher of tibb. His illustrious students included Najmulghanī Khān and Tayyib 'Alī, under whose name pharmaceutical laboratories in Indore and Karachi were set up (Zillurrahman, 1999–2000).

A'zam Khān is best remembered for two authoritative works on unani tibb in Persian: *Iksīr-i A'zam* ('The elixir of A'zam'), on therapeutics, and *Muḥīṭ-i A'zam* ('The ocean of A'zam'), a comprehensive work on simple drugs. The four-volume *Iksīr-i A'zam* was completed in 1868, arranged according to a classical format, with diseases arranged from head to toe, and with description of the types of disease, diagnosis, and outlines of methods of treatment in that order. His efforts at comprehensiveness and his place in unani learning are reflected by his reference to 175 sources and numerous physicians. The work was presented by Tukojī Rāo to King Edward VII upon his visit to Indore. The four-volume *Muḥīṭ-i A'zam* on simple drugs included many local and indigenous drugs and the author's own experiences with them in treatment. Both of these works are considered masterpieces of unani tibb. A'zam Khān died at the age of eighty-nine, and the unani profession was continued in the family by subsequent generations until two of his great-great-grandsons became medical doctors, signaling the shifting terrain of prestige and professional opportunities in the medical professions in India during the mid-twentieth century.

Bibliography

Primary: 1871–73. *Iksīr-i A'zam* 4 vols. (Kanpur and Lucknow); 1897. *Muḥīṭ-i A'zam* 4 vols. (Kanpur); 1939. *al-Iksīr* (trans. and abridged by Hakīm Muhammad Siddiq) (Delhi).

Secondary: Zillurrahman, Syed, 1999–2000. 'Hakīm A'zam Khān and His Dictionary of Synonyms: Asmā al-adwiya.' (trans. Asghar Ali) *Studies in History of Medicine and Science* 16: 53–65; Siddiqi, Tazim Uddin, 1980. 'Nazim-e Jehan Hakim Muhammad A'zam Khan.' *Studies in History of Medicine* 4: 229–279.

Guy Attewell

KHANOLKAR, VASANT RAMJI   (b. Quetta, Baluchistan, India [now Pakistan], 13 April 1895; d. ?, 20 October 1978), *cancer research, leprosy.*

Khanolkar was the son of Dr Ramji Dhondji Khanolkar, a successful doctor in Quetta, where he grew up learning German, French, Urdu, and Persian. He studied at Bombay and at the Medical School, University College London (1920–23). Upon his return to India, after completing his MD, MRCS, and LRCP in Britain, Khanolkar was appointed professor of pathology at Grant Medical College (1924–26) and then at Seth Gordhandas Sunderdas Medical College, Bombay (1926–41). As professor, he trained a number of pathologists and organized the central clinical laboratory in the adjacent King Edward VII Memorial hospital. He was elected founder president of the Indian Association of Pathologists (1950).

When the trustees of the Sir Dorabji Tata trust established the Tata Memorial Hospital in Bombay (1941), Khanolkar accepted the offer to take over the leadership of cancer research and became its director. By 1958, 40,000 cancer patients had been treated at the hospital. After India gained independence in 1947, he gave direction to cancer research as head of the Indian Cancer Research Centre (1952–63), and started the departments of applied biology, experimental embryology, human variation and statistics, endocrinology, biochemistry, enzyme chemistry, biophysics, and microbiology. The distinctive character of his contribution was that his work would take him from the routine hematoxylin and eosin section of a tumor, to a study of the habits and customs of the people and their way of life as it influenced their susceptibility to the disease.

In his book *A Look at Cancer* (1958), he explained the significance of the warnings of cancer and how to heed them, and called for more campaigners against the disease. He believed that the preponderance of one or another form of cancer in different people was attributable to genetics, 'so-called racial factors', environmental conditions, and habits and customs. His tissue culture laboratory was located alongside his laboratory for demographic studies.

Contending that ancient Indian physicians were conversant with the features of cancer, the growth of the tumor, and the tendency to form colonies, he believed that their 'sagacious injunctions' would be valuable even today. Khanolkar was thus a fine synthesis of investigator, natural historian, and epidemiologist. He served as president of the International Cancer Research Commission (1950–54) and the International Union against Cancer (1958–62); as vice chairman of the UN Scientific Committee on the Effects of

Atomic Radiation (1958–59); and as a member of the WHO Advisory Committee on Medical Research (1959–63). He had 118 scientific publications to his credit.

His work on the pathology of leprosy lesions—*Perspectives in Pathology of Leprosy*—made important observations on the transmission of the disease and its evolution in contacts. His findings formed the standard in the teaching of leprosy. He was a member of the committee set up to review the question of establishing a leprosy research institute, and of the WHO expert panel on leprosy (1952–57).

Khanolkar's research interests included reproductive biology, family planning, and the study of blood groups. He played an inspiring role as a mentor; many young men and women obtained subjects for their doctoral dissertations from casual conversations with him.

Medical education was another area of interest to him. He took an active part in discussions on the syllabi in the medical faculty and the senate of the University of Bombay. He subsequently became vice chancellor of the university (1960–63). He was appointed National Professor of Medicine (1963) and was instrumental in formulating the policy that led to the upgrading of research facilities in various medical colleges in India. Like many young Indians who grew up in the post–World War I period, Khanolkar had tremendous enthusiasm for the establishment of world peace, universal political freedom, social amelioration, and economic equality.

Bibliography

Primary: 1945. (with Suryabai, B.) 'Cancer in Relation to Usages: Three New Types in India.' (Classic Paper, reprinted) *Indian Journal of Medical Research* 99 (March 1994): 351–361; 1955. (with Sanghvi, L. D., et al.) 'Smoking and Chewing of Tobacco in Relation to Cancer of the Upper Alimentary Tract.' (reprinted) *National Medical Journal of India* 9 (3 May/June 1996): 145–150; 1958. *A Look at Cancer* (Bombay); 1963. *Fifty Years of Science in India: Progress of Medical Science* (Calcutta).

Secondary: 1963. *Professor Khanolkar Felicitation Volume* (Bombay).

Mridula Ramanna

KHLOPIN, GRIGORII VITALIEVICH (b. Dobrianka, Russia, 28 [16] January 1863; d. Batumi, USSR, 30 June 1929), *hygiene, chemistry, physiology.*

Born into a clerical family in Perm province, Khlopin was educated at seminary for the first four years of his primary education. His interest in the natural sciences inspired a transfer to a classical gymnasium for the remainder of his school years. Khlopin studied at the physics and math faculty at St Petersburg University (1882–86), where he specialized in chemistry and physiology and completed a thesis under I. M. Sechenov's direction. He completed his requirements in the midst of an arrest due to his participation in a leftist student circle, and was immediately exiled to Perm province.

His work as a chemist and technician in Perm's hygiene laboratory led Khlopin to pursue a medical education at Moscow University (1890–96). There he earned his MD under the direction of Friedrich E. Erisman, the Swiss physician who was a pioneer of experimental hygiene science in his adopted country. After Erisman was forced to leave Russia for political reasons in 1896, Khlopin accepted a university professorship in hygiene at Iuriev University. During his tenure at the institution (1896–1903), Khlopin successfully developed what had been a new department when he arrived. He received recognition for his ongoing research, accepting a Ministry of Internal Affairs Medical Department prize in 1902 for his study of coal-based paints and their harmful effects.

Khlopin taught and directed the hygiene faculty at Novorossiisk University in Odessa between 1903 and late 1904, when he was chosen to lead the Imperial Ministry of Education's new medical section for educational institutions. He continued his teaching and research throughout this St Petersburg period at the Women's Medical Institute (1904–29). He also spent several years teaching hygiene to practicing community physicians at the Princess Elena Pavlovna Clinical University (1906–18), and held a professorship in hygiene at the Military Medical Academy (1918–29).

Khlopin combined a productive research and teaching career with continued attention to practical health problems in the localities where he worked and in the Russian Empire at large. He participated in several government commissions aimed at studying sanitary conditions and organizing surveillance and control of significant outbreaks of infectious disease. During his tenure at Novorossiisk University, Khlopin was appointed chair of the public health trusteeship for Odessa's municipal port, and served as mediator between the city's population and the port administration on health issues. During his time in St Petersburg, his research and publications included extensive work on practical problems of the quality of channelized urban sewerage systems and the methodology of water analysis, both of which were of particular interest to the city health administration. After the introduction of chemical weapons in World War I, Khlopin's research interests turned to questions of chemical defense and medical response to chemical weapons, where he performed pioneering research and served as consultant to the Soviet army.

Khlopin was one of the most important contributors to the development of experimental hygiene science in Russia. He imbued the moral traditions of the generation of hygienists that preceded him with an even greater scientific basis, keeping chemical and physiological experimental methods close to the core of the activist and consultative work that he performed on practical public health issues of his day.

Bibliography

Primary: 1899. 'Materialy dlia ottsenki vozdukh i zhidkosti kanalizatsionnykh stokov v sanitarnom otnoshenii.' [Resources for the evaluation of air and liquid from channelized drainage flows, from a sanitary point of view] *Vestnik obshchestvennoi gigieny, sudebnoi i prakticheskoi meditsiny* 11: 680–687, 982–1021; 1920. *Khimicheskaia promyshlennost' i narodnoe zdorov'e. Ocherki iz oblasti professional'noi gigieny* [Chemical industry and public health. Essays from the field of occupational hygiene] (Petrograd); 1921–23. *Osnovy gigieny* [Fundaments of hygiene] (Petrograd).

Secondary: Rachkov, A. A., 1965. *Grigorii Vital'evich Khlopin: zhizn' i deiatel'nost'* [Grigorii Vital'evich Khlopin: life and career] (Leningrad); Perov, O. V., 1963. 'G. V. Khlopin—uchenyi vysokogo obshchestvennogo dolga i gumanizma (k 100-letiiu so dnia rozhdeniia).' [G. V. Khlopin: a scientist of great civic responsibility and humanity (in honor of the 100th anniversary of his birth)] *Sovetskoe zdravookhranenie* 22(8): 84–87; Vernadsky, V. I., 1930. 'Pamiati G. V. Khlopina.' [In memory of G. V. Khlopin.] *Priroda. Ezhemesiachnyi populiarnyi estestvennonauchnyi zhurnal* [Nature: Monthly popular natural science journal] 29(1): 94–95.

Lisa K. Walker

KING, FREDERIC TRUBY

(b. New Plymouth, New Zealand, 1 April 1858; d. Wellington, New Zealand, 10 February 1938), *psychiatry, pediatrics, infant welfare.*

King was the son of English-born Thomas and Mary (née Chilman) King, who were among the early British immigrants to New Zealand. Truby's father was a member of the first New Zealand Parliament and manager of the Bank of New Zealand at New Plymouth. At age fifteen King followed his father into banking, but soon decided that this held no interest. He left New Zealand to study medicine at the University of Edinburgh in 1880 and graduated MB CM (first class) in 1886. In his final year he was awarded the Ettles Scholarship as the most distinguished graduate of his year, and two years later he was the first person to obtain the new degree of Bachelor of Science in Public Health at Edinburgh. There followed a short stint as resident medical officer at both the Edinburgh and Glasgow Royal Infirmaries. While in Edinburgh he met and married Isabella Cockburn Bella, as she was known, who had been dux of the Edinburgh Educational Institution for Young Ladies. A month after their 1887 wedding, they set sail for New Zealand.

In 1888 King was appointed medical superintendent of Wellington District Hospital, and a year later became medical superintendent of Seacliff Mental Asylum, near Dunedin, the largest mental hospital in the colony. He was also appointed lecturer in psychology and mental diseases, and examiner in public health and medical jurisprudence, at the University of Otago. Treatment of mental patients at Seacliff under King, who remained as medical superintendent until 1921, consisted of fresh air, exercise, good diet, work, and recreation. Attached to the asylum was a large farm on which patients worked. King tried to classify patients, and introduced separate facilities for epileptics and 'inebriates'. In 1894 he returned to Britain to study

Sir Frederic Truby King with a young child, possibly his granddaughter. Photograph, 1930s. Hocken Collections, Uare Taoka o Hkena, University of Otago, Dunedin.

brain pathology, and was admitted as a member of the Medico-Psychological Association, London.

King's worldwide reputation arose, however, not from his work in psychiatry, but from his initiative in founding a model infant welfare movement in New Zealand. Managing the farm at Seacliff, King developed an interest in animal nutrition which led him to draw parallels with human nutrition. Also important in alerting his attention to infant nutrition was the poor physical state of his adopted baby daughter, and his wife's complaint that he spent more effort on the health of his cattle than his own daughter. A third factor was his interaction with a colleague at Seacliff, Alexander Falconer, who had studied public health at University College London, and had been impressed by G. F. McCleary's milk depot for infants in Battersea, London. King's interest in infant welfare was further kindled by his observations, during a visit to Japan in 1904, of Japanese infants and the beneficial effects of prolonged breastfeeding.

At a time when infant diarrhea was the major killer of infants, studies and policies relating to the feeding of infants commanded the attention of new specialists in pediatrics.

Like other infant welfare leaders such as Eric Pritchard in Britain, King never faltered in his belief that breast milk was the best food for newborns. The British infant welfare journal, *Mother and Child*, later claimed that he had 'hypnotised thousands of mothers into the belief that breastfeeding was the important factor in infant care'. Unlike pediatricians in America, he argued that almost all women could breastfeed and should be persuaded to do so. Nevertheless, where breastfeeding failed, he looked to work being carried out by American pediatricians in constructing a scientific method of bottle-feeding infants. King employed a nurse, and taught her to modify cow's milk by this method.

She was so successful in helping undernourished babies that a public meeting was called in 1907 to formalize a system of training nurses to help mothers with their newborn babies. This was the start of the Society for the Promotion of the Health of Women and Children, which eventually became known as the Royal New Zealand Plunket Society, thanks to the patronage of Lady Victoria Plunket, the wife of New Zealand's governor. The Society aimed to 'inculcate a lofty view of the responsibilities of maternity', promote breastfeeding, train nurses in maternal and infant care, and educate mothers in domestic hygiene. It established six infant ('Karitane') hospitals throughout the country which treated premature babies and infants with feeding problems, and also trained nurses. New Zealand women heartily embraced the Society and set up branches all over the country. By the 1950s the Plunket Society was overseeing the health of more than 90 percent of newborn infants in the country. European New Zealanders enjoyed the lowest infant mortality rate in the world—the result of a number of factors, but generally attributed to the work of the Plunket Society.

In 1913 King was appointed to represent New Zealand at an international infant welfare conference in London. He was invited back to London in 1917 to set up an infant welfare center under the auspices of the newly formed Babies of the Empire Society. This became the Mothercraft Training Society, which established a clinic in Earl's Court London, and in 1925 moved to larger premises at Cromwell House, Highgate. Under the patronage of the Duchess of York, later the Queen Mother, it grew to be an important model for infant welfare work in Britain. In 1919 King was invited, along with Sir Arthur Newsholme and H. R. Kenwood, to represent the British Empire at the Child Welfare Section of the Inter-allied Red Cross Conference in Cannes, organized by the American pediatrician, Emmett Holt. The same year, King was made an honorary member of the American Pediatric Society, a mark of his acceptance into the international community of pediatricians.

Back home in New Zealand, King was appointed (1921) director of a new division of child welfare in the Department of Health, testimony to the importance attached to child welfare at the conclusion of the World War I. This position lasted only until 1925, as King's domineering and headstrong character did not sit well within the Department.

Still, that year he was knighted for his work in infant welfare. Throughout the 1920s he continued to support the rapidly expanding Plunket Society, run by middle-class women and staffed by nurses, in the face of opposition from his medical colleagues who felt that nurses were interfering with medical practice. King believed the primary care of infants was a more appropriate activity for women and nurses than for medical practitioners. He also alienated his medical colleagues when he blamed them for the high maternal death rate, attributing it to 'meddlesome midwifery' on the part of the medical profession. He favored natural childbirth with as little medical interference as possible.

King's publications became the authoritative source of childrearing advice in New Zealand, Britain, and elsewhere. *The Expectant Mother and Baby's First Month* went through six editions, including two London editions (1924, 1933). Throughout the British Empire, King's name became synonymous with strict routines in child care ('feeding by the clock'); yet in promoting routines he was following the dominant pediatric advice of the time. Routine feeding of infants was primarily advocated in the prevailing medical belief that this would strengthen the digestive system, and also provide more rest and strength for the breastfeeding mother.

Those who promoted a new child psychology based on John Bowlby's 'maternal deprivation' theories in the post–World War II period exaggerated the rigidity of King's advice, and claimed that King's regime prohibited a loving relationship between mother and baby. In fact, King argued that an advantage of breastfeeding was the close relationship it fostered between mother and child, and that the absence of 'mothering' (or cuddling) could lead to rickets or 'wasting away with marasmus' ('failure to thrive'). He retained an interest in psychology throughout his life, believing that 'the first five years of a child's life are by far the most momentous years of existence, because during this period the whole future being—potentialities of body, mind and even character—are mainly determined'.

In 1927 King's wife and loyal supporter died; King never recovered from her death. By the 1930s his daughter described him as old and tired; he deteriorated mentally, and the Plunket Society asked him to withdraw from involvement. When he died on 10 February 1938, these declining years were glossed over, and he was heralded as one of New Zealand's icons, the originator of the now world-famous Plunket Society. His daughter received a telegram from the Queen, and King was the first civilian in New Zealand to receive a state funeral. In 1957, to celebrate the fiftieth anniversary of the founding of the Plunket Society, King became the first New Zealander featured on a postage stamp.

Internationally respected and a brilliant speaker who captivated audiences, King proved a powerful figurehead for the infant welfare movement in New Zealand, which helped the Plunket Society to survive challenges from the medical profession and the Department of Health. While the methods he advocated fell from favor after World War II, he was a powerful propagandist for infant welfare both in New Zealand and overseas during the first thirty years of the twentieth century.

Bibliography

Primary: 1913, reprinted annually to 1932. *Feeding and Care of Baby* (London); 1924. *The Expectant Mother and Baby's First Month: For Parents and Nurses* (London).

Secondary: Bryder, Linda, 2003. *A Voice for Mothers: The Plunket Society and Infant Welfare 1907–2000* (Auckland); King, M. T., 1948. *Truby King the Man* (London); *DNZB*.

Linda Bryder

KINYOUN, JOSEPH JAMES   (b. East Bend, North Carolina, USA, 25 November 1860; d. Washington D. C., USA, 15 February 1919), *bacteriology, public health.*

Kinyoun received an MD from Bellevue Hospital Medical College (1882). He pursued postgraduate studies at Johns Hopkins, in the laboratories of Robert Koch in Berlin and Elie Mechnikov in Paris, and obtained a PhD from Georgetown University (1896). In 1886 he joined the U.S. Marine Hospital Service, and in 1887 he was appointed director of a one-room bacteriology laboratory in the Marine Hospital on Staten Island. Subsequently named the Hygienic Laboratory, it eventually became the National Institutes of Health. Kinyoun resigned from the Service in 1902. From 1903 to 1907, he was research director of the H. K. Mulford pharmaceutical company. He later entered private practice and directed the bacteriology laboratory of the District of Columbia. At the time of his death, he was director of the Army Medical Museum.

During the first decade of its existence, the Hygienic Laboratory was staffed by Kinyoun alone. Although he was frequently assigned to routine duties, Kinyoun, nevertheless, conducted a number of important investigations. He was one of the first to isolate the cholera vibrio from cases during the epidemic of 1892. He also investigated the ability of New York Bay water to sustain cholera organisms, experimented with various disinfection gases, and conducted investigations of suspected microbiological agents of yellow fever. In 1894 he returned to the Pasteur Institute to study Roux's method of producing diphtheria antitoxin. When he returned to the Hygienic Laboratory, he organized training programs to instruct Service officers in bacteriology and Émile Roux's method of preparing antitoxin. Training activities by the Laboratory were continued and expanded after Kinyoun's tenure. For reasons unknown, in 1899 Kinyoun was transferred to a remote quarantine station on Angel Island in San Francisco Bay. There he became involved with the plague epidemic of 1900–04.

In March 1900 Kinyoun provided laboratory confirmation of plague in a number of San Francisco's Chinatown residents. Fearing quarantine, residents hid their plague-sick and dead compatriots and denied the existence of an epidemic. Similarly, the business community, newspapers, and, importantly, the Governor of California tried to cover up the epidemic, vilifying Kinyoun even to the extent of accusing him of fabricating bacteriological evidence. When the epidemic continued, and Kinyoun persisted in efforts to institute control measures, while being resisted by local forces, the Surgeon General sent a blue-ribbon Commission to San Francisco to confirm or deny Kinyoun's findings. When the Commission supported Kinyoun's position, the Governor struck a deal with the Surgeon General to suppress the report of the Commission. The Governor then agreed to the implementation of plague-control efforts. The price was removal of Kinyoun from the scene. After transfer to the quarantine station in Detroit and orders to proceed to Hong Kong, Kinyoun resigned from the Service.

In 1895 the H. K. Mulford Company became the first commercial organization to market a diphtheria antitoxin. Because of his background in antitoxin technology, Kinyoun became, in 1903, after his separation from the Marine Hospital Service, director of research for the company. In 1907 Kinyoun became chairman of the department of pathology and bacteriology of the George Washington University Medical School.

During the summers of 1913 and 1914, a young medical student named Thomas Parran (1892–1968) did internships under the direction of Kinyoun, who was at the time director of the District of Columbia public health laboratory. Parran subsequently became one of the leading Surgeon Generals of the U.S. Public Health Service during the twentieth century, attributing his interest and commitment to public health to his contact with Kinyoun.

Bibliography

Primary: 1904. 'The prophylaxis of plague.' *Journal of the American Medical Association* 42: 145–147, 232–239.

Secondary: Chase, M., 2004. *The Barbary Plague: The Black Death in Victorian San Francisco* (New York); Harden, V. A., 1986. *Inventing the NIH: Federal Biomedical Research Policy 1887–1937* (Baltimore and London); *DAMB*.

Warren Winkelstein, Jr.

KITASATO, SHIBASABURŌ   (b. Kitasato, Higo domain [now Kumamoto Prefecture], Japan, 20 December 1852; d. Tokyo, Japan, 13 June 1931), *bacteriology.*

Kitasato was a Japanese bacteriologist renowned for his pioneering work as a member of the Koch Institute in Germany, with regard especially to tetanus and diphtheria antitoxin, and for his discovery of the plague bacillus while in Hong Kong. In Japan, he rose to become a leading figure in the country's medical world, and exerted strong influence on its infectious disease policy.

Kitasato was born in a remote village near the Aso Mountains, now in the Kumamoto Prefecture, on the island of Kyūshū. As the eldest son of Kitasato Korenobu, the head of

Shibasaburō Kitasato (back row, second right) standing next to Robert Koch (see biographical entry) in Japan. Koch's wife center front. Halftone reproduction from Victor Robinson, 'Robert Koch, 1843–1910', *Medical Life* 1932, vol 39: 127–174.

the village, he received primary education in local private schools. Social transformation following the Meiji Revolution of 1868 provided additional opportunities for ambitious, talented young men in the provinces like Shibasaburō. Under the new Meiji regime, acquisition of Western knowledge and sciences was thought essential to modernizing the country at the national level, and to raising living conditions at the individual level. In 1871 Kitasato entered the newly established prefectural medical college in the city of Kumamoto, where he was introduced into medical sciences by C. G. van Mansvelt (1830–1912), a Dutch medical advisor to the college. Seeing Kitasato's ability and diligence, Mansvelt gave him private tutorials and suggested that he further his study in Tokyo. Kitasato took the advice. In 1883, after eight more years of medical education and training, he received a medical degree from the University of Tokyo. In the same year, he married Matsuo Torako, the daughter of Baron Matsuo Shigeyoshi. She was a niece to the owner of a dairy plant where Kitasato had worked part time to support his own living in Tokyo.

The University of Tokyo at that time was regarded as the supreme academic institution of the Meiji state. Its graduates were meant to form the country's foremost elite, and to lead its modernization in each field. After graduation, Kitasato chose to become a central public health official to fulfill this expectation, and entered the Sanitary Bureau of the Ministry of Home Affairs.

It was at the Sanitary Bureau that Kitasato developed his interest in bacteriology. In 1885 he became a research assistant to Ogata Masanori (1853–1919), the chief of the Bureau's new laboratory, who had just returned from Germany. After his study of hygiene in Munich under Max von Pettenkofer (1818–1901), Ogata, on orders from the Japanese government, had stopped over at Robert Koch's laboratory in Berlin, where he received an induction into

bacteriology from Friedrich Löffler (1852–1915) for six months. The Japanese medical officials were cautious at that time about the rivalry between the schools, which became evident during the controversy between Pettenkofer and Koch over the cause of cholera.

Ogata thus came home with basic bacteriological skills, as well as with experimental kits and samples. At the new laboratory in Tokyo, under Ogata's guidance, Kitasato succeeded in identifying the causative agent of a mysterious poultry epidemic in Tokyo as the fowl cholera bacillus that had been discovered by Louis Pasteur (1822–95) five years earlier. The report on this epidemic published jointly by Kitasato and Ogata in the government's official gazette is regarded as the first written work in bacteriology in Japan. Ogata later assumed the first professorship of hygiene at the University of Tokyo.

Berlin

Kitasato's work at the laboratory attracted attention from senior government officials. Given the remarkable emergence of bacteriology, Nagayo Sensai (1838–1902), the director of the Sanitary Bureau, decided to send Kitasato to the Koch Institute for a longer period than Ogata's stay. The Institute was now part of the University of Berlin, and was leading the world of bacteriology with a number of breakthroughs, including Koch's own discoveries of the tubercle bacillus (1882) and of the cholera bacillus, followed by Löffler's diphtheria bacillus (1884) and G. T. A. Gaffky's pure culture of the typhoid bacillus (1884).

Kitasato thus got the chance to learn the full range of the latest bacteriological methods and techniques from Koch and his leading disciples. Once he arrived at the Institute in January 1886, his early work was concerned mainly with the cholera bacillus, in particular its viability and resistance to heat. This choice of topic reflected his determination to help his native country. As a sanitary official he had been engaged in preventive measures against cholera, which had severely attacked Japan every two or three years since the late 1870s.

According to Koch's later recollection, his first impression of his Japanese pupil was not particularly special, but, as time went by, he came to notice Kitasato's extraordinary zeal and diligence. In December 1888, at the end of the fixed three years of his stay in Berlin, Kitasato felt that he still had a lot to learn and pleaded with his superiors in Tokyo for an extension, which was subsequently approved for two years. His breakthroughs came during those two years, namely the first successful cultivation of the tetanus bacillus in a pure state (1889), and the discovery of antitoxic sera (1890).

A specific organism had already been suspected as the tetanus bacillus. The German physician, Arthur Nicolaier, had injected soil samples including a rod-shaped bacillus into animals. Having observed tetanus-like symptoms in those animals, Nicolaier had concluded in 1884 that the organism should be the bacillus causing tetanus. But the conclusion had not yet been decisive, since no researchers, including Nicolaier himself, had succeeded in isolating the organism in pure culture. It had widely been thought that the isolation would be impossible, and some researchers had even assumed that the bacillus could exist only in symbiosis with other organisms.

Kitasato, supported by Koch, challenged this assumption. He applied the methods used in his earlier research on the resistance of the cholera bacillus to heat, and more recently on the anaerobic bacterium *Clostridium chauvoi*. He eventually found that Nicolaier's organism survived at 80°C while other germs perished. By heating a mixed culture with other germs and then recultivating it in a hydrogenous atmosphere, he succeeded in isolating the organism. Experimental injections into animals confirmed that it was indeed the tetanus bacillus, *Clostridium tetani*. Kitasato first presented the result at a meeting of the German Surgical Society in April 1889.

He went on with his tetanus study. He wondered why animals injected with the culture solution of *C. tetani* got generalized symptoms of tetanus, but he could find the bacilli only around the wounds of their dead bodies. He thereby suspected that the disease was due not to the spread of bacilli but to intoxication. By devising a special percolator to filter out the bacilli from culture solution, he demonstrated the existence of tetanus toxin. It was also found that animals injected with nonlethal doses of tetanus toxin gained immunity against the disease. That immune function was due to the action of 'antitoxin' contained in the serum. Koch was pleased with these results and suggested that Kitasato and Emil von Behring (1854–1917), who was engaged in research on diphtheria, should collaborate.

In December 1890 a brief communication on immunity to diphtheria and tetanus was published under the joint authorship of von Behring and Kitasato in the *Deutsche medizinische Wochenschrift* [German Medical Weekly]. It dealt mainly with Kitasato's research on tetanus, and announced that they had succeeded in producing immunity against tetanus artificially, by injecting the serum obtained from immune animals. The report caused a sensation in the medical world. This was indeed the dawn of serology, and opened up a new era of therapeutics. Following this joint paper, similar results for diphtheria were published separately by von Behring.

When the report brought worldwide fame to Kitasato, his two-year extension of stay in Berlin was about to expire. Koch appealed to the Japanese government for a further extension. He wanted Kitasato's assistance in his struggle for the development of tuberculin. The Japanese government was at first not keen, mainly for financial reasons. But Koch's renown and Kitasato's rising reputation moved the Imperial Court of Japan. Another one-year stay was eventually made possible by a special scholarship granted from the Meiji Emperor's purse.

Kitasato returned to Japan in May 1892. The government restored him to his old post, in the Sanitary Bureau of the Home Ministry. But there were disagreements among government departments over how to treat Kitasato, now a national hero. He had a strong aspiration to establish a fully equipped, brand-new bacteriological laboratory just like Koch's Institute. But the Education Ministry opposed the new establishment on the grounds that the University of Tokyo already had a well equipped laboratory under Professor Ogata's supervision.

In order to realize Kitasato's hope promptly, Nagayo, the former director of the Sanitary Bureau, avoided interdepartmental conflicts and personally exerted his influence on the Japan Sanitary Society, a quasi-official voluntary association for the promotion of public health. Nagayo's old friend, Fukuzawa Yukichi (1834–1901), the founder of Keio University, offered a site and buildings at Shiba on the west side of Tokyo City. Later that same year, the Institute for Infectious Diseases (IID) was launched under the Sanitary Society's ownership and Kitasato's direction.

Behind the Education Ministry's opposition was an emotional discord between Kitasato and the medical faculty of the University, which had arisen while the former was still in Berlin. At that time, Japan's leading doctors were engaged in a fierce controversy over the cause of kakke, or beriberi. While Takaki Kanehiro (1849–1920), a naval surgeon, pointed out a dietary deficiency, army and Tokyo university doctors insisted on bacteriological origins of the disease. Among the latter, Ogata announced in 1886 that he had discovered the 'kakke bacillus'. But in 1889 Kitasato, from Berlin, disputed this in a German medical journal by demonstrating that Ogata's bacillus was just a coccus unrelated to beriberi. In doing so, he set professionalism above his personal respect for the man whom he had once served as an assistant. This reflected his serious attitude to scientific research, but seemed rude to some of Ogata's supporters.

Plague

Bubonic plague, which had broken out in the Yunnan region of southern China, spread eastward and reached Hong Kong in 1894. It was the first full-blown outbreak of the disease in a major city under Western rule after the rise of modern bacteriology. The world was anxious to learn the nature of the unknown causative organism of the disease. The Japanese government decided to send two distinguished researchers from rival institutions: Kitasato from the new Institute, and Professor Aoyama Tanemichi (1859–1912) from Tokyo University. They arrived in Hong Kong with their assistants on 12 June. From the British colonial government of Hong Kong, J. A. Lawson, a naval surgeon in charge of colonial hospital services, welcomed the Japanese delegation. A room was allocated in the Kennedy Town Hospital, where Aoyama was engaged chiefly in clinical and anatomical work while Kitasato conducted bacteriological examinations.

Kitasato immediately observed a bacillus in the bubo of postmortem specimens. While suspecting that this was what he was looking for, he was cautious since the material was taken from a body some eleven hours after death, long enough for possible contamination. Then he examined a blood sample from a patient in a serious condition and found a similar bacillus. Under Lawson's initiative, procedures were set in motion for publication of the discovery. The selected medium was a British journal, *Lancet*. The editorial of the 4 August issue confirmed that 'Dr Kitasato has discovered and described a specific plague bacillus.' The next week's issue carried some illustrations of slide preparations sent by Lawson. Kitasato's own report appeared in the 25 August issue, stating that the bacillus he found was rod-shaped with round ends, similar to the fowl cholera bacillus. However, Kitasato's report did not show results of Gram's staining method, a common procedure in identifying the nature of a bacterium.

Several days after Kitasato's discovery, Alexandre Yersin, a French bacteriologist, also identified a bacillus causing plague in Hong Kong. His morphological descriptions published in a bulletin of the Pasteur Institute mostly accorded with those of Kitasato. It is thus generally accepted that Kitasato and Yersin independently discovered the plague bacillus in June 1894. Yet its Latin nomenclature, *Yersinia pestis*, reflects credit only for Yersin's discovery, suggesting that the medical world was not unanimous about Kitasato's share. Ultimately, the discredit resulted from his silence about results of Gram staining examinations in his first report. Yersin, in contrast, reported from the first instance that the bacillus he discovered was gram-negative.

Kitasato returned to Japan on 30 July with regrets, as he had to leave Aoyama and the assistants who had contracted bubonic plague during their anatomical work. Fortunately, Aoyama subsequently recovered and came home. It was Aoyama who first cast a fundamental doubt on Kitasato's discovery. Sometime after his return, Kitasato had come to insist that his plague bacillus was gram-positive, and therefore that Yersin's discovery was false. Aoyama, on the other hand, supported Yersin's gram-negative bacillus, pointing out that Kitasato confused it with a gram-positive streptococcus. Controversies continued between Kitasato and Aoyama's colleagues at the University of Tokyo, notably Ogata who supported Aoyama based on his own investigation of the plague outbreak in Taiwan in 1896.

In 1899 plague entered Japan from the port city of Kobe. For the researchers, it was a chance to settle the controversy through closer examinations of new samples collected in their own country. For Kitasato, however, it proved to be a moment of embarrassment. After examining samples from thirteen patients in Kobe and Osaka, Kitasato conceded that not his but Yersin's bacillus should be regarded as the causative agent of plague. The concession was made public at a meeting of the IID in December of the same year.

In view of his erroneous comments after returning to Japan on the Gram stain reaction, it is understandable that

some cast doubt over his discovery. But it is now generally believed that what he originally found in Hong Kong was *Yersinia pestis*, since his description in *Lancet* accords with its morphology. Reexaminations of the original strains that Kitasato had sent to the Koch Institute also indicated that he had isolated the right organism. Kitasato's share of credit in the discovery of the plague bacillus is therefore still valid. But his subsequent error is also undeniable. Researchers have speculated as to why he erroneously concluded that the bacillus was gram-positive. Some have suspected a contamination of subcultures with a gram-positive organism. Others have argued that Kitasato described a different organism after his return from Hong Kong. This might seem plausible, as there are pieces of evidence suggesting that Kitasato had wavered between two types of bacillus: one, taken from buboes of patients, was gram-negative; another, from blood samples, was gram-positive. At some point after his initial description, Kitasato may have taken the latter for the former.

Kitasato's Institute

Kitasato's disadvantage in the plague controversy did not affect his popularity among the Japanese public, nor senior health officials' trust in him and the IID under his direction. Since 1893 the government had provided financial subsidies for the IID. In 1899 its ownership was transferred from the Japan Sanitary Society to the Sanitary Bureau of the Home Ministry. The IID thereby became a national institution. Despite the transfer, the IID's internal management was left almost entirely in the hands of Kitasato as director.

The IID was primarily a research institute, and Kitasato was eager to foster young talent. His disciples included Shiga Kiyoshi (1870–1954) and Hata Sahachiro (1873–1938). In 1896 Shiga discovered the causative bacillus of dysentery, *Shigella dysenteriae*, at the IID under Kitasato's guidance. Shiga went to Germany after this achievement. Kitasato was aware that the heyday of bacteriological discoveries and of serological developments in which he himself had led the way would not last forever. As with Shiga, Kitasato encouraged his pupils to go abroad (mainly to Germany) and to keep in touch with progress in research worldwide. Biomedical sciences were indeed in transition around the turn of the century. Shiga and Hata both went to study under Paul Ehrlich, who pioneered studies on chemotherapy and, notably, Hata made an important contribution to the development of Salvarsan (1909). The works of such internationally active, younger researchers such as Shiga and Hata enhanced the reputation of the IID.

However, in Kitasato's view, the IID should not simply pursue highly scientific research within the laboratory. He eagerly promoted activities directly linked to preventive and curative measures against infectious diseases. One was the provision of introductory seminars. Many sanitary workers in military or local government services gained basic bacteriological knowledge and skills there.

Another was the promotion of serum treatments. Since their coauthored article of 1890, von Behring had proceeded with research on diphtheria antitoxin intended for practical use. Kitasato attempted to extend the scope of serotherapy to other diseases. He committed himself to research on serotherapy against cholera, although he eventually had to concede its ineffectiveness. Kitajima Taichi (1870–1956), who had studied (1897–1901) under von Behring, helped Kitasato in this field of activity. Notably, Kitajima succeeded in developing antitoxic sera against the venom of *habu*, a poisonous snake common in the southern islands of Japan.

At the time of its nationalization in 1899, the IID was able to produce sera for tetanus, diphtheria, and cholera from immune animals. It was the IID's ability to produce sera that persuaded the senior sanitary officials of the Home Ministry to proceed with its nationalization. Kitasato and Goto Shinpei (1857–1929), Nagayo's successor as the Director of the Sanitary Bureau, cooperated closely on this matter. By monopolizing production, they intended to maintain the quality of serum and vaccine products that circulated in the country. Subsequently, the list of the IID's products added smallpox vaccine, sera for typhoid, dysentery, plague, *habu* venom, and so on. Profits from the sale of these products helped the finances of the IID.

In the course of administrative reform in 1914, the Japanese Cabinet suddenly decided that jurisdiction over the IID should be transferred from the Home Ministry to the Education Ministry, with a view to a future takeover of the IID by the Medical School of the University of Tokyo. Serious discordance flared up again between the ministries, and between Kitasato and University professors. The battle was over the monopoly in serum and vaccine production. The Cabinet sided with the Education Ministry and the University. In protest, Kitasato resigned as director of the IID. What embarrassed the Cabinet was that, following Kitasato, almost the entire staff of the IID, including senior members such as Kitajima, Hata, and Shiga, also resigned. Without them, the IID could not function properly. Aoyama, who took over the directorship, encountered difficulties in meeting the country's demand for sera and vaccines.

Public opinion was sympathetic to Kitasato, who lost the IID that could not have developed without his devotion. Many donations were offered to him. Having obtained the Home Ministry's sanction for the production of sera and vaccines, Kitasato and his staff opened a new private institute in December 1914 at Shirokane in Tokyo City. It was named the Kitasato Institute.

Loyalties and Honors

Since he fought hard against the Cabinet and the Education Ministry during the IID turmoil of 1914, there was a public image of Kitasato as a man of defiance, representing the standpoint of the private sector. His commitment in 1917 to establishing the Medical School at Keio University, arguably the first private medical school comparable to that of the University of Tokyo, consolidated this image.

But whatever the circumstances, Kitasato's loyalty to the Japanese state seems to have been consistent throughout his career. One example can be seen in his commitment to antituberculosis activities. He did not forget his obligation to Emperor Meiji, whose special grant had enabled him to extend his stay in Berlin. Since the grant had been designated for his study of tuberculosis, Kitasato tried to repay it by committing himself to the prevention and treatment of pulmonary tuberculosis. At that time, the disease was emerging as the biggest health problem in Japan. With Fukuzawa Yukichi's help, Kitasato opened Japan's first sanatorium for tuberculosis patients in 1893. There he vigorously promoted the clinical use of tuberculin, invented by Koch. Kitasato's loyalty to Koch, his teacher, was also notable.

As the therapeutic effects of tuberculin became subject to deep suspicion at the end of the century, Kitasato's concerns were subsequently directed more to prevention. As a member of an advisory committee to the government, he influenced the legislation of the Pulmonary Tuberculosis Prevention Regulations of 1902.

In 1908 Koch and his wife visited Japan on Kitasato's invitation, and were enthusiastically welcomed not only by medical circles but by the Japanese government and various sections of the nation. Kitasato felt delight at the reunion, and showed the Kochs the famous sights in the country. The coming of the discoverer of the tubercle bacillus encouraged Japan's antituberculosis movement. At the welcome ceremony held at the Kabuki Theater in Tokyo, it was proposed to form a national antituberculosis organization, to memorialize Koch's visit. After a few years of preparation, the Japanese Association for the Prevention of Tuberculosis began its activity in 1913. Kitasato became its first director.

Koch died two years after his visit to Japan. In grief, Kitasato built a small shrine on the site of the IID for his teacher's memorial. Koch was his role model as a researcher. But Kitasato's actual career differed somewhat from his teacher's more purely research-oriented one. For one thing, he stepped more deeply into medical politics than Koch. Both differences in personality and in the circumstances in which they lived and worked seem to have mattered.

When the Japan Medical Association was established in 1923 as the first nationwide body for the interests of medical practitioners in Japan, Kitasato was elected its first president. In 1924 he was made Baron and a member of the House of Peers. Kitasato died of a stroke at the age of eighty on 13 June 1931 at his home in Tokyo. He had remained active as a researcher, educator, director, and medical politician until the day before his death.

Bibliography

Primary: 1977. *Collected Papers of Shibasaburō Kitasato* [in English and German] (Tokyo); 1978. *Kitasato Shibasaburō ronsetsu-shū* [Collected papers in Japanese] (Tokyo); 1890. (with

Behring, E. von) 'Ueber das Zustandekommen der Diphtherie-Immunität und der Tetanus-Immunität bei Thieren.' *Deutsche medizinische Wochenschrift* 16: 1113–1114. 1894. 'The bacillus of bubonic plague.' *Lancet* ii: 428–430.

Secondary: The Kitasato Institute, ed., 2003. *Seitan-150nen-Kinen. Kitasato Shibasaburō* (Tokyo); Odaka, T., 1992. *Densen-byo Kenkyu-jo* (Tokyo); Fujino, K., 1984. *Nihon saikingaku-shi* (Tokyo); Bibel, David J., and T. H. Chen, 1976. 'Diagnosis of Plague: An Analysis of the Yesin-Kitasato Controversy.' *Bacteriological Reviews* Sept.: 633–651; Howard-Jones, Norman, 1975. 'Kitasato, Yersin, and the Plague Bacillus.' *Clio Medica* 10: 23–27; Miyajima, M., ed., 1932. *Kitasato Shibasaburō den* (Tokyo); Bullock, W., 1931. 'Shibasaburō, Baron Kitasato. 1852–1931.' *Journal of Pathology and Bacteriology* 31: 597–602; DSB.

Takeshi Nagashima

KLEBS, EDWIN (b. Königsberg, Germany, 6 February 1834; d. Bern, Switzerland, 23 October 1913), *pathology, bacteriology.*

Klebs studied medicine in Königsberg, Würzburg, Jena, and Berlin. After practicing as a physician in Königsberg, he opted in 1859 for an academic career. From 1861 to 1866 he worked as Rudolf Virchow's assistant in Berlin, after which he became professor of pathological anatomy in Bern. During the Franco-Prussian war (1870–71) he served as a doctor. In 1872 and 1882 he accepted calls to chairs in Prague and Zurich, respectively. At the age of sixty he left Europe to live and work in the United States for six years, most notably as a professor at Rush Medical College in Chicago. After returning to Europe he continued his life as an academic nomad, and died in Bern in 1913.

Klebs was a leading pathologist and medical bacteriologist of the 1870s. His book on septic infections in gunshot wounds, published in 1872, put him among the leading medical bacteriologists of his time. While working in a clearing station during the Franco-Prussian war, he studied such wounds and, as a result, proposed a biological explanation of sepsis as an infection caused by a polymorphous microorganism which he called *Microsporon septicum*. Although Klebs did some animal and cultivation experiments, the principal basis of his knowledge of infectious disease etiology was the pathological anatomy of infected tissues.

In 1878, having identified the pathogens of numerous infectious diseases, he launched an attack on his former teacher, Virchow, and insisted that infectious diseases should be seen less as internal bodily processes of the organism than as externally caused conditions. Although, mostly due to his adherence to bacterial polymorphism, many of his early findings later became obsolete, his ideas on bacterial etiologies are the single most important source of Robert Koch's so called postulates. Klebs clearly stated that producing pure cultures of a suspected pathogen and using them in subsequent animal experiments was a means to give evidence of bacterial etiologies. He even invented his own culturing technique, called 'fractionierte Kultur', for that purpose. However, the steps to be taken were not postulates for Klebs, since he proposed experimental procedures to be applied only in cases where bacterial etiologies could not be directly based on the findings of pathological anatomy.

In the 1880s, having reconciled his bacteriology with Koch's, Klebs continued to be a productive researcher, and was one of the leading experts of his day on tuberculosis, against which he invented a host of medicines. In 1893 he even invented an improved version of Koch's tuberculin which he called tuberculocidin. Likewise, he continued to be a productive medical bacteriologist. He was among the first to identify the pathogen of diphtheria, and as early as 1879 established primates as an animal model for the study of syphilis.

Bibliography

Primary: 1872. *Beiträge zur pathologischen Anatomie der Schußwunden. Nach Beobachtungen in den Kriegslazaretten in Carlsruhe 1870 und 1871* (Leipzig); 1878. *Über die Umgestaltung der medicinischen Anschauungen in den letzten drei Jahrzehnten* (Leipzig).

Secondary: Carter, K. Codell, 2003. *The Rise of Causal Concepts of Disease: Case Histories* (Aldershot); Gradmann, Christoph, 2000. 'Isolation, Contamination, and Pure Culture: Monomorphism and Polymorphism of Pathogenic Micro-Organisms as Research Problem 1860–1880.' *Perspectives on Science* 9: 147–171; Stürzbecher, M, 1977. 'Klebs, Edwin' in Bayrische Akademie der Wissenschaften, ed., *Neue Deutsche Biographie*, Vol. 11 (Berlin) pp. 719–720.

Christoph Gradmann

KLEIN, MELANIE (b. Vienna, Austria, 30 March 1882; d. London, England, 22 September 1960), *psychoanalysis.*

Klein was born in Vienna, the daughter of Moritz Reizes, a physician, dentist, and Orthodox Jewish scholar, as the youngest of four children. Little affection was shown in the family. Her sister died when she was four; her brother when she was twenty. At the age of seventeen, she became engaged to Arthur Stephan Klein, a chemical engineer, whom she married in 1903. They had three children, the oldest of whom, Melitta, became a psychoanalyst later in life and who bitterly fought her mother in the British Psychoanalytic Association. The family moved repeatedly. Family life left Klein unfulfilled, and she repeatedly suffered from depression, for which she was, at times, institutionalized. In 1914, while she lived in Budapest, she read Sigmund Freud's (1856–1939) *On the Interpretation of Dreams* (1899) and became interested in psychoanalysis. She started analysis with Sandor Ferenczi (1873–1933), who, five years later, convinced her that she could contribute to psychoanalysis by making observations of young children, in particular observations of her own. Klein developed play analysis, in which she gave children as young as three years old a set of small toys and observed how they played with them. She was the first psychoanalyst to work with children on a therapeutic basis. The investigations of Klein encouraged psychoanalysts to pay much more attention to the significance of the mother in the emotional development of young children, a topic neglected by Sigmund Freud.

In 1920 Klein and her husband separated; in 1923 they divorced. In 1921 Klein moved to Berlin, became a member of the local Psychoanalytic Society, and was further psychoanalyzed by Karl Abraham (1877–1925), who encouraged her work with children. In 1926 she moved to London, where she was active in the British Psychoanalytic Society and developed her research on children further. Her highly original and creative work aroused great interest in England. Klein's views on the emotional development of young children differed significantly from those of Freud's daughter Anna (1895–1982). After the move of Anna and Freud to London in 1938, the rivalry between these two child psychoanalysts became increasingly intense, leading to sharp disagreements, rivalry, and hostility among British psychoanalysts.

In the views of Anna Freud, children could not engage in free association and could not be analyzed. According to Klein, the emotions of very young children were characterized by aggression, sadism, envy, hate, and destructiveness. Whereas Anna Freud presented an orderly process of developmental stages, Klein proposed a dynamic set of mental processes, emotions, and developmental stages, which occurred simultaneously and with turbulent intensity. Klein emphasized the role of unconscious fantasies, which she thought were based on instincts. She stated that in the first year of life, children occupied the paranoid-schizoid position, in which they counteracted strong anxieties with defense mechanisms such as splitting (in which the world and emotions are split in strictly separated good and bad parts), idealization, and projective identification. The next phase was the depressive position, in which children began to recognize the independence of individuals (in particular the mother) around them and to develop feelings of loss, guilt, and mourning. In this phase, children also developed reparative capacities, which could counteract these feelings.

Klein was known as an extraordinarily creative and original thinker with a strong and overbearing personality who demanded absolute loyalty in her followers. Her work is still highly controversial in psychoanalytic circles.

Bibliography

Primary: 1932. *The Psychoanalysis of Children* (Vienna and London); 1957. *Envy and Gratitude: A Study of Unconscious Forces* (New York); 1964. (with Rivière, Joan) *Love, Hate and Reparation* (New York); 1975. *Note of a Child Analysis* (London).

Secondary: Kristeva, Julia, 2001. *Melanie Klein* (New York); Grosskurth, Phyllis, 1986. *Melanie Klein: Her World and Her Work* (London); Segal, Hanna, 1973. *An Introduction to the Work of Melanie Klein* (London); *Oxford DNB*.

Hans Pols

KNOX, ROBERT   (b. Edinburgh, Scotland, 4 September 1791; d. London, England, 20 December 1862), *anatomy, ethnology.*

Knox was the son of Robert Knox, an Edinburgh teacher, and Mary Scherer. He was educated at Edinburgh High School (1805–10) and received his MD at Edinburgh University (1810–14), then in a period of intellectual stagnation after its Enlightenment heyday. After studying under John Abernethy (1764–1831) at St Bartholomew's Hospital, London, Knox traveled to Brussels as an assistant surgeon in the Duke of Wellington's army, where he cared for the wounded after the battle of Waterloo (1815).

In 1817 Knox was posted to South Africa. Here he became interested in ethnology and comparative anatomy and also began to expound his radical views on politics, race, and colonialism. After returning to Edinburgh in 1820, Knox wrote up his experiences for the Royal Society of Edinburgh. He spent 1822 in Paris, enlarging his knowledge of comparative anatomy under the acknowledged master of the discipline, Georges Cuvier (1769–1832). In 1824 he married Mary Russell and in 1825 was elected FRCSEdin.

Knox believed that an understanding of comparative anatomy was central to the successful teaching of medical anatomy. He used the technique in his own research on the eye, and he campaigned for the creation of a museum of comparative anatomy at Edinburgh, becoming its first Conservator in 1825. Much of Knox's early reputation was founded on his abilities as an engaging and learned lecturer. His classes on anatomy were the largest of their kind in Britain at that time (with four to five hundred students), and they attracted not only medical students but also lawyers, painters, and aristocratic dilettanti.

In November 1827 Knox began to buy bodies for dissection from two Edinburgh grave robbers, William Burke and William Hare. Most anatomists engaged in this practice: the only other source of bodies was the gallows. By the time of their arrest in November 1828, however, Burke and Hare had murdered twelve locals and sold their bodies to Knox. Although Knox was not involved in their trial, and Burke admitted that Knox had received the bodies with no knowledge of their origins, public feeling turned against him. He was vilified in print, most effectively by Sir Walter Scott, and in February 1829 a crowd hanged and burned an effigy of Knox outside his home. Although he retained the support of his students, Knox was ostracized by his University colleagues. He resigned from the Museum in 1831 and spent the next two decades working for various small anatomy schools. In 1841 Mary died after the birth of their sixth child.

In the mid-1840s Knox sought to reinvent himself as an anthropologist. In his lecture-tour, 'The Races Of Men', he argued that the human 'race' was in fact a collection of separate species, firmly fixed in their physical and intellectual characteristics. For this work he was made an honorary Fellow of the Ethnological Society of London in 1860.

Despite this success Knox's ostracism continued until his death: he was struck off the roll of FRSEdin in 1848 and was refused various official appointments.

Historians have argued that, despite the racist nature of his later work, Knox was attempting to synthesize his interest in comparative anatomy with his radical politics to attack what he saw as the evil of European colonialism. It remains the case, however, that interest in Knox is dominated by his involvement with Burke and Hare.

Bibliography

Primary: 1837. (published anonymously) *Edinburgh Dissector* (Edinburgh); 1850. *Races of Men* (London); 1852. *Great Artists and Great Anatomists* (London).

Secondary: Richards, Eveleen, 1989. 'The "Moral Anatomy" of Robert Knox: The Interplay between Biological and Social Thought in Victorian Scientific Naturalism.' *Journal of the History of Biology* 22: 373–436; Richardson, Ruth, 1988. *Death, Dissection and the Destitute* (London); Stephen, Kathy, 1980. *Robert Knox* (London); Lonsdale, Henry, 1870. *A Sketch of the Life and Writings of Robert Knox, the Anatomist* (London); *DSB*; *Oxford DNB*.

Richard Barnett

KOCH, HEINRICH HERMANN ROBERT (b. Chausthal, Germany, 11 December 1843; d. Baden-Baden, Germany, 27 May 1910), *bacteriology*.

The biography of Koch is linked to the rise of medical bacteriology in the late nineteenth century and the history of experimental hygiene in that period. He developed many of the principal tools, methods, and concepts of medical bacteriology, a discipline that arose during the time span of his career. Koch was interested in applications of the newly developed knowledge in the sphere of public health and hygiene. His career was closely connected to the founding and growth of institutions that were central to bacteriological hygiene as a discipline.

Koch was born in a small north German mining town. The family was petty bourgeoisie, with Koch's father working as a senior official at a local mine. While at school, apart from being attracted to observing and collecting plants and animals in a general way, Koch showed little interest in the microcosmos that he would later research. Of more relevance is that Koch, who spent much time on the road as an experimental scientist, showed a considerable passion for traveling, and nurtured dreams of emigration (to America) in his early years. Such plans and desires were not uncommon in the Koch family: six out of eight brothers emigrated from Germany, and Koch's own such plans were a continuous source of worry to his parents. His dream ended with Koch's first marriage in 1867 to Emmy Fraatz, who seems to have had a dislike for such adventures.

From 1862 Koch was a student in nearby Göttingen, starting in botany, physics, and mathematics. He became a medical student in 1863 and showed considerable talent,

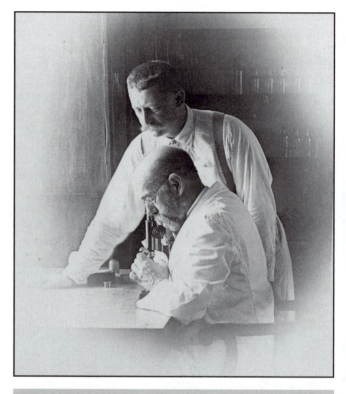

Robert Koch (at microscope) and Richard Pfeiffer investigating the plague in Bombay (1896–97). Photograph attributed to Captain C. Moss, 1897. Iconographic Collection, Wellcome Library, London.

finishing first in a prize essay competition with the topic, 'the existence and distribution of uterine nerves in the ganglia'. His doctoral thesis was on some particulars of urinary excretion. Koch's thesis-related research included a heroic self-experiment of consuming several kilograms of butter to test the presence of succinic acid in the urine. Results of this research were published in Jacob Henle's *Zeitschrift für rationelle Medizin* in 1865. The anatomist Henle, one of Koch teachers, had been a pioneer of medical bacteriology somewhat earlier, by giving a theoretical account of the possible existence and proof of pathogenic germs. However, later in his life, Koch explicitly denied having received any particular training for his career in bacteriology at university, and it seems that what he took with him upon graduating from Göttingen in 1866 was a sound training in microscopical anatomy and physiology that he received from Henle, the physiologist Georg Meissner, and the pathologist Karl Hasse.

Primarily thanks to the recent work carried out by French researchers such as Louis Pasteur, microbiology was becoming a fashionable issue in the 1860s, and it is likely that a cholera epidemic that hit Germany in 1866 gave Koch his first experience in working on pathogenic germs. As an assistant physician at a hospital in Hamburg, he seized the opportunity to investigate the microscopical pathology of cholera, probably observing those structures that came to be famous as the comma bacillus of cholera (*Vibrio cholerae*) almost two decades later.

However, there are no indications that Koch was heading for a scientific career at that time. After leaving university, he married and decided to establish a private practice to make a living. This turned out to be difficult to achieve and included several failed attempts, renewed plans for emigration, and practice as a military doctor in the Franco-Prussian war (1870–71) where he gained experience in wound infections and typhoid. Finally, in 1872 Koch became district physician (*Kreisphysikus*) in nearby Wollstein (today Wolsztyn, Poland), where he stayed as a successful and increasingly wealthy practitioner for the next seven years.

In Wollstein, Koch finally started his work in medical bacteriology. The starting point he chose was a veterinary disease, anthrax, that frequently occurred among local sheep populations. Starting from Casimir Joseph Davaine's research, which had proposed that the disease was caused by small rod-like structures in the blood, Koch succeed in describing the full life cycle of what became known as *Bacillus anthracis*, and to reproduce the disease in animal experiments. A crucial point in his proof of the bacillus's stability as a species and its pathogenic effects was the demonstration of a spore stage in its development. This provided evidence of the constant presence of the microorganism in infected animals; offered a new explanation concerning phenomena that had seemed to indicate pleomorphism or spontaneous generation; and explained the epidemiology of the disease, most notably the survival of the bacteria under unfavorable conditions. Thus Koch's achievement lay less in discovering a microorganism than in fully describing its life cycle, and in establishing a causal link of this bacterial species to a certain disease. He had applied knowledge about bacteria that had been developed by botanists such as Ferdinand Julius Cohn to the medical question of disease causation and disease definition. Finally, his work included a proposal of such hygienic measures that seemed suitable to prevent further propagation of anthrax epidemics, e.g. by properly disposing of cadavers, which he identified as a main source of future infections.

For publication of his results, Koch in 1876 turned to F. J. Cohn. Cohn, on whose bacteriological work Koch's approach relied, was a professor of botany at the University of Breslau. He enthusiastically greeted Koch's results (which provided fresh supporting evidence for his system of bacteria) and connected him to other local researchers in the medical faculty who crucially influenced Koch's future career. Carl Weigert introduced Koch to bacterial staining and to his nephew, Paul Ehrlich, who would later be one of Koch's most important collaborators and a master of staining technique himself. Equally important was the pathologist, Julius Cohnheim, an expert in experimental pathology and animal experimentation—methods that would be crucial for Koch's work.

Still in Wollstein, Koch spent three years expanding his experimental technology and methodology. In 1877 he published 'Verfahren zur Untersuchung, zum Konservieren und Photographieren der Bakterien', in which, among other inventions, he introduced microphotography of bacteria, which was not only a means of giving what was regarded by contemporaries as an objective image, but equally created the means of quickly spreading the newly acquired knowledge about bacteria. Later in 1877 he published a paper on the etiology of wound infections, and for the first time made systematic statements about criteria to be fulfilled in experimentally establishing disease causation. Much later, these statements came to be called 'Koch's postulates' by his colleague, Friedrich Löffler. In their classical form, these postulates include, first, the proof of a specific microorganism in infected tissues; second, its isolation and cultivation into pure cultures; and third, a renewed bringing about of the same disease by using these cultures in animal experiments. The term 'postulates' is, however, somewhat misleading, since the most constant trait of the various statements Koch gave on the issue was not the chain of identification, cultivation, and inoculation, but the flexibility with which he modified his methods upon any given case. Even though he mostly emphasized the crucial and indispensable character of animal experiments, he showed no hesitation to deny their necessity in other cases.

Koch's talent for polemics became obvious in 1877 when, on the occasion of a book review, he delivered a ferocious attack on Carl von Naegeli's theory of infectious diseases. Since Naegeli was the most prominent advocate of bacterial pleomorphism (the concept that among bacteria no distinct and fixed species could be found), the object of his polemic was well chosen. Medical bacteriology as it was devised by Cohn and Koch was entirely reliant on the specificity of bacterial species to which they linked constant pathological effects as one more property of such organisms.

Having started his career, Koch tried to leave Wollstein. Attempts by the Breslau faculty of medicine in 1879 to create an extraordinary professorship in hygiene for him failed. A subsequent attempt to move his medical practice to Breslau proved to be economically disastrous. One year later, in 1880, aided by Julius Cohnheim, Koch became an employee of the recently founded Imperial Health Office in Berlin, where he set up a small hygienic laboratory. His first collaborators in a quickly growing team were Ferdinand Löffler and Georg Gaffky. The next five years Koch spent at the Imperial Health Office were the most productive phase of his career, and laid the foundations for the fame that the 'Bacillenvater' (father of bacilli) would acquire. Initially, the team concentrated on methodology and technology, which resulted in Koch's huge paper, 'Zur Untersuchung von pathogenen Mikroorganismen', published in the first volume of the *Mitteilungen aus dem Kaiserlichen Gesundheitsamte*. Similarly, the team investigated disinfective measures, particularly the application of hot steam, which they showed to be superior to Lister's carbolic acid. A demonstration of Koch's new techniques at the 1881 International Medical Congress in London brought him favorable recognition and a personal acquaintance with Joseph Lister and Louis Pasteur.

In 1882 Koch demonstrated the powers of his methods on the single most deadly disease of the age, tuberculosis. He succeeded in establishing a bacterial etiology, thereby verifying older claims that tuberculosis was an infectious disease (most notably put forward by Jean Antoine Villemin in 1865), and leaving in ruins the complex theories that other German physicians, especially Rudolf Virchow, had developed on the subject of tuberculous processes. In the context of his work on tuberculosis, Koch came to develop a distinctive concept of infectious diseases as bacterial invasions that were defined by the presence, distribution, and behavior of bacteria in an infected organism. This concept included a profound disregard for clinical appearances as a means of identification of diseases, and an almost exclusive reliance on etiological arguments with regard to the definition of diseases. In the particular case of tuberculosis, this resulted in a redefinition of the disease's essence and boundaries by identifying phthisis, caeseous pneumonia, lupus vulgaris, etc. as a single disease.

Enthusiasm about bacteria was rising among professionals and the wider public. It culminated when in 1883–84, Koch went on an expedition to Egypt and India and identified the *Vibrio cholerae*, the 'comma bacillus', as the bacterial agent causing cholera. Koch's cholera expedition was first of all a public relations success. The Imperial government, on whose commission he was traveling, actively secured publicity that was all too easy, since the German team found itself in competition with French and British researchers. Even though the expedition was given a triumphal reception upon returning—with Koch and his fellow travelers being given financial donations and medals of war—the scientific results were inconclusive. Although pure cultures of the bacterium could be attained, and knowledge about the pathological anatomy of the disease was expanded, no satisfactory results were reached in animal experimentation. Koch had thus failed to meet his own standards. His bacterial etiology for cholera was instead based on epidemiological observations that might just as well have supported Max von Pettenkofer's miasmic theory of the disease. Nevertheless, Koch's bacterial etiology proved to be robust enough to be accepted by most members of the cholera commission of the German empire, where Koch's and Pettenkofer's opposing views clashed from late 1884 on.

National rivalry and chauvinism were important features in the relations between French microbiologists and German bacteriologists. This became obvious in the Koch-Pasteur controversy that started at the 1882 International Congress for Hygiene in Geneva. Even though the factual focus of the controversy was on questions of proper bacte-

riological technique, vaccines, and priority issues related to anthrax, it quickly became a highly politicized event in which the German public learned to consider bacteriological hygiene a matter of national pride. Apart from this, the controversy served to sharpen the theoretical concepts and methodology of Koch's school; the stress he put on bacterial specificity, his skepticism regarding virulence and Pasteur's vaccines, and finally the conviction that 'proper' bacteriological work required the methods and tools of his school, were amplified in the course of the conflict. Added to this was an undeniable element of jealousy in Koch's ferocious critique of Pasteur's vaccines, which had their spectacular appearance at the latter's famous demonstrations of anthrax vaccines at Pouilly-le-Fort. The results of these trials were published almost simultaneously with the outbreak of the controversy.

During the early 1880s Koch's institutional position constantly improved, and following the cholera expedition he was promoted to deputy directorship of the Imperial Health Office. The group of his collaborators and pupils was growing rapidly, as was the reputation of his methods and discoveries in expert circles and the public consciousness. Bacteria became widely regarded as very plausible embodiments of diseases, and Koch's public image acquired features of heroic dimensions.

Koch felt a need to improve his own institutional position in the period. However, plans for his own independent, federally funded Imperial institute for bacteriological research failed. Instead, in 1885 he found himself placed in a university chair without ever having had a Habilitation, when he became director of a newly created institute for hygiene at Berlin University. This was a fortunate happenstance for the institutional and disciplinary growth of bacteriological hygiene. The institute allowed for the inauguration of training courses in hygiene for physicians and civil servants. Koch's medical bacteriology became a standard method for many hygienists in these years. The discipline itself underwent changes in this process. When similar programs were set up in France at the Pasteur Institute, bacteriology that had previously been almost a secret science practiced in a few places, was now more and more publicized. The rapid increase in the number of people familiar with its methods also meant that, beginning in the late 1880s, the discipline became more pluralistic and discursive.

Independently of this institutional growth, however, Koch's own career ran into a crisis. The chair for hygiene at Berlin University had been created against stiff resistance by the medical faculty, and his position remained precarious. Extended routine duties such as teaching, conducting examinations, etc. annoyed him. Health problems imposed interruptions on his work, as did private problems, which in 1890 led to Koch's separation from his first wife.

Apart from this, Koch was facing a conceptual problem: his successes had so far relied on the introduction of new methods, and on the establishment of etiologies of major infectious diseases. Obviously, such a strategy was unlikely to continue to produce spectacular results indefinitely. Since everybody, including Koch himself, had taken the knowledge about bacteria to be almost a promise of their control, the next logical step to take was therefore into therapy of infected patients. However, the tools to fight diseases that German medical bacteriology had so far deployed remained restricted to preventive medicine and unspecific hygienic measures such as disinfection. Therapies of infected patients were nowhere in sight. Koch thus seems to have felt an enormous pressure to continue in this direction, a pressure that was certainly increased by Pasteur's spectacular rabies vaccine presented in 1885, which was a highly specific tool based on microbiological knowledge.

Koch failed to achieve his objectives. In his later career, despite substantial work, he never again came close to anything that equaled his early successes, and his quest for antibacterial therapies instead resulted in a medicine for tuberculosis that remained disputed during his lifetime and beyond. Koch presented his remedy against tuberculosis (that became known as tuberculin) in November 1890, triggering an unprecedented euphoria that lasted for about three months. Around the turn of the year, doubts arose about the therapeutic value of tuberculin. Worsening states among tuberculous patients and even fatalities were reported, and the euphoria gave way to a sad awakening. Koch had presented tuberculin, which was an extract from tubercle bacteria cultures, as a secret remedy; now he was harshly criticized because it turned out that the secrecy had served to cover a scientific premise that could only be called feeble. He had almost no idea about the precise contents of tuberculin, and only a speculative theory of its curative effects based on animal experiments that proved hard to reproduce. Above all, it became public that Koch had pursued plans to earn himself a fortune, and accordingly by the end of the affair he fell into public disgrace.

On the conceptual level the results were equally devastating: Although Koch never realized this, the failing of tuberculin eroded some of his thinking on the nature and pathophysiology of tuberculosis. Renewed discussions about heredity, constitution, and related issues that followed showed that medical bacteriology no longer seemed to give the ultimate answers to the problem of how to explain infectious diseases.

The short-lived euphoria over tuberculin, however, freed Koch from his unloved post at Berlin University. Prussian government officials seized the chance to push for the foundation of the huge Institute for Infectious Diseases (IID; today's Robert Koch Institute) in Berlin. Koch became director of the IID in July 1891, and in this period reorganized his personal life and research interests. He separated from his first wife, Emmy, and married Hedwig Freiberg in 1893, whom he had met in 1889 while she was a seventeen-year-old student of fine arts.

The Hamburg cholera epidemic of the summer and autumn of 1892 offered an opportunity for the IID (still under criticism) to demonstrate the skills of its director and staff. Furthermore, it was while combating cholera in Hamburg that Koch's research took a turn that would become central to his future work. Koch did not, as many of his pupils such as Ehrlich, von Behring, or Wassermann, enter the new field of immunology and serology. Instead, he supplemented his bacteriological work with an epidemiological interest.

Certain epidemiological observations that he made while working on the Hamburg epidemic forced him to modify his original model of infectious diseases as simple bacterial invasion. Phenomena such as subclinical infections, atypical infections and, most of all, healthy carriers, forced him to rearrange his ideas about infectious diseases. The final result was an increasing importance of epidemiological concepts of such diseases, and a stress on the behavior of diseases in populations instead of the infection of individuals on which he had focused so far. Koch had always been a dedicated traveler, and much of his work to come was related to epidemic parasitic diseases that he would work on during extensive travels to tropical countries.

There were, however, continuities. In the case of tuberculin, Koch continued to keep faith in its curative effect and never realized the erosion of his work that followed from its failure. In fact, his 1902 proclamation of the nonidentity of human and bovine tuberculosis still showed strains of the older conceptions, and was soon vigorously criticized. Koch's disregard of clinical evidence gave his critics a particularly good angle to attack his assumptions.

Koch's work on tropical diseases was diverse, and apart from the fact that it was almost exclusively on vector borne, parasitic diseases and focused on epidemiological questions, it is not easy to see the common motive in it. One important theme was a connection to eradication campaigns for which Koch devised plans or conducted himself. In 1896 he traveled to the South Africa on commission from the British Colonial Office to study and control rinderpest, and in 1902—again on a British commission—to Rhodesia to research East Coast fever, which at that time was tormenting local cattle farming. This and other research into parasitic diseases also reflected Koch's increasing interest in epidemiology, and the new measures to control epidemics in populations made possible by the definition of the carrier state.

In 1901 Koch was offered the chance for a large-scale demonstration of such methods on a human population at home. In close collaboration with military officials, he seized upon a few, isolated cases of typhoid in the Trier area to develop a large-scale eradication campaign that included the testing of local populations for healthy carriers of the disease. The area in question was, of course, one of the most important deployment areas of the Schlieffen plan, Germany's strategic plan for World War I. Eradication campaigns were thus needed to create sufficiently hygienic spaces for the deployment of huge, modern armies.

Another important focus of Koch's work was on malaria, which he researched on various expeditions to Italy, Africa, and New Guinea. His most important contributions were new information about the life cycle of the parasite to add to Ronald Ross's etiologic argument of its mosquito-mediated transmission, and epidemiological work on acquired immunity among local populations in New Guinea. In this case, as in some others, voices were heard that accused Koch of a self-interested style of scientific work, not always giving due credit to fellow workers and colleagues.

Koch's directorship of his Berlin institute had never been a particularly active one. After the mid-1890s he spent most of his life on extensive travels, and most of the day-to-day work was left to others, most notably to Richard Pfeiffer. In view of this, as well as his poor health, it was a logical move to go into retirement at the early age of sixty in 1904. Koch did not have to leave the IID upon retirement; he continued to have his own laboratory in the institute. His successor as director was to be Georg Gaffky, who had been his assistant in the early days at the Imperial Health Office.

Following retirement, Koch went on his longest expedition ever. He had earlier done work on trypanosomes and sleeping sickness, and in 1906–07 he traveled to East Africa for the purpose of therapeutic research on the disease. His trust in atoxyl as a means of therapy turned out to be an unfortunate choice. Instead of curing the disease, it led only to a temporary disappearance of the parasites of sleeping sickness, the trypanosomes, and at the same time about 25 percent of the patients treated lost their eyesight.

The twentieth century in particular saw a rising tide of decorations for Koch, and travels of a more private sort. He traveled to the United States and to Japan in 1908 and in both places received many honors. He received the Pour le mérite, Germany's most prestigious medal, in 1906; he was elected external member of the French Academy of Science in 1902, actually two years before he became a member of the Prussian academy of science! The rather late call to the Prussian academy was due to Virchow's delaying resistance, and it was ironic that Koch was elected to the French academy as Virchow's successor. In 1905 Koch was awarded the Nobel Prize, notably four years later than his former pupil, Emil von Behring, with whom he had been on bad terms for scientific and personal reasons since the late 1890s. Shortly thereafter, a foundation for fighting tuberculosis and a medal for outstanding medical research were named for Koch.

Robert Koch died of a heart attack on 27 May 1910 while staying in Baden-Baden. His body was cremated, and the urn containing his ashes was deposited in a mausoleum in the Institute for Infectious Diseases in Berlin. This burial place can still be visited in the Robert Koch Institute today. It seems fair to label Koch a founder of medical bacteriology

for his early work. He contributed essential methods and technologies of investigation, identified the pathogens of some major infectious diseases, and introduced key concepts to the field. Equally, the application of such knowledge was strongly associated with him. His fabulous career was closely connected to the growth of public health institutions and large-scale research in late nineteenth-century Germany. That after 1890 Koch failed to live up to the great successes of his early days is obvious. Still, his work indicates an epochal shift in medical science; all things considered, it was because of Koch's medical bacteriology that laboratory science finally entered everyday medical practice.

Bibliography

Primary: 1987. (Carter, K. Codell, ed. and trans.) *Essays of Robert Koch* (New York); 1912. (Schwalbe, Julius, ed.) *Gesammelte Werke von Robert Koch* 2 vols. (Leipzig).

Secondary: Gradmann, Christoph, 2005. *Krankheit im Labor. Robert Koch und die medizinische Bakteriologie* (Göttingen); Schlich, Thomas, 1997. 'Repräsentationen von Krankheitserregern. Wie Robert Koch Bakterien als Krankheitserreger dargestellt hat' in Rheinberger, H.-J., M. Hagner, and B. Wahrig-Schmidt, eds., *Räume des Wissens. Repräsentation, Codierung, Spur* (Berlin); Mendelsohn, John Andrew, 1996. 'Cultures of Bacteriology: Formation and Transformation of a Science in France and Germany, 1870–1914.' PhD thesis, Princeton University; Mazumdar, Pauline M. H., 1995. *Species and Specificity: An Interpretation of the History of Immunology* (Cambridge); Carter, K. Codell, 1985. 'Koch's Postulates in Relation to the Work of Jacob Henle and Edwin Klebs.' *Medical History* 29: 353–75; Brock, Thomas D., 1988. *Robert Koch: A Life in Medicine and Bacteriology* (Madison, WI); Möllers, Bernhard, 1950. *Robert Koch. Persönlichkeit und Lebenswerk 1843–1910* (Hannover); Heymann, Bruno, 1932. *Robert Koch. I. Teil 1843–1882* (Leipzig); DNB.

Christoph Gradmann

KOCHER, EMIL THEODOR

KOCHER, EMIL THEODOR   (b. Bern, Switzerland, 25 August 1841; d. Bern, 27 July 1917), *surgery, endocrinology.*

Born the second of six children of an engineer and a Pietist mother, Kocher studied medicine in Bern and Zurich. There, having come in contact with Theodor Billroth, and witnessed Thomas Spencer Wells performing Switzerland's first ovarectomy, he opted for surgery.

On a study trip (1865–66), he met Bernhard von Langenbeck and worked as a volunteer in Rudolf Virchow's laboratory in Berlin. In London, Spencer Wells was paving the way for surgical intervention in the abdominal cavity, previously avoided for fear of lethal infections. Wells's 'cleanliness-and-cold-water' surgery and frank statistics contrasted sharply with the 'dirty' surgery Kocher saw in Paris, where professors did not inform students about the fate of operated patients.

After graduation, Kocher became Bern University Surgical Clinic's (1866–69) sole assistant. An Anglophile, he was quick in applying Lister's antiseptic wound treatment (1867), thus reducing the clinic's mortality rate. It rose again after Kocher left to go into private practice because of his marriage (to a wealthy girl). Yet he managed to study hemostasis in animals. He also invented the 'Kocher maneuver' for reducing shoulder dislocations (1870). The first Swiss ever to hold a surgical chair, Kocher succeeded his former head, Albert Lücke, as professor of surgery (1872). He stayed in Bern, active until death, despite interesting calls to Prague, Vienna, and Berlin.

The breadth of this surgical giant's original work is enormous. Together with an assistant trained in bacteriology, he developed antisepsis by high-pressure steam sterilization (1880s). Kocher began resecting tuberculous bones and joints, a procedure later challenged by conservative high alpine climate therapy. He performed more than 4,000 goiter operations. Kocher's surgery, as that of most of his contemporaries, initially aimed at the removal of pathological tissue. However, his discovery of aftereffects from complete thyroid removal (1883) led him to consider functional viewpoints of surgical therapy and to resume physiological research, as did Johannes von Mikulicz-Radecki in Breslau. Kocher is now recognized as a pioneer of organ transplantation, because from 1883, he implanted human thyroid tissue, attempting to correct the loss of postulated thyroid functions which he later assessed by a blood test. He was awarded the 1909 Nobel Prize in Medicine for his contributions to physiology, pathology and surgery of the thyroid, i.e., for the practical beginnings of endocrinology.

Kocher's uniquely slow 'physiological' operating techniques, and painstaking hemostasis (with 'Kocher clamps') were adopted by his younger American friend, William Halsted. From the mid-1880s, Kocher combated operative 'shock' by administering warm 'physiological' saline intravenously, based on animal experiments of the Bern physiologist, Hugo Kronecker. This procedure was later adopted by another of his American visitors, George Crile.

Furthermore, Kocher contributed to clinico-diagnostic neurophysiology, publishing the first complete chart of human dermatomes (1896). He also wrote a monograph on brain surgery (1901) using results of experiments on endocranial pressure performed in Bern by Halsted's pupil, Harvey Cushing, who was also impressed by Kocher's intra-operative blood pressure measurements.

Kocher, in fact, created his 'system of safe surgery', described in five increasingly voluminous German editions of a textbook on surgical operations (1892–1907), translated into six languages. A world leader in the 'golden age of modern surgery', he was elected first president of the International Society of Surgery, founded in 1903.

In 1883 the unintended consequences of total thyroidectomy signified Kocher's harsh confrontation with the ancient ethical imperative of avoiding harm. He attempted to master the resulting conflicts scientifically, by promoting research, and morally, by falling back on his Christian faith.

He donated funds for a research institute, which, together with a street, still bear his name in Bern.

Bibliography

Primary: 1901. *Hirnerschütterung, Hirndruck, und chirurgische Eingriffe bei Hirnkrankheiten* (Vienna); 1907. *Chirurgische Operationslehre* 5th edn. (Jena). (English edns. 1895, 1903, 1911); 1909. 'Über Krankheitserscheinungen bei Schilddrüsenerkrankungen geringen Grades' in *Les Prix Nobel en 1909* (Stockholm) pp. 1–59.

Secondary: Modlin, I, 1998. 'Surgical Triumvirate of Theodor Kocher, Harvey Cushing and William Halsted.' *World Journal of Surgery* 22: 103–113; Boschung, Urs, ed., 1991. *Theodor Kocher* (Bern); Tröhler, Ulrich, 1984. *Der Nobelpreisträger Theodor Kocher* (Basel).

Ulrich Tröhler

KORÁNYI, FRIGYES (b. Nagykálló, Hungary, 10 December 1827; d. Budapest, Hungary, 19 May 1913), *medicine, medical education, medical scholarship.*

Korányi began studying medicine in 1844 at the university in Pest; he finally earned his doctor's degree in 1851, the delay a result of his having spent time as a student leader in revolutionary affairs in 1848. The following year he served as a surgical assistant in Franz Schuh's clinic in Vienna.

Korányi's activities brought him to the attention of János Balassa, in whose circle of medical reformers he became involved. After an innocent remark in a letter to another reformer, Lajos Markusovszky, was misinterpreted, Korányi was convicted of treason and barred from Vienna. Returning to Nagykálló, he practiced medicine with characteristic energy during twelve years of forced internal exile; he also began writing and publishing. Like Balassa and Markusovszky, he argued in favor of a more scientific basis for medicine. With them, he played a significant role in modernizing medicine and improving medical education in Hungary.

By 1865, the political climate had changed. Korányi was rehabilitated as Privatdozent for neural pathology in Pest, and a year later made professor of internal medicine. No one dominated the scene so completely during the more than four decades that Korányi taught at the university. An extraordinarily clear lecturer, he is said to have held his classes spellbound as he shared his knowledge and passion for the healing arts. At the time of his death, most of Hungary's practicing physicians had been taught by Korányi; all the leading members of the faculty had been his students. One, his son Sándor, was later also a highly successful professor of internal medicine.

Two examples of Korányi's influence stand out: he transformed the tiny, outmoded clinic for internal medicine in Budapest into a large, modern, scientific institute that could be favorably compared to such establishments elsewhere; and he almost single-handedly developed two modern sanatoria for patients with lung diseases and introduced prophylactic measures at a time when Hungarians were among the Europeans worst afflicted by tuberculosis.

In addition to being an activist physician, teacher, and public health worker, Korányi wrote more than 150 scientific papers on varied subjects: the displaced spleen (1857), hepatic hydatids (1876), pneumonia (1884), and the thyroid (1892). He won a prize for a paper on the treatment of *tabes dorsalis*, published in *Orvosi Hetilap* (1883) and abstracted in two German-language journals. He was among the first Hungarian physicians invited by non-Hungarian colleagues to collaborate (he contributed to several major texts), and was one of a small handful of Budapest professors who, by 1900, had a truly European reputation. Of fundamental importance within Hungary was the six-volume work he and two colleagues compiled on internal medicine. At nearly eighty, he devised new diagnostic techniques for several debilitating diseases, using spinal percussion, and published a long article on it (1906).

In 1886 Korányi was *Rector Magnificus* (president) of the university. He advised the King-Emperor on public health matters. Upon his retirement (1908) he was made a hereditary baron. A corresponding member of the Hungarian Academy of Sciences (from 1884) and president of the Royal Medical Association in Budapest, he was also an honorary member of the *Société de Thérapeutique* in Paris, and a corresponding member of the *Verein für innere Medizin* in Berlin.

Bibliography

Primary: 1870. 'Der Milzbrand.' *Handb. d. allg. u. spec. Chir.* i, 2. Abth., A, Nr. 7: 149–83; 1870. 'Rotz- und Wurmkrankheiten' *Handb. d. allg. u. spec. Chir.* i, 2. Abth., A, Nr. 8: 184–203 (Erlangen); 1878. 'Weitere Beiträge zu Pathologie u. Therapie des Echinococcus der Leber.' *Pest. med.-chir. Presse*, xiv, 53; 73; 257; 1896. 'Die Lungenschwindsucht in Ungarn.' *Pest med.-chir. Presse* xxxii: 394–397.

Secondary: Birtalan, Gőyző, 2000. 'Korányi Frigyes' in Albert, E., et al., eds., *Hires Magyar Orvosok* (Budapest) pp. 161–165; 1929–34. *Biographisches Lexikon der hervorragenden Ärzte aller Zeiten und Völker* vol. 3 (Berlin) p. 586; Királyfi, Géza, 1913. 'Nekrolog. Prof. Baron Friedrich v. Korányi.' *Wiener klin. Wochenschr.* 24: 996–998.

Constance Putnam

KORCZAK, JANUSZ (literary pseudonym of HENRYK GOLDSZMIT) (b. Warsaw, Poland, 22 July 1878; d. in concentration camp at Treblinka, Poland, probably August 1942), *pediatrics, education, literature*.

Today Korczak is often remembered as a martyr. Director of a Jewish orphanage, imprisoned in the Warsaw ghetto, his (reported) refusal to leave 'his' children and save his life became a symbol of heroism in dark times. It was immortalized in numerous art works, in spite of the uneasiness of some of his close collaborators with the reduction of a complex personality and multiple achievements to an iconic image. Korczak is also known as a pioneer of an innovative approach to education, and as a successful writer for adults and children. His *King Matt the First* became a classic of children's literature. But the writer and the educator Janusz Korczak was also the pediatrician Henryk Goldszmit (the name he signed on his medical publications). Korczak's medical career is frequently presented as a semi-accidental prelude to his true achievements as an educator. This is regrettable, since Korczak's innovative pedagogy was shaped by his experience as a medical practitioner.

Korczak's father, a lawyer, suffered from a mental illness, and died from its sequelae when his son was fifteen, leaving his family impoverished. The fear of 'dangerous heredity' followed Korczak throughout his lifetime and might have been one of the reasons that, his great love for children notwithstanding, he had no children of his own. Early in life, Korczak became revolted by social injustice, and as a medical student he started his highly successful literary career with stories on the plight of inhabitants of Warsaw slums. Back from military service in the Russian army (1904–05), Korczak worked at Children's Hospital, Warsaw. In 1907–08 he traveled to Berlin to specialize in pediatrics. Korczak rapidly became dissatisfied with hospital work, however, realizing that he cured children only to send them back to conditions that would make them sick again. He switched gradually to work with underprivileged children, first in summer camps, and then in orphanages. In 1912 he became the director of a Jewish orphanage (co-managed by Stefania Wilczynska), and a pedagogical counselor of a Polish orphanage directed by Maryna Falska.

Korczak's highly original pedagogical approach was grounded in his conviction that a child is not a 'future person', but is already a real person, no less entitled to respect and dignity than an adult. The orphanages he directed applied the principle of self management. The children's tasks and duties were defined by a 'children's council', while misbehavior was judged by a 'children's court'. Korczak's strong belief in the virtues of a progressive education was nevertheless coupled with a conviction that every child's potential is determined to a great extent by heredity. He submitted all the candidates for his orphanage to a battery of psychological tests destined to weed out mentally impaired or otherwise 'abnormal' children. In parallel, he tolerated the fact that psychologists who worked for him occasionally 'bent' the results of such tests, to help a child in distress. Interested in scientific studies of child development, Korczak was convinced that a precise and objective evaluation of such development is a pre-condition of a serious pedagogical enterprise. Korczak insisted on weekly weighing and measuring of all the orphanage children and the inscription of the results in individual charts, an activity he viewed as essential for the evaluation of the orphanage's achievements. The weighing and measuring routine was maintained in the Warsaw ghetto. Until the very end,

Korczak's mission as an innovative educator was intertwined with his role as a medical scientist.

Bibliography

Primary: 1992–98. *Collected Works* (in Polish) 12 vols. (Warsaw); 1992. *When I Am Little Again and The Child's Right to Respect* (Lanham, MD); 2003. *Ghetto Diary* (New Haven, CT).

Secondary: Grzegorzewska, Maria, 1989. *Souvenirs of Korczak* (in Polish) (Warsaw); Lifton, Betty Jean, 1988. *The King of Children: The Life and Death of Janusz Korczak* (New York); Newerly, Igor, 1966. *The Living Bond* (in Polish) (Warsaw).

Ilana Löwy

KORSAKOV, SERGEI SERGEEVICH   (b. Gus' Khrustal'nyi, Russia, 22 January 1854; d. Moscow, Russia, 1 May 1900), *psychiatry.*

Korsakov, the son of a provincial factory director, was sent to study in Moscow when he was ten years old, and graduated from the gymnasium with a gold medal in 1870. That autumn he entered the medical faculty of Moscow University, where he studied nervous and mental illnesses under the renowned neurologist A. I. Kozhevnikov (1836–1902). After his graduation in 1875, he was hired as a psychiatrist at Moscow's Preobrazhenskaia Psychiatric Hospital.

Korsakov's most lasting contribution to world psychiatry was his study of alcoholic psychoses. In his 1887 doctoral dissertation, 'Ob alkogol'nom paraliche' [On alcoholic paralysis], Korsakov described alcoholic patients who were unable to make new short-term memories, but did not loose their ability to reason. Most importantly, Korsakov was able to correlate this syndrome (later dubbed 'Korsakov's psychosis') with polyneuritis, a finding that participants at the 1889 International Medical Congress in Paris heralded as proof that mental disorders could ultimately be linked to lesions in neural tissue. (Subsequent research has established that patients developed the syndrome described by Korsakov due to a thiamine deficiency, a condition that can result from alcoholism, but has also been found in people who have suffered from famine or infection.)

In Russia Korsakov is remembered primarily as a founding father of Russian psychiatry, but in addition to his research, he was a prominent teacher and reformer. Korsakov began his teaching career in 1888, when he began to give a popular series of lectures on psychiatry, and he developed these lectures into the first edition of his classic textbook, *Kurs psikhiatrii* [A Course in Psychiatry] (1893), in which he offered students an engaging introduction to the fundamentals of Continental psychiatry. Like his contemporary, Kraepelin, Korsakov stressed the importance of studying the development of psychoses over time, rather than focusing on specific symptoms as they presented themselves at any particular moment. Korsakov, however, explicitly rejected Kraepelin's concept of dementia praecox, arguing that the condition should not be defined by its outcome. Korsakov continued to revise and expand his textbook until his death, and the second edition, which was published posthumously in 1901, served as the primary psychiatry textbook for several generations of Russian medical students.

Following his heroes, Pinel and Conolly, Korsakov used his influential position to argue that Russian psychiatric hospitals should abandon straitjackets and barred windows. 'Non-restraint', he argued, was inherently a more humane approach, but in addition, the hospital environment should be seen as an important therapeutic factor in its own right. A generation of young physicians employed by local government councils [*zemstvos*] adopted Korsakov's call for a more humane psychiatry and contrasted this approach with the tsarist government's allegedly outdated, repressive treatment of the mentally ill.

Korsakov's Soviet biographers praised him for his self-denying dedication to his work, but such single-minded devotion clearly took a toll on his health. He died of heart disease in 1900, at age forty-six.

Bibliography

Primary: 1887. 'Ob alkogol'nom paraliche *(Paralysis alcoholica, Paraplegia alcoholica)*' [On alcoholic paralysis] (Moscow); 1889. 'Neskol'ko sluchaev svoeobraznoi tserebropatii pri mnozhestvennom nevrite (Cerebropathia psychica toxaemica).' [Several cases of distinctive cerebropathia with multiple nephritis] *Ezhenedel'naia klinicheskaia gazeta* 5: 85–92; 6: 115–121; 7: 136–143; 1901. *Kurs psikhiatrii* [A Course in Psychiatry] 2nd edn. (Moscow).

Secondary: Banshchikov, Vladimir M., 1967. *S. S. Korsakov: Zhizn' i tvorchestvo* [S. S. Korsakov: Life and Works] (Moscow); Iudin, Tikhon I., 1951. *Ocherki istorii otechestvennoi psikhiatrii* [Studies in the History of the Homeland's Psychiatry] (Moscow); Kannabikh, Iurii V., 1928. *Istoriia psikhiatrii* [History of Psychiatry] (Moscow).

Benjamin Zajicek

KOSTIĆ, ALEKSANDAR Đ.   (b. Belgrade, Serbia, 18 March 1893; d. Belgrade, Yugoslavia [now Serbia], 19 January 1983), *histology, sexology.*

Born in Belgrade the son of a high state official, Djordje, and his wife Katarina, Kostić (Kostitch) began medical studies in France in 1912 at age nineteen. As a participant in two Balkan wars and World War I, Kostić organized courses on personal health and hygiene, and for the prevention and treatment of scurvy. He later published a collection of stories, *Priče iz strašne kuče* [Tales from the Horrible House] (1968), inspired by wartime traumas. Kostić earned a doctoral degree at Strasbourg (1921), with a thesis on the influence of alcohol upon the sperm cells, and became the assistant to the well-known histologist Paul Bouin. With the establishment of the

Medical Faculty at Belgrade, Kostić was appointed to the chair in histology. In 1927 he organized the Histological Institute, considered among the most modern of its kind in this part of Europe; the Rockefeller Foundation marked the occasion with a special publication (1928). The Institute included a museum of embryology, a terminology section, and a photography section, which produced the first microphotographs in the region. Kostić served as dean of the Medical Faculty from 1936 to 1939, and contributed to the establishment of the pharmacy department (1939), as well as of the faculty for veterinary medicine (1936).

As a histologist, Kostić specialized in two main fields: researching the impact of toxic materials and sulphonamides on testicles and spermatogenesis; and spleen function. The spleen was an organ that had been little studied. Focusing on the links between immunology and endocrinology systems, Kostić produced pioneering work in Serbian medicine, as well as in medical films. His film, produced in Belgrade (1946), was presented at the Royal Society of Medicine in London in 1950.

Kostić had researched medical terminology since 1913, and was an active participant in the WHO's terminology forums. The final version of his medical dictionary contains 140,000 comparative terms in eight languages, and was published in English as well as in several German editions. As a sexologist, Kostić became an extremely popular public figure in Serbia and greater Yugoslavia, publishing twenty books in the field and delivering more than 2,000 lectures before a total of 300,000 people. Apart from university textbooks of histology, he wrote *Osnovi medicinke seksologije* [The Basis of Medical Sexology] (1966), which was among the first books on the subject in Europe.

Also active in artistic photography, music, and poetry, Kostić founded a local history museum in 1978. His wife, Smilja A. Kostić–Joksić, was an international expert on BCG vaccination. During the time of the Communist repression after 1945, both were persecuted and expelled from the University. In 2001 both were posthumously rehabilitated. Kostić was awarded the Legion of Honor (1940) and many other decorations. His wife was also awarded the Legion of Honor (1952) for her achievements in the field of BCG vaccination.

Bibliography

Primary: 1966. *Osnovi medicinke seksologije* [The Basis of Medical Sexology] (Belgrade).

Secondary: Kostić, Vojislav A., 2004. *Život sa neprebolnim bolom u duši (Prof. dr Aleksandar Đ. Kostić 1893–1983)* (Belgrade); Bumbaširević, Vladimir, 2002. 'Aleksandar Đ. Kostić (1893 – 1983).' *Život i delo srpskuh naučnika* 9; Kostić-Joksić, Smilja A., 1968. *Osvrt na život i rad prof. dr Aleksandra Đ. Kostića.*

Jelena Jovanovic Simic and
Predrag J. Markovic

KRAEPELIN, EMIL WILHELM MAGNUS GEORG
(b. Neustrelitz, Germany, 15 February 1856; d. Munich, Germany, 7 October 1926), *psychiatry.*

Kraepelin studied medicine in Würzburg, Leipzig, and Munich. Early in his career he showed a strong interest in criminology and experimental psychology. After working with Wilhelm Wundt and Bernhard von Gudden, he was appointed professor of psychiatry in Dorpat in 1886. From there he moved first to Heidelberg in 1891, where he was professor and director of the university psychiatric clinic, and then to Munich in 1903. By the time he arrived in Munich he was one of the most influential figures in German psychiatry. His classification of affective disorders and his concept of 'dementia praecox' had gained increasing support among colleagues, and his expansive textbook was quickly becoming the standard introductory text for academic instruction. In 1917 he founded the *Deutsche Forschungsanstalt für Psychiatrie*, Germany's preeminent psychiatric research institute.

Kraepelin's famous nosology evolved in the context of two important developments within German psychiatry in the 1860s and 1870s. It was a response to both the dissolution of the concept of a unitary psychosis, and to the hypotheses advanced by cerebral pathologists. On the one hand, unitary psychosis—i.e. the theory that all psychiatric symptoms were manifestations of one single mental disorder—had become increasingly untenable following clinical studies by Karl Ludwig Kahlbaum and Ewald Hecker. Their work on catatonia and hebephrenia suggested the existence of various discrete psychiatric disorders. Consequently, Kraepelin discarded the concept of unitary psychosis and set about constructing a system of classification based on discrete disease entities. On the other hand, Kraepelin was highly skeptical of the claims of cerebral pathologists such as Theodor Meynert and Paul Flechsig. He criticized their efforts to link brain function with mental disease as speculative and lacking empirical evidence.

In search of alternatives, Kraepelin turned to Wilhelm Wundt's experimental psychology to study mental processes. In numerous stimulus-reaction experiments, Kraepelin's early research investigated the effects of various stimulants and exhaustion on mental functioning. His aim was to generate quantifiable psychological norms that could be used to diagnose mental deviance and delineate specific disease entities. Much of Kraepelin's and his students' work was published in the journal, *Psychologische Arbeiten*, that he founded in 1895.

Kraepelin also embarked on a major clinical research project in Heidelberg to study the long-term course of his patients' illnesses. He was convinced that careful longitudinal documentation would enable him to isolate specific disease entities. Consequently, he began systematically to collect and catalogue hundreds of patient histories. In the process, he developed elaborate institutional strategies and diagnostic instruments, including his famous diagnostic cards (*Zählkarten*). On the basis of this clinical research, Kraepelin crafted a nosology that exerted a powerful influence over psychiatric practice in the early twentieth century.

After the turn of the century, Kraepelin's interests turned increasingly toward larger public health issues. He became a fervent advocate of alcoholic abstinence, and was an early supporter of the racial hygiene movement in Germany. A convinced Social Darwinist, Kraepelin believed that social problems were often manifestations of forces that subverted the German people's biological 'struggle for survival'. Consequently, he supported eugenic measures to enhance public health, and advocated reforms to various social institutions (such as the welfare state and the education system) that he believed impinged upon processes of natural selection. The enormous losses inflicted by World War I saw his interests converge around the 'folkish existence' of the German people, whom he believed were poised on the brink of extinction.

Bibliography

Primary: 2000–2005. (Burgmair, Wolfgang, Eric J. Engstrom, and Matthias M. Weber, eds.), *Emil Kraepelin* 5 vols. (Munich); 2002. *Lifetime Editions of Kraepelin in English* 5 vols. (Bristol); 2002. (Steinberg, Holger, ed.) *Der Briefwechsel zwischen Wilhelm Wundt und Emil Kraepelin* (Bern); 1992. 'Psychiatric Observations on Contemporary Issues.' *History of Psychiatry* 3: 253–269; 1987. (Hippius, H., et al., eds., trans. Wooding-Dean, C.) *Memoirs* (Berlin and New York).

Secondary: Engstrom, Eric J.,Wolfgang Burgmair, and Matthias M. Weber, 2002. 'Emil Kraepelin's "Self-Assessment": Clinical Autography in Historical Context.' *History of Psychiatry* 13: 89–119; Hoff, Paul, 1994. *Emil Kraepelin und die Psychiatrie als klinische Wissenschaft* (Berlin).

Eric J. Engstrom

KRAFFT-EBING, RICHARD VON   (b. Mannheim, Germany, 14 August 1840; d. Graz, Austria, 22 December 1902), *psychiatry.*

Richard Freiherr (Baron) von Krafft-Ebing descended from a German Catholic family who had been ennobled by the Austrian emperor around 1800. Krafft-Ebing studied medicine in Heidelberg, where he lived in the home of his maternal grandfather, Carl Joseph Anton Mittermaier (1787–1867), a professor of criminal law. During an academic visit to Zurich he encountered the famous psychiatrist, Wilhelm Griesinger (1817–68), who drew Krafft-Ebing's attention to psychiatry. After completing his medical studies (MD 1863), Krafft-Ebing started training in psychiatry in Illenau, a progressive mental asylum in the duchy of Baden which had already begun implementing the non-restraint system in psychiatric care. In 1869 Krafft-Ebing decided to leave Illenau, and practiced as a neurologist in Baden-Baden, where his chief specialty was the treatment of bourgeois patients by using electrotherapy.

Krafft-Ebing's academic career started in 1872, when he was appointed adjunct professor of psychiatry at the University of Strasbourg. Only some months later, he left Strasbourg and accepted a professorship at the University of Graz, Austria (1873). This position was combined with the directorship of a newly established mental asylum in Graz. Whereas Krafft-Ebing's efforts to improve the situation of the patients in the asylum could not make much progress, he was able to concentrate on his scientific ambitions and on treating private patients. In 1886 he founded a private sanatorium (Mariagrün) where he treated middle-class and upper-class patients suffering from neuroses, such as neurasthenia or hysteria. In addition, he became increasingly interested in the study of contrary sexual feelings (the term 'homosexuality' was popularized by Krafft-Ebing with great success) and sexual perversions.

In 1889 Krafft-Ebing left his academic position once again. He moved on to the University of Vienna, where he succeeded Max Leidesdorf (1818–89) and, in 1892, Theodor Meynert (1833–92). In his capacity as professor of psychiatry at the University of Vienna, Krafft-Ebing could consolidate his position as a recognized expert in psychiatry, neurology and sexology. However, Krafft-Ebing retired prematurely in 1902 and returned to Graz with plans to concentrate on scientific writing. One year after his retirement, Krafft-Ebing died at the age of sixty-two.

Krafft-Ebing's work covered a broad range of topics, including psychiatry and sexology. In psychiatry, although at first under the influence of anatomical and physiological explanations of mental disorders, Krafft-Ebing stressed the importance of the knowledge of psychology in clinical and private practice. Accordingly, he experimented with several forms of hypnosis as a treatment form for nervous disorders. After having written the first systematic textbook of forensic psychiatry (1875), he also became a highly sought expert in that emerging field. However, to many of his contemporaries and later generations, Krafft-Ebing became prominent as a result of his work on sexual perversions. His monograph, *Psychopathia sexualis*, which first appeared in 1886, went through fourteen editions until 1903, and was translated into several languages. The first English translation (based on the second edition) appeared in 1893. On the basis of numerous letters from those who had read his work, and on a large number of case histories gathered from his psychiatric practice, Krafft-Ebing explained sexual perversions chiefly in terms of psychopathology. As a result, he introduced a number of new categories of sexual perversions, such as fetishism, masochism, and sadism. In contrast to moralistic or criminal views, Krafft-Ebing provided scientifically and liberally based thinking about sexuality, thus opening unprejudiced ways of understanding contrary sexual feelings and sexual variances.

Bibliography

Primary: 1875. *Lehrbuch der gerichtlichen Psychopathologie mit Berücksichtigung der Gesetzgebung von Österreich, Deutschland und Frankreich* (Stuttgart); 1879–80. *Lehrbuch der Psychiatrie auf klinischer Grundlage* 3 vols. (6th edn., 1897) (Stuttgart); 1886. *Psychopathia sexualis. Eine klinisch-forensische Studie* (17th edn., 1924) (Stuttgart); 1895. *Nervosität und neurasthenische Zustände* (Vienna).

Secondary: Oosterhuis, Harry, 2000. *Stepchildren of Nature: Krafft-Ebing, Psychiatry, and the Making of Sexual Identity* (Chicago); Klabundt, Per, 1994. 'Psychopathia sexualis—die ärztliche Konstruktion der sexuellen Perversion zwischen 1869 und 1914.' *Medizin, Gesellschaft und Geschichte* 13: 107–130; Hauser, Renate, 1992. 'Sexuality, Neurasthenia and the Law: Richard von Krafft-Ebing (1840–1902).' PhD thesis, University of London.

Hans-Georg Hofer

KRAUS, FRIEDRICH   (b. Weiher/Bodenbach, Böhmen, Germany, 31 May 1858; d. Berlin, Germany, 1 March 1936), *medicine.*

Kraus came from humble origins, and paid for his training and studies by being a student assistant as well as a servant in a boarding house. While studying in Prague (MD 1882), Kraus came into contact with the two leading figures in the field of the physiology of the senses, Ewald Hering and Ernst Mach, an encounter that led to a lifelong interest in scientific theory as well as related philosophical issues. During his studies, Kraus worked as an assistant in Karl Hugo Huppert's Institute for Physiological Chemistry. In 1885 he became an assistant to Otto Kahler at the II Medical Clinic, where, among other things, he embarked on chemical research into the blood's acids and bases in Franz Hoffmeister's laboratory, research that would form the basis of colloid chemistry. Having received his Habilitation in 1889, Kraus became the temporary head of the clinic after Kahler left. In 1890 Kraus left the II Medical Clinic in turn to follow his teacher to Vienna. When Kahler died in 1893, Kraus once again became the temporary head of the II Clinic, but was not appointed as a regular professor. In 1894 Kraus received the chair for internal medicine in Graz, and in 1902 he was appointed to the II Medical Clinic of Berlin University, despite having been ranked third in the application process.

Kraus was a committed partisan of the union between clinical medicine and experimental laboratory research. An active member of the 'Neo-Hippocratic' movement, he was deeply implicated in the struggle to overcome the perceived antagonism between the art of medicine and the reductive materialism of the laboratory sciences. The latter was being increasingly criticized at the end of the nineteenth century. By 1897, he had made a substantial contribution to contemporary constitutional pathology, in which the organism was regarded as an integral functional unit. The 'Unity of the Organism' would remain a central theme in Kraus's work, and his writings on the 'Pathology of the Person'

were intended to provide a theoretical foundation for this view, based on a synthesis of science and philosophy. Here, he integrated not only the new work on colloidal chemistry, but also Henri Bergson's philosophy. Despite his desire to cultivate an open-minded approach among his students and coworkers based on his own enthusiastic temperament, Kraus was inclined to use complex and often opaque methods of representation in his philosophical writings (e.g., he termed his theoretical models 'clinical syzygiology' and 'Tiefenperson'), which hindered its dissemination.

Under Kraus, the Berlin University Clinic became the center of a new form of laboratory medicine. When the Clinic moved to a new building in 1910, it included a large number of laboratories—in hematology and serology, chemistry, physics, and bacteriology, as well as laboratories for respiratory and calorimetric experiments, the analysis of gases, animal experimentation, and microscopy. Later, Kraus would promote the new medical uses of x-rays, and in 1910, when the string galvanometer had made the registration of cardiac activity possible, he, along with Georg Nicolai, developed the first plausible physiological interpretation of the meaning of electrocardiography that could be used in medicine. Nevertheless, Kraus did not regard laboratory research as a technical specialty; rather, in his more utopian vision of scientific medicine, he perceived it as one step in the process of coming to a holistic understanding of the human being.

Bibliography

Primary: 1897. *Die Ermüdung als ein Mass der Constitution* (Cassel); 1910. (with Nicolai, Georg) *Das Elektrokardiogramm des gesunden und des kranken Menschen* (Leipzig); 1919–1926. *Die allgemeine und die spezielle Pathologie der Person* 2 vols. (Leipzig).

Secondary: Lindner, Martin, 1999. *Die Pathologie der Person. Friedrich Kraus' Neubestimmung des Organismus am Beginn des 20. Jahrhunderts* (Berlin).

Volker Hess

KRETSCHMER, ERNST   (b. Wüstenrot, Württemberg, Germany, 8 October 1888; d. Tübingen, Germany, 8 February 1964), *psychiatry.*

Kretschmer was born into a family of Protestant theologians. After completing secondary school, he matriculated as a student of philosophy and history in 1906, but turned to medicine one year later. He attended medical school at the universities of Munich and Hamburg. Having graduated in 1913, he started his psychiatric training at the university department of psychiatric and nervous disorders at Tübingen University under Robert Gaupp. From 1916 until 1918, he directed a military ward for 'war neurotics', where among other methods he applied a therapeutic method combining suggestion and punitive elements.

In 1918 he completed his Habilitation thesis, entitled 'Der sensitive Beziehungswahn' [The sensitive delusion of reference], a study on the etiology of psychogenic psychoses. Three years later, he published his most influential book, *Körperbau und Charakter,* of which an English translation (*Physique and Character*) appeared in 1925. In this work, Kretschmer postulated a causal relationship between premorbid physical or psychological characteristics of an individual and the etiology of mental disorders. He outlined the triple typology of the 'leptosome', the 'athletic', and the 'pyknic' habitus.

In 1926 Kretschmer was appointed full professor and director of the psychiatric clinic of Marburg University (Hesse); from 1946 until his retirement in 1959, he held the same position at Tübingen University. In 1936, he was also elected a member of the *Deutsche Akademie der Naturforscher Leopoldina* in Halle. After his retirement, he directed the *Forschungsstelle für Konstitutions- und Arbeitspsychologie* [Research Program into Constitutional and Occupational Psychology], which investigated psychological developments in puberty and their impact on occupational aptitude. He was also cofounder of the reestablished *Kriminalbiologische Gesellschaft* [Association for Criminal Biology], and engaged in establishing professional bodies of physicians. Already in the late 1920s, he had been involved in initiating a form of psychotherapy which incorporated ideas of psychodynamic psychiatry, and sought to integrate them with methods of persuasion and behavior modification.

Kretschmer was a proponent of racial theories, but skeptical towards Nazi racial policies which he saw as interfering in the competence and 'ethos' of physicians. He nevertheless cooperated with the institutions of health and social policy of the Nazi regime, and in part complied with the sterilization program against those patients diagnosed as suffering from hereditary conditions. He also did not hesitate to apply his methods of 'active psychotherapy' in the context of German military psychiatry, and propagated a strict and authoritarian stance towards soldiers 'simulating' neurotic conditions. For the Nazi health authorities, he acted as one of the major coordinators of medical psychotherapy.

His scientific work was characterized by the following basic ideas: first, the somatic and the psychological are a priori coordinated, and changes on one side are accompanied by changes on the other side of this parallelism; second, psychological phenomena are not fixed realities, but dynamic processes grounded in, but not determined by, physical conditions; third, the psychological *Konstitution* is the potential of an individual for experiences and reactions, and is grounded both in hereditarian factors and in the individual's psychological development; fourth, diagnosis has therefore to be carried through in a multidimensional approach.

At the time of his death, Kretschmer's monographs had already been published in more than forty languages; in German, they totaled more than fifty editions.

Bibliography

Primary: 1918. *Der sensitive Beziehungswahn* (Berlin); 1921. *Körperbau und Charakter* (English edn., 1925) (Jena); 1922. *Medizinische Psychologie* (Leipzig).

Secondary: Müller, Roland, 2001. *Wege zum Ruhm: Militärpsychiatrie im Zweiten Weltkrieg—das Beispiel Marburg* (Cologne); Schmiedebach, Heinz-Peter, 1998. 'Ernst Kretschmer' in *Deutsche Biographische Enzyklopädie* vol. 7 (Munich) pp. 99–100.

Volker Roelcke

KUBLER-ROSS, ELISABETH (b. Zurich, Switzerland, 8 July 1926; d. Scottsdale, Arizona, USA, 24 August 2004), *psychiatry, thanatology.*

With the writing of a single book, Elisabeth Kubler-Ross transformed the public's perception of the process of dying and began a discussion of end-of-life issues that has since then become a constant theme in the dialogue of our time. Prior to her work, death was in general a hushed topic, hidden or neglected by the medical profession and feared to the point of quiet murmurings by the laity. But after the publication in 1969 of Kubler-Ross's surprising best seller, *On Death and Dying,* a new attitude replaced the previous hesitancy and apprehension, as physicians, families, and most especially, patients themselves entered into what has become an open forum on ways to understand the psychological manifestations of terminal disease and improve care during the final phases of life.

One sentence in the preface describes the intent and contents of the book: 'We have asked [the patient] to be our teacher so that we may learn more about the final stages of life with all its anxieties, fears and hopes.' The study began in 1965, when Kubler-Ross was an assistant professor of psychiatry at the University of Chicago Medical School's Billings Memorial Hospital. Several theology students had asked her for help in learning more about death, and she suggested that conversations be held with dying patients in order to know the nature of their anxieties and concerns. She herself conducted many such interviews, leading to her conclusion that individuals go through five psychological stages as they confront the certainty of their own mortality. Her description became the substance of the book.

The first stage, she pointed out, was frequently denial: it is difficult to acknowledge to oneself that life is coming to an end. As the disease process makes itself all too evident, denial is likely to be succeeded by anger that one has been singled out in this way. In time, patients frequently find themselves bargaining, for example, making promises to God or some force of destiny in return for more life. Though the stage of bargaining is less well-recognized than the others, the state of mind that follows it is the one most obvious: when it becomes clear that such stratagems are likely to be futile, depression commonly sets in. Many patients overcome this and reach a stage of acceptance. Kubler-Ross emphasized that this five-stage pattern varies and that not everyone passes through all parts of it, though it is common for several of them to be prominent.

Elisabeth Kubler was one of triplet girls born in Zurich to the wife of an executive in an office-supply business, whose aim for his two-pound daughter was that she would one day become his secretary. But by sixth grade, she had determined to be a doctor. After completing her work at the gymnasium, she volunteered at a large hospital in her home city and then obtained her MD degree at the University of Zurich. While there, she met an American student, Emanuel Ross, and she later married him and emigrated to the United States, where she took an internship at a community hospital in Glen Cove on Long Island and then became a research fellow at Manhattan State Hospital. It was there that her interests in improving the care of the dying, first aroused during her Zurich volunteer days, began to take shape.

In 1962 Kubler-Ross became a teaching fellow at the University of Colorado and continued to study dying patients. She was appointed assistant professor of psychiatry at the University of Chicago in 1965, and it was in that highly academic atmosphere that her work took on its eventual form, culminating in the publication of *On Death and Dying*. The book and the research methods on which it was based, being considered anecdotal and unscientific, caused so much controversy among members of the medical staff that her contract with the university was not renewed. But the worldwide acclaim after publication assured her of a huge audience for her theories, and she rapidly became a public figure, speaking and writing often and publishing eight additional widely read books.

In time, Kubler-Ross was awarded twenty-five honorary doctorates in spite of her gradual turning toward philosophies of death that seemed to many observers to resemble more of the occult than of rational hypothesis, embracing ideas of out-of-body experiences, visions of a happy afterlife, and a theoretical psychic energy. In her last years, she built a home in the Arizona desert. There she consulted with magical healers, expounded her by-then mystical notions of an everlasting soul and communications from the other side, and was watched over by her son Kenneth, having long been divorced from her husband. She died, still the center of controversy but now more for her metaphysical and spiritualistic notions than for the five stages, on 24 August 2004.

Bibliography

Primary: 1969. *On Death and Dying* (New York).

Secondary: Oransky, I., 2004. 'Elisabeth Kubler-Ross.' *Lancet* 364: 1120; Noble, H. B., 2004. 'Elisabeth Kubler-Ross Dies.' *New York Times*, 26 August; Nuland, S. B., 2004. 'Appreciation.' *Time*, 24 September, p. 20; Clark, D., 2004. 'Elisabeth Kubler-Ross: Facing Death.' *Journal of Palliative Medicine* 7: 481–482.

Sherwin Nuland

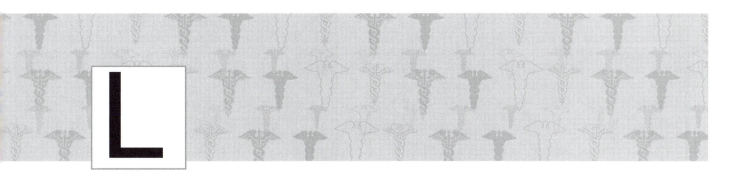

L

LA METTRIE, JULIEN OFFROY DE (b. St Malo, France, 19 December 1709; d. Potsdam, Prussia (now Germany), 11 November 1751), *materialism, medical philosophy.*

La Mettrie was the son of a textile merchant who gave him a good education. He attended the provincial colleges of Coutance and Caen, where he was influenced by Jansenism, before going to Paris in 1725 to study philosophy and natural science at the College d'Harcourt (the first to make Cartesianism central to its curriculum). La Mettrie then studied medicine at the University of Paris for the next five years but, to avoid high graduation fees, took his degree from the University of Reims. He found his education an insufficient preparation for medical practice and went to the University of Leiden to study with Herman Boerhaave, a renowned teacher of physiology and chemistry and an innovative clinical practitioner. Afterwards La Mettrie practiced medicine in St Malo and later served as the physician for a battalion of the French guard. He then focused on writing works dealing with medical reform and using medicine as a foundation for philosophical speculations.

As a medical student La Mettrie gained an awareness of professional issues that led him to write satires lampooning the ignorance and venality of Parisian medical practitioners. These texts supported the surgeons in their dispute with the Faculty of Medicine over surgical education and practice. But La Mettrie was also greatly interested in the theoretical foundations of medicine. He translated Boer-haave's most significant works, and, in his extensive commentaries, emphasized the materialistic strand he found in them. La Mettrie also wrote five medical treatises on specific diseases, including smallpox and venereal disease, and addressed public health issues. All of these works led La Mettrie to define the *médecin-philosophe* as embodying the astute empirical observation of surgeons, the thorough training in physiology of an idealistic physician, and the zeal of the reform-minded philosophe, and thus the most effective practitioner of critical analysis and reform.

La Mettrie's philosophical works applied this perspective. In *L'Histoire naturelle de l'âme* (1745), he discussed the animal and vegetative souls in conventional terms but posited a materialist view of the human, rational soul. This text led to his exile to Holland in 1745. In *L'Homme machine* (1747), he demonstrated the effects of the body on the soul and the comparability between men and animals using anatomical and physiological evidence. For this work even the tolerant Dutch exiled him. He sought refuge at the court of Frederick the Great of Prussia, where he remained until his early death in 1751. In *L'Homme plante* (1747) and *Le Système d'Epicure* (1751), he compared man to lower creatures and placed all creatures in the context of the unfolding of matter and motion in an evolutionary process. In *Le Discours sur le bonheur* (1750), La Mettrie examined the implications of materialism on moral values, questioning explicitly whether Christian morality corresponded to his physiological understanding of human beings; other thinkers rejected these radical views. In *Discours préliminaire*, written in 1751 to introduce a collection of his philosophical works, La Mettrie explicitly identified his work in medicine and philosophy with the reformist agenda of the nascent intellectual movement we now call the Enlightenment.

Bibliography

Primary: 1774. *Oeuvres philosophiques* 3 vols. (Berlin); 1743–1750. *Institutions de médecine de M. Hermannn Boerhaave traduites du Latin en française par M. le La Mettrie et avec une commentaire par M. de La Mettrie* 2nd edn. 8 vols. (Paris); 1746. *Politique du médecin de Machiavel, ou le chemin de la fortune ouvert aux médecins* (Amsterdam); 1750. *Oeuvres de médecine de M. de La Mettrie* (Berlin).

Secondary: Wellman, Kathleen, 1992. *La Mettrie: Medicine, Philosophy, and Enlightenment* (Durham, NC); Thomson, Ann, 1981. *Materialism and Society in the Mid-Eighteenth Century: La Mettrie's 'Discours préliminaire'* (Geneva); Vartanian, Aram, 1960. *La Mettrie's 'L'Homme Machine': A Study in the Origins of an Idea* (Princeton).

Kathleen Wellman

LACAN, JACQUES-MARIE ÉMILE (b. Paris, France, 13 April 1901; d. Paris, 9 September 1981), *psychiatry*.

The oldest of three children of Alfred Lacan, a prosperous merchant, and Emilie Baudry, Lacan received his *baccalauréat* at Collège Stanislas in 1918. He studied medicine and psychiatry at the Faculté de Médecine de Paris. He did clinical training at Sainte-Anne Hospital (1927–32) under Henri Claude, George Dumas, and Gaëtan Garian de Clérambault, among others. In 1932 Lacan received his MD degree. His thesis, *De la psychose paranoïaque dans ses rapports avec la personalité*, became his only book; *Écrits* (1966) was a compilation of journal articles and papers presented at congresses. Lacan lived his entire life in Paris. He married twice and had four children.

Lacan trained as a psychoanalyst (1932–38) under Rudolph Loewenstein, a member of the Société psychanalytique de París (SPP). Loewenstein later immigrated to the United States, where he became a main contributor to the psychoanalytical school of ego psychology criticized by Lacan for its 'deintellectualization' of American psychoanalysis; the school espoused the view that the individual should adapt to society and that the ego was the origin of psychic stability. Lacan promoted instead the 'return to Freud' and refounding psychoanalysis as a quest to decode the logic of the unconscious in pursuit of an 'ethics of desire'.

In the early 1950s theoretical conflicts in the SPP divided the society. Lacan, with others, founded the Société Française de psycoanalyse (SFP), and he taught a weekly seminar at Sainte-Anne Hospital (1953–63). The 'case of Lacan' became increasingly prominent in the tense relationship between the SFP and the International Psychoanalytic Association (IPA). Finally, Lacan was barred from the IPA for his unorthodox

ideas. In 1964 he founded the École freudienne de Paris (EFP), the first psychoanalytic institution separate from the IPA. In 1980 Lacan dissolved the EFP and founded the École de la cause freudienne (ECF), which remains dedicated to teaching Lacan's radical theory of subjectivity.

As a young psychiatrist, Lacan set out to reinvent psychoanalysis. From the French and German classics, he derived the idea of structure, and from linguistics, the notion of the signifier. This allowed him to apply a theory of language to the study of madness. Claiming the unconscious is 'structured like a language', he rethought Freud's notion of the unconscious as a structure based on language and speech rather than biology.

Two of Lacan's most famous and radical concepts were the Name-of-the-Father, which refers to the symbolic paternal function of prohibition, and the Mirror Stage, which denotes the genesis of self-awareness that begins when the infant sees the image of herself as both being and not being herself. This experience structures the prior chaos of sensations and perceptions, forming the nucleus of the ego and foreshadowing the evolution of the ego as an illusion. Lacan is also known for his concept of the three fundamental orders that comprise the subject—the Symbolic, the Imaginary, and the Real. The Symbolic (language and culture) order is the primary term of these three intertwined cognitive dimensions and refers to the notion that structures and law dominate us. The Imaginary order (sense perceptions and fantasy) begins with the prelinguistic experiences in the child-mother unit and is the locus of the ego as an illusion; it is restructured as the child enters language by the Symbolic order that supersedes the Imaginary and ties the subject to language. The Real remains outside language; it is what has not yet been, or resists being, symbolized.

Lacan developed a new psychiatric conception of paranoid forms of experience by denoting the importance of disordered speech and the position of the subject in relation to the Other's desire, that is, to the Other's desire as cause of the subject's desire. He believed that the subject's desire is set in motion as a function of the Symbolic order. According more importance to hearing than to speech, he allowed language to produce an effect on the patient. To separate the subject from its fantasized relation to the Other's desire, the analyst deciphers the patient's speech, as a commentator glosses over an original text.

Lacan's view of the ego as the seat of illusion—rather than the place of psychic integration—and the Symbolic order as the primary place for the formation of the subject have greatly influenced the humanities, in addition to the theory and practice of contemporary psychoanalysis.

Bibliography

Primary: 1966. *Écrits* (Paris).

Secondary: Roudinesco, Elisabeth, 1997. *Jacques Lacan* [translated by Barbara Bray] (New York); Fink, Bruce, 1995. *The Lacanian*

Subject: Between Language and Jouissance (Princeton); Schneiderman, Stuart, 1980. *Returning to Freud: Clinical Psychoanalysis in the School of Lacan* (New Haven, CT).

Cecilia Taiana

LAD, BHAU DAJI   (b. Manjre, Goa, India, 1824; d. Bombay, India, 30 May 1874), *medicine, leprology.*

Born Ramchandra Vitthal Lad Parsekar, Bhau Daji was the name adopted by this multifaceted personality, who was physician, Indologist, and social reformer. His father was of modest means, making and selling clay images in Bombay. Educated at the Elphinstone High School, Bhau Daji excelled in his academic career, won several scholarships and prizes, and subsequently was appointed an assistant teacher at the school (1843). Two years later, he joined the Grant Medical College and was among the first group of eight students to graduate (1851). After a short stint in the Bombay government service, as sub-assistant surgeon, Bhau Daji set up a private practice, which soon flourished and made him prosperous. His qualities as a physician and surgeon were lauded in *Lancet* (1855), and his practice was considered so successful that a medical man of his age in England would have been proud to be in his position. With his brother, Narayan Daji, also a graduate of the college, he provided free medical treatment to patients who came from all parts of Bombay Presidency at the Nagdevi charitable dispensary (1853–65). From 1858 to 1859 there were over 11,000 patients, to whom he prescribed a combination of Indian and Western medicines.

Bhau Daji was first vice president and then president (1855–56) of the Grant College Medical Society. In this capacity, he urged his fellow members to greater exertion, disseminating knowledge and popularizing smallpox vaccination. His papers, presented to the society, included 'Notes on Some of the Native Medical Drugs Used in the Nagdevi Dispensary' and 'Native Remedies Used in the Treatment of Poisons by Venomous Serpents' in addition to case notes on surgical operations he had performed. He researched a cure for leprosy in the 1860s and treated several patients with this remedy. Though the latter voluntarily wrote to the press acknowledging their cure, there was controversy as to the nature of the drug he had prescribed. His death in 1874 prevented the completion of his research. However, the drug he prescribed has been identified as *Hydnocarpus wightina*, also known as 'tuvarak' in ayurveda and mentioned in the ancient Indian text *Suśruta Saṃhitā.*

Bhau Daji was a keen botanist and was involved in the establishment of the Victoria gardens and museum in Bombay city. He contributed English and Latin synonyms to a Gujarati work on Indian plants.

As a member of the Students' Literary and Scientific Society, started by students and teachers of the Elphinstone Institution (1848) he was associated with its efforts to disseminate knowledge, stimulate scientific inquiry, and promote the education of women. Connected with the Native Improvement Library, he lectured frequently at the Mechanics Institute. Even as a student, he had written a prize-winning essay on the horrific practice of female infanticide. He was against social obscurantism, and advocated widow remarriage and the removal of caste taboos on foreign travel. It was his medical testimony that helped the case of social reformer Karsandas Mulji, who was campaigning against the immoral activities of religious leaders.

Traveling to different parts of the country, Bhau Daji studied inscriptions, coins, and monuments as sources for the reconstruction of ancient Indian history. He contributed papers on his findings to the *Journal of the Royal Asiatic Society of Bombay,* which were commended by Max Muller. As secretary of the Bombay Association, he was associated with a petition submitted to the British parliament demanding a greater share for Indians in the administration. A member of the Board of Education (1852–56), he was the prime mover of another petition, which led to the establishment of the Bombay University (1857). He twice served as sheriff of Bombay (1869, 1871).

Bibliography

Primary: 1854–55, 1855–56. *Reports of the Grant Medical College* (Bombay).

Secondary: Ramanna, Mridula, 2002. *Western Medicine and Public Health in Colonial Bombay, 1845–1895* (New Delhi); Mainkar, T. G., ed., 1974. *Writings and Speeches of Dr. Bhau Daji* (Bombay); Priolkar, A. K., 1971. *Dr. Bhau Daji* (Bombay); Karnataki, S. N., 1930. *Dr. Bhau Daji Lad* (Bombay).

Mridula Ramanna

LAENNEC, RENÉ THÉOPHILE HYACINTHE   (b. Quimper, Brittany, France, 17 February 1781; d. Kerlouarnec, Brittany, France, 13 August 1826), *medicine, pathology.*

Laennec was the eldest of three children. His mother, Michelle Guesdon, died in November 1786, possibly of tuberculosis, although her death came just two days after a stillbirth. His father, Théophile-Marie Laennec, was a magistrate and a poet, unable to keep a job and incapable of looking after his children. They were sent to the care of various aunts and uncles, including Guillaume Laennec, physician at Nantes.

Education

The young Laennec began the study of medicine under the tutelage of his uncle. But the strife of the Revolution soon brought violence and disorder to the region. Many brutal executions and murders took place in Nantes, and the uncle moved the family out of town to escape the carnage. All medical schools in France were closed, and the hospitals were underfunded, with their botanical gardens neglected. Still an adolescent, Laennec served as a medical cadet in the

Revolutionary army. These events deeply disrupted his education and home life, and they indelibly marked his spiritual and political views: he would always oppose the atheism and republicanism that characterized the leaders of the new medical intelligentsia.

In 1801 Laennec went to the newly reopened École de Santé in Paris. He studied with Jean Noel Hallé and Baron Jean Corvisart des Marets, personal physician to Napoleon and a staunch supporter of the new order. A gifted clinician, Corvisart had stumbled upon a little manual of percussion, published by Leopold Auenbrugger in 1761. This technique of physical examination involved tapping on the chest to determine the state of the organs contained therein. Corvisart correlated the sounds emanating from the chests of living patients with the findings at autopsy. After twenty years of experimenting with percussion, he published a treatise on heart disease (1806), in which he described the significance of the mitral thrill and provided an expanded translation of Auenbrugger's original work (1808).

A precocious and confident student, Laennec witnessed Corvisart's clinical investigations and excelled in what he called the 'new science' of pathological anatomy. He taught dissecting courses privately to his fellow students and began to write a treatise on the subject. He also worked on Corvisart's *Journal de Médecine* as a scientific journalist and editor with special interests in pathology, parasitology, ancient medicine, music, and language, especially Greek, Latin, and Breton. One of his many contributions to pathological anatomy was a lengthy, original article on the newly recognized tissue-based disease of peritonitis. He also served as a demonstrator for the teaching of the slightly older Guillaume Dupuytren. The two engaged in a priority dispute over a new classification of cancerous tumors. Laennec was convinced that Dupuytren had stolen his ideas.

While still a student, Laennec espoused conservative ideals. Influenced by fellow students M. F. R. Buisson and Gaspard-Laurent Bayle, he joined the Congrégation, a clandestine group of devout Catholics. His medical thesis was an unorthodox interpretation of certain passages in Hippocrates that reconciled the 'father of medicine' with the new anatomo-clinical ideals. At his graduation in 1804, Laennec took several prizes and fully expected to obtain a position in the Paris school.

Early Career

Despite his early successes, Laennec was repeatedly passed over for academic jobs, possibly because of his political and religious conservatism. Out of necessity and with little enthusiasm, he entered clinical practice in order to sustain his research in pathological anatomy and to support his father, an unmarried sister, and a brother ailing of tuberculosis. Eventually several cousins came from Nantes to live with him while they pursued their studies; he provided for them too. Because of his open support of royalism and reli-

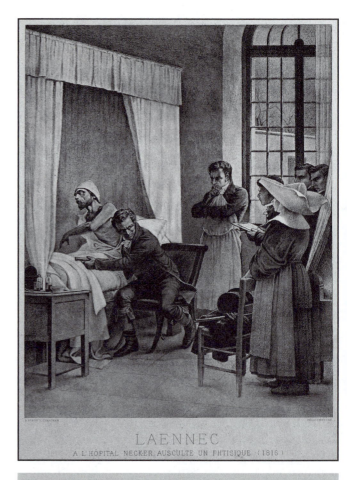

René Théophile Hyacinthe Laennec uses stethoscope on a tubercular patient at the Necker Hospital, Paris, 1816. Heliogravure after a painting by Théobold Chartran. Iconographic Collection, Wellcome Library, London.

gion, he became the physician of choice for clerics, Bretons, and returning émigrés; among his clients were Cardinal Fesch, René de Chateaubriand, Félicité de Lammenais, and Victor Cousin. Anonymously, he authored a royalist pamphlet on feudalism under various regimes.

In this period of clinical endeavor, Laennec was active in Société l'École de Médecine (which would reemerge as the Académie de Médecine). There he presented several papers on pathology and on parasites, including at least one collaboration with Georges Cuvier. In 1812 he read an important essay on angina pectoris, in which he cited the coronary artery theory of English authors. In the same year, he published a lengthy dictionary entry on the classification of anatomical lesions, together with a justification for the importance of anatomy in bedside medicine.

Laennec's hopes for a faculty position were raised again in 1810–11, when the chair of Hippocratic medicine fell vacant with the death of the dean, Michel Thouret. He might have been a credible candidate, but other faculty members seemed not to favor him; in the end, the chair was abolished. Always nostalgic for Brittany, Laennec now formulated a plan to return, hoping to derive an income from the rents on his farms and to write his treatise on pathological anatomy. At this time he developed a keen interest in agricultural practices, architecture, and engineering. He restored the dilapidated old manor of Kerlouarnec that had been used as a barn. A plan to enlarge his property by emptying a swamp resulted in a system of dykes and drains. But major political events and his famous discovery changed these plans; the lands reverted to marsh and the treatise of pathological anatomy was never published.

Discovery

Following the restoration of the French throne to Louis XVIII in 1815, Laennec was rewarded for his long-standing royalist sympathies with a position in the Necker Hospital. Later he would be named to the faculty now restored to its original name, École de Médecine de Paris. These political and personal changes in fortune coincided closely, if not inextricably, with his discovery of 'mediate auscultation': breath and voice sounds emanating from the chest that can be heard through a 'mediator'. This discovery led to the invention of the stethoscope.

Laennec wrote only briefly about the first moment of auscultation (1819; 1: 7–8). He had been consulted by a young female whose plumpness made percussion virtually useless. He did not reveal her age. Seized with a desire to listen to her heart, he was equally aware of how inappropriate it might seem to lay his head on her chest. He rolled up his notebook, applied one end to her chest, the other to his ear, and was amazed at the clarity of the heart and breath sounds. Without more research, however, the sounds were meaningless; this discovery needed interpretation to be complete.

The hospital provided a living laboratory for testing the new invention on many patients, some of whom were also examined postmortem. As his teacher Corvisart had done, Laennec correlated the sounds heard in illness with the morbid findings of the autopsies. This research into the nature and interpretation of the physiological sounds of heart and lungs, in both health and disease, resulted in an entirely new vocabulary of signs that would reveal the organic changes inside a patient's body before the patient died.

The exact date of the first observation of transmitted sounds was not given; probably it took place in the autumn of 1816. By 1817 Laennec was investigating heart sounds and murmurs; later that year, his focus had transferred to the lungs. He described and named the diagnostic sounds for pulmonary edema, pneumonia, bronchitis, tubercular cavity, and pleural effusion. Key to this research, as Mirko Grmek has shown, was his discovery of the exaggerated sound of the patient's voice heard over a cavity in the lung: 'pectoriloquy'. Wherever he heard that sound, he would eventually find a cavity in the lung. His appreciation of the reliability of this 'pathognomonic' finding inspired further research.

Laennec's early version of the stethoscope was a rolled up notebook sealed with gummed paper. Soon it became a hollow tube of wood, with an obturator at the patient end, which he called the 'cylindre'. Later he coined the word 'stethoscope' (derived from two Greek words for 'chest' and 'exploration').

The first edition of Laennec's two-volume treatise, *De l'auscultation mediate*, appeared in 1819, less than three years after his discovery. It contained fifty full case histories, most with autopsy findings, as evidence for his claims. By 1821 John Forbes had published a partial translation in English, and, within five years, auscultation was widely practiced in Europe and North America.

Continued Research

Although he was deeply engaged in clinical work, Laennec's investigations in pathology continued unabated. With his work on auscultation, he unified phthisis from the multiple symptom-based diseases it had been to a single entity characterized by the presence of the anatomical tubercle. He also wrote lucid clinico-pathological descriptions of bronchiectasis, emphysema, asthma, and pulmonary edema. His name is eponymously associated with cirrhosis of the liver because of a dictionary entry and a footnote in the treatise of auscultation. Indeed, he coined the name 'cirrhosis', from a Greek word for 'tawny-color', but he was not the first to describe this condition.

Laennec's research extended to physiology and physics. Keeping a lathe in his apartment, he investigated different woods and different shapes for building stethoscopes. He extended his auscultatory research to skeletal muscle contraction, acoustics, and dissection of living animals. With David Barry, he witnessed the vivisection of horses at a slaughterhouse in an attempt to sort out the meaning of the heart sounds. In keeping with the preoccupations of the experimentalists in the Paris school, he thought of this work as physiology: the lungs and heart of a dead body are silent. An expanded second edition of his treatise appeared in 1826, just a few weeks before the author's death; Forbes published a faithful translation of the new edition in 1827.

In his clinical research, Laennec used the new method of numerical medicine to assess the value of antimony potassium tartrate, a controversial old treatment for pneumonia. The drug was associated with vomiting, diarrhea, dehydration, and collapse, sometimes leading to death. Used in high doses, Laennec claimed, this drastic remedy could cure more pneumonia cases than all other methods.

In an eclectic combination of ancient and new, Laennec also applied the numerical method to assessing the Hippocratic notion of crisis and coction. With his long-standing confidence in Hippocrates, Aretaeus, and other ancient writers, he tried to find a formula for determining the date of onset of illness in order to identify the critical days and days of crisis when therapeutic intervention would be ideal.

Critics, Organicism, Royalism, and Vitalism

Auscultation was adopted by many clinicians in Paris, some of whom went on to found a medical philosophy called 'organicism'. This philosophy held that all diseases would eventually be reduced to and identified by changes in the organs. The exponents included François Broussais, François Magendie, Léon Rostan, and Jean Bouillaud, all of whom vigorously opposed Laennec, even as they embraced his new invention of the stethoscope. The reasons for their hostility were as much intellectual as they were political and social.

By 1822 Laennec had accepted the chair of clinical medicine at the Collège de France, which had been vacated by the death of his old professor, Jean-Noel Hallé. His selection was the result of royal intervention and in opposition to the votes of the other professors. He also took up a position as court physician to the Duchesse de Berry. Infamy for enjoying these royalist favors combined with further notoriety for willing participation in a reactionary sweep of the medical faculty. His medical enemies envied the successes, they resented the pious conservatism, and most of all, they denigrated the antiquated ideas that he expounded in his clinic and from his position at the Collège de France.

Laennec's lectures at the Collège de France were a two-year cycle, delivered twice from 1822 to 1826. To relatively small audiences containing a number of foreigners, Laennec revealed his views, not only of chest disease, but of all diseases. Citing many medical writers, he contended that the human body was made up of solids (organs), liquids, and life force. He thought that an alteration in any of the three components—solid, liquid, or life force—could lead to physical disease.

The life force, or vital principle, was an ancient notion that Laennec traced to antiquity. He knew that some colleagues were contending that it did not exist because they could not see or measure it. He pointed out that gravity could not be seen, yet its existence was not in doubt. Laennec admitted that diseases of solids are easiest to detect and classify; for these reasons he agreed that anatomical pathology should form the basis of disease concepts, or medical epistemology. However, he criticized the rising trend toward organicism, which he said was narrow-minded and arrogant. He began a project to identify changes in the state of the life force inside his patients by using the stethoscope. He discovered the sound 'puerile respiration', which was normal for children, he believed, but was an indicator of an increased 'need for oxygen' in adults with psychic distress. He often spoke of the importance of emotional well-being for the health of the body. In particular, he announced that tuberculosis, the disease of the anatomical tubercle, was caused by misery, poverty, and hard living conditions. From his personal correspondence, it is clear that this opinion was bolstered by his own experiences with chronic illness: his health improved whenever he took a vacation or went back to Brittany.

These ideas about a life force made Laennec appear to reject the very trend that his own research had helped to launch. He asked his physician cousin, Mériadec Laennec, to publish the lectures as a four-volume treatise on medicine, but the project was never completed. Some evidence suggests that it was actively suppressed.

Having corrected the proofs for the second edition of *De l'auscultation mediate* in the late spring of 1826, the seriously ailing Laennec raced to his beloved Breton home, Kerlouarnec, hoping for a remission; he died there just a few weeks later. No autopsy was performed, but the presumed cause of death was tuberculosis. He was survived by Jacquemine Argou, his wife of just two years; she was a distant cousin who had been his housekeeper. They had no children. Laennec was buried in Ploaré cemetery north of Quimper. His eulogy at the Académie de Médecine was not read until after the death of his greatest rival, Broussais, thirteen years later.

Impact of Auscultation

In the decades following his death, Laennec's popularity began to rise in the medical establishment of Paris. George Weisz has shown how his posthumous reputation owes much to the eager ambitions of French pathologists striving to create a distinct profession within academic medicine. Perhaps as a result of their efforts to venerate certain aspects of his research, Laennec was thought of as a pathologist by Michel Foucault and many other historians. He, however, saw himself as a clinician with research interests in both anatomical pathology and physiology.

Laennec's stethoscope not only increased the relevance of pathological anatomy to bedside medicine, it contributed to a reconceptualization of diseases, from clusters of symptoms as they were described by the eighteenth-century nosologists, to products of organic changes detected objectively by physicians. With this tool, Laennec could distinguish between mild and dangerous illnesses, and he could detect signs of disease even when his patients felt entirely well. As a result, auscultation endorsed a paradigm shift in medical epistemology—not only for chest diseases, but for all diseases—from patient-based to physician-based diagnosis. Although the stethoscope has been credited with the triumph of anatomical science in medicine, it also was the first instrument of medical technology to distance and diminish the role of the patient in her own illness experience.

Laennec Manuscripts

Hundreds of manuscript pages of notes for Laennec's Collège de France lectures have been preserved, together with dozens of patient records, in several archives, most notably the Bibliothèque Interuniversitaire de Médecine de Paris, and the Musée Laennec of the Université de Nantes. A vast collection of personal letters is owned by various family members who are descended from first cousins; recently some of these letters have been offered for sale on the Internet. Fortunately, most of the letters were transcribed faithfully by Alfred Rouxeau for his biography of Laennec (2 vols., 1912 and 1920); the typewritten transcriptions reside in the municipal library of Nantes and have been the subject of five medical dissertations at the Université de Nantes.

Bibliography

Primary: 1802–03 (An X and XI). 'Histoires d'inflammation du peritoine receuillies à la clinique interne de l'école de médecine de Paris sous les yeux des professeurs Corvisart et J. J. Leroux.' *Journal de médecine* 4: 499–547; 5: 3–59; 1804. *Propositions sur la doctrine d'Hippocrate relativement à la médecine pratique* (Paris); 1812. 'Anatomie pathologique' in Panckoucke, C. L. F., ed., *Dictionnaire des sciences médicales* vol. 2. (Paris) pp. 46–61; 1815. [as Anon.]. *De la Féodalité, ou mémoire sur cette question, le rétablissement de la féodalité étoit-il plus à craindre sous le gouvernement du Roi que sur l'Empire de Buonaparte?* (Ghent); 1819. *De l'auscultation médiate ou traité du diagnostique des poumons et du coeur* 2 vols. (Paris); 1823. 'Extrait du discours prononcé par M. Laennec à l'ouverture de son cours de médecine au Collège Royale de France.' *Archives générales de la médecine* 1: v–xx.

Secondary: Duffin, Jacalyn, 1998. *To See with a Better Eye; A Life of R. T. H. Laennec* (Princeton); Maulitz, Russell C., 1987. *Morbid Appearances: The Anatomy of Pathology in the Early Nineteenth Century* (Cambridge); Weisz, George, 1987. 'The Posthumous Laennec: Creating a Modern Medical Hero, 1826–1870.' *Bulletin of the History of Medicine* 61: 541–562; Lesch, John E., 1984. *Science and Medicine in France: The Emergence of Experimental Physiology, 1790–1855* (Cambridge, MA); Boulle, Lydie, Mirko D. Grmek, Catherine Lupovici, and Janine Samion-Contet, 1982. *Laennec: catalogue des manuscrits scientifique* (Paris); Grmek, Mirko D., 1981. 'L'invention de l'auscultation médiate, retouches à un cliché historique.' *Revue du Palais de la Découverte* no. spécial 22: 107–116; Rouxeau, Alfred, 1978. *Laennec [1912 and 1920]* 2 vols. (Quimper); Ackerknecht, Erwin H., 1967. *Medicine at the Paris Hospital, 1794–1848* (Baltimore).

Jacalyn Duffin

LAGUNA, ANDRÉS

(b. Segovia, Spain, *c.* 1511; d. Guadalajara, Spain, *c.* 28 December 1559), *medicine.*

Laguna's Jewish-converted father was the personal physician of the Bishop in his native city. He studied arts for two years at the University of Salamanca. In late 1530 or early 1531 he moved to Paris, where he took the arts degree and studied medicine. In 1534 Laguna obtained the title of bachelor of medicine at the Sorbonne, and eleven years later (1545), that of doctor at the University of Bologna. During his sojourn in Paris Laguna was taught medicine by outstanding humanist teachers such as the professors of anatomy Jacques Dubois (Jacobus Sylvius) and Günther von Andernach, and that of surgery Jean Tagault. In addition he studied Greek and philosophy at the Collège Royal and took lessons on *materia medica* from Jean de la Ruelle.

From 1535 on, Laguna's life was that of an ambitious fortune-searching physician who traveled to many European countries in pursuit of patronage, protection, and professional promotion from powerful court circles such as those of Emperor Charles V and of popes Paul III (1534–49) and Julius III (1550–55). Yet, except for his being contracted as a municipal doctor by the imperial city of Metz (1540–45), Laguna's major aspirations were not fulfilled until later in his life, when he was honored as a chamber physician to Pope Julius III (1550). Meanwhile, he presumably made a good living through his varied and distinguished professional clientele and the profits from his books. At all events, Laguna's career was conditioned by his Jewish origins, and his determination to become noble by buying Roman titles in the 1540s might have been intended to eradicate the stigma.

Laguna wrote many works, all of them first published in his lifetime. Most of them deal with medicine. His written production entirely fits the pattern of humanist scholarship. Thus, he edited, translated, abridged, annotated or commented on a great many works by ancient scholars, both Greek and Latin.

Laguna's early works consisted largely of Latin translations of Greek texts, but from the 1540s on his humanist scholarship focused on editing, abridging, and annotating ancient medical works. He published two different *Epitomes* of Galen's works, along with some *Annotationes* to Galen's editions by other humanist translators (Venice, 1548). Laguna's Spanish commented version of Dioscorides' Greek encyclopedia of *Materia medica* (Antwerp, 1555), which heavily depended on the Italian version by Pietro Andrea Mattioli (1544), is regarded as his most influential work (seven new editions before 1700). One year before, Laguna had published some *Annotationes* (Lyon 1554) to Dioscorides' Latin version by Jean de la Ruelle (1516). As was typical at the time, all his annotations were intended to show off his own learning at the expense of other humanist scholars.

In addition to translations, Laguna produced original works such as the *Anatomica methodus* (Paris, 1535), an early anatomical study resulting from his dissecting practice as Tagault's medical student in Paris; a plague tract, first published in Latin (Strasbourg, 1542) and then in Spanish (Antwerp, 1556, abridged version) on the occasion of two epidemical crises; a short health regime (Cologne, 1546); and two clinical works on joint pain (Rome, 1551; Italian translation: Rome, 1552) and urethral outgrowths (Rome, 1551).

Last but not least, Laguna's discourse *Europa* (Colonia, 1543) collects a lugubrious political declamation that he pronounced at the University of Cologne in support of Emperor Charles V's determination to keep—despite the confrontations among the Christian princes and nations—the politico-religious unity of Europe in the face of the Ottoman Empire, which was then perceived as the common enemy. Highly influenced by Erasmus' Irenical thought, this humanist declamation shows Laguna's political thoughts and concerns, but it might also be seen as an outstanding example of his eagerness to gain the emperor's favor.

Bibliography

Primary: 1535. *Anatomica methodus . . .* (Paris); 1542. *Compendium curationis, precautionisque . . . precavendae atque propulsandae febris pestilentialis* (Strasbourg; Spanish abridged version: Antwerp 1556); 1548. *Epitomes omnium Galeni Pergameni operum . . .* (Venice); 1555. *Pedacio Dioscorides Anazarbeo, acerca de la materia medicinal y de los venenos mortíferos* (Antwerp); reedited in Salamanca (1563, 1566, 1570, 1636) and Valencia (1651, 1677, 1695).

Secondary: García Hourcade, Juan Luis, and Juan Manuel Moreno Yuste, eds., 2001. *Andrés Laguna: humanismo, ciencia y política en la Europa renacentista* (Valladolid); González Manjarrés, Miguel Ángel, 2000. *Andrés Laguna y el humanismo médico* (Salamanca); Granjel, Luis S., et al., 1990. *Vida y obra del Dr. Andrés Laguna* (Salamanca).

Jon Arrizabalaga

LAING, RONALD DAVID (b. Glasgow, Scotland, 7 October 1927; d. St Tropez, France, 23 August 1989), *psychiatry.*

Laing, son of an electrical engineer, received his education in Glasgow and graduated from the University of Glasgow Medical School in 1951. He spent a year at the Glasgow and Western Scotland Neurosurgical Unit in Killearn, worked as an army psychiatrist for two years, and was associated, from 1953 to 1956, with the department of psychological medicine in Glasgow. In 1956 he moved to London to undergo psychoanalysis while he worked as a registrar at the Tavistock Clinic and Institute, the most innovative center in psychiatry and psychoanalysis in the United Kingdom. He finished his psychoanalytic training in 1960, after which he remained at the Tavistock as research associate. During this period, he advocated the view that schizophrenia was not an illness but a reaction to the pathological relationships within the family or a strategy to survive in an unlivable situation. He criticized psychiatry for blaming the victim by medicalizing this condition. Instead, he claimed that schizophrenia constituted an authentic experience while normal individuals could be considered 'mad'. Because of these ideas, Laing has often been labeled as an anti-psychiatrist, and he became something of a cult figure of the 1960s counterculture. In his writings, he described the subjective experiences of individuals suffering from schizophrenia, in an attempt to make madness comprehensible.

In 1965 Laing was one of the founders of the Philadelphia Association, which established and ran residential communities in which individuals diagnosed with schizophrenia were assisted in making their authentic journey through madness without suffering the alienating effects of conventional psychiatric intervention. The most famous (or notorious) of these was Kingsley Hall, which operated from 1965 to 1970, where patients were given the freedom to regress and engage in artistic activities. No limits were set on their behavior, with the expectation that this freedom would enable them to find their true, authentic, and integrated self. The atmosphere was anarchic throughout. Kingsley Hall was eventually closed because of neighborhood opposition and the inability of Laing and his colleagues to settle their disagreements.

Inspired by his interest in mysticism, Laing traveled to Sri Lanka and India (1971) and became a monk, acquainting himself with Buddhism and practicing meditation. After his return, he distanced himself from his earlier views and colleagues. His attitude toward the family became much more positive, which led to criticism by former admirers. His writing became more obtuse and speculative. His writings on the consequences of prenatal experience and, in particular, the uterine trauma he experienced eight days after conception were received with incredulity. He unsuccessfully tried to reinvent himself as a psychotherapist, poet, and entertainer and was frustrated by the lack of success of his artistic, musical, and theatrical efforts.

Laing was a striking person who was charismatic, photogenic, and unusually well able to boost his own popularity by relating his work to the ideas of the 1960s counterculture, which viewed him as a guru. He was arrogant and mercurial, and he craved fame and attention. He experimented with illegal drugs, was at times an alcoholic, and dabbled in mysticism and Eastern philosophy. He was a highly gifted pianist. He also was one of the most controversial psychiatrists of the twentieth century. He married twice and had ten children.

Bibliography

Primary: 1960. *The Divided Self: An Existential Study of Sanity and Madness* (London); 1967. *The Politics of Experience and the Bird of Paradise* (Hammondsworth); 1970. *Knots* (London).

Secondary: Burston, Daniel, 1996. *The Wing of Madness: The Life and Work of R. D. Laing* (Cambridge); Mullan, Bob, 1995. *Mad to Be Normal: Conversations with R. D. Laing* (London); Laing, Adrian Charles, 1994. *R. D. Laing: A biography* (London); *Oxford DNB*.

Hans Pols

LAMBO, THOMAS ADEOYE (b. Abeokuta, Nigeria, 29 March 1923; d. between Lagos, Nigeria, and Geneva, Switzerland, 13 March 2004), *psychiatry, international health.*

Lambo's birthplace of Abeokuta, considered a focus of Egba identity, is an important center of Yoruba culture and has been home to a variety of Nigerian dignitaries since the middle of the nineteenth century. Abeokuta was an important focus of missionary enterprise and competition in precolonial and colonial Nigeria, which endowed the town with well-developed schools and a high profile in Nigerian society. Lambo was a son of the Chief Basil Olamboasiri-Ajagba, the Otunbade of Igbore, Abeokuta, and Felicia Bolawa Lambo (née Akintolan). He was educated at St Paul's Primary School, and, from 1934 to 1939, the Baptist Boys High School in the town. He passed the Cambridge certificate examination with exemption from the London Matriculation and proceeded abroad for his university education.

Psychiatrist

Lambo left Nigeria to study in Britain in 1941, surviving a shipwreck off the coast of Senegal. He married Dinah Violet Adams, a British woman, in 1945. Lambo studied at the University of Birmingham Medical School, qualifying MB ChB in 1948. He worked as a house physician in the General Hospital and Midland Nerve Hospital, Birmingham, before returning to Nigeria in 1950. He worked as a medical officer in the Colonial Medical Service in Lagos, Zaria, and Gusau before deciding to specialize in psychiatry. Despite resistance from colleagues who had felt an internal specialism more appropriate to Lambo's skills, his choice of psychiatry was both encouraged and facilitated by Sir Samuel Manuwa, chief medical adviser to the colonial government.

Between 1952 and 1954, he carried out postgraduate psychiatric studies at the Maudsley Hospital and Institute of Psychiatry in London, earning the DPM in London, and the MD at Birmingham for his thesis 'Observation on the role of cultural factors in paranoid psychosis among the Yoruba tribe.' This thesis provided a powerful critique of John Colin Carothers's influential *The African Mind in Health and Disease*, which contended that cultural factors had led to under-development of the frontal lobe in Africans.

On his return to Nigeria, Lambo was appointed specialist-in-charge of the Neuro-psychiatric Hospital at Aro, Abeokuta. Lambo was the first African psychiatrist to practice in Nigeria, and the Aro hospital, which he was largely responsible for setting up, was Nigeria's first full-scale hospital for the mentally ill, replacing the system of incarceration in refuges and prisons that had so poorly served African patients diagnosed with mental illness. Colonial concern with mental illness and its social effects had been mounting since the 1930s, and Lambo's energy and sense of urgency were critical in developing institutional capacity at Aro.

The hospital buildings were not completed until 1958, but Lambo's practical approach to patient care and his strong local roots helped ensure that Aro's singular contribution to the practice of community psychiatry in Africa and further afield were fully in place long before then. His major innovation was the development of the Aro Village System. This system involved placing patients diagnosed as mentally ill with residents in local villages, in exchange for

Lambo in his office at Aro Hospital evaluating questionnaires during the Cornell-Aro Mental Health Research Project. Reprinted from *Psychiatric Disorder among the Yoruba*, edited by A. H. Leighton, T. A. Lambo, C. C. Hughes, D. C. Leighton, J. M. Murphy, and D. B. Macklin. Copyright © 1963 Cornell University. Used by permission of the publisher, Cornell University Press.

rent, nursing, and sanitary services, and other public-health enterprises. Lambo was assisted by his wife, Dinah, in the design and implementation of the system, which was administratively distinct from the hospital, though medical services and treatments provided by the hospital were available to those placed in the villages.

Lambo's system was in essence a social form of treatment, endowing unfamiliar psychiatric practices with familiar cultural and community-based resonances. It was a novel solution to practical cost-based problems in the practice of medicine and psychiatry in Africa, and it also helped to promote the integration and understanding of mentally ill patients and their conditions. Lambo and others later acknowledged the precedent of the Geel village model operating in Belgium from the fifteenth century, and similar schemes were being examined by Tigani el-Mahi in Khartoum and by Alexander Leighton in Navajo areas in Arizona. The range of significant scientific studies undertaken at Aro (beginning with Leighton, Lambo, et al., *Psychiatric Disorder Among the Yoruba*, which employed methodologies developed at Cornell University in the Stirling County study to examine psychiatric diagnosis and care) set it apart as a groundbreaking enterprise in culturally appropriate modern psychiatric care.

The Leighton, Lambo, et al. study demonstrated that patterns and prevalence of psychiatric disorders in the United States and in Nigeria were strikingly similar, undermining the basis of studies that propounded a distinctive racial character to the African brain and mind. However, the Aro Village System proposed a radically different approach to the treatment of mental illness. Controversy was excited by the use of traditional medical practitioners in the treatment of psychiatric illness. Lambo emphasized the psychoanalytic content of much of the care traditionally offered by locally designated healers, and he sought to harness their expertise in expanding the reach and capacity of the Aro Hospital. In dialogue with traditional practitioners who ran social and group aspects of care, Lambo sought to gain a greater understanding of the pathology and dynamics of psychiatric illness in his patients. From 1956, he was consultant psychiatrist at University College Hospital (UCH), Ibadan, and associate lecturer at the University of Ibadan (UI), though most of his time was spent at Aro.

Administrator

After Nigerian independence in 1960, Lambo became senior specialist to the Western Region Ministry of Health's neuro-psychiatric center, and, in 1961 he was a founder of the Association of Psychiatrists in Africa, convening the first Pan-African psychiatric conference at Abeokuta in November 1961. This conference attracted delegates from thirteen countries, who presented over fifty papers, in addition to a photographic exhibition and film presentations. Lambo's contributions, besides convening and chairing the conference, focused on psychological aspects of the growth of African children and on outlining important areas of research in tropical neurology. He became professor and head of the department of psychiatry and neurology at UI in 1963. His research in these years focused on the links between psychiatric disorder and infectious disease (notably trypanosomiasis), on psychiatric epidemiology (continuing the Aro-Cornell lines of enquiry), on drug addiction and criminal homicide, and on the development of psychiatric services in Africa.

He became dean of the medical faculty in 1966, and in 1968 was named vice-chancellor of the university, succeeding the historian Kenneth Onwuka Dike, who had resigned in 1967 as a consequence of the Nigerian civil war. His stewardship coincided with the foundation of the Behavioural Sciences Research Unit at UI, funded with assistance from Lambo's contacts at the Ford Foundation. A dispute over catering, which led to an outbreak of violence among UI students, encouraged Lambo to end his tenure as vice-chancellor and take up a position as assistant director general at the World Health Organization (WHO) in 1971.

Statesman of Global Health

While working at the WHO, Lambo continued to foster an interest in the study of psychiatry in Nigeria, developing interests in crime and substance abuse, which he had pursued in the 1960s. His initial appointment with the WHO encompassed special responsibility for the divisions of Mental Health, Non-communicable Diseases, Therapeutics and Prophylactic Substances, and Health Manpower Development. By 1973 he had been promoted to deputy director general of the WHO, and moved to Geneva. There he initiated a range of programs aimed at emphasizing

tropical disease training, treatment, and research, and establishing WHO collaborating centers in countries worldwide. He promoted the importance of recognizing mental health as a crucial component of the organization's Health for All programs, working closely with Norman Sartorius in developing mental health initiatives and programs with global reach. He continued to reassess the relevance of his earlier medical work to psychiatric care in contemporary Africa.

He set up the Lambo Foundation to promote research, training, and patient care in a multidisciplinary medical setting, and mooted an African Health Consultancy to target medical expertise toward combating African health and social problems. Lambo served on the Commission de Coordination Technique en Afrique au Sud du Sahara (CCTA) in 1957, was made OBE in 1962, and received the Haile Selassie Research Award in 1970, as well numerous honorary doctorates from around the world. He was awarded Nigeria's National Order of Merit Award in 1979. He retired from the WHO in 1988 and returned to Lagos. Lambo died while traveling from Lagos to Geneva for medical treatment in March 2004.

Bibliography

Primary: 1955. 'The Role of Cultural Factors in Paranoid Psychosis among the Yoruba Tribe.' *Journal of Mental Science* 101(423): 239–266; 1961. (ed.) *First Pan-African Psychiatric Conference: Abeokuta, Nigeria* (Ibadan); 1963. *African Traditional Beliefs: Concepts of Health and Medical Practice* (Ibadan); 1963. (with Leighton, Alexander H., et al.) *Psychiatric Disorder among the Yoruba* (Ithaca, NY); 1965. 'Psychiatry in the Tropics.' *Lancet* ii: 1119–1121; 1973. 'Changing Patterns of Mental Health Needs in Africa.' *Contemporary Review* 222 (1286): 146–154; 1981. 'Mental Health of Man in Africa.' *African Affairs* 80(319): 277–288; 1990. (with Day, Stacey B., eds.) *Issues in Contemporary International Health* (New York).

Secondary: Odeboye, Femi, 2004. 'Obituary: Thomas Adeoye Lambo O.B.E.' *Psychiatric Bulletin* 28(12): 469; Famuyiwa, Oluwole O., 2004. 'Tribute: Lambo Once Survived a Shipwreck!' *This Day* (Lagos) 24 April; Sadowsky, Jonathan, 1999. *Imperial Bedlam: Institutions of Madness in Colonial Southwest Nigeria* (Berkeley); Jegede, R. Olukayode, 1981. 'Aro Village System of Community Psychiatry in Perspective.' *Canadian Journal of Psychiatry* 26: 173–177; Asuni, Tolani, 1967. 'Aro Hospital in Perspective.' *American Journal of Psychiatry* 124(6): 763–770.

John Manton

LÁN ÔNG 懶翁 **(aka LÊ, HỮU TRÁC** 黎有㽪, **HẢI THƯỢNG LÁN ÔNG)** (b. Văn Xá, Vietnam, 11 December 1720; d. Bầu Thượng, Vietnam, 17 February 1791), *Vietnamese traditional medicine, epidemiology, hygiene, medical ethics.*

Lán Ông was a famous physician who lived and practiced medicine in Vietnam during the civil wars of the eighteenth century. He had Taoist leanings and Taoist connections, and these shaped his medical and political response to the troubles of the time in which he lived. Lán Ông's real name was Lê Hừu Trác, but he is generally referred to as Lán Ông (懶翁). This name is often translated as Mr. Lazybones; it is a pseudonym with strongly Taoist overtones indicating avoidance of worldly matters. Sometimes Lán Ông is also referred to as Hải Thượng Lán Ông, meaning Lán Ông native of Hải Dương Province, the province where he was born; of his father's native region, Thượng Hồng; and of his mother's native village, Bầu Thượng.

Early Life and Education

Lán Ông was born into a distinguished family that had been producing excellent scholars for three generations by the time of his birth. His mother's family included Lán Ông's maternal grandfather, who was a famous doctor and a member of the military medical corps for the royal court. As many of his male relatives had performed very well on the imperial exams, most of them were also government officials, and the family was thus quite well-known. Lán Ông was his parents' seventh child, and his childhood nickname was Chiêu Bảy, meaning Mister Seventh. He had a very close relationship with his father, and from a young age he was allowed to accompany his father to the capital, present-day Hà Nội, to study with famous teachers in preparation for the imperial exams. He became well-known as a bright young scholar, as a poet, and as a martial artist.

This experience of living with his father in the capital exposed him to many of the struggles and intrigues at court. It was probably during this period that he acquired the disdain for fame, wealth, and titles that characterized his adult life and which is forcefully expressed in his writings. Sadly, Lán Ông's father died when Lán Ông was just twenty years old. After this, although he was accepted three times as a candidate for the imperial exams, he refused a career as an official, and eventually the death of one of his brothers caused him to return home to care for his mother.

Medical Career

Partly due to concern for his mother's health and partly due to a chronic affliction of his own, Lán Ông decided to study medicine. He felt that he could best contribute to the world and to his countrymen and women by avoiding the worldly trappings of the royal court and devoting himself to health care. Lán Ông consciously made the decision to practice medicine in the rural areas near his home rather than to seek a position as a doctor in the royal court, which his scholarship and family connections would undoubtedly have acquired for him (Lê Trần Đức, 2004, pp. 88–89).

Lán Ông devoted himself to the study of the Chinese medical classics and to the works of Tuệ Tĩnh with even more enthusiasm than he had shown for the Confucian texts required for the imperial exams. He also based his study of

Statue of Lán Ông at the National Institute for Traditional Medicine, Hanoi, Vietnam. Photograph Mark de Fraeye, Wellcome Photo Library, London.

medicine on long hours of clinical observation through working with other well-known local doctors. He went beyond the usual methods of medical education at the time by studying and correlating medical texts kept by local healers of various sorts and the records kept on health issues by local and regional government offices and by Buddhist pagodas, which at that time were almost universally involved in public health care.

Lán Ông came to have a very great interest in epidemiology and a belief that diet, hygiene, and education could prevent many diseases and could ease the discomforts associated with old age and obstetrical and gynecological conditions. It was during this period of his life that he wrote his two most important medical treatises. The *Vệ sinh yếu quyết* [Hygienic Principles] extensively discusses diet, housing, clothing, and personal hygiene as factors in preventing disease and bodily deterioration. In this work Lán Ông also voices his opinions on the mental, physical, and social activities that he felt contributed to overall health—not just of individuals but of whole families.

Lán Ông's second text written during this period, *Hải Thượng Lán Ông Y Tông Tâm Lĩnh* [The Medical Treatise of Hải Thượng] contains sections on hygiene, but it also devotes attention to many other medical subjects. This enormous work includes sections on clinical observations of patients suffering from a variety of complaints, drugs, epidemiology, geriatrics, hygiene, medical ethics including doctor-patient relationships, and professional relationships between and among professional healers, obstetrics, gynecology, and pediatrics. The subject of medical ethics to some extent dominates the text and clearly occupied much of Lán Ông's attention. For virtually every section of the book and every situation he describes, Lán Ông states very firmly the responsibility of the physician toward patients of various types and with regard to any other healers who might be involved in the case. He also recommends very highly not only charitable work in connection with direct patient care but also assistance, financial when appropriate, with lifestyle and familial problems. In other words, one can say that he viewed physicians as also responsible for what today would be called social work. Lán Ông finished writing this text in 1770, and handwritten copies of it soon circulated around Vietnam. However, it was not printed until 1865, nearly a century after Lán Ông's death.

Lán Ông's social concerns also dominated his third major work, which is as much travelogue and political commentary as medical text. In a sense, this adds to its historic value. The *Thượng kinh ký-sự* [Relation of a Journey to the Capital] is a detailed commentary by an intelligent, trained observer on the physical, economic, and mental condition of the people of northern Vietnam, after they had endured decades of civil war. The health issues are obvious. Lán Ông wrote this text as a memoir of his last journey to the capital city where he had spent his youth.

In February of 1782, Lán Ông was summoned to the royal court to treat the illness of the young son of the regent. His journey covered some 300 kilometers, and while the author enjoyed the sights as he traveled, he noted (phrased in the guise of medical commentary) the condition of the people in the countryside in what should have been the richest agricultural area of Vietnam at that time. The book is also a commentary on the life of the court itself, as Lán Ông attributes the sickness of the young child to the rich and idle life he led and to the hovering-over treatment of the royal physicians. Lán Ông stayed with the court for some eight months, and then returned home in the turmoil of yet another palace coup.

Lán Ông lived and practiced medicine near his home for another nine years, during which time he wrote his memoir of the journey to the capital. He also composed one more book, this one specifically on local plants with medicinal uses. The *Lĩnh nam bản thảo* [Herbal of Vietnam], like his book on hygiene, was composed in the Vietnamese language and written in a poetic form that made it easy to memorize. It describes the appearance, preparation, and usage of 722 indigenous plants. Along with his other works, Lán Ông's last work remains essential reading for practitioners of Vietnamese traditional medicine.

Bibliography

Primary: 1742–70. *Vệ sinh yếu quyết* [Hygienic Principles]; 1770. (first printing 1865) *Hải Thượng Lán Ông Y Tông Tâm Lĩnh* [Medical Treatise of Hai Thuong]; 1782–91. *Lĩnh nam bản thảo* [Herbal of Vietnam]; 1782–91. *Thượng kinh ký-sự* [Story of a Journey to the Capital].

Secondary: Lê Trần Đức, 2004. 'Hải Thượng Lán Ông Lê Hữu Trác (1720–1791)' in *Renowned Vietnamese Intellectuals prior to the 20th Century* (Thế Giới) pp. 87–95; Hoang Bao Chau, 1993. 'Overview of Vietnamese Traditional Medicine' in Hoang Bao Chau and Huu Ngoc, eds., *Vietnamese Traditional Medicine* (Thế Giới) pp. 5–29; Nguyễn Trần Huân, trans., 1972. *Lán Ông, Thượng Kinh Ký-Sự* [Relation d'un voyage à la Capitale] (École Française D'Extreme-Orient).

C. Michele Thompson

LANCISI, GIOVANNI MARIA   (b. Rome, Italy, 26 October 1654; d. Rome, 20 January 1720), *medicine, malariology, cardiology, hygiene, anatomy.*

Son of Bartolomeo, a native of Borgo S. Sepolcro, and of the Roman Anna Maria Borgiani, Lancisi lost his mother in the delivery and was brought up by an aunt, a nun in Orvieto. When the aunt died, Lancisi returned to his father's home in Rome, at age twelve, and went to the Collegio Romano, an outstanding school because of the high quality of the teachers, to study philosophy, literature, and botany. Then he studied medicine at the Medical School La Sapienza, where he took his MD in 1672, a month before his eighteenth birthday.

After a contest, in 1676 Lancisi became an Assistant Physician at l'Ospedale di Santo Spirito in Saxia, under Giovanni Tiracorda, first physician of the hospital and doctor of Pope Innocent XI. Tiracorda had played an important role in fostering Georgio Baglivi's (1668–1707) attitudes and professional career.

In 1678 Lancisi was admitted to the Collegio Piceno di S. Salvatore in Lauro, an institution that selected young physicians with talent for study and research. During the five years he spent in this institution, Lancisi produced research in many different fields and left many scientific manuscripts, preserved in twenty volumes at the Biblioteca Lancisiana in Rome.

In 1684 Lancisi was appointed lecturer in anatomy at La Sapienza, and his lectures were attended also by Malpighi and Luca Tozzi. Then, in 1689, he moved to the chair of theoretical medicine, and from 1702 to 1718 he took also the chair of practical medicine.

In 1688 Lancisi was appointed by Pope Innocent XI as Medico Ordinario e Cameriere Segreto Partecipante. This pope died in 1689, and Lancisi performed the autopsy. The following pope did not confirm Lancisi's position, but luckily, in the same year Cardinal Altieri named Lancisi his vice-regent, a very high professional position in Rome, and upon the death of Altieri, Cardinal Spinola confirmed the appointment. Subsequently, he was appointed physician by Pope Innocent XII (1691–1700). He assisted the Pope on his deathbed, and the College of Cardinals asked Lancisi to become Medico del Conclave. The elected Pope, Clement XI

(1700–21), confirmed Lancisi in his position and, when cured of a renal calculus, appointed him as a canon of the church of St Lorenzo, named him Protomedico (First Physician) of the Pontifical States, and conferred upon him Roman nobility.

Lancisi was a member of many academies, including the Accademia dei Fisiocritici Siena, the Accademia delle Scienze in Bologna, the German Academy Naturae Curiosorum, and the Royal College of Physicians in London. With the name of Ersilio Macariano, Lancisi was also admitted in the literary academy of the Arcadia. A medical library, which now bears his name, mainly based on his collection of books, opened with a solemn ceremony on 21 May 1714, and in 1715 he organized a new medical academy in Rome, which included representatives of all the medical institutions in Rome. At this occasion Lancisi delivered an essay titled *De recta medicorum studiorum ratione instituenda* (published in 1715), supporting the reform of the medical teaching according to the model established by the Dutch school in Leiden, insisting on 'rational medicine', practical observations, and experiments.

In 1700, while he was physician of the conclave, Lancisi started to write a book on cardiac physiology and pathology, on which he worked for the rest of his life. The book, *De motu cordis et aneurysmatibus*, was published posthumously in 1728 by P. Assalti.

The first part of the work was devoted to anatomo-physiology, whereas the second part described many clinical observations and pathological anatomy. Lancisi distinguished clearly between hypertrophy and dilatation of the heart (characterized respectively by thick and thin walls), observed abnormal growths on heart valves, and explored the mechanical causes of heart enlargement, recognizing the relation of heart alterations to valvular stenosis within the heart and chronic lung lesions outside it. Lancisi also underlined the importance of violent emotions, palpitations, and excesses as causes of aneurysms, and he provided the first description of syphilitic aneurysms (*aneurysma gallicum*), describing the vascular changes produced by syphilis.

In this book Lancisi suggested also an iatrophysical explanation for the etiology of aneurysms, on the basis of many experiments performed on dogs. He had tied the iliac artery, observing the appearance of dilatation as a consequence of the alteration of the dynamics of the blood, resulting from the mass of the blood, the strength of the heart, and the conformation of the vessels.

During the years 1705–06, Rome experienced an extraordinary increase in the number of sudden deaths, and Pope Clement XI charged his physician Lancisi to find the cause of this kind of epidemic. Lancisi found that the 'epidemic' touched almost exclusively wealthy men with immoderate habits; poor people and those who had sober behavior in relation to food, alcohol, and sexual activity seemed to be exempt. Prevention was therefore possible, and 'as shown by our father [Hippocrates] the man of the art acquires the sta-

tus and admiration reserved to a good physician, when, unable to cure, he can at least prevent and predict'. At the level of anatomical observations, Lancisi showed that lesions were limited to the heart, even if he could not isolate a single cause of the deaths. In some of the cases, he attributed the death to mechanical causes—for example, the rupture of an aortic aneurysm, a hemorrhagic stroke, the presence of cardiac hypertrophy and dilation of the heart, or various kinds of valve defects. However, in other cases there was no apparent cause, and Lancisi postulated a chemical cause, such as a deviant fermentation, which, according to his iatrophysical models, was necessary for the correct functioning of muscles and organs.

This first clinical analysis of sudden death, which was a central preoccupation in the eighteenth century and the resulting treatise *De subitaneis mortibus* (1706), became quickly a classic of cardiac pathology and a model for forensic medicine.

In the field of anatomy, Lancisi described the medial longitudinal striae of the *corpus callosum*, an organ that he considered the seat of soul. Lancisi also was successful in persuading Pope Clement XI to acquire Eustachi's unpublished anatomical tables, which he edited in 1714.

In the years 1711–15, an epidemic of 'cattle plague' exterminated the European bovine population. The heavy economic losses caused reactions, and the most important Italian doctors of that time were charged to investigate the issue and to suggest preventive measures. The epidemiological analyses showed that the outbreak of the disease in the Italian countries was initiated by a herd of oxen for slaughter, which had been shipped from Dalmatia to Venice and then transported to Padua. Despite market restrictions, the disease spread throughout Venice, the Habsburgian possessions, and the Papal state.

Bernardino Ramazzini (1633–1714), professor at the University of Padua, played a significant role in the study of this event. In a work commissioned by the doge of Venice, *Contagiosa Epidemia, quae in Patavino Agro, & tota ferè Veneta Ditione in Boves irrepsit* (1711), he described the general state of knowledge about rinderpest and proposed twelve measures against it, some of which were adapted in the decrees of Maria Theresa.

The main debate concerned the nature of the disease. Could this disease be considered a true plague, that is, a highly contagious disease? Many great clinicians remained committed to the classical humoral, chemical, or mechanical explanations, but Lancisi, in 1715 in the treatise *De bovilla peste*, stated that reason and experience showed that this disease was a 'true plague' (*veram pestem*) and a 'pestilential fever' (*pestifera lues*), specific to cattle, and its origin (*originis que principium*) was an infection transmitted by contagion. The plague was produced by a ferment, involving the proliferation of small corpuscles (*semina*) that irritated, corroded, and damaged the animal machine. He left it open whether the process involved microscopic animals or an inanimate miasma.

On this theoretical basis, Lancisi suggested a series of practical measures to avoid the spread of the disease, including the method of 'stamping out'—that is, the designation of infected zones, intensive surveillance to identify infected animals, immediate slaughter of all susceptible animals in the whole infected area, and interring of all carcasses and other potentially infected materials. Because of his authority, Lancisi's suggestions, which were called 'Lancisi's method' for several years, were rapidly transformed into decrees, and everybody, including the clergy, had to follow the strict rules, a model of hygienic policy.

Lancisi also devoted attention to another 'popular' disease, which was particularly important in Rome: malaria. He studied five malaria epidemics occurring in Rome between 1695 and 1715, and he related the prevalence of malaria with the presence of swampy areas. In 1716 Lancisi first described a characteristic black pigmentation of the brain and spleen in the victims of malaria, which only in the nineteenth century became the pathognomic sign of the disease. In 1717, in his monograph entitled *Noxious Emanations of Swamps and Their Cure*, he linked malaria with poisonous vapors of swamps or stagnant water. Observing that swamps are *seminaria insectorum*, he echoed the old theories of Varro and Columnella by suggesting that malaria was due to 'minute bugs' or 'small worms' that enter the blood and thereby revived the old idea that mosquitoes might play a role in the causation of the disease. He considered that the most dangerous marshes were those in which one could find a large number of *vermiculi* (small worms), which later become *stridulos culices* (noisy mosquitoes).

Lancisi proposed two ways in which mosquitoes or other flying insects might spread malaria. In the first hypothesis, the insects deposited microscopic organisms in uncovered food and drink, and the disease resulted from the consumption of this contaminated material. The second hypothesis was closer to modern knowledge; Lancisi wrote that the insects 'always inject their salivary juices into the small wounds which are opened [by them] on the surface of the body'. Because their viscera are 'filled with deleterious liquids . . . no controversy can arise among men of science concerning the deleterious effect which the insects of the swamps, by mixing their injurious juices with the saliva . . . inflict upon us'. Lancisi noted that the noxious nature of mosquito bites was not produced by the bite itself, but was the result of a *venifico liquido* (a poisonous liquid) injected through the wound (*infuso per vulnus*). He noted also that the living exhalations (*effluvia animata*) of marshes acted not by themselves (*per se ipsa irritando*), but by mixing their poison with the liquids of the human body (*pravo suos succos cum nostris liquidis permiscendo*). At the prophylactic level, therefore, he recommended, without much success, swamp drainage. He suggested avoiding the stings of insects by staying indoors until sunrise, and he protested also against the cutting of the forest in the Agro Pontino because he considered that the trees created a barrier against the diffusion of the poisonous *effluvia animate*. He

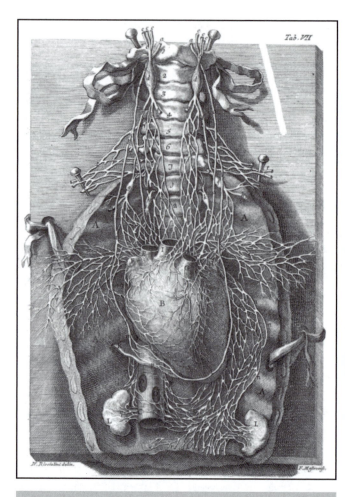

Anatomical dissection showing the coronary vasculature. Engraving from *De motu cordis et aneurysmatibus . . .* Rome, 1728. Rare Books, Wellcome Library, London.

produced in this context beautiful maps of the Pontine marshes, showing the position of the swamps.

At the therapeutic level, because of his practical experiences during the Roman epidemics, he was strongly in favor of the use of cinchona as a specific remedy against intermittent fevers.

Bibliography

Primary: 1707. *De subitaneis mortibus, libri duo* (Rome); 1712. *Dissertatio historica de bovilla peste* (Rome); 1715. *Dissertatio de recta medicorum studiorum ratione instituenda.* (Rome); 1717. *De noxiis paludum effluvis eorumque remediis.* (Rome); 1728. *De motu cordis et aneurysmatibus, Opus postumum in duas partes divisum* (Rome, English edn. 1952).

Secondary: Ongaro, Giuseppe, 1974. 'Lancisi, Giovanni Maria' in *Scienziati e tecnologi dalle origini al 1875*, vol. 2 (Milan) pp. 243–245; De Angelis, P., 1965. *Giovanni Maria Lancisi, la biblioteca lancisiana, l'accademia lancisiana* (Rome); Bacchini, A., 1920. *La vita e le opere di Giovanni Maria Lancisi (1654–1720)* (Rome); *DSB*.

Bernardino Fantini

LANE, WILLIAM ARBUTHNOT (b. Fort George, Scotland, 4 July 1856; d. London, England, 16 January 1943), *surgery, health education.*

Lane, of Irish descent, was the eldest of eight children born to Benjamin Lane, an army surgeon, and Caroline Arbuthnot Ewing. At age twelve, after a childhood abroad, he returned to school in Scotland. When the family was posted to the Royal Military Academy, London (1872), he studied medicine at Guy's Hospital (1872–77), serving house positions at Guy's and the Victoria Hospital for Children while studying for his MB (1881), MS (1883), and FRCS (1882). He married Charlotte (Lottie) Jane Briscoe on 25 October 1884. Both were engaged to others when they met and fell in love, and they went on to have three daughters and a son.

Lane was appointed assistant surgeon to the Hospital for Sick Children, Great Ormond Street (1886), and to Guy's (1887). As a pediatric surgeon, he modified flap techniques to repair cleft palates, popularized rib resection to drain empyema, and radicalized mastoid surgery in middle-ear infection. He was interested in skeletal anatomy, recognizing that functional repair of simple fractures in weight-bearing limbs was inadequate for dock laborers to resume work. Perfect anatomical alignment, he believed, could only be achieved with 'internal splinting' and he intra-operatively wired, screwed, and plated broken bones. Aware of the risk of bone infection, he adopted a scrupulous aseptic 'no touch' technique using steam sterilized drapes and long-handled instruments. Internal fixation jump-started orthopedics and was adopted in Germany and the United States. The BMA vindicated Lane's methods but recommended they be adopted only by experienced surgeons (1912).

With Lane recognized as a superb and dexterous operator, it was said that patients were more likely to survive abdominal surgery under his hands than anyone else's, and this reputation contributed to a successful private practice (£20,000 p.a. by 1925). Yet it was for abdominal surgery, notably colectomy, that he was most criticized. Although not originating the concept of autointoxication arising from constipation—James Paget (1814–99) and Elie Mechnikov (1845–1916) were enthusiasts—he was unique in applying such a radical remedy. He described the individual with 'chronic intestinal stasis': clammy palms, blue-tinged ears and nose, and no sexual appetite (1909). He himself took a thrice-daily dose of liquid paraffin. Lane removed colons for tuberculosis, thyrotoxic goiter, trigeminal neuralgia, and rheumatoid arthritis, publishing about 189 articles on chronic intestinal stasis. The procedure was discredited by the Royal Society of Medicine (1913), the year in which he received a baronetcy for performing abdominal surgery on a royal princess.

Lane was well received in America (1906, 1911), performing colectomies and fracture surgery to large audiences. He befriended the Mayo brothers and paid tribute to Alexis Carrel (1873–1944), whose transplantation experiments he had pre-empted by (unsuccessfully) employing rabbit femurs in human bone grafts (1899). During World War I he organized the plastic surgery unit at Queen Mary's Hospital, Sidcup, Kent, where Harold Gillies (1882–1960) pioneered facial reconstruction. In the postwar era of vitamin discovery, eugenics, and national fitness, he campaigned for public education in diet and lifestyle, believing that many diseases, including cancer, were linked to civilization. He founded the New Health Society (1925–37), attracting such notables as Lloyd George, Henry Wellcome, and Caleb Saleeby. In *Secrets of Good Health* (1927), Lane advocated wholemeal bread, fruit, and vegetables, a 'back to the land' policy, and a chair in nutrition like that at Johns Hopkins University, USA. Press articles publicizing the society's views resulted in Lane being censured by the BMA ethics committee for 'indirect advertising'. After arguing the case for doctors' involvement in health promotion, he resigned his BMA membership.

Although many of Lane's ideas were controversial, he avoided professional confrontation. Soft-spoken, he was charming to patients and was a good dancer. He enjoyed a relaxed family life, and he and Lottie regularly entertained. When she died (1925), he married Jane Mutch (1925), whose physician brother, Nathan, was involved in the New Health Society and married to his daughter Eileen. Lane's personal creed, 'If everyone believes a thing it is probably untrue,' defined his lifelong individualism.

Bibliography

Primary: 1904. *Operative Treatment of Chronic Constipation* (London, 2nd edn. 1909, 3rd and 4th edns. published as *Operative Treatment of Chronic Intestinal Stasis*, 1915 and 1918); 1905. *The Operative Treatment of Fractures* (London, 2nd edn. 1914); 1905. *Cleft Palate and Hare Lip* (London, 2nd edn. 1908, 3rd edn. 1916); 1909. 'Civilisation in relation to the abdominal viscera, with remarks on the corset.' *Lancet* ii: 1416–1418; 1927. *Secrets of Good Health* (London); 1929. *The Prevention of Diseases Peculiar to Civilization* (London); 1935. *An Apple a Day* (London); 1935. *The New Health Guide* (London).

Secondary: Dally, Ann, 1996. *Fantasy Surgery, 1880–1930: With Special Reference to Sir William Arbuthnot Lane* (Amsterdam); Morrice, Andrew A. G., 1994. '"The Medical Pundits": Doctors and Indirect Advertising in the Lay Press 1922–1927.' *Medical History* 38: 255–280; Layton, T. B., 1956. *Sir William Arbuthnot Lane, Bt., CB, MS: An Enquiry into the Mind and Influence of a Surgeon* (Edinburgh); Ogilvie, Heneage, 1954. *Surgical Leadership: In Memory of Arbuthnot Lane* (Bristol); Tanner, W. E., 1946. *Sir W. Arbuthnot Lane, Bart., CB, MS, FRCS: His Life and Work* (London); *Oxford DNB.*

Carole Reeves

LANE-CLAYPON, JANET ELIZABETH (b. Boston, Lincolnshire, England, 3 February 1877; d. Seaford, Sussex, England, 17 July 1967), *physiology, epidemiology.*

Lane-Claypon, daughter of banker William Ward Lane-Claypon and Edith Margaret Stow, received her primary and secondary education by private tutelage at her home, in Wyberton, Lincolnshire. In 1898 she matriculated at University of London College of Medicine for Women, receiving her BSc in physiology with first class honors in physiology (1902), DSc (1905), MB (1907), and MD (1910). She was designated a university scholar, received a gold medal, and is memorialized, with other outstanding women medical students, on a plaque hanging in the Royal Free Hospital, London. She was the first woman to receive a British Medical Association research fellowship. With this award, she carried out research, in the laboratory of physiologist Ernest H. Starling (1866–1927), on the development and function of the interstitial cells of rabbit ovaries and hormonal control of lactation. This seminal research was extensively referenced in the first textbook of reproductive physiology (Marshall, 1910). In 1907 Lane-Claypon joined the research staff of the Lister Institute of Preventive Medicine, where she carried out bacteriological and biochemical studies of milk.

In 1909 Lane-Claypon received the prestigious Jenner Research Scholarship from the Lister Institute. With this award, she toured Europe studying maternal and child health programs. Subsequently, she joined the Local Government Board, where she conducted a study of the comparative nutritive value of breast milk and boiled cows' milk (Lane-Claypon, 1912). In this study, Lane-Claypon demonstrated that infants who were fed breast milk gained significantly more weight than infants who were fed boiled cows' milk during the first 208 days of life. Her study was the first to utilize the historical cohort design, to consider and analyze the data for confounding, and to employ Student's T-test, introduced in 1908 by W. S. Gosset, to evaluate differences between data based on small samples (Winkelstein, 2004). These 'firsts' are integral components of modern epidemiological research.

In 1913 the newly established Medical Research Committee (forerunner of the Medical Research Council) commissioned Lane-Claypon to prepare a comprehensive report on the hygiene of milk. The report, in book form, received wide distribution in Britain and America (Lane-Claypon, 1916).

In 1916 Lane-Claypon was appointed dean of King's College for Women and its department of household and social science. During her tenure, she encouraged research and established a BSc to replace the former diploma in household and social science. However, harassment by the chairman of her advisory committee led to her resignation (1923) and return to the Ministry of Health. There she conducted a series of studies on various cancers, two of which may be considered classics.

Her case-control study of breast cancer, with 500 cases and 500 controls, identified most of the risk factors recognized today, including benign proliferative disease of the breast and failure to lactate (Lane-Claypon, 1926). Her study of survival after mastectomy according to stage of disease at operation introduced competing risk analysis—namely, accounting for intervening mortality from other causes—and survival analysis, namely application of life-table analysis to assess the impact of mortality over time (Lane-Claypon, 1928).

During her career, Lane-Claypon published thirty-one reports and three books. She married in 1930 and was, thereby, forced to retire from the civil service.

Bibliography

Primary: 1912. *A Report to the Local Government Board upon the available data in regard to the value of boiled milk as a food for infants and young animals* (London); 1916. *Milk and Its Hygienic Relations* (New York and London); 1926. *A Further Report on Cancer of the Breast, with Special Reference to Its Antecedent Conditions* (London); 1928. *A Report on the Late Results of Operation for Cancer of the Breast* (London).

Secondary: Winkelstein, W., Jr., 2004. 'Vignettes of the History of Epidemiology: Three Firsts by Janet Elizabeth Lane-Claypon.' *American Journal of Epidemiology* 160: 97–101; Marshall, Francis H. A., 1910. *The Physiology of Reproduction* (London); *Oxford DNB*.

Warren Winkelstein, Jr.

LANFRANC OF MILAN

(b. Pisa, Italy, early thirteenth century; d. Paris, France, *c.* 1306), *surgery.*

Little is known about the life and academic career of the physician Lanfranc. It is certain that he studied medicine at the University of Bologna as William of Saliceto's pupil and practiced medicine in Milan, before political disorder obliged him to escape to France (1290). He practiced medicine for some years in Lyon. He wrote *Chirurgia parva* [The little surgery], a surgical summary divided into sixteen chapters for his sons' education. He then moved to Paris (1295), where he enjoyed remarkable success as a practitioner and teacher. In France he completed his most famous work, *Chirurgia magna* [Great surgery] (1296), dedicated to King Philip IV (the Fair). In Paris, he probably had contact with professors at the Faculty of Medicine, since his work seems in some aspects to have been conceived for an academic public.

Chirurgia magna is a broad work, divided into five treatises dealing with the general rules of surgery, healing wounds, and fractures, following the traditional anatomic hierarchic scheme from head to foot (*de capite ad calcem*). Loyal to the organizational model of knowledge his master adopted, Lanfranc devoted a chapter to anatomy at the beginning, immediately after the description of the nature and goals of surgery. For this reason he defined surgery as a science founded on theory and not a mere manual art. He described various anatomical details, connected to wounds in different parts of the body. Lanfranc's text has a taxonomic characteristic that was not found in any other Latin texts about surgery, but that later became a model constantly used. The final pages of *Chirurgia magna* have an antidotary (*antidotarium*), that is to say, an outline of drugs that the surgeon can use to clean, corrode, soften, or regenerate the tissues: Lanfranc describes the general properties of such drugs, their preparation, and their specific applications. He introduced some novel ideas concerning the description of concussion of the brain and of the symptoms of skull fracture. In most cases, he recommended the use of trusses instead of a radical operation.

With his treatise Lanfranc—like his Italian colleagues William of Saliceto, Theodoric Borgognoni, and Roger of Salerno—contributed to surgery and to the establishment of a doctrinal tradition, the creation of an 'educated', didactic, medical literature that highlighted how the need for starting a more regular and methodical teaching of this discipline was developing. *Chirurgia magna* represented a step forward in surgical knowledge in the late Middle Ages, both for its methodical exposition, strictness, and use of clinical examples and news, and also for the ideas expressed. While reflecting the basic notions of Greek-Arabic medicine, largely those of Galen, Avicenna (Ibn Sīnā), and his master, William of Saliceto, Lanfranc suggested a certain originality accompanied by broad experience.

Through Lanfranc the new Italian surgery became known widely in Europe. Not only his book, but also the didactic activity he carried on in Paris passed on to French physicians the idea of considering medicine and surgery as a single scientific discipline. Among his pupils and followers were the French physician Henry of Mondeville and the Flemish Jan Yperman, who in 1320 published an outline of his master's teachings.

Chirurgia magna was the first surgical work in English, being translated first in 1380 and again in 1420. It was also translated in French in 1490.

Bibliography

Primary: 1498, 1546. *Chirurgia magna, Chirurgia Parva in Collectio Chirurgica veneta* (Venice).

Secondary: Tabanelli, Mario, 1965. *La chirurgia italiana nell'alto Medioevo. Guglielmo–Lanfranco* vol. 2 (Florence) pp. 801–1053; Sarton, George, 1931. *Introduction to the History of Science* vol. 2 (Baltimore) pp. 1079–1081.

Romana Martorelli Vico

LANGENBECK, BERNHARD VON (b. Padingbüttel, Hannover, Germany, 8 November 1810; d. Wiesbaden, Germany, 29 September 1887), *surgery.*

The son of a Lutheran clergyman and nephew of the surgery professor Konrad Langenbeck, Langenbeck studied medicine at the latter's university of Göttingen. He won a travel grant for a two-year study trip to France, England, the Netherlands, and Belgium on the merits of his MD thesis

(still in Latin) on the structure of the retina. He was most impressed by Astley Cooper and William Lawrence in London. Having returned to Göttingen, he qualified as Privatdozent for anatomy and physiology (still one subject) in 1838. Inclining increasingly toward surgery, he was appointed to that chair at the University of Kiel (1842). After participating in the first Danish War (1848), he ultimately went to Berlin (1848). During his thirty-five years as their head, the university clinics at Ziegelstrasse became a continental center in the first stage of modern operative surgery that was based on pathological anatomy, anesthesia, hemostasis, and antisepsis. Theodor Billroth (1826–94) was among Langenbeck's pupils. His method of surgery was considered 'scientific' in that as a young man he had already worked experimentally on cancer and hemostasis. He succeeded in generating pulmonary cancer in animals by injecting cancer cells intravenously. As did Thomas Spencer Wells in London, Langenbeck tested new operations on animals prior to conducting them on humans. In his later Berlin years, he supported the experimental and practical work of his ingenious pupil, Themistocles Gluck, on tissue replacement by homeotransplants of tendons and bones and by implants made of ivory or metal. Gluck was eventually dismissed by Langenbeck's more authoritarian successor, Ernst von Bergmann.

Langenbeck's tenotomies and myotomies of the 1840s and his plastic facial operations, such as resections of tumors, hare-lip, cleft palate, and nose corrections (around 1860), were typical of the pre-antiseptic era when operative surgery was still chiefly restricted to the surface of the body. He tried to improve postamputation healing of extensive wounds by frequent warm baths (1855). Based on anatomo-physiological insights, he innovated sub-periosteal and sub-synovial bone and joint resections in order to avoid mutilating amputations after injuries and in diseased (e.g., tuberculous) bones or joints of the extremities. He created a posterior exposure of the hip joint, developed later by Theodor Kocher of Bern, currently known as the 'Kocher-Langenbeck Surgical Approach'. Later he extirpated the pharynx for cancer. Characteristically for his generation, he also invented new instruments. The knee-joint retractor still bears his name. As a result of additional war experience (Denmark 1864, Austria 1866), Langenbeck directed the Prussian Army Medical Services in the Franco-Prussian War of 1870–71 as surgeon-general. He was knighted for his merits in military surgery in 1864. An apparently uniquely ingenious operator, Langenbeck brought a pronounced sense of duty to patient care in his clinic, which depended extensively on his own efforts. As a young foreign visitor, von Bergmann was disappointed that Langenbeck demonstrated brilliant interventions in his lectures but did not discuss diagnoses, postoperative treatment, or outcome of his interventions. Langenbeck was a humane doctor, shocked by the harsh treatment of patients witnessed by foreign visitors in Paris and London.

He remained rather modest and never amassed a fortune. Langenbeck was cofounder, with Billroth and Ernst Gurlt, of the first surgery periodical in German, *Archiv für klinische Chirurgie* (1860; today *Langenbeck's Archiv . . .*), in which he published many observations and analyses. He never wrote a textbook. With Billroth he initiated the world's first national surgical society, *Deutsche Gesellschaft für Chirurgie,* and chaired it as uncontested leader (1872–85). The Langenbeck-Virchow-Haus in Berlin has been its seat since 1892.

Bibliography

Primary: 1862. 'Die Uranoplastik mittelst Ablösung des mucösperiostalen Gaumenüberzugs.' *Archiv für klinische Chirurgie* 2: 205–285; 1874. *Chirurgische Beobachtungen aus dem Kriege* (Berlin); 1882. 'Ueber Zungenamputation mittelst des Thermocauters.' *Archiv für klinische Chirurgie* 27: 162–179.

Secondary: Mehlman, Charles, Ludwig Meiss, and Thomas DiPasquale, 2000. 'Hyphenated-history: The Kocher-Langenbeck Surgical Approach.' *Journal of Orthopaedic Trauma* 14: 60–64; *Neue Deutsche Biographie* 12: 580–582.

Ulrich Tröhler

LAPEYRONIE, FRANÇOIS DE (b. Montpellier, France, 15 January 1678; d. Versailles, France, 20 February 1747), *surgery.*

The son of a master barber-surgeon, Lapeyronie received a liberal education from the Jesuits and the University of Montpellier. Something of a prodigy for a surgeon of the time, he studied mathematics, natural history, and medicine, while he acquired practical experience in anatomy and surgery. Admitted to the surgeons' guild at nineteen, an exceptionally early age, he enjoyed the patronage of Pierre Chirac, also from Montpellier and future chief physician to the regent, Philippe d'Orléans. Chirac obtained a post for his protégé in Paris under the tutelage of Georges Mareschal, chief surgeon of the Charité hospital, who would himself a few years later become surgeon to Louis XIV. Lapeyronie then returned to Montpellier to become chief surgeon of the Hôtel Dieu hospital, served as military surgeon-major in the campaign against the rebels of the Cévennes, and performed a series of remarkable operations on important personages.

In 1715 Lapeyronie returned to Paris. Within two years, again with Chirac's help, he rejoined Mareschal, now chief surgeon to the regent, as Mareschal's designated successor. Lapeyronie seems to have overshadowed his senior (and unlettered) surgical colleague well before he officially succeeded Mareschal as chief surgeon to Louis XV in 1736. Drawing upon royal patronage, the king's surgeons were able to obtain unprecedented benefits for their profession in Paris and subsequently in the major cities of France. The monarchy established and generously endowed a school or college (1724) and a learned academy (1731), thus providing a venue for elite surgeons to carry on teaching and research.

The college enrolled students from all over the kingdom and beyond, while the academy had provincial and foreign associate members and correspondents.

In 1743 (more than coincidentally, the same year as the publication of the first volume of the Academy of Surgery's *Memoirs*), Lapeyronie secured a royal edict requiring all Paris master surgeons to take a prior university degree and prohibiting their work as barbers. By the time of his death, Lapeyronie had become a virtual king of surgery, possessing letters of nobility and enormous wealth, including his own chateau at Margin. More important, he brought together hundreds of disparate surgical guilds under his central authority, in effect (and in legal terms) raising the standards and status of French surgery to those of a liberal profession. Despite protracted opposition by the Paris Medical Faculty, this status received formal confirmation at mid-century. By then Lapeyronie, a bachelor, had made his final contribution to his life's work. His will specified that his immense fortune would endow surgical academic institutions in Paris and Montpellier.

A consummate administrator, elegant courtier and man of culture (his personal library contained nearly 1,400 titles), Lapeyronie was also highly skilled in surgical technique. He performed operations for strangulated hernia in which he removed a segment of gangrenous bowel and sutured together the two ends; his study of malformations of the penis (Peyronie's disease) proposed corrective surgery. Lapeyronie's animal experiments and clinical observations on the exposed brain were cited by Diderot. Reasoning from anatomy, Lapeyronie proposed a location in the brain for the 'seat of the soul'. His remarkably successful career epitomized new aspirations for surgeons of the Enlightenment. A modern hospital in Montpellier commemorates his name.

Bibliography

Primary: 1743. 'Mémoire sur quelques obstacles qui s'opposent à l'éjaculation naturelle de la semence' in *Mémoires de l'Académie royale de chirurgie* vol. 1 (Paris) pp. 425–433; 1743. 'Observation sur un étranglement de l'intestin, causé intérieurement par l'adhérence de l'épiploon au-dessus de l'anneau' in *Mémoires de l'Académie royale de chirurgie* vol. 1 (Paris) pp. 693–696; 1746. *Mémoire pour le sieur François Lapeyronie . . . contre les doyen et docteurs-régents de la Faculté de médecine de Paris* [attributed to François Quesnay] (Paris); 1748. *Testament du sieur de Lapeyronie, premier chirurgien du roi* (Paris).

Secondary: Gelfand, Toby, 1980. *Professionalizing Modern Medicine. Paris Surgeons and Medical Science and Institutions in the 18th Century* (Westport, CT); Forgue, Emile, 1934–36. 'La Peyronie' in Genty, Maurice, ed., *Les biographies médicales* (Paris) pp. 289–320.

Toby Gelfand

LAQUEUR, ERNST (b. Obernigk, Germany, 7 August 1880; d. Oberwald-Gletsch, Switzerland, 19 August 1947), *pharmacology, endocrinology.*

Laqueur, who was born in a wealthy Jewish family, was trained as a physician at the universities of Breslau and Heidelberg in Germany. After completing his PhD thesis in 1905, he became Privatdozent in Königsberg in 1907. In 1914 Laqueur was appointed lecturer in Groningen, where he worked with the well-known physiologist Hartog Jacob Hamburger. Shortly afterward, he volunteered to serve as a physician in the German army in Belgium. In 1917 he was appointed professor of pharmacology and physiology in Ghent. In 1920 he became professor of pharmacology and director of the Pharmaco-Therapeutic Laboratory of the University of Amsterdam. Under his leadership, this laboratory evolved into one of the leading research groups in the emerging field of endocrinology. In the 1920s and 1930s, Laqueur and his coworkers developed new biological assay techniques to isolate and synthesize the pancreatic hormone (insulin) and gonad (or sex) hormones. In 1930 his group was among the first three research groups to isolate a pure crystalline estrogenic hormone, and the first to isolate the male sex hormone testosterone. Laqueur also played an important role in developing the field of endocrinology in Europe, and trained many of the leading scholars working in this field between the two world wars.

In memorials, Laqueur is usually described as an excellent manager, a scientist who did not shine so much in laboratory experiments but who was a brilliant organizer of scientific labor. He was one of the founding fathers of Organon, the Dutch pharmaceutical firm that was the major producer of estrogens throughout the world until World War II, and is still one of the major firms on the world market for hormonal contraceptives. In 1923 he became one of the three members of the board of directors, specifically in charge of the scientific and medical management of the company.

Bridging the two worlds of academe and industry, Laqueur made important contributions to the research and development activities of the Dutch pharmaceutical firm. In 1923 he moved equipment from his laboratory in Amsterdam to Organon in Oss to set up the firm's first research laboratory. In the following years, research on sex hormones took place both at Organon's laboratory in Oss and Laqueur's laboratory in Amsterdam. Organon's laboratory staff was trained at Laqueur's laboratory. Moreover, the hormone preparations produced by Organon were controlled for quality in the laboratory in Amsterdam. Laqueur had the right of veto over hormone preparations that were not passed by his laboratory. He thus provided Organon with access to procedures for testing, standardization, and quality control, which enabled the young firm to develop into a major science-based industry.

The alliance with Organon also brought benefits to Laqueur. The company provided his group with access to large quantities of organic material required for research on hormones. Organon paid well for his expertise, thus enabling Laqueur to expand his laboratory staff. This close cooperation between academic scientists and pharmaceutical companies was of central importance to the research on sex hormones. Scientists who succeeded in making arrangements with pharmaceutical industries formed the leading research groups in sex endocrinology.

World War II was a very difficult time for Laqueur. In 1942 the Germans deprived him of his professorship and forbade him access to his laboratory because of his Jewish background. Despite these restrictions, Laqueur remained very active in helping colleagues and friends to survive the war years.

Bibliography

Primary: 1925. (with Grevenstuk, A.) *Insulin. Seine Darstellung, Physiologische und Pharmakologische Wirkung mit Besonderer Berücksichtigung seiner Wertbestimmung* (Munich); 1927. (with Hart, P. C., and S. E. de Jongh) 'A Note on the Preparation and Properties of a Female Sexual Hormone (Menformon) in Water-Soluble Form.' *Lancet* i: 1126–1128.; 1935. (ed.) *De Endocrine Ziekten en haar Orgaan- en Hormoontherapie* 2 vols. (Leiden and Amsterdam).

Secondary: Knegtmans, P. J., 2000. 'Laqueur, Onderzoeksleider en Ondernemers' in Knegtmans, P. J., and A. J. Kox, eds., *Tot Nut en Eer van de Stad. Wetenschappelijk Onderzoek aan de Universiteit van Amsterdam* (Amsterdam) pp. 90–94; Oudshoorn, N., 1994. *Beyond the Natural Body. An Archeology of Sex Hormones* (London and New York); Sneader, W., 1985. *Drug Discovery: The Evolution of Modern Medicines.* (Chichester).

Nelly Oudshoorn

LARDIZÁBAL DUBOIS, VICENTE DE (b. San Sebastián, Spain, 1746; d. San Sebastián, 23 August 1814), *medicine.*

Lardizábal's precise birth date and the place where he studied medicine are not known. He appears to have received a sound education and knew Latin, French, and English. He began his work in the medical profession in San Sebastián and in 1772 became a physician with the *Real Compañía Guipuzcoana* of Caracas, a company that enjoyed a monopoly over trade with Venezuelan ports from 1728 and sent at least two ships per year until 1784. Subsequently, in 1775, he entered the *Real Sociedad Bascongada de Amigos del País*, a philanthropic institution imbued with the ideals of the Enlightenment (development of education, wealth, culture, and general progress of the country).

His research focused on the two areas in which he carried out his professional activity: naval health and hygiene, and medical practice in the city of his birth.

He wrote his papers on the health of sailors in a period when commercial voyages were on the rise. His aim was to improve the understanding and training of naval surgeons, who were the only personnel responsible for health on board. He based his studies on the best authors and writers of the time, expressly citing papers by Herman Boerhaave, Andrés Piquer, Sanches Ribeiro, Louis Rouppe, and James Lind.

In line with the neoenvironmentalist and miasmatic theories of the time, his health discourse centered on ventilation and water potability. His proposals for the former were based on a good knowledge of gas physics, the pneumatic chemistry of Boyle, and the experiments of Hales and Watson; he finally opted for the method of Samuel Sutton, in which air is circulated using the heat produced by the ship's boiler. He addressed the water potability issue on the basis of the chemistry of the time, giving rise to the use of quicklime to preserve the quality of the water, which was then boiled before drinking, a method that had been successfully applied by the Scotsman Charles Alston.

Scurvy was the subject of his second paper on naval medicine, published in 1772. The author knew of Lind's experiments with citrus fruits and their proven efficacy against the disease, to which he referred throughout the text. Armed with his knowledge of John Bachstom's experiments with fresh vegetable diets, Lardizábal attempted to demonstrate similar anti-scurvy properties for a marine plant, sargasso, which could easily be gathered during a voyage. Although the experiment bore no fruit, Lardizábal supported recommendations to include fresh vegetables in the diet of seafarers.

With regard to his professional practice as a physician in the city of San Sebastián, Vicente de Lardizábal wrote a paper praising the virtues of chocolate as a dietary complement to mineral baths, which he fervently supported, and he participated in the smallpox inoculation controversy. He also published reports on cases of anthrax in the rural Basque area.

At the end of his life and after the destruction of his native city in 1813 by the English-Portuguese army led by Wellington, he reported on a typhoid fever (pestilence) epidemic in the first and only volume of the *Periódico de San Sebastián y de Pasajes,* which he published in 1814.

Vicente de Lardizábal has historical importance as a fine exponent of the medical Enlightenment and a pioneer in research on Spanish naval medicine and hygiene.

Bibliography

Primary: 1769. *Consideraciones Político-Médicas sobre la salud de los navegantes* (Madrid); 1772. *Consuelo de navegantes* (Madrid); 1788. *Memoria sobre las utilidades del chocolate* (Pamplona).

Secondary: Astrain Gallart, Mikel, 1992. *La medicina del mar. Sanitarios y sanidad naval al servicio del Rey de Utrecht a Trafalgar (1712–1805)* (Granada); Lloret, Martí, and Juan Bautista, 1970. *Vicente de Lardizábal, médico donostiarra de la Ilustración* (San Sebastián).

Mikel Astrain

LARREY, JEAN DOMINIQUE   (b. Beaudéan, France, 8 July 1766; d. Lyon, France, 25 July 1842), *surgery, military medicine, medical literature.*

Larrey has remained the most famous of French military surgeons, admired both for his expertise and his humaneness. Born into a family of surgeons, he was at first guided by his uncle Alexis Larrey, chief surgeon at the Hôpital St Joseph de la Grave at Toulouse. He then perfected his skills under the direction of two leading Paris surgeons, Antoine Louis and Pierre-Joseph Desault. Impatient for action, he enlisted in the royal navy on the frigate *La Vigilante* in 1787, voyaging to Newfoundland. But he preferred firm land to sailing, and the wars of the French Revolution and Napoleonic Empire gave him ample opportunities to try his skills. He joined the Rhine Army in 1792, rose to become its surgeon-in-chief, and then served in this same capacity during the Italian and Egyptian campaigns, and in Spain, Germany, Russia, and at Waterloo. He also headed the medical service at the Hôtel des Invalides and in Napoleon's Imperial Guard, and taught surgery at the Val-de-Grâce military medical school.

The soldiers, including Napoleon, admired his surgical skill. His success in amputations or resections was often due to speed and helped by freezing temperatures. Since anesthesia was unknown, operative speed was essential to saving lives. But he also earned the soldiers' esteem because his priorities were clear: he would operate first on the most serious cases, regardless of rank or nationality.

Larrey's concern for the wounded led him to collaborate with Pierre-François Percy in the introduction of stretcher-bearers (*brancardiers*) on the battlefield. But his most famous innovation was the 'flying ambulance'. Light and maneuverable, it was able to pick up casualties during battle, administer first aid, travel back to a field hospital, and return quickly into the melee to retrieve more wounded. In the Egyptian campaign, Larrey supplemented ambulances with stretchers carried on camelback. He wished in vain for a well-organized army medical corps with physicians and surgeons who would enforce hygiene and teach preventive measures. But Napoleon was highly skeptical of medicine and thus, under the Empire, army medicine remained subordinated to the quartermaster.

While abroad, Larrey used his organizational skills to reform the medical schools at Padua and Milan according to the French Republican model and create a surgery school in Cairo, and in 1832 he accepted the invitation of King Leopold of Belgium to create that country's military medical service.

During his long life Larrey kept notes that constitute his five-volume *Memoirs*, an invaluable source of information. Napoleon rewarded him with the Legion of Honor and a baronetcy; he was elected to the Academy of Medicine in 1820 and to the Academy of Sciences in 1829—so late, it was said, because of political animosity against Napoleon, who admired Larrey, calling him 'the most virtuous man I have ever known'.

Bibliography

Primary: 1814. *Memoirs of military surgery, and campaigns of the French armies on the Rhine, in Corsica, Catalonia, Egypt, and Syria; at Boulogne, Ulm and Austerlitz; in Saxony, Prussia, Poland, Spain, and Austria* (trans. Hall, Richard Willmott) (Baltimore); 1832. *Observations on wounds and their complications by erysipelas, gan-*

grene, and tetanus, and on the principal diseases and injuries of the head, ear, and eye (trans. Rivinus, E. F.) (Philadelphia); 1936. (ed. Pallardy, Paul) *Les rapports originaux de Larrey à l'armée d'Orient* in *Mémoires de l'Institut d'Egypte* vol. XXX (Cairo).

Secondary: Willemot, J., 2000. 'Larrey, Jean Dominique' in *Dictionnaire de biographie française 19*: 1087–1089; Weiner, Dora B., 1993. *The Citizen-Patient in Revolutionary and Imperial Paris* (Baltimore); Weiner, Dora B., 1969. 'French Doctors Face War: 1792–1815' in Warner, Charles E., ed., *From the Ancien Régime to the Popular Front: Essays in the History of Modern France in Honor of Shepard B. Clough* (New York).

Dora B. Weiner

LASÈGUE, CHARLES   (b. Paris, France, 5 September 1816; d. Paris, 20 March 1883), *medicine, psychiatry.*

The son of a botanist, Lasègue initially considered a career in literature and philosophy. After taking a licentiate degree in letters, he taught at the lycée Louis-le-Grand, where the poet Baudelaire was one of his students. Lasègue's friendship with Claude Bernard and B.-A. Morel, at the time interns at the Salpêtrière hospital, sparked an interest in the study of mental diseases. He received his degree from the Paris medical faculty in 1846. Six years later he became chief resident under Trousseau at the Hôtel Dieu. In 1862 the medical faculty appointed Lasègue to teach a new course in mental diseases. Although formally designated as a 'complementary clinical course', the new offering was hampered by the mental hospitals' refusal to provide patients for instruction. Lasègue was named to the chair of general pathology and therapy in 1867 and, two years later, he succeeded Andral as professor of clinical medicine at the Pitié hospital.

Lasègue took a strong stand in favor of an objective clinical approach to mental disease. A confirmed organicist, he believed that lesions of the brain, usually the result of various kinds of trauma, left patients susceptible to recurrent bouts of mental illness. He called such individuals 'les cérébraux', a term that gained wide currency. Lasègue's remark that hysteria had never been defined and never would be was frequently cited. Nonetheless, he published original accounts of various somatic manifestations of hysteria, beginning in 1852 with an article on the 'hysterical cough'. He is best remembered for his account of anorexia, which he classified as a hysterical disorder most frequently seen in adolescent girls. Unlike his British counterpart, William Withey Gull, who had noted a hysterical disorder of gastric function, Lasègue's conception of anorexia (1873) emphasized psychological factors, in particular, the dynamics of conflict within the patient's family.

Most of Lasègue's publications appeared in the *Archives générales de médecine,* a leading periodical that he edited for thirty years and in which he took the opportunity to indulge his literary talents in editorials and reviews on medical biography, history, and philosophy. Lasègue took a special interest in German medical psychology.

It is instructive to contrast Lasègue's career with Jean-Martin Charcot's. Nearly ten years older, Lasègue became a leading authority on hysteria during the Second Empire while his more famous rival flourished during the Third Republic. Lasègue's eclipse by the leader of the Salpêtrière School was due in part to his not building a comparable hospital-based specialty with a devoted group of followers. Although a popular, highly cultured, and eloquent professor, his courses were neither for beginning students nor the general public. Lasègue remained involved with all areas of medicine and, unlike Charcot, his expertise extended beyond the neuroses to include major forms of mental illness.

Lasègue's original contributions to psychiatry included the identification of persecution delirium. He published articles on exhibitionism (a term he imported into psychiatry) and department store kleptomania, attributing both to cerebral deficiencies. Together with Jules Falret he introduced the notion of 'folie à deux' in reference to a shared psychosis transmitted from one individual to another. Lasègue also published on general paralysis of the insane and alcoholic psychosis with delirium tremens. For more than twenty years, he was physician to the Paris prefecture of police, where he became an authority on determining responsibility in criminal cases of insanity.

Lasègue married Marie-Victorine Perrotin with whom he had several daughters. Although he appeared robust to contemporaries, he died from the complications of diabetes.

Bibliography

Primary: 1884. *Études médicales* 2 vols. (Paris): 1971. (Corraze, J., ed. and intro.) *Écrits psychiatriques* (Toulouse).

Secondary: Chabrol, Henri, and Jacques Corraze, 2001. 'Charles Lasègue, 1816–1883.' *Am. J. Psychiatry* 158: 28; Semelaigne, René, 1932. 'Lasègue (Ernest-Charles)' in Semelaigne, René, *Les pionniers de la psychiatrie française avant et après Pinel* vol. 2 (Paris) pp. 40–49; Ritti, A, 1885. 'Eloge de Lasègue.' *Ann. Méd.-psych.* 7 ser. 2: 88–121.

Toby Gelfand

LAVERAN, CHARLES LOUIS ALPHONSE   (b. Paris, France, 18 June 1845; d. Paris, 18 May 1922), *parasitology, tropical medicine.*

Laveran, by his father Louis-Théodore Laveran, belonged to a medical dynasty and, by his mother Marie-Louise Anselme Guénard de la Tour, to a military family. As a child, he went with his father on his postings in Algeria. He later entered the military medical school of Strasbourg. In 1866, as an intern, he submitted a thesis on nerve regeneration. After working at the military hospital of Saint-Martin in Paris, he experienced the consequences of epidemics in the army during the Franco-Prussian War of 1870, and in 1874 he published an authoritative *Traité des maladies et épidémies des armées.*

Sent to Algeria in 1878, he headed wards in Bône, Biskra, and Constantine, where he observed the pigment accumulated in the spleens of soldiers dying of acute fevers. Although he used a microscope of limited power, he noted, differing from pigment particles, the presence of small bodies, some of them crescent-shaped, either included in red blood cells or lying between them. On 6 November 1880, at Constantine, in a patient's blood he saw filaments bulging out violently and striking the surrounding cells, suggesting a flagellate organism (this was shown later to be the sexual form of the parasite). When he returned to Paris, he demonstrated the phenomenon in a soldier's blood to Louis Pasteur and Emile Roux, whom he convinced that he had discovered the material parasite.

Yet Laveran's first description of a parasite inside red blood cells was initially far from unanimously accepted, and his new parasite had to compete with bacteria claimed by other authors. How was malaria transmitted from man to man? Laveran was led to incriminate mosquitoes because of the coincidence of their season with the onset of fevers. When Ronald Ross solved the enigma, he paid homage to Laveran for anticipating the idea.

It is still debated today which parasite Laveran actually observed, *Plasmodium falciparum*, the agent of pernicious fever, or *vivax* or *malariae*. As for Laveran, he did not admit the existence of species. In his 1884 treatise on malaria, he attributed the variations in the course of the malady, the rhythm of fever fits and relapses, to the geographic context. The book popularized the microscopic diagnosis of malaria and detailed the effects of the wonder drug quinine, which, ingested or injected, cleared the blood of its parasites.

When in 1902, after neglecting his research and advice on malaria prophylaxis in colonial expeditions, the army offered him a purely administrative position, Laveran resigned. For the remaining twenty years of his life, he worked at the Pasteur Institute. He found in the zoologist Félix Mesnil a congenial partner, and together they founded the Société de Pathologie Exotique with its organ the *Bulletin*, still extant today.

In 1907 Laveran was awarded the Nobel Prize for his work on the role of protozoa in diseases. With the prize money he equipped a laboratory at the Pasteur Institute. There Laveran relentlessly explored disease-causing protozoa, from African trypanosomas (sleeping sickness) to Leishmanias (agents of the deadly kala-azar and mutilating sores). He helped turn the Paris Pasteur Institute into an international center of research in tropical medicine, thanks to its overseas branches.

Laveran married Sophie-Marie Pidancet and had no children. His sudden death interrupted the course of a life entirely dedicated to research. It seems that he worked until the very last day.

Bibliography

Primary: 1880. 'Sur un nouveau parasite trouvé dans le sang de plusieurs malades atteints de fièvre palustre.' *Bulletin de l'Académie de Médecine* 9: 1268; 1907. 'Protozoa as causes of disease.' in *Nobel Lectures, Physiology and Medicine*, 257–274 (Amsterdam, 1967); 1903. *Trypanosomes et trypanosomiases* (Paris) [English edn., 1907].

Secondary: Smith, Dale. C., and Lorraine B. Sanford, 1985. 'Laveran's Germs: The Reception and Use of a Medical Discovery.' *American Journal of Tropical Medicine and Hygiene* 34: 2–20; Phisalix, Marie, 1923. *Alphonse Laveran, sa vie, son oeuvre* (Paris); Roux, Émile, 1915. 'Jubilé Laveran.' *Annales de l'Institut Pasteur* 29, 405–414; *DSB*.

Anne Marie Moulin

LAWRENCE, WILLIAM (b. Cirencester, Gloucestershire, England, 6 July 1783; d. London, England, 5 July 1867), *surgery, physiology.*

Lawrence was the eldest of the four sons of the surgeon William Lawrence (1753–1837). He studied at Elmore Court, Gloucestershire, before being apprenticed to the London surgeon John Abernethy (1799–1801), who appointed Lawrence his demonstrator of anatomy (1801–13). Lawrence was elected assistant surgeon to St Bartholomew's Hospital (1813–25) and also served as surgeon to the London Infirmary for Diseases of the Eye and to Bethlem Hospital (1815–67). He rose to surgeon at St Bartholomew's (1824–65) and there lectured on surgery (1829–62) after a period teaching anatomy at the Aldersgate School, London, which he was instrumental in establishing.

Lawrence made numerous technical contributions to surgery, in particular his *Treatise on Hernia* (1807) and his work on testicular tumors. However, it was his lectures as professor of anatomy at the RCS that attracted notoriety. In his first lecture (1816), the opportunistic Lawrence criticized Abernethy's exposition of John Hunter's (1728–93) theory of vitality. Drawing on French medical thought and seeking to break from what he saw as reactionary science, Lawrence asserted that life was a resistance against an inanimate state, not a consequence of peculiar vital powers, and that doctors should explain function solely on the observation of life. Lawrence's views were not original: his call for an empirical approach to physiology was in line with European developments, and others shared his rejection of appeals to mind, soul, or ephemeral vital powers. However, many saw his ideas as heretical not least because of his controversial support for French institutions in the aftermath of the Napoleonic wars. Abernethy criticized Lawrence's reductionist views in his 1817 lectures at the College. In 1819 Lawrence published *Lectures on Physiology, Zoology and the Natural History of Man* in response. He reiterated his basic philosophy and scandalized those who regarded life as a separate entity from the material organism. However, to protect his position at St Bartholomew's, Lawrence was forced to withdraw his book when it was deemed blasphemous. He remained unpopular at the RCS given his support for medical reform, but by the 1830s he had begun to retreat from his earlier stance, following his inclusion in the College's ruling elite. In 1846 in his Hunterian Ovation, he defended the actions of the College to a hostile audience, raising a storm of dissent.

Lawrence was an authoritative figure in the early development of ophthalmology, publishing *A Treatise on the Venereal Diseases of the Eye* (1830) and *Treatise on the Diseases of the Eye* (1833). These showed the new specialism as thoroughly modern and placed the treatment of ophthalmic disorders on a sound footing. In his treatise Lawrence called upon Enlightenment claims of the epistemological importance of sight, arguing that ophthalmology had to be seen as part of a general practitioner's duties. In asserting the importance of ophthalmology, he attempted to gain the high ground for a branch of medicine traditionally associated with quackery. With most of his work confined to the Royal Ophthalmic Hospital, Moorfields, London, Lawrence defended the need for eye hospitals at a time when specialist hospitals were widely attacked.

He was clear that medicine could only be advanced by men 'of extensive anatomical knowledge, and of great insight into disease' (Lawrence, 1833, p. 6). He adopted this approach in his teaching at St Bartholomew's. Lawrence stressed the value of demonstration and practice, given his faith in Marie François Xavier Bichat's (1771–1802) attack on onotology. For Lawrence, hospitals were the arena in which surgery was learned and teaching in the wards was praised. He stubbornly remained attached to St Bartholomew's and continued to give the same lectures, which, when published (1863), were described as uneven and outdated. When Lawrence finally resigned after his first stroke, *Lancet* noted that it was 'a direct benefit conferred upon the profession' (*Lancet*, 1867, i, p. 635).

Bibliography

Primary: 1816. *An Introduction to Comparative Anatomy and Physiology* (London); 1819. *Lectures on Physiology, Zoology, and the Natural History of Man* (London); 1830. *A Treatise on the Venereal Diseases of the Eye* (London); 1833. *Treatise on the Diseases of the Eye* (London).

Secondary: Lawrence, Susan C., 1996. *Charitable Knowledge: Hospital Pupils and Practitioners in Eighteenth-Century London* (Cambridge); Desmond, Adrian, 1989. *The Politics of Evolution: Morphology, Medicine and Reform in Radical London* (Chicago); *DSB*; *Oxford DNB*.

Keir Waddington

LAYCOCK, THOMAS   (b. Weatherby, Yorkshire, England, 12 August 1812; d. Edinburgh, Scotland, 21 September 1876), *neurology.*

Laycock was the son of Thomas Laycock, a Wesleyan Methodist minister, and his wife, the daughter of a landed gentleman in the district. He attended the Methodist Woodhouse Grove School. His religious upbringing and education remained important to him throughout his life. His medical education followed the usual pattern for a general practitioner in northern Britain. At the age of fifteen, Laycock was apprenticed to surgeons in Bedale, William and John Spence, with the financial assistance of the Wesleyan community. Toward the end of his indenture, he worked in the Bedale dispensary.

Laycock's father died in 1833, and he received financial assistance from his maternal uncle, an alderman in York, to study medicine at the newly established London University. He spent three years there, studying anatomy with Jones Quain (1796–1865) and Richard Quain (1800–87), materia medica with Anthony Todd Thomson (1778–1849), chemistry with Edward Turner (1798–1837), surgery with Samuel Cooper (1780–1848), practice of medicine with John Elliotson (1791–1869), comparative anatomy with Robert E. Grant (1793–1874), and botany with John Lindley (1799–1865). He also became a pupil at the Middlesex hospital. In the summer of 1834, he spent twelve weeks in Paris, studying with Pierre Charles Alexandre Louis (1787–1872), Alfred-Armand Velpeau (1795–1867), and Pierre Joseph Manec (1799–1884). In 1835 he passed the examination to become MRCS, and after an additional fourteen months at the Westminster General Dispensary, he became an LSA. These two degrees, the MRCS and LSA, were generally accepted as the standard qualifications for a provincial medical practitioner.

Laycock returned to northern Britain, where his family connections helped him receive an appointment as house apothecary to the York County Hospital. This was an excellent start for a young practitioner, but Laycock felt 'degraded' by the political maneuvering—'flattering, lying, and electioneering in every possible way'—necessary to obtain the position (Barfoot, 1995, p. 12). Though he could not avoid 'electioneering' in future, he began to search for other, less demeaning ways of distinguishing himself. In 1839 he left the York County Hospital in order to obtain a degree from Göttingen University, an unusual choice suggesting that he had already developed an interest in the philosophy of the mind. In 1840 he published *An Essay on Hysteria*, which, he stated, most frequently appeared as 'direct derangement of the functions of the nervous system' (Laycock, *Essay*, 1840, p. 3). He had observed two cases at the York County Hospital, and his essay drew together a number of similar cases in the medical literature, allowing him to provide a detailed analysis of the presenting symptoms. In his analysis, Laycock relied on three guiding principles. The first was that hysterical symptoms were produced by a physical disorder of the nervous system, though Laycock noted the existence of what he called 'Imitative Hysteria', in which symptoms such as pains and vomiting could rapidly spread around a hospital ward among patients with completely dissimilar physical ailments. The second principle was that hysteria was a disease of women, who were affected by it because their nervous system was more susceptible to stimuli of all kinds. The few males whose cases Laycock diagnosed as hysteria were either 'a small delicate youth' or 'fat, pale-faces, effeminate looking men' (Laycock, *Essay*, 1840, p. 102). The third principle was that women were especially susceptible to hysteria in youth and early adulthood, 'at a time when the sexual organs are performing their peculiar functions' (Laycock, *Essay*, 1840, p. 99). Laycock's *Essay* influenced nineteenth-century research on hysteria and neurasthenia; it also, unfortunately, fueled medical and lay assertions concerning the weakness of the female nervous system and the extent to which women's reproductive organs defined their identity.

In 1842 Laycock was appointed visiting physician to the York Dispensary. From 1846 to 1855, he lectured on the theory and practice of medicine at the York Medical School. All his life, he alternated between regarding other medical men as members of an informed elite, which he wished to join, and regarding them as rivals, with whom he openly competed. As a result, he was frequently embroiled in vituperative medical controversy. He joined the York Medical Society (1839) on his return from Göttingen, but in 1840 a quarrel with Thomas Simpson, as well as other influential and well-regarded practitioners in York, forced Laycock to resign.

In 1855 the position of professor of the practice of medicine became vacant at Edinburgh University. Among the top candidates was John Hughes Bennett (1812–75), already well established in Edinburgh, but James Young Simpson (1811–70), one of the most influential men in the University, invited Laycock to apply and personally introduced him to the Town Council members who had the decisive vote in the decision. Somewhat to his own surprise, Laycock received the appointment. In 1856 he became FRCPEdin.

As professor of the practice of medicine, Laycock also gave lectures on clinical medicine and published *Lectures on the Principles and Methods of Medical Observation and Research* (1856). This was not intended as a handbook of clinical medicine, but instead was intended to inculcate habits of observation and reasoning in students. Influenced by Francis Bacon's *Nouvum Organum: or indications respecting the interpretation of nature* (1620), Laycock began by pointing out fallacies that impeded medical reasoning, such as fallacies of therapeutic theories and anatomical etiology. He then moved on to general methods of bedside observation. Though he acknowledged that instruments, such as microscopes and stethoscopes, could be useful, he emphasized that no new equipment could make up for deficiencies in the practitioner. Similar warnings to students and young physicians of the value of thoughtful observation over gadgetry have been echoed in clinical teaching up to the present day.

Laycock began a series of extramural lectures on medical psychology (1857), and in 1860 he published his most substantive publication, *Mind and Brain*. He drew from philosophy, physiology, and Christian teaching to provide a systematic overview of the operations of thought, volition, sensation, and instinct. The book gives a clear depiction of the physiologically grounded psychology of the mid-nineteenth century, relying on many of the same materials later read by Sigmund Freud (1856–1939), though to a very different purpose.

Laycock was appointed physician in ordinary to the Queen in Scotland in 1869, and in the same year he was president of the Medico-Psychological Association. He died in his home in Edinburgh, of pulmonary consumption.

Thomas Laycock. Half-tone reproduction from John D. Comrie, *History of Scottish Medicine to 1860*, London, 1927. Wellcome Library, London.

Bibliography

Primary: 1840. *An Essay on Hysteria* (Philadelphia); 1856. *Lectures on the Principles and Methods of Medical Observation and Research* (Edinburgh); 1860. *Mind and Brain: or, the Correlations of Consciousness and Organisation* (Edinburgh).

Secondary: James, F. E., 1998. 'Thomas Laycock: Psychiatry and Neurology.' *History of Psychiatry* 9: 491–502; Barfoot, Michael, ed., 1995. *To Ask the Suffrages of the Patrons: Thomas Laycock and the Edinburgh Chair of Medicine 1855* (London); Leff, Alex, 1991. 'Thomas Laycock and the Cerebral Reflex: A Function Arising and Pointing to the Unity of Nature.' *History of Psychiatry* 2: 385–407; *Oxford DNB*.

Lisa Rosner

LAZAREVIĆ, LAZA K. (b. Šabac, Serbia, 13 May 1851; d. Belgrade, Serbia, 10 January 1891), *medicine, public health, neurology*.

Lazarević was born to a merchant family in Šabac. Although his father (Kuzman) died when he was a child of nine, his mother (Jelka) succeeded in sending him to study law in Belgrade. In 1872 Lazarević was awarded a state scholarship in Berlin, where he studied medicine under Virchow, Helmholtz, and Du Bois-Reymond. In 1876 Lazarević interrupted his studies to volunteer as a medical assistant in the war against the Turks. The following year he published his first article, concerning wartime disinfection of makeshift hospitals that had been converted from schools. Lazarević was awarded his doctorate in 1879; the review of his dissertation was published in *Repetitorium der Analytischen Chemie* (III Jahrgang, 8), and the thesis itself is highly regarded.

Upon returning to Belgrade, Lazarević became involved in the struggle against the typhoid epidemic, serving as a municipal physician. At this time he also took a strong public stand against the advertising of false medicines, publishing a strong criticism on the front page of the main daily newspaper, *Srpske Novine*, in 1879. From 1881 Lazarević focused on reforming work at the General State Hospital by introducing clinical methods, laboratory examinations, and physical medicine.

Lazarević's most important work, on the cause of sciatica (1880), appeared in *Srpski Arhiv za Celokupno Lekarstvo* and was reprinted in *Allgemeine Wiener Medicinische Zeitung* four years later. It explains how sciatica pain derives from a strain to the ischiadicus nerve and its roots, rather than from muscle compression as previously understood. Lazarević believed that the pathognomonic sign had not been described. Known today as Lasègue's sign, Serbian scholars often refer to it as Lazarević's sign. Ernest Charles Lasègue recognized this sign in 1864; his student, Forst, published these findings in 1881, a year after Lazarević's paper (see Lazarević's contribution in works of Dimitrije Davidović and R. Wartenberg). In his neurological research, Lazarević focused on paralysis agitans, sclerosis medullae spinalis, neuralgia n. supraorbitalis, and aphasia. Regarded as the first Serbian neurologist, Lazarević was also a pioneer in the field of geriatrics, establishing a special ward for older patients at the General State Hospital in 1881. He died from tuberculosis at age forty. As the first Serbian writer to apply a psychological approach to his stories, Lazarević is highly regarded in the history of Serbian literature.

Bibliography

Primary: 1880. 'Ischias postica Cotunnii—Jedan prilog za njenu diferencijalnu dijagnozu' [Ichias postica Cotunnii—a Contribution for Its Differential Diagnosis] *Srp. Arh. Celok. Lek, odeljak prvi* 7: 23–35.

Secondary: Kanjuh, Vladimir, and Budimir Pavlović, 1998. *Život i delo srpskih naučnika* [The Life and Work of Serbian Scientists] vol. 4 (Belgrade); 1972. *Spomenica Srpskog Lekarskog Društva* (Beograd); 1962. *Medicinska enciklopedija*, 6 Komb-Min (Zagreb); Wartenberg, R., 1953. *Diagnostic Tests in Neurology* (Chicago); Dimitrijević, D. T, 1952. 'Lasegue Sign' *Neurology* 25(5): 453–454; Wartenberg, R., 1951. 'Lasegue Sign and Kernig Sign; Historical Notes' *Arch. Neurol. and Psychiat.* 66(1): 58–60.

Jelena Jovanovic Simic and
Predrag J. Markovic

LE CLERC, DANIEL (b. Republic of Geneva [now Switzerland], 4 February 1652; d. Republic of Geneva, 8 June 1728), *medicine, history of medicine.*

Le Clerc's father, Etienne Le Clerc (1599–1676) was a physician and a humanist who taught both Greek and ethics at Geneva's Academy. Little is known about Daniel's early years. Administrative records inform us that he finished his secondary studies at Geneva's College (Collège) in 1667. He then set out to study medicine in different European universities, stopping at Montpellier and Paris before qualifying as doctor in medicine in Valence, France, in February 1670, less than three years after having started out on his studies.

After his return to Geneva, Le Clerc married Charlotte Vernet-Chenaud and started to practice medicine, an enterprise in which he was rapidly successful. His first biographers insisted that he only used the simplest and most assured remedies and that his prime quality was the excellence of his diagnosis. As his reputation grew, patients came from afar to seek for his advice. The king of Sicily and the future king of Sardaigna (Sardinia), Victor-Amédée II, came himself to Geneva in 1715 in order seek the famous physician's advice.

As with many physicians of his day, besides his medical practice, Le Clerc was also a prolific medical writer. His *Bibliotheca anatomica*, written with his fellow physician Jean-Jaques Manget (1685), is an important compilation of the anatomical knowledge of the time. A second book, a *Historia naturalis et medica latorum lumbricorum* (1715), was considered by Albrecht von Haller to be the most important contribution on the subject.

Today Le Clerc is remembered for his *Histoire de la medicine* (1696), which is justly considered a landmark in the development of the field of medical history. At the time this book was written, there was little difference between medical knowledge and medical history. Le Clerc was conscious of the importance of the medical tradition in medical practice, but considered as he put it in his foreword that each generation of medical writers take only what is agreeable to them in older medical texts: 'Tis not so with this History, which is obliged to penetrate into the very soul of the age, and ev'ry Author; to relate faithfully and impartially the thoughts of all, and to maintain every one in his right, not giving to the Moderns what belongs to the Antients, nor bestowing upon these latter what is due to the former; leaving every body at liberty to make reflections for himself upon the matters of Fact as they stand related.'

Le Clerc was also an active citizen of Geneva, serving as a member of the Republic's parliament (from 1680) and then of the more restricted Council of LX (1704). He was a founding member of Geneva's first Medical Society (1713) and director of the library of Geneva's Academy (1610).

Bibliography

Primary: 1685. (with Manget, Jean-Jacques) *Bibliotheca anatomica, sive recens in anatomia inventorum thesaurus locupletissimus: in quo integra atque absolutissima totius corporis humani description*

(Geneva); 1699. (Dr Drake and Dr Baden, trans.) *The History of Physick or an Account of the Rise and Progress of the Art* (London).

Secondary: Barras, Vincent, 1991. 'L'histoire de la médecine à Genève.' *Cahiers de la Fondation Louis Jeantet* 6; Röthlisberger, P. von, 1964. 'Daniel Le Clerc (1652–1728) und seine *Histoire de la médecine' Gesnerus* 21: 126–141; Gautier, Léon, 1906. *La médecine à Genève jusqu'à la fin du 18e siècle, Mémoires et documents publiés par la société d'histoire et d'archéologie* (Geneva) pp. 251–253.

Philip Rieder

LEISHMAN, WILLIAM BOOG

(b. Glasgow, Scotland, 6 November 1865; d. London, England, 2 June 1926), *parasitology, tropical medicine.*

Leishman, the son of William Leishman, regius professor of midwifery at the University of Glasgow, and Augusta Selina, attended Westminster School and the University of Glasgow, graduating MB CM (1886). He joined the army and graduated fifth in his class at the Army Medical School at Netley (1887). He spent most of his early career in India. Leishman returned to Britain in 1899 to work at the Victoria Hospital, Netley. He also assisted Almroth Wright (1861–1947), professor of pathology, at the Army Medical School. The experience was crucial to Leishman's research career. It stimulated his interest in bacteriology and helped his appointment as assistant professor of pathology at the School (1900).

Leishman's first major contribution to tropical medicine was his improvement of the Romanowsky stain (1901). The simplified method greatly facilitated research on malaria. In 1902 he successfully devised a technique for measuring the phagocytic power of leucocytes. Leishman's crowning achievement was his discovery of the protozoan that caused kala-azar, also called Dum Dum fever, after the name of the army barracks in India where the disease was prevalent. In 1900 Leishman conducted a postmortem examination on an Irish soldier from Dum Dum who suffered from kala-azar and died at Netley. He examined the smear taken from the enlarged spleen under his microscope and saw numerous oval or round parasites, which he considered a species of *Trypanosome*. Leishman did not publish this finding until 1903, when Charles Donovan (1863–1951) of the Indian Medical Service observed the same parasites independently. Leishman later noticed that the parasite that caused kala-azar was very similar to the parasite found in the lesion of the so-called Delhi Sore, a tropical ulcer. It is now understood that different species of genus *Leishmania*, transmitted from animals to humans by the sandfly, can cause different forms of leishmaniasis (a term coined by Ronald Ross, 1857–1932), such as cutaneous, mucocutaneous, and visceral leishmaniasis.

Leishman married Maud Elizabeth, daughter of Lieutenant-Colonel Edward Gunter, in 1902. He was promoted to professor of pathology when the Army Medical School moved to Millbank, London (1903). There he worked on relapsing fever and an antityphoid vaccine. The vaccine was put to great use during World War I. Leishman was knighted (1909) and made honorary physician to the King (1912), KCMG (1918), and KCB (1924). He was elected to FRS (1910) and FRCP (1914). Leishman left the Army Medical School in 1914 to take up the post of expert in tropical diseases for the Army Medical Advisory Board. He became an original member of the Medical Research Committee, the precursor of the Medical Research Council. In 1914 Leishman was posted with British troops to France and Belgium to organize pathological research. He also presided over the committee investigating trench fever. Leishman was made the first director of pathology by the War Office (1919). After the war, he resumed his research on *Spirochaeta duttoni*, the parasite causing relapsing fever and transmitted by the African tick *Ornithoodoros moubata*. Leishman elucidated the life cycle of the spirochaeta, publishing the results in 1920. He was promoted to the rank of lieutenant-general and received the post of medical director-general of the Army Medical Service (1923).

Bibliography

Primary: 1901. 'Note on a simple and rapid method of producing Romanowsky staining in malarial and other blood films.' *British Medical Journal* ii: 757–758; 1902. 'Note on a method of quantatively estimating the phagocytic power of the leucocytes of the blood.' *British Medical Journal* i: 73–75; 1903. 'On the possibility of the occurrence of trypanosomiasis in India.' *British Medical Journal* ii: 1252–1254; 1920. 'Horace Dobell Lecture on an experimental investigation of *Spirochaeta duttoni*, the parasite of tick fever.' *Lancet* ii: 1237–1244.

Secondary: Anon., 1929. 'Obituary.' *Journal of Pathology and Bacteriology* 29: 515–528; Oxford DNB.

Shang-Jen Li

LEMNIUS, LEVINUS

(b. Zierikzee, the Netherlands, *c.* 1505; d. Zierikzee, 1 July 1568), *medicine, astrology, botany.*

Lemnius was born as Lieven Lemse in the province of Zeeland. He received a classical education at one of the Latin schools in nearby Ghent. On 23 December 1521, he matriculated at the University of Louvain (which then was the only academic institution of the Low Countries). He is believed to have studied at the famous Collegium Trilingue of the Faculty of Theology and later on at the faculty of medicine. In the older literature on Lemnius, Vesalius and Dodonaeus are mentioned as his teachers, but this is highly improbable. After completing his studies, Lemnius obtained his MD, presumably in Italy, around 1526. Here, he certainly did meet Vesalius. Around the same time, he reportedly visited the naturalist Conrad Gessner in Zurich. On return of his *iter italicum*, Lemnius settled as a physician in his native town Zierikzee in 1526 or 1527. Contemporary sources describe him as an affable practitioner who cheered up his patients with jokes. The learned Lemnius was a pious man who, while Protestantism was rapidly spreading in the Low Countries, remained faithful to the church of Rome. When his wife died (at an unknown date), he was appointed canon of the St Lievens cathedral, which is where he was later buried in July 1568, shortly after the outbreak of the revolt in the Netherlands.

Lemnius's fame mainly rests on his work on the occult miracles of nature. Lemnius was a typical representative of sixteenth-century humanist medicine and was highly fascinated by the hidden virtues of things. In 1554 he published *De astrologia liber unus,* in which he was somewhat critical of contemporary medical astrology. Five years later, Lemnius published the first edition of his *Occulta naturae miracula.* This book, which he later reworked and expanded, was to become a classic in the genre of the 'books of secrets'. It consists of a collection of physiological, physical, medical, religious, and moral topics, attempting to explain the wonders of nature. Based on a thorough reading of Pliny's *Natural History* and all other relevant classical sources, Lemnius discusses such topics as *aqua vitae* or brandywine, basilisks, the effect of human saliva, numerology, the hidden powers of minerals, whether it is better to sleep with the mouth closed or open, the meaning of comets, the influence of the weather on human affairs, the virtues of magnets and asbestos, and so on.

Like the writings of many of his contemporaries and kindred spirits, such as Pierre Boaisteau, Antoine Mizault, and Girolamo Cardano, Lemnius's writings are based more on written sources and speculation than on observation and experiment. The explicit aim of Lemnius was a religious one: he wanted to evoke admiration for the wonders of nature, while at the same preserving the presence of God in creation against the rising tendencies to naturalize miracles. Like St Augustine before him, Lemnius pointed out that everything in nature is a miracle of God: 'For in the smallest works of nature the Deity shines forth, and all things are good and beautiful'. Although later scholars have called Lemnius's work 'a disorderly miscellany of little value', the book was an enormous success. During Lemnius's lifetime, it was reprinted in a revised version in 1561, 1564, and 1567. In the following century, numerous reprints, editions, and translations appeared. The book was frequently quoted by later authors on the wonders of nature, such as Robert Burton and Thomas Browne.

Bibliography

Primary: 1554. *De astrologia liber unus, in quo obiter indicat, quid illa veri, quid ficti falsique habeat et quatenus Arti sit habenda fides* (Antwerp; many reprints); 1559. *Occulta naturae miracula, ac varia rerum documenta, probabili ratione atque artifici conjectura duobus libris explicata* (Antwerp; many reprints and editions); 1561. *De habitu et constitutione corporis, quam Graeci krasin, triviales complexionem vocant* (Antwerp); 1566. *Herbarum atque arborum quae in Bibliis passim obviae sunt* (Antwerp).

Secondary: Eamon, W., 1994. *Science and the Secrets of Nature. Books of Secrets in Medieval and Early Modern Culture* (Princeton); Hoorn, C. M. van, 1978. *Levinus Lemnius 1505–1568. Zestiende-eeuws Zeeuws geneesheer* (Amsterdam); Thorndike, L., 1923–1958. *A History of Magic and the Experimental Sciences* (New York) vols. 5 and 6.

Eric Jorink

LERICHE, RENÉ   (b. Roanne, France, 12 October 1879; d. Cassis, France, 28 December 1955), *surgery.*

The son of a long line of physicians from Lyon, Leriche studied medicine in this big city of southeastern France, specialized in surgery, and received his degree in 1906, with a thesis on the resection of the stomach as treatment for cancer. In 1913 he visited the United States as guest of his fellow Lyonnais surgeon Alexis Carrel at the Rockefeller Institute, and he met other American surgeons, including William Halsted at Johns Hopkins. Despite witnessing their virtuosity in dramatic surgical procedures, Leriche continued to practice 'moderate surgery'.

After war broke out, Leriche first operated on the front and then directed two military surgical services in Paris. In 1917 the French government created a hospital near Reims for training army surgical teams in the most recent developments in the treatment of war injuries and reconstructive surgery. Leriche perfected techniques of elbow resection and trepanation. After the war Leriche was named surgeon in the Lyon hospitals, where he studied occlusion of the aortic bifurcation (Leriche syndrome), sympathectomy to treat arteritis, and hypotension of spinal fluid, the importance of which was finally recognized in 1942.

In 1924 Leriche was named to the clinical chair in surgery at the University of Strasburg, where he introduced the idea of nontraumatic surgery into the curriculum and his surgical service. He opposed the anatomical school then dominant in French clinical medicine, demonstrating the importance of vasomotor reactions in pathology; in these situations functionality was more important than anatomy. During his work at Strasburg, Leriche did research on sympatic surgery, gastric and neurovascular physiology, and the origins of ulcers and chondroma, which led to the treatment of angina by excision of the stellate ganglions (stellectomy). Leriche advocated conservation of blood, and a deft touch, refusing to do a dramatic operation if it was radical and likely to produce a risky postoperative condition. Growing out of this was his concern with the problem of pain, a subject to which he devoted a considerable amount of attention.

In 1936 Leriche succeeded Charles Nicolle (a Pasteurian and Nobel laureate in 1928 for his work on typhus) as Chair of Experimental Medicine at the Collège de France. The Chair at the Collège, however, had no hospital affiliation, and because Leriche was a surgeon at the Hospitals of Lyon, he could have no affiliation with the Mecca of French clinical medicine, the 'Assistance publique de Paris'. After the armistice in 1940, Marshal Pétain apparently offered Leriche the post of Minister of Health, which the surgeon declined, but Leriche accepted the offer to be President of the Ordre National des Médecins, established by the Vichy regime in 1941. This organization asserted the control of the state over the profession of medicine by insisting on its right to establish restrictions, including exclusion of Jews and foreigners from the medical profession. After the Liberation, this ostracism practiced by the Ordre des Médecins during the

Occupation resulted in a reprimand of Leriche by the medical establishment, and in 1945 he accepted an appointment as chef de service at the American Hospital in Paris. After his retirement in 1954, Leriche was editor of a compendium and volumes on medicine such as *l'Encyclopédie française* (from 1940), where he suggested that medicine had entered a post-Pasteurian phase. 'The specificity of causes and effects in pathology has ceased to be fundamental,' he said. 'As a result, therapy must be devoted to detecting and healing neuro-humoral imbalances that determine disease conditions based on chemical components.'

Bibliography

Primary: 1937. *La chirurgie de la douleur* (Paris); 1955. *Souvenirs de ma vie morte* (Paris).

Secondary: Rey, Roselyne, 1993. *Histoire de la douleur* (Paris); Clarke, Robert, 1962. *René Leriche. Savants du monde entier* (Paris).

Jean-François Picard

LETTSOM, JOHN COAKLEY (b. Little Vandyke, West Indies, 22 November 1744; d. London, England, 1 November 1815), *medicine, philanthropy.*

Lettsom was the son of Edward Lettsom, a Quaker plantation owner, and Mary née Coakley. He was the sole survivor of seven successive pairs of twins, and his parents advisedly sent him to England at the age of six, to the Rawlinsons, a Quaker family of Lancaster who had business interests in the West Indies. He at once came to the attention of Samuel Fothergill (1715–72), a famous Quaker preacher who lived in Warrington. Samuel arranged for Lettsom's education at the Friends School at Penketh. On Lettsom's father's death, Samuel became his guardian and in 1761 arranged for him to be apprenticed to Abraham Sutcliffe, a Quaker apothecary of Settle in the Yorkshire Dales, who was a friend of the Fothergill family. Under Sutcliffe's supervision Lettsom learned the rudiments of the medical art; he studied botany and made collections of dried plants from the neighborhood, also learning Latin and French. After five years, he went to London with a warm recommendation by Samuel Fothergill to his brother John Fothergill (1712–80), a famous Edinburgh graduate who had by now achieved great success and was one of the most distinguished physicians in the capital. So began a friendship that lasted until Fothergill's death in 1780. As Lettsom later put it, 'As a medical man, my character was solely reflected from the patronage of Dr Fothergill … I can scarcely recollect a week without some instance of his affection and friendship.'

Early Years and Education

Lettsom took a one-year course at St Thomas Hospital, where Fothergill had also trained, studying as a dresser with the surgeon Benjamin Cowell. He was unimpressed by the haughty manners of the physician Mark Akenside. In 1767

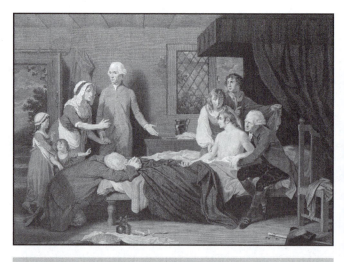

A man recovers from near drowning after resuscitation by John Coakley Lettsom (standing) and William Hawes, Royal Humane Society, 1787. Engraving by Robert Pollard after Robert Smirke, Iconographic Collection, Wellcome Library, London.

he returned to Tortola to take possession of what remained of his family property. Most of what he owned was Negro slaves, whom he at once set free, probably influenced by Fothergill, a strong opponent of slavery. 'I could no longer withhold from them', he wrote, 'the natural privilege of freedom, which Heaven had conferred on me'.

In Tortola he undertook medical practice, attracting crowds of patients. In the space of five months, he acquired nearly £2,000. One half of this he gave to his mother, and then he set off for England. Here, welcomed again into the Fothergill household in 1768, he was advised to attend courses in Edinburgh under William Cullen (1710–90). He visited Paris and Leiden, where he graduated MD (1769), with a thesis on the medical qualities of tea. Soon back in London, his patron wrote perceptively to William Logan in Philadelphia that his young protégé was likely to make a considerable figure in the metropolis. He soon became licentiate of the College of Physicians and in 1773, at the early age of twenty-nine, was elected FRS.

Practice In London

In 1769 Lettsom set up practice from a house in Basinghall Street in the City. He was at once successful. After Fothergill's death in 1780 and the demise of another Quaker physician, Thomas Knowles, in 1786, he became one of the most sought-after physicians in the capital. He was indefatigable. By 1791, he observed, 'During the last nineteen years not one holiday have I taken.' In 1800 his earnings had reached as much as £12,000 annually. He married Anne Miers on 31 July 1770. They had a large family. One son, Samuel Fothergill Lettsom, and two daughters survived him. Several of his children died before he did, including his eldest son, John Miers Lettsom, a young physician of great promise in whose education Lettsom had been particularly involved.

Although a Quaker throughout his life, he was never the strict member of the Society of Friends that the Fothergills were. He was highly sociable, entertaining a wide circle of friends at his home, Grove Hill, Camberwell. He was received by the king, George III, and maintained a correspondence with physicians such as Benjamin Rush (1745–1813) and Albrecht von Haller (1708–77), as well as with his patron's close friend, Benjamin Franklin (1706–90). Despite the pacifism of the Quakers, Lettsom became, in September 1803, physician to the Camberwell Volunteer Force. There were those who, envious of his remarkable lifestyle, considered him a social climber, with the *Westminster Magazine* in 1782 portraying him as Dr Wriggle in a piece entitled 'Dr Wriggle, or, The art of rising in physic'. A considerable number of verses were penned to describe Lettsom and his foibles during his lifetime. One of the best known, written by his friend and patient Lord Erskine, ran as follows: 'Whenever patients comes to I, / I physics, bleeds and sweats 'em; / If, after that, they choose to die, / What's that to me? I Letts 'em.'

The Dispensary Movement and the Medical Society of London

Unquestionably, Lettsom's most important contribution to the medicine of his day was the foundation of the dispensary movement. The eighteenth century had witnessed a great extension of hospitals both in London and throughout the land. But the hospitals did not provide care for the poor or for those afflicted with infection. In 1770 Lettsom, at the early age of twenty-six, joined with others in founding the General Dispensary in Aldersgate Street, the first of its kind. Here a physician, surgeon, and an apothecary attended to give free treatment to the poor, and they also undertook visits to the poor in their own homes. Lettsom himself was appointed physician to the Aldersgate Dispensay in 1773, and it was not without risk. Lettsom's own son, John Miers Lettsom, died of a fever contracted during a domiciliary visit. The venture attracted the support of the great and the good and spread throughout the capital and more widely to other cities. The first president of the Aldersgate Dispensary was the Earl of Dartmouth, friend and patient of John Fothergill.

It soon became clear that the men who staffed the newly founded dispensaries in London had no place to meet, given that many were nonconformists debarred from the Fellowship of the College of Physicians. It was for this reason that Lettsom founded the Medical Society of London, where physician, surgeon, and apothecary could meet for their mutual benefit and to discuss the medical matters of the day. It was the first society in Britain to bring the professions together in this way. Contemporary hierarchies recognized physicians as the elite of the medical world and saw surgeons as mere technicians, and the apothecaries trailed far behind. As a Quaker,

Lettsom was a leveler and would have recognized no such distinctions. He gave a freehold house in Bolt Court, Fleet Street to the new society and an extensive library, as well as funds to found a gold medal (called the Fothergillian Gold Medal after his patron), to be awarded annually for a medical essay. William Falconer of Bath first won the medal; other winners included Robert Willan (1757–1812), founder of modern dermatology, and Edward Jenner (1749–1823). The society went through various vicissitudes, but it continues to this day. In 1805 it was a splinter group of the Society that founded the Medico-Chirurgical Society, which later became the Royal Society of Medicine. The founder of the Medical Society of London is remembered by the Lettsomian Lectures, which are given at the society.

There were other important causes that owed much to Lettsom's support. He assisted William Hawes (1736–1808) and others in founding the Royal Humane Society (1774), designed to resuscitate the drowned, and he was the major supporter of the Royal Sea-bathing Infirmary in Margate when it was founded in 1791. It was specifically designed to provide convalescence for tuberculous patients. Both these institutions have lasted into the twenty-first century.

Hints to Promote Beneficence

Throughout his life, Lettsom was a prolific writer, constantly extolling the benefits of useful knowledge and giving medical advice and moral exhortation. Pamphlets poured from his pen. In 1772 he argued that tea drinking made people enervated and effeminate. He was a constant supporter of improving projects—soup kitchens, education, and the management of boarding schools. He produced books and papers against drunkenness and its attendant ills. He also wrote on beehives in his *Hints for Promoting a Bee Society* (1796). He considered that 50,000 beehives might be maintained within twenty miles of London.

By 1802, now approaching his sixties, he saw fit to bring together his collected essays in three volumes of *Hints Designed to Promote Beneficence, Temperance and Medical Science*. The subjects covered included poverty, discharged prisoners, prostitution, infectious fevers, crime and punishment, wills and testaments, deaf mutes, blind people, Sunday Schools, hydrophobia, and the use of Indian corn for making substitute bread, as well as hints to masters and mistresses. At the same time, he was writing letters of exhortation to all and sundry. Most remarkably, much of his writing was done while driving about to see his patients in his carriage.

Lettsom had other scientific pursuits. He followed Fothergill in his interest in botany, and after Fothergill's death, many of the plants from his famous garden at Upton in Essex found their way to Lettsom's greenhouses at Grove Hill. He was also interested in minerals and sent more than seven hundred specimens of metallic ores, crystals, and the like to professor Waterhouse at Harvard, which are preserved to this day. He was also deeply concerned with scientific agriculture and strongly supported the introduction of the mangel-wurzel. He grew the seed himself and distributed it widely to farmers in Britain as well as in Europe, America, and the West Indies.

Controversy

Lettsom was no stranger to controversy. He was a supporter of inoculation against smallpox from his earliest days and wrote a pamphlet on the desirability of introducing general inoculation. Baron Dimsdale, famed for having inoculated the Empress Catherine of Russia, objected, claiming that the practice would simply spread smallpox. When vaccination was introduced in 1798, however, Lettsom became a fervent supporter of Jenner.

He also had no hesitation in attacking those he considered to be quacks. He waged a newspaper war against the German quack uroscopist, Theodor Myersbach, whose claim to diagnose disease simply by examining the urine was clearly spurious. He was less successful in seeking to expose William Brodum, whose 'nervous cordial' was in Lettsom's opinion responsible for the death of thousands. On this occasion, Brodum sued, and the case had to be settled out of court, with Lettsom paying costs. It was a case that illustrated that the exposure of a quack could not be achieved by mere denunciation. As Lettsom's friend John Haygarth (1740–1827) showed in Bath in 1800, in exposing the claims of Perkins' metallic tractors, science was much more effective.

Last Years

Lettsom was philanthropic, charitable, and benevolent. He once commented, 'Who will thank us for dying rich?' But in his last years, his financial affairs were greatly troubled. Largely as the result of undertaking financial responsibilities for a relative, straitened circumstances made him part with Grove Hill, together with his museum, library, and botanic garden. Shortly before his death, he inherited a West Indian fortune bequeathed to him by the widow of his son Pickering Lettsom. He did not live to enjoy his good fortune, dying at his house, Sambrook Courth, Basinghall Street. He was buried in the Quaker burial ground, Coleman Street, Bunhill Row, where George Fox, founder of the Society of Friends, also lies.

Bibliography

Primary: 1772. *The Natural History of the Tea Tree with Observations on its Medical Qualities, and the Effects of Tea Drinking* (London); 1773. *Hints on the Establishment of a Medical Society of London* (London); 1774. *Medical Memoirs of the General Dispensary* (London); 1802. *Hints to Promote Beneficence, Temperance and Medical Science* (London).

Secondary: Lawrence, Christopher, and Fiona Macdonald, 2003. *Sambrook Court. The Letters of J. C. Lettsom at the Medical Society of London* (London); Abraham, James Johnston, 1933. *Lettsom. His Life, Times, Friends and Descendants* (London); Pettigrew, T. J., 1817. *Memoirs of the Life and Writings of the Late John Coakley Lettsom* 3 vols. (London); *Oxford DNB*.

Christopher Booth

LEWIS, THOMAS (b. Cardiff, Wales, 26 December 1881; d. Rickmansworth, England, 17 March 1945), *medicine, cardiology, clinical science.*

Lewis was born to Henry Lewis, a colliery owner and mining engineer who played a leading role in the South Wales coal trade, and Katherine Hannah Davies. He was educated mainly at home until the age of sixteen, although he spent more time playing in the woods than attending to his studies. Lewis was fascinated by magic tricks. Because he knew two family doctors who conjured, Lewis saw medicine as a means to become an expert conjurer. Although he initially failed the London matriculation examination, he reapplied himself to his studies and is reported to have failed no further examinations. Lewis performed three years of preclinical work at University College, Cardiff, where he impressed his professors enough that he was asked to coauthor medical papers with them. His clinical training started at University College Hospital, London in 1902, which, other than during wartime service, was to remain his medical base for the rest of his life. He qualified for the university gold medal in 1905 and then worked with two distinguished mentors, as house surgeon to Sir Victor Horsley (1857–1916) and house physician to Sir Thomas Barlow. In 1908 Lewis met Sir James Mackenzie (1853–1925), a renowned physician who had made a name for himself in the study of the pulse. Mackenzie had a strong influence on Lewis's career. The two remained both professional colleagues and close personal friends until Mackenzie's death. In 1910 Lewis received the first Beit Memorial Fellowship. In 1911 he was appointed lecturer in cardiac pathology, and that same year, he was named to head the new cardiographic department at UCH. In 1914 he was medical consultant to the London Zoo, a position that provided him with specimens with which to study comparative anatomy of the heart. He continued in private practice until 1916, when he was named to the staff of the Medical Research Committee, becoming the first person in England to hold a full-time research post in clinical medicine.

Electrocardiography

Thomas Lewis is today best remembered for his role in the development of the electrocardiograph machine. Prior to the invention of this tool, clinicians who wanted to study the heartbeat relied on careful examination of pulses in the neck, chest, or extremities. They were aided to some extent by the invention of the polygraph, an instrument that recorded those pulse waves. In 1902 Willem Einthoven (1860–1927), working in the Netherlands, invented the electrocardiograph machine, an instrument that could easily record the electrical action associated with the heartbeat. Lack of ready access to a medical setting hindered his ability to demonstrate the clinical efficacy of the new tool—it was Lewis who later, through his research and writings, transformed the electrocardiograph machine from a specialized tool for research investigation into a standard clinical tool for patient care. Einthoven realized the importance of Lewis to that transformation. Shortly after receiving the 1924 Nobel Prize in Physiology or Medicine for his invention, Einthoven wrote Lewis to say that 'without your steady and excellent work . . . there would have been in all no probability to question of a Nobel Prize for me.'

In 1908 Lewis visited Einthoven in the Netherlands and returned to London with an electrocardiograph machine. Lewis's initial focus with this new device was related to his earlier work. His first physiological research paper had been a detailed analysis of problems inherent in analyzing heart rhythms with pulse tracings. Not surprisingly, his first major analyses with the electrocardiogram machine were also directed toward abnormal heart rhythms. He examined the irregularly irregular pulse caused by a disorganized, ineffectual contraction of the upper chamber of the heart, atrial fibrillation. Lewis described the characteristic electrocardiographic changes of the abnormal rhythm and then postulated the mechanism, a 'circus like' movement of the contraction wave around the atrium. He also used the electrocardiograph machine to map out the origin and spread of the initial impetus to the heart's contraction in dogs, which he published in a series of detailed, careful papers. Lewis went on to study a wide range of cardiac arrhythmias. In 1911 he published the *Mechanism of the Heart Beat*, a comprehensive book that served as the standard reference for many years. He also distilled the key elements of electrocardiography into a slim volume, *Clinical Disorders of the Heartbeat* (1912), intended to supply the practitioner with key findings of cardiac disease without burdening the reader with the experimental evidence. The next year, he published another slim volume, *Clinical Electrocardiography*, which did not include 'practitioners and students' in its full title. Both of these books went through many editions. Lewis summarized his early work in a three-part article in the 1912 *British Medical Journal*, in which he concluded that 'no examination of the heart' would be complete without use of the electrocardiograph.

Soldier's Heart and the Effort Syndrome

During World War I, Lewis was preparing to command a Welsh Military Hospital in Mesopotamia when he was tapped by the Medical Research Committee to evaluate soldiers suffering from what was termed the 'effort syndrome', or 'soldier's heart'. This was a major problem—heart disease was the third leading cause of discharge from the British army during the war and a leading cause of pensioning (and thus expense) thereafter. Lewis was appointed to the permanent research staff of the Medical Research Committee in 1916 and started to study soldier's heart at UCH; the work was later transferred to a special unit at Mount Vernon Hospital in Hampstead and in 1917 to Colchester. Lewis did not find the rather cumbersome electrocardiograph machine to

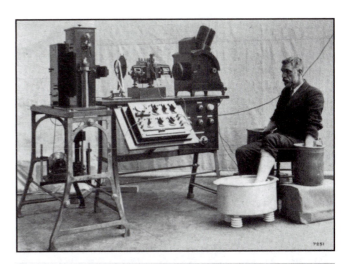

The Cambridge complete electrocardiograph as used by Sir Thomas Lewis, 1912. Halftone reproduction from S. L. Barron, *The Development of the Electrocardiograph . . .* London, 1952. Wellcome Library, London. Reproduced with permission of D. J. Unwin Archive.

be of value in differentiating soldiers with and without significant heart disease. Instead, he advocated a series of progressive exercises and proposed changing the name to the 'effort syndrome'. He laid out the results of his investigations in *The Soldier's Heart and the Effort Syndrome* (1918). For this work, Lewis received the CBE (1920) and was knighted (1921).

Inventing Cardiology

Lewis did not consider himself a specialist and did not like the term 'cardiologist'. Nonetheless, he played a key role in the development of the specialty of cardiology.

One way to define a specialty is with a journal. In 1909 Mackenzie encouraged Lewis to found a new journal, *Heart*. Intended not for the clinician but for the scientist (physiologists and pharmacologists outnumbered clinicians on the editorial board), the journal provided a conduit for Lewis and his colleagues to publish. He authored three of the eighteen papers in the first volume, with another thirteen from UCL. Overall, Lewis was either an author or coauthor of about a quarter of the papers. Not surprisingly, the topics reflected Lewis's interests. When he refocused his priorities away from the heart, the journal was renamed *Clinical Science* in 1933 (*vide infra*).

Lewis was a central figure in training those who were to become cardiologists, including people who later became leaders in the United States, such as Paul Dudley White (1886–1973), Alfred Einstein Cohn (1879–1957), and Frank Wilson (1890–1952). Lewis's textbooks were to be key resources for many years.

Another way to make a specialty is with a society. Those people who worked on soldier's heart during and after the war became the cardiologists of Great Britain. Although Lewis played far less of a role studying heart disease in soldiers after the war, as they went about forming the first cardiology society, the men who gathered to focus on soldier's heart saw Lewis as the central figure. Lewis was in the chair for the first meeting of the Cardiac Club in 1922. He was also asked to introduce the first volume of the *British Heart Journal* in 1939, but he did so clearly from the perspective of an honored outsider—for Lewis had left cardiac research in the 1920s, declaring that 'the cream is off the top'. He did not forget totally about the subject, however. Even though by then he had turned his research efforts in a different direction, in 1933 Lewis published a widely acclaimed text for practitioners and students, *Diseases of the Heart*.

Vascular Reactions of the Skin; Pain

From around 1924 Lewis took a different turn with his research and began examining the vascular reactions of the skin. He studied disease characterized by abnormal vascular reactions, such as Raynaud's disease. He studied the pain of intermittent claudication and showed it to be due to a substance released by the muscles, in a manner similar to the cardiac pain of angina pectoris. Later, he became interested in the causes of cutaneous pain and studied the response of the skin to injury, at times using himself, family, or friends as experimental subjects.

Clinical Science

Lewis became convinced that physicians must conduct experiments on people and that physicians needed to know how to use experimental methods to study clinical science. In 1930 he changed the name of his department to the 'Department of Clinical Research' and founded the Medical Research Society. In 1933 Lewis changed the name of the journal he had founded from *Heart* to *Clinical Science*. In 1934 he wrote an excellent book, *Clinical Science, Illustrated by Personal Examples*, in the hope of encouraging 'young men . . . to contemplate Clinical Science' as a 'field of fruitful and interesting life work'. He took 'Clinical Science' as the topic for his 1933 Harveian Oration. Near the end of his life, Lewis became intensely interested in medical education, especially in teaching students how to appreciate the nature of scientific practice, and it is noteworthy that one of his last publications, 'Exercises in Human Physiology Preparatory to Clinical Work' (1946), was a guide to help students move from preclinical to clinical studies.

In 1941 the Royal Society awarded Lewis the Copley medal. Only one other clinician—Joseph Lister (1827–1912)—had received the medal before.

Personal Life

In 1916 Lewis married Lorna Treharne James. They had three children: Patricia, Christopher, and Philippa.

Starting when they worked together at Colchester during the war, Lewis developed a close friendship with the University of Michigan physician Frank Wilson. They shared not only an interest in electrocardiography (Wilson was to take up the

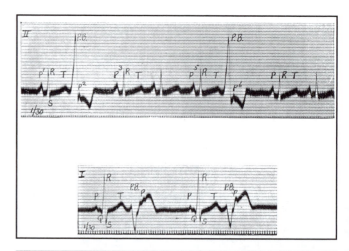

Electrocardiogram depicting a heart arrhythmia. Halftone reproduction from *Clinical Electrocardiography*, London, 1913. Wellcome Library, London.

baton from Lewis and lead electrocardiogram research for the next several decades), but also a keen interest in bird watching and bird photography. Lewis's only nonmedical paper is a paper on the breeding habits of the lesser tern, based on observations Lewis made while at Colchester. Lewis visited with Wilson in Ann Arbor in 1922, ostensibly to receive an honorary degree, but some suspected the underlying reason was to see the black tern, which had become rare in Great Britain.

Bibliography

Primary: 1911. *Mechanism of the Heart Beat* (London); 1912. *Clinical Disorders of the Heart Beat: A Handbook for Practitioners and Students* (London); 1913. *Clinical Electrocardiography* (London); 1918. *The Soldier's Heart and the Effort Syndrome* (London); 1934. *Clinical Science, Illustrated by Personal Experiences* (London).

Secondary: Hollman, Arthur, 1996. *Sir Thomas Lewis: Pioneer Cardiologist and Clinical Scientist* (London); Howell, Joel D., 1985. '"Soldier's Heart": The Redefinition of Heart Disease and Specialty Formation in Early Twentieth-Century Great Britain' in Bynum, W. F., C. Lawrence, and V. Nutton, eds., *The Emergence of Modern Cardiology* (*Medical History* Supplement 5); Howell, Joel D., 1984. 'Early Perceptions of the Electrocardiogram: From Arrhythmia to Infarction.' *Bulletin of the History of Medicine* 58: 83–98; Drury, A. N., and R. T. Grant, 1945. 'Thomas Lewis 1881–1945.' *Obituary Notices of Fellows of the Royal Society* 5: 179–202; *DSB*; *Oxford DNB*.

Joel D. Howell

LEYDEN, ERNST VON (b. Danzig, Prussia [now Germany], 20 April 1832; d. Charlottenburg, Berlin, Germany, 5 October 1910), *medicine*.

Leyden was born into the family of a prominent Prussian lawyer, but embarked on a career in military medicine because of the financial difficulties that followed the premature death of his father. In 1849 he went to study medicine at the

Friedrich-Wilhelms-Akademie in Berlin, and during his practical training as an intern at the Charité, Leyden came into contact with Ludwig Traube, who would later be appointed director of the Propaedeutic Clinic (which would later become the II Medical Clinic). After graduating and receiving his medical license in 1853, Leyden served as a military physician in Düsseldorf, Königsberg, and Gumbinnen. In 1859 he was ordered to return to the Charité for more scientific training, and he entered Traube's clinic as an intern. Thus, it was Traube who introduced him to the working of the experimental laboratory. In 1863 Leyden received his Habilitation with work on the spinal cord, and in 1865 he was appointed ordinary professor for pathology and therapy as well as director of the Clinic for Internal Medicine in Königsberg, at which point he was discharged from his military service.

Leyden's reorganization of the Clinic in Königsberg, which included the introduction of scientific research, as well as his skill as a clinical teacher earned him an appointment at the newly founded Imperial University at Strasbourg in 1872, which had been conceived as a showcase establishment for the recently unified Imperial Germany. After only four years at this post, Leyden, like many of these appointees to Strasbourg who were exhausted by the hard work of building up a new university from scratch, left to inherit the chair of his teacher Traube at the Propaedeutic Clinic in Berlin. After Frerich's death, Leyden then moved to the I Medical Clinic.

Leyden's research covered many areas of internal medicine, as is documented in his publication *Deutschen Klinik am Eingange des 20. Jahrhunderts*. In collaboration with Frerichs, Leyden founded the *Zeitschrift für klinische Medizin* in 1879 and the Verein für Innere Medicin zu Berlin in 1881. Leyden used this latter organization to combat the dominance of surgery within the profession. Similarly, the introduction of the first Congress for Internal Medicine in 1882 was a strategic move that began with a survey of hospital directors and the heads of clinics. One particularly significant contribution made by Leyden was establishing dietetics on a scientific basis. Under his leadership, researchers at the Berlin clinic conducted numerous studies into the set of problems regarding nutrition and eating disorders. In collaboration with Alfred Goldscheider, Leyden also founded the *Zeitschrift für diätetische und physikalische Therapie*, which provided a scientific forum to discuss practical applications and uses for new discoveries made in the biochemistry and physiology of nutrition.

Leyden was equally convinced of the need to provide therapy for tuberculosis. He was a committed supporter of the introduction of Lung-Sanatoria, which could cater to the less well off, and in 1895 he was one of the founders of the Zentralkomitees zur Errichtung von Lungenheilstätten in Deutschland [Central Committee for the Building of Lung-Sanatoria in Germany]. Leyden was one of the first to recognize that cancer would constitute a new problem area in medicine in light of the difficulty of achieving therapeutic success. Not only did he contribute to the founding of a Cancer Committee in 1900, but he also installed the first specialized cancer department at the Charité three years later. Even today, the crystals of phosphate found in the sputum of asthma patients, which he was the first to describe, are known as Leyden-Crystals.

Bibliography

Primary: 1874. *Die Klinik der Rückenmarks-Krankheiten* (Berlin); 1898. *Über den gegenwärtigen Stand der Behandlung Tuberculöser und die staatliche Fürsorge für dieselben* (Berlin).

Secondary: Dönitz, Dagmar, 1980. *Zur Biographie Ernst von Leydens unter besonderer Berücksichtigung seines Wirkens auf die soziale Medizin*, Thesis (Berlin); Lohde-Boetticher, Clarissa, 1910. *Ernst von Leyden. Lebenserinnerungen* (Stuttgart and Leipzig).

Volker Hess

LI, GAO 李杲 (aka LI, DONGYUAN 李東垣 or LI, MINGZHI 李明之) (b. Zhending, Hebei province, China, 1180; d. Zhending, China, 1251), *Chinese medicine.*

Li Gao was a Jin dynasty physician, one of the *Jin Yuan si dajia* 金元四大家 [Four Masters of Medicine in the Jin Yuan Periods], which included Liu Wansu (劉完素), Zhang Congzheng (張從正), and Zhu Zhenheng (朱震亨). These four physicians elaborated on the theories of the ancient canons of medicine and established four different etiologies of disease, giving rise to distinct schools of medical thought.

Li came from a wealthy family and followed the usual trajectory for people of his stature, studying the Confucian classics before becoming an official. When he was still young, his mother became sick. The family invited several physicians, but none could help or provide a diagnosis. His mother died. This motivated Li to devote his life to medicine. He studied under the famous physician Zhang Yuansu 張元素 (1151–1234) for a number of years, paying a substantial sum of money for his patronage. Li was a prolific writer and compiled many works, nine surviving to the present.

Li's contribution to the development of Chinese medicine was twofold. First, he systematized the pharmacology of the materia medica literature according to the terminology of systematic correspondence of classical medicine, developed in the context of cosmological doctrines and acupuncture. Second, he thoroughly discussed the nature of internal disorders, developing a specific etiology of disease, which made him the founder of a school of medicine.

Li effectively bridged the gap between drug therapy and classical medicine. Traditional Chinese drug therapy was based on categorizing drugs according to their *qi* 氣 [thermo-influence] and *wei* 味 [sapor], qualities that would determine the nature of their influence on the patient's body. In classical medicine, the body is categorized according to Yin and Yang, the circulation tracts, and the internal viscera. Li provided a framework for merging both approaches of medicine by interpreting the *siqi* 四氣, 'four thermo-influences' of drugs (hot, warm, cold, and cool), and the *wuwei* 五味, 'five sapors' (pungent, sweet, salty, sour, and bitter), in terms compatible with the general cosmological foundation of classical medicine: Yin and Yang, Heaven and Earth, Five Agents, and the Six Climatic Configurations. He enabled physicians who diagnosed the patient according to classical medicine to decide which drug to prescribe based on the underlying doctrines and not only on the observed symptoms.

Li lived through Genghis Khan's invasion of North China in 1232. Hundreds of thousands of people died during the siege, and many perished from the hunger and epidemics that followed. Utilizing his medical knowledge to help the ordinary people provided valuable experience. While treating the sick, he began to identify and formalize two basic types of disease of external and internal origin. Those of external origin contracted mainly from *shanghan* 傷寒 [cold damage] disorders, as first conceived by Zhang Zhongjing in Han times, produced febrile diseases and epidemics. The others were due to internal injury of the viscera.

Li's writing reveals a physician preoccupied with the effects of lifestyle on the body's organs, immoderation and intemperance principally affecting the spleen and the stomach, which he considered the root of the *yuan qi* 元氣, the original *qi*. Li based his treatments principally on medicinal formulas.

He is most famous for establishing a tradition, later known as the 'School of Spleen and Stomach' or 'the School of Warming and Replenishing'. In *Treatise on Spleen and Stomach*, Li claimed the set of functions associated with the spleen and stomach were predominant to all the other viscera, and thus, 'if the spleen and the stomach are deficient, this is the origin of hundred disorders' (preface to *Pi wei lun*). He reasoned that the spleen and the stomach, according to Chinese medicine, were the organs responsible for nourishing the whole body. As a result, if the *qi* of the spleen or the stomach was deficient, the body's constitution and its original *qi* would be harmed, leading to numerous diseases. In order to treat this type of problem, a physician had to focus on supplementing the *qi* of the spleen and the stomach.

Bibliography

Primary: 1180–1251. *Zhen zhu nang zhi zhang bu yi yao xing fu* 珍珠囊指掌補遺藥性賦 [Clarification and Addendum to the Pearl Purse [of Zhang Yuansu] and properties of drugs in verses]; 1231. *Nei wai shang bian huo lun* 内外傷辨惑論 [Treatise on clarifying ambiguities of inner and outer injuries]; 1249. *Pi wei lun* 脾胃論 [Treatise on spleen and stomach].

Secondary: Goldschmidt, Asaf (forthcoming). *The Evolution of Chinese Medicine: Northern Song Dynasty, 960–1127* (London); Unschuld, Paul, 1985. *Medicine in China: A History of Ideas* (Berkeley, CA) pp. 154–188.

Asaf Goldschmidt

LI, SHIZHEN 李时珍 (aka LI DONGBI 李东璧, LI BINHU 李濒湖 [by the lake]) (b. Waxiaoba, Hubei, China, 1518; d. Waxiaoba, Autumn 1593), *pharmacology, Chinese medicine, herbals, taxonomy.*

Li Shizhen, author of the monumental herbal encyclopedia *Bencao Gangmu* [Systematic Materia Medica] (completed 1578, first published 1593), is celebrated as 'the greatest naturalist in Chinese history' (Needham, 1986, p. 308) and one of the fathers of China's scientific research tradition.

Li Shizhen is now a household name, although very little is known of him from contemporary sources. He lived his life in relative obscurity, and until the twentieth century, interest was focused on the work rather than the man. No contemporary portraits of him exist—in fact, the now-familiar image of the gaunt, benign old scholar is based on a commemorative stamp issued in 1955. Wang Shizhen 王世贞 (1526-90), who met him in 1580, succinctly described him as a slender man with a scholarly face and as an excellent conversationalist. But during the 1950s, he was adopted as an iconic figure of the heroic socialist doctor in the service of the masses. In 1956 a popular biographical film was made about him (*Li Shizhen*, directed by Shen Fu, Shanghai Film Studio). Meanwhile, in Europe, Joseph Needham and others hailed him as the 'Prince of Pharmacists' and 'worthy of comparison with the best of the scientific men contemporary with him in Renaissance Europe' (Needham, ibid.). Despite the retrospective adoption of Li as a father of scientific enquiry, what more accurately characterizes his work is the eclectic and inclusive spirit with which he gathered remedies.

Family

Li Shizhen was the younger of two sons of a family of hereditary physicians of Waxiaoba 瓦硝坝, just outside the town of Qizhou 蕲州 in present-day Hubei province, in the Yangzi river area of central China. Qizhou was a communications hub and a distribution center for medicinal herbs, so it must have provided a stimulating environment for the young Li Shizhen. It was particularly renowned for the quality of the local artemisia (the herb used for moxibustion), on which his father, Li Yanwen 李言闻 (?–1564), published a monograph (*Qi ai zhuan* 蕲艾传). Li Shizhen grew up in times of rapid technological and mercantile development and considerable social mobility. His grandfather, who died when he was an infant, had been a traditional itinerant healer—a 'bell doctor', his father, an educated professional physician who published several books on medicine. Unlike his elder brother, Li Guozhen 李果珍 (?–c. 1581), it appears that the clever second son was not initially destined for a medical career, but intended to consolidate the family's social ascent by passing the challenging series of competitive examinations that would admit him to the elite class of scholar officials.

He had one sister, whose name is not recorded, though we know from an aside in *Bencao Gangmu* that she married a man named Liu Qiao 柳乔, whom Li Shizhen treated successfully for a severe illness.

Early Life

Under his father's guidance, Li Shizhen undertook a comprehensive study of the classics, with special emphasis on the *Erya* 尔雅—an encyclopedic dictionary compiled in the second century BCE, which must have fed his interest in the description and classification of the natural world.

He also had a mentor and role model in Gu Riyan 顾日岩, another local boy some eight years Li Shizhen's senior, who passed the examinations at the highest, metropolitan level (*jinshi* 进士) in 1538 and went on to pursue a distinguished official career.

However, Shizhen's early studies were hampered by ill health. Moreover, it has been suggested that he found work for the examinations arid and futile. He subsequently described himself as a sickly child and poor student, although he later 'became addicted to the pleasures of books, which were as sweet to him as sugar-cane candy'.

He passed the examination at the local level in 1531 at the age of fourteen, gaining the basic *Xiucai* 秀才 degree, but made three unsuccessful attempts at the triennial district exam (*Juren* 举人), probably in 1534, 1537, and 1540. At the second attempt, he was still recovering from a serious feverish illness contracted the year before. His third failure was the turning point in his life.

Maturity

Renouncing any bureaucratic ambitions, Li Shizhen decided to take up the family calling. He apprenticed himself to his father and embarked on a prodigious course of reading, which took in not only medicine and pharmacology but also all the other main branches of learning, including fiction and poetry. According to several sources, 'he did not stir from his home for ten years', although this must be something of an exaggeration because he also managed to make a name for himself as a gifted doctor.

His reputation as a physician came to the attention of a local aristocrat, the Prince of Chu, who appointed him physician and administrator to his court in the provincial capital, Wuchang. He seems to have held these posts for several years, from the late 1540s to the mid-1550s. Then in 1556 he was selected to join the Imperial Academy of Medicine in Beijing. Presumably, however, the life of an official in the metropolis did not appeal to him: he resigned on the pretext of ill health after just one year. But during that year, he must have had access to rare and restricted books, as well as access to rare drugs, which would have been invaluable for his research for *Bencao Gangmu.*

By the 1540s Li Shizhen was married. He and his wife, née Wu 吴, had four sons—Li Jianzhong 李建中 (?–?), Li Jianyuan 李建元 (1544–1598), Li Jianfang 李建方 (?–?), and Li Jianmu 李建木 (?–?). The younger three all seem to have followed their father into the medical profession, but Li Jianzhong was more successful than his father at the bureaucratic examinations, gaining the degree of juren, and he became a magistrate. The youngest son, Li Jianmu, was adopted as an heir by Li Shizhen's elder brother Li Guozhen, suggesting that the latter had remained childless.

In 1552 Li Shizhen began work on the project that was to dominate at least the next three decades of his life: *Bencao Gangmu.*

Bencao Gangmu

Li Shizhen was a respected physician and the author of various medical books, as well as at least two collections of poetry. His treatise on the pulses, *Binhu maixue* [Binhu's Sphygmology], based on his father's work, remains a standard text at Chinese universities. However, his fame rests primarily on his magnum opus, *Bencao Gangmu* [Systematic Materia Medica], the 'culmination of traditional Chinese pharmacology'.

The materia medica—herbal or pharmacopoeia—genre in China is an ancient one, dating back at least to *Shennong Bencao* [The Divine Farmer's Materia Medica], a compilation made around the first century. However, no official materia medica had been issued during the Ming period. A major new work, *Bencao pinhui jingyao* [Materia Medica Containing Essential and Important Material Arranged in Systematic Order], was commissioned by the Ming emperor Li Zong in 1503, but remained unpublished because the editor-in-chief, Liu Wentai, had fallen into disgrace. In Li Shizhen's time, the standard text was the *Zhenglei Bencao* [Classified Materia Medica] by Tang Shenwei, first published at the end of the eleventh century. In the course of his medical studies, Li Shizhen came to feel that an updated materia medica was urgently called for.

Previously, teams of full-time scholars had composed such works, by imperial commission. Li Shizhen set out to produce nothing less than the definitive encyclopedia of pharmaceutics and natural history on his own, with limited means, and initially at least, while still in other employment. For twenty-seven years, he immersed himself in scholarly research and also carried out meticulous fieldwork over a wide area of China.

The resulting work runs to fifty-two *juan* [volumes or fascicles] of text and two *juan* of illustrations. It contains entries on 1,892 substances, including 374 added by Shizhen himself, and 11,096 prescriptions, 8,161 of which he claims to have personally collected. The bibliography lists 981 titles, including not only theoretical works, but also novels and poetry. As well as quotations from the pharmacology literature, there are ethnographic observations, anecdotes, and explanations of technological processes and even culinary recipes, which makes it a treasure trove for later scholars. It is a monument not only to Li Shizhen's formidable scholarship but also to the breadth of his interests, sympathies, and enthusiasms and to his keen eye and his sharp, critical mind.

His stated aims were to remedy the errors, redundancies, lacunae, and arbitrary and inconsistent classification of previous materia medica texts and to offer an accurate presentation of the facts. His own method of classification, which has been much admired and compared to Linnaeus's, was based on a hierarchy of beings, which in turn has been linked with Darwin's theory of evolution.

His status as an independent scholar undoubtedly allowed Li Shizhen to give free reign to his skeptical, critical spirit. Much has been made of his critical attitude toward Daoist alchemical medicines and in particular toward the ingestion of highly toxic metals in the quest for immortality at a time when Daoist alchemists enjoyed marked imperial favor. The Jiajing emperor (r. 1522–1566) protected and advanced Daoist alchemists, and his death has been attributed to the ingestion of highly toxic 'elixirs of immortality'.

Li Shizhen acknowledged all four of his sons and four of his grandsons as contributors to the book—as proofreaders, illustrators, etc. However, it is not clear to what extent they actually collaborated on the work or whether this was rather a matter of courtesy.

The work was finally completed, after three revisions, in 1578, although it is likely that Li Shizhen continued to revise it over the next decade. In 1580 he approached Wang Shizhen, one of the most significant figures in the cultural and intellectual life of Ming dynasty China, for a preface. Wang Shizhen must have been impressed because he obliged with a warm and eloquent tribute to the breadth and depth of Li Shizhen's erudition and also the literary merits of the book. He may also have been instrumental in getting the first edition—the Jinling (Nanjing) edition—published, by the printer Hu Chenglong 胡承龙 of Nanjing.

Sadly, Li Shizhen was never to see his book in print: he died in the early autumn of 1593, just before it went to press. However, most of the blocks were engraved before his death, so he at least knew that his life's work was about to come to fruition.

Li Shizhen and his wife were buried on the bank of Rain Lake (*Yuhu* 雨湖) at Qizhou, where his mausoleum now stands.

In accordance with their late father's wishes, Li Shizhen's sons submitted a copy of *Bencao Gangmu* to the Emperor in 1596 in the hope that it would be selected for official publication by imperial decree. This was not to be, however. Whatever the Emperor's original intentions, the Imperial library (Wenyuange 文渊阁) burned down the next year, and all such projects were abandoned. In any case, the book became a best seller, even without the benefit of imperial sanction. A new edition, with improved illustrations, was published in 1603, under the aegis of the Inspector General of Jiangxi, Xia Liangxin 夏良心 (the 'Jiangxi edition'). Numerous editions of *Bencao Gangmu* followed, many of them incorporating Li Shizhen's works on the channels and pulses, and it remained an essential work of reference until well into the twentieth century.

Bencao Gangmu also reached an international audience. The first copy was brought to Japan in 1607, and it was subsequently reissued there many times, both in the original Chinese and, from the mid-seventeenth century onward, in Japanese translation.

It reached Europe a century later. A partial French version by Julien Placide Hervieu was incorporated into Jean-Baptiste du Halde's *Description géographique, historique, chronologique, politique de l'empire* (1735), which successively appeared in English, German, and Russian translation. *Ben-*

Duruo (*Pollia japonica*), Chinese medicinal plant. The root and stem can be made into a drug considered effective for replenishing kidney *qi* and treating conditions such as back pain and injuries from knocks and falls. Hand-colored woodcut from *Jing hui wuse tu zhu Ben Cao Mu*, 1655. Library of Zhongguo zhongyi yanjiu yuan/Wellcome Library, London.

cao Gangmu was certainly known, whether directly or indirectly, to both Darwin and Linnaeus.

Bibliography

Primary: 1593. *Bencao Gangmu* 本草纲目 [Systematic Materia Medica] (completed 1578, first published 1593); 2002. (Liu Hengru 刘衡如 et al., eds.) *Bencao Gangmu (Xin jiaozhu ben)* 本草纲目 (新校注本) (Beijing); 2004. (Luo Xiwen, trans. and ann.) *Compendium of Materia Medica (Bencao Gangmu)* (Beijing).

Secondary: Subhuti, Dharmananda, 2003. 'Li Shizhen Scholar Worthy of Emulation,' http://www.itmonline.org/arts/lishizhen. htm; Qian Yuanming 钱远铭 et al., 1988. *Li Shizhen shishi kao* 李时珍史实考 (Guangdong); Needham, Joseph, et al., 1986. *Science and Civilisation in China*, vol. 6: *Biology and Botanical Technology*, part 1 *Botany* (Cambridge) pp. 308–321; Goodrich, L. Carrington, and Chaoyang Fang, eds., 1976. *Dictionary of Ming Biography 1378–1644*, vol. 1 (New York and London) pp. 859–865; Zhang Tingyu 张廷玉 et al., ed., 1974. *Mingshi* 明史 vol. 25, juan

299 (Beijing) p. 7653; Lu, Gwei-Djen, 1966. 'China's Greatest Naturalist; A Brief Biography of Li Shih-chen.' *Physis* 8: 383–392; Chang, Hui-chien, 1960. *Li Shih-chen—Great Pharmacologist* (Beijing); *DSB*.

Penelope Barrett

LICEAGA, EDUARDO   (b. Guanajuato, Guanajuato, Mexico, 13 October 1839; d. Mexico City, Mexico, 13 January 1920), *public health.*

Liceaga was born in Guanajuato, a small provincial city. Although his father was a physician, his was a low-income family. Because there was no university in Guanajuato, Liceaga went to the capital city to study medicine. He finished his studies with the aid of the government, his father having died when he was quite young. Liceaga was a nephew of Casimiro Liceaga, the first Director of the establishment of Medical Sciences. This is an important detail because in 1833 the establishment adopted the program of study that was followed at the School of Medicine in Paris. In early nineteenth-century Mexico, the approach to medicine was still rather scholastic and anachronistic, little changed from the way medicine had been taught during the three centuries of Spanish domination. Clinical instruction was nonexistent. Liceaga's uncle was one of the modernizers of medical training in Mexico.

Liceaga was an excellent student, with high grades that earned him awards. He was highly respected by his professors and especially by the director. This experience turned out to be highly beneficial for two reasons: the director invited him to musical evenings at his home, where Liceaga associated with politicians who would later be very useful to his career. In addition, he was fond of music and participated in the founding of the Mexican Philharmonic Society (1867).

Diverse Positions and Activities

Liceaga was a versatile physician who stood out in several areas in addition to his chosen field of public health. He was the first to establish a consulting office where he received patients; the custom had always been for doctors to attend the sick in their homes. He served as director of the two most important hospitals in Mexico City in the late nineteenth century: the Maternity and Infancy and San Andrés hospitals, pioneering institutions in the area of clinical instruction.

Liceaga was president of the National Academy of Medicine in 1878 and again in 1906. He stimulated scientific research by offering a financial award for the best project designed to increase knowledge of yellow fever. He also served as president of the National School of Medicine on two occasions, where he succeeded in improving academic levels. In addition, he directed the Superior Council of Health from 1885 to 1914, and his ideas marked the path of health policies for almost thirty years.

Liceaga was an excellent clinician and surgeon, qualities that earned him a position as professor of surgical medicine at the National School of Medicine. He developed the technique of thoracoplasty to treat chronic empyema; used tuberculin in the treatment of tuberculosis patients; wrote about inguinal aneu-

Eduardo Liceaga. Photomechanical reproduction, courtesy of the National Library of Medicine.

rysms, chronic nephritis, and bladder cancer; and proposed the use of potassium bromide in the treatment of epilepsy.

Liceaga also elaborated the project for the General Hospital that replaced the Hospital San Andrés and brought it to fruition. This institution became a leader in the teaching of medicine in Mexico in the first half of the twentieth century, and it was there that medical specializations were structured. He was also instrumental in the construction of the Hospital de la Castañeda (1905), devoted to caring for mental patients. The creation of these two institutions meant an enormous leap toward modernity in Mexican medicine.

When Liceaga visited the Pasteur Institute in 1888, Emile Roux gave him a rabbit's brain that had been inoculated with the rabies virus. This allowed Liceaga to undertake the process of elaborating the antirabies vaccine in Mexico.

Public Health and Sanitation

During the sixteenth, seventeenth, and eighteenth centuries, medical care in Mexico was based on Christian charity and was provided by religious orders. By the mid-nineteenth century, private beneficence coexisted with charity, but the government soon began to take responsibility for the health of the society, first through a model of public assistance and later through concepts of public health. Liceaga became interested in public health and hygiene at an early age and was a protagonist of this paradigm change.

Liceaga considered hygiene to be the basis of public health and used this belief as the foundation for his activities as head of the emergent federal Mexican health system. According to him, every healthy Mexican was a productive element, whereas the ill not only represented losses, but also became a burden on society. Infant mortality, meanwhile, meant the death of future, productive, individuals. For these reasons, the State had the obligation to look after the health of the people and to encourage preventative medicine.

Liceaga promoted the construction of storm sewers, domestic sewers, and the infrastructure needed to supply potable water to the residents of Mexico City. It must be remembered that in the late nineteenth century the capital city had only open tanks for water (called *atarjeas*) on the main streets, special wagons collected waste materials at night, and a system based on aqueducts carried potable water to points where water-bearers (*aguadores*) distributed it to private homes. Liceaga also succeeded in blocking the construction of new neighborhoods until a potable water system, sewers, electricity, and gardens were installed.

Liceaga did brilliant work in the areas of disease prevention and social hygiene. During this period, vaccinations were administered against diphtheria, whooping cough, and the plague; epidemics such as cholera and smallpox were studied; and outbreaks of typhus (1876) and bubonic plague (1904) in the northeastern city of Mazatlán were successfully combated. Liceaga thought that diseases should be prevented and that municipalities were responsible for providing potable water, removing human waste and garbage, and paving streets. He circulated specific instructions designed to prevent the contamination of food and to install doors and windows to prevent the entrance of mosquitoes. Although these measures may seem simple, we must remember that in early twentieth-century Mexico, diarrheic illnesses and malaria were still major causes of death. In the case of yellow fever, the State became responsible for supervising commerce, navigation, and communications, all in an effort to improve hygiene.

Liceaga also enjoyed an international reputation given that he was a member of the U.S. American Public Health Association. Moreover, he was president of the Association (a position that had been also occupied during the turn of the twentieth century by another Latin American, Carlos Finlay). In addition, Liceaga organized two meetings of this association in Mexico City (in 1892 and 1906). He also played a crucial role in the organization of the international sanitary agency that eventually became the Pan American Sanitary Bureau.

Politics

Liceaga was a scientific politician with two particularly important characteristics: first, he considered the country as a totality that could not depend exclusively on the central government in the capital; and, second, he assumed that Mexico formed part of the world community in terms of hygiene and public health. With regard to the first point, people in the provinces frequently complained that regulations designed for Mexico City were inapplicable because their geographical and sanitary conditions were different from those of the places for which the regulations had been designed. During Liceaga's time, the Sanitary Code was finalized, dividing sanitary administration into local and federal branches and establishing rules and obligations for both. Using these ideas as a guide, Liceaga vigorously encouraged studies of the conditions in different areas of the nation. As part of the festivities for the Centennial of the Independence Wars from Spain, he organized an analysis of the hygienic conditions of the Republic. He sent questionnaires to each state, and though not all replied, the results allowed him to obtain, for the first time, a more-or-less accurate panorama of the sanitary state of the country.

Liceaga considered it very important that Mexico participate in the worldwide concern for sanitation. He was vice president of the American Public Health Association, he attended the International Congress in Moscow, and his labor in inter-American meetings was a precursor to modern organisms of international cooperation. Thanks largely to Liceaga, Mexico was the first country in Latin America to codify sanitary conditions.

Liceaga wrote his autobiography, which was published posthumously as *Recuerdos*. This book is a recounting of his work as a hygienist, his trips abroad as a delegate representing Mexico, and his experiences in the field of public health. It also mentions a few details of his private life and other activities in which he participated in the area of general medicine.

A Congressman in various legislatures, Liceaga was a man of humble origins who progressed thanks to his hard work. He met President Porfirio Díaz and became his personal friend and *compadre*. Díaz was president of Mexico for thirty years (1880–1910), and his government developed the political and social problems typical of authoritarian regimes. However, his firm belief in the utility of science, which he considered a kind of 'passport to modernity', led him to support Liceaga's proposals to improve the population's living conditions. Liceaga's relationship with power allowed him to carry out projects in the areas of public health and to introduce modern ideas into Mexican medicine. He occupied the highest positions in his field, and his prestige was so solid that he maintained his political-scientific leadership even after the fall of President Díaz in the second decade of the twentieth century. Liceaga retired from public life in 1914.

Bibliography

Primary: 1905. 'Plan de campaña para combatir la fiebre amarilla en la República Mexicana.' *Revista de Medicina Tropical* 6(2): 39–

42; 1908. 'Tercera Convención Sanitaria Internacional de las Repúblicas Americanas.' *Boletín del Consejo Superior de Salubridad* 13(8): 275–284; 1911. *Algunas consideraciones acerca de la higiene social en México* (Mexico City); 1949. *Mis recuerdos de otros tiempos* (Mexico City).

Secondary: Carrillo, Ana María, 2002. 'Economía, política y salud pública en el México porfiriano: (1876–1910).' *História, Ciências, Saúde-Manguinhos* 9: 67–87; Viesca Treviño, Carlos, 1998. 'Eduardo Liceaga y la participación mexicana en la fundación de la Organización Panamericana de la Salud.' *Revista Cubana de Salud Pública* 24(1): 11–18; *DSB*.

Ana Cecilia Rodríguez de Romo

LILEY, ALBERT WILLIAM   (b. Auckland, New Zealand, 12 March 1929; d. Auckland, 15 June 1983), *obstetrics, fetal research.*

Liley, known as 'Bill', the son of Albert Harvey Liley, an Auckland painter, and Zilla Jean Cook, attended Auckland Grammar School, topping New Zealand in the University National Scholarship in 1947. He attended Auckland University College and Otago University, where he had a distinguished undergraduate career, winning the Gold Medal for Anatomy and a Senior Scholarship in 1950. At Otago he worked with Nobel Prize–winning neurophysiologist J. C. (later Sir John) Eccles. Following graduation (MB ChB, 1954), he took up a research scholarship in physiology at the Australian National University and continued to study neuromuscular transmission. After completing his PhD, he returned to Auckland as a Sandoz Research Fellow in 1957, and in 1958 he was awarded a Medical Research Council of New Zealand Research Fellowship in Obstetrics. In 1968 he became professor in perinatal physiology at the founding of the Auckland University Medical School. His only period of extended overseas leave was in 1965, when he took up a position at Columbia University College of Physicians and Surgeons in New York.

Liley became famous for conducting the first intrauterine blood transfusion in the world in 1963, thus greatly advancing fetal medicine. He accomplished this at Auckland's National Women's Hospital, set up as a Postgraduate School of Obstetrics and Gynecology following World War II. From 1954 its head and professor was Harvey Carey, who successfully created a climate and facilities for research. When Liley returned to Auckland as a final-year medical student in 1954, Carey earmarked him for 'his intellectual qualities, his capacity for lateral thinking, enthusiasm and depth of compassion' (Scott, 1997). Carey successfully wooed him back to the hospital as its first research fellow in 1957, and Liley remained associated with the hospital for the rest of his life.

Rhesus blood incompatibility was recognized as a major cause of stillbirth and hemolytic disease of the newborn around the time of World War II. Much attention was devoted to this problem in the 1950s, and exchange transfusions of babies' blood immediately after birth became common practice. Liley refined prenatal diagnostic techniques and popularized amniocentesis. Obtaining samples of amniotic fluid by passing a needle into the uterus, he demonstrated that heavily jaundiced fluid indicated the fetus would be stillborn. A chance needling of a distended fetal abdomen led him to consider transfusing the fetus, which he eventually achieved in 1963. This was the baby of a mother, pregnant for the fourth time, who had lost the previous two to hemolytic disease. The baby, Grant Liley McLeod, was successfully delivered at thirty-four weeks on 20 September 1963 and made world headlines.

Liley argued that from conception the fetus was an individual, or a patient to be looked after. In 1970, together with gynecologist Hugh Patrick Dunn, he founded the New Zealand Society for the Protection of the Unborn Child, to fight against liberalization of the laws on abortion, and became its foundation president. In 1974 he gave testimony to the United States Supreme Court in a case to determine whether abortion infringed the constitutional rights of unborn children.

He became a Fellow of the Royal Society of New Zealand (1964) and of the Royal College of Obstetricians and Gynaecologists (1971). The significance of his work was recognized with a CMG in 1967 and KCMG in 1973. He had married Helen Irwin Hunt in 1953, and they had two sons, three daughters, and one adopted daughter with Down Syndrome. Sir William died prematurely, at age fifty-four.

Bibliography

Primary: 1963. 'Intrauterine transfusion of foetus in haemolytic disease.' *British Medical Journal* 2: 1107–1109.

Secondary: Hawgood, Barbara J., 2005. 'Professor Sir William Liley (1929–1983): New Zealand Perinatal Physiologist.' *Journal of Medical Biography* 13(2): 82–88; Scott, Sir John, 1997. 'Sir Albert William Liley.' http://www.rsnz.org/directory/yearbooks/ybook97/obitLiley.html; Foundation Genesis, 1984. *Sir William Liley: A Tribute to the Father of Fetology* (Strathfield, NSW).

Linda Bryder

LIM, BOON KENG (aka LIN, MENG QIN)   (b. Singapore, 18 October 1869; d. ?, 1957), *medicine, social reform.*

The second son of Lim Thean Geow, Lim had his English education at the Cross Street Government School and Raffles Institution. The first Chinese recipient of the Queen's Scholarship (1887), he read medicine at Edinburgh University, Scotland, graduating in 1892 with first class honors. He undertook postgraduate research in pathology at Cambridge University with publications in the *Philosophical Transactions*.

Returning to Singapore in 1892, he had a medical practice at Telok Ayer Street and operated the first Chinese dispensary. In December 1896, Lim married Margaret Wong Tung-Keng, the eldest daughter of Wong Nai Siong (1849–1924), the pioneer of the Foochow settlement in Sibu, Sarawak.

Four boys were born to this union: Ko Seng (Robert), Ko Beng, Ko Leng, and Ko Liao. Margaret died in 1905. Lim then married Grace Yin Pek-Ha and had two more children, Ena and Peng Han.

In 1895 the British colonial government appointed Lim a member of the Straits Settlements Legislative Council. He was also a Justice of the Peace, Municipal Commissioner, and a member of the Chinese Advisory Board, the latter a body to assist the colonial government in dealing with the Chinese community. With Song Ong Siang (1871–1941) and Wu Lien-Teh (1879–1960), Lim edited and contributed to the *Straits Chinese Magazine* (1897–1907), a quarterly publication on sociocultural issues. In 1897 he founded the Chinese Philomathic Society, the Chinese Recreation Club, and Weekly Entertainment Club in Singapore.

Lim was one of the leading advocates in the anti-opium movement in the Straits Settlements (Penang, Melaka, and Singapore). The Anti-Opium Society (1906) heightened public awareness of the baneful effects of opium smoking. Lim, together with Song in Singapore and Wu in Penang, rallied support for the abolishment of opium's import, sale, and consumption in terms of Chinese nationalism and patriotism; opium was undermining the strength and vigor of China and the Chinese: therefore, all Chinese nationalists should support the anti-opium movement as an act of patriotism.

As one of the movers in establishing the King Edward VII College of Medicine, Lim taught pharmacology and therapeutics (1907–10). His writings on tuberculosis and the baneful effects of opium smoking were published in the *Journal of the Straits Medical Association.*

With foresight, Lim, together with Tan Chay Yan (1871–1916) of Melaka, invested in rubber planting in 1896 and enjoyed the first rubber boom a decade later. With his foray into banking having begun when he was the inaugural chairman of the Chinese Commercial Bank (1912), he established the Overseas Chinese Bank (1919) in partnership with Oei Tiong Ham of Java, and in 1921 he was appointed a member of the standing committee of Ho Hong Bank. He was a director of Overseas Assurance Corporation and Singapore Rubber Limited and founding member of the Singapore Chinese Chamber of Commerce (1906).

A strong advocate of reforms to build a modern China, Lim in 1899 initiated a 'cut-the-queue' campaign among the Chinese in Singapore. He facilitated the visit of the reformist Kang Yu-Wei (1858–1927) to Singapore in 1900. Despite his Western education and Christian faith, as a cultural nationalist he felt strongly for the Chinese language (Mandarin) and Confucianism, leading the Confucian revival movement and lecturing on Confucianism in the Straits Settlements (1894–1919). He intended Mandarin to mold Chinese identity ('Chineseness') and unite the disparate overseas Chinese dialectism and parochialism. He succeeded in persuading the Chinese Association (Tiong Hua Huai Kuan) of Batavia to adopt Kuo Yu (vernacular Mandarin) as the medium of instruction in the hitherto Chinese dialect schools. A cham-

pion of female education, Lim had a role in the opening of the Singapore Chinese Girls' School (1899).

Notwithstanding his reformist leanings, the Imperial Ching (Manchu) government appointed Lim in 1911 to be medical adviser to the Ministry of the Interior; he later became inspector-general of the hospital in Beijing. He represented China in two international medical conferences in Paris and Rome. After the Chinese Revolution (1911), he held the dual appointment of confidential secretary and personal physician to Sun Yat-Sen (1866–1925), the Chinese Republic's inaugural president. His appointment in 1913 as head of the Board of Health was short-lived. When Yuan Shih-Kai (1859–1916) assumed the presidency (1913–16), Lim tendered his resignation.

Upon the invitation of his longtime friend Tan Kah Kee (1874–1961), Lim assumed the chancellorship of Amoy University (now Xiamen University) (1921–37). As a staunch Confucianist emphasizing morality over politics and ideology, he was at odds with students belonging to the May Fourth (1919) generation that demanded a more radical transformation of society and nation.

Lim received honors, awards, and fellowships from various quarters, including the Order of the British Empire (OBE) (1918), an honorary Doctor of Law (1919) from the University of Hong Kong, and the Chia Hu Chang (Second Class) and Wen Hu Chang (Second Class) from Nationalist China.

Bibliography

Secondary: Yong, C. F., 1992. *Chinese Leadership and Power in Colonial Singapore* (Singapore); Yen, Ching-Hwang, 1986. *A Social History of the Chinese in Singapore and Malaya 1800–1911* (Singapore); Song, Ong Siang, 1923. *One Hundred Years' History of the Chinese in Singapore* (London).

Ooi Keat Gin

LINACRE, THOMAS   (b. Canterbury, England, 1460?; d. London, England, 1524), *medicine, classical scholarship.*

Nothing is known for certain about Linacre's early life; even the place of birth is uncertain, being based on a supposed early association with a later patron, William Selling (*c.* 1430–90), who taught at the Benedictine priory of Christ Church in Canterbury from 1468. Linacre was in Oxford by 1481 and was elected to a fellowship of All Souls (1484). In 1487 he was invited to accompany Selling on the mission to thank the Pope for his dispensation to Henry VII (1457–1509), which had allowed Henry to marry Elizabeth of York (1466–1503) in 1486. Linacre perhaps dropped out of the mission on the way, given that he seems to have been in Florence in 1489, studying Greek under Politian (1454–94) and Demetrius Chalcondylas (1423–1511), translator of Galen. He enrolled at the University of Padua about 1492 and earned his MD in 1496. At this time, he became closely involved with the editing of the so-called Aldine edition of

Aristotle's works in Greek, undertaken by the humanist and publisher Aldus Manutius (1449–1515). Linacre's first publication—a translation of the *De sphaera* of Proclus (fifth century)—appeared from the Aldine press in 1499. Linacre also began collecting books and manuscripts while in Italy.

On his return to London in about 1499, Linacre incorporated his MD at Oxford and became a leading member of the group of English humanists, which included John Colet (1467–1519) and Sir Thomas More (1478–1535). In 1509 he was appointed physician to Henry VIII (1491–1547), and he began to build a practice of wealthy and important clientele. Rather than build a large practice, however, Linacre took holy orders and, with the help of his connections, acquired a number of ecclesiastical 'livings'—that is to say, Church posts that, though not burdensome, provided annual salaries. This ensured that he had time to pursue his scholarly interests, in particular his translations of Galen into Latin. The first of these, Galen's *De sanitate tuenda*, appeared in 1517. Linacre subsequently acquired a European reputation, and his translations were frequently reprinted until about 1550. He favored those Galenic texts that were important for the practicing physician, and his translations contributed to the improvement in understanding of Galen, which medical humanists hoped would lead to a reform of medicine.

Linacre did not confine his attempts to reform medicine to classical scholarship, however. In 1518 he was one of the prime movers in the establishment of the College of Physicians of London as a medical licensing and controlling body within a seven-mile radius around the city, and he was the organization's first president until his death. With the College of Physicians modeled on Italian institutions, the hope was that by licensing only university-trained physicians, the institution could improve the standard of medical treatment. Unfortunately, a number of institutions opposed the monopoly of the College, including the Company of Barbers and Surgeons, Parliament, and both English universities. Caught in a vicious circle in its early existence, the membership of the College remained too hopelessly small to provide adequate medical coverage for London, consisting of twelve members at Linacre's death and only eighteen in 1537.

In the year before his death, Linacre began planning for the establishment of medical lectureships at Oxford and Cambridge, to remind able men that the Church was not the only way to make a reputable living and to encourage more to turn to medicine. Again Linacre's reformist ambitions were thwarted. The inertia of the universities and the pre-existing low level of interest in medicine at these two universities proved to be insurmountable obstacles, and the lectureships failed to make significant improvements in medical education. Even so, the lectureships, and of course the College of Physicians, remain his most enduring legacy.

Bibliography

Primary: 1517. Galen, *De sanitate tuenda*, trans. into Latin (Paris); 1519. Galen, *Methodus medendi*, trans. into Latin (Paris).

Secondary: Maddison, Francis, Margaret Pelling, and Charles Webster, eds., 1977. *Essays on the Life and Work of Thomas Linacre c. 1460–1524* (Oxford); Clarke, George, and A. M. Cooke, 1964. *A History of the Royal College of Physicians of London* (Oxford); Johnson, John Noble, 1835. *The Life of Thomas Linacre, Doctor of Medicine* (London); *DSB*; *Oxford DNB*.

John Henry

LIND, JAMES   (b. Edinburgh, Scotland, 4 October 1715; d. Gosport, Hampshire, England, 18 July 1794), *naval medicine.*

Lind was the son of James Lind, merchant, and his wife, Margaret Smelholme (Smellum), who came from an Edinburgh medical family. (The younger Lind's cousin was named James Lind as well and was also an Edinburgh-born naval surgeon and later physician.) Lind attended grammar school in Edinburgh and in 1731 was apprenticed to George Langlands, an Edinburgh surgeon. In 1734 he attended Alexander Monro *primus*'s anatomy course at the University of Edinburgh. He became a royal naval surgeon in 1738, serving until 1748. Most of this time was spent aboard ship in the English Channel during the war of the Austrian Succession (1740–48).

When Lind left the navy, he returned to Edinburgh and graduated MD (1748) with a thesis on venereal disease. He probably practiced as a physician in Edinburgh or nearby during the following ten years. He was elected FRCPEdin in 1750 and was made the College's treasurer in 1756. During these years, Lind wrote his famous *A Treatise of the Scurvy*, published in 1753. A French edition appeared in 1756. In 1757 there appeared *An Essay on the Most Effectual Means of Preserving the Health of Seamen in the Royal Navy*. Two papers on fevers and infection read before the Philosophical and Medical Society of Edinburgh followed in 1763. He was elected a fellow of the Royal Society of Edinburgh in 1783, and at some point not ascertained, he married Isabel Dickie (d. 1797).

In 1758 Lind was appointed physician in charge of the Royal Naval Hospital, Haslar, a position probably obtained for him by Lord Anson, first lord of the Admiralty. Anson, as was well known, had had a disastrous, scurvy-ridden, four-year circumnavigation. While at Haslar, Lind published (1768) *An Essay on Diseases Incidental to Europeans in Hot Climates*. Several editions of this work, like the work on scurvy, appeared. In 1783 his son John succeeded Lind in the post at Haslar.

Widely cited and much esteemed, Lind seems to have been a reticent man. Little is known of his life except for what can be gleaned from his publications. It was largely the efforts of those who valued his works and authority, and not his personal interventions on deck or at the Admiralty, that effected reform in the navy. With the rise of ideas of disease-specific causality, the discovery of vitamins, and clinical trials, aspects of Lind's work have assumed a size disproportionate to their eighteenth-century significance.

As described in the *Treatise*, Lind, on HMS *Salisbury*, famously divided twelve seamen into six groups of two and gave them different remedies purported to cure scurvy. Lind came out in favor of lemon juice. In fact, this 'trial' was buried deep in the book, and neither Lind nor his contemporaries made much of it. There were a number of reasons for this. First, although scurvy was a disorder recognizable by its natural history (lassitude, stiff joints, loose teeth, and later subcutaneous bleeding and possibly death), it was also seen as closely related—clinically, etiologically, and pathologically—to other disorders, notably the putrid fevers, and was therefore seen as having similar means of prevention and cure. In 1790 in *An Essay on the Scurvy*, the naval surgeon Frederick Thomson observed that 'most of the means of prevention [of scurvy] . . . will apply to other diseases incident to seamen' (p. xiii). Second, although scurvy had an 'ideal' natural history, it was also recognized that it varied, like the fevers, according to a variety of factors, such as meteorological conditions and geography. Third, and crucially, the causes of scurvy were deemed multiple. For scurvy to occur, all authors agreed, a conspiracy of factors had to be present, notably the following: improper diet, excessive moisture, impure air, lack of exercise, and, not least, indiscipline or moral laxity among the crew. Various authors stressed these factors differently, but most, including Lind, noted how local circumstances determined which was the most important. Thus, a vegetable diet that might, on one occasion, prevent scurvy in a ship in, say, the West Indies might be of no use in another arena, for instance, the Pacific (and vice versa).

In the first edition of the *Treatise*, Lind emphasized the importance of diet and atmospheric moisture in generating scurvy. The noxious by-products of digesting a poor diet, he claimed, could not be evacuated by perspiration in wet weather, and scurvy then ensued. It was in this context that the famous 'trial' was reported. In his practice at Haslar, Lind's treatment of scurvy varied, and he remained a skeptic about making positive assertions regarding any aspect of therapeutics. To other observers, other remedies for scurvy worked equally as well as lemon juice. The immensely successful and relatively disease-free voyages of James Cook (1728–79) seemed to prove the value of sauerkraut and 'wort' (fermented malt), as recommended by the naval surgeon James McBride. The circle around Sir John Pringle (1707–82), when he was president of the Royal Society from 1772 to 1778, promoted water impregnated with fixed air (because of its acidic nature) as a valuable remedy for, and preventative of, scurvy. Lind stated that the preservation of water by fixed air needed a public trial. The introduction of a ration of citrus juice into the navy was largely owing to the lobbying of Gilbert Blane (1749–1834) and Thomas Trotter (c. 1760–1832). Both men esteemed Lind highly, but neither held a theory of scurvy substantially different from those of their contemporaries and certainly nothing like a modern one.

A

TREATISE

OF THE

SCURVY.

IN THREE PARTS.

CONTAINING

An inquiry into the Nature, Causes, and Cure, of that Disease.

Together with

A Critical and Chronological View of what has been published on the subject.

By *JAMES LIND*, M. D.

Fellow of the Royal College of Physicians in *Edinburgh*.

EDINBURGH:

Printed by SANDS, MURRAY, and COCHRAN. For A. KINCAID & A. DONALDSON,

MDCCLIII.

Title page of *A Treatise of the Scurvy*, 1753. Rare Books, Wellcome Library, London.

Bibliography

Primary: 1753. *A Treatise of the Scurvy, in Three Parts. Containing an Inquiry into the Nature, Causes, and Cure, of That Disease. Together with a Critical and Chronological View of What Has Been Published on the Subject* (Edinburgh); 1757. *An Essay on the Most Effectual Means of Preserving the Health of Seamen in the Royal Navy* (London); 1763. *Two Papers on Fevers and Infection. Which Were Read before the Philosophical and Medical Society, in Edinburgh* (London); 1768. *An Essay on Diseases Incidental to Europeans in Hot Climates. With the Method of Preventing Their Fatal Consequences . . . To Which Is Added, an Appendix concerning Intermittent Fevers. To the Whole Is Annexed a Simple and Easy Way to Render Salt Water Fresh, and to Prevent a Scarcity of Provisions in Long Voyages at Sea* (London).

Secondary: Lawrence, Christopher, 1996. 'Disciplining Disease: Scurvy, the Navy, and Imperial Expansion' in Miller, David Philip, and Peter Hanns Reill, eds., *Visions of Empire: Voyage, Botany and Representations of Nature* (Cambridge) pp. 80–106; Carpenter, K. J., 1988. *The History of Scurvy and Vitamin C* (Cambridge); Lloyd, Christopher, and Jack L. S. Coulter, 1961. *Medicine and the Navy. Volume 3—1714–1815* (Edinburgh and London); *DSB*; *Oxford DNB*.

Christopher Lawrence

LINNAEUS, CARL   (b. Råshult, Småland, Sweden, 23 May 1707; d. Uppsala, Sweden, 10 January 1778), *natural history, medicine.*

Carl Linnaeus (ennobled in 1757 as Carl von Linné, which is the name usually used in Sweden and other non-Anglo-Saxon countries), was the first son of a vicar in the Lutheran church of Sweden in the province Småland, close to the border to what up until recently had been Danish territory, in the parish of Råshult. Soon after his birth the family moved to Stenbrohult, a nearby vicarage. What too often has been described as an idyllic childhood was shaded by the poverty of the region and the breakdown of Sweden's era as a great power.

Between Sweden and Holland

Linnaeus studied at the gymnasium of Växjö in order to become a clergyman like his father. However, a senior teacher, Johan Rothman, inspired Linnaeus to move into medicine, especially botany. Rothman seems to be the one who taught Linnaeus about the sexuality of plants. Linnaeus spent one year at the University of Lund (1728), where he was tutored by the professor Kilian Stobaeus and allowed to use the professor's library. Arriving in Uppsala in 1729, he was given support by Olof Rudbeck *fil*, one of the two professors in medicine, but he also became close to the other, Lars Roberg. Maneuvering between different possibilities to find a career, he approached the local scientific society and acquired a grant to travel into Lapland in 1732. This journey led Linnaeus to travel along the Baltic coast and move west over the fiords to the coast of the Atlantic. He not only found new plant species but also encountered the Laps and their, to his mind, natural and ideal way of living, an example to which he often returned in his dietetic writings. A journey into Dalecarlia in 1734 gave him knowledge about the miners' occupational diseases.

In 1735 he went to Holland in order to obtain his doctoral degree in medicine, which he was given in Harderwijk with a thesis about the ague. Linnaeus stayed in Holland for more than three years, working as the gardener to George Clifford, a rich banker. During this period he was also intensively occupied by publishing different texts treating botanical taxonomy as well as his seminal *Systema naturae* (1735), where man is included within the zoological system. Again

Carl von Linné. Line engraving by P. Tanjé after Ehrensverd. Iconographic Collection, Wellcome Library, London.

and again Linnaeus stated his belief that man scientifically should be seen as an animal, a fact that the physician should also consider. During this period Linnaeus also made short visits to Paris, London, and Oxford. Despite never using any foreign language other than Latin, he renewed natural history terminology. Back in Sweden, he settled in Stockholm as a naval physician and married Sara Lisa Morea, by whom he had one son, his successor Carl, and four daughters.

Medicine or Natural History

In 1741 Linnaeus became professor of medicine in Uppsala, succeeding Rudbeck; he exchanged the responsibility for anatomy with Nils Rosén, his colleague and a pioneer of pediatrics. It was mainly in this period that Linnaeus published on medicine. He lectured on materia medica (often on botany) and natural history in general. Especially popular were his dietetical lectures, sometimes attracting several hundred students. Traveling into different Swedish provinces (to Gotland and Öland in 1741, to Västergötland in 1746, and to Skåne in 1749), he observed local diseases and folk medicine. Around Linnaeus's charismatic person, an inner circle of students gathered, his so-called apostles whom he sent out into the world in order to make *Systema naturae* complete, but also to test different acclimatization strategies. Several of these students died abroad in martyrdom. Others reached fame, such as Daniel Solander and Anders Sparrman, who both traveled with James Cook, and Carl Peter Thunberg, who taught European medicine to the Japanese and later on became Linnaeus's successor. No less than 186 students defended a master's or doctoral thesis under the presidium of Linnaeus. These dissertations should be considered as written by Linnaeus—with the exception of fewer than ten—and not by the different candidates. Linnaeus was one of the founders of the Royal Academy of Science in 1739, where he acted as its first president. Thus, he became a central figure in Swedish science and medicine, a successful entrepreneur, an early proponent of big science, and also a naturalist courtier who inspired king and queen to participate in this popular craze. His international success is obvious from many international honors.

A System of Diseases

By and large Linnaeus was an autodidact. He obtained his knowledge from reading, correspondence, and fieldwork. His early student years showed influences from hermetic writings that pop up late in life. His eclecticism allowed Hippocrates and Nature to be the foremost Doctors while he also adhered to the iatrophysical school, as did many physicians in his day. Its central proponent, Herman Boerhaave in Leiden, was a father figure to Linnaeus. Linnaeus's main medical contribution, however, was to medical taxonomy or nosology. His dissertation *Genera morborum* (1759, extended version 1763) could have been used as a handbook for the clergy in how to label diseases in their reports to the national statistics (Tabellverket). Linnaeus's ambitions were to transplant his botanical system into medicine with classes, orders, genera, and species as well as binary nomenclature. In this undertaking he was inspired by his correspondent in Montpellier, Boissier de Sauvages. He never published any full text on this topic, but in lectures he also treated disease at the species level. This nosology inspired many, William Cullen among others, up to the 1820s. One aspect of his nosology was his opinion on 'living contagion', put forward in *Exantematha viva* (1757), as physical causes of disease. Similarly, in *Systema naturae* (12th edition of 1766) and *Mundus invisiblis* (1767), he peeped into the world of microorganisms, called by him a *Regnum chaoticum*, or a fourth kingdom of Nature.

How to Live Well

A great teacher and organizer of science, Linnaeus showed a keen interest in the economical aspects of science—which should be understood in the context of the general ideological climate of mid-eighteenth century Sweden. His interest in occupational medicine and the importance of a simple and healthy life were characteristic of mercantilist ideology. On the other hand, in his lectures, following the old concept of *sex res non naturales* (the Six Non-Naturals), Linnaeus addressed the health of the individual rather than the collective, discussing how one should live a happy life in marriage, at the table or in one's study. All this means that Linnaeus's lectures on dietetics were rich in cultural content. As a botanist he wrote extensively about different medical cures: China cortex or Cortex peruvianus, Tartaric Rhubarb, Qwassia, and Opium, for example. To him, wild strawberries (*Fraga vesca*, 1772) were the best remedy against 'podager' or gout. For Linnaeus medicine was a part of natural history—and not the other way around. One example is the dissertation *De Taenia* [On the tapeworm, 1748], in which he explained the reproduction of one of the great enemies of man during the age of Enlightenment. Linnaeus's dissertations, which were collected in different volumes called *Amoenitates academicae*, meaning 'academic pleasures', include many similar observations.

Linnaeus's Medical Last Will

Linnaeus's materia medica centered around ideas of *sapor et odor*, taste and smell, a polarity that characterized *Clavis medicinae duplex* (1766), a small tract declared to be his medical last will and perhaps not possible to understand until a distant future—a period we do not seem to have reached. The combination of materia medica, popular ideas of electricity as the very essence of life, and his theory of a 'fatherly' formative 'cortex' and a 'motherly', electric, and god-like spiritual 'medulla' makes *Clavis* a most singular text. Dedicated to the foremost medical scholars, it did not impress anyone. However, it remains an interesting testimony to the difficulties within European Enlightenment medicine of finding a road between a mechanistic and an organic interpretation of life.

Linnaeus's contribution to the history of medicine is mainly connected to his epoch-making work as a taxonomist, making botany and natural history a major interest also in medicine. Likewise, his stress on order and cataloging every aspect not only of nature but also of human life, what could be called 'linnaeanism', has been important. Today, it seems natural to emphasize his role as networker and entrepreneur. From his position within Swedish medicine, he could rule through Uppsala University and the Royal Academy of Sciences and through friends such as Abraham Bäck at the Board of Medicine. And Linnaeus's impact was not only local. Because of his contact with the Swedish and East India Company, his students arrived at distant shores, broadening our knowledge of mankind and its conditions. His vision of a universal catalog of life in all its forms still lingers.

Bibliography

Primary: 1749–98. *Amoentitates academicae* vol. 1–10 (different editions and places); 1766. *Clavis Medicinae duplex* (Holmiae); 1759, 1763. *Genera morborum* (Uppsala); 1907. (Lindfors, A. O., ed.) *Dietetik or Lachesis naturalis* (Uppsala); 1957. (Uggla, A. H., ed.) *Diaeta naturalis 1733* (Uppsala).

Secondary: Koerner, Lisbet, 1999. *Linnaeus: Nature and Nation* (Cambridge, MA); Hövel, Gerlinde, 1999. *'Qualitates vegetabilium', 'vires medicamentorum' und 'oeconomicus usus plantarum' bei Carl von Linné* (Stuttgart); Lindroth, Sten, 1994. 'The Two Faces of Linnaeus' in Frängsmyr, Tore, ed., *Linnaeus* (Berkeley); Broberg, Gunnar, 1976. *Homo sapiens L. Studier i Carl von Linnés naturuppfattning och människolära* (Uppsala); Berg, Fredrik, 1957. *Linnés Systema morborum, Uppsala Universitets Årsskrift* vol. 3 (Uppsala); Hjelt, O. E. A., 1907. 'Linné som läkare och medicinsk författare' in *Carl von Linnésbetydelse som naturforskare och läkare* (1907) (also German edition); *DSB*.

Gunnar Broberg

LISTER, JOSEPH (b. Upton, Essex, England, 5 April 1827; d. Walmer, Kent, England, 10 February 1912), *surgery.*

Joseph Lister was the second son and fourth child of Joseph Jackson Lister (1786–1869), a wine merchant and microscopist, and Isabella Harris. The Lister household was affluent and studious. They were Quakers and shared the respect for learning that is characteristic of the Society of Friends. The young Joseph was greatly influenced by his father's scientific interests. Joseph Jackson Lister had made a very significant improvement in the design of the microscope (eliminating the problem of spherical aberration) and had used his new instrument to make a number of fine studies. He was, for instance, the first to measure accurately the diameter of red blood cells. Joseph's education was begun at home, but at the age of eleven, he was enrolled at the local school in Hitchin. Two years later, he was sent to Grove House School, Tottenham. By this time, Joseph had acquired a strong interest in natural history. He enjoyed collecting, dissecting, and preparing specimens of various kinds. He made many drawings, becoming, like his father, an accomplished draftsman, skilled in the use of the camera lucida. According to his nephew, Rickman Godlee (1849–1925), Joseph decided to become a surgeon while still at school, despite the Lister family having no tradition of doctoring. Medicine was a respectable and useful profession in which scientific interests could be expressed, with surgery perhaps having the added attraction of involving manual skills. Although his relations with his parents and siblings were warm and mutually supportive, Lister was socially isolated as a school and college student, partly owing to his studious and industrious habits and partly because of a speech impediment. Throughout his life, he retained a reputation for being socially awkward and aloof with his peers.

In 1844, at age seventeen, Lister entered University College, London, as a student in the Faculty of Arts. He was evidently developing his medical interests because he was present at the first operation performed under anesthesia in England. On 21 December 1846, in the operating theater of University College Hospital, Robert Liston (1794–1847) amputated the leg of a patient rendered unconscious by the application of ether. It might be said that Lister had witnessed an innovation that was to have crucial implications for his own career prospects. The contrast between the experienced surgeon and the prospective one is telling. Liston was extremely strong and very dexterous. Tough-minded, confident, and a very fast operator, he was well-suited to the arduous task of operating on conscious patients. Lister, on the other hand, was shy and sensitive; his operative technique would always be slow, steady, and cautious. It is unlikely that he would have progressed in surgery as far as he did if he had had to work in the rough conditions that prevailed before the introduction of anesthesia.

Lister graduated the following year with the degree of BA. However, he missed the next academic session. The hiatus was the result of a severe personal crisis. He contracted smallpox and, during his convalescence, experienced serious religious doubts, a cause of much angst to such a devout young Victorian as Lister. He also came to question whether he was suited to his planned career in medicine. Lister seems to have had a nervous breakdown, which was followed by some months of idleness as he recovered.

In October 1849 Lister resumed his medical studies at University College. The College's Medical School was small, but unlike its counterparts elsewhere in England, it based its curriculum firmly on the basic sciences. The governing ethos, at least in the early years of the course, was that the biological sciences, and especially experimental physiology, should form the basis of medical education. With the training he had received from his father and his background in natural history, Lister found the character of the curriculum to be particularly congenial. He was especially impressed by the professor of physiology, William Sharpey (1802–80), a leading figure within British microscopical and experimental physiology. Sharpey and Lister got on well together and the professor directed some of the student's earliest researches. Another influential teacher was Thomas Wharton Jones (1808–91), professor of ophthalmic medicine and surgery. Jones was a skilled and dedicated microscopist, and his investigations provided Lister with an important model for his own research work in this area. He also attended William Jenner's (1815–98) chemistry lectures. Throughout his later career, Lister never wavered from the belief, formed at University College, that scientific knowledge and research provided the best foundations of medical practice and offered the key to the improvement of surgery.

At medical school, Lister, who had previously been relatively academically undistinguished, began to excel. His skill in drawing assisted his investigations in dissection and microscopy, and he was awarded gold medals in pathological and comparative anatomy and silver medals in surgery and medicine. Lister was also elected president of the college's student medical society. He graduated MB (1852) and passed the fellowship examinations of the Royal College of Surgeons.

Sharpey happened to be an old friend of James Syme (1799–1870), professor of clinical surgery at Edinburgh University's Medical School. Fifty-four years old, Syme enjoyed an international reputation as a bold, skilled, and innovative surgical operator. In September 1853, at Sharpey's urging, Lister traveled north to visit the Edinburgh Royal Infirmary and observe Syme's surgical practice. Armed with a letter from his old professor, Lister introduced himself to Syme and was very quickly impressed with the surgeon's formidable and original intellect. Lister succeeded in having himself taken on as Syme's dresser. He quickly assimilated Syme's methods and was shortly appointed his house surgeon, a post he held for a year. Lister then began to teach in the extramural school of surgery and, in 1856, became assistant surgeon to the Infirmary.

In 1856 Lister made what was universally regarded in Edinburgh medical circles as a good career move. On 23 April he married Syme's eldest daughter, Agnes. In deference to the custom of his bride and her family, Lister left the Society of Friends and became an Episcopalian. Nevertheless, he continued to receive much moral, intellectual, and financial support from his father, with the financial aid in particular allowing him to devote considerable time to his scientific interests. The Listers' honeymoon was a three-month tour of the Continent, during which Joseph visited many famous hospitals and medical schools. Agnes took a keen interest in her husband's work and assisted him in many of his investigations. She was largely responsible for maintaining his research notebooks. The Listers had no children.

During his early years in Edinburgh, in addition to establishing himself as a practitioner and teacher of surgery, Lister conducted an intensive series of physiological and microscopical investigations. His first research papers, one on the muscular nature of the iris and another on the musculature of the skin, appeared in the *Quarterly Journal of Microscopical Science* (1853). By this time, he had begun an experimental investigation of the function of the lacteal vessels. This was shortly followed by a series of experiments on inflammation and the clotting of the blood, the results of which were later to play an important role in the development of his surgical innovations. In 1857 he presented a paper to the Royal Society entitled 'The Early Stages of Inflammation', in which he described his observations of experimental wounds in the membrane of a bat's wing and the web of a frog's foot. He chose these tissues as experimental objects because they were transparent and, thus, allowed the clotting of blood and other processes associated with healing and inflammation to be visualized with the microscope. As a result of these investigations, Lister was elected FRS (1860).

Also in 1860, Lister secured the post of professor of surgery at Glasgow University. An appointment as a surgeon to the city's Royal Infirmary followed the next year. By the time of Lister's appointment, Glasgow's Infirmary had about six hundred beds. A new Surgical House, in which Lister had his beds and operating theater, was opened in 1861. Like many large hospitals at this time, especially those situated in the industrial cities, Glasgow's Infirmary had a problem with periodic outbreaks of diseases such as erysipelas and gangrene. Postoperative morbidity and mortality were high, largely because of wound sepsis. From the time he took up his chair in Glasgow, Lister focused his experimental work on the problems of suppuration and inflammation. He sought to make observations that could be applied to improving the clinical management of accidental and surgical wounds.

The health problems of the Victorian era were not confined to the hospitals. There was a high incidence of fevers, both epidemic and endemic, among the general population. The problems of hospital morbidity and those of poor urban public health were seen as related, the underlying cause of both being ascribed to the accumulation of decomposing organic matter. Surgical sepsis was held to be due to the putrefaction of dead tissue in the wound, whereas zymotic disease was a product of the insanitary condition of the urban environment, which allowed sewage and refuse to accumulate and decay, producing pestiferous miasmata. What the exact mechanisms of these processes were, however, was a matter of considerable scientific debate. In 1865 Lister's colleague Thomas Anderson (1819–74), a professor of chemistry, drew Lister's attention to the work of Louis Pasteur (1822–95). Pasteur claimed that microscopic living organisms, carried from place to place by the air, caused putrefaction. Lister read the French chemist's publications with great interest and repeated several of his experiments in Glasgow. Lister was especially interested in Pasteur's famous series of investigations with S-necked flasks. The curvature of the neck excluded atmospheric air from the main chamber of the flask. Organic fluids in the flask (Lister used urine) remained fresh for as long as the neck was intact. But if the neck was broken, allowing entry to the air, fermentation and putrefaction followed shortly. Lister saw an analogy between this effect and the cutting of the patient's skin in surgery or by accidental injury. In particular he compared the broken flask to the condition of compound fracture, where the bones protrude through the skin and were thus exposed to the air and the noxious agents it was held to carry. The survival rates of compound-fracture victims were poor, with most of the deaths at this time following from wound sepsis.

Lister became convinced that Pasteur was right—living 'germs' of fermentation and putrefaction were carried in the air. He thus concluded that the causative agents of surgical sepsis must also be present in the atmosphere. Accordingly, Lister sought to exclude air from the surgical wound and also to kill any 'germs' that were already there. He sought, in other words, to interpose a barrier, both chemical and physical, between the air and the cut flesh of the wound. Lister learned of the use of carbolic acid to deodorize sewage and decided to experiment with its application to surgical wound management. Early in 1865, he employed carbolic acid for the first time, in the course of treating a compound fracture of the lower leg of an eleven-year-old boy, James Greenlees. Lister first infused the wound with carbolic and then covered it and the surrounding area with a layer of lint soaked in the acid. The boy made a complete recovery. Shortly afterward, Lister also used this method for the treatment of septic abscesses.

Between 1867 and 1869, Lister published a series of papers in *Lancet* and the *British Medical Journal* in which he articulated his new 'antiseptic system' for the management of surgical wounds. In the first of these papers, he described the successful treatment of several cases of accidental compound fracture. Only two patients in a series of eleven had died, an excellent result by contemporary standards. Lister emphasized that his method was based on the best scientific principles and, in particular, was derived from Pasteur's work on fermentation and his own microscopical and physiological investigations of suppuration and inflammation. This was an unusual way for a nineteenth-century surgeon to adduce support for a technical innovation. Most of his colleagues saw themselves as empirical practitioners, working within and incrementally improving upon a craft tradition.

Lister's views on wound management occasioned much criticism. His claim to the scientific high ground should not obscure the fact that many other surgeons were also attempting to prevent and control surgical sepsis at this time, and a number of different chemicals had been experimented with to assess their potential as antiseptic wound dressings. Lister distanced himself from these trials by maintaining that, to him, carbolic acid was not merely a wound dressing in the conventional sense, but an integral part of a broader antiseptic method. It was, however, generally agreed that carbolic acid irritated the skin around the wound, and Lister himself sought more emollient alternatives.

Several surgeons claimed to have achieved considerable success in the prevention of sepsis by simple but rigorous cleanliness. One of Lister's most formidable and aggressive opponents was Robert Lawson Tait (1845–99), another protégé of Syme, who was now based in Wakefield. In 1868 Tait reported a series of twelve cases of compound fracture, all of which had successfully healed without suppuration except the two he treated using Lister's methods. Some London surgeons reported comparable results. In 1879 Tait moved to Birmingham, where he joined forces with another convinced opponent of Lister's ideas, Sampson Gamgee (1828–86). Tait was a more radical operative innovator than Lister and achieved remarkable success in abdominal surgery without the application of Listerian techniques. Other critics pointed out that, in salubrious environments, wounds exposed to the air often healed without any suppuration or inflammation whatsoever. Veterinary surgeons never adopted the antiseptic method, but achieved good results nevertheless.

The next fifteen years saw intense debate over Lister's system of antiseptic surgery. A retrospective assessment of this controversy is rendered problematic by the fact that surgical mortality was probably falling spontaneously at this time. Wound sepsis is, to some extent, a host-factor disease, and by the 1870s, with improvements in the conditions of trade and employment, the industrial working classes were better nourished and housed than they had previously been. Improvements in hospital hygiene, standards of nursing, and general cleanliness doubtless also played a part.

In 1869 Lister was appointed to the chair of clinical surgery at Edinburgh University. During his years in the Scottish capital, he constantly developed and refined his methods. From his first employment of antisepsis, Lister had insisted that surgical instruments, and anything else that came in contact with the wound, should be immersed in carbolic acid, for a period of time, prior to the commencement of surgery. He also recommended a thorough cleansing of the patient's skin in the vicinity of the wound. However, applying the principles of antisepsis to sutures and ligatures presented Lister with problems that proved time-consuming to resolve. Victorian surgeons used a variety of materials, including silk, horsehair, and silver wire, for ligation. One end of the knot was generally left long enough to protrude from the wound, allowing subsequent removal. But this practice was unacceptable to Lister because, in his view, the corridor created by the strand exposed the depths of the wound to the dangers of sepsis. At first, he experimented with silk threads that he had impregnated with carbolic acid, leaving them buried in the closed wound, in the hope that they would remain inert. But this provided unsatisfactory. Often the wound had to be reopened because of irritation caused by the silk.

Lister undertook a number of animal experiments to find a satisfactory alternative. He knew that surgeons had previously tried using catgut, which was strong, flexible, and cheap. These trials had, however, been disappointing. Catgut softened and lost its strength after about twenty-four hours in the wound. Also, the material was absorbed by the surrounding tissue too quickly to be of clinical use. Eventually, after much trial and error, Lister devised a method of treating catgut that rendered it aseptic, preserved its strength and flexibility, and delayed its absorption. Fresh catgut was steeped in a dilute mixture of chromic and carbolic acid for forty-eight hours and then stored in carbolic oil. Thus treated, catgut ligatures persisted in the body for two to three weeks, which was long enough for most surgical purposes. Lister published the results of these investigations in 1881. Suitably prepared catgut ligatures and sutures quickly came into general use. This was a major technical advance.

In 1871 Lister introduced the carbolic spray apparatus, with the intent to kill germs in the air of the room in which surgery was taking place, before they could reach the wound. His conviction that the causative agents of surgical sepsis were present in the atmosphere was strengthened in the 1870s by the publication of experiments by the eminent physicist John Tyndall (1820–93), in which Tyndall revealed the presence of large numbers of microbial organisms in air-borne dust. Carbolic acid is, however, a metabolic poison, and breathing it in on a daily basis was deleterious to the health of the surgical staff.

Another problem with the antiseptic method was that carbolic dressings could produce sterile necrosis in a wound. Thus, it was often the case that a patient treated by Listerian methods recovered more slowly than one treated more conventionally. The resulting longer bed occupancies did not endear the professor of surgery to the governors of either the Glasgow Infirmary or the Edinburgh Royal Infirmary. Lister spent many years experimenting with different dressings, hoping to find one that would exclude the air and kill microbes in the wound without irritating intact skin or damaging healthy flesh. He introduced dressings based on carbolized putty and carbolized shellac, eventually arriving, in 1889, at the 'double cyanide of mercury and zinc' plaster, which consisted of eight layers of treated gauze covered with an impermeable coating. This remained the standard antiseptic dressing for many years.

In 1877 Lister left Edinburgh to become professor of surgery at King's College, London. He had already antagonized many London surgeons with his criticisms of the manner in which surgery was taught in London. This controversy was an expression of the tension between those who advocated a scientific, experimental approach to surgery and those who defended the craft-based, empirical tradition. Lister returned to London as a proselytizer. On accepting the chair at King's, he insisted that he be allowed to take with him a team of assistants from Edinburgh, in order to ensure that the antiseptic method be performed and taught correctly in London. Notably among the group that went south with Lister was his houseman, William Watson Cheyne (1852–1932), who became a famous surgeon in his own right and one of Lister's most loyal protagonists. Lister's time at King's seems to have been difficult, at least at first. The faculty were sharply divided between supporters and detractors. He attracted few students, and his reforms were said to have been obstructed by the nursing staff. Nevertheless, he gradually developed such a national and international reputation, particularly in Germany, that it became impossible for the London surgical elite not to embrace him. He relinquished his chair in 1892 and retired from practice after the death of his wife (1893).

In the period between his first use of the antiseptic method in 1865 and his retirement, Lister's views on the nature of wound sepsis evolved considerably, as the germ theory itself developed. Lister had not initially regarded the 'germs' of surgical sepsis as distinct pathogenic species but rather as nonspecific entities associated with the processes of putrefaction and decay. In 1867 he had also accepted the orthodox view that the presence of pus in a wound was a matter for concern only if it smelt unpleasant, indicating putrefaction. Pus had formed in eight of the cases of compound fracture described in the first *Lancet* paper without Lister associating this with microbial

activity, or regarding it as a failure of the antiseptic method. Lister also continued to hold the traditional belief that, in constitutionally susceptible individuals, erysipelas could be produced by local irritation, such as exposure to cold, in the absence of microbes. However, by the mid-1870s, influenced in particular by the researches of John Scott Burdon Sanderson (1828–1905) that had demonstrated that pathogenic bacteria were not carried in the atmosphere, Lister acknowledged that the germs of sepsis were transmitted by contaminated surfaces rather than by the air. In 1875, he concluded, 'All that would be needful would be to purify the surface of the skin of the part to be operated upon by means of some efficient antiseptic, to have my own hands, and those of my assistants, and also the instruments, similarly purified; and then the operation might be performed without the antiseptic spray . . . and no one would rejoice more than myself to be able to dispense with it.'

By the early 1880s, a new version of the germ theory, based more upon the work of Robert Koch (1843–1910) than on Pasteur's research, began to gain general acceptance in Britain. Koch attributed the different infectious diseases to the invasion of the body by specific microbial pathogens. Lister's followers, notably Cheyne, were initially reluctant to accept that this version of germ theory applied to surgical sepsis, but by the late 1880s, the specific pathogen hypothesis had become generally accepted. By this time, moreover, following the example of the German surgeons, surgery was increasingly being practiced not on antiseptic principles, but on aseptic principles. The emphasis of the aseptic method was on ensuring that the surgical environment was free of pathogens rather than focusing on the sterility of the wound.

Lister's followers claimed that the aseptic method was simply an extension of the principles expounded by their master. It might indeed be argued that the introduction of the carbolic spray was aseptic in intent given that the aim was, in effect, to sterilize the surgical environment rather than merely the wound. On the other hand, Lister had begun to abandon the spray, whenever circumstances were favorable, in the late 1870s. It might, perhaps, equally be argued that Lawson Tait and the London surgeons, with their emphasis on general cleanliness, anticipated a major tenet of asepsis. One might also maintain that the Listerian method, as it evolved through the 1870s, became more similar to 'cleanliness and cold water' than it had originally been. Late in his career, Lister acknowledged that a regime that advocated strict cleanliness was antiseptic in intent and effect, if not in scientific principle.

Whatever the rights and wrongs of the matter, Lister and the Listerians bagged much of the credit for the improvement in the safety of surgery in the last decades of the nineteenth century. Surgery certainly benefited from the increased confidence that surgeons gained from their conviction that surgical sepsis could be prevented. The surgical repertoire expanded rapidly. Lister came to be regarded as a hero, almost as a secular saint. He was loaded with honors, both at home and abroad. In 1880 he was elected to the council of the RCS. He would later have been President, had he wished. In 1883 Lister was made a baronet and, in 1897, raised to the peerage. He was the first British surgeon to be ennobled, a potent indication of how the status of his profession had improved in the last decades of the nineteenth century. In 1895 he was elected president of the Royal Society, and in 1896 he was president of the British Association for the Advancement of Science. In 1902 Lister was inaugurated as one of the twelve original members of the newly founded Order of Merit. Upon his death (1912), he would have been buried in Westminster Abbey had he not expressed a wish to be interred beside his wife in Hampstead Cemetery.

Although not a radical surgical innovator in the class of Syme, Tait, or his own protégé, William Macewen (1848–1924), Lister modified several surgical procedures and invented some new methods of treatment. He improved the operations of lithotomy, mastectomy, varicotomy, and the excision of the wrist and led the way in the elective opening of knee and elbow joints. His work on the wiring of fractured patellae was particularly important. As well as introducing absorbable ligatures, he pioneered the use of wound-drainage tubes.

The key to Lister's fame and his lasting reputation lies in his advocacy, by practice and precept, of a scientific approach to surgical problems. He always based his claims on experimental evidence, much of which derived from his own researches. The pioneers of the germ theory in France and Germany recognized Lister as a colleague and a peer. His testimony to the Royal Commission on vivisection, which reported in 1876, was influential. He was one of the founders of the British Institute of Preventive Medicine, modeled on the Pasteur Institute in Paris, and he became its first chairman in 1891. In 1903 it was renamed the Lister Institute, in his honor. In Britain, Lister was adopted as a champion by those who campaigned for science to be accorded a greater role, not only in medicine, but also in industry, education, and the life of the nation as a whole. It is very significant that he was president of both the Royal Society and the British Association simultaneously. The two organizations were the twin pillars, exclusive and inclusive, respectively, of the pro-science movement in the late Victorian period. Lister's achievement was to raise the prestige of both surgery and science, hugely and irreversibly.

Bibliography

Primary: 1909. *The collected papers of Joseph, Baron Lister* 2 vols. (Oxford).

Secondary: Worboys, Michael, 2000. *Spreading Germs: Disease Theories and Medical Practice in Britain, 1865–1900* (Cambridge); Pennington, Thomas Hugh, 1995. 'Listerism, Its Decline and Its Persistence: The Introduction of Aseptic Surgical Techniques in Three British Teaching Hospitals, 1890–99.' *Medical History* 39: 35–60; Granshaw, Lindsay, 1992. '"Upon This Principle I Have Based a Practice": The Development and Reception of Antisepsis in Britain, 1867–90' in Pickstone, J., ed., *Medical Innovations in Historical Perspective* (London) pp. 17–46; Lawrence, Christopher, and Richard Dixey, 1992. 'Practising on Principle: Joseph Lister and the Germ Theories of Disease' in Lawrence, C., ed., *Medical Theory, Surgical Practice: Studies in the History of Surgery* (London) pp. 153–215; Gibson, Thomas, 1990. 'Evolution of Catgut Ligatures: The Endeavours and Success of Joseph Lister and William Macewen.' *British Journal of Surgery* 77: 824–825; Hamilton, David, 1982. 'The Nineteenth-Century Surgical Revolution—Antisepsis or Better Nutrition?' *Bulletin of the History of Medicine* 56: 30–40; Godlee, R. J., 1917. *Lord Lister* (London); *DSB*; *Oxford DNB*.

Malcolm Nicolson

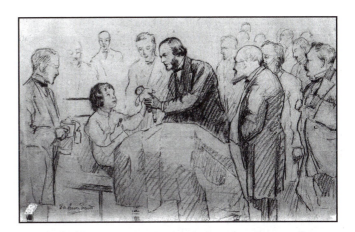

Joseph Lister at the bedside of a sick child. Drawing by Leeson Everette. Wellcome Library, London.

LISTON, ROBERT   (b. Ecclesmachan, Linlithgowshire, Scotland, 28 October 1794; d. London, England, 7 December 1847), *surgery*.

Born in the manse, Liston was the eldest son of the Rev Henry Liston, minister of the parish, who principally educated him. In 1808 he entered the Arts Faculty of the University of Edinburgh. In 1810 he transferred to the Extra-mural Medical School as assistant to John Barclay (1758–1826), the distinguished human and comparative anatomist and physiologist, and remained with him until 1815, when he was his senior assistant and prosector. Liston undoubtedly gained his love of anatomy from Barclay. From 1814 to 1816, he was employed in the Edinburgh Royal Infirmary as surgeon's clerk first to George Bell and then to Dr Gillespie.

He moved to the London Hospital in 1816 and worked under Sir William Blizard and Mr Thomas Blizard. In 1816 he obtained his MRCS diploma and later attended Abernethy's lectures at St Bartholomew's Hospital. He then rejoined Barclay, and during 1816–17 taught anatomy with his distant cousin James Syme (1799–1870). In 1818 Liston passed the FRCSEdin examination with a thesis entitled 'Strictures of the Urethra and some of their consequences'. After a disagreement with Barclay, Liston and Syme set up their own anatomical teaching class, although difficulties were encountered in obtaining adequate numbers of subjects, and many had to be obtained from London and Dublin. Liston later withdrew from teaching anatomy to undertake full-time surgical practice, leaving his class to Syme. The friendship that formerly existed between them soon turned to animosity. Syme eventually gave up teaching anatomy in about 1826 to concentrate on the teaching and practice of surgery.

Liston's appointment to the Infirmary was terminated in 1822 after a series of quarrels with the management and some of his colleagues. However, in 1827, after Liston apologized for his earlier behavior, he was reinstated to the surgical staff and in February 1828 was appointed an assistant surgeon. When James Syme, rather than Liston, was appointed to the Edinburgh chair of clinical surgery in 1833, Liston took this personally and decided to leave Edinburgh. In 1834 he accepted an invitation to become a surgeon to the hospital attached to London University (later University College Hospital). In 1835 he accepted the chair of clinical surgery there. In 1840 he became a Member of the Council of the RCS, and in 1846 he was elected to their Board of Examiners. In May 1841 he was elected FRS.

He was possibly the most dexterous surgeon in the pre-anesthetic era and had a profound knowledge of anatomy. When he amputated, it was said that the gleam of the knife was followed instantaneously by the sound of the bone being sawn, so that the two actions appeared almost simultaneous. Liston also carried out the first major operation under ether anesthesia undertaken in Europe. This was carried out at University College Hospital, London, in December 1846 and was a mid-thigh amputation of the left leg on a patient for chronic osteomyelitis of the tibia. This operation was successfully performed, and the patient recovered with no awareness that the operation had been performed. Liston died of a ruptured aneurysm of the arch of the aorta and was buried in Highgate Cemetery. He was not a scientific surgeon and was a relatively poor speaker. He wrote a number of textbooks on surgery as well as numerous pamphlets and case reports.

Bibliography

Primary: 1831. *Elements of Surgery* (London and Edinburgh, 2nd edn. 1840); 1837. *Practical Surgery* (London, 2nd edn. 1838, 3rd edn. 1840, 4th edn. 1846).

Secondary: Stanley, Peter, 2003. *For Fear of Pain: British Surgery. 1790–1850* (Amsterdam); *Plarr's Lives*; *Oxford DNB*.

Matthew Howard Kaufman

LITTRÉ, ÉMILE   (b. Paris, France, 1 February 1801; d. Paris, 2 June 1881), *history of medicine, philology, philosophy, politics.*

Littré's father, Michel-François Littré, had been a staunch republican during the French Revolution, as was his mother, Sophie Johannot. Émile attended the lycée Louis-le Grand.

A shoulder injury and a dislike of mathematics prevented him from continuing on to the École Polytechnique as he had planned.

In 1823 Littré decided to study medicine at the École de Médecine, and two years later, he earned a post of hospital intern. He also spent much time in Pierre Rayer's anatomical laboratory. Although his medical studies lasted seven years, including four as an intern, he never submitted the required thesis to obtain a medical degree. Broader scholarly interests and the untimely death of his father in 1827 led Littré to earn money teaching languages. He mastered classical and oriental languages, including Sanskrit. In 1844 he began to work on a dictionary of the French language based on historic usages of words, which was finally completed in 1874. A supplement appeared from 1877 to 1882, winning him lasting fame as a philologist. In 1839 he was made a member of the Académie des inscriptions et belles lettres.

That same year, Littré published the first volume of his monumental ten-volume translation of and commentary on the works of Hippocrates, in which he depicted Hippocrates as an opponent of superstition in medicine. Around 1840, Littré met Auguste Comte and became a devoted follower of Comte's positivist doctrine. The young physician Charles Robin, who adopted Littré's form of scientific positivism, was instrumental in founding the Société de Biologie in 1848, dedicated to those principles. Littré was elected an honorary member. Robin joined Littré in publishing the *Dictionaire de Médecine* (a reworking of Nysten's dictionary), which appeared in 1852. This caused a scandal when they defined 'soul' as 'a term which in biology, considered anatomically, designates the complete functions of the brain and the spinal cord and physiologically, the entire function of awareness'. They also defined the human as 'mammiferous animal, of the order of primates, family of bimanes, characterized in taxonomy by a skin covering on which hair is scant'. Littré's contribution to the history of medicine led to election as an associate member of the Académie de Médecine in 1858. At his country home in Mesnil-le Roi, he put his knowledge of medicine to work by treating the complaints of the local peasants without charge in association with a local physician.

When Littré was proposed for the Académie Française for the first time in 1863, he was vehemently opposed by the Bishop of Orleans, Monsigneur Félix Dupanloup, and his candidature failed. When he was proposed again in 1875, Dupanloup again opposed him, claiming that a vote for Littré was an endorsement of 'materialism and socialism'. Times had changed, however, and Littré was elected.

Politically, Littré was a staunch republican, though never radical. He participated in the 1830 revolution, and during the 1848 revolution, Littré became a member of the Municipal Council of Paris but resigned when Louis Napoleon was named president of the republic. He returned to politics after Napoleon was deposed during the Franco-Prussian war. He was elected a deputy of the Seine in February 1871 and senator in 1875. That same year, Littré was inaugurated as a Freemason into the lodge Clément Amitié. He died six years later after a long and painful illness.

Bibliography

Primary: 1839–1861. *Oeuvres d' Hippocrate* 10 vols. (Paris); 1852. (ed., with Robin, Charles) *Dictionnaire de Médecine* (Paris); 1872. *Médecines et Médecins* (Paris).

Secondary: Hamburger, Jean. 1988. *Monsieur Littré* (Paris); Rullière, Roger. 1982. 'Les études médicales d'Émile Littré, Actes du colloque du centenaire de la mort de Emile Littré. *Revue de Synthèse* 106–108, 255–262 (see also other contributions in this issue by G. Canguilhem, A. Petit, etc.); Aquarone, Stanislas. 1958. *The Life and Works of Emile Littré* (Leiden).

Joy Harvey

LIU, WANSU 劉完素 (aka LIU, SHOUZHEN 劉守真, LIU, HEJIAN 劉河間) (b. Hejian, Hebei province, China, 1110 or 1120; d. Hejian, China, 1200), *Chinese medicine.*

Liu Wansu was a Jin dynasty (1115–1234) physician, one of the 'Four Masters of Medicine' of the Jin Yuan Periods, which also included Li Gao (李杲), Zhang Congzheng (張從正), and Zhu Zhenheng (朱震亨). These four physicians elaborated on the ancient canons of medicine and established four different etiologies of disease that gave rise to separate schools of medical thought.

Liu came from a poor family. Early in his life, his mother fell ill and died because of the lack of medical help. This motivated Liu's interest in medicine. He apparently devoted his life to treating the common people. Three times, he refused official civil service positions offered to him by the Jin emperor, Zhangzong, preferring to practice medicine by combining the doctrines of the *Inner Canon* with the pragmatic reality of everyday clinical practice.

Liu claimed that the contemporary practice of prescribing heating medicines was inappropriate to the pathologies he observed. The correct course of action should be to administer cooling medicines. Accordingly, he was later considered the founder of the Cooling School. He stressed that the origin of most diseases arises was in two organs—the spleen and stomach—and claimed that of the Six Climatic Configurations, fire was the most prominent.

When Liu was twenty-five, he focused on the *Inner Canon.* He studied the text for many years, and it became the basis for his medical practice. Unlike many of his predecessors, he did not annotate this ancient canon. He used contemporary medical knowledge to adapt the doctrines of classical medicine to contemporary practice. He presented his new exposition of medical knowledge and practice in a book titled *Profound Model of Disease Origin According to the Basic Questions.* Here he used all the existing commentaries of the *Suwen* volume of the *Inner Canon, materia medica* collections, and the *Shanghan lun* 傷寒論 [Treatise on Cold Damage Disorders] to compile a new text integrating ancient and contemporary knowledge on the origin of diseases.

Liu is also known for comprehensively integrating the Five Transformations and Six Climatic Configurations (*Wuyun liuqi* 五運六氣) into medical theory and practice. This doctrine concerned the correspondence of changes in the world and in the body based on the Five Agents, Yin and Yang, and the four seasons. So long as the seasonal changes and characteristics appeared at their proper time, the body should correspond to the changes; however, when climatic factors appeared off schedule, e.g. a heat wave in the middle of winter or a snowstorm in spring, these untimely changes promoted diseases. Based on his studies of the *Inner Canon* and the effects of the climatic changes on the body, Liu claimed that disease arose predominantly from the fire pathogen. Thus, the preferred course of treatment was cooling therapy, which used cool or cold natured drugs.

The renaissance of the Five Transformations and Six Climatic Configurations began during the early decades of the twelfth century when the Song dynasty emperor Huizong (r. 1101–26) endorsed it in two of his medical compilations. Liu took the use of this doctrine to another level. He proclaimed that seeking to study medicine without understanding the doctrine was futile and that, although existing texts used diagrams and elaborate discussions, they never applied this knowledge in real clinical settings. According to Liu, treatment should be determined according to the physical location of the patient—i.e. the environmental influence—and the specific season when the disease was contracted. Liu also stressed both the patient's physical constitution and symptoms when determining the correct treatment. In subsequent generations the doctrine of Five Transformations and Six Climatic Configurations pervaded every aspect of medical theory and practice.

Bibliography

Primary: 1182. *Suwen xuanji yuanbing shi* 素問玄機原病式 [Profound model of disease origin according to the Yellow Emperor's Basic Questions]; 1186. *Huangdi suwen xuanming lun fang* 黃帝素問宣明論方 [Proclaiming and discussing formulas according to the Yellow Emperor's Basic Questions]; 1186. *Suwen bingji qi yi bao ming ji* 素問病機氣宜保命集 [Pathogenesis, proper *qi*, and maintaining life according to the Yellow Emperor's Basic Questions].

Secondary: Goldschmidt, Asaf (forthcoming). *The Evolution of Chinese Medicine: Northern Song Dynasty, 960–1127* (London); Unschuld, Paul, 1985. *Medicine in China: A History of Ideas* (Berkeley, CA) pp. 154–188.

Asaf Goldschmidt

LIVADAS, GREGORY ACHILLEA (b. Cephalonia, Greece, 8 January 1894; d. Athens, Greece, 5 October 1977), *public health, malariology.*

Gregory, the son of physician Achilleas Livadas of Cephalonia and his Italian wife, Ermelinda, attended school in

Cephalonia before studying medicine at the University of Naples, Italy. He graduated, with honors, in 1915.

He returned to Greece, joined the army's medical service (1916), and participated in Greece's ill-fated Asia Minor campaign (1919–22) before undertaking postgraduate studies in microbiology and parasitology at the universities of Naples and Rome (1923–24) and at the Superior School of Malariology in Rome (1928).

The year 1928 provided a turning point in Greece's public health efforts. Newly reelected, Premier Venizelos declared his willingness to modernize Greece's archaic medical services and combat the country's ancient scourge, malaria. He was instrumental in securing the assistance of both the League of Nations and the Rockefeller Foundation toward that aim.

Livadas was drawn into this ambitious program. He served as assistant to the Foundation's representative in Greece (1931–36). During the same period, he benefited from a Foundation fellowship by studying for the MPH degree at the Johns Hopkins University (1934).

In 1936 he became director of the division of malariology at the Athens School of Hygiene. Two years later, General Metaxas's regime created an autonomous Malaria Service within the School. The Service became responsible for undertaking antimalaria work across Greece. Livadas, by now the School's dean, became director of the Service and, effectively, leader of Greece's antimalaria efforts. The Service's very promising work came to a halt when the Axis powers occupied Greece (1941).

At the time of liberation (1944), Livadas and UNRRA officials identified malaria as a problem that had to be solved for progress to take place in Greece. In 1945 pilot studies confirmed the effectiveness of newly imported DDT; Greece was, in 1946, the first Balkan country to launch a nationwide antimalaria campaign. The campaign, jointly undertaken by Livadas's Malaria Service and UNRRA, coincided with the Greek Civil War. Although the conflict troubled antimalaria work, activities had succeeded, by 1949, in reducing malaria morbidity and mortality figures to a small fraction of their prewar values. DDT's effectiveness greatly contributed to the campaign's success.

In 1949 the Ministry of Social Welfare became responsible for antimalaria work and the School's Malaria Service was dismantled. Livadas, disappointed with this development, resigned his position as School dean.

In 1951 he played a highly important role in an experimental scheme that aimed at investigating the feasibility of interrupting house-spraying activities, without compromising the outcome of antimalaria work, in areas where several years' intensive antimalaria work had taken place. Two areas participated in the scheme: Crete and the Peloponnese. Preliminary results suggested that the interruption of the house-spraying program was possible.

In the same year, Livadas reported to the WHO the identification of the phenomenon of anopheline resistance:

Greece's *Anopheles* had started to develop resistance to DDT, which soon extended to other insecticides. In the following years, Livadas and coworkers described their findings on the phenomenon in the Greek and international medical press.

The WHO took both the increasing importance of anopheline resistance and the preliminary results of the Crete-Peloponnese experiment into consideration while shaping its malaria eradication policy of the 1950s.

Livadas retired from the Athens School in 1959. In the following years he offered his services to the WHO—as a consultant he contributed to the antimalaria efforts of, among others, Cameroon, Jordan, and Afghanistan. He received numerous awards during his career including, that of Greece's Royal Order of the Phoenix (1953).

With his wife, Aphrodite, he had one daughter.

Bibliography

Primary: 1940. (with Sphangos, J.) *Malaria in Greece, 1930–40* (Athens); 1973. 'The History of a Great Achievement: The Eradication of Malaria.' *Akadimaiki Iatriki* 37 (no. 9, 409): 1–64 (in Greek).

Secondary: Vassiliou, Maria, 2005. 'Politics, Public Health, and Development: Malaria in 20th Century Greece.' DPhil thesis, University of Oxford.

Maria Vassiliou

LIVINGSTONE, DAVID (b. Blantyre, Scotland, 19 March 1813; d. Chitambo's Village, Zambia, 1 May 1873), *missionary medicine.*

Livingstone (originally Livingston) was born to a working-class family in Blantyre, Scotland, the second of seven children. The family shared a room in a tenement building owned by the mill company, where Livingstone started working at the age of ten. He was taught to read and write by his father, and in addition to schooling in the evenings provided by the company, he taught himself Latin and developed a love of natural history. At the age of nineteen, he was promoted, and with his increased wages, by 1836 he had saved enough money to enter Andersonian University, Glasgow, to study medicine, where he was taught by Andrew Buchanan. Two years later, he suspended his course and spent a year at the London Missionary Society in Chipping Ongar, Essex. He moved to London in 1840 to complete his medical studies at the British and Foreign Medical School, the Aldersgate Street Dispensary, Charing Cross Hospital, and Moorfields Hospital, and at the end of the year, he qualified as a Licentiate of the Faculty of Physicians and Surgeons of Glasgow. The same month, he was also ordained a missionary in London, setting sail in December for South Africa and the mission station at Kuruman as a missionary doctor.

From 1841 until his death in 1873, Livingstone explored the interior of central and southern Africa. His initial aim was to spread Christianity and bring commerce and 'civilization' to these regions, but his later missions were more concerned with exploration, first of the Zambesi and its tributaries, and later to find the source of the Nile. During this time he returned to Britain only twice, in 1856 and in 1864.

Livingstone was one of the first medical missionaries to enter southern Africa and the first in central Africa, and he was often the first European to appear to local tribes. He won their trust as a healer and medicine man and gained such a reputation among the villages he visited that he eventually had to limit his treatment to those with serious illness. He was particularly sought for his skills in obstetrics, the surgical removal of tumors, and ophthalmology.

Livingstone was a keen and accurate observer; he was also a prolific writer, and his journals, letters, and published narratives provide some of the earliest observations on diseases in Africa such as tropical ulcer, scurvy, and malaria. He was one of the first to administer quinine correctly, and thus, unlike previous expeditions in Africa, his parties of explorers suffered a comparatively low death rate from malaria. The recipe for this remedy, known as 'Livingstone's Rousers', was recorded in his travel writings and subsequently manufactured in tabloid form by Burroughs Wellcome and used until the 1920s. More than thirty years before Ronald Ross established the link between mosquitoes and malaria, Livingstone had recognized an association: 'Myriads of mosquitoes showed, as probably they always do, the presence of malaria' (1865, p. 368). In 1854 Livingstone also observed the association between relapsing fever and the bite of the tampan (tick). Additionally, his experience in Africa led him to make connections between the environment and climate and diseases such as pneumonia, typhoid, and dysentery.

During his final years, Livingstone was beset with health problems, but despite ill health, he refused to leave Africa, where he died in 1873. Livingstone's posthumous fame was largely owing to the efforts of the journalist Henry Stanley. After his death, his body was returned to Britain for burial in Westminster Abbey.

Bibliography

Primary: 1857. *Missionary Travels and Researches in South Africa including a sketch of sixteen years' residence in the interior of Africa.* (London); 1865. (with Livingstone, Charles) *Narrative of an Expedition to the Zambesi and Its Tributaries, and the Discovery of Lakes Shirwa and Nyassa, 1858–1864* (London).

Secondary: Jeal, Tim, 1973. *David Livingstone* (London); Gelfand, M., 1957. *Livingstone the Doctor* (Oxford); *Oxford DNB.*

Sharon Messenger and
Caroline Overy

LLOYD, JOHN URI   (b. West Bloomfield, New York, USA, 19 April 1849; d. Van Nuys, California, USA, 9 April 1936), *pharmacy, pharmaceutical manufacturing, sectarian medicine, eclecticism.*

Despite his places of birth and death, Lloyd moved with his parents, Sophia Webster and Nelson Marvin, to Boone County, Kentucky, in 1853, and it was in the Cincinnati/Northern Kentucky area that he would spend most of his life. An indifferent student, his penchant for constructing homespun chemistry experiments with his mother's kitchen appliances caused his parents to suggest a career in pharmacy. After apprenticing to W. J. M. Gordon in Cincinnati for two years, he joined George Eger for further training. Although apprenticeship was typically all most pharmacists had for a professional education, Lloyd augmented his practical apothecary studies with chemistry lectures under Roberts Bartholow at the Ohio Medical College.

Lloyd soon secured a position with H. M. Merrell, a pharmacist specializing in botanical preparations for eclectic practitioners. Eventually, a series of mergers transformed the Merrell firm into a partnership owned and operated by Lloyd and his two younger brothers, Nelson Ashley and Curtis Gates. Established as Lloyd Brothers in 1885, the company manufactured botanical medicines (the most popular being 'Lloyd's Specifics') until its posthumous sale to the S. B. Pennick Company in 1938. This lucrative business allowed Lloyd to devote himself to amassing books on pharmacy and pharmacognosy. His collection eventually grew into one of the largest in the United States.

But Lloyd's manufacturing concerns were but one aspect of his varied career. Despite his devotion to sectarian medicine, Lloyd rose to become one of the leaders of mainstream American pharmacy. He was a teacher and a scholar serving on the faculty of the Eclectic Medical Institute from 1878 to 1895, lecturing on chemistry and pharmacy. He contributed hundreds of articles to the *Eclectic Medical Journal,* the *Proceedings of the American Pharmaceutical Association,* and other pharmacy journals of the day; his *Chemistry of Medicines* (1881) was a popular textbook that ran through eight editions. In 1887 he was elected president of the American Pharmaceutical Association (APhA). Three times he won the coveted Ebert Prize, given by the APhA for outstanding original research, and in 1920 he was awarded pharmacy's highest honor, the Remington Medal. Along with manufacturing and scholarship, Lloyd was responsible for numerous medical and pharmaceutical patents—e.g., 'Cold Still Extractor', 'Percolating and Concentrating Apparatus', an improved 'Medicine dropper or Syringe', an atropine sulfate used by the U.S. Army for eye wounds during World War I, and others.

Equally eclectic in the vernacular sense, Lloyd became a literary figure of some note. His *Etidorpha, or, The End of Earth* (1895) was an early sci-fi thriller before such a name was even applied to the genre, and his Stringtown series (six novels published from 1900 to 1934) were popular local color stories that caught the attention of other important literati like James Lane Allen and William Henry Venable. Lloyd's acceptance within the day's small circle of cultural elites is established by the fact that he shared the dinner table with Mark Twain's daughter at the literary giant's seventieth birthday party.

Nevertheless, Lloyd is best remembered for his contributions to pharmacy and his role as the most prominent and honored of American medical eclectics. The financial trust established by the brothers in 1917 has perpetuated the Cincinnati library, which bears their name to the present day. It remains one of the largest pharmacognosy libraries in the world and is a lasting testament to this leading American eclectic.

Bibliography

Primary: 1881. *The Chemistry of Medicines* (Cincinnati); 1882. 'Precipitates in Fluid Extracts.' *Proceedings of the American Pharmaceutical Association* 30: 509–518; 1921. *Origin and History of All the Pharmacopoeial Vegetable Drugs* (Washington, DC).

Secondary: Flannery, Michael A., 1998. *John Uri Lloyd: The Great American Eclectic* (Carbondale, IL); Simons, Corine Miller, 1972. *John Uri Lloyd: His Life and His Works* (Cincinnati); *DAMB*.

Michael A. Flannery

LOCKHART, WILLIAM (b. Liverpool, England, 3 October 1811; d. Blackheath, London, England, 29 April 1896), *surgery, missionary medicine.*

Lockhart studied medicine at the Meath Hospital in Dublin and Guy's Hospital in London and became a member of the Royal College of Surgeons (England) in April 1834. The London Missionary Society sent Lockhart to China as a medical missionary in 1838, and on the ship he met Catherine Parkes, whom he married in 1841. She was a sister of Sir Harry Parkes, a diplomat who played important roles in several Sino-British negotiations. Catherine was then traveling to Macao to visit her cousin Mary, the wife of the missionary Karl Friedrich Gützlaff.

After a brief stay in Canton, Lockhart proceeded to Macao to open a hospital in March 1839. Due to the looming Sino-British conflict, Lockhart left Macao for Batavia in September 1839. Lockhart moved to Chusan in June 1840 after British forces captured the island. In Chusan he opened a hospital, where about 3,500 Chinese patients were treated. He also witnessed a large number of British troops suffering from dysentery and fevers. Lockhart was compelled to leave for Hong Kong in February 1841 after the troops withdrew. He supervised the building of a missionary hospital in Hong Kong and returned to Chusan in June 1843 before moving onto Shanghai later in the year. Lockhart established a missionary hospital in Shanghai and stayed there until his return to England in 1857, when he was elected FRCS.

After the Anglo-French joint expedition, the Chinese government was compelled to open Peking to foreign residence in 1860. Seizing the opportunity, Lockhart returned to China and established a hospital in the capital in October 1861. He reported a successful medical practice with a large number of Chinese patients from all walks of life. He also conducted medical topographical observations of the city and concluded that its locality was healthy. Lockhart returned to England in 1864, leaving the hospital in the care of John Hepburn Dudgeon, a fellow medical missionary of the London Missionary Society.

Besides being the first British medical missionary to China, Lockhart was renowned for his account of the early history of Protestant medical missions to that country. In his book, Lockhart robustly defended the use of medicine in missionary enterprise. He argued that medical missionaries should be laymen with proper medical qualifications rather than ordained ministers with limited medical training. Unlike most medical missionaries, Lockhart held favorable opinions about Chinese medicine. Although he was critical of its theoretical principles, Lockhart claimed that Chinese medicine contained useful information about medicinal substances. Lockhart also praised Chinese physicians for being observant, experienced, and prudent, and he acknowledged the benefits that Chinese medical techniques such as moxa brought to the patients. Lockhart's interest in Chinese medicine prompted him to translate a Chinese treatise on midwifery into English, which was published in the *Dublin Journal of Medical Science* in 1842.

After returning to England, Lockhart continued to practice medicine in Blackheath and regularly attended the Board meeting of the London Missionary Society, donating his collection of Chinese books to the Society in 1892.

Bibliography

Primary: 1841. 'Report of the Medical Missionary Society's operation at Chusan in 1840–1' in *The First and Second Reports of the Medical Missionary Society in China* (Macao) pp. 21–33; 1842. 'A Treatise on Midwifery, a New Edition published in the Fifth Year of Taou Kwong (1825)' translated from the Chinese by W. Lockhart, Esq. M.D. (communicated by Dr. Churchill). *The Dublin Journal of Medical Science* 91: 333–369; 1861. *The Medical Missionary in China: A Narrative of Twenty Years' Experience* (London); 1863. *The First Report of the London Missionary Society's Hospital at Peking* (Shanghai); 1864. *The Second Report of the London Missionary Society's Hospital at Peking* (Shanghai).

Secondary: Sibree, James, 1923. *London Missionary Society: A Register of Missionaries, Deputations, etc. from 1796 to 1923* (London); Legge, James, 1896. 'Obituary. William Lockhart, FRCS.' *The Chronicle of the London Missionary Society* (n. s.) 5: 139–140; *Plarr's Lives.*

Shang-Jen Li

LOGHEM, JOHANNES JACOBUS VAN (b. Amsterdam, the Netherlands, 10 April 1878; d. Amsterdam, 31 October 1968), *bacteriology, epidemiology, hygiene.*

Born as the son of Martinus Gesinus Lambertus van Loghem and Sara Geertruida de Bruin, van Loghem studied medicine in Amsterdam between 1895 and 1902. In 1903 he defended an anatomical thesis—supervised by Louis Bolk—cum laude. He continued his education in Paris (with Elie Mechnikov at the Institut Pasteur), Prague (with Hans Chiari), Strasbourg (J. Forster), Liverpool (Ronald Ross), and

Amsterdam (Pieter Ruitinga and Rudolph H. Saltet), where he was appointed lecturer of bacteriology in 1907.

Keen on increasing his bacteriological and epidemiological knowledge and experience, van Loghem and his wife—Johanna Christina Wilhelmina Pouw—moved to the Dutch East Indies in 1908, where he was appointed substitute director of the Pathological Laboratory in Medan, Sumatra. His main interest was in the health conditions of Chinese and Japanese immigrants working on the Sumatra tobacco plantations under bad circumstances. In 1911 the Dutch government put him in charge of the fight against a plague epidemic on Java. Van Loghem's approach emphasized improving living conditions, in an attempt to prevent contact between man and rat. In 1912 van Loghem was appointed director of the department of tropical hygiene of the Colonial Institute in Amsterdam; four years later, he became extraordinary professor there, presenting an inaugural address called 'Klimaat en ziekte' [Climate and disease]. In 1919 he was appointed extraordinary professor of tropical hygiene at Wageningen Agricultural University; this time, his address was on 'Ziekte en parasitisme' [Disease and parasitism]. In 1923 van Loghem succeeded his teacher Saltet as full professor of Hygiene and Medical Police at the University of Amsterdam, resigning from his post at the Colonial Institute. In the same year, he became a member of the Health Council, the independent advisory board of the Dutch government in health matters. In 1948 he retired as professor, and two years later, he retired as a member of the Health Council.

Van Loghem shaped the discipline of hygiene in the Netherlands, theoretically as well as institutionally. Having great admiration for the work on the variability of species by Hugo de Vries and Martinus Beyerinck, he did much research on the variability of microbes in different cultures. Van Loghem concluded that microbes had strong adaptive qualities that enabled them to change shape, chemical qualities, antigenetic structure, and virulence. Contrary to de Vries and Beyerinck, however, van Loghem argued that these changes were not related to the genotype, but rather to the phenotype. Crucial to his work on the variability of microbes was the concept of opportunistic infection: infections need not be the result of contagion following contact, but may be caused by microbes and viruses already present, causing disease only under special circumstances. The concept played an important role in his understanding of natural antibodies, in his approach to catching a cold, tuberculosis, meningococcemia, or the El Tor strain of cholera, and in his approach to other topics. Having also traveled in North Africa and the Middle East, van Loghem published on the etiology and the epidemiology of such diseases as the plague, cholera, typhoid fever, and dysentery.

Van Loghem's hygienic interests had a practical component. Strongly convinced of the value of sanitary measures, he advocated sanitary training for general practitioners. In the 1920s, he made study trips to the United States, Great Britain, and Denmark to inform himself about educating sanitary workers. In 1926 the first course of the new curriculum—put together by van Loghem and Anna Charlotte Ruys, his later successor—started, paying much attention to microbiology, immunology, statistics, nutrition, sanitary measures, and the fight against contagious disease. Even though the curriculum was discontinued after a few years because of lack of interest, van Loghem was important for the Dutch field of hygiene. In 1919 he joined the editorial board of *Nederlands tijdschrift voor geneeskunde* [Dutch journal of medicine]; he was to remain a member of the board for nearly fifty years, until he was ninety years old. His wide-ranging hygienic expertise led him to publish a handbook on the topic in 1935, *Algemeene gezondheidsleer* [General hygiene], which went through a sixth edition in 1956.

Bibliography

Primary: 1920. *Vraagstukken der Indische hygiëne* (Amsterdam); 1929. (with Brenkman, C. J., and A. Ch. Ruys) 'De Amsterdamse leergangen tot opleiding van hygiënisten.' *Nederlands tijdschrift voor geneeskunde* 73: I, 469–477 ; 1933. *Tropische gezondheidsleer* (Amsterdam); 1935. *Algemeene gezondheidsleer* (Amsterdam); 1951. *Inleiding tot de geneeskunde* (Haarlem).

Secondary: Loghem, J. J. van, Jr., and J. van der Noordaa, 2002. 'Johannes Jacobus van Loghem (1878–1968), Microbioloog-hygiënist' in Kaandorp, C. J. E., et al., eds., *Erflaters van de geneeskunde. Beroemde Nederlandse artsen beschreven door hun (kinds)kinderen* (Alphen aan den Rijn) pp. 128–137; Ruys, A. Ch., 1968. 'Prof.dr. J. J. van Loghem negentig jaar.' *Nederlands tijdschrift voor geneeskunde* 112: I, 712–713.

Frank Huisman

LOMBROSO, CESARE (b. Verona, Italy, 18 November 1836; d. Turin, Italy, 19 October 1909), *psychology, anthropology.*

Lombroso, son of Aronne Lombroso and Zefora Levi, was born into a wealthy Jewish family. Though having in his youth philosophical and literary interests, in 1852 he followed Paolo Marzolo's advice and enrolled in the Medical Faculty of the University of Pavia. Like many of his contemporaries, he also went abroad to learn about the most recent scientific and medical theories and techniques. After a short stay in Padua, he visited Paris and Vienna. On 13 March 1858 he took his degree in medicine. In 1859, during the war of the Italian Risorgimento, he enrolled in the Military Medical Corps, jotting down numerous observations on the soldiers. He also participated for three months in the campaign against banditry in Calabria. In 1864 he was appointed to teach a course of clinics in mental diseases at the University of Pavia (1864–67), later becoming professor (1867–75). In 1871 he was also director of the asylum of Pesaro (1871–73), which constituted another rich source for original experiences. In 1876 he was called to the University of Turin, to the chairs of forensic medicine (1876–1903) and then psychiatry (1890–1909). In 1907 the chair of criminal anthropology was created for him.

In 1870 Lombroso married Nina De Benedetti. They had five children; two of them, Gina and Paola, later wrote biographical accounts of their father. When Lombroso died at the age of seventy-two, he was one of the most well-known Italian scientists. He was a prolific writer, and books such as *Genius and Madness* (1864), *The Criminal Man* (1872), *The Forensic Medicine of Alienation* (1873), *Anti-Semitism and the Modern Sciences* (1894), and *The Social Function of Crime* (1896) departed from strictly academic circles and enjoyed great editorial success, numerous re-editions, and translations into various languages.

Lombroso's lifelong project was dedicated to the creation of a natural history of humankind and all its extreme psychological manifestations. Besides these scientific goals, he aimed at an application of his results on social politics and reforms of the judicial and prison system. His work was characterized by his ability to assimilate the ideas circulating in mid-nineteenth-century European science, adapting them to new fields of scientific investigation. The community of European anthropologists, psychologists, psychiatrists, and criminologists, however, was split between strong advocates and harsh opponents.

Dreams, Madness, and Genius

In the 1850s Italy was still under Bourbon, French, and Austrian domain. Pavia, however, was the most open and progressive Italian university and anticipated many of the future epistemological and institutional transformations of Italian science. Anatomist Bartolomeo Panizza awakened Lombroso's interest in neurology, and Paolo Mantegazza, professor of general pathology in Pavia and pioneer of Italian anthropology, instructed his students to consider psychology as a 'physiology of the brain'. In 1859 Lombroso read Jakob Moleschott's *Der Kreislauf des Lebens*, which he later translated into Italian (1869). Moleschott and his materialism were a source of great inspiration for the young generation of Italian philosophers and scientists, and they confirmed Lombroso's somatic conception of psychological phenomena and of the necessity of an 'experimental and synthetic' approach. In the trail of emerging positivism, he was determined to eliminate all kinds of philosophical explanations and to found psychology on objective data, hence measuring the living matter instead of carrying out introspection.

Lombroso's first scientific work (1853) treated the influence of the encephalic functions on the general physiology of insects. He then turned his attention to man and to the study of madness and dreams (1854–57). Inspired by Louis-Ferdinand-Alfred Maury, pioneer of the exploration of dreams, he attributed to dreams the importance of 'forgotten records, buried in the unconsciousness'. For Lombroso dreams were the point of junction between physiology and pathology and thus were appropriate for the study of madness. In *Su la pazzia di Cardano* [On the insanity of Cardano, 1855] Lombroso tried to explain the causes of madness by applying the contemporary concepts of teratology and embryology.

In the 1890s Lombroso was particularly attracted by the phenomenon of genius. His first sketches went back to the 1860s, when he gave a paper that was published in 1864 as a small volume. During the following three decades, his original ideas developed, and the size of the book steadily increased, becoming 743 pages in 1894. Lombroso reduced the phenomenon of genius to a form of mental pathology, in particular, epilepsy. Known personalities, among them Charles Darwin, were described as neuropaths with symptoms of epilepsy, obsessive manias, and some 'degenerative' characteristics such as a short nose and big and long ears. The social status of genius, however, was radically different. In contrast to criminals, Lombroso considered the genius to be the 'protagonist of evolution', affected by an alienation that was at the same time an extraordinary force of innovation, a psychotic that could succeed in changing the history of the world. The six Italian and eight foreign editions largely contributed to the nineteenth century's identification of genius and madness and to Lombroso's national and international fame and popularity.

The Criminal Man

Like many anthropologists of his time, Lombroso expressed in *L'uomo bianco e l'uomo di colore* (1871) his conviction of the constant inequality of the different human races. He classified the races and investigated their somatic and behavioral characteristics and the determining climatic and ecological factors. More innovative was the link he made between contemporary races and their arrest at different stages of embryological evolution. And for the first time, he alluded to the relation among atavism, the diversity of the man, and criminal tendencies that became explicit five years later in his most famous work, *L'uomo delinquente*. Lombroso was an original and attentive observer. Wherever he went, he observed. During his stay in Calabria, he studied the language and folklore of the Calabrians, and during his stay at the asylum of Pesaro, he spent much time recording interesting material. Lombroso's interest in identifying the traits of criminals was raised during his activity as a military physician, when he observed and classified the tattoos of soldiers and related them to their psychological traits. Lombroso's later experiences, however, were rarely direct, depending mostly on material and reports that were sent to him by others. He interpreted the huge amount of information within the framework of several scientific currents of the mid-nineteenth century: comparative anatomy, anthropological classification, embryological theories of recapitulation, pre-Mendelian debates on atavism, teratology, Joseph Gall's phrenology, Darwinian and pre-Darwinian evolutionary theories, the treatises of Bénédict-Auguste Morel and Henry Maudsley on moral degeneration, and positivism.

The first outline of Lombroso's theory was made public during a session of the Istituto Lombardo di Scienze in 1871. In his lecture 'Esistenza di una fossa occipitale mediana nel cranio di un delinquente', he reported on his investigation of the cranium of a criminal. 'Brigand Villella' presented a median occipital fossa, a characteristic of the cranium almost absent in humans but frequent in lemurs and rodents. Like the phrenologists of the first half of the nineteenth century, he did not investigate the brain itself, but deduced its constitution from the form of the cranium. Lombroso was convinced that Villela's cerebellum corresponded to that of an adult rodent and that of a five-month-old fetus—and hence represented a regression to a primitive phylogenetic stage. This was clamorous proof for the correlation between the presence of primitive somatic traits and criminal attitudes.

In *L'uomo delinquente*, Lombroso elaborated this idea by presenting the somatic traits of 832 criminals, describing also their morality, their intelligence, their habits, and their slang. He considered criminals a distinct class of human individuals, characterized by physical and mental peculiarities that could be identified and measured by the means of anthropometry and statistics. Both types of characteristics, somatic and psychological, were intimately linked because both resulted from the reappearance of 'atavistic' forms, reminiscent of earlier evolutionary stages. The anomalies—stigmata—that distinguished criminals from respectable people became morphologically evident as abnormal forms or dimensions of the skull and jaw, asymmetries in the face and of other parts of the body, excessive forms of hair, behavioral tendencies, etc. The more the morphological elements represented atavistic trends, the more the individual was thought likely to be violent. Thus, criminal behavior did not depend on the will of the individual, but corresponded to the degree of biological regression. In years of cultural optimism, Lombroso explained criminal behavior as primitive, degenerate behavior.

Lombroso's theory of 'criminal atavism', though not considerably changed, was developed and enriched in the course of the following years, responding to the numerous critiques that were put forward. Sustained by its enormous editorial success, the size of *L'uomo delinquente* increased steadily: the number of pages in the second edition (1878) had nearly tripled, the fourth (1884) was edited in two volumes, and the fifth (1896–97) appeared in three volumes and included a 'criminal map'.

Based on his theory, Lombroso also made several proposals to reform the judicial and prison system. Because criminal behavior did not depend on one's will, it was a 'social duty' to protect society's sane majority. Lombroso differentiated various categories of criminals according to the presence of determinate anatomical, physiological, and psychological elements: born criminals, alienated criminals, occasional criminals, professional criminals, and later also the political criminals. The born criminal was irretrievable

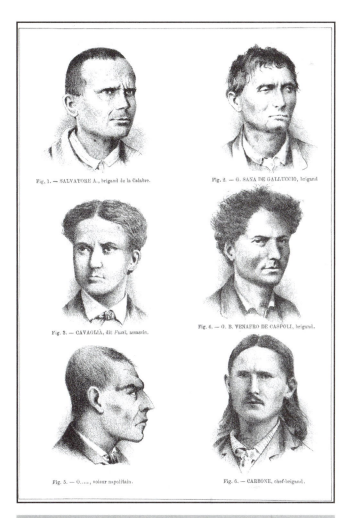

Fig. 1. — SALVATORE A., brigand de la Calabre.

Fig. 2. — G. SANA DE GALLUCCIO, brigand

Fig. 3. — CAVAGLIÀ, dit *Fusti*, assassin.

Fig. 4. — G. B. VENAFRO DE CASPOLI, brigand.

Fig. 5. — O....., voleur napolitain.

Fig. 6. — CARBONE, chef-brigand.

Criminal 'types' as portrayed by notorious villains. Lithograph from *L'Homme Criminel*, Rome, 1888. Wellcome Library, London.

and, in the name of public security, had to be shut up forever; the others could be reeducated.

The Museum of Criminal Anthropology

From his youth, Lombroso cultivated a great passion for collecting crania, brains, skeletons, and other objects of people from all regions of the Italian Kingdom. In time the collection was integrated with samples coming from abroad. He dedicated special attention to the compilation of numerous albums with photographs portraying criminals. In 1878 Lombroso's collection became part of his laboratory at the University of Turin. In 1884, on the occasion of the Great Exhibition at Turin, Lombroso showed part of it, attracting a large number of visitors. This experience encouraged him to put forward a project to establish a Museo di Antropologia Criminale. It was officially inaugurated in 1892 and recognized with the status of a scientific institution. Lombroso's dream to create a national center for the inventory and conservation of criminological objects seemed to be realized when the Ministry of Interior gave advice to the directories of the Italian jails to send all objects of scientific interest to the Museum in Turin. In 1909 it also received the skeleton, the cranium, and the brain of Lombroso himself.

Bibliography

Primary: 1995. (Frigessi, D., F. Giancanelli, and L. Mangoni, eds.) *Delitto, genio, follia: scritti scelti* (Turin); 1864. *Genio e follia. Prelezione ai corsi di antropologia e clinica psichiatrica presso la R. Università di Pavia* (Milan, 2nd edn. 1872, 3rd edn. 1877, 4th edn. 1882, 5th edn. 1888, 6th edn. 1894) [English: *The Man of Genius*, 1891 (London)]; 1871. 'Esistenza di una fossa occipitale mediana nel cranio di un delinquente.' *Rendiconto del R. Istituto Lombardo di Scienze e Lettere* 4: 37–41; 1876. *L'uomo delinquente studiato in rapporto alla antropologia, alla medicina e alle discipline carcerarie* (Milan) [5th edn. 1896–97 (Turin)].

Secondary: Castelnuovo Frigessi, Delia, 2003. *Cesare Lombroso* (Turin); Colombo, Giorgio, 2000. *La scienza infelice: il Museo di antropologia criminale di Cesare Lombroso* (Turin); Pancaldi, Giuliano, 1991. 'Cesare Lombroso and Social Darwinism' in Pancaldi, Giuliano (trans. Ruey Brodine Morellii), *Darwin in Italy. Science across Cultural Frontiers* (Bloomington, IN) pp. 142–151.

Ariane Dröscher

LONG, CRAWFORD WILLIAMSON   (b. Danielsville, Georgia, USA, 1 November 1815; d. Athens, Georgia, USA, 16 June 1878), *anesthetics, surgery.*

Long, son of James Long, a planter and merchant, and Elizabeth Ware, was educated at the University of Georgia in Jefferson, Georgia. He graduated with honors in 1835, and after teaching at the University for a year, he entered its faculty of medicine. After a year, he transferred his studies to Transylvania University, Kentucky. He moved again in 1838, this time to the University of Pennsylvania, and received his MD in 1839. After working in various hospitals in New York, Long returned to Jefferson in 1841, where he took over Grant's post as lecturer in medicine and local physician. In 1842 he married Caroline Swain.

'Laughing gas frolics'—the inhalation of nitrous oxide to produce intoxication—was a popular party game at this time. When a friend asked Long to make a quantity of nitrous oxide for a frolic in the winter of 1841, Long suggested he substitute the cheaper and more widely available sulfuric ether. When he attended an ether frolic, Long saw that the participants suffered cuts and bruises, but did not notice the pain. Minor surgery formed a large part of Long's work, and he decided to try ether inhalation as a means of obtaining pain relief. On 30 March 1842, he gave ether to James Venable, a local farmer suffering from a large benign tumor on his neck, and cut away the tumor. Venable remained unconscious throughout the procedure, and on waking, he reported no pain.

Long continued to experiment with ether as an anesthetic, and by 1846 he had performed eight successful operations under ether and had given it to Caroline during the birth of their second child. Despite this apparent success, Long did not report his experiences in print until 1849. It appears that his workload as a rural physician, his wish to gain as much experience as he could before revealing his method, and the enthusiasm in the American medical press for mesmerism as an 'anti-aesthetic' all contributed to this diffidence.

Long's first account of his technique was given in a lecture to the Medical College of Georgia in 1849, and a paper describing his technique was published in the *Southern Medical and Surgical Journal* in 1849. By this time, however, both the surgeon Henry Bigelow and the dentist William Morton had published accounts of ether anesthesia. In 1849 Morton made a claim for recognition and compensation for his work to the U.S. Congress, and this prompted several rival claimants to come forward. Although it became clear that Long was indeed the first to use ether anesthesia, the fact that he had not been the first to publish confused the issue, and Congress did not act. In 1851 Long moved to Athens, Georgia, where he continued to work as a general practitioner for the remainder of his career. Although he opposed the secession of the southern states, he worked during the Civil War (1861–65) as a surgeon in the Confederate Hospital in Athens and served in the Georgia Home Guard.

Long was undoubtedly the first to use ether as an anesthetic for surgery. He was also renowned among his colleagues as an excellent surgeon. However, the confusion caused by his delay in publishing has served to obscure the nature of his life and work.

Bibliography

Primary: 1849. 'An Account of the First Use of Sulphuric Ether by Inhalation as an Anesthetic.' *Southern Medical and Surgical Journal* 5: 705–713.

Secondary: Duncum, Barbara M., 1994. *The Development of Inhalation Anaesthesia* (London); Young, Hugh, 1942. 'Crawford W. Long: The Pioneer in Anesthesia.' *Bulletin of the History of Medicine* 12: 191–225; Long Taylor, Frances, 1928. *Crawford Williamson Long and the Discovery of Ether Anesthesia* (New York); *DAMB*.

Richard Barnett

LÓPEZ ALBO, WENCESLAO   (b. Santander, Spain, 6 November 1889; d. Mexico City, Mexico, 28 December 1944), *neuropsychiatry, neurosurgery, hospital organization.*

Born into a wealthy family, López Albo studied medicine in Valladolid and Madrid between 1905 and 1912. He showed an early interest in brain function and in 1912 and 1913 attended the teaching of Cajal's disciple, Nicolás Achúcarro, at the Laboratory of Histopathology of the Nervous System. He completed his training at the Ciempozuelos mental asylum under the supervision of the psychiatrist

Miguel Gayarre and obtained his doctorate in 1914. The same year, he went to Germany to broaden his training in neurosciences at Berlin University and became interested in neurosurgery. In 1915 he opened a private surgery practice for neurological and mental diseases in Bilbao, and in 1916 he was appointed head of surgery of these specialties at the Civil Hospital of Basurto, Bilbao. Between 1920 and 1923, he benefited from new postdoctoral studies abroad, mainly in Paris, where he collaborated, among others, with Pierre Marie at La Salpêtrière. In 1925 he was appointed head of the Zaldivar mental asylum.

López Albo was a member of a generation of neuropsychiatrists who exerted an important influence not only in the scientific life but also in the social and political scene of the last years of Primo de Rivera's dictatorship and of the Second Republic, through their professional association (*Asociación Española de Neuropsiquiatría*) and the League of Mental Hygiene. These bodies worked on proposals for psychiatric reform that the new republican administration immediately adopted as its own.

In 1928 López Albo accepted the invitation of the philanthropist Ramón Pelayo, marquis of Valdecilla, to take charge in Santander of the scientific organization of a new hospital that in López Albo's hands would become alien to the hospital tradition of Spain: the *Casa de Salud Valdecilla* (literally, Valdecilla House of Health). He was appointed scientific and economic director of the institution and head of the psychiatric pavilion that included neurological and neurosurgical sections, where he continued his research on brain parasites. The Valdecilla Hospital was the most important professional achievement of López Albo's life. An active member of the medical section of the Basque General Workers Union (UGT) and personal friend of the socialist leader Indalecio Prieto, López Albo believed in the power of science as a tool of social transformation. In the organization of the new hospital, he saw opportunities for putting into practice his ideals for a just social order, ruled by scientific principles, inside and outside the hospital. The organization and structure of the Valdecilla Hospital were inspired by discussions of the International Hospital Association that López Albo attended as the official Spanish representative. The daily and professional press stressed the hospital's uniqueness within Spanish hospital culture at the time.

The turbulent political atmosphere conditioned López Albo's work as director of the hospital, and in September 1930, the Board, dominated by the local conservative oligarchy, forced his resignation. He resumed his private practice in Bilbao until September 1936, when he was reinstated as director of the Valdecilla Hospital. When the entry of pro-Franco troops into Santander was imminent in August 1937, López Albo left the city hurriedly by sea, to reach Barcelona through France. There he became professor at the Universidad Autónoma (Autonomous University) in 1937–1938 and held various posts in the republican health organization. When Barcelona fell in 1939, he went into exile in Mexico and continued with his clinical work, teaching and conducting research, first in Monterrey and then, from 1942, in Mexico City, where he died in 1944.

Bibliography

Primary: 1928. 'Proyecto de un Pabellón Psiquiátrico, Dispensario Psiquiátrico e Instituto de Orientación Profesional para la "Casa de Salud Valdecilla".' *Revista Clínica de Bilbao* 3: 581–586; 1932. *Planteamiento y organización de un hospital moderno* (San Sebastián); 1945. *Aspectos clínicos de la cisticercosis del sistema nervioso central* (Mexico City).

Secondary: Salmón, Fernando, Luis García Ballester, and Jon Arrizabalaga, 1990. *La Casa de Salud Valdecilla* (Santander).

Fernando Salmón

LOUIS, ANTOINE   (b. Metz, France, 13 February 1723; d. Paris, France, 20 May 1792), *surgery.*

Louis came from a surgical family with frustrated noble ambitions. Schooled by the Jesuits, he trained under his father, who was chief surgeon of the military hospital in Metz. After working in his turn as an army surgeon, Louis moved to Paris in 1743. There, he sought the patronage of François Gigot de Lapeyronie, who was first surgeon to Louis XV and the leading advocate for surgical reform. Two years later, Louis won the post of *gagnant-maîtrise* to the Salpêtrière hospital, where, in exchange for six years as resident surgeon, he earned his mastership. He then worked at La Charité between 1757 and 1761. During the Seven Years War, he served as a surgical consultant for the Rhine army.

Louis steered an ambitious career path. Like C.-N. Le Cat and François Quesnay, he wanted to improve surgery's social and scientific prestige. Once in Paris, Louis participated in the pamphlet war between surgeons and physicians over a royal decree that stipulated that surgical candidates must take an arts degree from a French university. Louis himself learned Latin and received his master's degree in 1749. During this period, Louis showcased his philosophic and physiological learning. In 1747 he wrote a short book on the mind–body problem, and two years later he participated in the Academy of Dijon's contest about hereditary disease (the latter work remained the standard reference on this subject until the early 1800s).

In 1764 Louis became permanent secretary of the Royal Academy of Surgery. As part of his responsibilities, he published the annual memoirs, gave elegies for deceased members, and adjudicated conflicts between members and associates. Louis often balanced innovative and conventional surgical practice. On the one hand, he was a judicious voice for curricular improvement, and he was a patron for talent, such as in the case of Pierre-Joseph Desault. On the other hand, his surgical approach was relatively conservative, though he followed new techniques involving neural and facial operations, caesarians, the forceps, and, most famously, tracheotomies.

Louis made important contributions to legal medicine. After his appointment to the Royal Academy, Louis took a law degree and became a member of the Paris Parlement. He commented on a variety of public scandals that included premature burial, late births, abortion, drowning, infanticide, impotency, strangulation, and suicide. In 1763 Louis became involved in the case of Jean Calas, a Protestant who was accused of murdering his converted son and was executed in 1762. Corresponding with Voltaire, Louis experimented on hanging victims and presented the forensic evidence needed to rehabilitate Calas in 1765. Denis Diderot commissioned him to write about seventy articles for the *Encyclopédie*, and he assembled the surgical plates for the illustrated volumes.

During the French Revolution, Louis served alongside Jacques Tenon and Félix Vicq d'Azyr on the National Assembly's health committee. In 1792, following Ignace Guillotin's suggestion, Louis designed the French model of the guillotine. Assisted by Philippe Pinel and Pierre Cabanis, Louis performed experiments on cadavers and animals and officially launched the new machine. Parisians first called the decapitating device the 'Petite Louison', though the word 'guillotine' (a rhyme between Guillotin and 'la machine') quickly replaced it.

Louis left an important legacy in Enlightenment medicine because he helped transform surgery from a craft guild to a liberal profession and a science. More broadly, he promoted the belief that medicine itself had scientific and social utility, though he opposed the unification of medicine and surgery during the French Revolution. Through his work on jurisprudence, Louis gained public support for forensic medicine, and he influenced later specialists such as Paul Mahon and Fodéré. For many contemporaries, Louis embodied the ideal of the so-called *médecin-philosophe*—the enlightened physician.

Bibliography

Primary: 1772. *Dictionnaire de Chirurgie* 2 vols. [Collection of articles in the *Encyclopédie* of Diderot] (Paris); 1788. *Oeuvres diverses de Chirurgie* 2 vols. (Paris).

Secondary: Milanesi, Claudio, 1991. *Mort apparente, mort imparfaite: Médecine et mentalités au XVIIIe siècle* (Paris); Gelfand, Toby, 1980. *Professionalizing Modern Medicine: Paris Surgeons and Medical Science and Institutions in the 18th Century* (Westport, CT); Huard, Pierre, and Marie-José Imbault-Huart, 1972. *Biographies médicales et scientifiques, XVIIIe siècle (Astruc, Louis, Desault, Bichat)* (Paris); Sue, Pierre, 1793. 'Éloge de Louis' in Dubois d'Amiens, E.-F., ed., *Éloges lus dans les séances publiques de l'Académie Royale de chirurgie de 1750 à 1792* (Paris) pp. 416–454.

Sean Quinlan

LOUIS, PIERRE-CHARLES-ALEXANDRE (b. Aï, France, 14 April 1787; d. Paris, France, 22 August 1872), *medical statistics, pathological anatomy.*

Louis's father, a wine merchant in the Champagne region, died when his son was six. After abandoning the idea of a law career, Louis began medical studies in Reims and worked as an assistant to a hospital physician. He returned to Paris with a recommendation to Théodore-Nilammon Lerminier, a native of Reims and a physician at the Charité hospital. Louis submitted his doctoral thesis in 1813. His early attempts to practice medicine in Paris were unsuccessful, and he returned home. A chance encounter with Count Armand de St Priest, an émigré Frenchman and governor of the region of Kherson, in southern Russia (now the Ukraine) resulted in Louis becoming the Count's personal physician. He remained in Russia for seven years and developed a flourishing medical practice in Odessa. In 1820 he returned to Paris.

Now financially independent, Louis undertook a project that he had long contemplated. Giving up private practice, he gained access to patients at the Charité hospital, thanks to his friend Auguste-François Chomel. For six years, Louis studied the case histories of all the patients on Chomel's wards, collecting more than two thousand observations. His approach of meticulous observation, systematic record keeping, analysis of large numbers of cases, and verification of diagnosis through autopsy became known as 'the numerical method'. He sought to move beyond the details of individual case histories to discover what was common to specific diseases.

Louis's first important publication, *Recherches anatomico-pathologiques sur la phthisie* (1825), concerned phthisis or tuberculosis, the dominant chronic disease of the time. Based on the records of 167 patients, Louis determined that the primary location of tubercular lesions was at the top of the lungs. If tubercules were found in other organs, tubercules would always be found in the lungs. This work secured Louis's election into the Academy of Medicine. His monograph went through several editions and translations.

Louis next turned his attention to febrile diseases. He distinguished typhoid fever as a specific disease on the basis of characteristic pathologic alterations produced in the large intestine. Louis also served on the government commission that traveled to Gibraltar in 1828 to study the outbreak of yellow fever.

The third area for which Louis is known is his application of the numerical method to determine efficacy of therapy. His research and writings on the ineffectiveness of bloodletting, brought together in 1835, helped to bring about the decline of this long therapy. Louis tended to be skeptical of most traditional therapies. His book challenged François Broussais's reliance on bloodletting in his theory of 'physiological medicine'. Much debated in the Academy of Medicine, the numerical method raised the issue of how mathematical rules might be applied to clinical medicine and therapeutics.

In 1829 Louis became physician at the Pitié hospital, where his clinical conferences attracted many students. Although he never became a professor at the medical faculty, he was extremely popular with foreign students—above all, with young American physicians such as James Jackson Jr. of Boston, who extolled Louis's clinical-pathological lessons in letters to his physician father. In 1832 Louis founded the Société Médicale d'Observation to promote the numerical method.

Louis's later years were blighted by the early death of his son Armand in 1854. He largely retired from public life as a result. After years of decline, he died at age eighty-five.

Bibliography

Primary: 1825. *Recherches anatomico-pathologiques sur la phthisie* (Paris) [trans. Cowan, Charles, 1836, *Pathological researches on phthisis* (Boston)]; 1829. *Recherches anatomiques, pathologiques et thérapeutiques sur la maladie connue sous les noms de gastroentérite, fièvre putride, adynamique, ataxique, typhoïde, etc.: comparées avec les maladies aiguës les plus ordinaires* (Paris) [trans. Bowditch, H. I., 1836, *Anatomical, Pathological, and Therapeutic Researches on the Disease Known under the Name of Gastro-Enterite* [etc.] (Boston)]; 1835. *Recherches sur les effets de la saignée dans quelques maladies inflammatoires, et sur l'action de l'émétique et des vésicatoires dans la pneumonie* (Paris) [trans. Putnam, C. G., 1836, *Researches on the Effects of Bloodletting in Some Inflammatory Diseases* (Boston)].

Secondary: Matthews, J. Rosser, 1995. *Quantification and the Quest for Medical Certainty* (Princeton, New Jersey) ch. 2, 4; Béclard, Jules, 1878. 'M. Louis' in *Notices et portraits, éloges lus à l'Académie de Médecine* (Paris) pp. 227–257.

Caroline Hannaway

LOWER, RICHARD (b. Tremeer, Cornwall, England, 1631; d. London, England, 17 January 1691), *medicine, anatomy, physiology.*

Evidence suggests that Lower's prominent and wealthy Cornish family had strong religious sympathies. Lower's younger brother, Thomas, was at one point imprisoned with George Fox (1624–91), leader of the Quakers, and Lower himself lost his prominent position at court as royal physician after the succession of the Roman Catholic James II (1633–1701). Lower left money to help Protestant refugees from France and Ireland.

Lower entered Christ Church, Oxford (1649), and took his MA in 1655. He studied medicine extramurally under Peter Stahl (d.1675?), but received the DMed in 1665 at the recommendation of the Chancellor of the University, Edward Hyde (1609–74). He became a member of the remarkable group of experimental natural philosophers brought together by Robert Boyle (1627–91), which included Thomas Willis (1621–75), William Petty (1623–87), and Christopher Wren (1632–1723). The most fruitful outcome of this period can be seen in Willis's *Cerebri anatome* (1664), a major work on the anatomy of the brain, which was illustrated by Wren and based on the meticulous anatomical skills of Lower. Lower went into print under his own name in the following year, when he published his *Vindication* (1665) of Willis's theory of fevers against the attack of the traditional Galenist, Edmund O'Maera (d. 1680). It was also during these productive years

that Lower performed the first direct blood transfusions, between two dogs.

In 1666 Lower married Elizabeth Billing (d. 1704), so bringing her family's considerable Cornish estate into the Lower family, and moved to London to set up medical practice. In spite of a rapidly burgeoning practice, he managed to continue with his physiological research. He became a fellow of the Royal Society in 1667 and played an active part in the work of the Society over the next few years. Almost immediately, for example, he extended his experiments on transfusion by direct transfusion from a sheep into one Arthur Coga, who fortunately survived. The instigation here was not entirely philosophical; prominent members of the Society had been outraged by the recently reported human transfusions of the French natural philosopher Jean-Baptiste Denis (1640?–1704), which the Society claimed were inadequately described.

More importantly, Lower began to collaborate with Robert Hooke (1635–1703) in vivisections to investigate cardiopulmonary physiology. Lower now became convinced that the change causing the difference in color and consistency between venous and arterial blood took place in the lungs, not in the left ventricle of the heart, as was usually supposed. Lower attributed these changes to a 'nitrous spirit of the air'. The important results of this research were published in *Tractatus de corde* (1669) and made Lower's name. Willis abandoned his own ideas about a ferment in the left ventricle and adopted the new theory; and John Mayow (1643–79), who was to make the next major contribution to the physiology of respiration in his *Tractatus quinque* (1674), always acknowledged his indebtedness to Lower.

From now on, however, Lower began to concentrate on his medical practice. He published only one more work, the *De origine catarrhi* (London, 1672), which laid to rest the old idea that phlegm descended to the nose from the brain. In 1675 Lower succeeded Willis as royal physician and was finally acknowledged as the finest doctor in London. This did not last. He actively opposed James's policies and lost his position at court. He seems to have retreated to Cornwall and lost his London practice. After the revolution of 1688, he evidently returned to London. He died of pneumonia there but was buried in Cornwall.

Bibliography

Primary: 1665. *Richard Lower's* Vindicatio: *A Defence of the Experimental Method* [1983, Dewhurst, Kenneth, ed. (Oxford)]; 1669. *Tractatus de corde item de motu et colore sanguinis et chyli in eum transitu* [Reprint 1932, with English translation in Gunther, R. T., ed., *Early Science in Oxford*, vol. 9 (Oxford)].

Secondary: Frank, Robert G., 1980. *Harvey and the Oxford Physiologists* (Berkeley, CA); Hoff, Ebbie C., and Phebe M. Hoff, 1936. 'The Life and Times of Richard Lower, Physiologist and Physician.' *Bulletin of the Institute of the History of Medicine* 4: 517–535; *DSB*; *Oxford DNB*.

John Henry

LUDWIG, CARL FRIEDRICH WILHELM (b. Witzenhausen, Germany, 29 December 1816; d. Leipzig, Germany, 23 April 1895), *physiology.*

Ludwig completed his medical studies and finished his dissertation at Marburg University (1840). After spending some months in Robert Bunsen's chemical laboratory, he obtained a position as a prosector in Ludwig Fick's Anatomical Institute (1841–46). There, supported by Fick, Ludwig succeeded in his first substantial scholarly work, an investigation of the function of blood vessels in the kidney. The results appeared in Ludwig's *Habilitationsschrift* (1842) and went into the chapter 'Nieren und Harnleitung' that he was invited to contribute to Rudolph Wagner's prestigious *Handwörterbuch der Physiologie* (1844). In 1846 Ludwig was appointed university professor at Marburg's medical faculty.

In late 1840 Ludwig focused his research interests on cardiovascular physiology and hemodynamics. He expanded his knowledge in mathematics and physics and developed the 'kymograph'. This graphical recording and inscription device, made up of a mercury manometer and a smoked metal cylinder, enabled blood pressure experimentation on living animals. Soon after the 'machine' was described in *Müllers Archiv* (1847), it became a widely spread standard device in contemporary laboratories. Kymographic curves virtually became emblematic of the mechanistic approach to the understanding of life and its functions.

Ludwig's textbook *Lehrbuch der Phyiologie des Menschen* (vol. 1, 1852; vol. 2, 1856) was a programmatic milestone in the history of modern physiology and its task to analyze living phenomena through the methods of physics and chemistry, mathematics, and the extensive use of laboratory instruments and experimentation. Major parts of the book Ludwig wrote at the University of Zurich, where he worked as a professor of anatomy and physiology from 1849. In 1855 he went to Vienna. In his laboratory at the Josephinum, an academy where Austria's military doctors received their education, Ludwig devised a modified mercurial pump to remove the mixture of respiration gases from a given quantity of blood.

In 1865 Ludwig accepted a call to Leipzig. Supported by the King of Saxony, he immediately began to develop a highly sophisticated building for physiological research. This institute, unique worldwide in size and equipment, opened its doors in 1869. In Leipzig, Ludwig's international reputation as a brilliant experimenter and scientific instructor attracted students from all over Europe, Russia, and the United States. Together with his assistants and collaborating technicians, Ludwig maintained his fame as a creative inventor of laboratory apparatus. Most successful was an in vitro device he made for the investigation of the isolated and perfused frog heart. Another innovative instrument was the flowmeter (Stromuhr). It measured regional blood flow and cardiac output in living animals.

Ludwig was also pathbreaking by making the new developments in engineering and urban technology productive for his institute. 'As in a factory', as his friend Emil Du Bois-Reymond said, all workrooms were provided with water, gas, and mechanical power from a combustion engine. Another novelty was Ludwig's style of management and work organization. In terms of both space and personnel, he divided research work among three specialized divisions for chemistry, physics, and anatomy.

Ludwig's institute marked a point of departure into the modern age of laboratory work in physiology. Taking Leipzig as the most important model, the institutional revolution in nineteenth-century life sciences reached the level of large-scale research undertakings in factory-like laboratories.

Bibliography

Primary: 1852–1856. *Lehrbuch der Physiologie des Menschen* 2 vols. (Heidelberg); 1869. *Rede beim Beginn der Vorlesungen in der neuen physiologischen Anstalt* (Leipzig); 1879. *Die wissenschaftliche Tätigkeit in den physiologischen Instituten* (Leipzig).

Secondary: Zimmer, Heinz-Gerd, 1999. 'The Contributions of Carl Ludwig to Cardiology.' *Canadian Journal of Cardiology* 15(3): 323–329; Lenoir, Timothy, 1988. 'Science for the Clinic: Science Policy and the Formation of Carl Ludwig's Institute in Leipzig' in Coleman, William, and Frederic L. Holmes, eds., *The Investigative Enterprise. Experimental Physiology in Nineteenth-Century Medicine* (Berkeley, CA) pp. 139–178; Schröer, Heinz, 1967. *Carl Ludwig. Begründer der messenden Experimentalphysiologie 1816–1895* (Stuttgart); *DSB*.

Sven Dierig

LUST, BENEDICT (b. Michelbach, Germany, 3 February 1872; d. Tangerine, Florida, USA, 5 September 1945), *naturopathy.*

The son of Johannes Lust, a farmer, and Louise Rieger, Lust received a grade school education in Germany and then immigrated to New York City (1892). Soon after arriving in America, however, he developed a severe illness (which he believed to be tuberculosis) and, despairing of his life, returned to his homeland to undergo the therapeutic regimen known as Kneippism. Father Sebastian Kneipp operated a celebrated water cure in the Bavarian town of Worishofen, where chronic invalids were treated with a combination of various applications of cold water and herbal remedies. There Lust slowly regained his health, and he then determined to serve as a missionary of Kneippism to the New World.

Lust returned to New York (1896) and immediately set about expanding the Kneippist system by adding a range of other natural therapies that included dietetics, massage, musculoskeletal manipulation, exercise, sun bathing, and electrical stimulation. This eclectic orientation to healing was manifested as well by his pursuit of formal training in several unorthodox healing practices: he obtained degrees from the Universal Osteopathic College (1898), New York Homeopathic College (1907), and the Eclectic Medical College of New York (1913). To this collection of treatments he applied the name naturopathy, a term he began using in 1901.

Although strictly speaking, naturopathy means 'nature disease', Lust intended the term to denote the employment of natural substances and agents to encourage nature's efforts to heal the disordered body. Naturopathic therapies were supposed to support and strengthen the *vis medicatrix naturae*, the body's own innate recuperative power. Similarly, disease was interpreted to be the result not of bacteriological infection or effects of other external irritants, but rather of unnatural living practices that undermined the strength of the *vis medicatrix*: improper diet, insufficient exercise, inadequate rest, and the like. The foundation of naturopathic care, therefore, was educating the sick on how to live in accord with nature.

To that end, Lust operated a health resort he called the Yungborn, or Fountain of Youth. Opened in 1896 in Butler, New Jersey, the Yungborn was an institution at which guests were placed on a vegetarian diet and put through various forms of open-air exercise while also encouraged to take river baths, sun baths, and mud baths in the nude. In 1913 a second resort (Qui-si-sana) was opened in Tangerine, Florida. Lust also opened one of the first health food stores in America, in New York (1896).

Lust founded and edited the chief naturopathic periodical, begun in 1901 under the name *Naturopath and Herald of Health*, then renamed *Herald of Health and Naturopath* (1916), and finally called *Naturopath* (1923). A magazine directed toward lay readers, *Nature's Path*, was introduced by Lust in 1925. He established the fledgling profession's first educational institution, the American School of Naturopathy, in New York City in 1901. The following year, Lust organized the Naturopathic Society of America, renamed the American Naturopathic Association in 1919. He was the organization's first president and was reelected to that office annually until 1921, at which time he was elected president for life.

Although Lust's encouragement of exercise, fresh air, and dietary moderation represented sound judgment, he was often remarkably naïve in his ready acceptance of any and all treatments that could be construed to be 'natural'. 'Nature is perfect in every way and everywhere', he proclaimed; 'the new art of natural healing expects everything from nature' (1900, p. 120), and thus endorsement was given to such natural treatments as eating sand to cure constipation, rectal manipulation to relieve headache, and eight-hour-long shower baths to eliminate all ailments whatever and to extend the human lifespan to several centuries.

Lust's interpretation of natural medicine also involved rejection of the recently developed germ theory that was revolutionizing orthodox medical practice. To his mind, germs were the product of disease, not its cause, and parasites were able to establish themselves only in bodies that had been made corrupt by impure living. Consequently, he was violently opposed to the antitoxins and vaccines, particularly the smallpox vaccine, which physicians employed to prevent infection. Naturopaths were leading participants in the antivaccination movement of the early twentieth century, and for good measure, they joined in the antivivisection movement as well.

Hydrotherapy fountain of Aesculapius at Bad Wörishofen, Bavaria. Color lithograph by Friedrich Rehm, 1902. Iconographic Collection, Wellcome Library, London.

Early naturopaths' most vigorous opposition to orthodox medicine was on the political front, where frequent and vitriolic attacks were leveled against the campaign to establish a national department of health within the federal government. Through such organizations as the American Medical Liberty League and the National League for Medical Freedom, Lust and fellow naturopaths fought to save the country from the 'medical trust' they believed was set on enslaving Americans to a single system of therapy.

Preserving the public's freedom of choice of healing options was also a major factor in naturopaths' struggle to win licensing legislation from the individual states. In the opening decades of the century, hundreds of naturopaths were arrested for practicing medicine without a license, receiving fines, jail sentences, or both. Lust himself was arrested on a number of occasions (once being fined as much as $500), and he recognized licensing laws as critical to his young profession's survival. California became the first state to license practitioners of naturopathy (1909), and over the next decade, nine more would fall into line, usually recognizing the system under the heading of 'drug-less healing'.

Naturopaths were hardly the only drugless healers, of course; there were osteopaths, chiropractors, mind curers, and a swarm of others who claimed to heal without the use of pharmaceuticals. Naturopathy employed the broadest array of nondrug methods, however, and Lust regarded his system as the logical agency for uniting all drugless approaches into a single front of resistance against the monopolistic ambitions of the medical establishment. He was instrumental in the 1912 founding of a National Association of Drugless Practitioners, and in subsequent years he issued repeated appeals to chiropractors, osteopaths, and others to drop their constant sniping at one another and join hands with naturopaths to provide the American public with an integrated program of nonpharmaceutical care. But as his calls went unanswered, he eventually abandoned the dream of a single system of drugless healing. By the 1920s, in fact, he had become openly critical of chiropractic care, dismissing it with such terms as 'fad' and 'hoax'.

In 1901 Lust married Louise Stroebele, who took up the practice of naturopathy also, supervising the women's departments at his health resorts in New Jersey and Florida until her death in 1925. They had no children. In 1943 Lust was overcome by smoke when a fire broke out at his Florida resort, and though he survived, he never recovered his former vigor and remained convinced until his death two years later that his compromised health was the result of sulfa drugs given him while he was still unconscious after the fire.

Those same sulfa drugs had a depressing effect on naturopathy in general, the introduction of first the sulfas in the 1930s and then antibiotics in the 1940s serving to impress the public with the superiority of modern pharmaceuticals over drugless methods. Even so, the decline in public support experienced by naturopathy in the mid-1900s was due in equal measure to dissension within the ranks. To be sure, factionalism had disturbed naturopathy from the beginning, yet had been contained until Lust's death. But at that point, the field fell into disarray, rival groups becoming so contentious that soon there were no fewer than six national organizations claiming to represent the profession. Such confusion inhibited the recruitment of new practitioners to such a degree that by the late 1960s there were fewer than 600 naturopaths practicing in the United States.

During that same decade, however, a movement took shape to rejuvenate the system by subjecting its traditional treatments to more rigorous scientific evaluation and by accepting those advances in biomedical science that could be adapted to the principles of naturopathic philosophy. The culmination of that movement occurred in 1978, with the establishment of the John Bastyr College of Naturopathic Medicine in Seattle (now Bastyr University). By the end of the century, Bastyr was enrolling more than 1,000 students annually, and other naturopathic schools were operating in the United States, Canada, and Australia. There was, moreover, only one organization representing the profession nationally, the American Association of Naturopathic Physicians, organized in 1980.

Naturopathic medical practice is still made up of therapies presumed to heal by supporting the body's innate recuperative power. Among the most common treatment categories are clinical nutrition, botanicals, physical medicine (massage, heat and cold, electricity), homeopathy, hydrotherapy, spirituality, and lifestyle counseling. These are much the same categories as those combined by Lust to create naturopathy in the 1890s.

Bibliography

Primary: 1900. 'Art versus nature in the process of healing.' *Kneipp Water Cure Monthly* 1: 120; 1918. *Universal Naturopathic Encyclopedia, Directory and Buyer's Guide Year Book of Drugless Therapy for 1918–19* (Butler, NJ); 1923. *The Fountain of Youth* (New York); 1926. *The Crime of Vaccination: A Foul Blot on America's Liberty* (Butler, NJ).

Secondary: Whorton, James, 2002. *Nature Cures: The History of Alternative Medicine in America* (New York) pp. 191–217; Cody, George, 1999. 'History of Naturopathic Medicine' in Pizzorno, Joseph, and Michael Murray, eds., *Textbook of Natural Medicine* 2 vols. (New York) vol. 1, pp. 17–40; Kirchfeld, Friedhelm, and Wade Boyle, 1994. *Nature Doctors* (Portland, OR) pp. 185–220; Baer, Hans, 1991–92. 'The Potential Rejuvenation of American Naturopathy as a Consequence of the Holistic Health Movement.' *Medical Anthropology* 13: 369–383.

James Whorton